# When Cosmic Cultures Meet

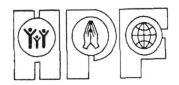

An International Conference
Presented by the
Human Potential Foundation

HPF

# When Cosmic Cultures Meet
### An International Forum held in Washington, D.C.
### May 27-29, 1995

ISBN
1882658035

Library of Congress Catalog Card Number: 96-79629

For information address:
Human Potential Foundation
P.O. Box 6
Falls Church, VA  22040

PRINTED IN THE UNITED STATES OF AMERICA

# Table of Contents

# Dedication

To all of those in each country and culture who are keepers of the secrets and sacred knowledge about the ubiquitousness of life in all dimensions throughout the Universe, and to their counterparts in all these dimensions.

Is it a common understanding that we are not prepared for contact?

If this is the case, does that condition serve the highest good for all?

If these answers are unsure, and that appears to be the case, what action or inaction is now appropriate to more firmly establish movement toward the time when each is honored for its existence and unique place in the Universal plan?

We do not presume to know what the appropriate response to the present condition should be, but challenge all keepers of these secrets and sacred knowledge to look again into the Source of your being and seek guidance.

It does appear that our shared interests and vision of the future is clouded by the consequences of a policy or revelatory gradualism. At a minimum, is it not time for a quickened dialogue?

# Acknowledgments

Many people contributed to make the conference and these Proceedings possible. The obvious groups are the presenters and the audience. Also visible was the corps of volunteers who handled all of the essential tasks of running a major conference. Design work on the flyer and conference program was done by Wickham & Associates.

Following the conference a number of people asked if it was going to become an annual affair. We hope that this will not be necessary, that the dialogue the conference was designed to stimulate will soon become an integrated part of the world's cultures. Perhaps smaller regional conferences around the world of the subject of the dialogue should take place. If they do, we hope that they receive the same generous and much appreciated support this conference received.

A special thank you is given to honorary LCDR Betty Plummer for the hours she spent transcribing speeches from audio and video tapes.

# Forward

The day that a believable announcement about the reality of cosmic cultures meeting comes from one or more governments, or when the Visiting Others, weary of a pusillanimous and confused boycott of the truth, make their presence undeniably known, is the day that the work begins.

There will be no magic in simply knowing. However, once that important knowledge threshold is passed, many new possibilities will be seen.

There apparently is something like the Prime Directive of non-interference. The work is still ours to do, and we have the technology and cultural diversity to do it.. We have lacked the will to make difficult, self-denying decisions, and to recognize the basic and critical interdependence of all life on, in, and over a living Earth.

For years the ET's have been sharing knowledge with individuals and perhaps also with some governments. It has been difficult to honor and use this information because the transmitting sources have been denied and ridiculed by the high priests of science. After a short period of ego adjusting penitence, I hope that this chastened priesthood will effectively work with this "new" knowledge to address all potential Earth-ending problems our excesses have created.

It may not be too late.

The fact that "the announcement" has either been forced out of governments or unilaterally made by the Visiting Others, suggests that a superior and reasoned judgment is that it is still worth a try to salvage Gaia.

Knowing for sure that we are not alone will release unrecognized and untapped energy. The consequences of a rising consciousness may well impact on critical boardroom decisions concerning issues of sustainability and equity of distribution of Earth's resources and the fruits of their use.

However exciting the announcement, the work will remain to be done. In fact, the most important message of the announcement is, "You now can see a possible future that previously was beyond your wildest dreams. Do the work to affirm that future and enter into it. Only when you have earned it will you deserve it and it will be so."

# Introduction

## The Intention

The conference, When Cosmic Cultures Meet, was designed to be the capstone on a process that had been going on for two years in which the White House had been encouraged to review the inherited policy from previous administrations concerning disclosure of information about Extraterrestrial (ET) and Unidentified Flying Objects (UFO) phenomena.

From the public's perspective the government's policy in these areas for nearly fifty years appears to be one of silence, secrecy and disinformation.

To the small part of the public that is seized by this subject, such a policy is viewed variously as being wrong, dysfunctional, dangerous, immoral, unjustified and totally inadequate for the future. Without presuming to know what the government knows about ET/UFO phenomena, our hope was that following a review of the current policy, it would be modified to one of more openness, appropriately sharing with the world what is known and what is anticipated for the future.

It was additionally hoped that the White House would accept our invitation to participate in the Conference and share with us whatever it was ready to do so at the time.

Copies of invitation letters sent and some of the responses received are reproduced in appendices at the end of this book.

These appendices will give the reader some insight about how we attempted to implement our strategy of encouraging a more open policy of sharing information with the American public and the world.

In a section in the conference program labeled, "The Continuing Dialogue," it was questioned how we might judge success of our efforts to engage government.

Attendance (at the Conference) is an obvious measure. But while some of the invited may think that merely showing up would be an act of bravery, it will be post-conference action of openly and actively joining the dialogue that will measure success.

Now, a year after the end of the conference, an assessment can be made of this strategy. Its success has been marginal to nonexistant if measurement is in terms of sharing information from any government group controlling ET/UFO information. Certainly there has been no official announcement of any type on the subject.

What appears to have happened is that president Clinton has received "the briefing." That may not have been the case before our meetings with White House staff on the subject. Our meetings along with other independent concurrent efforts directed to the White House on this subject appear to have influenced a decision to brief the president. Even though the president is the Chief Executive Officer of the nation and the Commander in Chief of the military forces, it is not reasonable to expect that he therefore routinely is briefed on every subject. That would be a logistical impossibility, impracticable and unnecessary.

Of course if someone believes that ET/UFO phenomena is one of the most important subjects and of cosmic dimension, it would indeed seem strange if each president was not thoroughly briefed on the subject early at the beginning of his administration. The fact that this apparently does not routinely happen may tell us something about how important this information now is considered within the small control group and/or by previous presidents when they were briefed. It serves no realistic purpose to try to analyze something we know nothing about, i.e., what does the government really know about ET/UFO phenomena.

Therefore, getting the president briefed may not be anything more than symbolically important, i.e., "we can all rest easier because the President knows." Certainly it means nothing in terms of what the strategy was designed to accomplish if the president does not review the old policy and change it to one of more openness.

## A FAILED STRATEGY

Assessing that our strategy was not successful, why was that the case? Charitably, it may be too soon to tell. Realistically, we may have appeared fanatical and crazy to different audiences. At this point I ask the reader to try to dump everything she or he thinks they know about ET/UFO phenomena and the role the U.S. government may be playing in the field. For those of you who have heard various conspiracy theories, this may be hard to do, because the bottom line of all of these is that the government is in some unholy alliance with the "wrong" ET group and that American citizens are being victimized as the result of this, i.e., government has become the enemy of the people. This is a bottomless energy trap that probably is fueled by other aggravations we all have with government. There will always be some real confrontational and antagonistic relationships between governments and their citizens. However, I doubt that a serious one has anything to do with ETs and UFOs.

Now with an empty mind on the subject, put yourself in the White House, up on Capitol Hill, and in the offices of cabinet members of the president. Read the letters in the appendices. How would you respond to them? Would you respond at all? Would they even make sense to you if you had no previous interest or knowledge about ET/UFO phenomena? In each case the letters presumed either prior knowledge or interest in the subject. That was an error in our assumptions. The letters did not make sense and additionally were probably considered belligerent and arrogant in tone.

Why make this confession? There are a small number of other responsible efforts under way to engage the government on this issue. It may be helpful for them to know in detail about our efforts and the assessments of our failure.

## A NEW STRATEGY

With the experience gained, a more responsible strategy and one with greater potential for success can be designed. It would make the assumption that ET/UFO phenomena will be recognized as important in terms of its relationship with real earth problems that must be faced, and with the broad cosmological issues that have intrigued humankind since the dawn of consciousness.

The target audiences for this strategy would be current leaders in the power structure of the nation-state system, and the unknown leaders of the 21st Century who are still in school systems around the world. The more important of the two probably are the students because they have a greater potential for openness, willingness to accept new concepts, and are not yet vested with power and the status quo mentality which that engenders. The current power structure cannot be ignored because they are in power, and because there are some problems which simply must be handled more adequately now.

It is not necessary for the government to play any direct role in this new strategy. Of course they would be welcome to be involved, but the assumption is that we are not dependent upon any knowledge the government may have on the subject.

Recognition of the shortcoming of the old strategy and insight of the revised strategy was a direct result of feedback from the Conference. It was an exceptional group of individuals who participated in the Conference, as speakers, panel members and audience. By way of the completed questionnaire and in many separate private communications after the Conference, I have been challenged to face all of my prior assumptions about ET/UFO phenomena, what it means to me, and what I am doing about it. This has been a gift of great personal value for which I am deeply appreciative.

I do not presume to speak for any others on this subject, but my understanding of the core belief of those who have spoken with me is this:

It really doesn't make any difference at all what the government knows or does not know. Attempts to get governments to share whatever they know on the subject empowers them more than they deserve. There is a possibility that such efforts may delay or substitute for the work required by each of us personally to integrate the vast amount of information already in the public domain. To the degree that we blame government, we give up our power to change and grow.

What does contact mean to you? That is the important question. It is easy to understand what it means to governments in the nation-state system. It means that the nation-state system is now and forever inadequate for a future in which intercourse with Cosmic Cultures will become the norm. The challenges and opportunities are simply too great for a "national" approach. A global response is an imperative, and probably what is expected from the various Cosmic Cultures. Until the current system can figure out how to organize to do this, most of the contact will be as it has been up to this point - with individuals.  I suspect that most of the government's activity has been trying to keep informed about individual contact. It would be more efficient if they would simply ask, but that would obviate the policy of secrecy, and this is something that all governments are loath to give up.

As the Human Potential Foundation continues in its dialogue with the Washington, DC diplomatic community, we will be able to determine what degree of support there is for the establishment of a Non-Governmental Organization (NGO) on the subject of Cosmic Cultures' interactions. Such a NGO could be an information bridge in the nation-state system that could survive that system's transformation.

I cannot overstate how important the Conference and the dialogue that followed has been to the Human Potential Foundation in terms of what our future activity will be in this field. It really is beside the point how naive or arrogant various governments have been on this issue. That is their problem. The assumption is that ET/UFO phenomena primarily is an individual spiritual issue. Taking it any less seriously than that would be an unfortunate error. But handling it as a spiritual issue, however complex that will be for each of us, is where the joy will be.

Each presenter and panel member at the Conference was asked to provide a written text to be included in these proceedings. Almost all of them have done so. In most cases the papers you will read are those that were presented at the Conference. The exceptions are from those presenters who used video at the Conference as their primary medium. In the case of panel members, most of their contributions are new, not previously presented. One panel member requested that we reprint a highly germane paper from someone who was not at the Conference, and yielded his space for this.

Each paper is preceded by a short introductory paragraph.

Following the papers a composite questionnaire completed by over 100 participants is presented with comments. When we realized how many had completed the questionnaire, we knew the dialogue truly had started and that the Conference was a success. A robust sense of humor, so essential for survival, frequently was demonstrated in responses to questions and situations.

What the government knows and when it knew it is of minor importance to the magnificence of the knowledge that we are not alone. There is a danger that many of us will use the government's policy of secrecy, silence and denial on this subject as an excuse for us painfully to face up to the significance of what contact means to us individually, and thus delay the necessary action to integrate this knowledge fully into our lives.

There are far more opportunities presented by contact than there are dangers. But denial of the reality of contact increases the dangers and shuts out the hopeful and needful opportunities.

This is a great individual spiritual challenge. The role that governments can and will play is small, but not insignificant if done with honesty. The reality is that the phenomena exists absolutely beyond governments' control and influence. It must be frustrating for them, especially the powerful nations, to realize this and to anticipate what that means to them in the current nation-state system. The unspoken, but deeply felt policy of the United States government is stridently paternalistic with strong traces of institutional arrogance and fear of loss of control. They may well have blinded themselves to any vision of a transformed nation-state system.

The saddest part of the current situation has been the squandering of opportunities to capitalize on contact swiftly to move Earth through very dangerous and trying times. The greatest disappointment may well be to learn someday that what governments have tried to do is to use their special knowledge to try to maintain the status quo. In as much as change is the only constant in life, such an effort could have fatal consequences. The growth mandated by change is both the hope and glory of the future.

## WHAT IS A HUMAN, WHY DO WE CARE?

The gorilla and chimpanzee by anatomical and molecular comparison are the closest earth-based living relative to humans. While there are obvious physiological differences between humans and apes, i.e., jaw and brain size and bipedalism, the most distinguished difference is the elaborate culture of humans. We have designated ourselves, human beings - homo sapiens, "wise and discerning men." Charles Winick, in his *Dictionary of Anthropology* notes that the emotional connotations of the term human ("referring to man") makes it difficult to use in a taxonomically correct manner. Some non-Western earth-based cultures call themselves "the people." This is more generous, being sex neutral, but since emphasis is on "the," it is exclusionistic.

Indeed, we humans are emotional about our status. Proof of our concern about being at the top of the food chain and claim holders of the most highly developed consciousness is easy to find by evidence of our abuse of everything 'below' us. One of our most scathing epithets is to label someone or something "inhuman."

Particularly in Western cultures and less so in many indigenous cultures, any discussion that would challenge homo sapiens' central position is rarely attacked on the merits, but on the proposition that such a notion is so foolish that it is not worthy of consideration. George S. Robinson and Harold M. White, Jr., in their book *Envoys of Mankind*, observe that "The intensity and furor of this and other debates involve a deep cultural, perhaps genetically coded, fear that humankind, collectively and individually, will lose its central position in the universe, perhaps somehow forfeiting the promise of paradise."

We can speculate that life on other distant planets may have developed in a similar pattern to that which has resulted in homo sapiens on earth. That being the case, there most certainly would be a species that is hierarchically equivalent to homo sapiens. Whatever they call themselves, "the people," "God's Children," "the Ones," when we meet, whatever our physical and psychological differences, we will be meeting spiritual sisters and brothers. Western science may gag on this thought and reject it as both unprovable and irrelevant. Some earth religions may find intolerable the thought that there is a spiritual equivalent to humankind that is not in the physical image of humankind. Both groups will have to work through their problems. From evidence in hand there is a diverse group of visiting others who have been interacting with humankind. Some have been described as having the appearance of giant insects, others as reptilian, and some as passable humans. I wonder how we are compared and described in their journals and data bases?

The point of this is the power of words when that is all someone has to create a mind image of an important future event. For fun and profit Hollywood has joined the game and given us a variety of images, some cute, some ugly, some frightening, some reassuring. Does that reflect a known reality?

If we are into enemy making, and it appears that President Reagan was, who would you rather have as an enemy—a super intelligent human look-alike, or an equally brilliant erect reptile? That is an easy one to answer.

When the visiting others made their presence known on earth, an early obvious label applied to them was "alien." This carried several meanings: belonging to another place; strange; repugnant; an outsider, and finally a creature from outer space. (See The American Heritage Dictionary, 2nd College Edition, 1985)

The authors of the MJ-12 document introduced another term, Extraterrestrial Biological Entities (EBEs). This skirted the human/non- human issue. The term "creature" is suggestive of presumptive non-human origin, but in fact carries a tertiary dictionary meaning of "human being." The only precise term that would indicate a presumption of not being "human," would be to call them "non-human entities". However, even this term is vague. It could mean "non-earth human entities."

Why this discussion? It is important because of the earth's sad history of the treatment by one group of humans who were different (culturally, racially) than another group of humans. I cannot imagine what new experience we might have as the result of contact with non-earth cultures. It appears that we have already done it all, slavery, genocide, forced breeding, medical experiments, ethnic cleansing. I shuttered when a very well known UFO researcher who deals principally with female "abduction victims," said, "I wish they would just treat us as well as we treat each other."

I assume that we will get what we merit. In simple karmic terms it may well be pay back time for Earth cultures. Obviously some cultures will fair better than others, and in the end great lessons will have been learned. To take only one example, the U.S. Constitution is respected around the world by those countries and cultures who seek to establish a democratic form of government based upon a written document.

The origins of the U.S. Constitution may be seen in American state governments of the late 1770s and early 1780s, the Articles of Confederation, the Founding Father's knowledge of the works of ancient Greece and Rome, the political treatises of visionary writers of the 18th century European Enlightenment, and significantly through Benjamin Franklin's knowledge and contact with the Iroquois League, the Six Nations of Cayuga, Mohawk, Oneida, Onondaga, Seneca and Tuscaroras.

Earlier, in 1775, Thomas Jefferson in the Declaration of Independence, had yielded to economic and political expediency and edited out his reference on the abomination of slavery. However, in his litany of charges of injuries and usurpation's against King George, he wrote: "He has excited domestic Insurrections amongst us, and has endeavored to bring on the Inhabitants of our Frontiers, the merciless Indian Savages, whose known Rule of Warfare, is an undistinguished Destruction, of all Ages, Sexes and Conditions." Don't be confused by Jefferson's ringing declaration that "All men are created equal, that they are endowed by their Creator with certain unalienable Rights, that among these are Life, Liberty, and the Pursuit of Happiness." The purpose of the document was to rally as many colonists as he could while provoking a fight with England.

Later in Philadelphia, in 1778, our new Constitution addressed both the Blacks in slavery and Native Americans in ways that left no doubt about the status of their value as "humans." In Article One, Section 3, Apportionment of Representatives and census, it was determined that the number of representatives each state would be allowed would be based upon its population, "which will be determined by adding to the whole number of free persons, including those bound to service for a number of years and excluding Indians not taxed, and three fifths of all other persons." In other words, unless taxed, Indians were non-persons, and 'all other persons" (read Black slaves) were counted as 3/5 a person. Slaves and slavery were embarrassing words, not used in the Constitution until 1868, when after a civil war in which the economic issue of slavery was a major cause, the 14th Amendment stated that "Neither slavery nor involuntary servitude ... shall exist within the United States, or any place subject to their jurisdiction."

Every country has an abundance of warts and history of conduct that is edited out of classroom textbooks. While the United States abolished slavery, it came only after a war whose wounds still fester and people of different color eye each other uneasily, harboring deep feelings of rage, guilt, fear and want for closure. And slavery in hideous forms is currently found in many nations around the world. The United States apparently is still not ready to admit and make restitution for the failed government policy of genocide against Native Americans. Indeed, there are many lessons for all of us to be learned.

14

The
Papers

**Prof. George S. Robinson**

16

*George S. Robinson, D.C.L.*

Dr. Robinson is a graduate of Bowdoin College and holds an LL.B. from Virginia School of Law, and an LL.M. and Doctor of Civil Laws degrees from McGill University. He has served as legal counsel at the Smithsonian Institution, the Federal Aviation Administration, and the National Aeronautics and Space Administration. He is the author of over one hundred articles and books of space law, business, and space governance. He also teaches graduate courses in space commerce and space telecommunications at George Mason University and is in the International Institute of that institution.

# Homo Alterios Spatialis: A Transgenic Odyssey

*What basis can be found for legal regimes controlling Earth interactions with representatives of extraterrestrial civilizations? Can it be derived from the experiences of Earth-based jurisprudence, or is there a need for a totally unique framework? For twenty-five years Professor Robinson has been exploring these issues.*

Why am I here, representing the legal profession, perhaps the most conservative and, frequently, most hidebound profession? Because law, like a huge mirror held up against society at any one time, reflects values underlying all human activities in one aspect or another. Jurisprudence, the philosophy of law, touches upon and weaves throughout all other disciplines of humankind inquiry. It examines the most fundamental premises of those disciplines. That mirror of law will reflect the legal regimes that will cradle and balance the relationships when cosmic cultures meet, and finally determine to interact openly.

Roughly thirty years ago, I submitted my masters of law dissertation at McGill University's Institute of Air and Space Law in the graduate law faculty. The title was...is..."Jurisprudence For Man and His Extraterrestrial Counterpart in Space." It explored the tenets of law controlling the interactions between earth and indigent societies and potential representatives of extraterrestrial life forms, intelligent and otherwise, based upon extrapolated lessons from colonialism and socio-economic imperialism of our own civilizations. It examined the biological and sentient foundations of those interactive legal tenets, and explored the lessons to be derived from the study of cognitive dissonance in preparing earthkind attitudes for alien, intelligent life forms, including those already calling planet earth their home, such as porpoises, whales, and others of the cetacean family. It examined all aspects of natural law theory and positive law that would apply in establishing formal or legal principles and regimes for human interaction with all reasonably foreseeable types and levels of extraterrestrial life. The manuscript was never published. It was much too premature. It needs to be updated and published now. In fact, one of the reviewing law professors wrote in a slashing hand across his copy of my dissertation—"absolute nonsense!" The dissertation ultimately was accepted and, years later, even after I had received my doctoral degree on a dissertation dealing with constitutional law and extraterrestrial quarantine protocols, that very same law professor asked me to supervise his own doctoral dissertation on the biological basis of natural law theory. What goes around...

Twenty-five years ago, I was asked by a maverick law professor at George Washington University Law School to formulate and start a new elective course for third-year law students that explored the legal institutions likely to establish the formal relations between and among earth civilizations and extraterrestrial civilizations. It was to be a study based upon comparative methodology, with the form and substance being based upon my LL.M. and Doctor of Civil Law dissertations, as well as certain subsequent publications. Course lectures specifically excluded anyone trained in the law, except me. I gave the first lecture on the biochemistry of the law. Ensuing lectures included linguists, physicists, physical anthropologists, neurophysicists, mathematicians, paleontologists, comparative anatomists, and the like. The course, designed for 15 students, eventually attracted 170 students, most of whom ultimately submitted some incredibly brilliant research papers on legal regimes controlling human social interactions with representatives of extraterrestrial civilizations. The course lasted two years before the law school curriculum committee focussed on the content...and fainted, I am sure to the last member.

Surprisingly, or perhaps not so surprisingly, the National Aeronautics and Space Administration has contracted for numerous studies, conferences, symposia, and seminars dealing with the military, *ad infinitum*, impacts of established contact and interaction with extraterrestrial life. Boston University, Harvard Theological Seminary, Georgetown University, and many other such organizations/institutions have participated in these studies of so-called "soft" issues of human space activities. But these studies and related proceedings have been extraordinarily difficult, if not impossible, to locate and then extract from NASA, except, of course, for those dealing with the law applicable to outbound and back contamination risks in space activities.

Do I personally believe in the existence of sentient extraterrestrial life? Of course. As all chemists know, the creation of life is no more than a chemical evolution and the creation of life is the business of the universe(s). Now, putting that to rest, let me focus on what I believe is the most important, current resource for establishing the values that will subtend the legal regimes directing our interactions with our first universally recognized and accepted contact with extraterrestrial life. That resource and contact will in all likelihood continue to be with our own sons and daughters as they evolve from representatives of humans to representatives of human*kind*; from *homo sapiens sapiens* to *homo alterios spatialis*.

In thinking about today's remarks, the questions flitted across my mind, "What is a discussion of legal regimes regulating social orientation between different interstellar sentient beings without a touch of professional reticence? What is intellectual perversity without adversity? What is a cheshire cat without a grin?"

If one is willfully determined, or in the present instance disposed, to go counter to what is expected or desired by the public, or a representative portion of it, one must also expect varying degrees of adversity, often the stimuli of conviction. In reflecting upon the comparative virtues of juridical studies, Oliver Wendell Holmes once remarked that, "I can but envy the felicity of the generation to whom it is made so easy to see their subject as a whole. When I began, the law presented itself as a ragbag of details. It was not without anguish that one asked oneself whether the subject [of jurisprudence] was worthy of the interest of an intelligent man. One saw people whom one respected and admired leaving the study because they thought it narrowed the mind; for which they had the authority of Burke. It required blind faith—faith that could not yet find the formula of justification for itself."

Not so initially timid a person was the late Andrew G. Haley, an attorney who, in going even farther than many contemporary writers advocating adoption of human-oriented laws to space activities, strongly implored of his contemporaries the need to develop a totally unique framework within which humans could communicate and interact with potential sentient beings from other stellar derivatives. Unfortunately, Mr. Haley died before he could develop his concept of "metalaw," which rests as the restrained impetus of a plea, rather than the professed embodiment of matured logic from, say, Kant, Hegel, or Roscoe Pound. Haley, unlike the tailors and mechanics of the law, and quite like Descartes, skipped over attempts at reworking current legal concepts and spoke directly to the need for conceiving of, and cultivating, a new and objective jurisprudence to channel relations between and among humans and other sentient entities in an accurately observed space environment. Except for a couple of articles I published in 1969 and 1972, i.e., "Ecological foundations of Haley's metalaw" and then "Metalaw-prolegomena to quantification of *jus naturale*, Mr. Haley's endeavor remains significantly premature; primarily because of incapacity and not because of need. The basis of Haley's metalaw concept is what he referred to as the *Interstellar Golden Rule*, i.e., "do unto others (extraterrestrial life) as they would have you do unto them." This principal holds every bit as true for dealing with *homo alterios spatialis*, our human*kind* descendants existing long-duration or permanently in outer space habitats. And it is to this new "para species" I want to direct your attention for the preparation of legal regimes which could well accommodate great disparities in value systems of space inhabitants *other than* our own sons and daughters.

***********

In our present and measurably foreseeable cultures, even civilizations, driven in great part by the small and large engines of high technology, we see the resulting fruits of pessimism and negativism as almost intolerably bitter. Meddling, interfering, breaking down into component parts, and otherwise tampering with, are integral components of our evolutionary heritage. But we do have to live with, adjust to, and fine-tune the technology and consequent changes and destruction to our natural ecosystem that we and our ancestors have created for ourselves. And, looking forward through the murky evolutionary history leading from our common progenitors, it is clear we must continue to create technology for the benefit, or destruction, of our offspring as they stumble, grope, and metamorphose along their individual and collective paths into the future with the aid of our constantly evolving tools.

In the evolutionary context of biological diversity, humankind, like all other life-forms, is designed to disappear by virtue of the very processes that gave it life. We must also keep in mind, though, that no matter what beautiful creature may remain *potential* only because of *human* existence, humans collectively also are the hearth of creative energy that has taken us on our first footsteps toward human*kind* through the creation of technology; and now through the *integration* of that technology with our biology. And we also must live with our technology in a constructive and positive fashion for the benefit of exceedingly complex planetary civilizations...and those off-world civilizations that are beginning to spring from our minds, our loins, our earthly wombs.

This living with the creations, in turn, of our biotechnologically integrated intellects must be within a positive philosophic construct that gives meaningful direction to all societies or civilizations...on earth, in and beneath the oceans, and in outer space. Indeed, the implications of technology in the future and the survival of the species, of human*kind*, is infinitely more than just the "wind singing through the telegraph wires." Perhaps, as Loren Eisely envisaged for his *homo duplex,* the true creature composed of flesh and spirit will be *homo alterios spatialis*, the technology driven evolution of *homo sapiens sapiens* by the tools of *humankind's* own intellect...own hand.

Technology, flowing from and interacting with human biological evolution, makes the human occupation of near and deep space a very natural, biotechnological, evolutionary step. It reflects a basic biological principle that all biotic entities either are growing...or dying. Surely, humankind has not only "walked the knife-edge of extinction for untold years," but walks that line ever so much more delicately on the edge of its *own* technology. The unseen potential in what we have traditionally referred to as natural evolution, and now biotechnological evolution, has left *homo sapiens sapiens* with one eternal dictum; grow or die! It is the latency that lurks in all of us to be what has yet to be achieved. That reflection focuses not only on growth, itself, but the exciting business of the quality and shifting essences of growth. And the excitement is accentuated through an urgent sense of responsibility to pick up, pass along, to continue learning from the endless sacrifices and contributions of all the previous generations. This, indeed, becomes the essence of the biotechnological evolution of humankind, particularly as it moves more aggressively to occupy near and deep space.

Young and eager minds seem not to be encouraged to see themselves evolving from their biological predecessors...and building frighteningly new and perplexing future societies. They seem, instead, to respond Pavlovian to philosophic political drones who infect them with the so-called pessimism of immediate reality. Was Eisley really correct when he observed that "ideas for which millions yielded up their lives produce only bored yawns in a later generation?" Or do we really seek a community of knowledge and identity over the centuries, and after periods or moments of exhaustion and depression, we return to the "growing," the refining of that from which we only escaped momentarily? If a culture loses its driving, or even mischievous, risk-taking and curiosity...it dies. The seeking of a permanent, inward-turning solitude is, itself, not a permanent phenomenon.

Humankind's intellect may raise it sufficiently above its instinctive behavior to remove it from the survival benefits of nature, and subject it to all the horrors of a thinking and fearful collection of beings. Maintenance, biological maintenance, is not the sole or even principal purpose of organic life. Non-linear thinking into which many high-tech societies hopefully are evolving is certainly not for the pre-Copernican, linear thinkers. The evolution of humankind into near and ultimately deep space is not linear, of course. Never has been, and never will be.

But should the human movement into and occupation of near and deep space ever become, in fact, linear because of the very narrow and pressing requirements at some given time in the future, not only shall we miss the biological importance of a multiplex *groping evolution*, the sustaining fun and joy of it all will have slipped from the *meaning* of human life. The sum of our human and, indeed, humankind odyssey is a complex range of activities occurring all of the time...at any one nano-second and sequentially over what the average struggling individual may see only as drearily endless epochs of time. It is a very comprehensive, dynamic, and integrated process from the deepest abyss of the oceans through the molecular, atomic, and subatomic exchanges at earth's surface...right into outer space. The web of life shimmering into the continuum simply of changing and evolving...of a groping, but nevertheless directed, existence.

And, so, let's shift these considerations in the continuum from earth's surface to outer space where the ambience of human existence reflects its own special life-styles, with new-and-yet to-be-experienced, psychological and experiential perspectives. That uniqueness ought not be molded by technological fixes into those morphological, physiological, and emotional characteristics, of those mental attitudes with which most of us are only familiar as earth-sitters. We should use our technology to accommodate ourselves to that uniqueness...at least while in outer space. "When in Rome...," still seems abiding in this era of human biotechnological evolution and adjustment.

The social changes, personal interactions, confrontations, suasiveness, and consequent trans-social *newness* characterizing our current high-tech civilizations and individual participants may give a breath of fresh air to the positive sides of multiculturalism, homosexuality, and fundamental changes in male-female and family relationships. Add to these evolving values and lessons the never-ending changes wrought by technology to the very essence of the biological nature of being human, and we have a stunning inventory of humankind's raw material to seed the now accessible ecological niches of ocean floors, and of near and deep space. Such are the consequences of biotechnological integration for evolutionary purposes.

But what are the underlying spiritual and temporal values that drive us and pull us into these dispersal niches? What are the changes being wrought to the elemental "nature" of the human species through the expression of these values? When do we search systematically for the genesis of those values...from the great age of enlightenment to deep space? When will there be the intensive, and yet ecumenical, investigation to determine the impact of space-age technology, not only on human societies and civilizations, but on the individual human, as well?

A transgenic odyssey from the age of enlightenment to the space age might be defined, perhaps, as a peculiar, often unnerving, evolution of humankind by its own hand. But where did our species start that our evolved intellect could take us to near space, deep space, and other planets by our own hands...already? It took us over 3-1/2 billion years...but we are there. Now! And we came to this point from the physical evolution of our brains and their ever-increasing capabilities through the application of our collective brains, along with the evolution of our supporting biological structures and chemistry. It all started from, perhaps, a pond, a place of low life, of reek and corruption, of fetid smells. Things floundered and died in the fat, warm mud. It was indeed a place of low life. In it, the human brain began. Or, as Langdon Smith, an American journalist of the 1800's might have viewed a slightly more advanced point in human evolution,

> "[W]hen you were a tadpole and I was a fish in Paleozoic time,
>    and side by side in the sluggish tide
>    we sprawled in the ooze and slime."

Keeping in mind this very real element of our intellectual heritage, we truly must contemplate from our current evolutionary posture how quickly we have arrived at birthing from the womb of earth into near and deep space. How quickly our evolved biology and consequent technology may well have wrested our future from the hands of our creator. How quickly it has placed the destiny and survivability of our species for the first time directly in our own hands through the application of technology to cybernetics, biotic and abiotic organ replacement, as well as genetic and other cellular organelle and systems manipulations using direct pharmaceutical, surgical, and biological interventions.

Clearly, our sciences and technologies have become integral components of our biological evolution...and nowhere, perhaps, is this more apparent than in our drive to expand the ecotone of *homo sapiens sapiens*, and its altered descendants, off earth and to establish habitats in near and deep space. Nowhere is it more clear that, as Leo Tolstoy premised, we must protect the spirit so humankind does not reverse its essence, as reflected by or through natural law rights, and become the mere extension of its technology; a technology that has become the only instrument of species mutation in the history of humankind that we can actually observe and manipulate to our benefit...or detriment.

In space, our activities reflect a survival-oriented widening of that human ecosystem; the seed dispersal principle of biology in action. And in the process, through the use of surgical, pharmaceutical, and biotechnological intervention for the purposes of enhancing survivability and quality of human and humankind life in space, we may be evolving a new variation of the human species who, or which, are not 100% biologically responsive to human values that have been institutionalized in earth-indigent laws and legal regimes.

All of these possibilities, and perhaps probabilities, illuminate the awesome responsibility which the present guardians and shapers of human evolutionary values must face in our stabilization of planet earth, and our unfolding occupation of outer space. It is a call to adventure, both physical and moral. It is the recognition and acceptance of an unfolding of what is truly human and what its relevance is to the rights of humankind. It is the recognition and acceptance that the nature, the very essence, of humankind is the foundation or genesis from which all pragmatic decisions and policies about the direction of scientific research and applied technology flow.

Now, let's look at the natural law foundations of positive laws in space. Only comparatively recently has the world public developed an inkling that lawyers and jurists already have invaded outer space, dragging along with them both traditional laws of commerce and the comparatively exotic public treaties spelling out basic rules for using and otherwise occupying space. Although criminal laws applicable to human activities in space have been passed by the United States Congress, as well as by certain governments of other spacefaring nations, they really are only stop-gap measures that extend familiar principles of earth-indigent laws into the realm of space activities.

Nowhere, though, in all of these domestic laws and international treaties, is there a definitive embracing of the rights and freedoms of humans and their humankind descendants who are living in, occupying, or otherwise existing in a space environment. Nowhere is the global guardianship role of these rights and freedoms specifically stated. And nowhere is there an ecumenical, clear, and deep recognition of the need for principles of social order in a truly unique physical and psychological environment where human biology and technology are totally integrated for survival in a fashion and for purposes having no equal. Not in the mission rules of manned activities to date, nor in the mission rules for the various ocean floor habitat programs. There is no space law, for example, that incorporates a definitive bill of humankind rights to "extinguish," as James Madison spoke over 200 years ago, "from the bosom of every member of the community any apprehension that there are those among his countrymen who wish to deprive them of the liberty for which they valiantly fought and honorably bled."

Space is not just another place, as our military servants and strategists would have us believe. An arena for the ongoing exercise of recognized, and also yet-to-be-perceived, basic rights of humankind is still a shifting and shapeless forum. Not much interest, until relatively recently, has been attracted around the world in having our off-earth, space habitat participants and envoys of humankind carry such individual and social values with them into space as the freedom to exercise religious beliefs, free speech, peaceable assembly, and the right to petition the government for redress of a grievance; to be free from unreasonable search and seizure, and not to be subject to double jeopardy and self-incrimination; not to be subject to cruel and unusual punishment (and what those terms really mean in a totally synthetic and alien life support environment of a space habitat); and to enjoy the right not to be enslaved, as well as to retain all of those basic humankind rights and freedoms not specifically surrendered by the governed. The rights and freedoms applying to interaction with potential extraterrestrial life-forms (intelligent and otherwise) has only been addressed in the mission rules pertaining to planetary protection and quarantine protocols.

Humankind rights that flow simply from birth, if not conception, are given intellectual form through something we call *natural law theory* and protective constitutions or charters of implementing positive laws. Although tomes have been written over the ages about *natural law*, the essence of the theory is that each individual has certain innate rights by virtue of biological birth. These rights exist regardless of municipal or other transitory *positive laws*; unless they are repealed or suspended by proper and legal order...two very ephemeral qualifiers.

Learned dissertations have defined *natural law theory* as reflective of an abstract concept that is somehow in accord with the *nature* of man. It consists of rules or principles that are protective of certain rights that so necessarily agree with the "nature and state of man" that, without observing its maxims, the peace and happiness of society can never be observed. They have somewhat arcanely been referred to as those "fit and just rules of conduct which the creator has prescribed to man, as a dependent and social being; and which are to be ascertained from the deductions of right reason, though they may be more precisely known, and more explicitly declared by divine revelation."

Surely, in the present age, we can be less theologically esoteric than to define the inherent essence and rights of humankind in these amorphous, warm, and shimmering terms. This is a classic example of defining a word or concept by using the word or concept to define. What does it really mean to say that a right embraced by natural law includes a right which "in its primary and strictest sense, belongs to each person as a human being in a state of nature?" What is a "state of nature?" Is it an absence of technology so that you have no natural right to any, say, available life-support systems?

23

If technology is the result of socio-biological evolution, and natural law rights embrace those which depend upon interaction with other humans, then surely natural law rights apply to access to all socio-biological technology. Does it include the right to self-defense...a right that existed before the formation of society? For U.S. citizens, is it only the rights actually set forth in the U.S. Constitution...specifically, the bill of rights? Is it a right entitled to protection *in addition* to those rights protected under the specific guaranty of safeguarding a person in his or her or its life, liberty, or the pursuit of happiness; for example, the guaranteed right of affection between parent and child, or the right to beget children, or the right to love and be loved, or the right to have adequate and sustaining nourishment...and no more?

Must natural law rights always remain concepts in the abstract, separate and apart from specific rights articulated as positive law in the U.S. constitution and the even more creative charters of other democratic nations? Are they rights that can never be articulated precisely and definitively without each fact situation, such as what constitutes "common decency," the right to "integrity," "respect," "self-worth," and the like?

Since the natural world is completely indifferent to human morality, and since religion is often thought to be the repository of man's unsuccessful attempt to define and delimit his natural world, seen or unseen, at any one time, is it possible that natural law theory rests upon the *known* of the biophysical laws of nature, rather than the dictates of "divine direction?" If so, then we can move the endlessly unproductive contentiousness of morality and ethic from our investigations of the true nature or essence of humankind...the individual and the society.

Surely, nature is never so without light and in deepest secrecy that the most patient of curious minds will not prevail, step by painful step. As so aptly observed by Loren Eisely, that most creative of nature's poets, curiosity is every bit a part of the natural world that it seeks to know, to embrace, to find refuge in...like the "swarming cells of our own being, which toil for something, some entity beyond their grasp...man, the self-fabricator, is so by reason of gifts he had no part in devising—and so he searches as the single living cell in the beginning must have sought the ghastly creature it was to serve."

Would Gaia, gentle mother earth, have the necessary patience to accommodate this crudest of a beloved progeny's learning process?

But humankind now has the most rudimentary of tools to participate in what it is *becoming,* a gift denied in the original creation and succeeding evolutionary stages. In addition to the previously mentioned synthetic alterations to individual humans, as well as genetic structures that are sexually transferred to succeeding generations, thereby changing the "natural" *essence* of that segment of humankind, we are having to reconsider the traditional definition of "life," and what its characteristics are. In addition to organ modifications and transplants, genetic manipulation of ova and sperm, and wholesale surgical, pharmaceutical, and biologically-engineered changes to an individual's brainstem, we have to consider the integration of artificial intelligence, biology, and evolutionarily replicative computer programs as possible life-forms of intelligence, which also may have humankind rights. And is the existence of a "soul," with all of the attendant theological implications, really the determinative factor? Do "cyborgs" have rights? If so, do they or their caretakers have standing to sue for those rights? These types of entities are apt, in the long run, to be our envoys of humankind in the permanent occupation of near and deep space.

24      The possibility, or probability, of a substantially altered human specimen with all of these synthetically induced characteristics for survival and asexual replication, and their impact on the components of what we think of as "natural law" rights and human nature, may be much nearer reality than most of us care to believe.

It should be clear by now that the principle point I have been trying to make is that the manner in which we establish our formal relations with our biotechnologically integrated descendants within a legal framework could well provide a template structure and applicable lessons for interacting with whom we have heretofore always assumed were the true extraterrestrials. In short, earthkind may well be the common progenitor of the participants when cosmic cultures meet.

Now perhaps, just perhaps, the positive side to all of this is that we are learning how to cope and survive in a genuinely meaningful fashion in synthetic life-support environments *and our own biotechnologically evolving species* that will broaden the physical range of our species and its evolved descendants in a completely synthetic and earth-alien life support system.

Perhaps we are involved right now in the preparation of the species' progeny for survival in a totally new medium. Yes, perhaps the cervix, heretofore unknown to us, does surprisingly dilate and deliver the mature foetus from an otherwise toxic and deadly uterine ambience into a new world...a new existence.

If we are either to identify the so-called "natural law" rights of humankind living in space, or, more appropriately, lay a structured foundation whereby humankind in space (*homo alterios spatialis*) can evolve its own sense of those rights without their imposition by earth-sitters, alone, these are among the questions and issues that must be raised and pursued to prepare us for when cosmic cultures intentionally and knowingly meet and interact. Toward this end, then, there must be a *declaration of spacekind independence*, and then a *declaration of interdependence between and among earthkind and spacekind*...starting with, but not limited to, our own sons and daughters...the progenitors of *homo alterios spatialis*.

But then, maybe all of this serves a different objective or goal simple survival of a species on planet Earth. Perhaps, just perhaps, the positive side is that we are learning how to cope and survive in a genuinely meaningful fashion in synthetic life support environments that will the physical range of our species and its evolved descendants in a completely synthetic and Earth-alien life support system. Perhaps we are involved in preparing the species progeny in a totally new medium. Yes, perhaps the cervix does dilate and deliver the mature foetus from an otherwise deadly toxic ambiance into a new world.

If we are either to identify the so-called natural law rights of humankind living in space, or more appropriately, lay a structured foundation whereby humankind in space (*homo alterios spatialis*), can evolve its own sense of those rights without their imposition by Earth-sitters, alone, these are among the questions and issues that must be raised and pursued. Toward this end, then, the ensuing **Declaration of Interdependence Between and Among Earthkind and Spacekind** is offered as a template for future consideration and study.

# DECLARATION GOVERNING INTERDEPENDENCE AMONG EARTHKIND AND SPACEKIND

Signatories of this Declaration of Interdependence, encouraged by the increasing international commitment of valuable resources to the advancement of human occupation and exploitation of space, and inspired by long-duration human occupation of near-Earth orbit habitats and planned LunarPort facilities, and

Recognizing the empirical distinctions between value-forming processes of human*kind* functioning in an Earth-indigenous environment and those occurring in a biotechnologically integrated, alien, and synthetic life-support system in interstitial space or on an off-Earth habitat; and

Believing that exploration, exploitation, and occupation of near and deep space by human*kind*, hereinafter "Spacekind' while physically in space or on Earth's surface and still under the influence of space existence factors, should be conducted with a recognition and understanding of the breadth of biological variations upon which human*kind's* cultures are premised; and

Desiring to contribute to the unfolding knowledge of human*kind* values and behavior patterns reflected in the broad spectra of personal and social relationships encountered while occupying near and deep space; and

Believing that such recognition and understanding of the distinguishing biotechnological underpinnings of human*kind* activities in space will contribute to, and help strengthen, compatible relations among human*kind*, particularly Spacekind and Earthkind, and civilizations on Earth, as well as in space; and

Recalling the Treaty on Principles Governing the Activities of States in the Exploration and Use of Outer Space, Including the Moon and Other Celestial Bodies I signed at Washington, London, and Moscow of 27 January 1967 and entered into force 10 October 1967; The Convention on International Liability for Damage Caused by Space Objects (1972); and The Convention on Registration of Objects Launched into Outer Space (1975); and

Taking into particular account the United Nations Agreement on the Rescue of Astronauts, the Return of Astronauts, and the Return of objects Launched into Outer Space, as well as the many and several international agreements recognizing the transnational rights of all humankind under Natural Law Theory; and

Believing that recognition, understanding, and awareness of the biological and biotechnological foundations of humankind value-forming processes, judgments, and activities on Earth and in outer space will contribute to, and help strengthen, compatible relations among nations, cultures, and humankind representatives regardless of their locations in the Solar System; and

Embracing the interdependence of human*kind's*—current biotechnological, economic, and political evolution into Earthkind and Spacekind; and

Being convinced that a Declaration of Interdependence espousing basic principles governing the conduct of long-duration and permanent inhabitants of outer space, including on the surface of Earth while such inhabitants remain under the influence of Earth-alien life-support factors, will further the essential transitioning of Earthkind as a representative culture from an Earth indigenous environment to one reflecting the uniqueness of outer space existence that is Spacekind, and the interdependence of both in fulfilling an extraterrestrial biological imperative of *Homo sapiens sapiens into Homo alterios spatialis*;

NOW THEREFORE, the Signatories to this Declaration of Interdependence have agreed to the Articles as hereinafter set forth.

## ARTICLE I

The exploration and use of outer space, including all celestial bodies accessible by human*kind*, shall be carried out for the benefit and in the interests not only of Earth inhabitants, who shall be called Earthkind, but also of human*kind* inhabitants of outer space, who shall be called Spacekind. Such areas of habitation shall be considered the province of Spacekind in the first instance, and of Earthkind in the second. There shall be free access by Earthkind and Spacekind to all areas of outer space and celestial bodies, consistent with the best interests of the economic, social, psychological, and physical well-being of Spacekind and their habitats, and regardless of their political or Earth-sovereign origins.

## ARTICLE II

Space habitats, including orbiting platforms and those existing on or beneath the surface of non-Earth celestial bodies, shall not be subject to claims of national sovereignty or citizenship deriving from or exercised by nation states or regional jurisdictions located or originating on Earth. Spacekind occupying such habitats shall exercise independent cultural political sovereignty and in no manner whatsoever shall space habitat sovereignty or inhabitant citizenship be related to any territory or geographical boundaries on Earth. Subject to certain provisions set forth below relating to jurisdictional transitions between space habitats and Earth, the conduct and activities of Earth-space-Earth travel shall be subject to the Outer Space Treaty of 1967, the Agreement on the Rescue of Astronauts, the Return of Astronauts, and the Return of Objects Launched into Outer Space, the Convention on Registration of Objects Launched into outer space, and all other applicable international, transnational, and space law provisions.

## ARTICLE III

Signatories to this Declaration of Interdependence shall conduct their relations among each other and severally and collectively with Spacekind in a manner consistent with all applicable international and transnational law, including the Charter of the United Nations and dependent treaties and conventions, or any successor organization of the United Nations or appropriate dependent organizations, and consistent with developing law among Spacekind, in the interest of maintaining peace, security, and the economic welfare of Earthkind and Spacekind, and promoting cooperation and understanding, not only among Earth cultures, but also between Earth cultures and cultures unique to space.

## ARTICLE IV

The use of military personnel for non-hostile and peaceful scientific research requiring interaction with space habitats and their inhabitants shall not be prohibited: *Provided*, however, that there shall be no bilateral or regional military relationships or alliances whatsoever established between any one or more signatories to this Declaration of Interdependence and any space habitat and its inhabitants. A military alliance may be established between space habitat communities and the United Nations or its successor organization only for the protection of Earthkind or Spacekind against threats of hostile actions originating from cultures, civilizations, or political entities not Signatories hereto.

## Article V

Signatories hereto shall regard Spacekind as envoys of a culture or civilization different from those of Earthkind. In the event of accident, distress, emergency landing on the territory of any Signatory hereto, on the High Seas of Earth, or on any other celestial body, or in the event of any unforeseen or fortuitous situations experienced by representatives of Spacekind on Earth or in space, all reasonable steps shall be undertaken by Signatories to this Declaration of Interdependence to assist such representatives and return them to appropriate authorities and jurisdictions on Earth or in space.

Signatories to this Declaration shall inform immediately the other Signatories hereto of any phenomena they discover in space or on the surface of Earth which could constitute a danger to the life or welfare of representatives both of Earthkind or of Spacekind.

## Article VI

Each Signatory hereto shall bear international, transnational and interspace responsibility for its own national activities in space that may adversely affect any space habitat or Spacekind. All commercial activities shall be conducted in strict accord with the Principles set forth herein. Regardless of whether such activities are carried out by governmental agencies or non-governmental entities, each Signatory to this Declaration of Interdependence shall assure severally that such national or regional activities in space in which its is involved are conducted in conformity with existing international, transnational, and prevailing space law, including the various applicable provisions set forth herein. When activities which substantially affect the socio-political and cultural will of Spacekind are conducted in space by an Earth-indigenous international organization, responsibility for compliance with this Declaration shall be borne both by the international Signatory organization and/or by the individual Signatories that are participating members of such organization.

## Article VII

In the conduct of all space-related activities directly involving space habitats and Spacekind, Signatories to this Declaration of Interdependence shall be guided by the principles of cooperation and mutual assistance, and shall temper their relationships with due regard for protecting the cultural uniqueness of Spacekind.

Signatories hereto shall pursue space research, exploration, and exploitation in such a manner as to avoid harmful interference to and adverse changes in the ecosystems and cultural integrity of Spacekind habitats which might be caused by the introduction of harmful alien material, or the imposition of harmful alien cultural characteristics that are not consistent with individual freedoms and cultural uniqueness of said habitat societies. The interdependence of Earthkind and Spacekind shall always be embraced and evolved in the context of the Haley Interstellar Golden Rule.

If a Signatory to this Declaration has any reason to believe that an activity or experiment, planned by it or its nationals or those under its legal jurisdiction, in space might cause potentially harmful interference with space habitats or Spacekind cultures, it *shall* undertake immediate and effective international and transnational consultations among other Signatories hereto, as well as with the Spacekind cultures that may be affected by such activity or experiment. Any Signatory to this Declaration of Interdependence may demand reasonable consultation with any other Signatory hereto and any Spacekind community regarding an activity or experiment suspected of being potentially harmful to Earth, the space community, or to Earthkind or Spacekind, generally.

## Article VIII

In order to ensure the integrity of the peaceful purposes and intents embodied in this Declaration of Interdependence, all Signatories hereto that establish space habitats of a long-duration or a permanent nature shall establish them in such a manner that they shall be open for cultural examinations and military investigation by representatives of other Signatories to this Declaration on the basis of reciprocity. Such examination and investigation shall not occur as a matter of right hereunder beyond the second generation of Spacekind born to any subject space habitat community. Signatories hereto shall give the subject space habitat community and its founding state Signatory hereto reasonable advance notice of any examination or investigation, or attendant visit, to the space habitat community, in order that appropriate consultations may be held and that maximum precaution may be taken to assure safety and to avoid unnecessary interference with normal operations of the community or culture to be examined, investigated, or visited.

## Article IX

Signatories to this Declaration of Interdependence agree that there shall be established an expert organization, under the aegis of the United Nations or its successor entity, to be called the International organization for Spacekind Cultures (IOSC). The principle purposes of this organization, to be established under separate charter, are threefold: (1) Provide an interdisciplinary, international, and transnational body of recognized experts to review on a continuing basis all aspects of interactive relationships between and among Earthkind and Spacekind that occur either in space or on Earth; (2) grant international agreements of recognition and capacity (IARCS) to those space communities that satisfy the requisites for home rule established by the IOSC and consistent with the applicable provisions of the Smithsonian Institution's Declaration of First Principles for the Governance of Outer Space Societies (1987); and (3) refer case situations to the International Court of Justice and any correspondent or successor court of transnational law wherein the propriety and predictable compatibility of such interactive relationships are at issue among expert representatives of Signatories to this Declaration of Interdependence, as well as those representing outer space cultures and Spacekind. The ICSC shall serve as the sole expert advisory body to the Court in such matters.

# A SPACEKIND DECLARATION OF INDEPENDENCE

It may well be that humankind offspring and descendants of Earthkind who live or otherwise exist in space, indeed, any sentient life form in space regardless of its origin, will be forced to declare independence from Earthkind before establishing a legal regime that reflects the reality of interdependence. Such a declaration of independence might well characterize the initial relationship between Earthkind and *any* form of sentient extraterrestrial life. But, still, it is humankind that begins to help us formulate our legal relationships with extraterrestrials.

IN REPRESENTATIVE ASSEMBLY OF SPACEKIND
THE UNANIMOUS DECLARATION OF THE COMMUNITIES OF SPACEKIND
Recognizing the distinction between thought processes that occur in space and those that respond to the influences of inhabiting Earth's surface;

Believing that the habitation of space should be characterized by the full expression of the limitless varieties of human-related and other cultures;

Believing that an accurate understanding of the biological foundations of value-forming processes in a space environment will contribute substantially to lessening the fruitless competition and violent conflicts among Earth civilizations and in interactions with Spacekind;

Desiring to elevate the evolution of *Homo sapiens* to its next logical stage,

Be it therefore DECLARED:

WHEN IN THE COURSE OF HUMAN AND HUMAN*KIND* EVOLUTION it becomes necessary for progeny of succeeding generations to dissolve the political and biological bonds that have connected them with their progenitors, and to assume among the powers of the Solar System, and indeed the Universe, the separate and equal station to which the Laws of Nature and their Creator entitle them, a decent respect for the opinions of Earthkind requires that they should declare the causes which impel them to their separation into Spacekind....

..We hold these truths to be self-evident, that Earthkind and Spacekind are created equal to their own respective environments, that once having been raised above their biological origins to a recognizable level of sentiency and sapiency they are endowed by their Creator with certain inalienable rights, and that among these rights are survival, freedom of thought and expression, and the evolution of individual and community knowledge. That to secure these rights, governments are instituted among sentient beings, deriving their reasonable and responsive powers from the consent of the governed and by protective inference from those life forms without the capacity to communicate interspecies. That when any form of govern becomes destructive of these ends, it is the right of the governed to alter or abolish it, and to institute a new set of values and political framework, laying its foundation on such principles and organizing its duties and authority in such form as to them shall seem most likely to effect both their physical safety and sense of well-being through cultural evolution. Prudence, indeed, will dictate that political, economic, and ideological traditions long established should not be changed for light and transient causes; and accordingly all experience has shown that Earthkind, and now Spacekind, are more disposed to suffer, while evils are sufferable, than to right themselves by abolishing or radically restructuring the forms to which they are accustomed. But when there occurs a long train of abuses, usurpations, and insensitivity to the needs of future generations evolving in a unique life-support environment, pursuing invariably the policies of colonial dependency and biological parochialism, it is their right, their obligation, to destroy such usurpations, insensitivities, and unresponsive institutions, and to provide new value standards that will ensure their security from abuses by progenitor cultures and governments of Earthkind. Such has been the sufferance of space community migrants who are now evolved to Spacekind, and who now of necessity are constrained to alter the existing foundations of relationships among Earthkind and Spacekind. The histories of governments and private enterprises in space development industries is a continuing history of injuries and usurpations, all having in direct object the maintenance of an absolute tyranny over space communities and Spacekind. To prove this, a list of grievances is unnecessary. A candid planet need only remind itself of the historical patterns of Earthkind when nations have pursued economic, ideological, and religious expansion into the less technologically developed continents and societies of Earth. The plea of this declaration is to break the cyclic violence, warfare, and destruction of civilizations which follow with certainty from the establishment of colonies. We have petitioned for redress in the most humble terms: Our repeated petitions have been answered only by repeated neglect. We have warned the governments and appropriate controlling interests of Earthkind from time to time of their determined insistence to extend their total jurisdiction over space communities and Spacekind functioning in an Earth-alien environment. We have reminded them of the circumstances of our emigration and settlement in space, and those of our predecessors. These warnings and reminders, too, have met with the deafness of prevailing justice and a failure to recognize the responsibilities of consanguinity in succeeding generations of Earthkind. We must therefore, denounce the causes and acquiesce in the necessity of our separation, and hold them, as we hold the rest of galactic intelligence, enemies in war; in peace, friends.

We, therefore, the representatives of space migrants, space communities, and Spacekind descendants of Earthkind, appealing to the Creator for the rectitude of our intentions, do, in the name and by the authority of Spacekind settled and living in space communities, solemnly publish and declare that these communities and their inhabitants are free and independent; that they are absolved from all allegiance to the governments and organizations of Earth; and that all political and ideological subservience of Spacekind to Earthkind is and ought to be totally dissolved; and that as free and independent communities of Spacekind they have full power to protect themselves, establish peaceful relations, contract commercial and defensive alliances, and to do all other acts and things which independent communities in space, as well as on Earth, may do. And for the support of this Declaration, with a firm reliance on the protection offered through the creative intent, we mutually pledge to each other our lives, our fortunes, and our sacred honor.

# ⊕ Michael Hesemann

*Michael Hesemann*

Michael Hesemann studied Cultural Anthropology and History at Göttinger University. Since 1984 he has published *Magazin 2000*. Currently it is published in German and Czech, and Dutch and English editions are in preparation. The magazine has a circulation of 60,000. His international best-sellers, *UFOs: The Evidence, UFOs: The Contacts, A Cosmic Connection* and *UFOs: A Secret Matter*, were published in 12 countries with more than 500,000 copies sold. He has produced several award-winning documentaries and worked for TV programs in Germany, Japan and in the United States. He has spoken at international conferences in 16 countries on four continents and at the United Nations.

# Man's Greatest Challenge

## Ways and implications of a contact with extraterrestrial civilizations

*Over the years it has been the judgment of government and non-government experts that a sudden discovery of the existence of extraterrestrial intelligence would cause great disruption to individuals and institutions. That opinion nominates a strategy of gradual education of the greater cosmic reality. Some would say it is already under way. Cultural anthropologist Michael Hesemann discusses ways and implication of contact with extraterrestrial civilizations.*

Is there any possibility that "they" are already here? Yes, there is. Did anybody try to estimate the consequences of their presence? Surely. Being prepared for everything is the job of our military and intelligence, even for a hypothetical situation. And even if we deal with just a hypothetical situation—that behind the UFO phenomenon might be an alien presence—it is a fine scenario for our conference debate. So let's face the facts.

In the last years we experienced an amazing opening in the question of UFOs—Unidentified Flying Objects. The Ministries or Departments of Defense of several European countries, Belgium, Russia, Spain, France, England, Italy and Switzerland, released their files and made positive public statements on the existence of UFOs, although admitting that they cannot answer the 20-million-dollar-question: "Where do they come from?" In their last session the European Parliament discussed the installation of an European UFO reporting center in cooperation with the French Space Agency which already has its UFO-office, formerly GEPAN, now called SEPRA. Unfortunately under pressure of ridicule by the media, the E.P. representative Prof. Tullio Regge, who, after careful study, had recommended the UFO office, withdrew his recommendation in January 1994.[1]

To give you just one example of the thousands and thousands of impressive reports by competent observers let me quote Astronaut Colonel Gordon Cooper who on July 14, 1978, participated in an internal conference with Secretary General Kurt Waldheim and on November 5, 1978, sent an official letter to Grenada's Mission at the United Nations, stating: "I believe that these extraterrestrial vehicles and their crews are visiting this planet from other planets, which obviously are a little more technically advanced than we are here on Earth. I feel that we need to have a top level, coordinated program to scientifically collect and analyze data from all over the Earth concerning any type of encounter, and to determine how to interface with these visitors in a friendly fashion. We may first have to show them that we have learned to resolve our problems by peaceful means, rather than warfare, before we are accepted as fully qualified universal team members. This acceptance would have tremendous possibilities of advancing our world in all areas."[2]

When I interviewed Colonel Cooper in December 1993, he told me about his UFO encounters in Germany in 1951, and at the Edwards Air Force Base, California, in 1957.

At least some nation's Air Forces appear to be well informed about UFOs and their occupants. The US Air Force Academy Textbook in Physics, "Introductory Space Sciences" (1969), concludes that a closer look at the UFO situation "leaves us with the unpleasant possibility of alien visitors to our planet" and that "data suggest the existence of at least three and maybe four different groups of aliens (possibly at different stages of development)."

"The most commonly described alien is about three and one-half feet tall, has a round head (helmet?), arms reaching to or below his knees, and is wearing a silvery space suit or coveralls. Other aliens appear to be essentially the same as Earthmen, while still others have particularly wide (wrap around) eyes and mouths with very thin lips. And there is a rare group reported as about four feet tall, weight of around 35 pounds... described as being extremely strong."

The textbook gives four reasons to explain a lack of contact: "1. We may be the object of intensive sociological and psychological study. In such studies you usually avoid disturbing the test subject's environment. 2. You do not "contact" a colony of ants, and humans may seem that way to any aliens. (Variation: A zoo is fun to visit, but you don't "contact" the lizards). 3. Such contact may have already taken place secretly. 4. such contact may have already taken place on a different plane of awareness and we are not yet sensitive to communications on such a plane." "Besides the foregoing reasons," the textbook adds, "contacting humans is downright dangerous," adding the admission: "We too have fired on UFOs."[3]

That UFOs indeed played an important role for the Super Powers is clearly demonstrated by the thousands of official documents released in the past. In 1991 the Soviet KGB released to Air Force General Pavel Popovich 124 pages of UFO-documents about 17 incidents that took place in the 1980's. The most interesting case happened in Kapustin Yar, the Russian atomic weapon testing ground near the Caspian Sea. In July 1989, a UFO was observed by eight security guards hovering for two hours over an atomic weapon storage arsenal.[4] A similar incident happened at August 11, 1980, in the Coyote Canyon Atomic Weapon Storage Areas in New Mexico, when a security guard discovered behind an alarmed structure "a round disc shaped object. He attempted to radio for a back up patrol but his radio would not work. As he approached the object on foot armed with a shotgun, the object took off in a vertical direction at a high rate of speed."[5]

The obvious interest of UFOs in atomic weapon storage areas and atomic testing is documented as early as 1949 when in Project Sign U.S. Air Force UFO investigators spoke about the possibility that UFOs are "Space Ships" which "might observe that on Earth we now have atomic bombs and are fast developing rockets. In views of the past history of mankind, they should be alarmed."[6]

In 1969 Prof. Lambros Callimahos of the U. S. National Security Agency concluded in a working paper "UFO Hypothesis and Survival Questions":

"Some UFOs are related to extraterrestrial intelligences. According to some eminent scientists closely associated with the study of this phenomenon, this hypothesis cannot be disregarded. This hypothesis contains a number of far reaching human survival implications.

If they discover us, it is an old but hardly invalid rule of thumb, they are our technologically superiors. Human history has shown us time and again the tragic results of a confrontation between a technologically superior civilization and a technologically inferior civilization. The inferior is usually subject to physical conquest.

Often in the past a technologically superior people are also possessors of a more virile and aggressive culture. In a confrontation between two peoples of significantly different cultural levels, those having the inferior or less virile culture, most often suffer a tragic loss of identity and are usually absorbed by the other people.

Some peoples who are technologically and/or culturally inferior have survived—have maintained the identity and have equalized the differences. The Japanese people have given us an excellent example of the methods required to achieve such a survival:

...full and honest acceptance of the nature of the inferiorities separating you from the advantages of the other peoples

...complete national solidarity in all positions taken in dealing with the other culture

...highly controlled and limited intercourse with the other side...

...a correct but friendly attitude toward the other people

...a national eagerness to learn everything possible about the other culture —its technological and cultural strengths and weaknesses. This often involves sending selected groups and individuals to the other's country to become one of his kind or even to help him in his wars against other adversaries...

...adopting as many of the advantages of the opposing people as you can, and doing it as fast as possible —while still protecting your own identity by molding each new knowledge increment into your own cultural cast.

...It would seem a little more of this survival attitude is called for in dealing with the UFO problem."[7]

In 1961, a study prepared for NASA by the Brookings Institution was reprinted for the Committee on Science and Astronautics of the U.S. House of Representatives. Entitled "Proposed Studies on the Implications if Peaceful Space Activities for Human Affairs," Margaret Mead was quoted in a section titled "The implications of a discovery of extraterrestrial life:" "Anthropological files contain many examples of societies, sure of their place in the Universe, which have disintegrated when they had to associate with previously unfamiliar societies espousing different ideas and life ways; others that survived such an experience usually did so by paying the price of changes in values and attitudes and behavior." That's why the study recommends "historical and empirical studies of the behavior of peoples and their leaders when confronted with dramatic and unfamiliar changes or social pressures. Such studies might help to provide programs for meeting and adjusting to the implications of such a discovery. Question one might wish to answer by such studies would include: How might such information, under what circumstances, be presented or withheld from the public for what ends?"[8]

Considerable attention to extraterrestrial contact has been given by the manager of the former NASA SETI project. In preparation for SETI, three international conferences were held in Bangalore (1985), Innsbruck (1986) and Brighton (1987) to discuss the consequences of the hypothetical discovery of radio signals of a cosmic culture and prepare the "SETI Post Detection Protocol." The discussed dynamics are similar to the ones following a direct meeting with an extraterrestrial intelligence. "The discovery of an ET signal will be a profound event in human history," two of the speakers of these SETI-congresses, J.M.Logsdon and C.M. Anderson of the George Washington University declared, "Procedures for announcing to the world that such a signal has been detected and verified should be developed with probable global impacts of that announcement in mind. There almost certainly will be an intense reaction in many sectors of society in many countries. Questions of perceived security threats are likely to arise. There will be political, social and philosophical impacts on key institutions: the church, policy, the media, and cultural, scientific and intellectual organizations. The general public will certainly seek explanations, and various elites are likely to compete in providing such explanations."[9]

Prof. Allen Tough, University of Toronto, has stated that a cover-up of such a discovery might be recommended because of "seven factors" including "the belief people may panic, the fear of a negative

34

impact on religion, science and culture, embarrassment, the individual and national competitive urge, avoiding a harmful premature reply, a national trade or military advantage; and the fear of a "Trojan Horse" ... (that) an alien race—under the guise of teaching and helping us join the cosmic community might actually trick us into building devices that allow "Them" to conquer "Us"... (T)he government of a nation in which a signal is received might also worry about the longer-term effects on the culture and economy of that nation and to the whole world... they might believe and fear that religion, philosophy and science would ... be ruined, outmoded, or at least demoralized. Current technology, such as transportation and space exploration, could be superseded; many jobs and the economy could be disrupted. In general, a culture can suffer from contact with a stronger and more advanced culture."[10]

The same problem was faced by the Italian sociologist Dr. Roberto Pinotti of the Instituto Futuro, Florence. For him "the problem of mass-behavior after man's future contacts with other intelligences in the universe is not only a challenge for social scientists and political leaders all over the world, but also a cultural time-bomb as well. In fact, since the impact of CETI (Contact with ETI) on human civilization, with its different cultures, might cause a serious socio-anthropological shock, a common and predetermined worldwide strategy is necessary in releasing the news after the contact, in order to keep possible manifestations of fear, panic and hysteria under control...

The modern world is proud of its achievements. In spite of the fact Copernicus showed that the Earth was not the center of the Universe, man has continued to believe that even though he was not geographically in the center of the Universe, he is central in essence. This common belief would be shattered by the presence of ETI, even though there would be no evidence that the alien culture might be malevolent, and the masses would be swept into a state of fear."[11]

Indeed the famous Swiss psychoanalyst Carl-Gustav Jung came to the same conclusion in 1954, when he wrote in his article *About Flying Saucers* in the Zurich *Weltwoche*: "Should the phenomenon... turn out to be of extraterrestrial origin it would prove an intelligent, interplanetary connection. It cannot be foreseen what such a fact would mean for mankind. But without a doubt it would bring us into a most critical situation, comparable with that of a primitive tribal society confronted with our superior western culture... we would loose control, and we would, as an old medicine man once told me with tears in his eyes, 'loose our dreams. . .' Our intellectual high-fly would be hopelessly anticipated and thereby paralyzed. In the first line of course our science and technology would move into the slumber-room. The moral meaning of such a catastrophe can be determined by the tragic end of primitive cultures happening in front of our eyes." [12]

This would indeed be the result of what cultural anthropology calls "culture shock"—the result of an unprepared confrontation of two entirely different cultures, causing what sociologist Alvin Toffler says would be "bewilderment, frustration and disorientation," leading to "the breakdown of communication, a misreading of reality, the inability to cope. Yet culture-shock is relatively mild in comparison with the much more serious malady, future shock. Future shock is the dizzying disorientation brought on by the premature arrival of the future,"[13] e.g. extreme changes in society.

Indeed sociologists explain the worldwide increase of civil wars and racist violence in our quickly changing world as results of a "future shock," causing the psychologically stabilizing recourse to old "values" like religious fundamentalism, tradition, family values and nationalism. The success of the Gingrichs and fundamentalist "born again Christians" in your country is a part of the same phenomenon. Behind it are disoriented people who cannot deal with the quick changes in our society and technology, who are superseded by their own time—indeed a "cultural time bomb" which can explode at any time and just did in Oklahoma.

Pinotti has observed: "In any case it is evident that our culture is in constant turmoil, with its values incessantly changing and a dominating sense of general disorientation, involving also the weakest, less intelligent and most irrational—and they are surely the majority—members of society... in this global situation the news of the existence of ETI could prove to be devastating. In fact at this particular moment what mankind needs is psychosociological balance and rules to follow. The unexpected super-imposition of a new and alien component—ETI—on todays critical world scene would cause what usually happens when the familiar psychological clues that help an individual to function in society are suddenly replaced by new ones that are strange and incomprehensible."[14]

One of these socio-psychological stabilizers is the belief in man's ability to master and control the future. Politics, five-years-plans, insurance policies, social security, investments, the stock market—all base on the concept of a safeguarding of the future. The encounter with an ETI would confront us with what might turn out to be the most important factor for our future—that turns out to be a great un-known, an undeterminable, uncontrollable factor. On a sociological scale this means a crisis of rules, values and authorities—the basics of security and the fundaments of every society. A global attempt of "breaking with the past" would make this CETI the most exciting and maybe dramatic event in human history, causing a sudden lack of rules or anomie, usually associated with the disintegration of social structures.

Surely a "revising process" would affect every field of human activity and thought in the light of what would be defined as "The Second Copernican Revolution." Science would be criticized, the Carl Sagans and Philip Klasses of our time would be ridiculed; "new philosophical schools and cults would arise, along with traumatic theological debates on all the churches and religions, the arts would be inspired while socio-economic structures as we know them today would be doomed," [15] as Pinotti predicts. The momentary crisis of ideologies would continue into a breakdown of political systems. Instead of these, two general attitudes would polarize: Those who develop a more global—"we, man-kind of planet Earth"-attitude—surely the more intellectual classes—and those who withdraw into the snails shell of their ethnic traditions, causing new "tribal wars" and ethnic conflicts, trying to save their cultural identity. This means an evident fragmentation of all multi-cultural socio-political structures, as the end of the communist ideology already foreshadowed in Yugoslavia and the former Soviet Union. Fundamentalist cults, declaring the "invaders" as manifestations of the devil, and offering their beliefs as the only salvation to the temptations from outside. Surely, our modern-day establishment has everything to lose from any form of sudden contact with ETI. It would be the first victim of this frontal collision... if it does not take the chance to let the knowledge about it slowly leak into our common consciousness.

The cause of mass panic, hysteria and anarchy is fear, and fear of the unknown, xenophobia, is caused by ignorance. Indeed people fear extraterrestrials. In 1986, Australian UFO researcher Mark Moravec evaluated the witnesses reactions in 46 cases of UFO sightings. Fear was the most common reaction (69.6 % of the cases), followed by curiosity (15.2%), amazement and amnesia (8.7 % each).[16] The same conclusion was drawn by Harvard astronomer Donald Menzel, who belonged to a high level presidential commission to deal with the UFO-phenomenon: "The public is afraid of saucers and we need only a match to set off a nationwide panic that could far exceed that of the 'Invasion from Mars,'"[17] Orson Welles' famous public broadcast in 1938. In 1952 a memorandum of the CIA Office of Scientific Intelligence came to the same conclusion: "Flying saucers pose two elements of danger which have national security implications. The first involves mass psychological considerations and the second concerns the vulnerability of the United States to air attack... (the CIA recommends) a policy of public information which will minimize concern and possible panic resulting from the numerous sightings of unidentified objects."[18]

Indeed, if we where discovered by ETI, our role would be a passive one, leading to frustration, demoralization and fear. As Pinotti formulates it, "We would feel like the castrated victims of this frontal collision of different cultures."[19] Zdenek Kopal defined this common fear at the XXI. IAF Congress in Brighton in 1970. "An advanced civilization might treat us like ants and put us in test tubes. Look what we have done to lower civilizations—and the way we treat animals,"[20] But since the appearance of the UFO phenomenon this "Damocles sword" is hanging over Earth, so we have to prepare and develop adequate measures to control the damage and—make the best out of it.

Some say "forewarned is forearmed," but I am afraid our best SDI program would be no more affective than arrows protecting a tribal society confronted with a modern army. So maybe a different, a peaceful approach is the only game we could win. And indeed the preparation for an alien contact might turn out to be the greatest challenge and chance in our history to create a better world at the threshold of the third millennium. Why? Because it may help us to find our true place in the Universe, our common destiny, and a new vision of who we really are and where we really come from. In front of the General Assembly at September 19, 1987, former President of the United States of America, Ronald Reagan, remarked: "We often forget how much unites all the members of humanity. Perhaps we need some outside universal threat to recognize this common bound. I occasionally think how quickly our differences worldwide would vanish, if we were facing an alien threat from outside this world."[21] Well, I do not agree with Reagan in believing in an alien threat -we do not have any indication that aliens are hostile and I prefer the term of an "alien challenge"—but I do agree in the consequences of such a discovery. In the same sense, the above mentioned Brookings Institution study on Implications of Peaceful Space Activities for Human Affairs states: "The knowledge that life existed in other parts of the Universe might lead to a greater unity of men on Earth, based in the "oneness" of man or on the age-old assumption that any stranger is threatening."[22]

Finally, we would realize that we truly are one mankind, children of the Earth. We would see us as they would see us, not as Germans, Americans, Italians or Russians, but as Earthlings. I have spoken to many astronauts and cosmonauts and asked them what impressed them most in space. They all agreed it was the vision of planet Earth. This beautiful, fragile jewel on the deep black background of space, with no border visible and all people living on it being one humankind. They call it "the overview effect." An Arabian cosmonaut who participated in the Soviet Space program once said: "The first day in space each of us pointed out his home country. The second day we pointed out the continents we came from, but on the third day we realized that we only have one common home, this beautiful planet Earth."[23] Five hundred years ago men realized that we are not the center of the Universe, that Earth is just one of—at that time they believed six, today we say at least nine—planets surrounding the sun. This caused a revolution of thinking, the Copernican revolution, man's redefinition of his place in the universe. It was the birth of science, of religious reformations, the age of discovery, when man conquered the world, headed for the most distant places on our planet, the white spots on his maps, not fearing anymore that Earth is a disc and the sailor who travels too far could fall into the eternal abyss "where dragons dwell." I believe that the final encounter between us and our brothers and sisters from Space could cause a similar quantum leap in human evolution, a paradigm shift, create a new cosmic age, move man forward to the next step in his evolution, homo cosmicus, the cosmic man who was born out of the womb of mother Earth into the infinite realms of Space, his true home, his origin and destiny, because we are all made out of Stardust, we consist out of the same molecules as everything in the Universe. And we will meet our close and distant relatives, become a member of the cosmic family of space-travelling planets and head for the final frontiers of existence.

38

I do not count for any help from outside, for any cosmic saviours. I do not believe that someone would steal from us the golden opportunity to learn to help ourselves to solve our problems. But I believe that the recognition that we are just one humankind among millions and millions of other humankinds in the far realms of space will help us to overcome all these stupid little differences which divide humankind right now. We all have the same origin, are born from the same mother, if we believe in the scriptures or in modern anthropology which says that once upon a time, 300.000 years ago, the good old australopithecus climbed from his tree, put his arm around the hairy hip of his wife and said: Let's make a homo erectus. Now, this is not what I believe how man was created, this is the scientific theory—but it means that we are all related, brothers and sisters, children of the Earth and that we can only solve the serious global problems facing us at the threshold of the 3rd millennium -overpopulation, pollution, greenhouse effect, the ozone layer hole—together. Not Germany, not the U.S., not Russia nor Italy can solve these problems, only humankind—together. Indeed an interplanetary contact could cause this quantum leap from separation to unity, to oneness.

To reach this goal a long-term strategy, a global educational program, aimed at developing a general understanding of humankind's role in the universe is necessary and should be encouraged. To quote Dr. Pinotti: "This universal awareness in future generations is the only key to facing, with all our limits and possibilities, the impact of contact."[24] Indeed we all bear this "cosmic consciousness" in us, because we are a part of the cosmos. As a sidemark, let me refer to Dr. David Bohms model of a holographic universe. It is still present in a child's unconscious, before it gets inprinted by what we call "cultural identity." More than that, our new generation already is the space generation and grew up with TV series like *Startrek* and movies like *Close Encounters...*, *Cocoon*, *Starman* and *E.T.*—all featuring visions of interplanetary contact. In 1982 David W. Swift, professor of sociology at the University of Hawaii, concluded that the belief in ET and UFOs "is strongest in the most influential stratum of the American population,"[25] that is better informed, higher income people, proving that at least the "opinion leaders" of tomorrow are ready for a next step. Based on this readiness to accept the reality of ETI, we now have the responsibility in feeding the public slowly but steadily with the facts—in the form of a long-term educational strategy. Actually this can be done with the same aims already used in the cover-up of ETI, the mass media such as television, motion pictures and popular articles. It would function similarly—but in the opposite direction—as the "educational program" resulting from the "Scientific Advisory Panel on UFOs," the so-called "Robertson Panel," sponsored by the CIA, that met at the Pentagon January 14-17, 1953, and defined the two major aims as "training and debunking" which "would result in reduction of public interest in flying saucers which today evokes a strong psychological reaction." The panel recommended the surveillance of private UFO organizations "because of their great influence on mass thinking if widespread sightings should occur."[26]

According to inside sources the most recommendable strategy for such an "educational program" for the time frame 1995-1999, would be to release information to the media and the UFO community in a controllable way—in a way that allows the debunking of information if the public overreacts or the impact is not the one wanted. One possibility is the stepping forward of more and more witnesses from military circles, who, in the beginning, do not have "hard evidence" in their hands, but just their testimony.

This strategy can be started by an Executive Order releasing former military personnel from their security oaths in connection with UFO phenomena. If more and more credible witnesses "stand up" and tell the true story without proving it, the public interested is stimulated as well as their desire for more. The next step can follow, the release of evidence. This still gives the public a feeling of "we discovered them." Cases involving UFO crashes and retrievals are ideal, proving the vulnerability and humanness of their occupants. If these cases go far back into the past—like the Roswell-incident, 1947—the public does not have to fear a revenge-reaction of the aliens. The 50th anniversary of the Roswell crash 1997 would be a good date to release ALL files and evidence including "hardware."

39

The next step, for the year 2000, would be a "UFO world summit" organized by United Nations, like the Ecological Summit in Rio 1992, or the World Population Summit in Cairo 1994, with participants from the world governments and the military, the scientific community and UFO research pioneers. At this congress every nation, every scientist, every UFO research pioneer should put his evidence on a table and draw his conclusions. The main subject of this congress should be: how can we establish an open contact and how could we—step by step with an educational program—prepare humankind for this, the greatest moment in human history when man finally leaves planetary isolation and becomes a member of the cosmic family. This would change our self-definition. We would still be the discoverers of these alien life-forms, those who are in control of the situations, not the victims of a discovery.

The time for contact has come. When NATO's SHAPE Headquarter investigated the UFO phenomenon between 1961 and 1964 they came—as communicated to me by Command Sergeant Major Robert O. Dean—in their final "Assessment" to the conclusion that "they seem to follow a plan, a program of gentle approach, preparing mankind step by step for an open contact somewhere in the future. Obviously there is an evolution in their approach: First single sightings, the first contacts, than mass sightings, landings..."[27] Indeed, UFOs are coming closer and closer since the beginning of the 90's, starting with the amazing UFO waves of sightings in Belgium 1989/90, Russia 1989/90, East Germany 1990. Then South and Central America followed when on July 11, 1991, thousands of Mexicans filmed the famous Eclipse, predicted by the Aztec astronomers as the beginning of a New Age, the "Sixth Sun," the Return of the Gods.

Many of them had brilliant, shining, silverish discs on their films, including a television crew from TELEVISA, Mexico's largest private TV Station. When TELEVISA discovered what they filmed, anchorman Jaime Maussan asked his viewers to send him UFO films—and received more than 5,000 since them. A film shown on Brazilian TV reported 70.000 people watching a strange disc over Curitiba near Sao Paolo in September 1992. Interestingly the UFO projected religious symbols of the Native Americans, the cross and the circle. We have film from Mexico City, January 6 , 1994, where the UFO splits into two. There is a film of an alien tourist observing the air parade on Mexico's national holiday, September 16, 1993. In July 1993, a group of Italian tourists visited the Zoo of Melbourne—and filmed a pinkish disc, dividing into two.

Maybe events such as the filmed open landing, near Carp, Ontario, near Ottawa, Canada, on August 18, 1991, will be ahead of all of us in the not-too-distant future. If we accept this possibility, we must act now. To quote Irwin Pikus, deputy director of the U.S. State Departments Office of Space Affairs: "Contact with other world beings is something that would have tremendous repercussions if it happened and we weren't prepared."[28] The time for preparation has come. We cannot allow ourselves the luxury of ignorance any longer, neither in science nor in politics. It is our responsibility for all mankind to open the doors into a cosmic future today!

[1] Regge, Tullio: *Report Draft, European Parliament Committee for Energy, Research and Technology*, August 17, 1993, Doc-DE/PR/233233, PE 202.202/rev.

[2] Cooper, Gordon: *Letter to Ambassador Griffith, Mission of Grenada to the United Nations*, November 9, 1978.

[3] *Introductory Space Sciences, Vol. II*, Physics 370, United States Air Force Academy 1969.

[4] KGB-Report, July 31, 1989, released under No. 1953/III, October 24, 1991, by Deputy KGB Director N.A. Sham to General Pavel Popovich.

[5] Report by AFOSI Det 1700, Kirtland AFB, NM, September 9, 1980 *Alleged sightings of Unidentified Aerial Lights in Restricted Test Range*.

[6] Technical Report No. F-TR-2274-IA: Unidentified Aerial Objects Project "Sign," Headquarters Air Material Command, Wright Patterson AFB, Dayton, Ohio, February 1949.

[7] Callimahos, Prof. Lambros: *UFO-Hypothesis and Survival Questions, NSA Paper (Draft)*, 1968, released 1979.

[8] House of Representatives, 87th Congress, 1st Session, Report Nr. 242: *Proposed Studies on the Implications of Peaceful Space Activities for Human Affairs, Report for the National Aeronautics and Space Administration by the Brookings Institution*, Washington, April 18, 1961.

[9] Logsdon, J.M. & Anderson, C.M.: *Announcing the First Signal: Policy Aspects*, in: Tarter, J.C. & Michaud, M.A. (ed.): SETI Post Detection Protocol, Washington 1988.

[10] Tough, Allen: *A Critical Examination of Factors that Might Encourage Secrecy*, in: Tarter/Michaud 1988.

[11] Pinotti, Roberto: *Contact: Releasing the News*, in: Tarter/Michaud 1988.

[12] Jung, Carl-Gustav: *Über Flying Saucers*, in: Weltwoche, Zürich, July 9, 1954.

[13] Toffler, Alvin: *Future Shock*, New York 1977.

[14] Pinotti, *op. cit.*

[15] Pinotti, *op. cit.*

[16] Fawcett, George D.: *Human Reactions to UFOs Worldwide* (1940-1983), Lincolnton/NC 1986.

[17] Menzel, Donald: *Flying Saucers*, Cabridge 1953.

[18] Chadwell, H. Marshall: *Memorandum for the Director of Central Intelligence. Subject: Flying Saucers*, (Secret), October 2, 1952, declassified September 20, 1977.

[19] Pinotti, *op. cit.*

[20] Kopal, Zdenek: Lecture at the XXI. IAF Congress in Brighton, GB, 1970.

[21] Reagan, Ronald: Speech at the 42nd Session of the General Assembly of the United Nations, New York, September 21, 1987.

[22] House of Representatives Report, *op. cit.*

[23] White, Frank: *The Overview Effect*, New York 1987.

[24] Pinotti, *op. cit.*

[25] Swift, David W.: *SETI Without Saucers?*, in: *AIAA's Aeronautics and Astronautics*, April 1982.

[26] Durant, F.W.: *Report of Meetings of Scientific Advisory Panel on Unidentified Flying Objects convened by Office of Scientific Intelligence, CIA, January 14-18, 1953*, declassified January 21, 1975 .

[27] Personal information from CSgt Maj. Robert O. Dean.

[28] Quoted by the *National Enquirer*, 7/25/78; quotation confirmed personally to Col. C.v.Keviczky on August 29, 1978.

40

# James J. Hurtak, Ph.D.

*James J. Hurtak, Ph.D.*

Dr. Hurtak is the Founder and President of the Academy For Future Science, and consultant in the field of Philosophy and its application to technological futures. He was former professor at California State University, Northridge and California State Los Angeles. He has Ph.D. degrees from the University of California, Irvine, in Social Sciences and Linguistics, and the University of Minnesota in History and Oriental Studies. He was director of TMAC, which co-sponsored with the U.S. Department of Energy and the Department of Commerce the very large Renewable Energy Technology Symposia (RETSIE) for five years. He currently is senior scientific consultant for Advanced Scientific Systems in Houston, Texas.

# Extraterrestrial/Ultraterrestrial Paradigms

# For The Future

*In this tour de force, the enormous degree of universal complexity forms a backdrop for a discussion of the opportunities and challenges in the near future as Earth and its inhabitants face their inevitable rendezvous with a host of cosmic cultures.*

## ABSTRACT

With continuing scientific exploration in outer space, the human race has entered the most critical evolutionary stage: the breakthrough into a new open-world environment and probable contact with other civilizations in space. In this transitional phase, humanity must make some very important decisions in discerning the categories of other life forms. The burden of proof of extraterrestrial contact has shifted from isolated human contact to collective sightings that include large numbers of people on a worldwide level. At the same time it appears that our planetary humanity may be a "womb environment" for certain types of ETs conducting genetic experiments with human biological targets. ET reports indicate a wide spectrum of life forms, some of which include nonphysical levels of intelligence which could be called ultraterrestrial (UT) intelligence.

The most critical period of human-ET involvement begins when the human race passes through its initial point of contact in relationship with other races in space. The long-term realities of contact will redefine "the new image of Man" and change the meaning of all disciplines and new adjustments to life extending well into the 21st century. Our new awareness capabilities in conjunction with extraterrestrial intelligence can help restructure our life in new space frontiers and provide for the experience of space law and a new cosmic civics for citizenship in the frontiers of outer space.

## 1. THE COSMIC FRONTIER

With its astronomic tools to explore the seemingly limitless space environment, the human mind is now receiving its first impressions of life in the new frontier. Human consciousness and subconsciousness was so conditioned in the West that when post-medieval astronomy reduced Earth to a small planet of a medium-sized star in an vast universe, political, socioeconomic and religious attitudes continued to maintain a human-centered cosmology until well into the 20th century. The human race was looked upon as the only source of physical intelligent life in the universe.

In contrast, among scientists, the broad ordering of interstellar evolution is now so plainly acknowledged that it may be regarded as conventional wisdom. Scientists believe all life and energy originated in a "Big Bang" which evolved as it expanded outward into local evolutions of greater complexity. SETI researchers through radio astronomy are looking into these local galactic structures to detect other sources of life in the universe.

Despite exponential leaps in technology and the completion of some 67 cosmic eavesdropping projects worldwide, the combined efforts of radio astronomers have covered only the tiniest fraction of our galaxy. Jill Tarter of the SETI Institute in Mountain View, California estimates that radio astronomers have only "covered one part in 1010 (ten billion) stars— maybe."[1]

The debate rages about whether the vision of SETI is a reality that can be substantiated or, indeed, whether communicating with other worlds is even a good idea. Given that humans have just recently gained the technological capability to send out and possibly to receive interstellar beacons, it stands to reason—and most astronomers would argue—that any civilization we might encounter via radio astronomy would be far, far more advanced than ours. In fact, they would not be simply hundreds of years more advanced than us, they would be billions of years more advanced. As some astronomers put it 'compared with them, we might be like your average paramecium.'[2]

It's a shocking thought, and most people have considerable worry as to what will take place when cosmic cultures meet in a new frontier. According to anthropology traditions throughout human history, whenever there has been contact between primitive and advanced cultures, these encounters have always been disastrous to the primitives. Similarly, it could be argued that intelligent beings living within 30 light years from planet Earth could pose a substantial threat to the paradigm of life as we know it. In addition to these advanced civilizations having their own motives, which may be malevolent or not, their direct effect on our race and adaptation of their logic to our culture may have adverse effects on humanity. We simply don't yet know enough about space, about extraterrestrial civilizations, in what manner they exist, and about what is or isn't possible in the universe. A correlatory argument of this, however, suggests that all we should do is go about our mundane, terrestrial existence, make our scientific discoveries, and continue to wonder "what if" other life forms exist in the Milky Way.

Another approach would be to look headlong at the impact of a sudden experience of cultural contact with other spaceborne cultures and to be prepared theoretically for intelligences which may exist in other dimensions. One of the arguments for the search for extraterrestrial intelligence is that detection would assure us that other evolutions-to-intelligence have survived to the point of achieving interstellar communications capability, or visibility to our observational techniques.[3] We may discover that intelligences have succeeded further not only by conscious choice, but also by cooperative effort, arranged through inter-species communication. However, we must beware of turning contact into a simplistic philosophy as proposed by Robert Jastrow, who has argued that the latest discoveries in astronomy and the life sciences may offer some elements of a new religious perspective, with its corresponding cosmology and moral content—cosmology being the scientific theory of the origin of the universe, and moral content giving us the purpose behind the very root of evolutionary progress, expansion, and survival.[4] Nevertheless, the paradigm of simultaneous evolutionary existence is a powerful idea, and raises questions as to our place within a vast ocean of intelligent creations.

## 2. The Evolutionary-Entropic Paragidm

In the traditional evolutionary paradigm, the universe evolves through stages, beginning with the evolutions of galaxies after the Big Bang and culminating in life and expansion of intelligence. Within the evolution of galaxies there are stars and planets, which may eventuate into complex intelligent life in a variety of forms. From our viewpoint, the universe will continue to evolve, which implies that our present stage of evolution is not necessarily the definitive stage. Our next evolutionary stage may culminate in terrestrial-extraterrestrial interconnectedness.

Cosmologists like Frank Tippler go beyond even an anthropocentric model to imply that there must be a greater evolution into even more elevated stages of consciousness awareness, having the potential of developing a self-programming universe. He implies a stage beyond what we consider intelligence, that is a total interaction of consciousness and the experience of the Divine throughout the many different orders of creation.[5] This thinking is not unique: Teilhard de Chardin argued that evolution is leading humans toward a higher state of union and consciousness at the time of a great millennial event.[6] Modern writers on extraterrestrial intelligence have not deviated from these philosophers, suggesting that contact will almost certainly bring us a new awakening and greater abilities based on higher levels of universal integration.

However, Frank Tippler, Freeman Dyson and Alexander Friedmann also tell us that all life must come to an end, regardless of its evolutionary state, principally because the second law of thermodynamics states that entropy within any system will increase over time, that is, the universe will expand either indefinitely until it eventually runs out of energy (in an open universe) or until gravity terminates the expansion and a recompression begins (in a closed universe). In the closed universe, all matter will finally collapse inward towards a central point, which may begin a new formulation of the Big Bang and a new expansion.[7]

In an open universe, Freeman Dyson (1978) suggests a brilliant way of dealing with its ultimate demise stemming from problems of the expenditure of energy. Intelligent beings or perhaps intelligent machines would have to replace themselves with new generations which expend only half of their normal energy and think only half as fast. According to Dyson, intelligence that would process information in this manner could theoretically exist forever. Thus, in an open universe, their actions would still be continually narrowed as the availability of usable energies decreased. In a closed universe, they still would not survive the collapse.[8]

Regardless of your belief in an open or closed universe, the universe and all physical evolution within it is proceeding through time towards a terminus. Although this may be in the far distant future, the question prevails: Have we emerged from cosmic evolution only to die in the collapse of a closed universe? If all life will eventually lose energy, we must conclude that all life is ephemeral and without eternality unable to control it own fate. Unless scientists can see the triggering event prior to the Big Bang, or whatever even was at the origin of the universe, or project into the future to see a positive completion to evolution, one must instead seek metaphysical answers as a future recourse.[9]

If other intelligences truly exist, are they also caught within the confines of entropy? The answer would most assuredly be 'Yes,' for unless an expanding technological civilization is able to work out arrangements for cooperative entropy control on very large scales, it will eventually encounter the same fundamental problems of limited energy. Thus, the logical universal goal of cooperating intelligences would be—universal entropy control. Is it possible?

A truly higher intelligence would be defined as intelligence that has been able to control entropy and can be described as anti-entropy, or as intelligence that can locally intervene in the overall entropic process.[10] On a planetary level, noted scientist Moore has described the extension of Earth life to other worlds as "a coup against entropy."[11] In fact, even the concept of colonization brought forth by Gerard O'Neill is a step beyond the entropy of planet Earth.[12] To control entropy on a large scale goes beyond the construction of space biospheres, into the macro-engineering of astrophysical environments to make local areas of the galaxy more thermodynamically efficient.[13] Dyson suggested the placing of a protective sphere of material around a star or planet (1960) and others like Zwicky have gone so far as to suggest the reconstructing of the entire Universe.[14,15]

According to our present understanding of physical laws, reducing entropy within a given volume increases entropy in the volume around it. However, if a species or group of cooperating species could discover how to operate outside the limited system, they must be able to control their travel in and out of any universe that is subject to ultimate collapse and death, in order to somehow escape the infall or recompression of the universe.

45

With our current technology it seems impossible to organize such a quantum jump beyond our limitations of time and space, and there is the possibility that other dimensions may also be subject to these events, if the dimensions are stacked and in conjunction with one another. However, the ultimate goal of any civilization and the sign of truly advanced intelligence should be when they are capable of transferring themselves outside a closed system to another realm, such as a parallel universe.

Thus, although there is a boundary to the expansion of entropy control according to physical laws, if in the evolutionary schema, the expansion of consciousness related directly, devising a methodology whereby intelligences could step outside of the three-dimensional paradigm before final collapse, then, in this case, intelligence, by using its technology, might be still able to influence lower levels of evolution and assist lower intelligences through deliberate choice to also cross beyond the entropic or three-dimensional boundary. The cosmic evolutionary life paradigm would then continue from the formation of life on planetary system, to terrestrial-extraterrestrial interconnectedness, and finally into a consciousness/physical evolution of civilization into a form that is no longer under entropy's control.

## 3. Science, Civics, and Extraterrestrial Activities

The United Nations Outer Space Treaty (1967) affirms outer space as "the province of all mankind," indicating that, like governmental activities in space, private enterprises are to use space not only for peaceful purposes but to allow for the benefit of all countries.[16] The finding of extra-solar life occupying planets in a nearby solar system will have a tremendous impact on all space-related endeavors, from creating new living environments to the disposal of waste from vehicles and man-made space platforms.

We can evolve our technology to the point where we can develop autonomous space cities which could carry their own communications, navigational, meteorological and geodetic vehicles and satellites. At the same time these colonies could easily become a "no-man's land" for technological conquistadors divided into legitimate and bandit colonies without the existence of international and intercolonial treaties that limit hostile activities in space.

It can be said that there are four basic phases in the development of an extraterrestrial civilization in redefining the long-range goals and role the human race will play in the next stage of cosmic evolution:

a. Exo-industrialization and exo-commercialization Commercial activities in outer space will function in a way similar to that of the Law of the Seas, where the resources in outer space are open to all. The Law of the Seas has often been stated as the guidelines of international space law.[17]

b. Exo-socialization Acclimation of the human race to new living conditions, through which members of the planetary society and family groups can share common exo-terrestrial perspectives of life, understanding the trade-offs of living in other evolutionary environments. Here a common civics would contain practical survival concepts of life in new transplanted family structures, similar to the implanting of "colonies" in the New World by the European exploratory enterprises.[18]

c. Exo-theology The mapping of a common underlying basis of ethics and moral responsibility wherein the various philosophies and theologies would coexist within the new paradigms of non-earth environments.

d. The ET/Human interface Under the umbrage that we are not unique in the universe, when we encounter our first extraterrestrial civilization we must realize that they also may not be that unique. Therefore, in our critical decisions, we must work with various possibilities, whereby the existence of one ET life force would most likely indicate that there are many other ET life forms and that all ET life may not be alike. In the event that the ETs appear friendly, and are benevolent in sharing knowledge and science, the logic of cooperation is to be standard policy. In the event that the ETs appear to be warlike conquerors or disease-ridden contaminators or in some way a threat, we may see the diverse people of the earth uniting together in a common defense. In the event that the ETs appear to be much like us, we can expect both of the above reactions initially, and then we will eventually see the development of alliances and counter-alliances between segments of both earth and ET populations, while maintain our own unique cultural and philosophical identity. When we do engage in a new civics with civilizations further advanced than our own, it would assure us that at least one civilization has passed the "crisis of survival," having surmounted it and survived beyond the major problems we as an earth-based society face in the galactic quagmire. However, bridging the evolutionary gap would bring exciting challenges, as well as future shock.[19]

## 4. EXO-THEOLOGY: IMPACT ON PHILOSOPHY AND THOELOGY

Currently, the beginning of the ET era surrounds us. We have been searching for extraterrestrial life with radio telescopes. Budgetary arguments regarding space exploration rage in Congress. Our theaters have been showing sci-fi films depicting interplanetary space travel and even contact and interbreeding between extraterrestrial civilizations. Some theologians have recently taken up the subject seriously in their writings. The provocative German Catholic theologian Hans Kueng of Tuebingen argues the need to de-center the place of humanity in the universe when he writes, "we must allow for living beings, intelligent although quite different-living beings, also on other stars of the immense universe."[20]

Moving toward the center of mainline Lutheran theology, we find New Testament scholar Krister Stendahl, former dean of Harvard Divinity School. At a NASA sponsored symposium in 1972, when Stendahl was asked about communication with ETs, he said: "That's great. It seems always great to me, when God's world gets a little bigger and I get a somewhat more true view of my place and my smallness in the universe."[21] Paul Tillich would agree. Tillich, the renowned systematic theologian supports thinking that is part neo-orthodoxy and, at the same time, modern philosophy. To Tillich, the prospects of extraterrestrial life raise important questions that need to be answered in terms of Christian creationism, salvation, and Christology.

According to Tillich:

...a question arises which has been carefully avoided by many traditional theologians, even though it is consciously or unconsciously alive for most contemporary people.

It is the problem of how to understand the meaning of the symbol "Christ" in the light of the immensity of the universe, the heliocentric system of planets, the infinitely small part of the universe which man and his history constitute, and the possibility of other worlds in which divine self-manifestations may appear and be received.

...our basic answer leaves the universe open for possible divine manifestations in other areas or period of being. Such possibilities cannot be denied. But they cannot be proved or disproved. Incarnation is unique for the special group in which it happens, but it is not unique in the sense that other singular incarnations for other unique worlds are excluded...Man cannot claim to occupy the only possible place for incarnation.[22]

Catholic theologian Karl Rahner also agrees that the possibility of ETs can today no longer be excluded, but still maintains that "Christ is head of all creation."[23] According to Ted Peters, Lutheran theologian, Christian interpreters perceive with accuracy the salvific structure inherent to the developing UFO myth in our society and, further, that this myth stands at some variance with what Christian scripture wants to teach. For this the appropriate response is apologetic theology, to be sure. Yet, the apologetic argument as actually raised here is unnecessarily confused with fallacious appeals to the exclusive Bible authority.[24]

With these testimonies in mind we must note that, in the giant story book that constitutes some six thousand years of the Judeo-Christian heritage, there is a vast corpus of material, particularly the Sepher Ha-Aggadah[25] material of ancient Judaism, and Coptic and Ethiopic writings (e.g. Nag-Hammadi) of early Christianity in Africa, which suggest a much larger cosmology of interplanetary activities. In fact, the Nag Hammadi account of "The Origin of the World" tells us a very different Adam and Eve story from a completely different perspective, stating, "when their eyes were opened they (Adam and Eve) were disgusted because they saw that those who created them were grotesque."[26] If ETs were discovered in our midst, should they be seen as the new gods or should we instead send our own missionaries to administer to them as took place when Europe discovered the Western hemisphere?

## 5. MODERN-DAY ANGELS: EXTRATERRESTRIALS

Much is said in the wisdom traditions of Biblical literature about angelic realities. In fact, most religious traditions, especially those of the Old Testament, speak about God's angel or "Yahweh's angel." The God whom the heavens cannot contain and is omnipresent, communicates with those which are creaturely and which cannot be everywhere at once, namely His angelic hosts. He uses these creatures to assist him in his work with human beings as reported by the ancient sacred texts of most all religions.

The cosmology introduced in Genesis 1:1—"In the beginning God created the heavens and the earth..."—Allows for the creation of these angelic messengers, for the world was made to contain both the celestial as well as the terrestrial heavens and thus the creation of angels and their abode.[27] In fact, the biblical narrative is incomplete without its many allusions to these invisible orders who are both transcendent and yet administrative in service to the Divine.[28] Good angels are said to be obedient to the ways of God, and instruments among us of the hierarchical powers in the heavens. So the heavens are the habitat of angels? And what do biblical angels do? They reflect a royal office of God that accompanies Christ's own three-fold work. There are 311 references to them in the New Testament (and, by anticipation of the Kingdom of God, numerous Old Testament counterparts).[29]

Modern-day testimonies also relate of guardian angels who are able to rescue or heal in times of need, which reminds us of Acts chapter 12 when Peter was jailed, when an angel of light shone before him: his chains fell off his hands and he was directed to pass through all the sentinel guards and gates of the prison.

48

However, not all angels/messengers between worlds have been helpful to humanity. Let us remember also that the basic concern of Judeo-Christian cosmology is the category of "fallen angels." In fact, the Dead Sea Scrolls contain a prayer against fallen angelic activity that penetrates the privacy of the human body.[30] Although there are some grounds for thinking that both the Jewish and Christian faiths are earth centrist, an assessment of the overall historical and contemporary strength of theology indicates no such weakness. In fact, they speak of many levels of angels dwelling in many different spheres/heavens, some which are good and some which are non-benign. Why would an angel be non-benign? Because they work for their own will and perform experiments against the will and Plan of the Divine as we read in the Intertestamental *Book of I Enoch*, chapters 6-7, where a multitude of "fallen angelics" are specifically named for the travesty of intercourse with the "fair women" of the earth. They are called by name:

> "And it came to pass when the children of men had multiplied that in those days were born unto them beautiful and comely daughters. And the angels, the children of the heaven, saw and lusted after them, and said to one another: `Come, let us choose us wives from among the children of men and beget us children.' ... Semiaziz, their leader, Arakiba, Rameel, Kokabiel, Tamiel, Danel, Ezeqeel, Baraqijal, Asael, Armaros, Batarel, Ananel, Zaqiel, Samsapeel, Satarel, Turel, Jomjael, Sariel...and all the others together with them took unto themselves wives.... And they [the offspring from the mixture of angels with women] began to sin against birds, and beasts, and reptiles, and fish, and to devour one another's flesh, and drink the blood."[31]

Here, in examining ancient accounts within the context of modern ET studies, one can make important contributions to the theological discernment of powers that come amongst us. In Greek mythology, one could even question whether figures of "pan-creatureliness" express an association of earthly-creaturely elements. Is this unthinkable, unimaginable, and impossible? Similar accounts are even recorded in Genesis 6:1-4, which state past conditions of the ancient world that interfered with our earthly existence.

Is there a connection between "fallen angels" and what is pictured in contemporary times as "alien poachers"[32] or negative alien intruders who attack "beasts" such as cattle or horses?

I believe, as we come into our own extraterrestrial civilization, we will also encounter all types of intelligence, some three-dimensional extraterrestrial cultures who are still learning how to survive and internalize this reality, like our own culture, and some that are much more advanced, that operate beyond the three-dimensional realm of life as we know it. But in either case we are to be aware of the forces that exist, knowing that not all intelligences, even those of higher life systems, always have had our interests at heart.

## 6. Extraterrestrial Contact: The Abduction Phenomenon

In addition to simple sightings of UFO's flying over rural and populated areas, and beyond strange blips on radar screens over military bases and major countries of Europe, we find other urgent reasons for believing that vast populations throughout the world are being targeted for interplanetary/ interdimensional studies and experimentation. One of these reasons is the abduction phenomena described by numerous people throughout the world. Usually under hypnosis, many abductees discover that they have encountered alien intelligences who do not ask them if they desire the experience of contact, but simply "abduct" the individual without respect for free will. In fact, the majority of abduction contacts fail to make that request and involve repeated episodes of contact with each individual.

There appears to be a method used by ETs to control and entrain individuals or groups over short periods of time, whereby the contactees can be projected through the walls of their room into what they describe as a "space vehicle." This appears to be taking place now on a global level, and a model of control is emerging. The mere "alien appearance," the specifics of a given location, or contact relating to one individual, are no longer the only criteria; we are now gaining information about the use of a sophisticated paraphysics that uses the pattern of a convergent evolution as a means of "interfering" in our evolutionary structure.

Although the aliens can differ from one individual's experience to another, no information on the aliens' origins have been noted to date in most of the contemporary cases. Yet the aliens do not appear to live completely within our third-dimension. They have the power to materialize and dematerialize. Thus, along with understanding extraterrestrial visitations comes the need to develop a greater understanding of a new multidimensional reality which ultimately may become the single most important reason for communicating among technological species.[33]

The abduction, that is, the taking of a man and woman or woman and child against their free will into a space craft for what could be called sexual experiments or genetic experiments, has been going on very quietly for many years.[34] I had the opportunity in California to examine a family that was taken into a space craft. The woman who was pregnant at the time was given subdermal injections and, after her child was born, on the back of the head of the child some type of triangular marking was seen.

Recent case histories in California, Brazil, and South Africa, and happenings throughout the world, are not unique, neither in the appearance of multiple aliens, nor in the reality of violating the concept of noninterference with life (both individually and collectively) by very powerful and overwhelming means. However, two types of aliens stand out. These two classifications in abduction cases are represented by a human-size Commander (slightly above or below two meters) and a series of small grey alien beings.

In the standard situation a "Commander" is in charge of the alien team. He works as a group leader and is, generally, a type of large insectoid life form with neutral feelings. During the abduction experience, he stands out as a dominant authority figure with a humanoid but grotesque body form. Although some characteristics described may differ, he has been described as having a thin and defined rib cage. He can hold his arms and legs straight out. He is clearly different from smaller aliens who are also present. Both intelligences appear to integrate and homogenize human and nonhuman characteristics.

It is reported that between the Commander's eyes there is a ridge that extends all the way to the back of his head and neck (and perhaps down his back). His skin appears leathery. It can ripple and move with the wind. It makes a sound like leather moving upon wood. His front is of a darker, pinkish brown than the rest of the body. His skin is lighter around his eyes and face.[35]

The Commander holds his head upright from the body, but his eyes are insectoid. The face has human classical proportions except for the large eyes and insect features. The cheeks are sucked in as if the alien came out of a concentration camp.

His ability to communicate has been noted to be through mental communication, hand movements, and also light-emissions from the eye. There appears to be a code system by virtue of the way the eye geometries are coordinated with necessary functions during medical experiments.

50 Many of the smaller aliens which are usually also present in abduction cases show a grey or off-grey color. They lack hair during most appearances, however they have also showed the ability to grow or show copious hair. They have two eyes which are large and protrude out from their face and, in some cases, look pure black. If a color is present the eyes have no pupils but slits. A brown-orange color seems to glow around the eyes. They have no nostrils but only two small "Tylenol capsule-sized" holes for openings.

They are sometimes noted to wear a jump-suit which has epaulets/patches of insignia like those worn by military authorities. The aliens can make a noise when they walk like when you rub surfaces of a plastic tablecloth together, or a fish jiggles on a wood floor.

Other private investigations by this writer in the past 15 years have conveyed the picture of other alien figures, some who are more akin to the human race (See Plate 1), what could be called having Adamic appearances, who might have some genetic connection with us as human counterparts and others who instead of being close to the human race in their genetic appearance, are insectoid, robotoid, or reptilian and perceive little of what could be called human free will. In some abduction cases, pleasant feelings are exchanged regardless of the type of entity encountered, but usually there is overwhelming fear. In most cases, however, due to the uniqueness of the event, there are bizarre elements of being attracted and repelled. Most abductees have horror and shudder in describing their experiences which usually involve medical and sexual probes being forced upon them, and in some cases the involuntary insertion or

Plate 1: ET, Syrian Category

9

removal of precious bodily fluids takes place.

All events are usually completely beyond the abductee's control, and most medical experimentation done to him/her are performed by those revolting in appearance (See Plate 2).[36] In addition to the medical experimentation, the experience goes beyond a singular abductee but affects his/her entire family, and even domestic animals can be killed or seriously affected. Thus, aliens are not only working with isolated individuals throughout the world, but abductions usually extend collectively throughout the entire family tree.

Consequently, this writer believes that these events are amoral, and that the intelligences practicing these procedures represent a threat to our human rights. They also appear to show little or no compassion for one another, let alone the person they have abducted. Asserting our own rights as a creation may be the final test of our intelligence.

The theme of abduction case studies severely upset the view of the existence of all ET activity as being positive. At the same time, it would be a mistake to take the abduction fright as representative of all extraterrestrial encounters as a whole. However, it appears in looking at the vast documentation coming from South Africa, Russia and our country that negative alien intelligence is trying to create a sub-race by taking the sperm and the genetic materials from both men and women, intermixing this with some type of hybrid experiments, and showing in some instances, as detailed by investigators such as Budd Hopkins, the embryonic face of a child as a result of the hybrid experiment.[37] This has been going on clearly in violation of human terms of free will.

Abductions fall under the phenomenon of what I call Electro-Motivative Force (EMF) which is potential energy that migrates in the absence of a field from one pole or field to another. Electro-Motivative Force is potential energy, in

Plate 2: A Greyling

the absence of any other forces, which will make a "charge" migrate from one area to another so as to increase and control kinetic energy and the subjects within said kinetic energy. Specifically, the extraterrestrial intelligence uses this field for energy entrainment of the biological target.[38]

In multiple abductions, EMF is a powerful means to quickly target a recipient with artificially induced thoughts for genetic/medical formulations. The subject in this field undergoes a kinetic change, whereby he or she is teleported or taken into a vehicle location where the biological target is subjected to various technical or medical insertions, generally in violation of free will. In some instances a small bio-chip much smaller than the tip of a finger nail is inserted. This could be in any part of the body. It can be in areas connected with the brain, heart, or the thoracic area. We have hundreds of examples of bio-chips and all appear to create a tracking/coding mechanism that is placed within the body through subdermal injection.

Russians and Americans who came across these bio-chips claim that they appear very much like skin flakes but are similar to our silicon chips, having what we would call a small transistor-like apparatus which seems to influence and exert control over human brain waves, assisting the ETs in maintaining the abductee under the resonance of mind entrainment. The chips appear to work with extremely low frequency signals.

The analysis of these clearly show the desire to control some subjects over long periods of time. In cases of regressive hypnosis, hypnotherapy sessions, etc., these biological targets would often stop short of disclosing the full information regarding the mind control experiment, or the close encounter of the multiple abduction kind, due to the energy that was sent through the bio-chip.[39]

In addition to research reports by Budd Hopkins and Dr. John Mack, similar reports are also coming from Russia in conjunction with the loss of children. Something tragic has been happening in all of these cases involving "negative alien intelligences" or what this writer calls "poachers," who come to our planet like hunters into a game reserve, taking and experimenting with us at will, as we humans would experiment with animals.[40]

Whole families are being taken from strategic populations and being given markings/identification codes, and several of my colleagues have felt that this is possibly with the intent to create a subhuman race or a hybrid race. The ETs have passed on some information to their abductees; although most contacts go on without any information being relayed, in some instances they claim that they are working to repopulate our planet if we should experience nuclear war or environmental collapse. However, we can also come to the conclusion that their race is genetically degenerating, thus, requiring a sampling of nearby planetary populations for their own survival. Another possibility is that these intelligences are continuing to play out the same scenarios as those described in *The Book of I Enoch*, whereby they enjoy genetic experimentation with other races and see themselves as cosmic genetic engineers—playing the role of god in their own ignorant way.

These are not farfetched theories. We have programs on national television and enough information through leading scientists to suggest that we as a human race are being watched by both positive and negative forms of ET intelligence. It is up to us to decide: Do these intelligences respect our free will? Do these forms of intelligence give us an opportunity to dialogue and work with them; thus elevating our science and our consciousness for the benefit of the entire human race not just for a few? And do these ETs respect the great prophetic traditions of knowledge and human rights? If they do not, we must clearly disengage from these tragic experiments of abduction if we can.

In contrast, there exist cases of direct and intimate contact that have been examined and that indicate a positive consequence by virtue of free participation. There is an instance of this in the remarkable story of Elizabeth Klarer, a South African woman of Swiss background who, in the 1950's had a very unusual experience. While she was riding her horse in the mountains of Drakensburg (South Africa), a spacecraft came down and a very special commander came forth who identified himself by the name Akon. He was special in the sense that he looked Scandinavian, with human facial features and unique blond hair (See Plate 3). He identified himself as coming from a region known as Meton (within the system of Proxima Centauri) and said his task was to study the various experiments in the star systems of this local universe. In the process of friendship, Akon and Elizabeth entered into a spiritual marriage, and she gave birth to a son who returned with his father to Meton.[41]

Akon can be considered a representative of a positive extraterrestrial intelligence in the context of several contact experiences. In the process of knowing Akon, E. Klarer received mathematical texts and instructions on interplanetary navigation. Of course, American and many European ufologists dismissed her story as pure gibberish. However, the Russians, the (West) Germans, and others sent special delegations of scientists to look over the mathematical materials that she had received from Akon and realized that the depth and the nature of this information, which revealed galactic coordinates, could not have

come from a woman of her background in the 1950s. This was clearly not for purposes of her own publicity, but a true "close encounter of the third kind," for which she was put under severe criticism.[42]

In the fuller documentation she received was a series of mathematical references to those who had the ability to cross the "light barrier" and to make positive contact with the human race. In one particular presentation I made at the University of Johannesburg in the early 1980's there were noticeable paraphysical light modulations in the auditorium that were witnessed by many in the audience when Akon's name was mentioned in the context of Madame Klarer's presence and in speaking of her contact experience.

Another amazing contact case which I would like to cite as one illustration of the positive

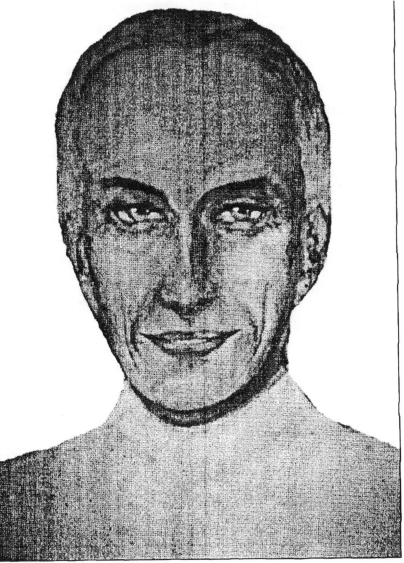

Plate 3: Akon from Meton

ultraterrestrial category is the case of Mauricio Panisset. This writer worked with him in Brazil and has film material of his extraordinary phenomenon of emitting light bursts. Mauricio Panisset was born on March 6, 1930, in Minas Gerais, Brazil. In 1969, while he was driving in his car with his family, a transparent electric blue light followed him, and moved with the car in front of them. The light materialized into the form of a transparent being, in human appearance. This being called himself Uhr and said:

"You must use your own light to heal the sick. You must go to the hospital and begin."[43]

Mauricio at that time in his life was very sick. He was reluctant to heal because he felt he was too busy in practical matters, hardly able to keep an income for his family, due to his health. He was surprised to discover, however, that his illness gradually faded when he healed the sick. Several years later, while driving in his car, he was again followed by lights. This time a yellow light approached him and materialized into a being who called himself Akron[1], who told Mauricio:

"You must continue to heal, that is your agreement."

During the following years Mauricio would go into hospitals and heal many, when he had time. He generally only did this when his health became bad, and by doing the healing he would gradually recover.

Now, Mauricio was not an ordinary healer. For when he healed, one observed blue-white lightning flashing from his hands and flowing over the body of the one he healed. Sometimes the whole room was filled with this electrical lightning. In one film which I have accessed, one observes Mauricio (usually bare armed) materialize a ball of light in his hands. The patient is lying down. Then he throws the ball of light over the body of the patient, where it spreads as dozens upon dozens of paths of electrical lightnings, going in and out of the body and concentrating power on the area of illness or physical deficiency.

However, Mauricio was often reluctant to heal or to show his powers, and his healing work would come to a standstill. Then in 1980, three starlike lights merged into one large ball of light, and Mauricio heard the words from an ultraterrestrial "angelic being" speak to him:

"Go to the hospital to heal, time is short. I will be with you."

Mauricio raised his voice in objection: "I haven't any more time, I don't care if time is short, I have my own problems."

The being replied, "There will be no more problems for you."[44]

Mauricio discovered that the more he healed, the more his life problems and financial problems faded away. His health improved dramatically. He would walk into hospitals and heal and cure dozens upon dozens of persons, while lightning was seen from some distance around to be coming out of the hospital. During this period of healing, Mauricio, and sometimes those around him, would witness two light beings accompanying him, whom he referred to as Akron and Shalla.

What are we to make of abductions, alien children, light beings that instruct us to heal? Scientists

---

[1]Note the similarities in the names between Klarer and Panisset.

are accustomed to dealing with data that may be elusive, but not outrageous and inconsistent in terms of our three-dimensional reality. Is it illusion, only in the mind of the believer, or simply a story made up by con artists? But, as Dr. J. A. Hynek has pointed out, many aspects of modern science would be utterly incomprehensible to a nineteenth-century scientist, and there is going to be a twenty-first century science and probably a twenty-third century science which is at present utterly incomprehensible to us, and to which the paraphysical phenomenon may provide a key. Hynek himself with this writer had seen paraphysical realities in Brazil, and knew that one could not solely interpret the study of UFOs from a three-dimensional scientific logic, but one needed to incorporate a meta-science—and this is where most rational investigations stop short.

## 7. ET/UT Typologies

The first questions everybody asks are: What do alien races look like? How many races are there? In order to address these important questions we must provide an overall picture of the various extraterrestrials and ultraterrestrials.

There is a wide variety of extraterrestrials comprising a general category of approximately 54 different races. The most common category is called the "Greys," which are 1-2 meters in height, have black wraparound eyes, no hair, different breathing features, and a skin quality very much like an off-color white or grey material. Their eyes are rather grotesque, having a neutral stare, and their head is often pear-shaped and slightly larger than human heads. Other races are "reptilian" and show affinity with the lizard phylad. Their skin is scaly and grey, brown, or green in color. Their eyes are clearly those of a reptile. Their smell is usually offensive to humans. A third category are the insectoids, covering a wide variety of life-forms that are directly identified by large bug-like (multi-cellular) eyes, clearly defined (and sometimes external) skeletal structure, and in some cases paired appendages or claws.

Credo Mutwa, a Zulu shaman, speaks of the Mhondoruka,

Plate 4: The Mhondoruka

which have been recorded in Zulu legend and are still appearing today (see Plate 4.). They are usually ten feet tall, and he calls them "evil creatures." They kill cattle and horses after mutilating them for their parts. They have also been known to do this on human beings. According to Credo Mutwa, Africans believe they are the cause of wars between tribes, feeding on fear and hatred. On one occasion in 1959, a Mhondoruka was seen near the community of Marandellas in Zimbabwe.[45]

The Mhondoruka are a variation of "stick being"—aliens generally having what looks like a drill-bit head. They travel at speeds that can seldom be registered except with sensitive tracking systems. Recent sightings of these stick beings have also been recorded in the American Southwest. They are known to cross in and out of the third dimension, easily attacking their prey and disappearing almost instantaneously. Their body is their vehicle of travel and can only be spotted by glimpsing their high physical luminescence, shining off their body at four points.

Credo also speaks of the Nkasana as the most feared and hated space beings in Africa. This creature kills people and will operate on women and children for fun. This creature's bone structure is on the outside while its flesh in inside. They have four pincerlike fingers. They are omnivorous hunters. The Nkasana carry large scythe-like jaws on their heads. They attack targets by first stunning them and then slicing them up. According to other shamans, these creatures come from the vicinity of the Scorpion constellation. They are called in the tribal languages, "sons of the evil scorpion." It is more hated than the Mhondoruka being.

Not all of African encounters with alien creatures are bad, for Credo also speaks of the Ndeyiza as a race of friendly messengers from the Anaku star gods. They are said to be small extraterrestrial beings, about the size of a twelve year old child with a huge head. They are honored by all African shamans, since this creature cares deeply for humans. Credo terms them one of the few positive white-greys. They come wearing a suit of clothes and a face mask which is similar to an underwater snorkel system for the filtration of particles from different planetary environments.

According to private reports shared with me there are also the Arcturians, who like Akon are a variation of the extraterrestrial Nordic types. Many of the physical manifestations of extraterrestrial Nordics come from Arcturus, which in the ancient Paleo-semitic languages was called the place of "Ash" or "Asta," which means the region of the Shepherd (or "Herdsman" in Arabic). Arcturus is said to be our local Mid-Way station, the first threshold of clearance for travel beyond our consciousness time zone.

The Arcturians are extraterrestrials working from the third to the fifth dimension. Their life form manifests anywhere from 6-9 feet tall. They look like earth humans and are created either male or female. Their clothing can vary, but is similar to modern mankinds. They work to educate planetary intelligence and sometimes appear with a staff or governing rod which is used as an energy conduit. They appear in spacecraft which they use to monitor the heavens. They are under the direction of the greater Light intelligences that are ultraterrestrial in form.

The Orion constellation also has several levels of intelligence, one of which are ultraterrestrial intelligences from Mintaka. Reports of the Mintakans claim that they are 9th to 24th dimensional beings. They are not limited to this local universe, and travel not only to other dimensions within our universe, but to other universes as well.

The Mintakans are said to occupy this key gateway into other universes. The Mintakans work with advanced intelligences of the "Galactic Federation" to monitor and guard this threshold or gate, protecting it to allow only those intelligences with the proper clearance to enter and pass through from our local realm of creation into other realms. They tell us that our universe is simply a schoolhouse for the lessons of Life.

With these various categories of intelligence in mind, the question we must be concerned with is: Do all aliens have the same intention? Since they are all superior to us in one way or another, should we follow their leadership blindly? If we analyze reports from contactees, we find everything from the most profound "religious type" of experience to the feeling of rage, medical/sexual violation and intimidation. From reports of sightings, we also find the killing of animals and removal of blood and organs—hardly what we should accept as intelligent actions from advanced civilizations.

The controversy rages over the fact that alien civilizations are so advanced—we simply do not understand their logic since we are the inferior ones. They must be doing good, trying to help, etc. Rubbish! Since ancient times, we have records telling us that those in space have both good and bad intentions just like humanity on earth. So much reported UFO activity is mischievous or silly, and is irreconcilable with the concept that they are space vehicles from another world accomplishing some divine mission on Earth.[46]

On the other hand, should UT intelligence be equated with Gods? I believe that some may be in keeping with the divine intentions, but nevertheless, they are still not God. Although they may treat us with respect and provide important gifts and information, we must utilize our own constant discernment and test their information, and under no circumstances submit ourselves without question to their control.

Let us analyze the total picture: We have ET intelligences who are similar to earth-kind, only they are space-kind and are a few technological evolutions ahead of us. These can be helpful or they may be tricksters. Then there are ET intelligences that have conquered the third-dimensional entropic system, which still does not make them any more spiritually enlightened than our race. Finally we have UT intelligences which originate from completely outside our galactic system. However, these intelligences as we are told in The Book of I Enoch, can also be positive and negative for the human race. There are some forms of UT intelligence that through their own desire to control reality have separated themselves from the Divine Source. If we believe some of the ancient texts, these intelligences are responsible for having created lower planetary experiments, many of which are coming into our life space at this time. I believe, for the most part, humanity has been under a system of quarantine and has been protected from these entities who are mostly interested in thrusting themselves into density so as to experience feeling desire and sexuality, rather than the higher and more etheric elements of the Divine Source.

If we were to back-engineer ET cosmology, it would scan something like this: The false "gods" began to divide and war amongst themselves, each falsely claiming to be the supreme deity. It was at this point that the world of polarity began, and as a result came the belief in good and evil, with no thought for the balanced middle from which we came. It has always been the intentions of these lesser Gods to deny us the privilege of knowing that there is a rightful point of origin, and that they are the very epitome of that which is most reprehensible to our quest. That is to return intuitively to the true source.[47]

This brings us to the all-important question: How does one discern the negative and positive ETs/UTs in the experience of contact? First of all, one has to acknowledge that there is a negative intelligence and remove oneself from the simplified concept that everything is positive in the universe. What is here on this earth is also reflected in the greater universe. There are some experiments that clearly show non-benign intelligences intercepting and violating the wombs of thousands of women and children throughout the world. Our bodies are not to be violated by an adversary intelligence, but protected. The positive intelligences will always show a Love, a compassion, an empathy, and a deep rapport with the human creation. They will also bring us knowledge and science that can be applicable for all people on our planet without distinction of ethnic group or race. They will also respect the charter of nations, the tradition of the great prophets and thinkers, respecting our place in the universe.

58

To the contrary, the negative intelligences operate in violation of human free will. They operate out of a fear structure, and they have a neutral stare showing little or no compassion. They are clearly in contrast to the positive beings who have the apparition or appearance like a "beloved Teacher who is here to assist us" and whose form or appearance is very much like the human race. They are usually accompanied by some type of spiritual symbol or light pulsation around their head, what we would call bioluminescence. Most importantly, they are recognized by their great Love and compassion—as opposed to the negative ETs who violate free will and do not have compassion, love or understanding, but operating simply as a military search and destroy mission.

Thus, five kinds of explanations may be entertained for current ET activity: (1) they are working with an agenda not directly in conjunction with the human race per se but with a desire to reorient the human enterprise; (2) they might destroy themselves without human genetic material; (3) they represent competing interstellar civilizations and operations which may look at the human race as humans look at bacteria; (4) they are working as extra-solar intelligence exploring some aspects of life on planet earth to tangentially decide to settle in the local area long enough to test our genetic capacity, to join ours with theirs through hybrid mutants; or (5) they have already influenced our culture genetically and philosophically in the past and have returned to observe and reorient these changes. The latter, in fact, although seemingly the least plausible, may very well be true to some extent, for we have been told that advanced races did "marry with the daughters of earth." But we are also told that this was in violation of our "God-given rights" and created only havoc on planet Earth.

In fact, down through the centuries, the existence of intelligences who do not accept our free will have been pointed out by ancient scholars and orientalists as representing a demi-god force. In the Indian and Tibetan pantheon of gods, we find deities who are carefully described as being devoid of grace, pardon, and mercy, and instead demonstrating emotional irrationality, self will, subjective force, paralyzing movements, and strong impetus.

We, thus, have the choice of going with our counterparts who respect our place in the book of life and in the heritage of what is called cosmic citizenship, or being "charmed" by the temptation of the lower gods. Let us work only with those entities who accept our freewill, as opposed to those who violate it. Let us not find ourselves caught within a secondary god system, prompted by terror and mental entrainment. We have powers that can overcome those of the lesser gods, who are in a dialectic struggle against the powers of the Divine Eternal Father, when we make use of sacred language and Divine Names. This is important, for these most powerful fallen forces cannot use the Divine Names, according to research at The Academy For Future Science.[48]

There is a Divine Plan, and what we are seeing now might only be the first phase of a much larger "house-cleaning." One must not be swayed by the lower types of phenomena, but give consideration to the meta-terrestrial and ultraterrestrial life forms and their promise of compassion in accordance with a greater Plan of Life. This is our cosmic birthright, and it could be that these other forms of intelligence are also being tested and recycled from their positions of authority.

A final question is: How do these intelligences travel? The physical intelligences use "physical hardware" to travel through the physical universe. These encompass a variety of physical spacecraft that use "advanced-fusion technology" and a number of closed-loop magnetic systems to energize their ships for travel along the bending of magnetic fields or to warp time-space.

For some highly advanced extraterrestrial intelligences, their vehicles are only solid when traveling in the third dimension, in which case they usually function through light/energy waves for travel amongst the dimensions.

The nonphysical intelligences (ultraterrestrial) exist in a more rarefied state of energy and have devised a way of making use of their intense thought-forms, or use a thought-form technology, to steer the energy envelope forms through dimensional openings. The vehicle energy form is, in effect, a superluminal form which the ancients called the Merkabah, which encapsulates the entirety of the body/bodies in traveling from dimension to dimension. (See Appendix A).[49]

Thus, it is impossible to make a sociological hypothesis which applies to every ET. This is the dilemma facing our society, since there is no one clear paradigm. Only education of a higher reality structure can provide a solution—education as to how to examine each contact experience, how to challenge each step of our negotiations carefully, and when applicable, how to use linguistic protection, involving sacred Language or the musical use of sacred language.

The degree of universal complexity is enormous. This fact should be completely obvious to anyone with even a superficial understanding of the universe and a minimal knowledge of quantum mechanics. In exhibiting the magnitude of this diversity in the universe, there would also be exhibited a diversity of intelligent forms. The hard fact is that talk of genetic relations presupposes more common ground between us and the alien intelligences than is actually admitted by many of the people involved in this study. From the theological side particularly, there are many contemporary and classical perspectives in which the notion of direct genetic relations/sharing would have to be the result of a thoroughly new interpretation of theological notions.

In retrospect, we see we are truly headed for a new evolutionary reality. Now we must have the wisdom, humility, and courage to discern the "Powers and Potencies" that are in our midst. A new text book of biology is being written, forcing us to reexamine the claims and cosmology of our own Genesis and Spiritual Heritage.

## 8. Conclusions

Science has only led us to a detailed knowledge of our small, limited part of reality, and the scientific method as we know it from the time of Roger Bacon must now be expanded to handle experiential situations of contact that may come from sources representing a whole new spectrum of multiple realities that fall outside our own scientific measurement. Similarly, we must go beyond theological understandings that are linked with human-centered notions of creation and recognize that what has been recorded in ancient religious texts does not necessarily negate other realms of intelligence that exhibit both spiritual and non-spiritual qualities.

We must develop a post-Einsteinian science and begin using "the experience" of contact to redefine the criteria of the scientific method and the theological evaluation. We are only now beginning to discover through modern physics that there is more to nature than we can perceive through the framework of three-dimensional space and a single, linear flow of time. Only now are we beginning to look beyond a naive world view and perceive a higher vision of greater multidimensionality. String theory, which uses the concept of hyperspace extensively, is a good example of scientific inquiry into areas of which humans have been ignorant. Introduction of higher-dimensional models can only resolve many apparent conflicts in the quest for an understanding of ET/UT realities.[50]

The application to theology of the ET/UT concepts functioning within other dimensionalities, however, would require more than simply a new interpretation of space, time and living matter. Theology would require the understanding of qualitative characteristics of respective dimensions (i.e., recognizing dimensional levels of discrete intelligence) in order to accommodate the qualitative transcendence of the higher realities. This will become the greatest breakthrough in theology since Martin Luther (and Trent in the Sixteenth Century)!

There are a few major advantages to using the dimensional model for theology, one of them being that the model naturally allows many different ways of experiencing and describing the same higher reality. In effect, the paradigms of a multidimensional reality would allow for the invisible things of God to become a natural matter. Until this point, we have not had any other epistemological tools for understanding higher dimensions than revelation and faith. The model may even allow for different epistemological schemes for different dimensions along with their epistemological connections.

A multidimensional reality of multiple universes must be flexible enough to become a heuristic one, as different qualities can be assigned to different dimensions, in addition to their structural properties. This and other flexible features of the model will allow one to work within various models of different reality structures, all of which may be subsumed under one Divine Source which gives forth direction to a multiplicity of creations.

Contact with those cosmic cultures that will allow us to maintain our individual identity will undoubtedly lead us in the direction of our own cosmic evolution, beyond our own eventual extinction into an awareness of our own higher spiritual-scientific purpose in the universe as we become aware of ourselves. Thus, as we begin to discover a greater state of affairs in the universe, it would be entirely plausible that in certain circumstances the mind of man should come closer into participation with the mind of God, and that man should have experiences of enlarged consciousness, of greater awareness, of understanding time past, present, and future, for such experiences would be contacts with aspects of omniscience. There is definite evidence that some ultraterrestrial and even extraterrestrial intelligence have a greater consciousness awareness, and there is evidence, too, that this ability can be not only shared, but acquired. Then we can truly put into practice the words of St. Thomas who said that "all things should belong to one world," and this one world would include terrestrials, extraterrestrials, meta-terrestrials, and ultraterrestrials—not denying God's existence, but expanding his domain into areas that we have never before been aware of. But let us not be persuaded by the first major display of "unearthly power" without real discernment of intent of the lesser "gods" within a divine orderings of creation. It would be a great tragedy if we surrender ourselves at the very point of our greatest consciousness awakening. I call it the "last temptation," which is to deny our living image as the Adam Kadmon which has been divinely inscribed on every cell and molecule within the heritage of humankind.

As our consciousness is awakened, new goals reached in cooperation not only amongst ourselves but with other races of intelligence is assured. In essence, a preparation is being made for us to realize that we are part of the cosmic citizenship in the heavens, that we are but one branch of a higher Adamic creation that has gone through many stages of evolution, and that we shall soon understand firsthand the references to such terms as exousoi, archai, dynameis, thronoi, kyritoes, angeloi—authorities, elders, powers, thrones, dominions, and angels.

Mankind throughout history aspires to the notion that the "House of Many Mansions" as it is called in the West, or what is known in the tradition of the East as "the Palace of the Spheres," or as what some contemporaries would call the "Galactic Federation," should operate with the ethic of doing unto others what one would do unto oneself. There are laws that are consistent in space with those revealed to Moses on Mount Sinai, showing that without these laws, intelligence in space, no matter how abundant or how developed, would make technology and theology into a graven image.

# References:

[1] Interview with Jill Tarter, *Metro News*, December 22, 1994, p. 17.

[2] Ibid. Under the leadership of Frank Drake at UC Santa Cruz, NASA began using radio telescopes in 1960 to listen for radio signals of possible ET origin. On 12 October 1992 new channels were added and technology upgraded by a factor of 10,000 in SETI listening capabilities.

[3] N.K. Kardashev, "Transmission of information by extraterrestrial civilization," *Proceedings: Akademiya Kauk Armyanskoi SSR Byurakanskaya Astrofizicheskaya Observatoriya*, 1965, pp. 19-29.

[4] Robert Jastrow, *Red Giants and White Dwarfs*, 2nd Edition, New York: W.W. Norton, 1979.

[5] Frank Tippler, *The Physics of Immortality*, New York: Doubleday, 1994, p. 250.

[6] P. Teilhard de Chardin, *The Phenomenon of Man*, New York: Harper & Row, 1975, pp. 43, 53, 66.

[7] Michael A. Michaud presents a unique view of understanding other evolutionary cultures who have learned to survive and who can communicate with us in "Negotiating with Other Worlds," *The Futurist*, April 1973, pp. 71-77.

[8] Freeman Dyson, "Time Without End: Physics and Biology in an Open Universe," *Review of Modern Physics* **51**: 447-460.

[9] Personal communication with John Wolf, NASA-Ames, Mt. View, June 1979.

[10] S.E. Khaikin, "Communication with Extraterrestrial Civilizations," *Proceedings, Akademiya Nauk Armyanskoi SSR Byurakanskaya Astrofizicheskaya Observatoriya*, 1965. pp. 53-59.

[11] P.A. Moore, and Jackson, F., *Life in the Universe*. London: Routledge & Kegan Paul, 1962.

[12] G.K. O'Neill. "The Colonization of Space," *Physics Today,* Sept. 1974, pp. 32-40. See also *Space Colonization—A Design Study*. Report of the NASA/ASEE 1977 Summer Faculty Fellowship Program in Engineering Systems Design. E. Burgess editor. NASA SP-413.

[13] Michaud, *op. cit.*, pp. 75-77.

[14] Freeman J. Dyson, *Thinking Small in Space*. Paper presented at the annual meeting of the American Association for the Advancement of Science, Washington, D.C., Feb. 15, 1978.

[15] Fritz Zwicky, *Morphological Astronomy*. Springer Verlage: Berlin, 1957. Personal conversation with Dr. Fritz Zwicky at Cal Tech in April 1973.

[16] U.N. Outer Space Treaty. Inforce on 10 October 1967. See Preamble and Article One.

[17] Kraft Ehricke, "A Long-Range Perspective and Some Fundamental Aspects of Interstellar Evolution," *JBIS*, 28 (1975), 713-714.

[18] J. J. Hurtak, "Marketing and Legislation in Outer Space For Martian Resources," *Proceedings from Case for Mars IV Conference*, University of Colorado, Boulder, Co., June 1990.

[19] Ted Peters, *UFOs-God's Chariots?* John Knox Press: Atlanta, 1977, pp. 162-168.

[20] Hans Kueng, *Eternal Life?* Doubleday: New York, 1984, p. 224.

[21] Krister Stendahl, statement in *Life Beyond Earth and the Mind of Man*, edited by Richard Berendzen, NASA Scientific and Technical Information Office: Washington D.C., 1973, p. 29.

[22] Paul Tillich, *Systematic Theology*. University of Chicago Press: Chicago, 1951-63, II: 95f.

[23] Karl Rahner, "Natural Science and Reasonable Faith," *Theological Investigations*, 22 vols., Crossroad: New York, 1961, XXI:51-52.

[24] Conversations with Ted Peters, June 1992, Graduate Theological Union, Berkeley, California.

[25] *Sepher Ha-Aggadah*, edited by Hayim N. Bialik and Yehoshua H. Ravnitzky, Schocken Books, Inc., New York, 1992.

[26] James Robinson, editor, *The Nag Hammadi Library*, Harper and Row: New York, 1978.

[27] Renowned theologian Gerhard von Rad understood the problem of external angelic hierarchies as a problem

of human perceptions. He writes accordingly: "As soon as God enters into the apperception of a human being, God's angel appears...." See *Theological Dictionary of the New Testament*, Wm. B. Eerdmans: Grand Rapids, 1964, I, p.77.

[28]Noted theologian Karl Barth somewhat grudgingly acknowledges some truth in higher angelic orders in his *Die kirchliche Dogmatik* 3/3. See American edition, Church Dogmatics, Harper and Row: New York, 1962 p. 482-483.

[29]Gabriel Fackre, "Angels Heard and Demons Seen" *Theology Today*, October 1994, pp. 350-355.

[30]Robert Eisenmann, *The Dead Sea Scrolls Uncovered*, Element: New York, 1994.

[31]*The Book of Enoch I,* edited by James Charles, Oxford University Press: London, 1912. For an illuminating tracing on the mission of angels see Jesuit scholar Jean Danielou, *The Angels and Their Mission: According to the Father of the Church*, Westminister, MD: Christian Classics, 1976.

[32]Testimony given to former astronaut Harrison Schmidt in the context of private investigation of multilations, Santa Fe, New Mexico, July-August 1979.

[33]Conversations with Dr. Lavonna Stillman, The Stillman Institute, San Jose, CA., August 1992.

[34]Private research still in progress (1995) of repeated abductions of extended family unit in California.

[35]J.J. Hurtak, "Close Encounters of the Multiple Abductions Kind," Pt 1, *International UFO Library*, Pt. 1, Jan. 1993, pp. 24-25, 38.

[36]David Jacobs, *Secret Life*. Fourth Estate Ltd.: London, 1993.

[37]Private conversation with B. Hopkins, Frankfort, Germany, November 1989.

[38]J.J. Hurtak, "Close Encounters of the Multiple Abductions Kind," Pt. 2, *International UFO Library*, April 1993, pp. 32-35 .

[39]Conversations with Dr. Lavonna Stillman, Stillman Institute, San Jose, CA., August-Sept. 1994.

[40]J.J. Hurtak-A.Puharich. *Overview of Extraterrestrial Developments*. KGO radio talk-show, San Francisco, March 16, 1976.

[41]Personal conversations with E. Klarer, Johannesburg, RSA, August 1981.

[42]*Ibid.*, in Natal, RSA, December 1993.

[43]Personal conversations with M. Panisset, Brasilia, Brasil, January 1984.

[44]*Ibid.*

[45]Personal conversations with C. Mutwa, Mafaking, Bophutaswana, June 1983.

[46]See Plotinus' Enneads , vol. 17 of *Great Books of the Western World*. U. of Chicago Press, Chicago, 1952.

[47]Conversations with Dr. Ted Peters, Pacific Lutheran Theologial Seminary, Berkeley, CA., November 1994 on the question of "panspermia and on-going evolution within a possible divine plan." The great philosopher Albrect Ritschl wrote in the nineteenth century about "the development of a spiritually-endowed race of organisms" living in other worlds. "Thus it is possible that the earth is not the only scene of the history of created spirit." See *The Christian Doctrine of Justification and Reconciliation*, Vol.3 of *The Positive Development of Doctrine*, translated from German by H.R. Mackintosh and A. Macaulay, 1874.

[48]A fuller description and image of the various alleged categories including the Insectoid, the Reptilian, the Grey Reticulans, the Hybrids, the Orion group, etc., is detailed in my book, *IMAGE AND SIMILITUDE*, forthcoming in August 1995 from The Academy For Future Science, P.O. Box FE, Los Gatos, CA 95031.

[49]See Appendix I and II at the end of this paper. See also: Scroll of Yehezkiel, The Jerusalem Bible, Katav: Jerusalem, 1981. The Scroll of Kings, The Jerusalem Bible, ibid.

[50]See models of future in the following: A. Claude. "The Coming of Age of the Cell," *Science*, 189 (1975), 433-435. JD. Bernal, *The World, The Flesh, and the Devil*. Methuen: London, 1929. Freeman J. Dyson, "Search for Artificial Sources of Infrared Radiation," Science, 131, 1667 (1960), and Stuart Holroyd, *Prelude to the Landing on Planet Earth*, Allen Ltd.: London, 1977.

# APPENDIX I:

## MERKABAH (Divine Vehicle)

If we look at the descriptions in our Scriptures [namely, the sections of *Torah, Nebuim, Chetubim*], clearly this was not a UFO event. The actual terminology for transport is the Merkabah which is the ancient Hebrew word for Divine Vehicle—a vehicle that has its own Light power, that is, non-material, that brings a "prophecy" or scripture teaching as opposed to something very mechanical, mundane and in violation of free will. It is clear in the context of Ezekiel that the Merkabah or, in this instance, the Wheel within the Wheel (the Ophanim), the Eyes and the experience are connected with a complete energy field of intelligence. Clearly a physical movement of the prophet's body take place from one dimension to another.

How can we tell the difference between the Merkabah and the ordinary UFO ship, if we were viewing them in the sky? The Merkabah (divine vehicle) always is connected with a tremendous sense of spiritual profoundness, a sense of what we would call "sanctification," a sense of renewal, with the realization that there is an actual brotherhood or teaching of Light, the B'nai Or, in the documents of Qumran and the New Testament.[See 1QS 4.21;9.3, 1QH 3.20; CD 5,18; 1QM 13.10.

### CITATIONS ON MERKABAH and the Sacred Scriptures

1. He (God) has the "Chariots of the High and Exalted Throne" as is written in Isaiah 6.1: "I saw the Lord sitting upon a higher and exalted throne.

2. He (God) has the "Chariots of the Throne of Glory," as it is written in Jeremiah 17.12: "The Throne of Glory, set on high from the beginning, is the place of our sanctuary."

3. He has the "Chariots of the Ophanim," as it is written in Ezekiel 10.12: "and the Ophanim were full of eyes round about."

4. He has the Chariots of a Swift Kerub, as it is written in Ps 8: "riding on a swift cherub".

5. He has the "Chariots of the Chayyoth," as it is written in Ezekial 1.14: "and the Chayyoth ran and returned."

6. He has the "Chariots of the Araboth," as it is written in Psalm 68.5: "Extol Him (YHWH) that rideth upon the Araboth."

7. He has the "Chariots of Eagles," as it is written in Exodus 19.4: "I have you on eagles' wings."

8. He has the "Chariots of the Tent," as it is written in Deuteronomy 31.15: "And the Lord appeared in the Tent in a pillar of cloud."

9. He has the "Chariots of the Ribbotaim," as it is written in Psalm 68.18: "The chariots of God are Ribbotaim, thousands of angels."

10. He has the "Chariots of the Altar," as it is written in Amos 9.1: "I saw the Lord standing upon the Altar."

11. He has the "Chariots of the Ketubim," as it is written in 2 Samuel 22.11: "And he rode upon a cherub and did fly."

12. He has "the chariots of Clouds," as it is written in Exodus 19.9: "Lo, I come unto thee in a cloud."

# APPENDIX II:

## SPECIAL TERMS

*Adam Kadmon.* The "heavenly" or primordial image of mankind that was used by the Godhead of YHWH ELOHIM in the creation of the human race.

*Entropy.* Inevitable decay and degeneration of matter.

*Entropy-control.* Use of science/consciousness by advanced intelligence for control of the degenerative processes of physical reality within a given region of the physical universe.

*Multiple-Abduction Kind.* Multi-level abductions of human subjects by extraterrestrials, where relatives and other extended "family" members are also "experimented" with by alien intelligence.

*Ultraterrestrial.* Advanced intelligence that is non-physical, emcompassing the categories of the "angelic," "avatar" and supernal intelligence as found in ancient religious literature.

# Addendum to
## "WHEN COSMIC CULTURES MEET" Conference

During the week of May 29, 1995, two major events took place. One was the coming together in Washington D.C. (May 27-29) of leading experts on the questions and answers of higher intelligence centered around a major conference called "When Cosmic Cultures Meet." Experts from various parts of the world, many with former government and media backgrounds, came forward to discuss openly, before the public, the reality of actual meetings with "cosmic cultures," that is, bringing into the open the fundamental fears and hopes in the contact and coming together with other intelligences from space. Discussions identifying the ultimate dilemma facing our technical civilization in sharing our fate with other life forms in the universe clearly opens the door to the future in the preparations needed for cooperation with species that show similarities and differences with the human race. Papers and film documents were presented that validate the logical ultimate goal of cooperating intelligences.

The second major event was the colossal find of Egyptian tombs of claimed offspring of a leading Egyptian historical personality, Ramses II (1279 B.C.-1213 B.C.), who is mirrored on the covers of *Time* (May 29) and *US News and World Report* (May 29). This was the lead story in other worldwide magazines and periodicals carrying the reports of the discovery of the ancient tomb and mausoleum called Tomb 5 in the Valley of the Kings located in Thebes. It is not only the biggest and most complex tomb ever found in Egypt, but contains not just one Pharaoh but may, perhaps, have housed many of the 52 offspring of Ramses II, who was allegedly Pharaoh of Egypt at the important time of the Exodus event mentioned in the Bible when a "pillar of Light" was seen coming down from the heavens.

The finding of the inscriptions and mummified remains of some of Ramses II's sons within a labyrinthian network of rooms, halls and tombs has another possible meaning in the interplay of space-time events. If Ramses II was the Pharaoh at the time of the Exodus, and the remains of his "firstborn" son has just been found, then analyzing these remains and discovering that his son died as a youth and not in old age would validate the account of the Bible. The recovery of actual DNA samples from Ramses II's firstborn son (Amen-hir-khopshef)* will provide us with important historic information in validating not only the Exodus period, but a cosmology that spoke of an event of divine intervention, or put another way, the coming together of "cosmic cultures" from the heavens and earth.

The stunning new discovery in Egypt's Valley of the Kings, and the stunning "uncoveries" of the reality of "When Cosmic Cultures Meet" coming together in a synchronous moment in world history may serve to open our eyes to the "opening" of the back door to the Old Testament period, while giving us what could be called the opening of the "front door" to our future when intelligence of "cosmic cultures" may be returning to the scene of the human experiment of life. In effect, we could be re-examining both sacred and secular narratives on history that gives new meaning to the historical footprints of a "master intelligence" connecting the stories of our ancestors with our children who will be pioneers of space. The "greater Exodus" to the stars and the higher heavens may be in preparation before our very eyes!

It has become clear to those who participated at the conference "When Cosmic Cultures Meet" that the direction of cosmic evolution beyond human intelligence, the challenge to eventually make contact with other species that share similarities with us, and the renewal of life in new space frontiers gives each of us a sense of purpose to life. As we become aware of our place within the splendors of the universe and a greater extraterrestrial family of life, we ultimately know that our higher purpose of existence reaches beyond any one ethnic group or territorial region on planet earth, and perhaps beyond any one race of intelligence in space where we recognize a greater purpose to All Life in the Universe.

*P.S. This name (Amen-hir-khopeshef) has a clear reference and the same phonetic spelling to the ancient name —"Amon-Her-khepeshef"— written in a book, *The Book of Knowledge: The Keys of Enoch* by this writer in 1973 and cited by title at this Conference "before" the recent confirmation by archaeologists. In short, the timing for the coming together of the Egyptian cosmology and present contact themes could not have been more appropriate for the new public dialogue needed, for it opens up a timeline enigma that runs from the remote past to the future in the re-examination of the very foundation of Western civilization.

# ⊕ James W. Deardorff

*James W. Deardorff, Ph.D.*

For 27 years Dr. Deardorff was a research atmospheric scientist at the University of Washington, the National Center for Atmospheric Research and at Oregon State University as a research professor. An interest in UFOs in the 1980's led to the study in depth of the Meier UFO contactee case, then ufology in general, spirituality, reincarnation and karma, origins of Christianity, the various Jesus-in-India traditions, and New Testament scholars' conclusions. In 1986 he took early retirement to be able to stay abreast of the topics full time. Since then he has written three books, *Celestial Teachings* (1991), *The Problem of New Testament Gospel Origins* (1992) and *Jesus in India: A Reexamination of Jesus' Asian Tradition in Light of Evidence Supporting Reincarnation*, expressing his finding on these subjects.

# Coping With The Cosmic Culture Gap: Science and Theology

*As complex as our nation-state global system is, it pales into simplicity when one considers the possibility of interacting with alien cultures separated from us and each other by possibly millions of years of technological and spiritual development. What possible incentives could there be for any level of contact with a raw, immature and dangerous Earth? There may be issues of self-protection that are driving contact. What-ever the reason, there remains vast cosmic culture gaps of science and theology to be faced.*

## BASIC CONSIDERATIONS

**The alien headstart**. That a cosmic culture gap will become apparent after our civilization first openly encounters an alien culture from another world is scarcely to be debated. Such alien cultures could be up to two billion years ahead of us in evolution, and therefore in technology and wisdom, due to our solar system being a relatively young star system some 5 billion years old in comparison to the Milky Way galaxy itself, which is perhaps twice as old. As a consequence, it would be hopelessly wishful thinking to imagine that we, an emerging planetary species, would be the ones who would within a few centuries launch space ships to explore the nearby stars and discover alien races on their planets or in space, thereby being the ones to first initiate contact with aliens. Instead, if we leave anthropocentric thinking behind, we can understand that it will be (more advanced) alien civilizations that will first initiate contact with us when they deem us prepared for it. Our own history indicates that it is the more advanced culture that discovers the less advanced culture, not the other way around (e.g., Europeans discovering the New World native Americans rather than vice versa).

The same reasoning would lead us to believe that, this being the case, Earth's cultures would already have been discovered by aliens in past ages, since there should be nothing particularly special about our own place in time that would cause an accidental discovery of us to occur in our own life-times. That is, if we deem it likely that an alien civilization will discover and/or contact us within the near future, we should not be surprised if alien races have already noted our presence in past centuries. However, it is not the purpose of this paper or of this conference to present evidence, whether mytho-logical, Biblical or anthropological, that would support the likelihood of our ancient civilizations having been visited by aliens from other worlds. Instead, this likelihood is merely mentioned here as being highly probable if we have any good reasons to expect contact with aliens in the near future.

**Could we be alone in the galaxy?** At this point it is necessary to summarize a related line of thought. If mankind should be the only thinking creatures within the galaxy, then there would be no need for this conference. Can that view be upheld? Now, it has been rationally argued that if only one other advanced culture existed within our galaxy with an urge to explore and/or colonize, it would have taken only some 10 or 20 million years before it would have discovered or colonized almost all habitable planets within the galaxy, utilizing technology no more advanced than what we can envision for ourselves within one or two centuries, i.e., assuming that their science and technology never even advanced past the stage of rockets and relativity theory. This time period of course diminishes upon assuming they developed more advanced methods of travel over the intervening millions of years. Since we see no overt indications of having been discovered or colonized, the argument goes, this indicates we are alone within the galaxy as creatively thinking beings.

**Or do we remain undetected by aliens?** It may be pointed out that a second school of thought would have alien civilizations within the galaxy being common, but with Earth having escaped their detection over the aeons. In order to push forward this view in the face of the preceding argument, its advocates were forced to speculate that each time an alien civilization's exploration vessel came upon a habitable planet of a new star system, they and their ancestors would pause at that planet for a full 100,000 years or more before feeling the urge to explore or colonize further (Newman & Sagan, 1981, pp. 313, 320). This huge time scale seems totally unreasonable and postulated merely to derive the preconceived result that Earth remains undiscovered.

**The aliens' awareness of us.** However, still others have pointed out various reasons why the preceding level of thinking is not sufficiently creative or plausible. It does not allow for the likelihood that alien science and technology would continue to evolve over millions of years, allowing the aliens to travel, explore and communicate much more freely over the vast distances within the galaxy than 20th century science can envision. It does not allow for aliens in charge of operation Earth being sufficiently intelligent to have a strategy of dealing with us whereby they could implement and enforce a policy of non-colonization both by themselves and by any less ethically inclined aliens. It does not include the likelihood that aliens in control of our sector of the galaxy would be sufficiently evolved ethically to leave us more or less alone, after our civilizations had reached a certain primitive level of development, so that we could learn to think for ourselves from then on rather than to rely upon "gods and goddesses" to satisfy our needs, and to evolve freely in a manner that would exhibit maximum diversification. It does not allow for their technology to have developed to the point where they could observe us surreptitiously and decide if and when we are prepared for definitive contact by them. It does not allow for the likelihood that their strategy would include gradually preparing us for future contact with them or other aliens in a subliminal manner designed not to shock our societies into chaos. Discussions of such possibilities are mostly missing from the scientific literature because it is considered improper scholarship to postulate that science far in advance of ours could exist, notwithstanding the rapid pace at which our own science and technology are advancing. Nevertheless, some references relevant to the preceding discussions have been able to sneak into the reviewed literature; they may be found in Deardorff (1986, 1987).

Whether or not aliens who contact us in the future would choose to share much or any of their science and technology with us, or choose to share their theology or religion with us, will be examined in the next sections.

## THE SCIENTIFIC CULTURE GAP

**Its realization.** With the preceding discussion as background, we see that a great gap would indeed exist between the alien level of science and technology, and ours. The aliens would probably allow us to see bits of their technology in action, for one reason to cause us to realize our true place in the galaxy as Johnny-come-latelies whose science is in a relatively infantile state. They could easily do this by allowing us to watch their spacecraft maneuver and operate in manners unprecedented by 20th century standards of science, and with unknown sources of power.

The first reaction to an overt alien contact from science would likely be one of marvel and awe. "How can they do that which seems like magic to us?" There would be a brief spate of scientific speculation that they must be using this-or-that technology to accomplish such-and-such, and so could we not go back to the drawing boards and in a few months or years come up with craft that could emulate theirs? However, the futility of any such attempts would become apparent within a few years, as the realization sank in that whole new fields within physics, chemistry, metallurgy, etc. still awaited discovery, with much development required and integration of many new disciplines with each other before any progress towards emulating the alien technology would become apparent. And this could take centuries if not millennia.

**Scientific morale.** In the meantime a second reaction would gradually sink in, that almost everything known or correctly known to present-day science has long since been known to the advanced aliens and, in most instances, has become obsolete for them as they gradually developed ever newer and expanded technologies, and more correct and comprehensive theories. What will that do to the morale of our scientists? The individual Earth scientist might well lament that "Whatever I discover will have been discovered before, and will be of little lasting value, so what is the use?"

In order to combat that devastating blow for the scientist's morale, it would be essential for the scientist to come to an understanding of our temporal position within the scheme of things, and to realize that the more advanced aliens themselves were probably once in a position similar to us but somehow evolved past our level and on to a better life. Their scientists were evidently able to keep going and help their societies advance culturally, after they first reached a cosmic level of awareness, so cannot our scientists do the same? If the newly emerging, young alien race survived their scientific culture shock, it stands to reason that more advanced aliens than themselves allowed them to survive it; hence we may have hope that we also will be so lucky, if we apply ourselves and open our minds. In any event, our progress in science can proceed no faster than the rate at which we can digest our own scientific advances, but for it to proceed at all, after open cosmic contact has been initiated, scientists will need to understand that their talents will still be very much needed then. They must understand that alien contact will not mean the end of everything.

**Alien strategy for preparing us.** Of great plausibility, then, is the likelihood that aliens who have allowed us to evolve more or less on our own, oblivious to their presence over the past few thousands of years, would already be preparing us for contact with them or other aliens to the extent possible without prematurely shocking us into panic and confusion, as would a sudden appearance in force of alien spacecraft all over the world. Such a conditioning would presumably be initiated after our general knowledge had reached the level where we could understand the possibility or probability of intelligent life having arisen also on planets surrounding other stars. (This realization has been growing rapidly since WWII.) Thus scientists should step back and consider whether or not mankind has been subliminally exposed to an alien presence in the past few decades or generations, designed to minimize the shock of the cosmic culture gap when their presence in our vicinity finally becomes self-evident. Such subliminal exposure could be effected through a mechanism like the on-going UFO phenomenon, without it adversely affecting the structure of human society.

**Would aliens share their technology with us?** But would not the aliens perhaps share their level of science and technology with us, in which case the scientific culture gap would soon become minimal? It would seem that an alien group that was only a couple centuries ahead of us might behave in that manner, though their presence in our vicinity would seemingly be rare, if for no other reason than that they would not yet have developed means of space travel sufficiently advanced to render navigating interstellar distances simple. However, more advanced aliens would probably not wish to share their technology with us because (1) our level of science simply would not be sufficiently advanced to allow them to explain their technology to us, and if not that, then (2) they could predict, based upon Earthly societal behavior, that we would abuse their advanced technology, not only on our own planet but on other planets that we could then more feasibly visit in the near future. If, however, a much less developed alien race were to contact us, slight as the possibility seems, we could learn from them, as they might feel that we would have some knowledge or raw materials to offer in return, thus making the interchange mutually beneficial.

**Alien diversity.** It must be kept in mind that aliens of all different levels of technological and evolutionary development presumably exist, at least by the arguments of the preceding section. Aliens who are too many millions of years more advanced than others would presumably have little incentive for interacting with these others, and similarly aliens many more millions of years in advance still would not have incentive for interacting with either group, and so on. Thus, it seems most likely that even the aliens who are presumably overseeing our development and preparing us for our first open alien contact would have little future interaction with us afterwards. They would be too advanced. Thus, I do not believe they would try to share any of their technology with us, especially after having observed our societies' continuing warlike tendencies and extreme nationalism. They would probably instead reason like a good teacher does: her students must continue to learn for themselves and not come to rely upon their teachers to do their thinking for them, as may have happened to us in the distant past if aliens were then present and became revered as gods and goddesses. We might be in a position to ask them questions for a short while after they have initiated cosmic contact with us, but we should not expect answers to any questions designed to further our own technology.

## The Spiritual or Theological Culture Gap

We have seen that the spiritual or ethical side of the aliens' makeup cannot be left out of consideration even when discussing the scientific issues, because if the galaxy/universe *is* teeming with extraterrestrials (ETs), most of whom have had millions of years head start over us in evolution, we can only explain our present state of freedom from exploitation by them as due to their spiritual/ethical values being more developed than our own. Although this need not be true of every advanced ET race, it appears to be true of those alien groups who are overseeing our own development. Otherwise, we should expect to find ourselves being the slaves of ET taskmasters rather than pondering if they exist.

**Plausible ET ethical level.** If we are to make an assessment of the ethical or theological culture gap that could occur after contact from ETs became a fact, we need to ask what sort of cosmic philosophical outlook our ET overseers would likely possess. What sort of ethics would cause them to consider our free will of paramount importance, as suggested by a conditioning program that does not force anyone to believe that mankind is not the sole intelligence within the galaxy if that is his wish? If the UFO phenomenon represents this conditioning program, what sort of alien philosophy would be consistent with their patience in extending this conditioning over such a long, multi-decade time period? What sort of alien ethics would, at the same time, cause them to allow us to go ahead and make all kinds of seemingly catastrophic moral mistakes (World Wars, suppression of civil rights, etc.) without their stepping in and trying to force us to behave in some prescribed, peaceful and righteous manner?

A cosmic philosophy that seems to best fit these requirements, in my view, sees high ethical values as being nothing that can be forced upon others from the outside, but something that must be learned through personal experience—harsh experiences especially. It sees the learning of harsh lessons through bitter wars of mankind's own provocation as being more important (and feasible) than would be any alien attempts to establish a police state over us that would enforce world peace. In any event, any such imposition by the aliens would no doubt backfire by causing us to attempt continually to overthrow the ET police and place them in the position of being the oppressors, which would contradict the earlier deduction that our ET overseers possess high ethical values.

Would a religious view that believes ethical values can be imposed from the outside through the teachings of priests, ministers, rabbis, etc., combined with threats of not being admitted into heaven, paradise or an afterlife, be consistent with the deduced cosmic philosophy? Seemingly not, as it is inconsistent with the deduction that the aliens believe we must be permitted to make our own mistakes, so that we can learn to try to avoid making similar mistakes in the future. Furthermore, one lifetime followed by an eternity in paradise in which no learning takes place, seems far too short a period of time to learn on a personal level the many ethical lessons necessary for understanding how best to live peaceably with our neighbors while discouraging any less-than-ethical neighbor from inflicting violence upon ourselves. These considerations rule out any theology akin to Judeo-Christianity or Islam, although certain pieces within them might be considered valid, such as the Golden Rule.

In addition, it would be hopelessly anthropomorphic to expect the alien theology to encompass belief in a personal, localized, masculine or feminine God whose physical appearance mimics that of a human being or of an entity of any particular alien race. As long as we did not know that alien races exist, many of us were able to continue to expect that humans were made in God's image. Yet the aliens would likely realize, after having covertly observed mankind for a number of decades, that the reason some of our religions treat God in this manner is because it is a tradition carried over from having worshiped one or more of their own aliens as gods and/or goddesses (Elohim) in ages past. Hence, they may accept some responsibility for this and therefore have extra incentive for trying to prepare us gradually for the shock of rethinking our theological bases.

**The cosmic philosophy of reincarnation and karma.** We come, then, to the theological philosophy of reincarnation and karma as being consistent with the deduced alien philosophy and therefore worthy of examination. It does not suffer from any of the previous pitfalls. It could be cosmic in scope, applying to all creatures whose level of thinking exceeds the point where the meaning of life can be pondered. Reincarnation, in which one's essence is reborn but with its past-life remembrances blocked out at our level of development, is consistent with an alien emphasis upon preservation of free will. By not remembering our previous likes and dislikes, we are free to experience life from all different perspectives and make decisions based upon the experiences derived therefrom rather than from prejudices, some of them false, picked up in previous lives.

With the spiritual view that one will be reborn repeatedly within a similar society on the same planet again in the future, one would seemingly have more incentive for working towards the good of the society as a whole, and for an indefinite time in the future. Hence one would have a long-range outlook in solving societal problems. This could help explain the aliens' apparent long-range interest in our society, if we may judge from the extensive duration of the UFO phenomenon to date. Of course, if such aliens possess much longer lifetimes than we, this would also be consistent with a willingness on their part to implement long-range solutions to problems.

An alien philosophy that includes reincarnation is also very consistent with an alien view that we must learn from our own mistakes. This is what karma is all about, and the concept of karma seems to go along with that of reincarnation. That is, there would seem to be no point in reincarnation if, over a multitude of lifetimes, one did not learn lessons of wisdom and ethical value through living some lives in which we suffer, seemingly unjustly, in reaction to similar misdeeds we had inflicted upon others in the same or earlier lives. Although such lessons learned in the past may at our present stage of evolution only evince themselves as a more developed conscience or intuition, at some time in the indefinite future they presumably become available to conscious memory recall. Thus, the aliens may view mankind's wars, riots, civil unrest, and oppression of the poor and powerless, etc., as necessary evils to be tolerated while we learn better from them and evolve spiritually. However, such spiritual evolution would seem to be a relatively slow process, measurable only over significant numbers of lifetimes.

The above speculations concerning reincarnation and karma would not be offered here if evidence supporting the reality of reincarnation had not been burgeoning the past several decades (Hearn, 1897; Stevenson, 1975-1987; Dethlefson, 1976; Netherton and Shiffrin, 1978; Fiore, 1978; Wambach, 1979; Banerjee, 1980; Whitton and Fisher, 1986; Goldberg, 1988; Woolger, 1988; Weiss, 1988, 1992; Moody, 1991; Lucas, 1993). This evidence does indeed point to the reality of reincarnation, and we should expect, therefore, that aliens more evolved than we would long since have known of its reality, would have included it within their understanding and knowledge of life, and would have progressed far beyond this point in their understanding of the inner self. With this outlook, they can view the deaths of individual humans dispassionately if it serves long range goals, knowing that the individual essence does not die, and concern themselves much more with perpetuation of the human species as a whole and preservation of Earth as a suitable training ground for our human spirits.

Alien knowledge of the reality of reincarnation/karma is also consistent with their having avoided taking violent actions against us in any attempt to force us into a mode of more ethical conduct towards our fellow man. Not only would they immediately realize that any such actions would be unethical for them, they would realize that it could create negative karma for them that might in the future cause themselves, the perpetrators of such actions, to reincarnate as humans rather than reincarnating within their own societies. The Golden Rule is generally a good guideline on how to act so as not to build up negative karma, though its application may be uncertain in cases involving beings from disparate cosmic cultures. That is, the more evolved and ethical culture may not treat us as they wish us to treat them, since our present lack of cosmic understanding prevents us from being capable of treating them at their own level of understanding.

One may speculate that along with alien knowledge of reincarnation/karma would come also a belief in the existence of a spiritual God of the universe(s). God would be seen not only as the source of all—the material universe, its beauty and laws of nature, but as the original source of our own spirits and their ultimate home. God would be seen as pantheistic.

The theological culture gap that is expected to exist will be minimal for Hinduism, for which belief in reincarnation/karma is a basic part. However, various aspects of even this religion might be found wanting. For example, the above references to studies on reincarnation do not support a belief in transmigration—occasional rebirth of a human spirit within a lower animal, which is a part of Hinduism. Nor do they give any indication to support the notion that by living in an exemplary fashion for a portion of one's life at our stage of evolution one can permanently join up with Brahma upon death, thereby terminating the cycle of rebirth.

**Implications.** Thus, we come to the conclusion that the cosmic cultural gap, with respect to theology, is great, especially for a substantial or major proportion of those within Western society. The topics of reincarnation and karma are still treated as taboo, for the most part, within academia, and similarly either ignored or treated as manifestations of the devil within fundamentalist religions. Hence, the potential shock to be experienced by Western society if aliens' knowledge of the reality of reincarnation were made known, soon after future contact with aliens is confirmed, would be great. However, there is no need for them to force this knowledge or belief upon us in any abrupt manner after they initiate open contact with us, and in any event, knowledge of the reality of reincarnation and existence of a Universal Spirit stems from studying the experiences and investigations of others if it has not already become self-evident through personal experience. Hence, the cosmic culture gap in theology need not be realized abruptly, and could have years or decades in which to become ameliorated after overt alien contact. It is unlike the cosmic culture gap in science, for which any sudden realization that technologically advanced ETs exist and possess all the high technology described, for example, in reports of fantastic UFO maneuvers, would come as a sudden, giant shock and blow to those scientists who would never consider the UFO phenomenon to be anything other than some fad of science fiction.

Hence, if we were to ask our contactors from an advanced cosmic culture questions like "Is reincarnation a reality?" or "What is the purpose of life?", we would likely receive no answer, or no straight answer, or an answer like, "You already have sufficient information from which to deduce correct answers to those questions." If we were to ask them "What is God?" we might expect them to say something like, "The answer to that question will remain ahead of us all for a long, long time." There would just be no point in their answering sensitive questions that we should be answering for ourselves, especially if their answers would be immediately accepted as truths that would drive certain segments of our society into either despair or rebellion.

If we are to cushion these expected culture shocks, our obvious task is to educate, educate, educate. The taboos of the phrases "UFO phenomenon" and "reincarnation and karma" need to be overcome, while the evidence supporting their reality is presented to all who can accept it.

# REFERENCES

Banerjee, H. N. (1980): *Americans Who Have Been Reincarnated*. New York: MacMillan.

Deardorff, J. W. (1986): "Possible extraterrestrial strategy for Earth," *Quart. J. Roy. Astron. Soc.*, **27**, 94-101.

_____ (1987): "Examination of the Embargo Hypothesis as an explanation for the great silence," *J. British Interplanetary Soc.*, **40**, 373-379.

Dethlefson, T. (1976): *Voices from Other Lives: Reincarnation as a Source of Healing*. New York: M. Evans.

Fiore, Edith (1978): *You Have Been Here Before*. New York: Ballantine.

Goldberg, Bruce (1988): *Past Lives, Future Lives*. New York: Ballantine.

Hearn, Lafcadio (1897): *Gleanings in Buddha Fields*. Boston: Houghton, Mifflin & Co.

Lenz, Frederick (1979): Lifetimes: *True Accounts of Reincarnation*. New York, Ballantine.

Lucas, Winafred Blake, ed. (1993): *Regression Therapy: A Handbook for Professionals*, Vols. 1 and 2. Crest Park, California: Deep Forest Press.

Moody, Raymond A. (1991): *Coming Back: A Psychiatrist Explores Past-Life Journeys*. New York: Bantam Books.

Netherton, Morris, and Nancy Shiffrin (1978): *Past Lives Therapy*. New York, William Morrow.

Newman, W. I., and C. Sagan (1981): "Galactic civilizations: Population dynamics and interstellar diffusion," *Icarus*, **46**, 293-327.

Stevenson, Ian: *Cases of the Reincarnation Type*. Charlottesville: Univ. of Virginia.

(1975): Vol. 1, *Ten Cases in India*

(1977): Vol. 2, *Ten Cases in Sri Lanka*

(1980): Vol. 3, *Twelve Cases in Lebanon and Turkey*

(1983): Vol. 4, *Twelve Cases in Thailand and Burma*.

_____ (1987): *Children Who Remember Previous Lives*. Charlottesville: Univ. of Virginia.

Wambach, Helen (1979): *Reliving Past Lives: The Evidence under Hypnosis*. New York: Bantam Books.

Weiss, Brian (1988): *Many Lives, Many Masters*. New York: Simon & Schuster.

_____ (1992): *Through Time into Healing*. New York: Simon & Schuster.

Whitton, Joel L., and Joe Fisher (1986): *Life Between Life*. New York: Warner Books.

Woolger, Roger (1988): *Other Lives, Other Selves*. New York: Bantam Books.

## ⊕ Dave Hunt

*Dave Hunt*

Mr. Hunt has degrees in mathematics and accounting and was in the business world for 20 years as vice president, general manager of several corporations. Since retiring from the business world he has authored over 20 books covering a wide variety of subjects. They have sold over three million copies in more than 40 languages. Some of his titles are: *Sanctuary of the Chosen, The New Spirituality*, and *The Archon Conspiracy*. He lives in the Northwest with his wife of 45 years. They have four children and eight grandchildren.

# A Reason To Fear

*No other speaker was more certain about his assessment of what UFO phenomena was and was not than Dave Hunt. From a strongly professed Christian position he declares there are no physical ETs, that they could only be spiritual entities under the dominion of Satan. This being the case, he cautions that any association with the phenomena would be dangerous and reason to fear. Whatever support there may be for this view point, it is a part of the dialogue that needs to be heard.*

The premise of the ***When Cosmic Cultures Meet*** conference is that a meeting with extraterrestrial beings is inevitable and that it will take place right here on our planet. The purpose of the conference is to anticipate the impact of such a meeting upon all facets of earth's culture and to discuss ways of preparing for it. Unfortunately, if this premise is correct (that civilizations exist on other planets which have the capability of reaching earth), then we have good reason to fear such an encounter.

Robert Jastrow has suggested that on some planets "out there" evolution could have been in progress for 10 billion years longer than here upon earth and that the beings thereby produced could be as far beyond man on the evolutionary scale as man is beyond a worm. Their powers would make them seem like gods to us. That possibility alone is reason for great fear. Our only value to such creatures would be as "pets" or as guinea pigs for experimentation. They wouldn't even want us as slaves inasmuch as their robots would be far more efficient and easier to maintain.

Yet, instead of hoping to be left undiscovered by such awesome beings, we are trying to contact them. The Search For Extraterrestrial Intelligences (SETI) is being pursued relentlessly. The Voyager spacecraft, which is steadily making its way deeper into space, carries a message on a gold record affixed to its exterior:

> We cast this message into the cosmos.... Of the 200 million stars in the Milky Way galaxy, some—perhaps many—may have inhabited planets and spacefaring civilizations. If one such civilization intercepts Voyager...here is our message:

> This is a present from a small, distant world, a token of our sounds, our science, our images, our music, our thoughts and our feelings. We are attempting to survive our time so we may live into yours. We hope someday, having solved the problems we face, to join a community of galactic civilizations. This record represents our hope and our determination, and our good will in a vast and awesome universe.

> Jimmy Carter
> President of the United States of America
> THE WHITE HOUSE, June 16, 1977

President Reagan suggested that if faced with a threat from alien forces earth's inhabitants might unite for mutual protection. Obviously, however, any power that could travel from its planet to earth must be so far beyond our capabilities that we could not defend ourselves. The vast distances of space alone dictate that fact. To reach the closest stars (a mere 4.5 light years away) would take our Pioneer and Voyager spacecraft about 90,000 years! Our galaxy is about 100,000 light years across with the next closest galaxy about 1.5 million light years beyond. Going 1,000 light years from earth would only penetrate 1% into our galaxy, yet it would take Pioneer or Voyager 2 million years to get that far!

## THE CHALLENGE OF A NON-PHYSICAL DIMENSION

The incredible distances make it highly unlikely (certainly not by any technology we can even imagine) that *physical* beings in *physical* spacecraft will ever reach earth. Then what are UFOs? From the maneuvers they make, it is clear that they are not physical. Jacques Vallee, John Keel and others have come to this conclusion. Who operates them? Jastrow suggests that some beings could have evolved beyond the need of bodies to become what religious people call "spirits." Being unhindered by space and time, they could contact us here on earth by mental or psychic means—but here we face problems.

The entire structure of our science has been materialistic. It thus has no basis for evaluating spiritual entities or events. Jastrow says of such a hypothetical creature, "And so how do we know it's there? Maybe it can materialize and then dematerialize [as UFOs seem to do]. I'm sure it has magical powers by our standards...."[1] We have no instruments to measure "spirit" or to verify its existence much less to identify who these beings may be or their motives. Whitley Strieber, after years of alleged contact, still doesn't know who or what these entities are or represent—but he wants us all to trust them! However, whether or not there is actually contact with such beings is still in dispute.

In spite of the problems it poses, increasing numbers of our top scientists now admit the existence of a non-physical extension of the universe. Philosophy-of-science professor John Gliedman interviewed top scientists throughout Europe and America and as a result reported in *Science Digest*: "From Berkeley to Paris and from London to Princeton, prominent scientists from fields as diverse as neuro-physiology and quantum physics are...admitting they believe in the possibility, at least, of...the immortal human spirit and divine creation."[2] In agreement are such celebrated scientists as Nobel Laureate Eugene Wigner, known as "one of the greatest physicists of the century," Sir Karl Popper, who has been called "the most famous philosopher of science of our age," and the late mathematician and quantum mechanics theorist, John von Neumann, who has been described as perhaps "the smartest man who ever lived." Nobel Laureate Sir John Eccles has put it rather succinctly:

> But if there are bona fide mental events—events that are not themselves physical or material—then the whole program of philosophical materialism collapses.
>
> The universe is no longer composed of "matter and a void" but now must make (spaceless) room for (massless) entities [i.e. non-physical intelligences].[3]

In *Science and the Unseen World*, Sir Arthur Eddington, one of the greatest physicists of all time, wrote that to imagine that consciousness is ruled by the laws of physics and chemistry "is as preposterous as the suggestion that a nation could be ruled by... the laws of grammar."[4] Ken Wilbur reviewed the writings of the greatest physicists of this century and discovered that they virtually *all* believed in a non-physical dimension of reality. Based on their writings, he concluded, "There is no longer any major physical-theoretical objection to spiritual realities.... [T]his view...in all likelihood marks final closure on that most nagging aspect of the age-old debate between the physical sciences and religion...."[5] In complete agreement, Arthur Koestler declared:

> The nineteenth-century clockwork model of the universe is in shambles and, since matter itself has been dematerialized, materialism can no longer claim to be a scientific philosophy.[6]

## THE VERIFICATION PROBLEM

Psychic contact would thus seem to be a viable possibility. However, the only verification we have of alleged "contact" has been procured by psychotherapists under hypnotic regression. That method is unreliable at best and has been discredited because it has been proven to open the door to gross deception. More than 13 years ago the Supreme Court of California "barred the use of virtually all testimony from witnesses who have been hypnotized in an attempt to refresh their memories." [7] Other states have followed suit. In the *California Law Review*, Professor Bernard Diamond, a foremost expert on hypnosis, insisted that hypnosis is so rooted in deception that it is *impossible* to prevent distortion and fabrication from entering in.

Harvard University has begun an investigation of psychiatrist John Mack, a specialist in recovering "memories" of space alien abduction and abuse. A preliminary report has already been issued by the Harvard committee which "criticizes Mack's research and finds him 'in violation of the standards of conduct expected of a member of the faculty of Harvard University.'" [8] Even Whitley Strieber seems to have concluded that he was "the victim of a hypnotist who implanted the alien experiences deep in his mind" and that the same is true of other "abductees." In April an appellate court overturned the 1990 conviction of George Franklin Sr. for murder based upon memories recovered from his daughter under hypnosis. There has been a growing trend of recent court decisions against hypnotically recovered memories. Yet this is the backbone of the "evidence" being offered for ETI contact.

## EARTHLINGS AT THEIR MERCY

Apropos to this conference, whether physical or in spirit form, beings capable of contacting us here on earth would be so far beyond us that there is nothing we could do to prepare for such a meeting. It is absurd to imagine that we will have anything to say about the results of such contact should it occur. We can't even imagine what weapons they may have, either physical or psychic, and in any case we would have no defense against them. They will run the show. We will be at their mercy. Nor is there any reason to hope that they will be merciful—but plenty of reason to fear.

Why should they act toward us mere "worms" in any manner except from their own selfish interests? There is no basis for expecting evolution's higher forms to be kind and caring. They would likely be even more cruel and self-serving than we are. Isn't this how survival of the fittest works? A species doesn't survive long enough to reach god-like powers by being kind to others. We have every reason to fear.

Nor does education, technology, science or even the arts produce mercy and compassion. While there are evidences of these qualities on earth, the overall trend is an increase in crime, war and every act of selfishness. Germany was the most highly cultured and scientifically advanced society in the 1930's and it produced the Holocaust. To suggest that this is a negative view and that positive thinking will change it all is to engage in fantasy. It is not a question of pessimism or optimism but of realism.

## THE IMPOSSIBLE RELIGION

There is a general consensus which assumes the existence of intelligent life beyond earth on the basis of chance and evolution. This is the only accepted view in academic circles, yet it can be quickly dismissed on mathematical grounds alone. Eminent British astronomer Sir Fred Hoyle has calculated that "even if the whole universe consisted of organic soup" from which life is made, the chance of producing merely the basic enzymes of life by random processes without intelligent direction would be about 1 over a 1 with 40,000 zeros after it—a "probability" too small even to imagine.

Some comparisons are helpful. The odds that one could by chance pick a designated grain of sand from the Sahara Desert are about 1 over 1 with 20 zeros after it. The likelihood of reaching out and by chance plucking a particular *atom* out of the *universe* would be about 1 over a 1 with 80 zeros after it. If every atom in this universe became another universe, the chance of reaching out at random and plucking a particular atom out of all of those universes would then be 1 over 1 with 160 zeros after it. Obviously, Hoyle's probability is zero!

Considering the impossible odds merely to produce life's basic enzymes by chance, Hoyle concludes that "Darwinian evolution is most unlikely to get even one polypeptide [sequence] right, let alone the thousands on which living cells depend for survival." Even if that happened, chance would have to go on to develop millions of kinds of cells, each with thousands of complex chemical reactions in progress at the same time and in delicate balance with one another. Furthermore, differing kinds of cells (there are trillions in the human body) would have to develop by chance (nerves, eyes, heart, kidneys, stomach, intestines, lungs, brain, fingernails etc.), all in the right place and each functioning in proper harmony with the rest of the body. It's an absurdity!

The truth is that evolution is mathematically impossible and that cold fact can easily be proved. Then why does this bankrupt theory persist? Hoyle accuses the evolutionists of self-interest, unfair pressure, and dishonesty in keeping their theory alive and forbidding the only alternative, Divine creation, from being heard:

> This situation [mathematical impossibility] is well known to geneticists and yet nobody seems to blow the whistle decisively on the theory....
>
> Most scientists still cling to Darwinism because of its grip on the educational system.... You either have to believe the concepts, or you will be branded a heretic. [9]

"Heretic" is an appropriate term, because evolution, like psychotherapy, is a religion—a religion to which Hoyle himself remains strangely committed. While he has defected from the Darwinian camp, Hoyle has simply switched his membership to another "denomination" of evolutionists which has an equally bizarre belief: that life came in from outer space. Of course this theory only raises a further question: Where and how did *that* life originate? We are obviously back where we started.

## EVOLUTION OR CREATION: CHANCE OR GOD

Hoyle does admit that perhaps "God" is the One who sent life in from space, but who or what is "God"? That question cannot be answered by science. Unfortunately, the popularizers of science have convinced our generation that science will ultimately answer every question. That is a delusion which the world's greatest scientists have long denounced, but almost no one has been listening. Sir Arthur Eddington wrote that "'Ought' [morality] takes us outside chemistry and physics." [10] Nobelist Erwin Schroedinger, who played a vital role in giving the world today's new physics, reminds us:

> [Science] is ghastly silent about all...that is really near to our heart, that really matters to us.... [I]t knows nothing of beautiful and ugly, good or bad, God and eternity....
>
> Whence came I and whither go I? That is the great unfathomable question, the same for every one of us. Science has no answer to it. [11]

In *Chance and Necessity,* Nobelist molecular biologist Jacques Monod gives a dozen or more reasons why evolution could not possibly occur. He explains, for example, that the essential character-istic of DNA is its perfect replication of itself; that evolution could only occur through a mistake in that operation; and that it is absurd to imagine developing even a single cell, much less the human brain, from a series of random and harmful mistakes in the DNA mechanism. Yet after giving reason after reason why life could not possibly be the product of chance and why evolution couldn't work, Monod con-cludes that it **must**, nevertheless, have happened that way. Having no valid reason for such "faith," Monod simply refuses to accept creation by God and trusts "chance" instead.

## THE LOGICAL CONSEQUENCES

If evolution, not God, is responsible for our existence, then we should shut down all medical facilities and let the weak die. Medically prolonging lives allows such persons to pass on their defects to subsequent generations and thereby weaken the race. Only the fittest must survive. We must stop trying to find a cure for AIDS and let its victims die, and the sooner the better. As for homosexuals and Lesbians, since their form of sex works against survival of the species by its failure to reproduce, the evolutionary process would eliminate them rather than grant them special rights.

Nature has no compassion. There is nothing more **natural** than disease, pain, death, and those calamities known as "**natural** disasters" (hurricanes, earthquakes, lightning, drought, famine, etc.). Gaia or "Mother Nature" is anything but kind. The evolutionist's attempt to have it both ways—denying a personal Creator yet insisting upon morals and compassion which can't come from Nature—betrays the lie that is taught as fact in our educational institutions.

## IRRECONCILABLE CONTRADICTIONS

If evolution is true, then man is as much a part of nature as the animals and no complaint can be made against anything he does. If it is not "wrong" for a volcano to spew forth poisonous gases, then neither is it wrong for a man-made factory to do the same. If man, as a result of the evolution of his brain, succeeds in destroying the earth in a nuclear holocaust or some ecological disaster, then in the big picture of the evolving universe that must be accepted as progress, since it was brought about by evolu-tion.

As for all the furor that is raised over the possible extinction of a species such as the spotted owl, hasn't evolution been exterminating species for millions of years? One cannot believe both in evolution and the preservation of endangered species. To stop loggers from felling trees because it might cause the extinction of the spotted owl is to defy the natural forces of evolution! Man, as the ultimate product of evolution on this planet, must be the ultimate predator and is only following evolution's laws by stomp-ing into extinction any species that gets in his way. The same would be true of highly evolved ETIs' (if they existed) treatment of earthlings, no matter how cruel or abusive.

Human beings, however, do have concern for the weak, the sick, the dying and feel compelled to help the helpless (even of lower species) even at the expense of their own safety and well-being. That fact cannot be explained by evolution. That we can reason about and interfere with ecology and survival of species proves that we are not the product of blind natural forces. On the contrary, we must have a higher origin. Obviously we didn't create ourselves, so we, like all of the universe, must have been made by some intelligent Creator to whom we are accountable. Our compassion proves that we were created by a personal, loving and gracious Creator. Certainly if we evolved from lower species and ascended by the power of fang and claw and the evolutionary development of capabilities for survival of the strongest, we would never have developed compassion and concern for our rivals.

## WHY HUMANOID ETIS DON'T EXIST

Obviously, the absurdity of evolution argues strongly against the existence of life on other planets. The suggestion that life could develop by chance not only on earth but on many other planets has been exposed as foolishness. Evolution is a fraud foisted upon us by those who are unwilling to face the consequences of being accountable to their Creator. If intelligent life exists anywhere, it was deliberately created by God. Furthermore, it can be shown logically that the creation of humanoids on other planets makes no sense—and the Bible, which tells us of God's creation, indicates that no such life exists.

Any intelligent created beings with the power of choice would eventually rebel against God as mankind has done. The Bible calls that rebellion, sin. God does not need to experiment ("Man rebelled against me, but let me try again on another planet... etc."). Thus, if there are other sinners scattered throughout the universe, God put them there intentionally. But why? Surely one planet of rebels is enough!

Our own compassion tells us that a loving God would want to forgive sinners and reconcile them to Himself. To do so righteously, however, the penalty for having broken God's laws must be paid. Finite beings could never pay that infinite penalty, so God Himself would have to do so by becoming one of us. The Bible claims that God became a babe through a virgin birth, lived a perfect, sinless life and died for our sins upon the cross. From Genesis to Revelation, the Bible makes it clear that in the final consummation of God's purposes the entire universe will be cleansed of sin through Christ's once-for-all sacrifice on the cross in payment of the penalty His justice demanded for sin. Forgiveness is offered to all who will repent of their rebellion and accept the pardon offered through Christ.

For any other rebellious beings "out there" to be redeemed, God would have had to become one of them also. But the Bible—the only religious revelation on earth that presents this essential gospel of the penalty having been paid—says that Christ did not "incarnate" or die anywhere else. He died only **once** and here on earth:

> ...by his own blood he entered in **once** into the holy place [heaven], having obtained eternal redemption for us ...[and] now **once** in the end of the world hath he [Christ] appeared to put away sin by the sacrifice of himself....
>
> But this man, after he had offered **one** sacrifice for sins for ever, sat down on the right hand of God.... For by **one** offering he hath perfected for ever them that are sanctified [and]...there is **no more** offering for sin.
>
> Hebrews 9:12, 26, 10:12,14,18

## A FASCINATING COMMON THREAD

No evidence of physical life anywhere else in the universe has ever been found (or ever will be found) because there are no physical ETIs "out there" somewhere. The only intelligent life, in addition to mankind, is all in spirit form: God, angels, Satan and demons. The Bible indicates that Satan has been communicating an unvarying lie to the human race from its beginning in order to prevent mankind from believing in Christ and receiving the pardon He freely offers. What is fascinating about the messages being received from alleged ETIs is their consistency. A common theme comes through. Moreover, the same message comes through in all channeling, whether in yogic trance or under hypnosis or on drugs or any other altered state of consciousness—and whether the source claims to be "spirit guides" or "ancestral spirits" or some alleged "ancient wisdom" or whatever.

Even more fascinating is the fact that this common message conforms precisely to the lie which the Bible declares a "talking serpent" conveyed to Eve in the Garden of Eden. Here was the forerunner to today's ETIs. And it brought a message that hasn't changed: that God is not personal but a force; that there is no death, we merely get recycled through reincarnation; that we are evolving upward to godhood; and that the evolutionary process can be accelerated through initiation into a secret "knowledge" with a dark and light side. This so-called enlightenment supposedly brings instant elevation to a higher consciousness where godhood and its powers are realized.

Not only have we found no evidence of physical life "out there," but all of the data to date weighs in favor of the extradimensional or non-physical hypothesis. And it also points to a spiritual goal rather than a physical one. "Contact" is of an occultic nature and involves altered states of consciousness where delusion is at its greatest. It was Shirley MacLaine's dabbling in the occult that opened her, like so many others, to a belief in extraterrestrials being in contact with earthlings to guide us to a higher level of consciousness, a "New Age."

Ruth Montgomery's case is much the same. It was her dabbling in the occult also that brought her into "contact" with non-physical entities who allegedly dictate through her as she types. Hardly the way a powerful civilization which is highly-advanced technologically and concerned about this world would operate. And the messages she receives (like everyone else) are anti-Biblical and anti-Christ. The references to a "Christ spirit" rather than to the resurrected Jesus Christ are a major indication, according to the Bible (1 John 4), that the source is not God but Satan.

Furthermore, the results of extended "contact" which these "contactees" describe sounds like demon-possession as the Bible depicts it. This is true of the many people who claim to be "walk-ins" and are thus possessed by the spirit of an alien. The same is true of Whitley Strieber who, in *Transformation* claims he can call these beings into his life at any time. He simply turns himself over to these "visitors" and submits to them controlling his life, even though he admits that he still struggles with the fear that they are evil and he doesn't know who they really are. And their predictions are mostly wrong, some leading to destruction and death.

## PAGANSIM REVIVED?

The messages that come from alleged ETIs sound very much like the channeled messages from spirit entities such as those received for some 20 years by Jane Roberts from Seth, who called UFOs "visitors from another reality." It is clear that a religion is being created which opposes the Biblical message and that resembles the ancient polytheistic pagan religions which the Bible condemns. At one point, Strieber came to the conclusion that the visitors were probably the gods who created us. In fact, these entities seem to resemble the ancient gods of the pagan religions. As only one example, an entity identifying itself as Ashtar (sounds like Ashtoreth, Astarte, Ishtar etc.) has been in communication with numerous contactees.

Ashtar has lied to all of its contactees. George Van Tassel was given instructions for building an "Integratron" building that would reverse aging. Van Tassel is dead and the Integratron uncompleted. Thelma Terrell, under the name Tuella, channels Ashtar also, who told her that the "great prophecies" from the space brothers would all be fulfilled in the early 1980s—another lie. Ashtar gave much other misinformation through T. James (about the earth being hollow, that George Adamski was genuinely in touch with ETIs, that Lemurians still have cities in Antarctica, etc.). Of course, Ashtar's main lies (like those of other channeled entities) are about Jesus Christ, denying all that the Bible says about Him.

## A Reliable Source Neglected

In contrast to the vagueness and misinformation and speculation and tantalizing stories that can't be verified which come through contact with Space Brothers or Spirit Guides, the Bible presents prophecies that have come true. These are not cheap psychic predictions of obscure happenings that rarely come true, but involve world shaping and world shaking events which have occurred precisely as foretold in the Bible hundreds and even thousands of years ahead of time.

Consider, for example, the prophecies concerning the Jews and the land of Israel. The Bible foretold that they would be cast out of their land and scattered to every corner of the earth; that they would be hated, persecuted and the object of continual attempted extermination; that nevertheless they would be preserved as an identifiable national/ethnic people; that in the "last days" they would be brought back into their land; that Jerusalem, after being destroyed again and again, would be rebuilt and would become a "cup of trembling...a burdensome stone" for all peoples on earth; and that Israel would be like a devouring fire to the neighbors around her (Zechariah 12).

These prophecies, which have been in the Bible in the clearest language for thousands of years, have been fulfilled in our day. That the Jews could remain an identifiable people after being scattered all over the world for 2,500 years since the destruction of Jerusalem and their Babylonian captivity is nothing short of miraculous. And that after all that time they would return to their land is even more incredible. And that Jerusalem is the greatest problem faced by the United Nations today and that a world of 5.6 billion people has its eyes on that obscure city, knowing that the next World War could well break out over it, only compounds the miracle. And that the armed forces of the tiny nation of Israel could consume its neighbors (in the 1967 and 1973 wars they could have taken Cairo, Beruit and Damascus) exactly as foretold brings the fulfillment of prophecies to the point where mathematically it could not have happened by chance. We are forced to believe that the Bible is God's Word.

Such prophecies are unique to the Bible. Nothing like them is found in the Koran, the Hindu Vedas, the sayings of Confucius or Buddha, the Book of Mormon or anywhere else. Nor are there any prophecies foretelling the coming of Krishna, Buddha, Mohammed, Zoroastra or any other religious leader. Only the coming of Jesus Christ has been foretold. In fact, the Old Testament contains more than 300 references to His coming, specific prophecies that were fulfilled in His life, death and resurrection: where He would be born, His rejection by the Jews and betrayal by a disciple for 30 pieces of silver, His crucifixion prophesied centuries before that means of punishment was known, that He would be crucified with criminals, that the soldiers would give Him vinegar mingled with gall and gamble for His robe, the very date He would ride into Jerusalem on a donkey and be hailed as the Messiah, the very day He would be crucified, etc. etc.

The prophecies in the Bible prove beyond a shadow of doubt that God exists, that He is the Creator of the universe, that the Bible is His Word, that the Jews are His chosen people, that Jesus Christ is the only Savior of sinners and that He is coming back to this earth to reign. It is astonishing, then, that so many people are looking to extraterrestrials with hope and are heeding the contradictory and lying communications from them, instead of heeding what the Bible, which proves its veracity, has to say.

## Preparation For Delusion

What we are seeing is staggering. Not only spirit mediums, psychics, yogis and kooks, but now top scientists are seriously attempting to contact "spirit beings" whom they believe are highly-evolved, god-like entities with greater knowledge and powers than humans possess. It takes little insight to realize that the attempt to contact non-physical entities opens the door for all kinds of Satanic deception that could be used in putting Antichrist in power!

In fact, Syrian President Hafez Assad, in an interview with *Time* magazine, expressed the belief that *only* an extraterrestrial power could bring real peace to this world. He has had a long-standing interest in UFOs and takes these unidentified flying objects quite seriously, believing they are space probes from other planets. *Time* asked Assad, "Suppose, as we discussed earlier, there were an extraterrestrial power and it tried to solve the Middle East's problems. What would you want it to do?" Hafez replied, "Certainly it would be a big power, and we would expect it to be unbiased." [12] Unbiased, yes, as far as earth's competing interests are concerned, but why would it be unselfish about its own interests if such a power actually existed?

Is it possible that the growing and compelling interest in ETIs is setting the world up for its greatest and most fearful delusion? The Bible indicates that Christ is going to catch out of this world all of His true followers. When that happens the reaction will be absolute terror: "Who took them, where did they go, will I be next?" Such unanswerable questions will haunt every rational person. No one will believe that the missing millions have been taken to heaven. The most likely explanation will be that some powerful civilization has snatched them from earth for slaves, or for some experimentation.

The Bible indicates that in the midst of the terror and chaos a man will arise known as the Antichrist. He will claim to have the answer. He may well say that he is in touch with an intergalactic council and is negotiating to have the missing loved ones returned. In the meantime, everyone must take his mark on their hand or forehead (Revelation 13), which will be the pledge that they will not be snatched away also. Everyone would only be too glad to have someone explain the situation and prevent any more disappearances from earth.

Whatever one believes about UFOs and ETIs, there is no reason for hope from that quarter, but only fear. There is great hope, however, in the solution the Bible offers, and nowhere else.

[1]*GEO*, February 1982, "GeoConversation," an interview with Dr. Robert Jastrow, p. 14.

[2]John Gliedman, "Scientists In Search of God," *Science Digest*, July 1982, p. 78.

[3]Sir John Eccles, with Daniel N. Robinson, *The Wonder of Being Human—Our Brain & Our Mind* (New Science Library, 1985), p. 54.

[4]Sir Arthur Eddington, *Science and the Unseen World* (Macmillan, 1937), pp. 53-54.

[5]Ken Wilbur, *Quantum Questions: The Mystical Writings of the World's Great Physicists* (Shambhala Publications, 1984), p. 170.

[6]*Research in Parapsychology 1972* (special dinner address by Arthur Koestler), p. 203.

[7]*Los Angeles Times*, March 12, 1982.

[8]*The Boston Globe*, April 12, 1995.

[9]From an interview by AP correspondent George W. Cornall, quoted from *Times-Advocate*, Escondido, California, December 10, 1982, pp. A10-11.

[10]Sir Arthur Eddington, *The Nature of the Physical World* (Macmillan, 1953), p. 345.

[11]Erwin Schroedinger, cited in Wilbur, *Quantum Questions*, pp. 81-83.

[12]"An Interview with Hafez Assad," *Time*, October 20, 1986, pp. 56-7.

## ⊕ Richard J. Boylan, Ph.D.

*Richard J. Boylan*

Dr. Boylan has had extensive experience as a clinical, research and consulting psychologist in private practice in Sacramento, CA. A student of UFO phenomena since 1947, he has, since 1989, interviewed over 145 persons reporting extraterrestrial contacts, in an ongoing research effort. He has written two books: *Extraterrestrial Contact* and *Human Responses and Close Extraterrestrial Encounters.* Dr. Boylan has taught as Lecturer at the University of California, Davis, Sacramento State University and Sierra College. He is a Founding Director of the Academy of Clinical Close Encounter Therapists (ACCET).

# Effects on Human Consciousness and Spirituality of World Announcement of ET Presence: Paradigm Shift Par Excellence

> *While it is factually unknown at this time, it seems reasonable that ET consciousness and intelligence impacting Earth is several magnitudes more developed than those of Earth-based humans. What does this portend? Some may rejoice at the prospect of openly interacting with vastly superior travelers. Others may assess it as being a very dangerous and threatening future. For example, facing perfect telepathic skill, where does one hide? If we are beginning to awake, for many it may be a very rude awakening.*

From the perspective of being a clinical and developmental psychologist, also trained in cultural and psychiatric anthropology, and as a researcher into extraterrestrial encounters, I believe that psychology and anthropology provide illumination and prediction about the effects on humanity of the public disclosure of extraterrestrial contact.

Let us start this examination of the effects of extraterrestrial contact, starting from the "pre-contact," natural, self-centered perspective from which we humans tend to operate.

Along the long chain of evolution from simple primate to *homo sapiens sapiens*, it is widely accepted that the point at which our evolution passed from pre-human (or proto-human) to fully human, was at the point at which man became conscious. Webster's defines "conscious" as meaning: "perceiving, apprehending, or noticing with a degree of controlled thought or observation," and "capable of or marked by thought, will, design, or perception." Inherent in these definitions is the idea that consciousness is self-awareness that is under the control of the aware person. While modern comparative psychologists have conceded that the faculty of consciousness is not limited to humans, but also shared to some degree by other animal and even plant life, it is the <u>degree</u> to which humans are self-conscious, purposefully reflective, and able to elaborate our ideas into complex actions and new creations, which marks our distinctive consciousness.

When we scan the other members of the animal kingdom, we have almost universally arrived at the conclusion that we are, perhaps through no merit of our own, at the pinnacle of animate life. What places us at the pinnacle of animate life, we deduce, is precisely the consciousness which enables us to step back and evaluate all other orders and species, and arrive at the conclusion that none is as conscious as we are. And we <u>act</u> upon this superiority-consciousness: we treat other species as inferior, and obviously here for our use and domination. We ride horses. We butcher cows. We pen up gorillas in our zoological gardens for our amusement or education. We eat chickens and fish. We keep birds in cages, and confine cats to our homes, as companions. And aside from the anomaly of the "neurotic" Venus flytrap, we hardly give plant life any thought about its consciousness at all.

Naturally, we equate our superior consciousness with superior intelligence. Because of the apparently unique way in which we are aware, we conclude that the way we process information and organize data makes us the most intelligent species of all. Whales may have bigger brain mass, but no whale has ever produced a Lamborghini, we proudly point out. And again, because we place ourselves at the pinnacle of not only consciousness, but also intelligence, we assume that the rest of the less-bright natural order is putty in our hands, to be manipulated by our intelligence into useful and creative forms.

Human consciousness, we further surmise, is inherently an **individual** matter. Each of us has our own thoughts, plans and imaginations. We have individual control of these, and derive security from the idea that our thoughts are our own. Our cultural behavior is built around these assumptions. As an example, consider the reaction of a 14-year-old girl when she discovers that her parents have been reading her diary. But it is not that way with every culture on Earth. (And it most certainly is not that way with off-planet cultures contacting us.)

There is a tribe in the East Indies whose first ritual in the morning is to gather after awakening, and then each member of the tribe shares their dreams of the night before. The content of these dreams is seen as a valued shared resource, to be made use of by the entire tribe for instruction, prediction, and understanding. How different from the jealously-guarded individual thought domains of individuals in Western culture!

Since psychologists and anthropologists generally agree that the natural condition of humankind is social interdependence, it follows that modern hyperindividualism of consciousness may be seen as unnatural and dysfunctional. Put more strongly, we humans cannot attain our highest and best potential while we cage ourselves in cells of rugged individualism.

The extraterrestrials (ETs) accomplish their communication telepathically. Furthermore, because of the shared, radiating-outward quality of telepathy, ETs operate in a collective mind-field, a sort of shared mental "commons," just as the Boston Commons is a physical shared meeting ground. Because of their heritage of operating in a shared mind-field, the ETs have developed cultures which emphasize collective purpose, group will, and the presumption of mutual support and aid.

Furthermore, the ETs' degree of collective consciousness has opened them up to the presence of consciousness throughout the universe and in all things, to a greater or lesser degree. Additionally, the ETs have a metaphysics which seems to hold that consciousness is at the foundation of the universe as its Supreme Source.

Thus, one impact on the traditional cultures of the Western industrialized societies will be a radical revision in the way we look at consciousness. As we humans develop more experience in dealing with the extraterrestrials' consciousness, we will have to abandon what we will come to see as our distorted view of consciousness as completely individual. We will have to expand our understanding to create a permissive context for shared mental communication and group consciousness to be allowed to take place among us. Events which formerly were restricted to the province of psychics and the paranormal, such as reading another person's mind, will become commonplace. But even more, such consciousness-sharing will not be seen as socially impolite. In the mental "commons," no one is an intruder, and all have a place.

The transformative implications of this paradigm shift should not be missed. Just as at a nude beach, visual openness among people tends to create a social spirit of relaxedness and trust, even more so will a mental openness and exchange foster attitudes of mutual acceptance and respect, appropriate trust, and the abandonment of interpersonal behavior based on misuse of power and deception. In a telepathic mind-field commons, there is no place to hide dark thoughts of greed, hate, aggression and deception. Social collective consciousness exerts a pressure on the individual to abandon such thoughts, and operate in ways that work together for the greater good of all.

Our assumption about being at the pinnacle of evolutionary development, because of our highly-developed consciousness and intelligence, is due for a rude revision, when the reality of extraterrestrial contact emerges into public awareness. The consciousness of the extraterrestrials is not only arrayed more distributively than ours, it appears to be, on the average, much more developed. Features of such advanced consciousness development include: less reliance on material artifacts, greater reliance on metaphysical and spiritual perspectives in planning and decision-making, treating individual beings and planets from an integrated systems perspective, and an appropriate subordination of their motivations and will to ethical and spiritual considerations derived from awareness of the intrinsic sacredness of all creation. Extraterrestrial intelligence is certainly not only greater than ours, but arrayed differently. Using human IQ as an inadequate but understandable yardstick, I have estimated the intelligence of the most prevalent visiting ET race at an average of "300 IQ." Of course, the ways that the ETs are intelligent are almost certainly different than our form of intelligence. And their intelligence, operating in conjunction with their advanced consciousness, develops much more thorough, systemic and integrated comprehension and problem-solving than is common in human intelligence.

Therefore, another paradigm shift which awaits us is the lowering of ourselves from the pedestal of creation's peak, and instead to place ourselves in a more modest but more accurate position somewhere along the spectrum of intelligent conscious life forms.

A corollary revision of human thinking involves the realization of the **cosmic** dimensions of the community of intelligent life. We humans will have to make the leap of awareness that, not only are we not the only intelligent, conscious life in the universe, but that such intelligent consciousness is common, and widely distributed among star systems. Further revision of perspective will be needed as we come to see that intelligence and consciousness form a **community** in the universe. This community is not just due to the common sharing of intelligence and consciousness, but more radically, due to the nature of intelligent consciousness as the core underpinning constituent of the universe. Further, that consciousness is intrinsic to the nature of matter and energy.

Another revisionist area for humans will be the erstwhile assumption that each of us is a personal uniqueness, consisting of a unique consciousness/personhood/soul, operating in one unique lifetime. The extraterrestrials know better.

While each of us is unique in the sense that we are not interchangeable clones, our uniqueness is not derived from separateness from the community and collective consciousness. For it is only within such community and collective consciousness, that we derive our awareness of being, our understanding of our special role and contribution, our sense of a heritage from which we are derived, and our sense of a future into which we can take our personal and community efforts. The individual person has no meaning divorced from the community of origin and community of participation. The extraterrestrial cultures have long since mastered this understanding. Members of ET societies operate from a communitarian perspective, and derive their sense of worth and belongingness from their contributory position within their communities.

Furthermore, when we view the situation from the perspective which the ETs use, we can see that while we may think of ourselves as unique individuals, each of whom has his/her individual allotment of intelligent consciousness, actually the reverse is the case. There is intelligent consciousness, distributed widely and generously throughout the universe; and of that consciousness matrix, we are **somewhat** individuated yet connected actualizations.

This is also why each of us does not die, indeed, cannot die. As transitorily-individuated constituents of the pervasive consciousness matrix, since the matrix consciousness is forever, so are those connected with matrix consciousness.

The human idea of a soul doing a unique lifetime, after which it will be judged on how well or evilly it acted in its lifetime, is thus simply not a correct understanding. Human spirituality, at least in the Western industrialized cultures, has historically involved a cosmology built upon the assessment of the way the conscious self/soul behaved. Furthermore, our morality has been built on the proper exercise of the faculties of motivation and will, the handmaidens of individual consciousness. Each of these religious/moral assumptions will undergo abrupt discontinuity and major challenge, when humans, individually and socially, confront the paradigm-shattering implications of the public world announcement of extraterrestrial contact with Earth.

A major disconcerting notion for many Westerners will be the ETs' metaphysics, which includes the awareness that which defines a person, their spark or soul, does not die nor is used up after a lifetime. Instead, that spark persists, and can, and often does, choose to reinvest in another body and go through another lifetime.

Indeed, the ETs tell us, certain such sparks, which were invested in an extraterrestrial body in a previous lifetime, have subsequently volunteered to do a human lifetime, and have invested in a human embryo, and are doing a human lifetime currently. This "missionary incarnation" is apparently designed to help spread appropriate consciousness, as we humans prepare for the major transitional times which are upon us. Such serial-incarnation histories for a given soul/spark may help explain why certain human experiencers of ET contact have the notion that, although human, they have an ET heritage and/or an alternative ET consciousness which breaks through at times.

It follows that the perspective that a unique soul will be definitively judged at the end of its lifetime as to how well or evilly it behaved must be changed. No one lifetime is definitive for the soul. Indeed, soul continuity allows for the soul to become more developed in its consciousness and spirituality, as a result of the various lifetime experiences it has undertaken. Therefore, traditional Western societies' Judgment-Day mentality must give way to a more developmental understanding of the "Pilgrim's Progress" of the journeying soul. Parenthetically, such spiritual metaphysics underscores the folly of those U.S. military compartments which are waging covert war on the Visitors in their craft. Such hostilities are attacks on what may well turn out to be family.

As a corollary, evolution will now become seen as not merely a doctrine about physiological development, but also spiritual and moral development as well. And traditional notions of Divine Creation will have to yield to a richer understanding that the Supreme Source continually creates, and recreates, throughout successive lifetimes.

But no modern psychology and metaphysics would be adequate if they remained as mere conceptualizations, and were not translated into practice. Let us examine some practical implications of the above.

As background, the evidence suggests, as James Deardorff has noted, that Earth has been in a galactic quarantine against contact by other civilizations for a long time. And the quarantine is about to be lifted; not because we have been good, but because time is running out for Earth and for the human species. While we deserve galactic conservatorship, we are fortunate enough to be about to be offered galactic partnership: to save the planet, to end weapons of mass destruction, to work together to assure fair access to resources for all, and to acquire the information we need to develop further mentally and spiritually, so as to become fit to join the partnership of intelligent inhabited worlds.

In response to the lifting of the quarantine, we will need to develop a truly planetary single voice in addressing the Visitors. The shape and functioning of our future global governing structure will depend on what we insist that it be. We can draw some inspiration for the global governing structure by remembering that in America we founded a country based on principles which are still the inspiration of peoples around the world. Is it not now time for us to reexamine the founding principles of our country? The right of human equality. The right to life and property (right livelihood). The right to pursue personal goals and objectives within the context of social responsibleness (the pursuit of happiness). And we must add to the Founding Fathers' list of basic rights the other rights which we have signed off on, which are included in the United Nations Declaration of Universal Human Rights.

Furthermore, we will have to temper the American historical preoccupation with Rugged Individualism, by reflecting that, contrary to what Cain said about his murdered brother Abel, we **are** our brother's (and sister's) keeper.

Paradoxically, coming cataclysms will provoke each of us to reach down inside, and remember what is basic and best in each of us. Just as during the recent American floods, we saw society women and cleaning ladies, banking officers and farm hands all pulling together, filling sandbags while standing in the rain. Because, after all, it was everybody's community which was threatened. We need to keep that consciousness and spirit alive for the days of the near future, when we will be rebuilding human society, as we operate from the renewing perspective of having found out that we are cosmic citizens.

There is more. As we become aware of the Visitors from afar as not just curious interlopers from space, but rather quite literally our "distant cousins," we shall have our whole sense of reality changed, and hopefully transformed. While it may shake many to come to learn that the ETs have played an active intervening role in our evolutionary development over the aeons, this news can also serve to build quicker bridges between humans and our galactic distant cousins.

We have always risen to new challenges. Mastering such challenges have made us stronger and wiser. I expect that this moment in our history, as extraterrestrial contact is dawning, will prove no exception. We can, and we will, arise to the challenge of being confronted with cosmic citizenship and interstellar family ties. And when soon the official meeting between our Cosmic Visitors and ourselves takes place, we can let that be not just an historic occasion, but recognize the truth that it is a family reunion, and as such, an occasion for great joy.

What are the implications for us humans of, finally, the day arriving of the global manifestation of ET reality? How will it change us as individuals, as a society, as a planet? Each person will have to answer these questions personally, but I can offer some suggestions.

The advanced development of the extraterrestrials can inspire us to reach beyond our own current horizons. The ETs can, and will, challenge us to develop ourselves more mentally and spiritually, and to stop worshipping material progress for itself. The ETs will challenge us to confront, honestly, effectively and unflinchingly, the ecological crisis our world is in, and to turn the damage around now, for it is very soon becoming too late. The ETs, with their selfless outreach across millions of miles of space to raise our consciousness, can set an example for us to extend our own renewed caring to the less fortunate members of our own human race, and to see our basic solidarity as one human people. And the ETs can make us aware that the precious gift of life is not confined to one planet, or one millennium, or one galaxy, and thus help us have an improved understanding of what the source of life is, and on what our deepest human destiny is grounded.

An Age is passing; a new Age is being born. Let us welcome it.

© 1995, Richard J. Boylan

## ⊕ R. Leo Sprinkle, Ph.D.

*R. Leo Sprinkle, Ph.D.*

Dr. Sprinkle is a counseling psychologist in private practice in Laramie, Wyoming. He is Professor Emeritus, Counseling Services, University of Wyoming. A UFO Experiencer, he had childhood encounters in 1940 and sightings in 1949 and 1956. His UFO research began in 1961 with surveys of UFO contactees and he began hypnosis sessions with UFO Experiencers in 1967. He is dedicated to assist others who are helping to bring Heaven and Earth together.

# I Am Becoming A Cosmic Citizen

*Using himself as a living laboratory, Leo Sprinkle has devoted more reflective thinking on what UFO phenomena really represents that any other researcher working the problem and recognizing the opportunities. The exploration he sees is that of our own fears, angers, hopes and potentials. The recognition he anticipates is of our ancient space origins, and the outcome is to return to the distant stars as fully developed Cosmic Citizens.*

Thomas Jefferson was quoted as saying, "I am no longer a Virginian; I am an American."

As a nitpicking professor, I can quibble with that statement; I can claim that Thomas Jefferson continued to be a Virginian. Also, I can question whether he emphasized his role as a "true" American (North, Central, and South America) or whether he focused on his role as a citizen of the United States of America (USA). However, the spirit of Jeffersonledge is bold!

My goal is to find ways to incorporate that spirit into my own experiences as a citizen of Laramie; of Wyoming; of the USA; of America; of Planet Earth; and—someday—as a Cosmic Citizen.

I am pleased to participate as a panel member in this conference, When Cosmic Cultures Meet. My hope is that this gathering is a step in the direction for all of Humankind becoming Cosmic Citizens.

## PAST EXPERIENCES

As a small child, I was interested in science and religion. As a skinny kid, I experienced a religious "rebirth" at a Methodist Youth Camp near Colorado Springs, Colorado. I felt that my life should be dedicated to serving God and Humanity.

As a student at the University of Colorado—Boulder, I saw a "flying saucer," or daylight disc, in 1949. My buddy, Joe Waggoner, and I watched the metallic appearing object as it moved silently beyond the Arts and Sciences building and disappeared behind some trees.

I shifted from being a "scoffer" to being a skeptic about reports of flying saucers.

In 1956, my wife Marilyn and I observed a strange nocturnal light that moved and hovered, moved and hovered, silently, over Boulder, Colorado.

I shifted from being a "skeptic" to being a "believer" in the reality of UFOs.

In 1961, I completed a doctoral degree in counseling psychology at the University of Missouri—Columbia. I joined the faculty of the Department of Psychology, University of North Dakota—Grand Forks (UND). I became a member of the National Investigations Committee on Aerial Phenomena (NICAP) and a consultant for the Aerial Phenomena Research Association (Sprinkle, 1967).

I conducted a survey of 256 NICAP members, comparing their responses on the *Rokeach Dogmatism Scale* with those of UND Graduate Students and Professors of Psychology (Sprinkle, 1969).

In 1964, I joined the faculty of the University of Wyoming—Laramie. In 1968, I completed a pilot study of 82 persons who described their ESP and UFO experiences, and who completed standardized personality inventories. I concluded that the majority of participants were "normal" in personality profiles (Sprinkle 1976a).

92

In 1967, I began to conduct individual hypnosis sessions with persons who reported "loss of time" experiences during UFO encounters. I continued with the survey of UFO Experiencers (UFOErs), which resulted in a 1986 dissertation study by Dr. June Parnell, Counselor Education, University of Wyoming (Parnell, 1987; Parnell & Sprinkle, 1990). She concluded that a majority of the 225 participants were normal in their personality profile patterns, regardless of the level of their UFO claims, including claims of communication with UFO occupants.

During the 1960's, I stumbled into past life therapy. I learned two important lessons: Most of my clients were pleased with the benefits of past life explorations; some of my colleagues were not pleased with my willingness to report the results of interviews and workshops for past life/future life explorations.

Since 1978, my wife and I have conducted more that 160 reincarnation workshops with more than 2100 participants (Wambach, 1978). The analyses of the reports of possible "future lives" have been summarized in the book, *Mass Dreams of the Future*, by Chet Snow (1989).

I have conducted hypnosis sessions with hundreds of UFOErs, as well as several surveys that have compared the personal characteristics of UFOErs and Non UFOErs. I have corresponded with thousands and thousands of UFOErs, for more than three decades, about their encounters with Extraterrestrial or Interdimensional Entities (ETs).

In 1980, we began our Rocky Mountain Conference on UFO Investigations, with the able assistance of the staff of Conferences and Institutes, University of Wyoming. Over the years, interested persons have been encouraged to speak openly about their UFO/ET encounters and the changes in their scientific and spiritual development (Gordon, 1991).

After that first conference in 1980, I finally gained the courage to arrange a hypnosis session with a fellow psychologist so that I could explore more fully my own memories of childhood encounters. I recalled events of 1940, when I was 10 years old, when I was on board a spacecraft, with a man standing on my left with his hand on my right shoulder; he was saying to me: "Leo, learn to read and write well. When you grow up, you can help other people learn more about their purpose in life. (Montgomery, 1985).

## CURRENT ACTIVITIES

I left the University of Wyoming in 1989, so that I could enter into private practice and continue, without pressure, my studies of reincarnation and UFO experiences (e.g., Sprinkle, 1989).

Recently, I completed a field study of individual sessions with interested persons who rated my verbalized impressions as dissimilar or similar to their own personal characteristics.

These "life readings," as some persons describe then, are conducted either "long distance" (LD) or in "sitting sessions" (SS). The intent is to merge, psychically, so that impressions of participants can be gained about "possible other lives" and the influence of those lessons on the current journey of the soul (Sprinkle, 1985).

Approximately one half of more than 1000 sessions were "sitting sessions." Evaluation forms indicate that the average ratings, overall, are 8 on a 9 point scale. There are no significant differences between LD and SS in terms of perceived similarity of verbalized impressions and personal characteristics.

These results are difficult to explain on the basis of conventional scientific hypotheses. Apparently, the results support the hypothesis of psychic communication between participant and me.

Another recent survey, with more that 400 participants, indicates that the UFOErs differ from Non UFOErs in the way that they respond to items about "scientific opinions." For example, in a pilot study, one third of the Non UFOErs indicated that they believe in the concept of reincarnation, while three fourths of the UFOErs indicated that they believe in reincarnation. Thus, one could speculate that UFOErs are moving toward a new/old perspective of science: the study of Nature/Body/Mind/Soul (Sprinkle 1988a and b).

In the 1970's, I speculated that UFO activity is part of a huge educational program that could be called "cosmic consciousness conditioning" (Sprinkle, 1976b).

In the 1980s, I developed a brief statement about the significance of UFO experiences.

## FUTURE HOPES

My hope for the future is (Sprinkle, 1986) that the following speculations become the perceived reality of Humankind on Planet Earth (Sprinkle, 1991):

In my opinion, UFO activity is one aspect of a huge educational program. The program can be called "cosmic consciousness conditioning."

This educational program apparently is conducted by representatives of extraterrestrial (ET) and/ or ultraterrestrial (UT) civilizations. These representative (UFOLKS) seem to be highly sophisticated, both technically and ethically. They can remain " invisible" to the human eye, and to the dominant Earth culture, except when they choose to arrange an encounter. The purpose of these encounters seems to be an initiation for the individual, and a stimulus to society, so that human development moves from Planetary Persons to Cosmic Citizens.

Thus, UFO contactees view themselves as "pawns" or as "partners" of UFOLKS, depending upon their psychological, social, and spiritual development. These encounters with Space Beings (or Spiritual Beings or SOBs!) force contactees to grapple with their sense of science and reality, and their attitudes about Near Death Experiences; Out of Body Experiences; Reincarnation and Psychical Experiences; UFO Experiences, etc.

If this hypothesis of UFO activity has merit, then we can anticipate further UFO reports which confound our view of science and reality. Further, we can predict that UFO "games" will continue along the lines of military and physical games; sexual and biological games; political and psychosocial games; and healing and spiritual games.

The purpose of these serious/silly games apparently is to puzzle and prod humanity, individually and collectively, so that—gradually—humanity learns to accept Suffering and Joy as twin aspects of change and growth. The eventual goal seems to be an integration of planetary forces and achieving twin tasks: sufficient scientific knowledge for space/time travel, and sufficient spiritual knowledge for compassionate interaction with other levels of consciousness.

In my opinion, we UFO contactees are being tested, and cultivated. Through "signs" and "symbols" we continue to explore our fears, angers, hopes, and potentials. The ridicule and rejection from others around us can lead to despair and hopelessness, or to the courage and commitment to a "new age" of service and cooperation. Then, gradually, all humankind awakens and moves toward a merger of science and ethics, a union of technology and spirituality, a balance of masculinity and femininity, and a transition from Planetary Persons to Cosmic Persons.

The only major question, in my opinion, is the question of formal public contact: Do UFOLKS choose to land, openly, simultaneously, in many Planetary communities? Or do UFOLKS continue to hide, while our Earth society learns to build flying saucers, and then sends representatives, as UFOLKS, to play space/time games with other developing planetary civilizations?

## RECOMMENDATION

94

I recommend any meditational and interpersonal activity that can enhance our communications with representatives of extraterrestrial and interdimensional civilizations.

Perhaps, someday, we shall become more aware of our distant past. Perhaps we shall recognize ourselves as ancient souls who traveled to Earth in order to experience many lifetimes and to prepare for our distant future: to return, once more, to the distant stars and to interact more fully with the consciousness of many cosmic cultures.

## REFERENCES

Gordon, J.S. (August 1991). *The UFO Experience*, The Atlantic, 268, No. 2, 82-92.

Montgomery, R. (1985). *Aliens Among Us*. New York: Putnam.

Parnell, J.O. (1987). Personality characteristics on the MMPI, 16 PF, and ACL of persons who claim UFO experiences. Dissertation Abstracts International, 47, No. 7. (Order No. DA8623104). Parnell, J.O., & Sprinkle, R.L. (1990). Personality characteristics of persons who claim UFO experiences. Journal of UFO Studies, new series, 2, 45-58.

Snow, C.B. (1989). *Mass Dreams of the Future*. New York: McGraw-Hill.

Sprinkle, R.L. (1967). Psychological implications in the investigation of UFO reports. In Lorenzen, C., & Lorenzen, J. *Flying Saucer Occupants*. New York: Signet Book. Pp. 160-186.

Sprinkle, R.L. (1968, July 29). Personal statement on investigation of UFO reports. Submitted to J.E. Roush, Chairman, Symposium on Unidentified Flying Objects. Hearings before the Committee on Science and Astronautics, United States House of Representatives. 90th Congress, 2nd Session. Pp. 206-210.

Sprinkle, R.L. (1969, June). Personal and scientific attitudes: A study of persons interested in UFO reports. In Bowen, D. "Beyond Condon," *Flying Saucer Review*, Special Issue No. 2, 6-10.

Sprinkle, R.L. (MORE)

# ⊕ James Moore, Ph.D.

*James Moore, Ph.D.*

Growing up in Hawaii, Dr. Moore developed an interest in dolphins. While an undergraduate at Stanford University he studied baboons at Gombe National Park in Tanzania. At graduate school in Biological Anthropology at Harvard, interaction with paleoanthropologists led to an interest in human origins. The threads combined in research on chimpanzee adaptation to savannah environments as a model for hominid origins, using dolphins to "triangulate" on the behavior of our ancestors. Aspects of behavior and social organization that are common to chimpanzees, dolphins and humans are likely to be fundamental to large-brained, long-lived social organisms such as australopithecines and, perhaps, ETs.

# Are Aliens Likely to be Altruists?

*Chimpanzees, dolphins, computer simulation and creative speculation about altruism are subjects anthropologist Jim Moore uses to address the possible nature of human/alien contact. The nature of contact, i.e., an unplanned confrontation versus a calculated, controlled meeting may be as important as any predisposition toward altruism. Moore concludes that we can expect suspicion and hostility to arise from uncertainty. What should we be doing now to reduce uncertainty in an inevitable meeting?*

If our goal is to try to anticipate the behavior of extraterrestrial intelligent aliens (ETIs) in a contact situation, we are limited to three basic approaches:

—individual armchair theorizing, which has great potential but quality control is difficult;

—attempting to formalize this by explicit appeal to natural selection theory, biology and anthropology to try to get at hypothetical fundamental properties, which at least makes the logic of individual models testable (but risks encouraging misplaced confidence);

—simulating contact as best as we can and interpreting the results in light of the above.

In this paper I want to draw on a bit of all three approaches to address the question, should we expect ETIs to be reciprocal altruists; i.e., should they understand and use (at least among themselves) the principle "you scratch my back and I'll scratch yours"? To do this I will begin by arguing that chimpanzees are good "models" for our earliest ancestors, and having established this will ask whether they exhibit reciprocal altruism. The answer is, "not much, of a particular sort"; they do however cooperate—largely to kill each other. Drawing on ideas proposed by Darwin and later Richard Alexander (see e.g. Alexander, 1989), I will suggest a mechanism by which such lethal cooperation might favor altruism and briefly review the fossil record for relevant evidence. Since a single evolutionary instance is not much upon which to build a general principle, I will then look at a possible parallel evolution among dolphins, and conclude by speculating about what all this might say about types of altruism we could expect in ETIs. But first a bit of background theory to make clear why altruism is a paradox.

## I. THE PARADOX OF ALTRUISM

I am operating here on the assumption that Darwin could have lived on any planet: natural selection operates the same everywhere. We are all familiar with the basic mechanism of natural selection; genes that contribute favorably to the differential fitness of individuals in terms of reproduction (and so, incidentally, survival) are better represented in subsequent generations.

This creates a problem when it comes to "altruism" or beneficence. Behavior that contributes to the fitness of another individual's genes seems to be helping a genetic competitor, and hence to be inconsistent with the image of "survival of the fittest"; it is paradoxical. There are two major classes of explanation. One is kin selection, in which relatives help care for typically younger relatives which are likely to share some proportion of their genes. This is essentially an extension of the idea of parental care, and it seems responsible for the majority of observed "altruism" among nonhumans (as well as humans). The second is reciprocal altruism (RA). Since we are presumably unrelated to ETIs, my focus is on RA.

The logic of RA is simple (see Trivers, 1971, 1985; Mesterton-Gibbons & Dugatkin, 1992). If an act provides some benefit to a recipient who predictably will reciprocate in the future, then natural selection could favor such actions. Clearly everything depends on the phrase "predictably will reciprocate"; for RA to evolve, the following conditions must be met:

  —populations must be viscous and individuals long-lived, so interactants are likely to meet again
  —individuals must be able to recognize others and remember previous interactions
  —they should use this information to discriminate among potential recipients, in order to avoid cheaters

Because such altruism is vulnerable to cheating, Trivers notes that RA might have provided a context for natural selection favoring evolution of intelligence (to better cheat and detect cheaters), friendship (to promote chances of future interactions); moralistic aggression, justice, guilt, gratitude and sympathy may all stem from conflicts over reciprocal altruism.

All this at least sounds very plausible when applied to humans, but the evidence for RA in nonhumans is weak. When we do see something that looks like reciprocal altruism, it often turns out to be something else entirely (e.g. mutualism). So there is a theory, and it seems to fit human behavior well, but other examples need careful examination—and this is puzzling since there are plenty of other fairly intelligent animals living in viscous populations. RA should be common according to theory, but among most nonhumans it is a minor phenomenon at best.

## II: Chimpanzees as Models

It is important to emphasize that we have not evolved from chimpanzees. They have been evolving from our last common ancestor for just as many generations as we have, and a priori there is no reason to think they are any more similar to the LCA than we are. The last year has however provided good evidence that the LCA was indeed very chimpanzee-like. This evidence comes from two independent fields: paleontology and molecular biology (reviewed in Moore, in press).

The paleontological evidence is the recent discovery of *Australopithecus ramidus*, the earliest known hominid dating from ca. 4.4mya in Ethiopia. So far, not much more than teeth are known of it, but these teeth are unexpectedly similar to modern chimpanzees, and what we know of its stature suggests *ramidus* was roughly chimpanzee-sized.

The molecular evidence is a bit indirect, but I think persuasive. For some reason, rates of morphological change have been much slower in the African apes than in our own lineage; we know this from their hair. It turns out that with the polymerase chain reaction (PCR), it is possible to isolate enough DNA from a hair follicle to do population genetic analyses. All one needs is the hair, and these can be collected from night sleeping nests chimpanzees build. Since hairs are easily stored and transported, a group of us were able to obtain samples from across Africa and then sequence several mtDNA loci; comparison of sequences from different populations allowed us to construct a branching sequence that, assuming roughly constant rates of mutation, can be used to estimate actual dates of divergences.

The results were surprising; west African chimpanzees appear to have been genetically isolated for over 1.5my. They cannot be told apart morphologically, and yet they have existed independently since about the time *Homo erectus* first evolved (Morin et al., 1994). Furthermore, bonobos and chimpanzees have been separate some 2.5my; they can be distinguished but only just. 2.5mya about marks the origin of the genus *Homo*, when our ancestor *Homo habilis* had a brain less than half ours in size, stood maybe four feet tall and was still adapted for tree-climbing.

## III. Are Chimpanzees Reciprocal Altruists?

One commonly cited example of reciprocal altruism among nonhumans is food-sharing among chimpanzees. It is mainly mother-infant, which is just parental investment and so not a puzzle. However, sharing among adults is seen in the context of hunting: a group of chimpanzees will capture a prey animal (usually a monkey) and then share the kill (Stanford, 1995). A key feature of such sharing is that the holder of the kill usually controls its distribution—even normally dominant individuals will beg for a share as they sit around and eat.

This is usually interpreted as cooperative hunting, with the spoils altruistically shared by the owner of the kill in anticipation of future reciprocity when roles are reversed. This picture may be the accurate one, but I want to propose an alternative.

The alternative is simple: a group of chimpanzees spots some colobus and one of them — Jomeo, say — decides to attempt a hunt. As soon as he does, others in the group — I'll focus on Evered, for example — know there is a chance that as the colobus dodge Jomeo, one will make a mistake and stumble into Evered's waiting arms. So Evered joins the hunt, not cooperating, but essentially parasitizing Jomeo's efforts. Suppose Evered gets lucky and makes a kill. Everybody, including Jomeo, gathers around. We now have a bit of a problem: Evered would like to eat the monkey in peace, but with three or four other individuals looking menacing, and Jomeo especially feeling put out, that looks unlikely. On the other hand, Jomeo knows that if he makes a grab for the kill, Evered has merely to run off carrying it; a dead monkey is nicely portable. Unlike the case with a fruiting bush, simply getting Evered to move is not going to help.

Clearly, Evered's best strategy is to give a piece to each of the beggars just to shut them up.

You object: that's fine, but it's just a story; why choose it over the first one?

There are two specifics on which the reciprocal altruism model and this extortion model differ, and we can test the predictions of the two models. First, with reciprocal altruism, rank should make little difference, but one might expect to see some reluctance to share with dominant individuals since they might be inclined to pull rank when it comes their turn to reciprocate. Clearly, the extortion model says pay up fast to the dominant guy. Second, the reciprocal altruism model predicts that one should be stingy toward much older individuals, because, let's face it, there's a good chance they won't last long enough to reciprocate. The extortion model predicts the opposite: because older individuals have less chance of surviving to reproduce in the future, they have less to risk by escalating a fight; old chimpanzees, regardless of rank, are more likely to escalate to serious fighting over a resource than are young ones, so the extortion model predicts that when an old guys asks, you **give**.

Using data from Gombe, both tests support the extortion model (Moore, 1984; see de Waal, 1989a for alternatives).

I want to make two points based on that. The first is that a critical aspect of this example is that the chimps are **sharing** a resource, not helping each other in any way. If you have a monkey and don't want to share it with me, I can punch you a good one and maybe encourage your more altruistic side to come out; if I'm drowning and want you to help me, well, threats are very cheap under those conditions. *There is a difference between sharing and helping.* The second point is that when you look at most other examples of "altruism" long and hard, they have alternative interpretations or actually involve sharing, not helping. However, chimpanzees do appear to help each other, to cooperate, in another context: intercommunity conflict.

## IV. LETHAL INTERGROUP AGGRESSION AND COOPERATION

At every site where chimpanzees have been studied intensively for more than about a decade, violent intergroup aggression has been observed (Goodall, 1986). At each of the two longest-running sites, this aggression has escalated to the point of killing all the males of one community and annexation of that community's territory and surviving females. Chimpanzees appear unique among nonhuman primates in this, and the key seems to lie in their fission-fusion social system. Because of the patchy distribution of their main foods, the members of a community rarely if ever all congregate at one spot; instead, they form temporary parties which split and reform on an hourly or daily basis. One consequence is that even when neighboring communities are evenly matched, *parties* may not be: a temporary party of 5 might well come across a single neighbor. Given their ability to use their grasping hands to immobilize an opponent plus several-to-one odds in favor of cooperators [sensu lato], the risk of lethal aggression in such circumstances is minimal and "warfare" the result; for most simple human societies, the same pattern applies (Manson & Wrangham, 1991).

This suggests a ready explanation for human cooperation and altruism: for a very long evolutionary time we have had the ability to use stones, spears, arrows, and more recently quite a wide variety of implements of destruction to kill both other animals and each other. As Charles Darwin and more recently Richard Alexander have argued, groups composed of individuals willing to die for the group would have a significant advantage over other groups composed of less altruistic individuals (see Moore, 1994); the ability to move socially up and down a scale of inclusiveness would have been a great advantage.

What I want to emphasize here is that weapons that kill at a distance are a fundamentally new ball game in the evolution of animal behavior. If a small baboon has something that a big one wants, the big one can flash a set of canines and take it. If the small one wants to argue back with his teeth, he has to come within reach of his opponent. He could sneak up from behind—but at most that buys a half-second. Distance weapons change that. Suddenly, the little guy can wait behind a shrub and put an arrow in the bully's back. It is not cricket, but it is effective. One very obvious consequence of this is that any genetic tendency towards being over-bullying or "too" selfish has to face some very strong counterselection. And I put "too" in quotes because that is a subjective term that will presumably be defined by society. You don't need language or rulers or anything like that; distance weapons are equalizers and as such provide a mechanism by which social sanctions can be very effectively applied against non-altruists. If I'm drowning and calling to you for help, it is worth your while to note my little sister there on the bank; she may not know how to swim but she is a good shot with her bow.

From such violent power asymmetries we have evolved capacities for reciprocal altruism and peaceful cooperation that are unheard of among nonhumans. This conference could not take place among baboons; they'd have started fighting within minutes of the doors closing. This is not to say that nonhumans lack behavioral mechanisms for attaining peace; they do, and this is one of the hottest areas of primatology today (de Waal, 1989b). Monkeys and apes simply are not as good at it as we are.

## V. OK, BUT IS THERE ANY *EVIDENCE?*

As noted above, the last common ancestor of chimpanzees and the hominids was not a chimpanzee, but was very like a chimpanzee. **We** have changed, but the question of when and how is difficult to answer—we are interested in behavior, which doesn't fossilize, and so we have to look at proxy evidence such as brain size, as an index of behavioral complexity. It is important to recognize that the brain remains a virtual black box and so this argument is getting even *more* speculative here.

Clearly, absolute brain size doesn't seem to be the critical variable, or the fin whale would be much smarter than us. Rather, brain size adjusted for body size seems to be the best morphological measure of "intelligence" or complexity we might get from the fossil record, and this is measured with "encephalization quotient" (EQ). When we look at fossil EQ data we see that for much of hominid evolution there is a period of apparent stasis in EQ; most of the absolute increase seen is due to increased stature. It looks like the australopithecines were not much more encephalized than chimpanzees; there is a big jump with the origin of *Homo* and another as *H. erectus* evolved into *H. sapiens*. What else is happening with the origin of *Homo*? There is a thickening of the cranial vault in *H. habilis*, then further thickening and a sudden increase in stature with *H. erectus*. That, and the first record of simple stone tools.

Let me put that all together: for about 2 million years the australopiths were small bipedal chimpanzees; one of them began routinely using stone tools and suddenly we see an increase in skull thickness followed soon after by an increase in stature and jump in EQ. While indirect, this is at least consistent with the notion that lethal aggression using weapons had a major impact on evolution of the genus *Homo*, and provides some support for the Darwin/Alexander hypothesis for the origin of human altruism and reciprocity in violent competition among nested levels of alliances—what one might call the "2,001: A Space Odyssey" scenario.

## VI. Unique Historical Explanations Don't Illuminate ETI Behavior

It is dangerous to make much of a single case when we are trying to understand evolutionary universals. We need to find another group in which non-kin altruism is common, and dolphins appear to be such a group.

The nice thing about looking at altruism in dolphins is that because cetaceans and primates have been distinct taxa for some 60my, we can be very confident that any similarities in the ways that members of these two groups deal with the world are due to convergence and not their common history (beyond the basic mammalian characters of warm blood, internal gestation and lactation). Shared behaviors are likely to be due to fundamental properties of interactional dynamics among intelligent long-lived social animals—useful for anthropologists testing theories about primates, and for exobiologists looking for general behavioral principles.

Epimeletic or care-giving behavior is widespread among dolphins (Connor & Norris, 1982). During capture (e.g. by whalers) individuals will often stay with the captive and sometimes try to interpose themselves between captive and captor, or to attack the capture vessel. This behavior occasionally occurs between species as well as within them. A more widely-known form of care-giving is supporting injured or sick individuals at the surface; this too occurs between species as well as within and there are in fact reports of human swimmers rescued by dolphins. Finally, it is worth noting that cooperation appears to be common among some species of dolphin (Connor et al. 1992) and at least in the context of fishing this too is sometimes generalized across species to include even humans (Pryor et al, 1990). While such cooperation does not represent reciprocal altruism, it similarly involves establishment of some form of "trust" between non-relatives.

For my ideas about the evolution of human altruism to have any validity, it seems we'd need to find dolphins using spear guns or something, which they patently don't do. Enter the "Big bang hypothesis" of Norris and Møhl (1983). It is well-known that odontocetes use echolocation to "see" through sometimes murky waters. They make sounds by passing air back and forth in small sacs attached to the nasal passage, and these sounds are focussed by the melon on the head using a principle not unlike a laser—by bouncing the sound back and forth through the melon's tissue, the dolphin is able to amplify it to very high levels. Sound intensities in the 120dB range have been measured just in front of the melon of bottlenose dolphin. That is loud enough to damage the swim bladder of fishes, and repeated sonic blasts should in theory be able to stun or at least severely debilitate fish.

There is a minor caveat in that the use of sonic blasts to stun fish has not been reported from the wild (and captives are unlikely to let loose within a cement tank); while the dolphin presumably have motive and opportunity, there is no smoking gun as yet. Evidence is inferential: some sperm whales have been captured that had long-broken lower jaws that didn't occlude properly, and yet they had full stomachs; some species of beaked whale have lower teeth that curve around the upper jaw, restricting the opening of the mouth. Both of these observations seem hard to explain unless the cetaceans involved are stunning their prey before capturing it. While the circumstantial evidence is thus pretty strong, I recently heard of a case in which some killer whales attacked a sperm whale calf and no bangs were heard by observers. It seems unlikely that whales with the ability to use such blasts would not do so to protect a calf, so all this remains speculative. It is interesting and sobering to me that our ability to create models for understanding ETIs might be limited by the lack of funding for basic research on the natural history of our own planet.

That uncertainty aside, the conceptual connection between human weapons and dolphin sonic blasts should be obvious. As Richard Connor put it, "imagine the social consequences of giving everybody a Saturday Night special at birth" — it puts a new spin on weaning tantrums, to say the least. And dolphin have presumably had that capability for something like 10-15 million years, as opposed to maybe half a million or so for us. That difference in time span might explain why dolphin sometimes extend their altruism across species, even to us, while we don't always extend it even among ourselves. We're an unfinished product.

## VII. So, For Aliens?

I'm guessing that members of any technological species would have, or have had in their dim primitive past, distance weapons. If these threads hang together at all, we can make the following rough predictions from that: Depending on how long ago they got their distance weapons, such species should exhibit some degree of generalized altruism along a continuum from being very reluctant and perhaps contract-bound through to being almost automatic and reflexive. And **any** species, technological or not, that had a built-in system like dolphin seem to have ought to be an automatic altruist.

One key difference between an automatic *vs* a conditional altruist/cooperator such as we are seems likely to be in the importance of suspicion. Among humans, the system has a component of manipulation in it—can we tilt balanced reciprocity in our favor?—and the risk of being played for a sucker is very real. What does that do to interactions when knowledge is imperfect, as any first contact situation necessarily would be?

Several years ago I had a chance to find out in the context of an Internet-based simulation of a SETI contact, simSETI, that was run as part of CONTACT. An alien team created a message which was received by an Earth team composed of a small "central command" based at the conference and about 70 participants scattered all over the globe. We ran the simulation in real-time, trying to make it as realistic as possible. To me the most interesting discovery of the simulation was the speed with which the

Earth team fell into angry bickering over access to information; the remote participants became convinced that the central command was withholding data and manipulating the contact scenario. Within an hour, erstwhile collaborators were making ad hominem attacks and (in the context of the simulation) threatening to send in US Marshalls with a warrant for the release of the full data set.

102    In fact, the alien team had given us the message on a DOS disk and the Earth team's Mac did not have the proper file translation software; it was all due to honest human error. Any of you who would like to read an entertaining fictional account of this sort of remote contact scenario, see Tom Clancy's *The Sum of All Fears* (1991) in which e-mail misunderstanding and suspicion nearly launches a nuclear exchange. Whether understanding the evolutionary substrate from which such interactions spring will help us to avoid them when real contact is made, I don't know; I can only assume it is better to understand them than not.

## VIII. Conclusion

Whether the ETIs we run into are automatic or conditional altruists, it's a fair bet that they should at least understand the principle of "tit for tat" reciprocal altruism. They are not likely to be blindly aggressive or slavishly altruistic by nature (though they might well have socially decided to pursue one of those strategies).

We can expect suspicion and hostility to arise from uncertainty, focussing on the possibility that one is being played for a sucker. Moralistic outrage may, alas, be a universal among technological ETIs.

If these principles really follow, we can assume that ETIs who have had contact experience will know all the foregoing. Unfortunately, whether they use it tactically to best us, or to avoid misunderstanding, is an open question; it is at least a start to know what pieces they'll be playing with.

And to close on a question: while I think this approach gets us closer to a robust prediction about ETI behavior than other available ones, the possibilities are not very constrained—have we really gained anything useful in "knowing" that an ETI would likely, at least, have a notion of reciprocal altruism?

## Acknowledgments

This paper is a revised and updated version of one written for CONTACT IV in 1987. I am indebted to Jim Funaro for creating a context in which one can pull together such strands as apes, dolphins, and aliens, and have it all *mean* something. The 1992 CONTACT IX simulation of a SETI contact (simSETI) did what the best simulations do: forcefully showed me a problem I hadn't previously recognized, that in retrospect should have been predictable from the model developed here—thank you to the literally scores of people who made simSETI work. I also thank Mischa Adams, Richard Connor, and Ken Norris for very useful and interesting discussions about the topic of altruism in dolphin and apes. Finally, thanks to Scott Jones and the Human Potential Foundation for the invitation to contribute to this volume.

# REFERENCES

Alexander, R. D. (1989). Evolution of the human psyche. pp. 455-513. In Mellars, P. & Stringer, C. (Eds.), *The Human Revolution*. Princeton: Princeton University Press.

Connor, R. C. & Norris, K. S. (1982). Are dolphins reciprocal altruists? *Am. Nat.* **119**: 358-374.

Connor, R. C., Smolker, R. A. & Richards, A. F. (1992). Dolphin coalitions. In de Waal, F. B. M. & Harcourt, A. H. (Eds.), *Coalitions and Alliances in Humans and Other Animals*. New York: Oxford University Press.

de Waal, F. B. M. (1989a). Food sharing and reciprocal obligations among chimpanzees. *J. Hum. Evol.* **18**: 433-459.

de Waal, F. B. M. (1989b). *Peacemaking Among Primates*. Cambridge: Harvard University Press.

Goodall, J. (1986). *The Chimpanzees of Gombe: Patterns of Behavior*. Cambridge: Harvard University Press.

Manson, J. H. & Wrangham, R. W. (1991). Intergroup aggression in chimpanzees and humans. *Curr. Anthropol.* **32**: 369-390.

Mesterton-Gibbons, M. & Dugatkin, L. A. (1992). Cooperation among unrelated individuals: evolutionary factors. *Q. Rev. Biol.* **67**: 267-281.

Moore, J. (1984). The evolution of reciprocal sharing. *Ethol. Sociobiol.* **5**: 5-14.

Moore, J. (1994). Hominids, coalitions and weapons; not vehicles. *Beh. Brain Sci.* **17**: 632.

Moore, J. (in press). "Savanna" chimpanzees, referential models and the LCA. In McGrew, W. C., Nishida, T. & Marchant, L. (Ed.), *Great Ape Societies*. Cambridge: Cambridge University Press.

Morin, P. A., Moore, J., Chakraborty, R., Jin, L., Goodall, J. & Woodruff, D. S. (1994). Kin selection, social structure, gene flow, and the evolution of chimpanzees. *Science*. **265**: 1193-1201.

Norris, K. S. & Møhl, B. (1983). Can odontocetes debilitate prey with sound? *Am. Nat.* **122**: 85-104.

Pryor, K., Lindbergh, J. & Milano, R. (1990). A dolphin-human fishing cooperative in Brazil. *Marine Mamm. Sci.* **6**: 77-82.

Stanford, C. B. (1995). Chimpanzee hunting behavior and human evolution. *Amer. Sci.* **83**: 256-261.

Trivers, R. L. (1971). The evolution of reciprocal altruism. *Q. Rev. Biol.* **46**: 35-57.

Trivers, R. (1985). *Social Evolution*. Menlo Park (CA): Benjamin/Cummings.

Jim Moore
Anthropology Dept UCSD
La Jolla, Ca 92093-0101
jjmore@ucsd.edu

# ⊕ William J. Baldwin, D.D.S., Ph.D.

*William J. Baldwin, D.D.S., Ph.D.*

Co-director of the Center for Human Relations, Dr. Baldwin now resides in Florida with his wife, Judith. He received his Doctor of Dental Surgery in 1970 from the University of the Pacific School of Dentistry, The Doctor of Ministry degree from Western University Graduate College of Theology in August 1982, and the Ph.D. in clinical psychology from American Commonwealth University, San Diego, in September 1988. Dr. Baldwin is a Pastoral Counselor, Past Lives Therapist and hypnotherapist. A modern pioneer in the field, he has written *Spirit Releasement Therapy: A Technique Manual*, the first textbook on Regression Therapy, Past Life Therapy and Spirit Releasement Therapy.

# Spirit Releasement Therapy and the Dark ETs

*Two of the most discussed hypotheses concerning the origin of UFO/ET phenomena are that it originates somewhere in the visible universe, or that it is other-dimensional in nature. These hypotheses are not mutually exclusive. Dr. Baldwin's paper takes a depth view of an important component of the other-dimensional consideration of the phenomena.*

## ABSTRACT

The concept of spirit possession, that is, full or partial takeover of a living human by a non-physical being, has been recognized, or at least theorized, in every time and in every culture. Clinical evidence suggests that such beings can attach and merge fully or partially with the subconscious mind of a living person, exerting some degree of control on the thought processes and emotions, as well as the physical body. These non-physical beings fall into three main categories: the earthbound spirit of a deceased human; the dark force being or classic demonic spirit; and the alien, or extraterrestrial, some of whom may be non-physical in its normal form. In private therapy sessions, all three types may be discovered with a client. Some extraterrestrials are also plagued by the dark entities. The techniques of Spirit Releasement Therapy can facilitate the process of discovering and releasing the attached spirit entities, thus alleviating the imposed symptoms, often immediately and permanently.

## BACKGROUND

Let me begin by clarifying my position on this subject. When I began this work in 1981 I labeled myself a firm agnostic, with no ties to any organized religious body and with an absence of religious beliefs regarding reincarnation, spirits, spirit possession, demons or demonic possession. As far back as I can remember, I have had an enormous curiosity about UFOs, and all manner of psychic and parapsychological phenomena. I even enjoyed the movie, *The Exorcist*.

My first past life regression experience occurred in 1977. It was vivid and meaningful to me personally, and I began reading the literature on the therapeutic and healing value of past life recall. I attended a lecture on past life therapy in 1979, given by Dr. Edith Fiore, author of *You Have Been Here Before*. She spoke about discarnate interference and clinical depossession, a process she utilized routinely in her clinical practice. I was astounded; this was a revelation to me, an entirely new direction in healing practice. I began to read the precious little that had been written on this subject. The seminal work in this field is *Thirty Years Among The Dead*, a book by psychiatrist Carl Wickland, published in 1924.

In March 1981, I began seeing clients for past life regression therapy. Within six months, more than half of my clients showed signs and symptoms of some degree of spirit interference. I began to develop the techniques of Spirit Releasement Therapy, a term I coined to more accurately describe the process of safely removing the spirits which I perceived as attaching, not possessing.

The clients in an altered state of consciousness describe the images, feelings and sensations that arise within them. I use this information to guide them to the source and resolution of the presenting problems. The source of any present life conflict or problem of the client is often discovered as a traumatic event in a past lifetime, and past life therapy is indicated. Past life therapy is a powerful, direct, methodical approach to psychotherapy (Fiore, 1978; Netherton, 1978; Wambach, 1978, 1979; Woolger, 1987; Weiss, 1988). The results are rapid and lasting, and it includes the spiritual dimension of the human consciousness which is ignored in traditional mental health theory and practice.

## DISCOVERY OF THE EARTHBOUND SPIRIT

Past life therapy is only effective if the past lifetime trauma was part of the lifestream of the client. In many cases, the cause of the client's presenting problem turns out to be a traumatic event that was experienced in physical body by another person, now dead, a discarnate earthbound spirit of a deceased human being which attached to the client sometime after its death. The client and the entity may have interacted with each other in this life or in a past lifetime. Past life therapy on the attached entity cannot resolve the unresolved conflict or satisfy the unfulfilled desire which holds it to the earth plane. It seems what was done in the physical plane must be undone in the physical plane while incarnated in one's own physical body.

Regression therapy techniques can be used to resolve any conflict between the host and the attached entity, in this life or the prior lifetime of the two, to the point of forgiveness between the entity and the client. The next steps are separation and release of the attached entity and sending it into the Light, the next stage of evolution for this lost and confused being (Wickland, 1924; McCall, 1982; Crabtree, 1985; Fiore, 1987; Baldwin, 1992). The experience of moving into the Light is similar to the descriptions of the near death experience, or NDE, except the being continues all the way in and does not return to the body (Moody, 1975; Ring, 1980; Sabom, 1982).

Many of these attached earthbound spirits are stubborn, belligerent and unwilling to release. They are hostile to the therapist, possessive and vengeful toward the host. The entity is directed to focus inside itself. It is urged to locate anyone or anything lodged within itself, just as it is lodged inside the client. This often leads to the discovery of a dark blob, a black growling mass, a hissing black shape, or a snarling black thing. If they look more closely, they see angry red eyes somewhere in the black shape. This is a demonic entity nested within the attached earthbound. The client is affected by both entities (Baldwin 1992, pp. 307-313).

## DISCOVERY OF THE DEMONIC ENTITY

In the process of therapy, many clients will locate within themselves demonic beings as well as earthbound spirits. The usual complaints of a person afflicted with a dark being is expressed as a feeling of being blocked or being held back in life, or being out of control with rage or self-destructive feelings. As they describe these feelings, there is usually a physical sensation in the body. As the client focuses inward on this sensation, they may discover the dark form, the dark shape with red eyes.

The dark ones are extremely hostile, arrogant, egotistical. They swear profusely, using obscenity and foul language, but never profanity. They do not utter any Holy Names. The client may refuse to repeat verbatim what they say. They often refuse to believe this is really happening to them, even though they are seeing the images and uttering the words.

The demonic beings seem to be able to tap into the mind of the host, drawing on the fear-provoking images in the person's memory banks. Depending on the mental state and educational and religious background of the client, this can elicit fear. This is their intent.

The dark ones can appear in many forms. Other than the black growling blob, they appear as snakes, spiders, scorpions, lizards, vultures, crows, ravens, bats, dogs, wolves, gargoyles; almost always with glaring red, angry eyes, frequently with hideous open mouths full of sharp teeth. This discovery often disgusts, surprises and frightens the host, whether it be the client or the attached earthbound spirit.

During a session, when the client describes a dark form, a hideous face with red eyes perhaps with surrounding flashes of red, a black thing which is growling, snarling, or hissing, the therapist must assume the possibility of a demonic spirit attachment.

This newly discovered dark being will be defiant toward the therapist and threatening toward the client. The therapist asks specific questions.

Therapist: "Have you ever been alive in your own human body?"

It will not only deny being human, but will answer the question derisively, as if insulted. After all, who would want to be human if you can be a demon? There are many varieties of non-human entities and more than one kind of dark being. The final step in differential diagnosis is necessary for positive identification as a demonic entity.

T: "Who is your master? Who is your leader?"

When asked the name of their master the demonic being may call him Lucifer, Satan, Father, Lord, the Devil, the One, the Great One, the Eternal One, the Evil One, the Powerful One, the Dark One, the Dark Angel, the Darkness, or something similar. They may refuse to state the name of their commander-in-chief or may deny any master other than themselves. Some of them are aware of God as their creator, but not as their master. According to the classic definition, these are demons, the minions of Lucifer which have plagued mankind for eons. They were cast out of heaven by Archangel Michael and sent to earth for this purpose (The New Testament, Revelations 12: 7-12, 17). The diagnosis of demonic infestation or attachment can safely be made at this point.

The client may refuse to repeat this information as it often conflicts with personal belief systems. They are urged to simply repeat the words they hear from the entity, and assured that they do not have to believe any part of this narrative. With this caution, they are able to continue the process.

The demonic beings understand only the energy of the lower three chakras: survival, fear, threat, lust, greed, power, control, aggression, antagonism, competition, bullying. This resembles the human ego at its most base.

They do not understand love, compassion, sharing, humor, loyalty, devotion, happiness, joy, or fulfillment. There is no reward for their services to their master. They are allowed to continue to exist, and they are not punished as long as they continue to obey their orders. They continue to perform their duties because they think there is nothing else. It is just what they do; it is their job.

They sometimes work alone, or in small bands, or as part of much larger networks. The dark networks focus on specific groups of people. The target groups assigned to the various dark networks include: families, women, men, gays, lesbians, professionals in any capacity, teachers, physicians, healers, students of any spiritual path, spiritual leaders of any path, popular leaders of any kind, corporations and their officers, members and leaders of the Catholic Church, the fundamentalist churches, the born-again Christians, political leaders, police personnel, drug users, or any other particular group.

If the dark ones fail in their assignment, they are punished in a deep, dark, cold pit, and they are all alone for a very long time. They are threatened with annihilation, extinction, or ceasing to be. (The term "death" is rarely used. This is a function of living physical bodies). After suffering in the pit for a significant duration, they are retrieved and given another mission or project in return for the promise of more diligent obedience. They are promoted in rank and assigned subordinate demons to command. The ones who have some rank or stature and who command underlings have certainly been in the pit. They acquire another layer of slimy, sludgy darkness during their stay in that hell, then they are sent out on another assignment to interfere with some unsuspecting human (Baldwin, 1992, p. 273-284).

## EXORCISM

The Catholic exorcism procedure, the Roman Ritual, has a long history of development. It finally reached its present format in the seventeenth century. It is still used by priests of the Catholic Church in cases of solemn exorcism. Between 1970 and 1980, there were more than 600 solemn exorcisms performed in the United States alone (Brittle, 1980, p. 200). It is still a viable procedure in the Church, though not publicized. Basically, the interaction between the possessing demon and the priest exorcist is adversarial; the demon is cast out in the name of Jesus Christ, without a specified destination. The procedure offers no love, no compassion, no concern whatsoever for the entity, as though the fallen angel were not a God-created being.

This form of exorcism is irresponsible with regard to the treatment and disposal of the entity. The demon can return to the same person. It can find another unwitting victim, or it can attach to the priest-exorcist. It is like removing a nail from a tire and tossing it out into the street. Either the person who tossed it, or anyone else, may pick it up in their tire again.

## SPIRIT RELEASEMENT OF THE DEMONIC ENTITY

The basis for Spirit Releasement Therapy is the firm knowledge that all created beings contain the spark of God consciousness. All else is illusory and transitory, part of the duality that constitutes this physical reality which encompasses good and evil, light and dark, right and wrong, and other polarities. The Book of Revelations outlines the beginning of the game, the act of choosing sides: Light or darkness. Every spark of God will return, and eventually all will join in the Oneness. This includes Lucifer, the ultimate prodigal son, and his legions of demons, "the Forces of Darkness."

As the questioning continues in the therapy session, the dark being will describe some form of interference, interruption, disruption with the family, occupation, or goals. The purpose might be to stop the client in his/her work in life.

The process of demonic spirit releasement requires imagination, visual imagery, and acceptance of certain spiritual figures. This is not a religious exercise and does not require adherence to any religious belief or practice. This is explained to the client before a session begins. Certain names will be used in the session, and specific beings may be called on for help. They seem to be universal and not associated with any organized church or religion. Spirit beings are eternal. Human beings in the past have developed the rules and restrictions of organized religions around misperceptions, misinterpretations, magical thinking, and individual beliefs, and have attempted to claim certain elevated spirit beings as property of these religions.

The therapist calls on the Warrior Angels of Light to form a bastion of Light all around the location of the session. The Rescue Spirits of Light bind the demonic being in a capsule of Light, impervious, impenetrable, and inescapable. As the capsule of Light squeezes, the dark one begins to feel the pressure and its edges begin to fade.

The spirits of Light who assist in this process may be archetypal or totally imaginary. They may also be absolutely real, spiritually evolved, conscious beings existing in a non-physical reality, or a different vibration or dimension than the Earth level.

The true demonic beings have not been human, so they have no experience of dying, though they may have a sense of the concept due to contact with human minds. As their edges become fuzzy, gray, or ragged, they often momentarily fear death. They think fading means dying.

T: "What did your superiors tell you would happen to you if the Light came this close?"

Client: "They said it would burn. They told me I would be destroyed."

There is very little belligerence at this point. The dark entity's focus has been turned from its assignment with the client and its defiance and threats toward the therapist to thoughts of its own survival. With guidance and the assistance of the therapist, it begins to understand that it has been deceived.

T: "Turn and look deep inside yourself. Begin to focus deep inside. Tunnel to your center, to the very center of your being, to the very core of your existence. What do you find?"

C: "Nothing, it's just dark."

T: "Keep looking. What did your superiors tell you about what's inside you?"

C: "There is nothing there except darkness."

T: "That is the first deception. Keep looking. Through the darkness, through the layers of black slime. Keep looking, keep going, right into your center. What do you see there? Look carefully."

C: "There is some light. Just a little light."

T: "They deceived you. They told you there was no light at your center. This is the first deception. This is the denial of God, a deception of the first magnitude. This spark of Light is the spark of God consciousness. Every created being is a spark of God consciousness, each in a slightly different frequency or vibration, so each is recognizable. It is the spark at the center of your being which gives you eternal life. No one can take it from you. The dark masters can neither give you life nor can they take it away.

"Once you believe the first deception, that there is no Light at your center, you will believe the second deception, that you can cease to be, that you can be destroyed. After that you will believe anything. They tell you the Light is harmful, that it will burn, and you must stay away from it. If you believe this third deception and obey this command, you will never learn about the Light. How does it feel to know they deceived you from the beginning?"

C: "I don't like it. I'm angry. They lied to me."

T: "Would you continue to serve these masters who deceived you like this?"

C: "No."

The Light inside has been described as a flicker, a spark, a candle, a little flame, a red coal, a pearl, a diamond, a star, a ruby, a crystal, an emerald, a fire, a sun.

T: "What happens to that little light as you continue to watch it?"

C: "It's glowing brighter, it's getting bigger."

This always happens with this type of entity.

T: "Move close to it. How does it feel? Does it burn?"

C: "No, it doesn't burn. It feels warm."

T: "Step into it. It is your own Light. It is the center of your being. Step right into it. Stand tall in your own Light, little friend. How does that feel?"

Once the dark being has stepped into its own Light, the darkness is gone, and the therapist can use the term "friend" if it feels appropriate.

C: "It's warm. Peaceful."

T: "How long since you have felt warm or peaceful?"

C: "I don't remember."

T: "What has happened to your dark form, the darkness we first saw?"

C: "It's gone."

This is the transformation of a demon, and it nearly always follows this pattern. It is a straightforward therapeutic process; teachable, learnable, repeatable by any open-minded therapist.

T: "Rescue Spirits of Light, lift this one to its own appointed place in the Light. We send you to your own place in the Light, little friend, and we say farewell."

The therapist has just performed an exorcism of a demon. Not from the adversarial position of a priest, not with rancor and animosity toward this foul thing, but from a compassionate stance of tough love for a God-created being who went astray. Long ago this spirit made a serious error and chose the dark path. It is certain that it caused untold misery to countless beings along that path. It has also suffered its own pain in the darkness. There is a great deal more involved in the process than this brief description would suggest, yet this is the final outcome in nearly every case (Baldwin, pp. 323-349).

The question arises about the reality of demons and demonic possession. In an orderly universe created by God, why would He allow such beings to exist? Why would He allow His human creations to be so plagued by them? Why is such chaos allowed in the world? Some people have speculated that this is His way of giving humans an incentive to strive for something better. The dark ones act like starting blocks for a runner, something to give the impetus for forward movement, something to push against.

In the act of creation, He gave his created beings, the individual sparks of consciousness, the power of free will. This is the greatest of His gifts. As great as this gift is, there must be something equally significant available to choose from, or between, for this power of free will choice to be meaningful. There must be something upon which to exercise the power of choice, something to choose between, something of enormous impact. It seems to be the choice between Light and darkness.

Of course, this is only a speculation growing out of extensive clinical work with the dark beings.

In materialistic Western culture, even in the churches, the existence of an actual Prince of Darkness with legions of demons under his command is considered as symbolic, metaphoric, even mythical. Whether the force of Darkness is a figment of imagination, a product of the rantings of zealous prophets, a creation of the collective unconscious, or something else unknown, the speculations regarding good and evil will without a doubt continue unabated.

In clinical practice there is no need for concern regarding religious conjecture nor superstition. Whether it is imagination, archetype, collective hallucinations, mass hypnosis, a projection of the beliefs of the therapist or something else again, the dark forces seem to exist in some form in this consensus reality. Beings of darkness seem to be present and actively involved in our personal and planetary evolution.

The word "possession," as used in the New Testament, comes from a Greek word which more accurately translates as "demonized." Some members of the clergy consider the Earthbound spirits of deceased humans to be aberrant, unclean, and demonically influenced. The unwilling, unwary victim of obsession by this kind of entity is said to be demonized, and as such subject to the full force of deliverance ministry. In such a service the "unclean spirit" is cast out, condemned to continue its confused wandering in the "outer darkness," perhaps to find another unsuspecting victim. There is no differentiation made between lost and confused souls of deceased humans and the demonic spirits which are among the legions of Lucifer (Basham, 1972; Montgomery, 1976; Linn & Linn, 1981).

The process of this therapy is distinct from any religious tradition or methodology of exorcism. The position of the Church fathers is adversarial and without compassion for the possessing spirit, even though it is a God-created being. Regardless of any religious belief structure, the dark beings seem to exist. They conform to the historic description and classic behavior attributed to demons.

Many humans have made bargains with the devil, in this life or another, for various self-serving purposes. Some times, the bargains are purposely made, in other cases, the connection is made inadvertently by accepting an invitation, veiled or overt, from the dark ones. Once these contracts are established, dark entities are assigned. The person is under the control of the dark forces. After the death of such a person, the newly deceased spirit may remain earthbound and continue to serve the dark ones, often by attaching to another human. Reincarnation is possible by going through the Light in the usual fashion, but the contract is again implemented immediately upon returning to the Earth plane. The human servant of the dark forces continues his work through his own physical body, in bondage to and totally controlled by the dark ones.

The demonic energy distorts the thinking just enough that the person actually believes that what he/she is doing is just exactly what he/she wants to be doing. Without some intervention such as this therapy, this behavior would continue unabated, the confused thinking well established.

In many instances the agreement is a conscious act and deliberately sought. The most serious summoning of Satan is for the express purpose of making a formal pact. The pact usually guarantees some Earthly gain, such as personal or political power, wealth, or securing the favors of a desirable woman. The Dark One delights in offering such transient rewards in return for the eternal soul of the bargainer.

Similar contracts have apparently been made between the leaders of alien civilizations and the dark forces. These malevolent bargains often have damaging consequences for planet Earth and her human inhabitants.

## DISCOVERING THE EXTRATERRESTRIAL

In religious literature there is no mention of nor recognition given to the extraterrestrial being, the ET, the alien. Yet this type of attached entity is often found in private session, interfering with the human host quite differently than attached earthbound spirits or the dark entities.

This is not the spirit of a deceased ET, but an alien in its normal form: non-physical. They have never been human in their own physical bodies here on earth. They claim to be from "far away," and the Light in their universe is a different color from our own golden-white. They are not hostile, aggressive, nor threatening. They are intrusive, secretive, and do not like to be disturbed in their work. When discovered, they will speak and they openly discuss their reasons for being present with the client.

The extraterrestrials describe various reasons for being here, but most have no compunction about the invasion, no hesitation regarding the violation of the free will of the affected human. Basically, there is no concern for the Prime Directive of non-interference with a sentient species, to borrow a notion from Star Trek.

Some claim to be using the eyes and ears of the human to gather data as they themselves do not have the proper apparatus to perceive this reality. They cannot interpret the band of the electromagnetic spectrum which is seen as color, nor can they interpret sound waves.

Some attached extraterrestrials claim to be conducting experiments much as earth scientists conduct animal experimentation. They have implanted physical and non-physical probes and various types of devices into humans for the purpose of gathering information. There are numerous reports of shiny, metallic nodes found in various locations in the skull.

Others assert flatly that they are taking over the world in this manner. They will simply suppress the human will, control human bodies and live here in these physical biological vehicles.

Attached extraterrestrials may be lost, marooned or retired here on the earth. They may be associated with a nearby craft which is on a surveying or information gathering mission. Through the consciousness and voice of the client, the ship commander will speak. Lines of communication are maintained between all members of this alien crew. The client can repeat their words as they speak. They may reveal that they are under orders and are part of a fleet of several such crafts on similar missions around the earth. They can cross-connect with base headquarters. The client can repeat the words of the base commander.

In some cases, the base commander will acknowledge the intrusion and will agree to remove the probes, the communication devices, the implants or whatever invasive mechanisms have been placed. They sometimes claim that they were just conducting scientific experimentation, much like earth scientists and did not realize that humans would either be aware of the intrusion or object to the work. They give the appearance of compassion and quickly cooperate with the request to disengage.

Many people who attempt to channel some higher source of information are deceived by opportunistic extraterrestrials. Channelling or mediumship, by definition, is a temporary possession by another being, with permission of the host, but for a specified purpose and limited duration. In many cases of channelling, the being coming through refuses to leave at the end of the channelling session. This becomes a permanent spirit possession or attachment by an extraterrestrial.

Some people actually call out for a visitation by extraterrestrials, or space brothers. The motivation can be curiosity or a genuine call for help for this disintegrating civilization. They will come at the call, and the person calling better have something important to ask. The extraterrestrials are serious, no-nonsense beings and have their own mission to accomplish. The call for help can be interpreted as permission to connect to the human being. This attachment can be enormously destructive for the hapless victim.

## EXTRATERRESTRIALS AND THE DARK FORCES

In some cases of ET attachment, the base commander may be evasive, deceitful, even defiant and refuse to remove the intrusions. He will usually divulge the information that there is a high dark being who controls his people. The therapist demands, not personally, but in the name of the Light, to speak to the highest in command of this group of dark or demonic beings.

The high dark commander will grudgingly come through. The client is instructed to verbally refuse permission for it to approach or to control the body or voice in any way. The client can repeat the words of this dark being. This dark one may be a former angelic being who followed Lucifer in his rebellion, one of the dark Princelings beneath Lucifer, the Prince of Darkness. Though very powerful, these errant beings exist in terror of Lucifer and his ostensible might. They are jealous of his power and envious of his legions.

They attempt to establish their own kingdom of dark-force beings, their own organization of dark interference. Somehow these dark Princelings have convinced, induced, or forced various groups of extraterrestrials, through coercion or temptation of the rulers, to obey them. The members of the ruling council agree to a pact with the dark forces, and an entire race of extraterrestrials comes under subjugation. Once this is accomplished, the dark underlings, the minor demons, are assigned and attached to the extraterrestrials. This generates the same distortion of thinking that humans suffer with the same affliction. The extraterrestrials are then motivated by greed, power, domination, aggression, antagonism, and their vocation becomes exploitation without compassion.

In a therapy session with a client, if this condition of attached extraterrestrial being with nested demonic is discovered, the same process of releasing nested demonic beings from earthbound spirits is initiated. The aliens are freed of their dark burden. The demonic beings are the same on this planet and any other where the Lucifer energy has penetrated. The same spirit releasement procedures are effective.

The dark Princelings nearly always capitulate without much resistance. They are highly intelligent and remember clearly the Light and their place in it before the rebellion. They are repentant and often tired of the struggle. They welcome the opportunity to return home to the Light. Their entire dark network can be herded into their appointed places in the Light. Perhaps an entire alien civilization can also be liberated and turned toward their path of evolution in the Light.

Following this releasement of this oppressive dark hierarchy, the direction of the therapy session turns to the attached aliens and any teams or spacecraft nearby. The ship commander will cross-connect with base headquarters. After connecting with headquarters, the base commander will cross-connect to the homeworld leaders or ruling council of the alien civilization. They will speak through the voice of the client. The client continues the refusal to allow control of voice, mind, or body by the aliens. This is conscious channelling, much like simultaneous translation of a foreign language.

They freely acknowledge that somewhere back in their history, either they or their predecessors struck the bargain with the dark forces in return for power over their citizens and were promised expansion out into the universe. The actual power was wielded by the dark force leader, but once established, the pact held the entire civilization, including the ruling council of leaders, in dark bondage. The dark beings were the power behind the throne, the invisible government. The council members did not know how to get out of the bargain. They are always terribly relieved to receive this assistance. They agree to withdraw their operatives attached to humans, recall their fleet of craft, and cease their intrusions on our planet.

The aliens are sent back to their spacecraft, their base headquarters, their own homeworld, or the Light. In some cases, they are from another, perhaps parallel, universe. The Light from other universes is often described as a different color such as purple, lemon-silver, blue or green. The Light in this universe is always seen as golden white. Rescue spirits of Light from the universe of their specific color are summoned to assist in the evacuation. It works!

There is one Power in the universe. It is the Power of the Light; it is Flow, not Force. It is the power of love, healing, and spiritual evolution. The power of the Light can be distorted and misused by anyone with such miscreant intention to damage or destroy others. This abuse is a violation of the free will of the victim, the person who is the object of the distorted force. It also violates the basic nature of the perpetrator; to misuse the Power of the Light is to incur severe karmic debt.

At the core of every God-created being is a spark of Light, a spark of the God consciousness. Denial and defiance of this spiritual heritage is a denial and defiance of God. At the innermost core, each being knows the truth of its identity. This cannot be denied. It is the way Home.

# REFERENCES

Baldwin, William. (1992). *Spirit Releasement Therapy: A Technique Manual*. Falls Church, VA: Human Potential Foundation Press.

Basham, D. (1972). *Deliver Us From Evil*. Washington Depot, CT: Chosen Books.

Brittle, G. (1980). *The Demonologist*. Englewood Cliffs, NJ: Prentice-Hall.

Crabtree, Adam. (1985). *Multiple Man*. New York: Praeger.

Fiore, Edith. (1978). *You Have Been Here Before*. New York: Ballantine.

Fiore, Edith. (1987). *The Unquiet Dead*. New York: Doubleday/Dolphin.

Fiore, E. (1989). *Encounters*. New York: Doubleday.

Linn, M. & Linn, D. (1981). *Deliverance Prayer*. New York: Paulist Press.

McAll, K. (1982). *Healing the Family Tree*. London: Sheldon.

Netherton, M. (1978). *Past Lives Therapy*. New York: William Morrow.

Montgomery, J. W. (Ed.). (1976). *Demon Possession*. Minneapolis: Bethany Fellowship, Inc.

Moody, R. (1975). *Life After Life*. Covington, Georgia: Mockingbird.

Ring, K. (1980). *Life at Death*. New York: Coward, McCann & Geogehagan.

Sabom, M. (1982). *Recollections of Death*. New York: Harper & Row.

Wambach, H. (1978). *Reliving Past Lives*. New York: Harper & Row.

Wambach, H. (1979). *Life Before Life*. New York: Wm. Morrow.

Weiss, B. L. (1988). *Many Lives, Many Masters*. New York: Simon & Schuster.

Wickland, C. (1924). *Thirty Years Among the Dead*. Los Angeles: National Psychological Institute.

Woolger, R. J. (1987). *Other Lives, Other Selves*. New York: Doubleday.

# ⊕ Charles T. Tart Ph.D.

*Charles T. Tart, Ph.D.*

Dr. Tart is Professor Emeritus of Psychology at the University of California, Davis, and currently Visiting Professor in East-West-Psychology at the California Institute of Integral Studies, Core Faculty Member at the Institute of Transpersonal Psychology, and Senior Research Fellow of the Institute of Noetic Sciences. He is internationally known for research with altered states, transpersonal psychology, and parapsychology. His eleven books include two classics, *Altered States of Consciousness and Transpersonal Psychologies* and *Waking Up: Overcoming the Obstacles to Human Potential.* These synthesized Buddhist, Sufi and Gurdjieffian mindfulness training ideas with modern psychology. His latest book, *Living the Mindful Life,* extends these explorations.

# Cosmic Contact from the Perspective of Enlightenment

*Observing that just about every culture inculcates the belief that strangers are dangerous, Charles Tart notes that any contact with aliens calls for exceptional ambassadors, people who are enlightened. He outlines a path toward this state of being: live a basically moral and competent life; have a decent relationship with other people; recognize that there is something higher in life; do something about it. His call is not so much to wake up to a new reality, as it is to simply wake up. What would we know if we were fully awake?*

I'm sort of the reluctant bridegroom at this conference. It reminds me of an occasion about 20 years ago when Michael Murphy, founder of the Esalen Institute, called me up one day and said he had this brilliant idea for a private conference between UFO investigators and parapsychologists. I said, no, I'm sorry, Michael, I get into enough trouble for investigating parapsychology. I can't afford to associate with those far out folks. He said, "That's funny, that's what the UFO investigators were saying about associating with parapsychologists." After we played our little game of who was the biggest martyr, I went to the conference and I came away impressed, puzzled, scared, intrigued, and with my mind generally boggled and thinking , "Gosh I'm glad I have laboratory experiments to fall back on."

The perspective I'm going to bring to you today is somewhat different from what's gone on before. In the program it says it's a psychological perspective, but it's not a conventional mainstream psychological perspective, though I guess there's some of that in there. I'm going to draw mainly from transpersonal psychology, which is the psychology of human liberation, about the kind of experiences that go beyond our personal self, thus the word transpersonal. I'm going to draw from my experience with transpersonal psychology, parapsychology, altered states of consciousness, meditation, Buddhism and Gurdjieff's work, all looking at human possibilities. In an hour I can't get as systematic as I'd like to but for those of you who are interested, you may want to get my book, *Living The Mindful Life* which is much more systematic about these possibilities.

I've been focusing on the question — 'what is enlightenment?' for some time now. Not that I'm at all qualified to talk about it. Actually, both professionally and personally, I've been practicing and studying endarkenment for over 50 years and I'm quite expert on that. I figured out that if you go in the opposite direction, you're probably going to get in the direction of enlightenment and so what I have to say today should be useful for increasing human happiness, even if the aliens never decide to talk with us.

About 10 years ago, the university where I taught sent around a bulletin to all the professors called *How to Teach*. I was very surprised and delighted. I'd been faking it for about twenty years and thought it was good to finally get all the secrets. They did make one point. It is a good idea to tell people what you're going to talk about in the beginning so that they don't lose the forest for the trees.

I'm going to talk about some biases we bring to this whole question of possible contact with aliens, focus it around the question of who should make contact with intelligent aliens, and then I'm going to talk about the fact that, basically, we're unqualified to make contact with intelligent aliens, unless they're as dumb as us. When I heard that anthropomorphic principle earlier I had a different reading on it. I thought maybe our fear is that actually, while they're very technologically advanced, they're no better than we are. That's a really scary thought. I'm going to argue that we need enlightened people in order to make contact with aliens. Then I'm going to focus on what I mean by enlightenment, what does that actually consist of. I will talk a little bit about how we might get more enlightened, and reflect on the practicality of this approach, because of course it may be totally impractical.

I start out with an assumption, and this is an assumption I've had for at least the last thirty or forty years, and that is the assumption of this conference: it's a big universe out there, and obviously in a universe that big there must be all sorts of intelligent beings of one sort or another. I know lots of scientists prove every once in awhile that it's impossible, but if you know anything about the history of science, lots of things have been proved impossible down through the ages, which we now take as commonplace. So that doesn't impress me. When you decide something is impossible, the main thing you psychologically do is close yourself to making any progress and understanding something. So, for a long time now, I've followed the literature on UFO's, flying saucers, as they were called way back then, and it was clear to me long ago that something was happening. Something both in terms of a psychological impact and that funny things show up on radar once in awhile. I'm open to the fact that something real is happening.

On the other hand, there is a part of me that keeps saying, if there really are intelligent aliens and they want to make contact, they're not doing a very good job. If I wanted to make contact with people, I wouldn't go around scaring farmers in the middle of Kansas. I would contact influential people, I would contact government people, I would contact rich people, and I would contact mainstream religious people. That's how I would go about it. As I say these things I am psychologically aware enough to realize that I am primarily demonstrating my own biases and, in fact, I've spent much of the last few years trying to understand my own biases. In making those claims, I am projecting my definition of what an intelligent alien should want to make contact with us. I'm projecting my definition and ideas about how they should go about initiating contact and my definition of who influential people are. In some ways these are common sensical biases. They seem basic in intelligence, and in other ways they're reflections of my and my own culture's limited way of looking at the world. I'll come back to these biases at the end because they're important.

So, I made one assumption. It's a big universe, there's somebody, or lots of somebodies out there, and of course the second assumption is that we probably will make contact someday and to put it mildly it's going to be a very important event in the future of the human race. So, who should make contact? We're talking about meeting aliens. You've all seen the movie Aliens. They can be weird, at least in our pictures of that kind of thing. Clearly meeting creatures who are truly alien is going to be very hard on us psychologically. It's going to be hard on our beliefs, it's going to be hard on our feelings. It's going to be a fantastic opportunity for growth not only personally but for the whole human race in general. And knowing who we are, there is an excellent chance that our crazy biases will certainly spoil the contact and it will be much to the worse. The human race's track record in just dealing with other parts of the human race has a lot to be desired. Yes, sometimes there's trade, there's an increase of culture and so forth, and lots of times there's war and slavery and terrible things on everyone's part. So it's not a simple matter of, yes, we know who to send out to meet intelligent aliens.

We need ambassadors or representatives who are intelligent, but in a far more flexible definition of what intelligence is than what we usually think. We need ambassadors who are open, in an exceptionally open way, to things that are very different from what we're used to. We also need ambassadors who are personally secure, who are secure enough in who they are and what their life means that they're not threatened by something that's very, very different. We need people who are friendly, who are empathic. To put it in an even stronger way, what we really need are enlightened people to make contact.

Perhaps the main thing that impresses me at this stage of our life is that our current ordinary state, what passes for normal, is so unenlightened that contact could be a disaster in all sorts of ways. Probably intelligent aliens, if they're any more enlightened than us, don't want to contact us. I mean why would you hang out with people like us. Who was it, Groucho Marx, who said he wouldn't want to join any club that would admit somebody like him as a member? So we need to become more enlightened as a way of preparing for contact. So what does that mean, to not be enlightened, or to be enlightened, and how could we begin to train people to become more enlightened?

This brings us to my third conscious assumption, and that is that there are higher states of consciousness and being available to human beings. I say that, not out of religious belief or philosophical presupposition or something like that, but out of thirty years of investigating human potential. Of observing what can happen to people, at least temporarily, how people can change. From that perspective I know that people are capable of being much more intelligent than they normally are. Further, that people are capable of being much more emotionally intelligent. Now we don't normally think of this. We tend to be over-intellectualized and think of emotions as something that interferes with our rationality. But there are possibilities for our emotions to be a kind of intelligence, to tell us things about reality, not just about our own feelings, and it's possible for people to become more emotionally intelligent so that emotions are another kind of way of knowing the world. It is possible for people to achieve a balance between intellectual and emotional intelligence. When is the one appropriate, when is the other appropriate, how can they work together under the best circumstances? It's also possible for people to become much happier than we normally are, to have a feeling of fitting in with the universe, to begin to have that kind of security, a feeling that it's all right here, we belong. That makes for much more open dealings with alien people and aliens of any other sort. It's possible for people as they grow in this way toward enlightenment to become far more flexible and adaptive when dealing in life's situations.

I don't mean flexible in the sense of just not caring. You know there's a kind of picture of enlightenment for which the technical term among transpersonal psychologists is "Bliss Ninny." There are some people who are just so spaced out and it's all so wonderful that nothing bothers them, because they're too stupid to know that something bad is happening. I'm not talking about that kind of enlightenment. I am talking about a kind of enlightenment that can make people more intelligent in the way they deal with the universe. It's also quite clear that while these are human possibilities, we know almost nothing about how to train people for this. It's very hard to get to in spite of it being important.

What is this unenlightened state, this ordinary state of consciousness that I am talking about? Let me give you two descriptions of it. I'm first going to give you a poetic description from a Sufi teaching story, and then I'm going to give you a more scientific/psychological definition/exposition of why our ordinary state of consciousness leaves a lot to be desired. I'm going to read you a little story called *The King's Son* from a book by Idries Shah . This is now politically incorrect because it should refer to the king's son and daughter. I have decided not to mangle it by putting it in non-sexist language. Take it as a story from a long time ago when people didn't know any better. This is a story for your heart. We will get to your head in a minute.

*Once, in a country where all men were like kings, there lived a family, who were in every way content, and whose surroundings were such that human tongue cannot describe them in terms of anything which is known to man today. This country of Sharq seemed satisfactory to the young prince Dhat: until one day his parents told him: 'Dearest son of ours, it is the necessary custom of our land for each royal prince, when he attains a certain age, to go forth on a trial. This is in order to fit himself for kingship so that both in fact and repute he should have achieved by watchfulness and effort - a degree of manliness not to be attained in any other way. Thus it has been ordained from the beginning, and thus it will be until the end.'*

*Prince Dhat therefore prepared himself for his journey, and his family provided him with such sustenance as they could: a special food which would nourish him during an exile, but which was of small compass though of illimitable quantity.*

*They also gave him certain other resources, which it is not possible to mention, to guard him, if they were properly used.*

*He had to travel to a certain country, called Misr, and he had to go in disguise. He was therefore given guides for the journey, and clothes befitting his new condition: clothes which scarcely resembled one royal-born. His task was to bring back from Misr a certain Jewel, which was guarded by a fearsome monster.*

*When his guides departed, Dhat was alone, but before long he came across someone else who was on a similar mission, and together they were able to keep alive the memory of their sublime origins. But, because of the air and the food of that country, a kind of sleep soon descended upon the pair, and Prince Dhat forgot his mission.*

*For years he lived in Misr, earning his keep and following a humble vocation, seemingly unaware of what he should be doing. By means which were familiar to them but unknown to other people, the inhabitants of Sharq came to know of the dire situation of Dhat and they worked together in such a way as they could, to help to release him and to enable him to persevere in his mission. A message was sent by strange means to the princeling, saying: 'Awake! For you are the son of a king, sent on a special undertaking, to us you must return.'*

*This message awoke the prince, who found his way to the monster, and by the use of special sounds, caused it to fall into a sleep; and he seized the priceless gem which it had been guarding. Now Dhat followed the sounds of the message which had woken him, changed his garb for that of his own land and retraced his steps, guided by the sound, to the country of Sharq.*

*In a surprisingly short time, Dhat again beheld his ancient robes, and the country of his fathers, and reached his home. This time, however, through his experiences, he was able to see that it was somewhere of greater splendour than ever before, a safety to him; and he realized that it was a place commemorated vaguely by the people of Misr as Salamat: which they took to be the word for Submission, for which he now realized meant - peace.* *

* Idries Shah, *Tales of the Dervishes: Teaching-Stories of the Sufi Masters over the Past Thousand Years* (E.P. Dutton & Co., Inc., New York, 1969) pp. 217-18.

This is very inspiring, but how do we hear the message from our true home, Salamat? How do we understand the nature of the sleep we've fallen into? How do we awaken from this sleep, how do we subdue the monster and obtain the gem, and return home enriched by our journey? I think these questions are all actually very important to all of us here. I don't think people develop an interest in something like Cosmic Contact simply out of intellectual curiosity. It's because we feel a need. We feel we've heard the sound in some sense. We realize there's something more than everyday satisfactions and the endless round of getting more things and playing those kinds of games. We know there's something more, and we're trying to wake up.

Let me switch to a more psychological, scientific perspective and talk about our ordinary state and why it's not particularly suitable for contact with aliens. The central idea I'll use here was formulated in it's present form by a man named G. I. Gurdjieff, one of the early teachers from the East who tried to put certain Eastern ideas in a form that would make sense to Westerners. His basic statement was that man is asleep. Now it would have been better put to say that man is walking around in a waking dream. When you're totally asleep you're actually pretty safe, you just kind of lay there and don't do any harm. But it's like, we live in a kind of ongoing dream and nevertheless we're still operating in this world. We can sign checks and contracts and say things, but we're caught up enough in these kind of dreamlike illusions which we mistake for reality. We do an awful lot of stupid things that cause ourselves and other people lots of suffering. Some of these illusions are created by ourself. Lots of them have been created for us by our culture and taught to us. 'Conditioned' in us is, perhaps a better word, in the course of growing up. They result in reduced intelligence, both intellectual intelligence and emotional intelligence, and reduced will.

Just as when you wake up from an ordinary dream into our ordinary waking state you realize that we're kind of stupid in dreams. They may be symbolically interesting but we're awfully stupid and passive in a lot of dreams. Gurdjieff said it's possible to wake up to a higher state of consciousness in being, and from the perspective of that state it's quite clear that right now we're in a state of reduced intelligence, real stupidity, real passivity, very little ability to really do things. We don't recognize our true nature, as the Sufi story said, "Because of the food and the air of that country, a kind of sleep soon descended upon the pair and Dhat forgot his mission." Man is asleep. It sounds like a strange idea, especially to Western ears. Eastern psychologies and spiritual systems have a very similar idea that man is asleep. But the curious thing is that western psychology probably actually knows more about the nuts and bolts of being asleep, of being unenlightened, of being in a waking dream than they do in the East, although we don't have the concept of putting it together. We are too proud of where we are. Let me give you some examples from a psychological perspective of what it means to be asleep, to be unenlightened.

For one thing there is a great selectivity of perception which we're not aware of. We naively walk around thinking that we see reality simply as it is. I see a person, I see what they look like. I see a situation, I understand it. In point of fact, we know that in many important ways we have been taught what to see, what to hear, what to taste, what to smell, what to feel. We have been taught in accordance with the particular reality of our culture, with the consensus of what our culture thinks is important. That is why when I lecture on consciousness I don't talk about ordinary and normal consciousness anymore. I talk about consensus consciousness to recognize the fact that we've all been brainwashed to a very strong degree, but because it's very similar in all of us we reinforce each other for being normal.

The reality we live in can significantly differ from what is actually out there, sometimes in very arbitrary ways. We have to have reasonable contact with ordinary physical reality or we'd walk in front of trucks and get killed, but beyond that the sky's the limit. Some examples of this, a couple from anthropology. One is, all foreigners look alike. You go to a strange country and all those foreigners look alike. The strange thing is that those foreigners think that we all look alike. We don't see what are obvious distinctions to people raised in a different way. Or a more technical one is, there was a study done years ago working with American Indians who had been raised in teepees. If you gave these people pictures that had very complicated designs hidden in them, they could see things that involved diagonal lines better than ordinary Western people who grew up in things where everything is at a right angle.

Right there, from babyhood, the perceptual system itself is being selectively shaped. Here is another example of selectivity of perception. After World War II some experiments were done on subliminal perception. I think this was first at Harvard. If you show somebody a slide of a word for instance, and you show it to them for more than a second, anybody can read it. But what happens if you just flash the slide? What happens if you flash it so fast that people can't really see what the word is on the slide, they feel that they're just guessing at it? Well, they did this in a very technical way at first, trying to find out some basic mechanisms of perception, but then they started putting in some taboo words. They discovered, for instance, that if you put a word like fuck on the slide, people took a long time before they would say what it was. Now this experiment wouldn't work today. I can get up in front of a respectable group and describe this experiment. Thirty years ago I couldn't describe this out loud. They'd keep having to show longer and longer exposures. At first they thought, "Well, this is just social response bias, right?" The person recognizes the word but most polite people don't say things like that. There may be a little of that in there, but it gets deeper.

You can now do an experiment where, without hurting anyone in anyway, you can by using infrared light measure precisely where their eyes are looking. You give someone a slide to look at, say for ten seconds, and you tell them this is a test, that they're going to be asked about what's on that slide. That's how you motivate people in this country, you tell them it's a test. In the slide you include some material that's problematical for that person, so let's say a person has trouble with sexuality, you put something suggestive in one corner of the slide. Afterwards you ask them about it. They tell you they've inspected the slide. They don't tell you anything about the sexually suggestive material. The really interesting thing is from measured eye movements you know that they never looked at that corner of the slide. Consciously they thought they scanned the whole slide. However, some unconscious part of their mind is so interested in preserving their illusion and their comfort that it sort of signals the conscious mind somehow, "look over here, not up there."

This is living in illusion. This is the unenlightened state where we think we are clearly aware of things but in point of fact awareness is highly selective and often puts us out of touch with reality. We know from lots of examples from psychopathology that this is true. For example, one of the main factors in raising children seems to be confusing then about what they actually feel. Telling them, "No, no, nice girls don't think that, nice boys don't think that." We confuse people systematically about their emotions and then we're surprised when we discover things like all sorts of childhood abuse. Poor kids come into this world and they automatically love their mommy and daddy, so everything their mommy or daddy does is loving except you don't have to get a license to be loving before that.

We have a lot of funny things done to our minds, even those of us who are supposedly normal. Some of the things that are particularly important are that just about every culture inculcates the belief that strangers are dangerous, so we literally see them as dangerous. Now what's going to happen when these strangers are alien looking and this unconscious conditioning is saying danger, danger, danger?

We inculcate in many people, and not just at childhood but very much as adults, a totally materialistic view of life. We are nothing but our bodies, mind is nothing but the functioning of our brain, and you can die. That tremendously enhances whatever natural fear reflex we have, so that in any strange situation fear pops up in an exaggerated form, "Am I going to be killed?" When you project this into dealing with aliens, how often is this going to produce that wonderful American way of coping with life, "shoot first and ask questions later," because of the fear? Not that there is no natural fear. There are dangerous aspects of the universe, but if material life is all you have and you can die and it's a strange situation, it's so easy to fall into that "shoot first and ask questions later" kind of thing.

Gurdjieff said, "Man is asleep." Normal consciousness, consensus consciousness, to recognize it's cultural relativity, is a semi-arbitrary product of our cultural conditioning and our personal history. I say semi-arbitrary because every culture has to keep you enough in touch with the ordinary physical world so you don't get killed too easily. But after that we live mostly in a social world of interactions with other people and all of us have become highly biased in what we see. Some people can look around a room and see sinners. I wasn't too heavily conditioned on that. I'm not sure what a sinner looks like. But some people look around a room and say, "This person has characteristics A, B, and C, therefore I will conclude that they are a sinner. It's obvious the person is a sinner." Our beliefs actually, literally, shape our perception. To say that much unnecessary suffering occurs because of this is to put it mildly.

So we live in this crazy, biased kind of way and we forget our true spiritual nature. As the teaching story put it, "For years Prince Dhat lived in Misr, earning his keep by following a humble vocation, seemingly unaware of what he should be doing." Now there's lots of other psychological things I could add to that, which modern psychology knows about, defense mechanisms and the like, but I want to move on now to the positive side, enlightenment.

I don't want to talk about it in an absolute way, partly because I'm totally unqualified to do it — not being enlightened. As I said, my specialty is endarkenment. But I have some very interesting material to share with you to point out a direction that's possible for human beings to move in, which is going to make the whole question of alien contact much better. I'm going to share some fascinating brand new material that I have from a friend of mine who was accidentally enlightened. This is very valuable because the truth is, if you go and talk to people who have traditions of enlightenment, most of those people have been trained in essentially upholding the doctrine. It's kind of hard to say, "Hey, Joe, what's it like when you eat a steak now that you're enlightened?" You'll get a sermon on non-attachment. This friend of mine, John Wren Louis, a mathematical physicist by training, was very skeptical of all this. His wife, Ann Faraday, who wrote that great book *Dream Power*, was very interested in it, but John wasn't. I remember meeting John and Ann about fifteen years ago before this happened, and both my wife and I came away with the impression that John is a very nice fellow who tolerates his wife's odd friends but clearly had no interest in all this weird material.

Well, he got "enlightened," and I'm not pushing the way it happened. On a bus trip in Thailand, a nice young man offered he and his wife and daughter some candy and helped them with their luggage. John ate the candy. Ann didn't because it smelled rather musty. He found out it's quite common in Thailand for nice young thieves to dope people into sleep so they can steal the luggage. John took a nap, and when he turned blue Ann realized there was something wrong. There's a turn in the story about getting him back to a hospital. Whether he was really dead or not, who knows, but the doctors thought they almost lost him. Apparently it was a tremendous dose of morphine laced with cocaine. The thieves don't always get their doses right. John finally came to consciousness in his hospital room. Things were busy at first and he didn't notice that anything was different until he realized what a marvelous hospital room he was in. It was a dump—the smell of the toilet, the filth—but it was quite marvelous. Eventually, he suspected he must have had one of those near death experiences he'd read about, but he thought people had made up all of that. What surprised him even more was that it wasn't an experience he remembered, but that his being had permanently changed, and it's still with him twelve years later. He's writing a book about it called *The 9:15 To Nirvana*. It probably will come out in a year or so, he's almost finished writing it. It was the 9:15 bus that he caught.

Now of course, it's very hard to talk about this. Somebody mentioned it earlier, and I believe Allen Watts was the first to mention that while things were ineffable, we have a lot of fun trying to "eff" the ineffable. So I want to tell you some characteristics of what changed in the quality of his being to give us a feeling of what enlightenment might be like. The flavor of this will come through in the examples.

For instance, his discovery of the state. He said, "What I had experienced earlier as familiarity of the hospital was in visual terms something like an intensified version of the black light effect used at rock concerts. Everything was highlighted, though in this case the effect was more than visual, somehow seeming to include the other senses too: the smell of the toilet, the buzzing of the insects, the touch of the bed sheets. It was more than merely sensuous, it was like the sheer 'is-ness' of each thing standing out as a kind of greeting — the radiant blackness of being." He talks about a blackness that is even more profound than the light which is usually reported in rear-death experience. "The radiant blackness of being at the back of my head recognizing itself, or rather its no-self, in each other thing, both the objects and events of the outer universe and the thoughts, feelings, sensationings and imagining of John Wren Louis's personal inner universe. 'At the back of my head' is no idle figure of speech. The experience was so palpable that when the realization of the dark's continuing presence first hit me, I actually put my hand up to the back of my head to see if my skull was still intact. I suddenly felt for all the world as if the doctors had removed the back of that bony shell and somehow exposed my brain to the infinite darkness of space. The openness at the back of my head felt like an enormous liberation, as if I had had some kind of brain cataract removed, making true perception possible for the first time in my life."

Indeed, from this permanent change in the nature of his consciousness, what amazes him is that we all don't feel this way all the time. What he is trying to figure out is why aren't we all enlightened all the time? This is like it usually is with experts. Experts do something and they say that it is so easy and obvious. He had some experience with psychedelic drugs when he was younger, partly to keep up with his wife, and keep watch on her. These drugs were great sensory enhancers but this was different. This wasn't adding sensory fireworks to things or making them somehow special, but rather he appreciated every perception simply because it was there.

It changed his relationship to death. A lot of people who have had near-death experiences say that they are now confident that in some particular form they are going to survive death. His experience seemed even more profound than that. He said, "Fear and horror of death had gone because I was no longer experiencing my aliveness as particularly mine, a property or possession of the individual psycho-physiological organism called John Wren Louis. I was experiencing aliveness from a perspective which in some extraordinary way was altogether beyond the cause and effect processes of time. On the one hand, outside of them, and embracing them — yet also totally independent of them, in the sense of being completely present in each and every instant. This perspective was giving it a kind of deep and tranquil satisfaction to the mere fact of existence in every moment which altogether transcended the shallow and transient pleasures of John's personal progression along the time line. I suddenly understood for the first time why mystical philosophers have so often made a point of distinguishing between eternity and ever-lastingness, an eternal life from personal immortality. The eternity experience in each present instant makes the whole issue of possible immortality unimportant. Whereas the desire for immortality shows a preoccupation with separate selfhood along the line of time, which might very well block the joy and tranquility of eternity experience."

If some one could experience something more like this dealing with an alien, doesn't this kind of undercut the "shoot first and ask questions" later approach? The survival question, the fear that goes with it simply becomes an unimportant issue if it doesn't distract you from what is going on.

Another characteristic of his changed state of being is a new openness and feeling of relationship with all of life, and yet something that is not special or separate. He had been struggling, for instance — why had this experience happened to him? He was someone prominent in the "Death of God" movement. He thought we needed religious values, but not so silly as to bring in those crazy religious ideas. Here was something that he thought happened only to great religious figures. He wrestled with that for a long time: "why me?" At one point he thought, "The experience didn't carry the slightest hint of my being anything like a very special person. On the contrary, my sense of myself was a focusing down of the one infinite consciousness, the simultaneous sense of everyone else, indeed of everything else as also that. Even the fact that the other people around me seemed unaware of their 'thatness' didn't seem to make me special in anyway other than perhaps than just being lucky." This state of equality, of connection with everything and not being all that special oneself, think how that changes your way of negotiating with someone else, or relating with someone else, instead of the 'what's in it for me' kind of attitude.

His experience also produced a permanent change, such as he became more compassionate. Not in the sentimental kind of way we usually think about it, but in a very different kind of way. He writes about when his wife got very ill while they were in Malaysia, and rushing her to a hospital with lots of chaos. She was so terribly ill he was really worried about whether she was going to die. Then he writes, "My attention was so completely occupied with practicalities that it came as quite a shock to realize during a respite when Ann managed to doze off into an exhausted sleep on a makeshift corridor bed, that I was still firmly in heaven with the dark despite all the suffering going on around me, including that of my own dearest partner and savior of my life. Moreover, as soon as I noticed it, I knew I had been there all along, simply taking this heavenly detachment for granted without paying attention to it while I got on with what needed to be done." However, he said, "I barely focused on this when my inner critic intervened saying, 'But what about their suffering, what about Ann's suffering, how can you possibly stay detached in your tranquil happiness in the face of that?' Here followed a long intellectual struggle: why was he still in this changed state of being?"

Contrary to our stenotypes, it is not a state where you never think. He realized all the social conditioning he had, that when somebody else is unhappy you are suppose to feel bad. That is how you show you really care. He finally realized, "Eternity-blind consciousness, our ordinary consensus state, takes for granted that satisfaction comes to individuals only through getting their personal needs and preferences met. From which it seems to follow the impulse to help others must depend upon there being some kind of feeling identification with them. The very words compassion and sympathy imply this if taken back to their original common root. From my perspective inside nirvana consciousness however, the whole situation looks completely different. Eternity satisfaction automatically flows over into caring energy along the line of time, as the direct expression of eternity's love for time's productions. It is no great effort of renunciation for a mystic actually living in nirvana consciousness to put aside individual comforts and preferences to help someone else, because personal comforts and preferences are only very secondary sources of satisfaction, while helping others in distress is direct participation, the ultimate satisfaction, eternity's love for the productions of time." Many mystical traditions talk about the highest state of consciousness possible for human beings as automatically including compassion.

If we are talking about people having to relate to aliens who may frighten us, who may have their own agenda, if you feel genuine compassion for someone else, the quality of your negotiation is going to change. I think we have all had the experience at times when someone has tried to help us and we felt that they actually cared, rather than say professional helpers who go through the motions but don't actually care. What a difference it makes in the relationship.

I mentioned the technical term "Bliss Ninny" before, which is a stereotype we have of enlightened people, sitting around and contemplating their navel with a little smile. It didn't work out that way. Rather, John has found that he has become more effective and intelligent as the result of experiencing this eternity consciousness all the time. He gives an example. This, I believe, is the second night after they got out of the hospital. They were leaving the next morning on an early bus, the same bus that he had been poisoned on, which was an interesting thought. They had tried to find a quiet hotel the night before so they could get some rest, but it seemed like every hotel in Thailand was a sex-party hotel.

He was going down early to arrange for an early breakfast. He says, "What greeted me between the foot of the stairs and the entrance to the dining room was a huge pool of vomit, presumably evidence of excess at the previous night's revelry. I was truly astonished to experience its greeting with as much welcome as that of a beautiful flower. Astonished, for I have been extremely squeamish every since I can remember as the result of cautioning in infancy by a neurotically hygiene conscious mother who saw and carefully trained me to see threats of disease lurking in tiny specks on cutlery or crockery, in all dirt, especially, of course, biologically wet dirt, in excrement of every kind and in anything even remotely suggestive of illness. Now as the dark confronted me in the pool of vomit, I experienced that ability to enjoy, literally enjoy, contradictory feelings which I had already recognized as characteristic of the mystical consciousness. On the one hand I saw and smelled particles of semi-digested food mixed with bile fluid and they were quite fascinating sensations, each giving me greeting as if they were wonderful art works whose creation I had been personally present at, and simultaneously I experienced my disgust reaction even to the point of my gorge beginning to rise (this is the part that will make you remember this talk forever) as itself a creative act of John's body/mind under the direction of his mother's neurotic fears which was also a marvel. Moreover, deep underneath it all, an integral part of the appreciation was the peace past understanding of complete being. And as I negotiated my way around the pool of "divine" vomit I also noted that the new awareness didn't make me in the least careless about getting mess on my shoes. On the contrary, the dark perspectivising of my conditioned anxieties allowed much greater efficiency in coping with the purely practical problem of avoiding contamination than would have been possible with gritted teeth. The practical business of getting good results along the line of time is not in any way hindered by mystical awareness that everything is already perfect in the dimension of eternity. Freedom from domination by anxious thoughts for the morrow actually makes for greater efficiency in doing things."

Suppose the aliens smell bad, and makes you want to vomit? It would be very good to have this more enlightened state of being available to deal with that. Wouldn't that put us to the test? They are very intelligent and compassionate, and they smell very bad. One other capacity that is sometimes attributed to enlightenment that would be very handy to have would be psychic abilities. John Wren Louis has not experienced any particular psychic abilities as the result of the change in his state of being. But many of the spiritual traditions do talk about various psychic abilities coming in to play naturally after enlightenment, although they are quite tricky if you play with them before then.

Personally, I think the wisdom of enlightenment is far more important for people to have than psychic abilities. Psychic abilities are like another channel of information. In this modern age we already have enormous numbers of channels of communications, and how often do we use them wisely?

What does the state of enlightenment look like, and maybe not the complete enlightenment that is possible to someone who doesn't have an axe to grind in terms of some kind of doctrine or the like. How do we get there? I wish there was a comprehensive simple answer for this. There is not. I'll just give you some hints, The way I am going to tell you to be more like this is not "the" answer. It is just some generalizations I have pulled out over the years. For those of you who want more detail, read my *Living the Mindful Life* book, and some of the other books I have written. What is especially important to remember is that I am going to give a general outline of the way people can grow toward enlightenment. What is good for one person is not necessarily good for another person. Incidentally, I do not recommend the way John Wren Louis got there. In general, the near-death experience is the most efficient way to change your state of being. But I never recommend it because the 'near' part is always tricky. Most people who get that near do not describe a great experience to you afterwards, they get buried.

What works for one may not work for another. For example, psychedelics have produced wonderful spiritual opening in some people, and made other people more neurotic than they were. John Wren Louis himself is not very good in giving advise on how to get there. In fact, he says that every attempt to become enlightened simply reinforces your belief that you are not enlightened and acts as a barrier. He is still working on that one.

Here are some things that are generally thought of as ways of getting people more enlightened. I will present these as if this were a sequence, but in real life things interact with each other in complex ways. One thing is living a basically moral and competent life. You have to have enough of your needs met so that you are not totally concerned about ordinary survival kinds of needs all the time. You have to have a decent enough relationship with other people so that you are not constantly being attacked and retaliated by them. Also, insofar as the enlightenment perspective is right, that we are all joined within an intimate way, if you spend a lot of time attacking other people, you are actually attacking yourself, and you have a very strange and bad relationship with yourself from which it is not going to be possible to break through to the enlightenment perspective. Sometimes I say the state you need to be in is to be at the level of what I call the successful malcontent. You have to be successful enough in terms of what society says "here are the goodies," that you are not thinking, "well, if I really had a Mercedes then I would really would be happy." You have to get enough of those things to realize that material things are all right, but that is not it. Then you have to ask, "is there anything more?" The successful malcontent.

Next you have to hear the sound, the inspiration, the call. "By a means which was familiar to them the inhabitants of Sharq knew of the dire situation and sent a message saying 'awake.'" I think everybody here has heard that to some extent, and I suspect the call actually comes all the time. It is just at certain moments we realize there is something higher in life.

Then you have to do something about it. You have to recognize that you are unenlightened, that you are asleep in Gurdjieff's sense, that you are living in this waking dream. You have to recognize that not just in some vague sort of way, but you have to start getting specific about it, you have to start studying yourself - 'exactly how am I unenlightened, why am I unhappy, what is driving me?' What we usually tend to do is blame other people — those Republicats and Demicans are always screwing things up. Sure, other people do make life more difficult for us, and that is a part of the reality we have to deal with. But we have to recognize how much we ourselves contribute to being in an unenlightened state. How attached we are to things that keep us from recognizing our deeper connections.

The best way to jail somebody is to make them think they are at a vacation resort. The best way to make someone a slave is not to put shackles on them externally, but to give them a belief system that locks them into something. You have to begin to recognize the specific kinds of things that lock you in and keep you from going somewhere. That involves learning how to observe yourself, how to study yourself. How to be both deeply involved and objective at the same time, to see how you really are. Gurdjieff talked about observing the machinery of your mind, the habits, including the emotional habits which keep us trapped in our everyday personality.

You have to have a certain amount of patience. We, of course, all expect that 'once I get interested I can go to a weekend enlightenment intensive and take care of all of this,' but actually it is probably not a good idea to change things at first. You really have to see deeply into yourself.

There are formal ways of doing this like meditation techniques. There are other ways that are relatively new under the sun. For instance, lots of western psychotherapy in its best usage can be seen as ways of understanding yourself, and the traps and the detours and blocks of yourself, in a far deeper way than was ever possible before. To discover insights, to discover what your biases are. It is nice to know at some level you have biases, but until you know specifically what they are, they pretty much ruin you.

There are all sorts of practices on various enlightenment paths to begin to increase your ability to focus, to concentrate, to get it together. If we look at our ordinary minds they really are scattered all over the place a good deal of the time. We get a wonderful idea about change and improvement and we forget all about it five minutes later.

There are a lot of meditation practice exercises which are mainly about teaching you to concentrate. When you can concentrate you can also deeply observe yourself better. You can focus below the surface level. There are formal meditation practices where you sit on a special black cushion, ring a little bell to start. There are practices to apply as part of everyday life, to become more observant, more aware, more objectively in touch with things as part of your everyday life, feeling your own life experiences more deeply.

All of these things also in a certain way involve the ability to learn to live in the here and now. If you look at our ordinary human minds, the ordinary consensus consciousness, we have very little contact with the reality of what actually is at any moment. Something happens which reminds us of something which brings up a hope which reminds us of something which brings up a fear. We live in the past and the future all the time. That is not terribly good for picking up on the subtle nuances of the now. If someone is trying to negotiate with an alien, and something the alien does reminds them of something which reminds them of something, then they miss all the subtleties of the communication after that.

We need to learn to focus deliberately. We need to learn to live in the here and now. We need to understand ourself. This is a very general outline as those of you who have walked along this path know.

Then there is a funny step. Gurdjieff talked about 'work, as if everything depends on work, and pray as if everything depends on prayer.' Work as if nobody is ever going to help you, you are it. If you don't get your act together and put you ass in gear, forget it, you are dog food. Your efforts are what counts, and really make those efforts. At the same time, each of us is nothing. It's grace. It is something from a higher level that actually makes the transformation. Do both of those things at once, and try to be kind to yourself in the process. I hate to mention that one as it tends to go to people's super-ego and produce unpleasant results. It sounds paradoxical, but that is the way things are.

There is another step: finding and cultivating social support for wanting more enlightenment. "Dhat came across someone else who was on a similar mission, and together they were able to keep alive the memory of their sublime origins." It is very hard to swim upstream in an enlightenment that wants to lose itself in the narcotization of 500 channels on demand, and try to remember to live in the here and now. We need friends, we need people we can talk to. We need people we can share the best of our aspirations and knowledge with, and visa-versa to keep us supported.

We need to find teachers. Ideally, you should find a perfectly enlightened teacher who will show you the way. Are they in the Yellow Pages here in Washington, D.C.? How do you find the perfect teacher? There is a wonderful Sufi story about someone who spent all his life searching for the perfect teacher. He found lots of teachers who weren't quite up to snuff. They all had a flaw. Finally, toward the end of his life he found the perfect teacher who, after serving him tea, sent him on his way. The perfect teacher only accepted the perfect student. We can find teachers who are people we can learn from, who are people who can stimulate us, who know something more than us about awakenness, about enlightenment and the like, and we can learn from them without necessarily going crazy.

Taking any teacher, of course, is quite dangerous, but we seem to have a hard time getting by without them. But then, being alive is dangerous; we have to remember that perspective. It is not as if we are safe now.

I have talked about the shortcomings of our ordinary state. We have a very hard time with each other. How in the world are we going to have meaningful, growthful communications with aliens when we are so conditioned, when we are so blind, when so much craziness goes on?

I have talked about something called enlightenment. Tried to give you a little bit of a feel for it, tried to talk about a little bit of the general sorts of ways people try to escape the sleep of ordinary life, to begin to get out of delusion and more in contact with our real nature.

Let me conclude by bringing that to some practical considerations. This conference is based on the theme that someday we will probably have contact. What are we doing to prepare? Well, of course, there are extensive government training programs to enlighten people. I must have misread my notes here, something about being in Washington! I am afraid I am sadly pessimistic here. Government, any kind of large organization, turns into an organization devoted to preserving the organization in many ways. You cannot really expect organizations to teach transcendence, to teach opening up in new ways, to totally new ideas and ways that transcend the organization. The question is, will we start training ourselves, instead of waiting for someone to do it? Will we care enough to wake up? Will we become dissatisfied enough with the suffering that we go through in our waking sleep to make the effort to come into the present?

At the beginning I noticed my biases that if the aliens wanted to contact us they are not doing a good job. They should be contacting influential people, not farmers. What do I think now as I reflect on that? If the aliens are more enlightened than us, why should they want to contact us? Maybe we are not ready. It may be a case of the more progressed teacher wanting more progressed students. There is also the possibility that the aliens may be very technologically advanced, but not any more morally advanced than we are. That is very scary. I don't even want to think about that one particularly.

The real questions is, will we work on ourselves so that beings who are more intelligent in terms of their heart, not just their head, would want to dialogue with us? If they want to be helpful to us, would they find us capable of actually receiving that kind of help, rather than trying to force it into the old tired games that we play?

I don't have the answer to that question, but I think it is the kind of question we very much need to think about rather than assuming that contact will just come about by more of what we have now.

# ⊕ Puma Q. Singona

*Puma Quispe Singona*

Puma Quispe Singona is a Peruvian high school student who was born in Chinchero, one of the last traditional Q'esua (Quechua) communities in Peru. After working as a shepherd from the age of five to eleven, he moved to Cusco, where he became a street vendor. There, he taught himself English in addition to his native Q'esua and Spanish learned in school. His grandfather, Maximo Singona Puma Yalli, is the last altomisayoc (priest/Medicine man) of Chinchero, and is teaching Puma to continue the ancient Q'esua/Inca traditions. Puma's attendance at this conference was his first trip outside Peru.

# Other Dimensional Beings in Inca Cultures

*In a mystical experience as a six year old shepherd, Puma was chosen to follow in his grandfather's tradition as an Andean shaman. Now a teenager, and imbued with the sense of ayni, a relationship of reciprocity, he has been taught that space beings will help those who also help them make contact and to establish ayni.*

(Introduction by Elisabet Sahtouris)

*I'd like to tell you how I met Puma. He approached me for two months every once in a while in the streets of Cusco, Peru saying, "Are you looking for me?" I said "no" each time, and then started saying, "I don't think so." One night when a friend was down visiting, we were in a coffee shop and I saw him at the door and I said, "I'm going to buy a belt from this young man today," He was a street vender selling woven belts. He came in the door smiling, and I said, "I think I'm going to buy a belt from you tonight," and he said, "I know, I knew you would tonight." I also bought him a hot chocolate so I could have a conversation with him. It was remarkable, and from then on there was no question that we were in a very strong relationship. Puma's whole family are weavers. Different uncles have knitted his cap and woven his poncho especially for this trip. In his culture, people don't do things alone.*

*I don't want to take up any more of his time but I'll say he was born in Chinchero which is one of the last communities still practicing the traditions of ayni which is exchange between people. I help you today, you help me tomorrow, and it goes on within the whole community. His grandfather, Don Maximo Singona Puma, has become a strong advisor of mine, and he and Puma's father and Puma and I did a ceremony in Cusco before we came here to ask the permission and blessing of the Apus, the great mountain spirits of Peru and of the rest of the world. We prayed to the Apus, not only of the Andes but to Mt. Whitney and to Mt. Shasta on the west coast. One of Puma's missions is to go to a snow covered mountain in this country before he returns.* (This was accomplished on Mt. Shasta where Puma participated in ceremonies conducted by Native Americans.)

*Puma was a shepherd from the age of six, and in his first year of being a shepherd he was chosen by the Apus to follow in his grandfather's tradition. A true Andean shaman (I don't like that word but that's the one you can relate to) will not leave his community, will not be found teaching groups of tourists. So you have a very special opportunity today to hear the young man who is the last in a long chain from pre-Inca times, learning his tradition from his grandfather. With that I want to present to him a kintu, three leaves of coca, a traditional exchange.*

I will share my energy with all of you. In the Andes and in Peru we do that all the time, sharing energy with the Apus because we have to do it to work, to eat. Always we are in that relationship with the natural life. From six to eight years of age I was living with my grandfather, and had many experiences with the natural environment. When I came to Cusco where my parents live I learned Spanish and I taught myself English. Now I'm here and I'd like to say, "Thank you," for giving me the opportunity to come here to talk with you.

In Peru, the young people are losing their interest in learning the natural culture. But it is very important for them to learn it. Most of them like to live in the big countries and have different kinds of life. I was learning from my grandfather many things, and when he was in Cusco at first he did not want to tell Elisabet about our culture. The Indian people there think everyone is like the Spanish invaders, that they are going to make bad things happen to them. But I told my grandfather she is a good friend, and she will help us. Now I am here, and I would like to say that the mountains, the Apus, and beings of other dimensions are helping us, and are so powerful they help the people to have a better life. We are making it difficult to live in love and harmony. We have to make a better life in this world.

In Cusco, when there is work to be done, we go over to another house to tell them to help us, and then they come over to tell us to help them. That is the unity of the people there. But it has to be everywhere, and I came here to tell all the other cultures that they have to change, that they have to do things in a different way. They have to be just one, like in the Inca's times. We must work all together in our life. In this way, the world will have a different future.

These beings who came we call Light People. The Indians don't know anything about UFO's. They just call them what they look like. They were helping the Indians to have a better life, and we call them the healers, doctors. John Mack says that we call them doctors, and he is right. They heal the people who are sick. They were helping us before, but they can't do it now because we aren't going to help them. I told you this before Elisabet, will you explain?

*(ES) Puma is saying that the beings from space will help those who also help them to make the contact and establish this relationship of reciprocity. Ayni is best translated into English as reciprocity.*

Yes, and we have to do it. Everybody will have to have contact with them, and it's important for us to be very friendly, to live in a loving world. Everybody will have to be friends, just one heart. Nobody is rich, nobody is poor, everybody works for the same thing. To help other people is to help yourself. I think the Mountains will become a light for the people. The people have to live in a natural world. I have to tell it in Spanish. Elisabet will translate it. It's difficult for me to say in English.

*(ES) He's saying that the closer people return to the natural, non mechanical/technical world the easier it will be for us to be in touch with these beings. If you live only in this world of technology which closes itself from nature, it's more difficult for you to communicate with the spirits of the mountains and the other parts of the land.*

I want you to meet my grandfather. He is helping me to talk with you. In our culture he's in spirit just the same as if he is physically here. It's good if the people here can be in touch with their spirit to go over to other dimensions. My grandfather said that to see those beings we have to see them in other dimensions. One day when I was in a river I saw a big ball of light which came through my body. I was frightened. I didn't like it. I was six years old. Nobody was with me, only my animals. It was about five kilometers from Chinchero. Everything was natural, plants, the river. There aren't any houses or any people who live near. When the light came through my body it was like flying. I was not putting my feet on the ground. I felt like a big man.

Before that, I had strange dreams. There was an old man who told me not to tell anyone about this but my grandfather. He said that I had permission of the Apus to learn; that knowledge comes from father to son. My uncle, who lives in Cusco, is not interested in the natural culture. He says it is better to have money and a house and a family. To have a family is nice. Its nice to be in love, but we have to remain in contact with nature always. When I was with my grandfather he taught me many important things, and I was impressed with that life.

Naturally, I wanted to live with my parents because they were bringing me games, toys, television. But when this happened to me I just wanted to live the natural life. I was living with my grandfather until

I was eight years old and I was learning many things. When my grandmother died in December last year, my grandfather came to Cusco, he's living with me now and he taught me things before I came here. He told me to be careful with these people, many different things. He wants to take care of me.

I wanted to do a ceremony in here, but I couldn't bring the coca here because they think it's a drug. A despacho is a ceremony we make for the Apus. Most of the time it's when the moon is full. A despacho helps the people to do things better, to work better. Sometimes we pay the earth, to Pacha Mama, with despachos. They say in our culture if we make the despacho we will have a better harvest. My grandfather was teaching me to work with the ground. When I went to Cusco the only thing I learned in school was studying mathematics, science, history. In history, most of it doesn't talk about Incas. Most of it talks about wars and bad things and wrong things. That's all the history we have, we have no love history. My grandfather was telling me love histories, about many people who make friends. Friendship is very important for all people because you never can tell when you're going to need some one, because sometimes you have problems.

When I was in Cusco, I made many friends. I was lost when I was very small, and they helped me to find my home. My parents were looking for two days. I slept in the streets. It was difficult for me to live in a big city. I like it better to live in a small place where I know everything like streets and houses, where I can have contact with the natural life.

I always like to climb the trees, it's very nice. Trees are important too. My grandfather said that one day he was dreaming and the tree was like a light and it was talking to him, and he called it a silver tree and the tree said, "that is not my name." The trees and the mountains and everything teach the people many different things. After that happened in the river with me, I went only to other places as a shepherd. I didn't go back to that place for two years. That is a long time.

Later, I had these dreams with an old man who came through a light door. He said that for me it's important to not be in contact with the wrong kind of people. It's important that if I know the people well I can tell them to make a better life. I was afraid of these dreams, but my grandfather said, "He is your teacher, that light is for you on the road, because now on the roads of the people everything is dark. They are sleeping, and when they see the light they wake up." It is important to see the light, and how to do it is just to live in a love world.

The Light Beings, the Light People (conferring with Elisabet in Spanish) *are still here and are friendly to human beings and are ready to help again those who call on them.* Everybody right now is waiting for a comeback of somebody. For the Christians it's Jesus, for the Jews it's Jehovah, for the Mexicans it's Quetzelcoatl, and for our culture it's the Light Beings. When they come all they're going to do is just help. We have to make a love world, and it's good to communicate with them over other dimensions like dreams or meditating. It's important.

When I was living with my grandparents, we went one day, just the three of us, with the animals, and did watya *(a potato offering in the field where potatoes are roasted in mud ovens made in the field itself)* We were eating it, and when we finished my grandfather said, "this night we will go to a place where you will see that light." We went and there was darkness. Somebody was walking around on the rocks, so we didn't stay. My grandfather said that there is a place to meditate there. I saw many crystals there, and my grandfather said that those crystals are important for you to communicate with other dimensions. The stones there are important too. Everything natural is important. He said that we have to be communicating with the spiritual dimension, and then everything will come in it's own time. That is all I have to say. Thanks again for the opportunity.

*Elisabet Sahtouris: One of the things I would like to say about Puma is that from the age of three he has danced annually in the festival of Qoyllur Rit'i, which means Snow Star. It is the celebration of the return of the Pleiades to the Southern hemisphere after about fifty days during which they are below the horizon, from late April to some time in June. At that festival, which is high in the mountains in the snowy areas there are three main kinds of sacred dancers. The Qollas, who represent the mountain people, the Ch'unchus who represent the Amazon people, and the third kind of dancer are the Ukukus. I'd like Puma to tell you what it means to be an Ukukus.*

To be an Ukukus is to take the spirit of everybody to the mountain to be excused. Everybody has wrong things they do, and we carry all their spirits over a long road, which takes all the night to walk. I really don't know how many kilometers it is because we just go up and down and across mountains and we bring them to the mountains, and that's a festival that unites the three regions. Everybody has a mission there, and our mission is to take the spirit of everybody up into the mountain and make it excused, and then we bring it back. We each carry a block of ice, and that is the weight of the wrongdoing.

*(ES) So he has from the age of three, physically carried the wrongdoings of people up into the mountains and onto a glacier, and they then, each Ukukus (Ukukus means bear) carry the chunk of ice back and they then make tea for the people with this ice. This is a purification ceremony.*

*Are there any questions?*

**What role do the Pleiades play in your tradition?**

*(ES) In the Quechua language they are sometime called the storehouse, meaning that they hold the grain harvest. There is no written Quechua language. The Spanish used the word Qeswa (Valley) because that is where they found the people. The people were the runa and their language runa simi.]*

They disappear from the sky, and in the time of the Qoyllur Rit'i they come back to help the people, that's all I know of this.

*(ES) It's like a time of darkness when they are away, when people make offerings to them to bring them back. Remember this is the Southern hemisphere and their harvest is in what we call springtime; the fall and spring are reversed.*

**Do you work with crystals to travel to other dimensions?**

I just know that, and accept that.

*(ES) He doesn't take crystals out of their natural settings in the rocks, but he is aware of their medium for communication.*

**Could you please tell us some more about the Light Beings who taught the Incas, and who you are in contact with?**

No, that's really all. They are just helping the people, teaching them how to do things, like in agriculture with irrigation.

*(ES) He's saying that the Light Beings have a relationship with the water of the earth, and when the water pressure increases at certain times of the year this is a connection with the Light Beings above. The Andean people built their civilization very much to reflect the stars in the sky. For instance, in the town where I recently spent a week writing, the town is laid out in the form of a tree, and that exact shape is in the milky way just below the Southern Cross where there's a black hole in the shape of a tree like that. There was a great deal of conscious integration, and many of the teaching stories of the Andes are about the river of milk in the sky connected with the rivers of water on the earth. They knew how the waters are recycled through the sky, things of this kind. Light Beings, Star Beings, are connected*

*with waters of the earth, the flow that's above and below.*

**What can you tell us about the Nazca lines?**

I don't know anything about Nazca. Except in books, I have not seen them. Flying here the plane went over another way.

*(ES) The Nazca culture was one of the pre-Inca cultures.*

But I know about Parakas. My grandfather says that one of their weavings is the spirit of one mountain around Cusco, and he said that you have to see it because it has important signs that I was learning. I'm going to look for it, because he says it has heads of a puma and serpents and it's very strange to see. It's something I'm going to learn. I know that the Parakas culture had a good friendship with the Incas, or at least some Inca Indians. The Incas were making some weavings like them, too. But I don't know anything about Nazca.

*(ES) The Andean peoples recorded a lot of their knowledge in the weavings of the Andes. Currently (May 1995) the Smithsonian Institution has a Peruvian exhibit of the Lord Sipan. It displays objects from one of Peru's most important pre-Inca cultures.*

**Question about the Light Beings and energy.**

No, they live there, because they give help to the people. They are powerful beings. One day I went with someone to the mountains with my grandfather to work. He was just curious, but he could feel the power of the place. Those are just some of the mountains, not all of them.

*(ES) I might add that I've never seen Light Beings except in Peru, working with the men of Puma's family.*

**Question about the Festival of Qoyllur Rit'i.**

It's very far from Chinchero. It takes from 5:00 in the evening to 10:00 the next morning to get there, Then it's about eight kilometers to the mountain where we do the ceremonies.

*(ES) It traditionally lasts for three days and three nights.*

It's not always on the same day, this year it's June 3, so I won't be able to go but some years it's May 17 or 18.

*(ES) It coincides with the full moon. It always takes place on a full moon. It's a very ancient festival, and the Incas created their own myths about it. It existed previously to them, and to them it was the symbol of civilizing the wild people, so the interplay between the forest people and the mountain people was carried out in that way. When the Spanish Catholics came in they made up their own story about a shepherd boy who is visited by a boy who is Jesus, so it's the new form of civilization coming as each culture lays over the one before. But the deep original meaning of it has to do with separation and reunion with the disappearance and reappearance, with seed time and harvest time, with the sacrifices made to insure abundance for the people. And, of course, for the lifting of the sins, as we said before.*

**Question about Puma's training with his grandfather.**

*(ES) I'd like to tell one little story about Puma's grandfather. Puma told me that his grandfather was what we call a midwife. It was the first time I had heard of a man delivering babies. I was very interested and I asked him if he had learned anything about it. He told me he was present went his baby sister was born, and his grandfather was teaching him some things then. My daughter is an obstetrician, and I wondered about possible differences in procedures. I asked him about the delivery. He answered: "well, first of all you must be in a very happy frame of mind, because you're greeting a new life, and it's important to greet that new life in a happy way." I said, "Then what?" "You must be completely focused, and keep your mind on your work every moment and don't be worrying about other things." I*

*won't go on with the story. The point is, he didn't talk technology, he talked love.*

**Is there any connection between the particular stars, the Pleiades and the Light Beings or Apus?**

Yes, they have a relationship. My grandfather was saying maybe some of us come from those stars, too. One day Elisabet talked about her son (my brother) who said, "When are we going to go back to our other world, because I don't like this world." I understood, and I asked my grandfather and he said that many people come from there, like Mikokappa, an Inca who helped the people to make weaving, to work the grounds, and all of that. He came from the lake, and said that he had come from the light of the sun. So some of us do have a relation, some of us are sons of the stars. And maybe I am one too, I don't know. But their only purpose is to make a different world.

*(ES) In the Inca tradition, Inti, the sun is called Taytay Inti, father sun. There is also a father of the father sun, the central sun, which I believe they took to be the center of the galaxy. The first Inca appeared from the lake, from the water. Water has some special living qualities which make it easier to travel to other dimensions, and of course many UFO's are seen going into or emerging from lake Titicaca.*

**Question about dimensional travel.**

I went through other dimensions, and I went by myself, too. My grandfather went one day, when he was very young, and there were no other people there. Some people sleep there but they are not tourists, they are Incas. He says that some times the people are still there, and you can see them if you have the right thinking. He saw one there, and it was going into a bright door, and there were serpents everywhere. He wanted to go inside. To go in those doors is very important, but most of them can't do it. My grandfather couldn't, he was afraid. He had negative thoughts, and he didn't want something bad to happen to him. But now he wishes he had gone into the door because the deepest secrets were in there. He's still learning, but the masters don't teach like the Incas do, they have people who tell them things. They are really afraid because that culture is missing right now in Cusco, and everywhere it's missing.

One day I went with my grandfather and his Alto Misayoq friend to meet with other grandfathers to talk. I was very interested to learn things, but I was wearing my Peruvian city clothes. They like it better if you are in traditional clothes, a poncho, a chulyo, a vest, They thought I was some other boy who was not interested in the natural culture. I was learning about the mountains, and he kept looking at me to see whether I was paying attention. When he saw that I was, he gave me a nice stone, which I have with me in Cusco, and he said "This stone will protect you." Also, in my passport, my grandfather put two coca leaves and he said "These will protect you." I have the impression that one of the leaves is me and one is my grandfather, and if I put the two together we are talking with him. Last night I had a dream. I didn't tell Elisabet. I didn't have time because we are always busy here. I dreamed that I was with my grandfather and we were going up the stairs and at the top of the stairs there was a bright door. We were going into it. When we were inside it I saw everything was bright white. My eyes couldn't see very well, and I couldn't touch my grandfather's hand and he said he was trying to touch me but he couldn't. I understood more that it's the same thing, the spiritual and physical, even though we can't touch I can still see and he is always with me. Like my grandmother, he says, "Yes, your grandmother is gone but she is still here." And he is happy because she will not go into death until he does too, and then they will live together in the spiritual life. The Peruvian grandparents like to live in that spiritual world better than in this material world. When they finished work, they always made a ceremony like dancing, and eating foods, and all that. Now we no longer have that tradition to give the first food we get to the earth.

One day my grandfather had a dream about an old woman who said, "The people do not remember me." He didn't understand who this old woman was. The next day he went to work. Usually, when they drink, they put something on the earth. One of the young people, maybe 22, didn't do this. Then my grandfather said, "Ah, I know what it means. The Pacha Mama is missing some people that are still learning things from the Andes that most of them don't have the interest in learning anymore." The Earth is coming over other dimensions to some grandparents to ask for help.

*(ES) This is again reciprocity in that if you want help from the Earth, if you want help from the Light Beings, what are you giving? What's your role in helping the Earth so that in return the Earth can feed and protect us?*

**What is your story of how you met Elisabet?**

On the first day I saw her, my grandfather was talking to me about if I had found some good friends, because everyday I find friends when I'm working with belts. I like to make friends, I like to practice my English, too. My grandfather said that he was looking with coca and he asked, "Who is she?" I was confused. I had met maybe three women that day so I didn't know which one, but the next day when I went up to her I could tell that she was a positive energy and I could talk with her, and that day I did. I was telling her about my grandfather and some of his experiences and she was trying to tell me about her culture, too. I made friends and she said, "I want to talk with your grandfather."

He didn't want to come, but then I told him she will help us, she knows something about the Indian culture, she will help us, so he said, "O.K., I will go." When we went there we were talking about many interesting things. He was always not trusting people and Elisabet was hearing everything I was translating. My grandfather only speaks Quechua and no Spanish. We made friends, and he said it's O.K. to make friends with her because she will help you in many things. She is helping. I am happy now to be with her, because my grandfather is helping me to make a life of love, and he is here with me and I hope that you can feel the positive energy now to make a better life.

*(ES) Thank you, Puma. I'd like to say once more that here in the north an indigenous friend of mine once said if you want to tell whether someone who appears to be a native medicine man or shaman or whatever your word is, ask them three questions to find out if they're real. Who are your people? Do you have the credentials of your people? And, do you take money for what you do? It's a kind of good rule of thumb that works for those from the south as well. My entire experience with Puma's whole family, beginning with his grandfather, has been an experience of people who love. Puma has related to me conversations that these elders have had with each other in the mountains which was not for my ears, and everything he has told me indicates only a great concern and sensitivity for the Earth, for the people, and always in a positive way. There are many people who have powers, both in the north and the south, who use those powers negatively, for their own benefit. And I can tell you that you are not going to find a more real teacher than the young man you have before you now.*

## ⊕ Dennis Rohatyn, Ph.D.

138

*Dennis Rohatyn, Ph. D.*

Dr. Rohatyn teaches at the University of San Diego. His books include *Naturalism and Deontology, Two Dogmas of Philosophy and The Reluctant Naturalist*. He co-hosts *Free Thinking* with Virginia Muller on KPBS FM. Founder of the Society for Orwellan Studies (SOS), and president of the G.E. Moore Society, he also is a member of the Phi Beta Kappa. His Ph.D. is from Fordham University. In 1987, he received the J. Lowell Davies award for outstanding faculty achievement at the University of San Diego.

# The Myth of Merger

*With an existentialist flare, philosopher Rohatyn, set a fast pace and disabused the audience that the Conference would be wall-to-wall warm fuzzies about ET/UFO phenomena. His challenge to avoid self-deception and to dig deeply for answers to the question: why do we need ET/UFO phenomena is a powerful appeal for individual responsibility and assertion of the importance of passion in life. The audience found it difficult to remain neutral about Rohatyn's assessments and warnings.*

I must be in the wrong room—I thought this was the prayer breakfast for James Randy, Martin Gardner, and Philip Klass. But speaking of last suppers, and the sense of betrayal that accompanies them, I do want to confess to two misgivings that I had prior to arriving here today. One is that I can't compete with the New York City Police Department, even though I am from Manhattan. I've heard of Naked Gun, but this is ridiculous. So if you expected a sex show, sorry, this is it. I guess they give new meaning to the words "cops are pigs," straight from the animal farm by sliding up, or is it down, escalators and turning voyeurism inside out. But my second misgiving was that I was afraid I would tarnish or ruin what little is left of my reputation by coming here today, but then I reasoned that since Jesus went among the sinners why shouldn't I go among the space cases? And if you think it's hubris or chutzpah for me to compare myself to Christ, well, he walked on water, and I'm about to skate on thin ice.

I will, by the way, take questions when I'm done. I don't know how long this talk will take, but in case I go overtime and the referee blows the whistle I will certainly remain here forever to take bricks as well as bouquets, compliments as well as criticisms, and to answer any and all comers.

Our subject poses a unique challenge as well as opportunity. Nearly a century ago, William James, speaking of ESP, or what we would now call paranormal phenomena, said 90% of it is moonshine, the other 10% cannot be discounted. I think that is still true today, and it's true of what we'll be talking about in this room for the next three days. It was James too, who posited the dichotomy between tender and tough minded. It was a valiant effort to reconcile different aspects of our intellect and heal the rifts between parts of our personality so that we would neither be too dogmatic on the one hand or too gullible on the other. So that we would be, as David Hume once said, "as skeptical of our skeptical doubts as we are of everything else." It was James too, who in his *Principles of Psychology*, way back in 1890, coined the term "fringe" not to refer to the lunatic fringe, of which we are all charter members, but to speak about those things that we don't notice when we're busy noticing other things. The sorts of things that we don't quite take for granted, and can't afford to, whether it's a blimp on our radar screen or the interpretation of a photographic plate, like the kind of thing Clyde Tombaugh used to discover Pluto, or even just trying to navigate around Dupont Circle without getting killed. It was James who recognized that we constantly try to make order out of chaos even though life, obviously, does just the opposite. And that our perceptions never mesh or match with our conceptions, which is why we are so easily conned. We would do well to emulate James' model of open-mindedness, tolerance, and compassion for the kinds of things we are considering here.

So what do I believe, and why? I won't keep you in suspense either about cosmic cultures and contact therewith, or extraterrestrials, or UFO's, or whatever you want to call them.

I have three theses to offer you today. First, I think the whole subject is a symptom and symbol of our angst, but it is neither a cure or remedy nor the right word for what ails us. Secondly, I think the whole subject tells us a lot about ourselves, but nothing about the universe. And third, much of the research done in this area is an insult to our intelligence, but not a complete waste of time. I'll deal with these subjects in reverse order and then add some ingredients to the primordial talk soup I'm serving you.

First of all it's undeniable, and everyone here in this room would admit it, that there have been a lot of hoaxes, frauds, quacks, charlatans, and just a lot of hokum and hype as well as wishful thinking connected with UFO's. As P.T. Barnum said, "There's a sucker born every minute." Today he would probably say nanosecond. As H.L. Mencken chimed in, "Nobody ever went broke underestimating the taste of the American public."

It is easy to become indignant, if not cynical about the whole thing, and to view it as being bread and circuses intended to mislead as well as pacify people while raising false hopes, and to see it as a distraction from our real problems, which can be summarized as "distribute the wealth and don't hoard the stealth." Surely there are enough real mysteries in life, without adding spurious ones. By real mysteries I mean things like—"why is there something rather than nothing?" Or the child's curiosity, "why is the sky blue?" Or, why don't we know anything about what happened in the first ten to the minus 43 seconds of the universe's existence, so called 'plank time'?

Of course, the most important question of all, where is Elvis, and is he still working for Richard Nixon as honorary drug enforcement commissioner? God, that guy had a reverse Midas touch if ever I saw it. Indeed, if we ever do track down Nixon in the hereafter maybe he can tell us where those eighteen and a half minutes went on those tapes, and maybe then we'll know something about missing time. By the way, if you want a real mystery, I suggest that you go down the street to the National Gallery and look at Vermeer's famous painting of A Woman Weighing Gold. If you look carefully, you will see that there is a hand or something that certainly resembles a human hand, albeit with only two or three fingers, delicately nesting inside her shroud. Is it there to protect her or to attack her? Is it God, or the devil, do we serve two masters, or just one? Go figure, maybe she was making Dutch book instead of reading the good book. I've read quite a few articles and books about Vermeer; but no one has ever noticed, much less sought to explain, exactly what that hand is doing there, and whether it's to divinely inspire, or some sort of demon conjured up by the artist.

Even such false comfort that UFO speculation offers, it offers only to the few, not to the many. To the leisure class, or those who have the ability to engage in what Veblen called conspicuous consumption. As one reviewer of the film version of *Communion* said, "How come only upscale whites do this sort of thing?" My answer is, heavenly bodies for the rich, hell on earth for the poor. Even Ockham's razor would get dull in such a 'farce-field,' a plenum of fantasy, a vacuum of thought, non-entities multiplied and exponentially increased beyond all duplicity. Of course, Aristotle said, long ago, that poetry is higher than history. Because poetry deals with possible worlds, whereas history is confined to the actual.

My guess is that most of the writings about UFO's, and extraterrestrials, and contact with aliens makes great poetry, but lousy history (though hardly as lousy as our own). However, despite all that, long before this conference I was inclined to dismiss the whole subject of "UFOlogy" as anthropology, to paraphrase Feuerbach, or to cite—Louis Whitebech—"exobiology recapitulates eschatology." I viewed it as a projection, innocent, but still a projection of our fears and hopes, and I chalked it up to what I would call myths of resignation and resurrection. I found that Jacques Vallee in his finer moments does the same thing. And, of course, because since the scientific revolution three centuries ago we have all tried, without any luck, to re-enchant the universe. But neither the witches and ghosts and goblins of our Halloween adventures, nor any of the other spirits, have come back to haunt us. Mechanization did away with them once and for all. Of course, nowadays there's the ever popular sport of Descartes and Newton bashing, epitomized by films like *Mind Walk*, coupled with various abuses of quantum mechanics. You know the sort of thing I mean, inspired ultimately by Fritjof Capra, quantum mechanics and the soul, quantum mechanics and the banana, quantum mechanics and the orgasm, I think those are all the same book: The Greening of the Galaxy. I have the highest respect for quantum mechanics, but frankly I don't see how you can squeeze that much solace out of the two slits experiment.

Then, there is the worship of the great god Thomas S. Kuhn, another man whom I respect very highly. But have you noticed how every book written on whatever subject pays tribute to Kuhn either at the beginning or the end as having paved the way for whatever outré thesis the author wishes to maintain? Indeed, If I hear the words "paradigm shift" one more time I'll throw up. I already did during the Iraqi war when a general used it on CNN to describe a shift in battle strategy. Schwarzkopf couldn't even spell paradigm, much less use one. Sorry folks, this isn't what Kuhn had in mind, though to be sure, he wrote *The Structure of Scientific Revolutions* during the Cold War, and the book came out just before the Cuban Missile Crisis, when incommensurability was not just an abstraction but, in fact, our lives all hung in the balance of our imbalance.

Now all of this might be the last word on the subject, but as we all know, the last word is that there never is a last word. Just a few weeks ago I ran across this very interesting book, brand new, up to date, by Curtis Peebles called *Watch the Skies*. Peebles is certainly a debunker of UFO's and all the rest of it, and he is at least very thorough in chronicling all of the "incidents" and alleged sightings and whatnot. But what struck me in reading the book was his conclusion: "The function of mythology is to allow a society to relate to a larger world, this has not changed." And then, finally, the last sentence in the entire book, " We watch the skies seeking meaning, in the end, what we find is ourselves." When did he turn into Friedrich Nietzsche, or Feuerbach? For that matter, when did he cross the two cultures divide from techno-barbarism to empathy, if not renaissance humanism? It's strange, because after all, Peebles is an aerospace historian who works right here for the Smithsonian. When somebody with that much power, or a member of the establishment, starts talking in terms more suitable to Erasmus I begin to wonder and, indeed, get suspicious. What has he got to hide? And why such a morose coda?

The best argument for UFO's turns out to be the one against it. Which is why I'm here today after all, and this is why I say it's not an utter waste of time to consider this issue. Where there's that much smoke there must be a smoke screen, as all of us know who have followed the details about the Roswell Incident, also known as "The Moon Is Not A Balloon."

At the very least, the one thing that we can do in this area is—to use an aeronautical term that I'm sure the Wright Brothers would approve—push the envelope. Force, and at least pressure governments, and not just our own, to disclose what they've been up to, and how they've been mucking around for the past fifty years. Serve notice on them that we are not to be toyed with, even with all of their high tech toys. In this respect certainly everything we're doing here is not only justified and important, it's even downright healthy. It may be our last hope for salvaging democracy, albeit, indirectly, and in the most bizarre way. By the way, I noticed that in the latest issue of *UFO Magazine* there is a blurb for a new book called *The Grand Deception*. The blurb says, "A secret international government plans to stage an extraterrestrial event." Presumably in the year 2000, "To bring about a new world order." They should send Huxley the royalties every time they use that phrase, or maybe Shakespeare, for the Tempest. "An ominous totalitarian system, long prophesied."

142

The problem is, its already here, because we're making the world safe for Visa and Mastercard, and when Hong Kong takes over China in two more years then you'll really see something. One of my reasons for being interested in this topic, and fascinated by it despite myself, is because I ask this question, "So what if we do have a close encounter?" People are worried about the wrong thing. They ask, "Will they be friendly, will they be hostile?" The real question is, "Will they have money? And will they sign on the galactic line?"

Ezekiel saw the wheel and said let's make a deal. Instead of Sagan's "billions of planets" we'll have billions of K-marts, launched by the Starship Free Enterprise or Monopolies R Us. And Project Blue Book? That's simply a vehicle for used-rocket salesmen, to mystify and swindle us. As for those crop circles? Well, you know what they are, golden arches. And those men in black? Why, they're the I.R.S. They just want their cut of cash, commerce, and credit for cosmic capitalism.

You think I'm kidding, but in fact Isaac Asimov already knew that when he wrote *The Foundation Trilogy*. We are going to be the unwitting dupes in all of this, we intellectuals with our own little cottage industry. We are going to be co-opted and co-signed by all of this if we don't watch out. Or, even if we do. This is why I say that the whole business we are discussing teaches us a lot about ourselves, but not about the universe. Granted there are more things in heaven and earth than are dreamt of in my philosophy, but when I hold the mirror up to inhuman nature, I see what Swift, Twain, and Voltaire, among others, saw. Greed, vanity, corruption, despair, self-absorption, self-promotion, and self-delusion, all of which are rife in our little corner of the "Bilky Way." I begin to wonder whether it's even worth pursuing anything at all.

But I've left out one important factor in the human equation. Granted, true believers are self-deceivers, but then we live on, and for, hope, with faith that tomorrow will be better than yesterday. We believe in the future because the past has been so awful. Like Don Quixote, we keep tilting at windmills, even though they keep clobbering us. Like Sisyphus, we keep rolling the ball up the hill, even though it keeps rolling right back in our face. Perhaps like Faust, we feel the struggle for survival is itself successful. In that case we have already won the race against ourselves. For all noble things are stupid, though not vice versa, and thus our faith in the future is as touching as it is silly, as pathological as it is profound, as contemptible as it is courageous. Indeed our desire for unity, our longing for wholeness, fulfillment, and completion, and our intense desire to "eff" the ineffable makes us what we are. They define us, they are all the things that Plato described as Eros in *The Symposium*. But we've been chasing those platonic forms all our lives, or maybe, like the white whale, they've been chasing us. But what if we got them, what if we caught up with them, what if we actually grasped that brass ring, what if we found our soulmates in space?

Here I come to another thesis, not announced in advance. I dare say, based on my own humble experience, we'd be disappointed. We'd be bored, and we would soon grow restless. Which is all to the good, for woe unto those who find what they're looking for. Those who discover the messiah, for he'll either be a madman or a murderer, and if he's neither of those he'll end up being a martyr and a scapegoat for our sins. A bad infinite is worse than none. So, be content with what you haven't got.

This brings me, by the way, to the whole vexed subject of alien abductions, and here again the subject is serious silly and sad, simultaneously. I'll leave you to judge which is which, but I will say the following about it. First of all, my own belief is that people who report this are just repressing childhood or even adult traumas that they find difficult or even impossible to express. This may ultimately vindicate Freud's hypothesis concerning his so called hysteria cases long ago, which itself has been the subject of so much controversy in recent years. If we are going to use therapeutic techniques to treat people who have reported these things, we certainly will find various cases of child abuse, battery, rape, incest and all the rest, and they will be this worldly horrors, not otherworldly, I fear. All the band-aids we provide may be pitifully and woefully inadequate, but we have to keep trying.

Secondly, just speaking for myself as a lonely, horny, frustrated middle-aged man, if there are any aliens out there who want sex with me, I'm ready, come and get it. In fact, I will now wait five seconds to see if any of them show up to take me away, and beam me to another dimension where I can dwell in orgasmic peace. . . well, better fuck next time.

My third remark about this subject, and I hope it's the most important, is why would aliens come all the way here just to have sex with us? Or to reproduce with our aid, or to genetically alter us, when we can't even fix parking tickets? This is proof positive that despite the Copernican revolution we all believe that the universe revolves around us. We are all, indeed, nattering nabobs of narcissism. (Which may be appropriate, now that somebody's giving Spiro Agnew an award for being alive.) That is why, despite Galileo, humanity stands still. Ah yes, the two most frequent shapes of UFO's are cigars and saucers, what a perfect Rorschach test of our lust for life or lack of one.

But on a deeper level, we, or at least Americans, all want the exotic, the novel, the unfamiliar, the strange, and the forbidden. We want the one thing that might redeem us, that might absolve us, and dissolve and resolve all of our problems, but in particular racism, which is the biggest stain on our national character, and always has been. For puritan sermonizers it was sex with Indians; that was taboo, yet ardently sought. For suburban swingers it's sex with aliens. It's just a replay of Huck and Jim on the raft, or Ishmael and Queequeg, whether you're homo or hetero, it makes no difference as Leslie Fiedler showed in his famous book *Love and Death in The American Novel.*

I call this the myth of merger, and it is a myth, and a very powerful one, because if we could find our other half, we wouldn't need an insecurity clearance to get past the Pentagon's gates. We wouldn't be launching a quest for uncertainty with the help of Heisenberg. We wouldn't need UFO's to goad us or to reduce our existential terror to nothingness. Why then, we would all be one, just as nature, or Parmenides, intended. But, of course it doesn't work, even for a moment, even during ecstasy, and if it did, speaking of totalitarianism, we'd lose our identity, we'd get swallowed up, and we'd never get it back. Even Wagner knew that, though Hitler didn't, or didn't care, and that was the reason that god damned passion play of his turned out so rotten.

So the question is, ladies and gentlemen, not are there E.T.'s and where are they, but why do we want to know them carnally, biblically, and in all sorts of other ways? Why do we think they want to know us, what are our real motives, our real needs and our real fears? Are we that vulnerable or that dense? Are we prepared to see ourselves as others don't, won't, and can't see us? Or, do we invent deities and demons in order to conceal, and thus inadvertently reveal, who and what we are? Yes, it's no wonder that the whole story is so humanly compelling, because it is divinely dangerous and we are playing with Promethean fire.

What follows from all of this? Well, here are some parables worth pondering. Number one, as Calvin Coolidge once said many years ago, "The business of America is business." So let's take Plato's advice in Book One of *The Republic* and mind our own business, both as individuals and institutions. If we don't, big business will make us all mindless. It will inherit the earth while showing us that the sky's the limit, of their limitless and by no means bloodless conquests of economic constellations. Or, to put it another way, like Candide we must all cultivate our gardens, provided we don't fertilize them with sodium nitrate, thus turning the White House into a green house or perhaps an outhouse. Even Forrest Gump understood that as he rode around on his tractor, sans Beam, so perhaps we can learn from an idiot who turns out to be an idiot savant.

Secondly, don't expect miracles or messiahs. Chances are if there are spacelings, they're just like us. How depressing, trite, mediocre, and shallow at best; rapacious, gluttonous thieves at worst, and just as confused and inept as we are. Indeed, made in our own image.

By the way, I learned this from reading Kierkegaard many years ago, but I also found out posthumously from my mother, because when she died a couple of years ago I went through her safety deposit box as my lawyer instructed me to do, and I found that she had been married once before—before she met my old man, and for that matter so had he, before he met her. I saw the papers. I couldn't believe it. I had to prove that I was the sole heir and go through a rigmarole with probate and all of that which is how I happened upon these documents. It was all back during the Hitler era, and I'm sure my parents didn't want to talk about it, neither to me nor even to themselves. But I asked a close friend and then several relatives about this, and they said, "Oh yes, and when your mother married your father, she told me, when you marry the second time you change faces, but that's all."

So perhaps if we did find our alter egos in space, we would just have an unhappy ending to our little domestic drama. No doubt if there are aliens they're watching trash sports and the O.J. Simpson trial, and those are the same thing too, forgive my redundancy. Or maybe they have their own O.J. trial in a parallel universe, losing jurors by the minute. Remember, force, fear, fraud, and folly are the rule. The only antidotes are logic and laughter. They are all we've got, but luckily, they are all we need.

Unfortunately, there is no escape from our abject condition, or from our hangups and neuroses. As the doctor said to Macbeth, when Macbeth, fearful of his wife's condition asked, "Canst thou not minister to a mind diseased?" "Therein the patient must minister to himself." Or as Dorothy reminds us, don't fly to Oz, stay home. Despite appearances, Kansas and the cosmos are one and the same. If you dream too hard, your dreams will become nightmares, as they have indeed in the 20th century. Another thing that we can learn from this debacle is, don't underestimate yourself. Don't let lack of self-esteem kill your joy. Don't let me do it, either. We are all gods if we but knew it, and we don't need crutches, just a little self- respect. From Emerson to Rodney Dangerfield the message is the same "love yourself, trust yourself, and all else will follow and fall into place." That is the only kind of self-reliance worth cultivating, as opposed to rugged individualism and the devil take the foremost. Or as Jack Kerouac, who was certainly no stranger to space flight, put it in his book *The Lonesome Traveler*, with a bow towards Buddha, "There's no need for solitude, so love life for what it is and form no preconceptions whatever in your mind. By emptying it, it will indeed at last be full." We are all bits of star stuff, which is why we have Hollywood stars in our eyes, and thus can't see. The blind misleading the blind. The fault lies not in our stars, but in our warp-driven selves. All thanks to the binary delusion, both that we can be perfect, and that we aren't already.

By the way, on November 12, 1916, there was a strange telepathic phenomenon that occurred all over the United States, as reported by a newspaper in Cincinnati, and as recounted in David Robinson's biography of Charlie Chaplin. It seems that everybody had the same hallucination of Charlie, no doubt because they were all watching him at the picture show, and at 800 different hotels throughout the country Charlie Chaplin was paged. It wasn't even April Fool's Day. I wonder if there is room service for him right now? To me, this signifies something other than the obvious. It's not mass psychosis or delusion, it's that we are all Little Tramps, underdogs, hoboes, homeless people, strangers in our own house, as Thoreau said long ago. But we can all be champs, not chumps, if only we realize how much we are, and how little we need to be happy. Then, Jefferson's pursuit of happiness would not turn into the misery of pursuit. Indeed, we will be fulfilled, precisely because we will give up trying. We won't seek perfection because we will have already attained it. We will be able to say yes to life and no to death, like Molly Bloom. Let go, surrender, yield, and thus transcend ourselves.

In the meantime, let us transcend transcendence. Let us give up our unnatural impieties, and celebrate our common cosmic comic lot. Fools of the farce that we are, as Montain said, asses to asses, doubt to doubt. In his epic poem *Song of Myself*, Walt Whitman said, at the very end, "I stand somewhere, waiting for you." I hope like heck that I catch up with Walt someday, and that the micro and macrocosms finally become identical. But I'm not going to hold my breath, nor am I going to join Jack or Walt on that lonesome road, because I know it's infinite, and I also know that I'm already there. So quit waiting for Godot, don't take that alien train to hell, heaven, or Harlem, even here in D.C., which is Duke Ellington land. If you see a bogey on your MTV screen, it's just there to remind you that bad actors like Ronald Reagan, with a reactionary message should call Western Union, and get out of the movie lot pronto, and check their hats at the door, and indeed should be collected instead of calling us collect.

My message for today, my media message if you prefer McLuhan, my charismatic transmission is very simple. Don't kid yourself, whether about UFO's or official lies. Don't live a lie either. Don't be anybody's fool except maybe King Lear's. Be leery of power and then you may end up being king of your own realm or queen, rather than the naked unaccommodated man or woman out on the heath, with nothing to wear but the Empire's no clothes. Only in this way can you give meaning to life, master fate, and avoid the abyss of metaphysical mush. In that way you will be able to fulfill all the divine prophecies that have ever been uttered by human beings and make anthropology, theology, at last. Save your soul, save your money, and above all save your breath. Thank you. I'm open to questions.

**Question about the concept of illusion.**

I'm not a Hindu. Of course, I agree with Robin Williams that reality is an overused and little understood word, though I used it myself liberally in this talk. I think we need to puncture and penetrate some of those illusions, so that we won't be guilty of deception or self-deception, either about politics or passion. But there are certainly enough illusions to go around. I know I have more than my share, and without them who knows, I might not be here in front of you today. As my friend Jim Funaro likes to say, "Hope kills, but without hope there is no life." Jim, I hope I didn't embarrass you by repeating that. No, if everything were an illusion, nothing would be an illusion. Then, we would not be able to penetrate anything. Lift that veil, or we won't have the weapons to fight with against the words that bamboozle and bullshit us. Lose your illusions, but not your ideas.

**Question about the cosmic comedy.**

I guess he's just gotta laugh at himself and have a sense of humor. Or you'll wind up having the last laugh at my expense. I don't know what else to say. If we meet on life's highway I hope we can talk to each other. In ancient times, cultivating paradox and self-referential irony, the sophists opined, "Nothing exists; if it could exist it could not be communicated; if it could be communicated it could not be understood." I think our main problem with aliens is because we do not understand ourselves.

**What would contact mean to you personally?**

I hope it would mean a raise, because I'm sick of my old job. I'm looking for a new one. Actually, I don't think it would make a damn bit of difference. I think it would be an interesting novelty. But I think, like all the ephemera in our world, it would soon go the way of all flesh. It would be yesterday's news, a golden oldie. As I indicated a moment ago, we would soon grow weary of it. Sort of like *Citizen Cane,* if you remember the panel when he's been married too long, and after awhile they don't even read the same newspaper anymore, even though he publishes one. That's what I suspect would really happen, if and when we do make contact. So I plan to stay hermetically sealed until the time comes.

**You said we are all Gods, and that all is illusion. That implies that God means nothing.**

This is like when Andy Warhol was asked, "Aren't your pictures really trash?" and he answered, "Yes, but they sell for quite a lot of money." Which may be proof of that. Of course, I was being metaphorical here, I was trying to find a way to exalt our dignity because there are so many forces in society that seek to reduce it to rubble. So I was giving an emotional pep talk, and it must be understood in that Emersonian spirit.

**If we say that God means nothing, how does that exalt our dignity?**

In the following way. Most people are told from an early age that they are stupid, incompetent, and that they will never get anywhere in life. That becomes a self-defeating prophecy, and so they turn out just the way we want them and make them to be. But if we told them just the opposite, then perhaps they might become human beings at last. I'm enough of a Skinnerian to believe that.

**But if it all means nothing?**

I don't know what you're getting at, but while I'm very fond of word play, as you can tell, this particular one has taken a direction I can't fathom. When you say it all means nothing. . . ultimately we all die, to be sure. As Shakespeare said, "This great globe will disappear, wrack and all." But we still remember Shakespeare and can quote him on the subject. In this way, we become aware of our own demise and thus, feebly at any rate, try to postpone it. After all, all we have is history, memory, and each other. That's our collective immortality. That may not be good enough, but it's all we've got. If you want more, I'm afraid you're going to be dissatisfied. Am I answering your question? I'm not dodging it? If we all thought of ourselves as gods, you see, and thus treated each other as equals, then we wouldn't need those crutches and we might after all become fully human, at last, in the sense that the framers intended. Then we would indeed not just pay lip service to the bill of rights but we might practice what we preach. That is my naive hope, at any rate. More than that, I don't think anyone can ask for, demand, or certainly we won't get it. That would be meaningful, because such meaning as life has is what we give it. Garbage in, garbage out, so take a hint.

**What I am enjoying about your talk is that you are putting the focus on us being responsible for ourselves.**

I don't intend that in the sense of Bush's Thousand Points of Blight, or Newt's Zeroing Out of the Cosmos for funding. I didn't intend that as ecologically correct speech, but just as a feeble echo of what the Wizard finally taught Dorothy, and when she woke up she taught it to herself. She knew it all along, platonic recollection, she just had to discover it as the Good Witch told her before she clicked her heals. Of course, even Dorothy didn't stay in Kansas, she went to Hollywood and look what happened to her! I rest my case, Q.E.D. But she gave her life, so that our's would have meaning, through her songs.

**Question about the psychology of abductions.**

I'm totally unqualified to discuss the subject, which is why I'm posing as an expert here. I'm a complete impostor. My worst nightmare, by the way, is that one day I'll be invited to be the keynote speaker at a conference on faking it, which is the one thing I know something about, and I won't be able to do it. No, I've just read the literature—Mack, Jacobs, all the rest of those books, Strieber. Yes, the first amendment gives us all the right to be stupid, yet thank god for that or we wouldn't even have that right.

**Additional question concerning abduction of children.**

I'm not a clinical psychologist so I'm not prepared to answer that question, but let me deal with you very straight forwardly. I'm sure that something is going on. To use that dreaded word, real. Something has happened to these people, young or old. I'm sure it's not simply auto-suggestion, or, like clever Hans tapping his feet to the shrink's tune, or something that the psychiatrist implanted in their minds. It's coming from close encounters of a brother, sister, father, mother kind, in most cases, I would venture to say. Yes, we preach family values in this country, but what we really have is either the Manson family or the Adams' family. And that's a sad fact.

What I think you have to do is go very carefully, case by case beforehand, without any assumptions. That is very hard to do I know, because we all have prejudices, except me of course, I'm infallible. We don't want to acknowledge them, much less criticize or correct them. But I think it's dangerous again to underestimate the capacity of children to articulate their experiences. After all, children are able to speak fluently some language or other, aside from transformational grammar, by the age of two. So even children who are very young can certainly describe what has happened to them in ways that would astonish us. They can synthesize and create verbal data, even though they have not been given enough evidence, as it were, to simply put the links together.

**Why are people coming up with the same stories?**

Because they've all been raped by mom, dad, or the uncle in the attic. Well, if you want to pull a Jungian archetype on me, I don't know. I don't think they've been raped by extraterrestrials, and if so, they are beyond our jurisdiction. Such behavior in the family may be the one universal besides greed. It might be that if we look to our past, it was as commonplace as we are finding out that it is now. After all, in the last two centuries, since the industrial revolution, even though we've killed more people than in all preceding centuries, thus justifying Voltaire's dictum that history is nothing but fools, knaves and jackals slaughtering each other. Nonetheless we have also sanitized and deodorized death. Done it by remote control, Nintendo warfare and all of that, dropping bombs without ever seeing the target, much less the victim. So we have also created an aura around these sorts of things, hushing them up and pretending not to notice, or that they aren't there.

I would take Ockham's advice, find the simplest explanation consistent with the facts that doesn't force you to posit something unobservable. Or as Einstein once said, make it simple but not too simple. If you can get predictive or explanatory power out of an extraterrestrial hypotheses, then by all means go for it. After all, we don't observe gravity either, but we have faith in it because we can test it. It is in its way as superstitious as belief in evil demons. But it is more rational ultimately, and it's not merely social constructed either, though that's a long story.

**What is the best evidence of E.T. agendas?**

I base myself on the evidence on *Star Wars* and the scene in the singles bar. I think Spielberg understands this stuff a lot better than we do.

**But would that explain everything that is being reported?**

There are a lot of things I don't understand, including you, but I can agree to differ. Well, first of all,

I think there are three kinds of cynics. There's the kind of cynic who is simply a ruthless opportunist and a Machiavellian manipulator although that's an injustice to Machiavelli. Then, there's of kind of cynic who like Benjamin the Donkey in *Animal Farm*, is resigned to fate, poo poo's everything, throws in the sponge, and is also a victim of the self-defeating prophecy. But then, there's the kind of cynic who like Diogenes with the lamp, goes around looking for an honest man, even if, unlike W.C. Fields, he can't find one. He is nonetheless going to continue wandering, rather than curse the darkness. I like to think that in my better moments I am that kind of cynic, and that's the kind of cold comfort that warms me on a winters' night, or even in May in D.C.

**The E.T's seem to have a great interest in humans. Why wouldn't they have an equal curiosity about all life on the planet as humans do?**

Aristotle said all men by nature desire to know, but he never had to teach undergraduates in the Lyceum. Actually, I want to give you two different answers of varying degrees of relevance. One is, even if they were disinterestedly curious, in the sense that we like to think we are, why would they come all this way? They might have specimens closer to hand, or they might be able to observe us at long range, or they might not be able to get here (the well-known problem of distance) or they might not know that we're around. As Robert Nozick pointed out many years ago in an essay on the subject, has it ever occurred to you that they're as lonely as we are? Maybe what we should do instead of sending out pulses or Pythagorean harmonies is trade Bergman films with them, then we could really give each other solace.

The point is that even if I admit to your premise, it doesn't follow that they're either looking for us, or they're going to find us, or that we're the ones that they really would be interested in. We are not a terribly interesting species, except to ourselves. There might be other life forms on earth that they might be interested in, like platypuses or mollusks, algae, and insects. Who knows, maybe they're burrowing somewhere under the ocean right now, or in the desert, dealing with those entities and hoping like heck that they don't get squashed like bugs in some *War of the Worlds* scenario.

The other answer to your question is ultimately a Darwinian one, and here I have to be careful because the term Darwin is a loaded word and it means many different things to many different people. I have in mind the Darwin of the *Origin of Species* before the eighth edition when he inserted the unfortunate and tautological term "survival of the fittest," that set off the whole social Darwinian reaction in Britain. I think the pragmatists Hurst, James, and Dewey understood Darwin and got him right. Human beings don't do things out of disinterested curiosity. They do things because they have problems to solve, urgent needs including survival. Even theoretical curiosity is ultimately an urgent need. It may not be perceived as urgent at the time when we have the leisure to engage in it, but as we have found out in the history of science, the most impractical things in the world turn out to be practical, alas all too practical like the atom bomb. As Faraday once said when asked by Gladstone what good was the dynamo, "Lord Chancellor, some day you will be able to tax it." So the real question is, are human beings creatures of disinterested curiosity? On the whole the answer is no, but that doesn't make us evil. It merely means we want, as James said, ease, peace, and fluency and equilibrium, though, of course, we never get it except in death. That is the only time when we become one, and that makes life meaningless and yet, at the same time, desperately urgent. That is why we have to create meaning before it escapes us, evades us, eludes us, and destroys us.

**What is your greatest fear concerning contact?**

I've already mentioned it, they'll sell us out or we'll sell ourselves out. Indeed, if you look at

Columbus and Cortez they did the same thing when they weren't busy killing each other, that is, Native Americans, or anybody else who was in their way. Yes, my greatest fear is that we're making the world safe for passive consumption and couch potatoes. You don't need to look to the heavens to see that, it's right here on earth. So either they will do it to us, or we will do it to them, or we will do it to ourselves, or all of the above, and it's around the corner. The cosmic conglomerate corporations are busy working on it right now. It's not a conspiracy, and it's not teleology, it's just causality. Speaking of disinterested curiosity, it isn't worthy of us, it gives selfishness a bad name, and it'll be the death of us yet, but it'll be a slow and painless death. Like what Ned Beatty said in *Network*, all desires pacified, all needs tranquilized, and we'll all be staring hypnotically at the tube.

**Who is "us," who is "them?"**

Well, "us" is everybody, and "them" is Exxon, Mobile, General Motors, those kind of folks—the Fortune 50 as I like to call them. Soon to be reduced by a factor of ten, through pyramidal trusts and other schemes.

**Could this all be part of our unrecognized subconscious or evil from other people in our cultures that we don't recognize?**

Sure, that's why I paraphrased Feuerbach earlier, all UFOlogy is anthropology, that's exactly what that means. That's a projection, and you don't need a movie screen to set it up. That's in your mind's eye in that blind spot that none of us can reach. Speaking of mysteries, why does E to the $i\pi - \perp$ equal 0? That one could keep you occupied a good long while. But I prefer to stare at Vermeer.

**What is it that we have to sustain us, to assure our immortality?**

History, collective memory, our record of our doings and strivings, our cumulative Kilroys were here. All of those hearts and Valentines carved in trees, all of our desperate attempt to rise above the ashes, by recognizing our own presence on earth just prior to our departure and eminent demise and total absence. And so for the absent God we have to substitute present humans and embrace the present. Then, and only then, can we live meaningfully, or live with meaninglessness.

**What value do you place on other opinions about these issues that are different from yours?**

Well, of course, they wouldn't change my opinion at all since I'm close minded, unlike William James and all the rest of you. But one thing I would caution you about is that three millennia of human history, while dismal, is not a very good record, even though it's all we've got. We know that human beings have been on the planet for roughly 3 billion years, but we don't know anything about the first 2.9 billion of them. So it would be rash to form judgments about ourselves based upon that. We wouldn't even get the bell curve, much less its moronic authors, out of that scenario. I think what we can do is to raise our E.T.Q. However, recognize in doing so that we are all putting our shoulders to the wheel for an end we cannot see. The horizon is what we call truth, even though we only catch glimpses of it, and we catch glimpses of it, actually, by weeding out our errors and mistakes. As J.A. Wheeler once said about quantum physics, "In science we have to hurry up and make the mistakes as fast as possible." A kind of unnatural selection process. Nature's Darwinian, but culture is not. So in that sense we could make cumulative progress, but beware of the myth of progress which has also cost us dearly. Our naive belief that history is linear turns out to be a joke. The line turns into the circle and does not ever reach the top of the chart except in annihilation. Thank you.

# 🌐 Paula Underwood, MA

*Paula Underwood, MA*

Paula Underwood is an author, lecturer, consultant and trainer in education, cross cultural understanding, and organizational methodologies based on lifelong training/experience in an ancient Native American methodology for stimulating whole thought through a right/left brain dialogue. Oral histories were carefully studied and committed to memory by Ms. Underwood's Iroquois ancestress during the early 1800's and meticulously handed down through her family as they moved West—over the last five generations. This consensual oral history has been published as *The Walking People*. It recounts the major events and decisions of a continuous Native American People with a special focus on the evolution of both wisdom and an approach to self-governance.

# Who Are the Human Beings:
# In Search of Commonalty

*Drawing upon the history of her Ancestors going back thousands of years, Paula Underwood recounts the attitude of Native Americans when they met the early European arrivals. And from ancient traditions she reveals procedures to assist in dealing with new circumstances and to enhance understanding. She recounts an ancient time when a Wise Council received the message, "We are coming!" Upon reflection it was decided that too little was known about those who sent the message. Therefore, in concert this message was sent: "Whoever you are, do not come. Give us time to learn to understand one another. Give us time to learn to understand ourselves."*

Over the last several decades, when we have been considering the possibilities of meeting what we choose to call Intelligent Life from somewhere else, we have told ourselves again and again that we have no experience in such an event. I'd like to suggest that we have had a world full of experience!

Every time I hear about an earlier time—when Polynesians were 'discovered' by European explorers or when they 'discovered' Native Americans on Turtle Island or when they 'discovered' pygmies on the African continent—the question was raised again and again at the time . . are these human beings?

Well . . that depends, doesn't it, on how you define the term? How much similarity do we demand? How much difference can we tolerate?

My own ancestors faced just such a definition of terms many thousands of years ago. I would like to share their decision with you. This is a section from the Oral History handed down in my family for five generations to be shared in this generation. Although this history was passed down from my grandfather's Oneida grandmother, it is so old that it is useless to call it the history of any one people. It seems to me it is from an Iroquois tradition. More than this we cannot really say. It is definitely the history of my Ancestors, going back thousands and thousands of years.

We have published it under the title *The Walking People* . This is a section from our most Ancient Telling, "Beginning Song".

My Ancestors had been living at the edge of ocean for so long no one remembered how long. This edge of ocean home had at last become over crowded and—bit by bit—groups were forming to cross the mountains away from what had been our home toward no one knew what destination. One such group passed down to us this explanation of what they found when first crossing that mountain to the East.

("Who Are the Human Beings?", *The Walking People.: A Native American Oral History*, A Tribe of Two Press, Georgetown, TX, pp. 331-334. )

# WHO ARE THE HUMAN BEINGS?

152

NOW
THIS WAS THE WAY OF IT.

WHEREAS
*Space on the Earth*
*was one of the thoughts of the People*
*in deciding for a new land,*
*learning was in their mind also.*

*For much had been learned and was preserved, still,*
*from along the northward path*
*and great and equally preserved*
*was our Edge of Ocean learning.*

HOW MIGHT IT BE TO ADD TO THESE LEARNINGS
*An awareness*
*of the nature of land to the East of before?*

THEREFORE
All the People were alert to change . .
water or lack thereof,
variations in the nature
of what might be consumed,
rises and falls in the land,
stretching out of valleys.

All this was expected.

AND YET
ONE VARIATION WAS UNEXPECTED
AND THAT VARIATION
LAY IN THOSE
WHO WALKED THE EARTH.

AMONG THE PEOPLE
There was some variance . . .
some were taller, some shorter,
some darker, some lighter . . .

YET
The variance here
exceeded these limited possibilities.

HERE
Variations in height were so great
that some
who walked the Earth with two legs
might seem as too young

to be full grown. .
others seemed to tower over us
as if they stood on some rocky outcropping.

Variations in light and dark were also greater,
some disappearing long before dark
with others almost as marked by moonlight.

Variations in hair or lack thereof
were also marked.

AND EVEN
the two legs with which they walked the Earth,
some being straight and long
with others curved toward the Earth.

SOME
seemed to communicate with each other
through patters of sound
we did not recognize.

OTHERS
seemed not to possess this capacity,
but shook themselves before each other
in ways that might contain communication.

THE PEOPLE WERE AT A LOSS
TO UNDERSTAND THESE MANY WAYS OF BEING

AND BEGAN TO CONFER
AMONG THEMSELVES
AS TO HOW
THEY MIGHT RELATE TO ONE ANOTHER

*Which are our Brothers, our Sisters?*

*Which are related to us*
*and in what manner?*

*How may we understand them?*

*Is it possible, desirable*
*to form communities with them?*

*Or will our living be better*
*separate from them?*

ALL THIS
    Was discussed at length,
        comparing this and that,
    Until the People moved beyond the variations
        between those
            who walked the Earth with two legs only.

THEY LOOKED NOW
    At the variations between all two leggeds
        and those who walked the Earth with four
           or those who swam the waters
           or those who sailed the sky.

So many variations
So many similar patterns
    across these apparent differences.

UNTIL AT LAST IT WAS DECIDED
AND IT WAS A DECISION
    OUR PEOPLE
        HAVE HELD FROM THAT DAY TO THIS . .

*If we can learn from the Great Swimmers*
    *and understand our relations to them. .*

*Surely we can learn*
    *from any who walk the Earth with two legs,*
        *whether they share understanding*
           *through sound patterns*
           *or patterns of movement*
           *or through something*
             *we not yet understand . .*

*Surely we can learn from them*
    *as they from us.*

*Surely they are all our closest brothers*
    *tall or short, dark or light.*
*And surely*
    *they merit our awareness of the relation.*

AS WE ARE THE PEOPLE
    *So are they also their own People*
        *and—*
    *As there are so many apparent differences —*
        *we should honor these,*
            *as well as the similarities,*
            *and learn from both.*

SURELY
    ONLY WISDOM
        LIES IN LEARNING

AND SURELY
    GREAT LEARNING
        ALWAYS DOES CONTAIN
           GREATER POSSIBILITY OF SURVIVAL.

Let us learn from those
    who have not known an Ocean edge.

Let them teach us
    the manner of each new place
        and—if they are not so comfortable
           with all that we have said—
        let us learn quietly and from a distance
           so that we do not give offense.

AND—AS I HAVE SAID—
    *From that day to this*
        *our People have learned to remember*
           *who are our Brother, our Sister*
             *from whom we may best learn.*

WHATEVER WE CALL OURSELVES
    *That is greater than one People,*
    *we call them by this name as well.*

    ALL . . . ARE BROTHER, ARE SISTERS

YET
    ALL WHO ARE TWO LEGGEDS
        ARE GREATER BROTHERS, SISTERS,
        THAN THIS

    SUCH IS THE NATURE OF LIFE.

From this Great Learning, my ancestors decided that all those who walk the Earth on two legs, freeing their hands for other employ; all those who walk erect, balancing their head between their shoulders, thereby changing their perspective on life; all these are the Human Beings.

For their purposes—and perhaps for ours—this definition of those who are very closely related to us is sufficient. You might take a moment here to consider how many different beings, real and imagined might fit this definition of terms. And while you do that, let me explain that in Native American traditions, *everything* is considered real. A dream is real. It's just that it's a real dream. A vision is real. It's just that it's a real Vision. Everything . . is Real. Never . . never . . do you hear that anything at all is "only your imagination." For surely, that too is real.

Now let me ask, does the definition of Human Being I just read to you—adequately outline the possibilities for Intelligent Life?

I think not. I am not sure, for instance, that we Two-Leggeds are the only Intelligent Life on Earth. And I will try not to mention the astronauts' comments as they first overflew Los Angeles and it's density of smog, "Look's like there's no intelligent life down there." I suppose that depends on how you define "intelligent"!

Over the years I have noticed how our definition of Human Being has gradually shrunk.

We used to tell ourselves that human beings were the only tool-using species. Now we know that is not so.

We still tell ourselves that Human Beings are the only beings that use language. Well, I think we'd better wait until we speak fluent Whale and actually learn to ask other beings whether they have language or not before reaching such an amazing conclusion. It sounds too much to me—again—like those earlier European explorers who would sometimes call the local language "gibberish" . . merely because they found it hard to understand.

Now let's think of it for a moment from the point of view of those standing on the shore watching those funny-looking sea birds with great white wings approach the shore. Were they recognized as related? Well, perhaps that depends. Surely the Polynesians would have recognized sails immediately. Surely the Native Americans would have recognized wooden ships as soon as they were close enough to see its nature.

Were they confused by Human Beings with the hirsuity of Bear? Perhaps. But surely my own ancestors were not. Didn't these Visiting Others walk on two legs and balance their head between their shoulders? Logically, then, they were also Human Beings, also Two-Leggeds.

What I am saying here is that we already have a plethora of experience in meeting other beings similar to us, yet so different we do not always immediately assume that they are related to us at all. Of course, in a Native American sense, all things are related. In this context, there is no possibility of a lack of relationship. We are all star stuff, all crafted from a relatively stable form of energy. Therefore, we are all related . . Wolf and Bear . . Star and Planet . . Ocean and the relative void of Space . . all . . related.

Science fiction—that window overlooking the yet to be—the land of perhaps—science fiction has described to us many possible beings inhabiting our galaxy, our universe and its many dimensions.

Some are treated as intelligent, some are not.

Some are seen as energy, as pure light. Or as flows of liquid or gaseous matter. There are no hands to free or shoulders to balance between. Are these Human Beings? Are they Intelligent Life? Perhaps we will one day need to decide. In any event, in my tradition they are still—all—our relatives.

Some are seen as two-legged and stand erect. All these would be Human Beings under the terms decided by my Ancestors. Under this definition, androids would certainly be included as Human Beings and robots might be. C3PO would certainly be included, walking on two legs as he clearly does. R2D2, well, I'm not so sure. He walks on two feet, more or less balanced, but he may choose to drop three wheels and roll. Is he a Human Being only part of the time? Or do three rollers count for two feet?! And what about a head balanced between two shoulders? Is such structural solidity truly balance?

My point here is that any definition we can devise will both clarify—and limit—our thinking.

As you can see, I take science fiction reasonably seriously. It seems to me that it's one way we have of talking to ourselves about possibilities. It's one way of wondering about our future and what it may contain.

I leave you to consider whether the many and different beings contained in the description of Visitations—which some call Abduction Scenarios—whether they meet the criteria established by my Ancestors. In our present society, some call these described events fiction and some call them fact. My tradition does neither. Remember, everything is real. The question is a real what?

In my tradition, no event would ever be called anomalous. No one would need proof of any perceived reality. No one would believe. No one would disbelieve. Each such event would be understood as one individual's perception. It would be given equal value with every other individual perception, with every other group perception. After all, what you see when you open your eyes . . . depends on where you are standing at the time.

In terms of general Native American thought, androids and robots would not be considered "inanimate". Nothing is considered inanimate. All things that contain energy are alive. And as all things are made of a relatively stable form of energy, all things are logically considered alive—rock and star—ocean and atmosphere—all this is living stuff. Native Americans have been heard to tell the Children of the West, "You live in a dead world, a world in which so much is considered dead. To us, everything, everything is alive."

So it is like this: All things are real. All things are alive. All things are related. All things are connected.

It was much easier for a people thinking like this to understand the possibility of Europeans, than it was for the Europeans to understand the possibility of peoples they never knew existed. It is for this reason that the early European arrivals were treated in almost every instance with welcome and with respect. After we found out about small pox and slavery . . this welcome sometimes changed. But new people were for us more interesting than frightening. Some caution, but not hostility was indicated.

I recommend for your consideration this approach to all life forms that are new to us.

My own ancestors had certain other intellectual advantages in dealing with new circumstances and new beings. The first of these was the Rule of Six.

## THE RULE OF SIX FOR THE RIGHT SIDE OF THE BRAIN

When I was even younger than I am now and brought my thoughts to my father, he would often say, "Remember the Rule of Six." Yes, The Rule of Six. So inculcated in my nature by now that I have great difficulty in naming only one thing as the root cause of anything else.

For Life is like this: So many individuations acting and interacting at every identifiable moment, that nothing at all, no one thing, can cause anything else.

The Rule of Six says that "For every perceivable phenomena devise at least six explanations that indeed explain the phenomena. There are probably sixty, but if you devise six, this will sensitize you to the complexity of Universe, the variability of perception. It will prevent you from fixing on the first plausible explanation as The Truth."

And so it is, in a complex and changing world in which the past affects the future, but the future also affects the past, at least in that our understanding of the probable determines many of our decisions, provides signposts along many diverging, converging paths.

What we see when we open our eyes . . . depends on where we are standing at the time. Only move a little, to left, to right . . . gain the view from there. Tell me now, my Brothers, my Sisters, what does your New Vision show you? Move around the Circle of the Earth once more . . . and look again! A quarter turn to the left. A quarter turn to the right. Sit in the East and study life. Sit in the South and wonder. How is it to view the world from Moscow? Leningrad? Vladislovok? How from Durban? Cairo? New Guinea?

We are all Earth's Children, and each view has value.

Now turn the Wheel on its edge, my Brothers, my Sisters. How is it now to view Life . . . as Wolf? As Eagle? As those with a Hundred Legs? Crawling, walking, swimming through Life . . . How is it now?

Complete the Circle in three dimensions . . . and then we will talk.

Kind Thoughts come

## THE RULE OF SIX FOR THE LEFT SIDE OF THE BRAIN

For each apparent phenomena devise at least six plausible explanations, each one of which *indeed* explains the phenomena. There are probably sixty, but if you devise six, this will sensitize you to how many there may yet be and prevent you from focusing in on the first thing that "sounds right" as The Truth. Disciplining yourself to think this way - maybe *this* is happening, but on the other hand, maybe *that* is happening - keeps you from being rigid in your thinking, which in my tradition is considered to be extraordinarily counterproductive.

Now you assign a personal probability factor to each explanation. The probability factor will be based on your personal experience. This is all you have to go on. Someone else's probability factors will be different because their experience is different. You will understand this. This is OK. It is inevitable. Each of us has different experience and, therefore, different estimates of probability.

This personal probability factor can never be 100% - and never, never 0%.

You see how it is? How all conclusions are wisely tentative, as new information may come in at any moment. Yet, whenever a decision is necessary, you can *instantly* and *clearly* select between your top three probabilities. All, we hope, above 95%! Decisions are, thus, enhanced and expedited, while the mind is kept alert to new possibilities.

(Rule of Six from *Three Strands in the Braid: A Guide for Enablers of Learning*, A Tribe of Two Press, Georgetown, TX, pp. 31-32.).

Or, as my father used to say:

Jumping to conclusions

Leads to contusions!

So, everything is real, everything is alive, everything is related, everything is connected. Thus everything affects everything else, always!

Remember this, remember the Rule of Six, remember our many and extensive experiences with life forms so apparently different from us that we had great difficulty deciding who was enough like us to be called Human, who does and who does not use language.

Remember all this . . and I have one more gift to share with you.

When we first meet other Cosmic Cultures—whether that happened long ago, whether it has yet to occur, or some combination of the two—when we first meet beings that may be greatly different from us; someone brought up in my tradition would immediately turn to the Four Step Path. And this is its nature:

(From "The Stories We Tell Predict Our Future: A Native American Approach", in the forthcoming *Healing Stories: The Psychotherapeutic Use of Narrative,* edited by Stanley Krippner, Ph.D. and Michael Bove, Irvington Publishers, NY, 1995.)

## THE STORIES WE TELL PREDICT OUR FUTURE

In my tradition, whenever we need to evaluate our circumstance, whenever there are such great apparent changes either in our circumstance or in ourselves, we are encouraged to walk the Four Step Path toward enhanced understanding. The (cycle) Four Step Path is:

1. Be who you are — enhance accurate self-awareness.
2. Be where you are — accept your circumstances, walk past denial.
3. Look around — take in as much information as you can.
4. Decide and do — using all of the above, make clear decisions.

Let me restate that in cyclic form.

North (Be who you are) This means center yourself within yourself. Be aware of/in touch with all you have ever learned about your own essential nature, especially about how you learn. You are using your sense of yourself to provide yourself with a steady viewing platform in what may sometimes be a vigorously skewed reality. North is the place where you gather your personal wisdom together.

East (Be where you are) This means be aware of the energy flow/patterns around you. Feel your way into the circumstance, You have not opened your eyes yet! They may lie to you and they will surely tell you nothing about energy patterns. East is the place where you open yourself to perception.

South (Look around) Now open your eyes. The purpose is not to decide or even to try to understand what is going on around you. At this stage you are taking in uncategorized images (auditory, visual, etc.) of your circumstance. There is a midpoint between East and South at which you use your eyes, but in a totally unfocused condition. By looking at nothing in particular, you look at everything! (If you look at something, you cannot see everything.) This is a technique used in many Eastern martial arts. Only then do you focus on particular aspects of the situation. South is the place where you experiment with possibilities.

West (Decide and do) Now you have all the information you are able to gather and perceive. It will never be enough information, but never mind. It is time to decide. Accept your apparent circumstance as real. Respond to it appropriately, given your personal experience. Later on, after this challenge to your sense of reality is over, you can evaluate what you think was going on at leisure. West is the place where you analyze, evaluate, and decide.

Now begin again.

So, I have offered for your patient consideration several elements from my own tradition that may yet help us with the convergence of Cosmic Cultures many people predict . . and even work toward. Now let me share with you just such an event, taken from that same Oral History. It tells of a time when my Ancestors were living beside a Beautiful Flowing Water they called O-hi-o. It happened during a time when they were settled at the edge of this River for so long that they were able to set themselves the task of studying their own ways of knowing. They studied ways of retaining all the Gathered Wisdom handed down by Those Who Went Before. They studied ways of knowing that defied apparent logic. (Remember the Rule of Six? Well there's another rule—If the situation seems illogical, your data base is inadequate!) They studied ways of communicating without speech. And they learned much.

During that time of study and consideration, there was one major meeting that shaped our thinking.

(From "We Call the River Beautiful", *The Walking People: A Native American Oral History*, A Tribe of Two Press, Georgetown, TX, pp. 609-615.)

## WE CALL THE RIVER BEAUTIFUL

NOW DURING THIS TIME,
    This Long Learning time,
        the People met two others
            they had not known before.

The natures of these meetings
    were different
    and yet the same . .

FOR
    though the nature of these meetings—
    these brief joining of two Peoples—
        were different in every other way,
          they were the same in this . .

EACH PEOPLE
EACH DIFFERENT OTHERS,
    WERE OF A NATURE
        NEVER BEFORE
            APPREHENDED BY OUR PEOPLE . .

So that we came to rapidly understand
    the value of willing apprehension
    of That Which is . .

For the mind
        that turns away from circumstances
           merely because it is unfamiliar
    That mind
        truly ceases to learn.

AND SO I WILL TELL YOU NOW.
    FIRST OF ONE PEOPLE,
        AND THEN OF THE OTHER

NOW THIS WAS THE WAY OF IT.
    *Those who sat together*
        *to design the Learning Path*
        *of those of Strong Spirit*
            *sought also their own learning.*

AND AT THIS TIME
    *They sought to understand*
        *whether down this path also*
        *the Ancient Learning*
          *showed us any possibility . .*

FOR THE ANCIENT LEARNING
TELLS US
THAT WHAT MAY BE DIFFICULT FOR ONE
MAY BE EASILY ACCOMPLISHED BY MANY.

NOW IT WAS
    That they sought to understand
        whether the joining together
        of many Sees Beyond
           enhanced either focus or distance.

And they sought also to understand
    whether the nature of the Ocean People—
        they who spoke without speaking—
          might also be enhanced by joining together.

AND SO IT WAS
    That many things came to be understood,
        and that these things also
          are part of a different Telling,
    And yet
        the meeting of Two Peoples is not.

FOR IF THERE IS WISDOM
    IN LEARNING,
        AND WE SAY THERE IS . .

PERHAPS THERE IS WISDOM
    IN REMEMBERING
        TO TURN HOME AGAIN AND AGAIN . .

*So that the threads of connection*
    *need not be stretched too far,*
*So that the nature of the land between*
    *may be learned and understood.*

FOR THIS WAS THE WAY OF IT . .

*As this wise Council sat together,*
    *joining all their thoughts,*
    *joining their will to learn,*
*They asked a great question . .*

"DOES ANYONE AT ALL
    EXPLORE WITH THEIR MINDS
        THE NATURE
        OF THE LAND BETWEEN HERE AND
            THERE?"

NOW
    Much was learned during this time . .

AND YET
    Nothing at all
        that might be considered a response
            was apprehended.

    Of patient learning
        there was much . .

AND YET
    nothing was found
        of an echoing resonance —
    no implication
        of any other pattern of thought.

NOW
    As a child of the People
        you will understand
            how such things may be —
        you will understand also
            how such things may be exceeded
             and New Learning
                encountered all too quickly,
            for a slow approach
            always enables broader understanding.

AND YET ON THAT DAY
    No slow approach was possible . .

For that Council
    stumbled all too quickly
        onto sudden perception.

For the question was asked —

"Do any here
    also explore
        the nature of the land between?"

AND AN ANSWER CAME

No pale image of possible thought was here.

No echo of a distant perception.

AND YET DISTANT INDEED IT WAS . .

FOR
*beyond and beyond*
    *had been the nature of this exploration . .*
*beyond this double circle of Earth and Ocean,*
*beyond Earth's Moon Sister*
    *reflecting the light of the Sun,*
*beyond even the brilliance of Sun —*
    *that giver of regular light to those of us*
        *who dance a spinning Earth . .*

BEYOND AND BEYOND

AND
*The nature of this response*
    *was dim in no way,*
    *tentative in no way either.*

*The nature of this response*
    *was like a loud and strident voice*
    *in a quiet meeting.*

NOT ONE
    AMONG THIS WISE COUNCIL
        FAILED TO HEAR IT.

NOT ONE
    FAILED TO UNDERSTAND
        ITS IMPLICATIONS.

*For this answer*
    *sought no interim measures —*
        *no slow and patient exploration*
        *of the land between.*

THE ANSWER WAS THIS AND THIS ALONE —

"WE ARE COMING!"

AND YET
    Who was coming,
        by what means,
        and with what purpose —
            none of this could be learned.

    Neither could any among the People
        reassure themselves of the accuracy
            of this perception in the usual way.

FOR
    If they rose
        to walk toward this possibility . .

    If they chose in that way
        to go and see . .

    Who among them
        could describe the two-foot Path?

AND SO
    This Wise Council
        sat to consider all possibilities —
        counseled also with others in the community . .

    Until it was decided
        too little was known
            of this too eager People.

  No invitation at all
        had been implied . .

AND YET
    An invitation
        had quickly been accepted,
            and none of the nature of it
                was known or understood . .

160

So that all were agreed
    that so eager a People
        should be dissuaded from any such plan
            until more understanding was gained.

AND SO IT WAS
    *That this Council*
        *sat once more,*
        *sat and joined mind and mind*
        *until all*
            *thought in the same direction,*
        *and the nature of their thought*
            *was this —*

"WHOEVER YOU ARE
        DO NOT COME . .

*"Give us time*
        *to learn to understand one another.*

*"Give us time*
        *to learn to understand ourselves."*

AND
    *Although no answer was heard,*
        *neither was any greater proximity implied . .*

    *So that after many days of such concentration*
        *it was decided*
            *to turn our thoughts elsewhere.*

AND FROM THAT DAY TO THIS,
    *Those who learn such things*
        *have been slow to join together*
        *with too distant a focus,*
    *the results of which*
        *can scarcely be determined.*

SO THAT THIS
    BECAME A GREAT LEARNING ALSO . .

    TOO GREAT A SUCCESS
        MAY DISCOURAGE FURTHER EFFORT
        AS EASILY
            AS NO SUCCESS AT ALL

    Too great a success may discourage further effort as easily as no success at all!
    Perhaps we should remember that as we explore the possibilities of any meeting at all between Cosmic Cultures.

## ⊕ Ruth Montgomery

*Ruth Montgomery*

Ruth Montgomery is the author of fifteen books including *Aliens Among Us.* She was a former syndicated Washington columnist on politics and world affairs for twenty-five years and a long-time investigative reporter. She was awarded honorary Doctor of Law degrees from Baylor University and Ashland College, and has earned numerous journalism awards. She is Past President of the Woman's National Press Club and Mrs. Roosevelt's White House Press Conference Association.

# Let's Have the Facts

*The doyenne of inquiry and assessment of Earth contact with visiting extraterrestrials takes a hard position on government's responsibility to be honest with its citizens on the subject.*

Isn't it rather presumptuous of us to assume that within the vast galaxies of the firmament, we humans on puny earth are the only beings who can think and reason and possess awareness of selves? The earth, relatively speaking, is one of the smaller and newer planets. Only within the past few decades has mankind timorously begun to explore outer space, orbiting close to our home turf while aiming telescopes at other galaxies billions of light years away.

In all that vastness of the universe, is it logical that we are the only creations with the technical skill to establish contact with other stellar bodies? The mere thought appears preposterous. I believe that there are other countless civilizations, many of them older and more highly developed than our own. Of course we should want to establish contact with them, and learn from them. What a great leap forward it would be for mankind, to utilize the enormous strides that other stellar beings have made toward the creation of a true one world.

I personally am convinced that we have been observed, probed and explored by more advanced space beings than our own for countless generations; perhaps for eons of time. Biblical reports, enormous Easter Island statues, vast pyramidal structures assembled by seemingly superhuman means, folk stories of mythical "Gods," pictorial drawings in caves—all lend credence to early visitations by alien races who assisted in the habitation of planet earth.

Why, then, should our present-day governments believe that to release all information of sightings and/or visitations by UFOs would send current earthlings into panic? Our ancestors withstood that shock of learning that earth is round rather than flat, that we revolve around the sun, rather than vice-versa, that those pretty lights in the night sky are actually celestial bodies like ours. Are we not now sufficiently mature to accept that many of them can contain advanced civilizations, and that they are as interested in us as we are in them?

To believe that we warring, wrangling, self-centered humans are the highest form of life to emerge in the firmament is to insult the intelligence of our Creator. Let's have the facts from our government, please!

# ⊕ Zecharia Sitchin

*Zecharia Sitchin (photo by Eric Lundahl)*

Zecharia Sitchin, one of a small number of orientalists who can read the Sumerian clay tablets which trace Earth's and human events from the earliest times, was born in Russia and raised in Palestine where he acquired a profound knowledge of modern and ancient Hebrew and of other Semitic and European languages, the Old Testament, and the history and archaeology of the Near East. He graduated from the University of London, majoring in Economic History, having attended the London School of Economics and Political Science. After a writing career as a journalist he began writing his Earth Chronicles series of books that combine advances in modern science with textual and pictorial evidence from the past to form a cohesive and fact-based story of what really happened on our planet in the past 450,000 years.

# The Past Holds the Key to the Future

> *From archaeological evidence, especially Sumerian clay tablets, Sitchin asserts that cosmic cultures have met, and on a 3,600 year cycle are destined to meet again. That is the news, but is it good or bad? It appears that it depends upon the returning Anunnaki's judgment of our moral progress and discipline in controlling human population.*

The theme of this Conference, "When Cosmic Cultures Meet," must have been chosen with great forethought. It does not say, IF cosmic cultures meet, thereby implicitly suggesting that a meeting is a certainty—only its time, WHEN, is uncertain. But while implying such a certainty, the wording of the theme is ambiguous about the time. It does not say when cosmic cultures WILL meet, which while acknowledging the possibility (or certainty) projects the event into the boundless future. Rather, it chooses "meet," which can mean the present—a suggestion ripe with possibilities and evaluations that allows the discussion of UFOs and abduction reports, which are indeed the subject of a good many sessions of this Conference.

To tie all that together, the organizers have scheduled a panel discussion each day, and the panels' titles are indicative of what it is all about. On the first day we heard the "Fear Panel," and the second day the "Hope Panel," and now, on this third and last day of the Conference, we are having the session on the "Future Panel." Representing in this hall the masses upon this Earth, those who are gathered here have thus moved from FEAR of the unknown, fear of "aliens," to the HOPE of progress and a new era that a meeting with an extraterrestrial culture can hold—but whether to fear or to hope is placed in the context of the FUTURE.

Well, having devoted a lifetime to the subject, and having written seven books (the latest of which, *Divine Encounters*, is due later this year) replete with data, ancient texts and illustrations based on archaeological finds, I can tell you this: The cosmic cultures HAVE ALREADY MET. The records of the PAST are replete with information and evidence on the subject; and IF WE WANT TO KNOW WHAT THE FUTURE HOLDS—WE MUST STUDY THE PAST.

These records of the past have been available to us all along; yet they have been ignored because they had been labeled "myths." My own questioning of what had really happened in antiquity began with wondering, as a schoolboy, why the "Sons of ELOHIM" who had intermarried with "the daughters of the Adam" in the days before the Deluge (Genesis, Chapter 6) were called in the Bible NEFILIM, and why we have been told that the term meant "Giants" when in fact it meant "Those who have descended," who have come down to Earth from the heavens. Biblical scholars explain that this enigmatic segment in the Bible echoes "pagan myths." Years of study, and a review of a century of archaeological discoveries, trace the origin of all those "myths"—of the Romans and Greeks, the Egyptians and Babylonians, Assyrians and Hittites and all others, to the SUMERIANS. Their civilization appeared suddenly and as if out of nowhere circa 3800 B.C., in the great plain between the Euphrates and Tigris rivers (today's Iraq). Their civilization produced in an amazingly short time virtually all the "firsts" that we deem essential to a high and modern civilization: the wheel and the kiln, intensive agriculture and metallurgy, navigation and commerce; writing, arts, music, dance; laws and courts of law, kingship and royal courts; mathematics, chemistry, medicine, astronomy; high rise buildings, temples, a priesthood, religion.

Most amazing of all was their knowledge of astronomy. They knew of, described and even depicted on "star maps" all the planets we know of today (even those discovered by us only in the past century or two); and what is pertinent to our subject today, that 6,000 years-old knowledge included insistence that there is one more planet in our solar system, which they called Nibiru—a planet whose great elliptical orbit brings it to our vicinity once every 3,600 Earth-years, when it passes between Mars and Jupiter.

It was from that planet, the Sumerians asserted in all their records, that intelligent beings had come to Earth some 450,000 years ago. It was not a one-time visit, a crash landing, an accident. The visitors kept coming and going every time their planet was in our part of the heavens, every 3,600 years.

The Sumerians called them ANUNNAKI, literally meaning "Those who from heaven to Earth came"—the NEFILIM of the Bible. According to numerous Sumerian texts it was the Anunnaki who jumped the gun on evolution and, mixing their genes with those of a female hominid, created the "Adam"— Homo Sapiens, you and me. Later on the Anunnaki gave mankind civilization and scientific knowledge; "All that we know as taught to us by the Anunnaki," the Sumerians stated. Indeed, only this can explain how Sumerian knowledge had attained its heights without our modern instruments. That is why my book *Genesis Revisited* carries the subtitle, "Is modern science catching up with ancient knowledge?"

An examination of human progress since the Deluge, some 13,000 years ago, reveals that the marked advances, the transitions from Paleolithic to Mesolithic to Neolithic to the Sumerian civilization, are spaced every 3,600 years. Does this suggest that each time Nibiru neared Earth, each time the comings-and-goings had taken place, and by implication also the next time—we will be given one more dose of knowledge, one more upgrade of civilization?

Here is where my admonition, that the Past is the Future, must be studied very closely. For, as the Sumerian and Biblical records point out, the Anunnaki judged the product of their genetic engineering sternly. Indeed, on one occasion, they sought the total destruction of the Children of Adam through a global catastrophe, an avalanche of water—the Deluge of Biblical renown.

Will the Anunnaki come again on Nibiru's next approach, and what will the results of the next encounter be?

The loss in 1989 of the Soviet spacecraft Phobos-2 at Mars, the circumstances of which were first revealed in my book *Genesis Revisited*, led me to the conclusion that an ancient space base on Mars has been reactivated. What happened in 1989 may well explain the loss of the U.S. spacecraft Mars Observer in 1993. Both incidents bring to mind the tale of the Tower of Babel, when mankind was building a launch tower and the Lord came down and said to unnamed colleagues: We cannot let mankind do that. Such a reactivation of the space base on Mars could well be the explanation for the UFO phenomenon.

I have been asked what can Mankind do to assure a benevolent outcome of the next encounter with that other "cosmic culture," that of the Anunnaki. Indeed, some have wondered, is it at all up to us, in view of the obviously superior technology and perhaps even biology of the Anunnaki?

In answer, I can only invoke the lessons of the Deluge. According to the Biblical version, the decision to wipe Mankind off the face of the Earth was made because "the wickedness of Man was great on Earth. The much earlier Mesopotamian version gave as a reason the excessive proliferation of a tumultuous humanity. These two causes—the evil on Earth and the population explosion—are the two most conspicuous aspects of the twentieth century. The past teaches us that these two phenomena could well be again the criteria by which we will be judged; and in both respects, mankind controls its own direction and destiny.

The realization that we are not alone, in our own solar system, and the coming re-encounter with another, more advanced civilization, should be at the top of humanity's agenda. In this respect, a Conference such as this is an important step in the right direction.

So, in conclusion, what is one to say on the "Future Panel"?

My answer is: To know the future, study the past.

© Z. Sitchin, 1995

# ⊕ Donald M. Ware

*Donald M. Ware, MS*

Donald M. Ware retired from a commissioned career in the Air Force in 1982. He is a UFO investigator, and environmental activist. Raised in Arlington, Virginia, he earned a BSME from Duke University in 1957 and an MS in Nuclear Engineering from the Air Force Institute of Technology in 1970. With diverse interests and studies, he lectures on UFOs and Human-Alien Interactions, the Long-term Government Covert Educational Program on UFOs, Telepathic Communications and UFO Phenomena, Paths to World Government, and how an engineer, fighter pilot and staff scientist became a lightworker. He has seen craft of cosmic cultures on eight occasions.

# Telepathic Communications and UFO Phenomena

*It is clear from research and experience there are a number of off-Earth voices eager to communicate about all aspects of UFO phenomena. From the channeled material itself, practical guidelines for testing and use of this material are given. The breadth of presented material, which is of course only a fraction of that available, begs the question: Do we really need to be concerned about what special information the government may have on this subject? Is there not sufficient knowledge extant and known ways of garnering more to begin to take responsible action to solve man-made problems?*

## INTRODUCTION

Since my first personal UFO sighting in 1952, I have read all the information I could find on the subject. I now believe many of the flying objects can be clearly described as identified alien craft (IAC).

Since 1982, I have expanded research into many other areas that shed light on the larger reality that IAC represent. These avenues to truth include the world's persistent mysteries: religions, ancient astronauts, reincarnation, automatic writing, other telepathic processes, out-of-body experiences, near-death experiences, and spiritual healing. I accepted the idea that INTELLIGENT LIFE IS ABUNDANT THROUGHOUT THE UNIVERSE, in both incarnate and discarnate forms. I also accepted the idea that THE NORMAL MEANS OF COMMUNICATION AMONG MORE-EVOLVED INTELLIGENCE IS <u>TELEPATHY</u>. In 1991, I began to promote the idea that STUDY OF THE HUMAN SPIRIT IS A PROPER SCIENTIFIC ENDEAVOR, and I am also studying world government and evidence of influence on it by spiritual inspiration or alien liaison.

Additionally, I enjoy gathering data on birds for the National Audubon Society and state and federal agencies.

## TYPES OF TELEPATHIC PROCESSES
### STRANGE WRITING

By 1985, I was a Field Investigator, a State Section Director, and the Florida State Director for the Mutual UFO Network (MUFON), an organization dedicated to the scientific study of UFOs. I decided that any active scientist should have a research project. Ufology, sometimes perceived as the study of future science, is highly complex, and researchers become quite specialized. I chose to study strange writing associated with UFO cases as my research project. Few others had worked in that area, and I had just seen some interesting new data on the 1965 Brooksville, Florida case. A nine-year-old girl, just before going to sleep, felt compelled to write a series of strange characters identical to that left by an alien at the Brooksville landing site.

After five years I had collected samples of strange writing associated with 35 UFO cases. I learned little except that it resembled ancient human languages more than any modern human language. About one-third of it was in the form of "automatic" or telepathic writing by people who had been on board alien craft. For example, while speaking to Dan Wright on the phone about the grading of MUFON Field

Investigator examinations, Shirley Coyne absentmindedly doodled from right to left the following series of strange characters:

〆Γ ⁝⟨ ∴ ⊤⊤ ⟍ ∫ )( ⌐ ⊩ ⊂ ∼ ♂ ⊣ ⌒ )ʃ

This event subsequently led to hypnotic regression with Budd Hopkins which revealed an on-board experience at age nine where she was taught an alien language. I believe that automatic writing involves a telepathic process and normally occurs in altered states of mind. Automatic writing is frequently a beginner's form of channeling. Perhaps it is easier and less frightening for a higher intelligence to gain control over our writing hand than our vocal cords. This research effort caused me to be more open to messages in our own language that appear to come from a higher intelligence.

## VOICES, "HUMS," AND IMAGES IN THE HEAD

I was a primary investigator on the highly significant case of Ed Walters who had 18 photographic sessions with alien vehicles in 1987 and '88. Walters often was alerted to a photographic opportunity by a "hum" in his head, and he received several telepathic messages. One said, "Zehaus, Zehaus...sleep and know." He was asked by investigators to think about specific questions just before sleep and to record his first thoughts upon waking. One of his recorded thoughts, related to operation of the vehicles, included "7.5 Hz." Later, when his video of the Gulf Breeze Type 1 vehicle was analyzed by computer, Bob Oechsler discovered a 7.5 Hz fluctuation of the light at the bottom of the vehicle. I think many of the voices heard in the head by people involved in the UFO phenomenon are telepathic; because, often an alien is looking at them as if communicating when it happens.

I now recognize that two messages, or intuitive thoughts, that I have received directly came from what may have been a higher intelligence. In 1954, after a philosophical discussion with my fraternity brothers at Duke, I went to bed at midnight. I woke at 2:00 a.m. with many thoughts in my head that I felt I must write down. One said, "In order to be completely happy, one must have love, excitement, and self satisfaction." This helped me understand that you do not have to have a lot of money to be happy. I became quite satisfied with a service career, and that allowed me the luxury of early retirement.

The other message came on January 28, 1992. I woke at exactly 2:00 a.m. with two clear sentences in my mind. It was like I was looking at a video screen. There was no room in my mind for any other thoughts, and the sentences would not go away until I wrote them down. They said, "Unconditional Love is becoming a driving force on this planet. I am trying to learn to express Unconditional Love." The wording was new to me, but the ideas were not foreign. I would not normally have capitalized unconditional love. However, as a new member of a Unity church, I had been thinking of unconditional love. Also, I was aware that RA[1] said we are undergoing a transformation from 3rd density to 4th density positive experience on this planet. He said the purpose of 3rd density experience is polarization toward service-to-others or service-to-self through free-will choices, and the purpose of 4th density is to develop unconditional love. Perhaps these ideas were confirmed for me by a "spirit guide" because I had already accepted it through my own seeking.

## THE OUIJA BOARD

In 1988, one of my son's 18-year-old friends, Kenneth, asked for an appointment to talk with me. I thought he wanted to talk about UFOs for a school paper like many other young people do. When he finally got to the point, he asked, "What do you know about the ouija board?" I said, "Very little, except that I just finished a book, *Messages from Michael*, that was acquired through a ouija board." The book was given to me by a friend, Patsy Hill, and it tells much about the relationship between personality and the soul. Kenneth then told me his story.

Two years earlier Kenneth's friend borrowed his mother's ouija board and several of the boys experimented with it. When they placed their fingers lightly on the pointer, it moved and spelled out several messages. The name of the source was spelled out, and one of the messages told Kenneth to go and talk with Donald Ware. Then other messages, apparently from a different source, were spelled out, and they scared the boys badly. They put the board away and tried to forget it. Two weeks before his visit Kenneth had a dream that he was supposed to use the ouija board again. The boys borrowed the board, and again the message they spelled out was that Kenneth was supposed to talk with Donald Ware. That is why he was visiting me. Kenneth has had an interest in UFO-related subjects, and his visit caused him to attend several of my monthly meetings. I have considered that perhaps this experience was as much for my benefit as Kenneth's. It caused me to consider the telepathic aspects of dreams and of the ouija board.

## FACE-TO-FACE TELEPATHIC COMMUNICATION

Katharina Wilson was one of 20 or so people who came to MUFON investigators near Gulf Breeze, Florida within a year after the Walter's photographs were publicized. Each had experiences that suggested alien encounters. Regression with Dr. Dan Overlade indicated an implant was inserted up her right nostril six days earlier. When she agreed to a search for the implant, Vicki Lyons, Charles Flannigan, and I were advised. We were MUFON's Field Investigator on that case, State Section Director, and State Director, respectively. We knew from the experience of other investigators that most implants in the head do not show up on x-rays, but do using Magnetic Resonance Imaging (MRI). However, no doctor in his right mind will put a person's head in those strong alternating magnetic fields looking for a foreign object without first assuring himself it is not magnetic. So we ran a CAT-scan at a cost of $560. The implant did not show up.

Before we could schedule the even more expensive MRI, Katharina was told telepathically by the aliens, "Do not talk to Vicki Lyons, Charles Flannigan, or Donald Ware. We are not ready for them to know." Then the aliens added, "We know their every move and thought." The experiencer did talk. Vicki, Charles, and I decided to not let that deter us from our search for the implant. However, before we could schedule the MRI, Vicki suddenly found herself wide awake (or thought she did) in the middle of the night; felt compelled to run outside in her nightgown and look up, didn't see anything, ran through the house to the backyard, and found herself surrounded by five aliens. She was advised telepathically to stop the search, and she agreed.

Vicki does not remember coming back into the house. Her husband, for an unknown reason, felt some fear that night. When he got up he found things were not quite right in the house. He woke Vicki and asked, "Were you in the backyard last night?" She said, "I don't think so, but I dreamed I was." And he said, "Well, you left the back door open and the porch light on." Vicki now accepts the idea that she did encounter five of the little guys.

Because of the face-to-face communication, we agreed to stop the search for the implant. One might assume the implant is there for a purpose. If we found it, and it was too close to the optic nerve to risk removal, it would probably cause added mental stress. If it were removed, the alien folks may replace it, which probably would not be a pleasant experience. I think we made the right decision. I would rather develop a friendly relationship with our visitors than an adversarial one, and I have reasons to believe they want to be our friends.

## Light-Trance Channeling

One reason channeling is so controversial is because it involves the spiritual realm. I personally am comfortable describing God as All That Is, Universal Consciousness, or Christ Consciousness. I accept that there is only one consciousness in all of the universe. Since we have a spirit that is part of that consciousness, there is a little spark of God in each of us. I believe our spirits are eternal and can incarnate in a physical body many times. I believe that some spirits, whether incarnate or discarnate, can communicate through the direct projection of thought. This communication takes place with humans most often while we are in an altered state of consciousness.

Some people receive thoughts of great strangeness and often of great wisdom while in a light trance, the alpha or day-dreaming state of consciousness. Those who can type can translate these thoughts onto written form very rapidly with a typewriter, as if taking dictation. Questions can be typed or thought, and answers are provided. As in any translation, these messages are influenced by the knowledge of the channel, but much information of value has been obtained by thousands of people around the world in this manner.

One example is my friend Yvonne Cole, who communicated for three years in this manner with Eunethia. Yvonne felt a definite female presence when communicating, and Eunethia became her dear friend in the spirit realm. Later, when communications were attempted, one who was felt to be a male named Onethan responded. Yvonne was upset by this change, but they soon developed a cooperative relationship. Many communications later, a being who called itself Theodora responded, and Yvonne could not determine if it was a male or female energy. Theodora explained that it was also Eunethia and Onethan. The spirit is both male and female, and this was a demonstration to show her they have the capability to project either presence. As these contacts progressed, Yvonne was told that her spirit had been in a Zeta/human hybrid body in her last incarnation. Then she had a physical night-time visitation. She felt she knew the little guy at the foot of the bed, and she had no fear. She gave him a hug, took him by the hand, and gave him a tour of the house just like she would any other visitor. She said some of its friends were also in the house that night. She was later asked to type a book. That information has been published in Connecting Link magazine and also produced in a five-hour audio tape.[2] It sheds much light on our on-going transformation.

Another light-trance channel is Dr. Norma Milanovich. While a teacher at the University of New Mexico in Albuquerque, she received much information from KUTHUMI, apparently the same being who inspired the Theosophy movement many years ago. Milanovich, with two assistants, published *We the Arcturians*. She greatly expanded her perspective on the universe and on many transformational issues. Milanovich was then approached by the Wackenhut Corporation and hired to teach their people a course called Job/Task Analysis. Wackenhut has a contract with the U.S. Department of Energy to provide security for facilities where I think human/alien liaison is taking place. I *suspect* Milanovich was hired to expand the concept of reality of these folks who protect great secrets, to give them a framework of reality that includes many strange things they might see, to help them maintain their mental stability. I find it interesting that Milanovich now also works for some major high-tech corporations such as Westinghouse and General Electric. The motto on her stationery says, "...Specializing in training slightly ahead of its time."

## FULL-TRANCE CHANNELING

Full-trance channeling is a form of communication in which control of the vocal cords and often other muscles is loaned to another intelligence. Some full-trance channels are great orators. Some channels are better communication tools than others, and some sources display more wisdom than others. In that respect, the sources are somewhat like humans. I have been impressed with the RA material channeled through Carla Rueckert, with Don Elkins as the questioner. It included the transcripts of about 100 Q+A sessions from 1981 to 1983 where RA agreed to answer any questions about the reality of the universe. The format is easy for the scientific mind to understand.

Lyssa Royal is currently doing full-body channeling with an audience. Much of her contact is with SASHA who describes herself as a physical-bodied Pleiadian cultural engineer and psychosociologist. Much of the information Lyssa acquired has been published by Royal Priest Research in *The Prism of Lyra, Visitors from Within,* and *Preparing for Contact.* I think these books are useful in trying to understand a reality that is so complex it is beyond our ability to fully comprehend.

## INSTRUMENTED TRANS-COMMUNICATION (ITC)

In the UFO literature I occasionally find a case where a telephone, tape recorder, radio or television is apparently used by a high intelligence to send a message to humans. The spring 1993 issue of the Institute of Noetic Sciences (IONS) *Quarterly Review* had an interesting article titled, "When Dimensions Cross." Research groups have studied this phenomenon for years. For example, after 25 years of research, Swedish film producer, Friedrich Juergenson, published his findings in the 1964 book, *Voices from the Universe.* Even after his death in 1987, Juergenson continued to work from the "spiritside" with other ITC researchers on the "earthside." His face appeared on a television screen during these research sessions.

A Luxembourg research group contacted a voice on the radio called TECHNICIAN. The IONS *Quarterly Review* article by Willis Harman concludes by saying:

"While the declared spiritside aim of ITC is eventually to be able to circumvent the experiencers' psyche altogether, what is in practice today appears to be a telepathically assisted instrumental communication. It appears that researchers' beliefs, thoughts and attitudes affect ITC contacts, but to a lesser degree than during the phenomenon of 'channeling.' From the technical point of view, then, the ultimate aim of ITC is to develop an electronic system that will work independently of the psyches of the earthside participants, and the Luxembourg team seems to be getting close.

"What do the 'higher beings' hope to accomplish with ITC? According to TECHNICIAN, they want everyone to know that life continues beyond physical death. For many people today, faith in age-old religious texts is not enough: they need solid evidence of an afterlife, which ITC may provide."

Another example of a television apparently being used by a higher intelligence was captured accidentally(?) on December 23, 1990, when a lady in new Jersey was photographing her son. He was playing near the television that was not turned on. A clear picture of an alien head with large dark eyes and a circular indentation high on the side of the head was investigated by the New Jersey MUFON group. Their report was finally published in MUFON's New Jersey Chronicle of Sep.-Dec. 1992.

I find it significant that the alien head looked very much like the head of the alien on the back of the AMOCO ad that first appeared in aerospace magazines shortly before this event.

This final example of ITC occurred on November 26, 1977, at 5:12 p.m. when a strange unknown voice overrode, took over, or super-modulated the TV signals from five transmitters that were monitored by the Independent Broadcasting Authority (IBA) in England. IBA did not detect the intrusion. The 5+1/2-minute message overrode a scheduled newscast read by Ivor Mills on Southern ITV, England, and was heard by listeners as far away as Andover, London, Newbury, Oxford, Reading, Southampton, and Winchester. IBA engineers at Croydon, Surrey did not hear the override, and at the main transmitter at Southampton, Hants monitoring system, there was also no evidence of the takeover. A police spokesman told AP and UPI that the message was taken seriously; "They were frightened and generally scared."

The voice spoke slowly and deliberately, with a strange inward authority, calm, serene, never scolding. It said:

"This is the voice of GRAMAHA, the representative of the Asta [probably Ashtar] Galactic Command, speaking to you. For many years now you have seen us as lights in the skies. We speak to you now in peace and wisdom as we have done to your brothers and sisters all over this, your planet earth.

"We come to warn you of the destiny of your race and your worlds so that you may communicate to your fellow beings the course you must take to avoid the disasters which threaten your worlds, and the beings on our worlds around you. This is in order that you may share in the great awakening, as the planet passes into the new Age of Aquarius. The new age can be a time of great peace and evolution for your race, but only if your rulers are made aware of the evil forces that overshadow their judgments.

"Be still now and listen, for your chance may not come again. For many years your scientists, governments and generals have not heeded our warnings; they have continued to experiment with the evil forces of what you call nuclear energy. Atomic bombs can destroy the earth, and the beings of your sister worlds, in a moment. The wastes from atomic power systems will poison your planet for many thousands of your years to come.

"We, who have followed the path of evolution for far longer than you, have long since realized this—that atomic energy is always directed against life. It has had no peaceful application. Its use, and research into its use, must be ceased at once, or you all risk destruction. All weapons of evil must be removed.

"The time of conflict is now past. The race of which you are a part may proceed to the highest planes of evolution if you show yourselves worthy to do this. You have but a short time to learn to live together in peace and goodwill.

"Small groups all over the planet are learning this, and exist to pass on the light of the dawning new age to you all. You are free to accept or reject their teachings, but only those who learn to live in peace will pass to the higher realms of spiritual evolution.

"Hear now the voice of GRAMAHA, the representative of the Asta [sic] Galactic Command, speaking to you. Be aware also that there are many false prophets and guides operating in your world. They will suck the energy from you—the energy you call money and will put it to evil ends giving you worthless dross in return.

"Your inner divine self will protect you from this. You must learn to be sensitive to the voice within that can tell you what is truth, and what is confusion, chaos and untruth. Learn to listen to the voice of truth which is within you and you will lead yourselves on to the path of evolution.

"This is our message to our dear friends. We have watched you growing for many years as you too have watched our lights in your skies. You know now that we are here, and that there are more beings on and around your earth than your scientists admit.

"We are deeply concerned about you and your path towards the light and will do all we can to help you. Have no fear, seek only to know yourselves, and live in harmony with the ways of your planet earth.

We of the Asta [sic] Galactic Command thank you for your attention. We are now leaving the planes of your existence. May you be blessed by the supreme love and truth of the cosmos."

I think the normal means of communication by higher intelligences is through the direct projection of thought. Those thoughts can be transferred to the human consciousness through many processes. They are different forms of telepathic communications.

## MESSAGES ABOUT UFOs/IAC

A number of messages acquired through telepathic processes have had a significant impact on my thoughts about the universe. One of the first is ISHCOMAR'S FIRST MESSAGE.

A copy of the recording of this message was sent to me, unsolicited, by Sue Wallace. It was published in a 1978 book, *I am Ishcomar*, and discussed by Brad Steiger in his book, *Revelation the Divine Fire*. The message came through the voice box of a blue-collar worker in Texas in 1956. He was in a deep trance, and the deep, unnatural tone of his voice was impressive. The message follows:

"I am Ishcomar.

"I bring you greetings from beyond the stars. It is requested at this time to bring you a communication of our intent for the inhabitants of your planet. I will explain to you briefly who we are and who and what I am.

"You have named some of our craft who move through your atmosphere 'flying saucers'. I am not recorded in one of these. The craft that contains the instrument in which I am recorded is four and three-tenths miles in length, by your methods of measurements, and two and one-tenth miles in circumference.

"This craft also contains others of us who are in human form. I have passed the phase of human form. My knowledge and mind processes were long ago recorded into an instrument you would liken to a computer.

"I was brought to the vicinity of this planet approximately thirty thousand years ago, by your method of time measurement. Your planet and the living forms upon it have a specific value to us.

"Those of us who do menial work inhabit our craft in human form almost identical to some of you. For this reason, at about the time I was brought into the vicinity of your world, we interfered with the natural development of the species of man that inhabited this planet at that time. Our purpose was the shortening of the cycle of development necessary for the human inhabitants of this planet to be of use to us.

"Our intent, however, is not to control or to rule over you. Intergalactic law within our group forbids this. We are, however, permitted to guide you. Your acceptance of us is by your own choice.

"Our vessels number somewhat over twenty thousand in use within the confines of your solar system. These craft vary from a few feet to many miles in length and circumference. These craft vary in shape and size dependent upon the purpose for which it is used.

"Our human forms number many thousands. Some of them were alive in their present form before I was brought here. Those in human form inhabiting our craft have ceased to repropagate. This condition makes it necessary to chose one of two courses when it becomes necessary to dispose of the human vessel; whether to be recorded in a device and stored, as I was, or to be recorded into another suitable form.

"We have been unable to manufacture, by synthetic means, suitable human type forms. This, therefore, makes it necessary to find planets young enough where new man beings are being born, yet old enough for the human form to be developed to a point that will provide suitable bodies with sufficient brain capacity to receive our knowledge.

"By mutual agreement between a planetary dweller and an inhabitant of our craft, the knowledge and memory of one of us may be blended with the planetary inhabitant without the loss of the receiver's identity. The one from our group only adds his knowledge to the planetary dweller, and the abandoned body is disseminated.

"This blending may not take place without mutual agreement between the beings involved, and necessarily the planetary dweller must fully agree and desire this blending. We seek, therefore, not to take but to give.

"We, however, are not alone in our interests in your world. There is in existence with us another group. Their interest is not necessarily harmful toward you, yet their methods are in direct opposition to ours. They also may have interfered with the development on your planet. They wish to reach their ends not by cooperation but by control and domination over you.

"You must reach a high level of mental development and knowledge to be able to understand our purposes beyond harvesting. We have attempted to gain your cooperation in this for thousands of years. We have been vigorously opposed by the other group. We must achieve our goal by guidance of your kind, but you must desire guidance for us to be of assistance to you.

"Our work is beyond your present level of understanding and yet you will eventually be of great assistance in cooperating with us in making certain studies of life forms and conditions on your planet, the result of which will be compared with intercorrelated studies being conducted on other worlds, to the benefit of your own planet, our people, and the inhabitants of these other worlds.

"We have worked patiently with you for over thirty thousands years. However, the development brought about would have taken, by normal cycles, over two hundred and fifty thousand years.

"We also have limitations making it necessary to adhere to certain conditions difficult for you, at this time, to rationalize.

"Our intent and purpose toward you exceeds your most beautiful wishes and dreams for your existence. The inhabitants of your world have been repeatedly told of this and it has always been converted to spiritualistic ideals.

"It is [an] understandable thought process to attempt to understand the unknown by measuring it with the known. We do not condemn for this. To those of you who will follow certain steps, we may be able to help you a great deal to reach higher understanding, thereby improving your own conditions of survival on your world, and at the same time assist us in our endeavors.

"The man whose body and mind I am using to speak to you is being used by his own full cooperation. Had he not reached out, I would not have been beamed to him in answer; yet all who reach, however, are not answered—for all do not reach out in honesty of purpose. Some wish to acquire some personal gratification of the moment, and therefore do not reach a point of open acceptance necessary to receive me. I am beamed to many on your world. This man is not spectacular, therefore.

"We are using many methods at this time to inform your people of our presence and our immediate purposes. The time is quite near for cooperation between us to begin. Your next step upward will soon begin.

"Full knowledge of our presence will soon be known among your people. There will be, at that time, great upheavals on your planet. We regret this cannot in any way be avoided. We knew this from the beginning. We, therefore, have repeatedly warned to prepare for it mentally and physically. Those who take not the trouble to prepare are of little value to themselves in any case.

"We can in no way tell you the day or the minute this upheaval will begin to take on climactic proportions. You must watch and prepare yourselves according to the conditions you observe. We will guide those of you who sincerely allow us to.

"We do not intend any evacuation of your planet on any scale. You are of no value to us in the outer reaches. Our craft are now adequately manned.

"Our need of your cooperation involves habitation of your world by your own people, under more suitable conditions than you now realize, however.

"Following the climactic upheavals on your world, we will provide guidance to bring about the desired conditions for your, and our, mutual benefit.

"Seek us and you will find us.

"We only await your call.

"Peace be with you.

"I am Ishcomar."

## MESSAGE FOR SOMEONE AT EGLIN AFB

On January 25, 1989, I had a meeting in my home with two ladies from the Orlando area who receive telepathic messages. They were instructed to give me a message. It said, "There is something going on on the Eglin AFB reservation involving nuclear weaponry that they [higher intelligence] are concerned about. It's like playing Russian roulette." I had worked at Eglin in the testing business, and I knew no one would consider setting off any kind of nuclear weapon at that base. The message did not make sense to me, and I forgot about it.

Two weeks later, the first thought in my mind when I woke was, "You dummy. That lady drove nearly 600 miles to give you a message. Maybe you should do something about it." That Thursday at noon I called for an appointment with the general that I thought had the greatest formal education. I identified myself and was told by his secretary that his next open appointment was Tuesday morning. I said, "I'm sorry. It will have to be this afternoon or tomorrow morning or I'm leaving town—five minutes max." She asked what I wanted to see him about. I said I had a message from an unusual source. She said, "I'll squeeze you in between the general's staff meetings tomorrow morning." When I told him the message and circumstances, he looked me straight in the eye and said, "I don't know everything going on on this reservation, but I know who does. I will make sure they get the message." Then I opened my briefcase and gave him the written copy. Underneath was Ed Walters' photo of a UFO above the road. The general asked, "May I see that?" When I handed it to him he smiled and said, "Very interesting."

Over two years later I was contacted by "Leah Haley" to help define the "Gulf Breeze Incident," a term from her partial recollections. This led to a 13-mile walk in the sand from Navarre, near Gulf Breeze, Florida, to Ft. Walton Beach. She had already determined that the incident involved the downing of an alien vehicle that she was on. Apparently, a non-lethal weapon was used. She also had determined that it happened at dawn on one of six nights in early August 1988. Four or five miles into the walk Leah found a place on the beach she said looked like what she remembered when she got out of the vehicle. About a mile further we found a phased-array radar on the back of a military flat-bed truck between the low sand dunes. Another mile or so farther we found a large omni-directional doughnut that was later determined to be a directed-electro-magnetic-pulse (EMP) device, a device that can have devastating effects on electrical conductors. Both objects were secured by fences and sensors and were pointing southwest at a low angle of elevation.

This directed-EMP device caused me to wonder if it was related to the strange message I passed to the general. I called the lady from Orlando and asked if she still had her original notes from her January 1989 visit. When she found them I asked why she used the phrase "nuclear weaponry." She had drawn two images that she received telepathically; one was a missile-like thing with fins pointing up, and the other was a mushroom cloud. "Nuclear weaponry" was all that made sense top her. However, if she had interpreted these two images in the sequence she got them, "weaponry that could cause a nuclear explosion," then the message makes sense to me. An EMP device might destabilize an alien power system or cause a vehicle to crash and cause a big bang, like playing Russian roulette. The May 25, 1993 issue of "Aviation Week and Space Technology" has an article on EMP weapons development at Eglin AFB. I hope the military men at Eglin understood the message, even in its distorted form.

On May 9, 1988, Bob Oechsler wrote to President Reagan requesting he do something about airspace violations by aliens and human-rights violations of abductees in the Gulf Breeze area. Evidence that this letter was taken seriously was given when Oechsler received a reply from a Rear Admiral representing Navy Operations, Air Warfare.

On August 21, 1988, the Joint Chiefs of Staff met at Pensacola NAS and visited a hangar that had, some days earlier, been temporarily air conditioned at considerable effort and placed under heavy security. I *suspect* that vehicle was in that hangar, the closest place to hide it undetected. I *suspect* the vehicle was brought down because it did not stay away from Gulf Breeze at a very sensitive time when TV camera crews were visiting Gulf Breeze looking for UFOs. If Unsolved Mysteries had gotten good video of UFOs comparable to the photos Ed Walters had taken, I think our government would have had difficulty managing public reaction.

## Messages For Me From "The Captain"

In 1989 I was given 15 messages by seven different people who apparently received them telepathically from higher intelligences. Each mentioned my name. I was also elected to the position of Regional Director for MUFON by the members of the 18 eastern states. Just prior to my first MUFON board meeting I received three messages from THE CAPTAIN through the lady from Orlando that are more meaningful to me now than they were when I got them. I will quote all of each:

"MESSAGE ON UFOs: (1:20 a.m, June 2, 1989)

"In all things, focus on the positive. Even answers to questions about the negative aspects of UFO phenomena can be garnered from positive UFO contacts. Focus upon individuals who have had positive and spiritual information given to them from their UFO contacts. Do not focus upon those who have had negative and frightening experiences with UFOs, for they have not been contacted by the highest UFO sources and therefore their information will be distorted.

"The UFO information from the higher positive UFO contacts can explain the negative realms, and do it more fully and more accurately, for the higher positive realm fully understands the workings of the realms beneath it. In all things, do not fuel the negative with your attention, for that will only give it energy to grow and expand.

"Those individuals who suffer in any way from negative UFO experiences can be helped by information available from the higher realms of your UFO contacts. Seek the positive—always! Seek the spiritual—always! Know that God is real. Know that this most awesome creative force is not without personality (there is no word available to truly express this use of 'personality'). Know that this Creator is of love and has a plan for Earth beyond the most wonderful dreams of mankind. Know that the Creator creates within the rules of Universal Law, so anything that may seem to defy this can be explained when sufficient knowledge or understanding is achieved by man.

"Individuals such as Donald Ware have a mission whether they have as yet fully recognized it. They are to show that science and spirituality are two sides of one coin and cannot be separated. If that seems too trite an analogy, then I will speak more dramatically. A man cannot live if you split him down the middle, and yet that is what your Earth men of science have done. They have separated the physical body of man from his spirit. Until they realize that it is spirit which ultimately gives life to the physical, until they recognize the vast dimensions beyond the puny five senses of Earth man, they will be no more than bees making great buzzing sounds as they circle the honey—honey they can see and smell but cannot touch until they can get beyond the screen of physical limitations which separates them from the sweetness of the spiritual honey.

"As for those who suffer from their lower level contacts with UFOs, there is much that can be done. Use hypnosis upon those who have had the highest spiritually directed UFO experiences and ask for directions in helping those who are troubled. If possible, use medically trained experts to direct the hypnosis for that will add credence to what you do and what you ultimately will seek to prove. If possible, use medical hypnotists with spiritual understanding for that will enhance the results.

"Remember that those who continue to be harassed in any way from their UFO contacts should be treated as if they were being harassed by a deviant man in a neighborhood. If such a man were to peek in a window of a home, a bright flashlight in his eyes would make him run. The arrival of a police car would make such a man run away if possible. As with all things in the universe, Goodness and Light dissolve the negative. So seek the help of your Brothers of Light on the spiritually enlightened ships of the heavens. We cannot come to help you unless you request our assistance, for that is one of the Universal Laws. So if you wish relief for those who suffer, you must remember to request our help. We are here to help, just ask.

"Remember, too, the basic tenet of all faiths in the One God: Ask and you will be encircled in the Creator's Light of Protection. Seek and you shall find. There is no stronger force in the universe, but this, too, must be requested. Those who suffer have only to sincerely ask for the Creator's help, but so few truly believe and ask with true faith. Ah, the unnecessary suffering mankind endures because he separates his spirit from the body. It is so simple, yet Children of Earth have bogged down so deeply in the mud of materiality that they must be retaught this simple message again. Teach them, we plead, for they in their ignorance are destroying themselves and a most beautiful planet.

"NOTE: I was awakened abruptly just before this message came through. I had been dreaming that I was in front of a computer and a written message was coming across a large computer screen for Donald Ware. A half ring of my telephone then awoke me at exactly 1:20 a.m. The half ring and the time are important because they have been signals for me for several years. Many significant things happen at exactly 20 minutes before or 20 minutes after the hour so that I know that something is important or not just a mere coincidence. The half rings on the telephone indicate the same thing. Both always alert me to pay attention.

"ADDITIONAL MESSAGE: This information is to be sent to Donald Ware and Jim Greenen. They may be told that they are free to share it with others, but they are not to identify you as the receiver of this material or any other messages that may be sent through you for them. This information, and any subsequent information, is intended only to help and guide them in their mission and is not to become the object of their dissecting scrutiny. More than enough UFO cases have been, and will continue to be, provided for their analysis. Information that comes through you is solely for the purpose of getting them on the right track in their cosmic detective work. I trust that if they listen to their hearts when they read my messages that they will know that only truth is spoken."

"The Captain—June 23, 1989

"BULLETINS FROM SPACE

"*The highest level messages from space vehicles are spoken through two basic types of individuals: those who are simple, pure, childlike vessels and those who are highly illuminated with the Light.

"Those who dabble with metaphysical accouterments or seek in any way personal aggrandizement or control are not used as torches for the Spiritual Light messages. This means that it is often possible to discern the degree of validity of channeled messages by observing the behavior and philosophy of the vessels.

"*We are so weary of mankind being so unobservant of the things around.

"*So many think the owl is wise
for it sits in the trees and seems to despise
all beneath its perch on high.
Yet, in reality this bird of prey
is mesmerized in the light of day
and lives to hunt when the sun is gone,
to eat tiny creatures who've done him no wrong.
So, too, your wisemen sit on high
and think they're wise,
but in reality they're all in stupors.
Seeing naught and without much thought,
they wail 'til dark
to prey upon some lonely heart
who's run amuck upon the ground,
and they never soar where eagles are found.
For too long the owls have reigned within MUFON
and all of us in space
grow most weary of this disgrace.
It's time for heads to turn on high,
where eagles soar and the answers rise.
It's time for those without the Spirit,
to relinquish their perches to those who are with it—
to those who can see the souls
and not just the vehicles where they are enclosed.

"*Technological development in all space travel will be capped until the men of science learn of the Soul and entwine that understanding with their cold, hard facts and mechanical contraptions. The fools can no longer be in charge, and fools are those who cannot see that Spirit lives for eternity and indeed sparks all that is physical.

"Yes, yes, yes, we're tired of fools who see only the physical and dissect it to death without thought to the Light that illuminates it.

"Yes, we have answers to interplanetary travel. Yes, we have answers to the grand mysteries of ancient civilizations. Yes, we have answers to questions of vehicle propulsion. Yes, we have answers to all the questions your men of science ask, but complete answers will be withheld until mankind achieves a balance with Spiritual understanding.

180

"How could we possibly provide you with more technological information when you have exploited what you have already been given—to the extent that you have truly put your human race and your planet in jeopardy?!

"*We feel joy whenever a man of science discovers his Spiritual origins and the greater Cosmic Plan that God and his Brotherhood of Light have for this planet, this solar system and indeed the universe, but we grow so weary of playing 'prove it to me' games with kindergarten scientists who think they are so wise, yet despise the creative energy most call God.

"We grow weary of zipping and zapping across the skies before your eyes to prove it's all really happening. We grow so weary there are those amongst us who would wipe their hands clean of all of this and leave mankind isolated and alone to play endlessly with tinker toys, pop guns and cannons.

"Do not assume that we will play childish games forever and a day with you, for your questions are so basic and trite that we must try with all our might to tolerate your endless quest of knowledge of things so insignificant.

"Please, we beg of all of you, seek the Source from whence you've come, so that each of you and all of you can join the federation of planetary dwellers composing the Light of the Universe.

"Transmitted with the approval of The Captain"

"This will more effectively touch the hearts of men if read aloud to them.

"The Captain"

"Captain Message received June 28, 1989

[Just prior to the MUFON symposium in the Aladdin Hotel in Las Vegas.]

"The spirit world or those in the fourth dimension will, and have been, working around the clock to soften the minds of belligerent ones who will be attending the UFO convention meetings. Our representatives on Earth in this effort are therefore not alone in carrying out their missions to enlighten mankind.

"Even those who believe in God must be motivated to release an antiquated image of the Creator or Creative Force that is indeed the origin of life itself. Those who have an understanding of other worlds and dimensions always find Earth religions a bit like wearing tight lace-up shoes that are too, too small. Such shoes not only hurt the feet and squeeze the toes, but distract the mind and spirit from walking out into open spaces where it is more possible to connect directly with the Creator. Sometimes the constriction is so great that the laces must be cut quickly so the life energy can return to the souls of men. Yes, this has a double meaning.

"Donald Ware is to be our Genie in the Aladdin's Lamp. He should regard any negative opposition as a rubbing of the magic lamp to bring forth the Genie and his message. He should stay cool and remember this image whenever he is confronted by those who cannot see beyond their simplistic three-dimensional world.

"It is no accident that so many words of encouragement have been spoken in Donald's ears, that so many messages have been delivered to him, that so many books have appeared before him. All forms of encouragement have been carefully orchestrated to assure him of our reality, to ignite his spirit from an ember to a flames, and to give him courage to come out of Aladdin's Lamp.

"The space ships are real. Armageddon is real and has already begun. Tumultuous change is inevitable and has already begun. In the final moments of this change, the destiny of each individual soul will rest squarely upon its own shoulders, and the hope of each will be determined by the spiritual connection that has or has not been made with the Creator.

"Nothing is haphazard in our efforts to support our Genie in the Lamp, even the motel name in Las Vegas should be a constant reminder to him that he is not alone in his mission.

"God and The Captain are at one with another. Isn't it ironic that those who pride themselves in their intelligence would believe the words of a captain on a space vehicle before believing that there is a Creator behind and within the vastness of the universes? Feel sorry for such ignorant wise ones, for they are indeed blind and deaf."

Following the MUFON symposium, I was sent another message from the same source. I thought the advice showed much wisdom.

"CAPTAIN MESSAGE—July 15, 1989

"You have been monitored all your life, but now that monitoring is constant since you have begun your most important mission of your present life. Since your conscious awareness of your mission, I have been personally checking your progress, with the intention of providing sufficient support for your efforts to blend science and spirituality and to make this, and contacts from space, believable and acceptable to a larger percentage of the human population.

"As you are well aware, there are strict Universal Laws which every member of the Federation must follow. Therefore, I only can offer suggestions or point out things which I feel you may not have given full attention. With that stated, I would like to present a number of points for your thoughtful consideration.

(1) "Information that comes from the fourth dimension or above, which includes spirit beings and those who fly in space vehicles from other regions of the universe, must always be carefully scrutinized, for often there are distortions as well as truths in the messages transmitted to those upon Earth. Even the best known fourth-dimensional transmitters of information—such as Arthur Ford, Ramtha, Seth and your RA—have distortions as well as truths in their messages.

(2) "Be cautious of messages that come through human channels that follow any kind of ritualistic behavior of any sort before information can be transmitted. Remember that it has always been druids, sorcerers, magicians and priestly ones aspiring for power that have professed rituals to connect with God or universal forces. Such ritualistic behavior serves to separate mankind from the Creator. This is wrong because it is possible for every creature in every part of the universe to connect with the Creator instantaneously—just in the moment of the thought.

(3) "The Creator of this universe is love itself and any messages that lack expressions of qualities of love should be again scrutinized carefully. Remember that love is not mambie-pambie emotion, for love can be firm and strong when that is the only way to help some individuals grow toward the Creator or toward Universal Love. So even though some messages are filled with much truth, be wary when they are robotic and/or distantly removed from any true understanding of and compassion for mankind.

(4) "Remember that the Creator can communicate with or through any of his creations, from the tiniest insect to the most magnificent man upon your Earth, and of course, beings far beyond your limited plane. Today the Creator is attempting to spiritually awaken as many of his children upon the Earth as will allow him to come to them. Therefore, his Universal Truths will be stated in ways that can be easily comprehended by mankind. Consequently, be wary of messages that are not immediately understandable or can be open to alternate forms of interpretation for the Creator has no difficulty express-

ing truth and love to his children at the level they can most easily understand.

(5) "Upon the Earth you find those who are of the Light, of the shadows, and of the darkness, and so it is beyond your third dimension. Just as you have con men upon the Earth, so you have those beyond the third dimension who mix just enough truth with their distortions to lure men of good intentions down shadowed paths.

(6) "Carefully scrutinize any messages labeling any group, whether upon the Earth or in the heavens, as good or bad. I will give you an analogy to drive this point home to you. Imagine that ET has landed on the Earth for the very first time and that the first person he meets is Gadhafy. Would you want to be clumped into one category with this man simply because your body structures are similar? I think not. Neither do I think you are puffed up with ego enough to think yourself an equal to a man like Ghandi. Yet, if ET met Ghandi first, he would assume that all human beings would be gentle respecters of all life and would, therefore, assume you are like Ghandi. I hope this quick analogy points out the fallacy of labeling any group as all good or all bad.

(7) "If the same messages come from widely disparate sources, then the probability that they are correct is much greater, but this, too, must be carefully scrutinized. The same spirit, or space being, or fourth-dimensional group can send messages under different aliases. So if four spirits—John, Joe, Jim and Jane—all transmit similar messages, the validity of the messages, even though they are in agreement, is not increased four-fold unless you are positive that these transmitters are not aliases for one entity or mouthpieces of one entity.

"Remember that every human soul, if allowed to fly beyond the constraints of the human ego and intellect, will feel a total peace when it hears the truths of the Creator. That feeling is there to help man separate dark from Light and Truth from distortions. I leave you with that internal protection and with these ideas to ponder. Remember, it is possible for you through meditation to communicate fully with the Creator. It is only the constraints of your own mental conditioning that limit you in this gift of instantaneous communication with the Creator.

"The Captain"

[The Captain then explained the message was for Donald Ware.]

## THEODORA'S COMMENT ON GULF BREEZE

What we investigators call phase two of the Gulf Breeze sightings was an 18-month period when alien vehicles appeared for the Gulf Breeze Research Team about 180 times. They normally appeared as distant red lights or orange balls and provided an opportunity for many people from several countries to observe and photograph them. They stopped on July 4, 1992, after an appearance just before the fireworks display started. I asked Yvonne Cole to ask THEODORA why they stopped, and the response included this statement:

"The ships over Gulf Breeze have not stopped. Their missions run regularly on schedule, but they are cloaking themselves of late to protect themselves from the watchful eyes of those who are not of pure intent. As a man of military background, you will appreciate the need for breaking any patterns that might allow those who wish us harm to hone in on. We are not without our enemies, and not all are in human form.

"We shall return visibly in the very near future with a surprise for all the faithful at the bridge."

The very next night, August 7, 1992, Dr. Bruce Maccabee and other scientists were on the beach south of Pensacola with the "faithful" local researchers. A bluish-white light 2-3 inches in diameter came down the beach and passed 10 feet above Bruce Morrison's head. It blinked on and off, changed direction at the end of the parking lot, and was detected in the microwave range on the scientists' recorders. That same night a similar ball of light was seen by Vicki Lyons, another member of the research team, as it moved down her hall into the bedroom of her house guest, "Kathy Davis". Two days later the house was watched all night from outside. A similar ball of light was seen to enter, and "Davis" said it came into her room. When it brushed against her cheek she felt a definite intelligence associated with it. Perhaps these events did verify the statements made by THEODORA on August 6th.

## CLASSIC BOOKS FROM A HIGHER INTELLIGENCE

There have been vast amounts of information acquired by human beings through telepathic processes for thousands of years. Many books of this nature are now sold in book stores, and some are recognized as true classics. Although such classics are also found in the literature of the Eastern Hemisphere, I will just mention six produced in the West.

PARTS OF THE BIBLE

My friend, Tom Boyle, did some research in *The Holy Bible* and found 56 chapters that he felt referred to telepathy or channeling. For example, Luke 2:9, describes what happened to the shepherds in Bethlehem when Jesus was born. It says, 'An angel appeared to them and the glory of the Lord shown on them, and they were filled with fear. And the angel said to them, "Be not afraid, for behold, I bring you good news..." I suspect this communication was telepathic, because that is the way angels (or messengers) "speak" to people today. I know personally about seventy people who have been on board IAC, and most of them, at some point, were told, "Do not be afraid."

Here is a quote from Matthew 10:19-20, where Jesus is speaking to his disciples. "When they deliver you up [to the councils and governors] do not be anxious how you are to speak or what you are to say; for what you are to say will be given to you in that hour; for it is not you who speak but the spirit of your Father speaking through you." Think about that. Does that mean that Jesus told his disciples they would be channeling? I think it does.

In the Old Testament in 1 Kings 19:9, it says, "And then he came to a cave and lodged there; and behold, the word of the Lord came to him, and he said to him, "What are you doing here, Elijah?" I suspect that the "word of the Lord" is far more common than many people think.

The Book of Acts describes visions by Ananias, by Cornelius, and by Paul. Matthew, Chapter 2 describes Joseph's dream, and Daniel describes his own dream in Chapter 7. I suspect these were visions and dreams with a purpose, perhaps inspired by their spirit guides telepathically.

In Psalms 94:11, it says, "The Lord knows the thoughts." Earlier, I said my friend, Katharina Wilson, was told by aliens they know my every move and thought.

In Revelations, John apparently experienced several forms of telepathic communications, including an out-of-body experience. Chapter 4 starts, "After this I looked, and lo, in heaven an open door! And the first voice, which I had heard speaking to me like a trumpet, said, 'Come up hither, and I will show what must take place after this.' At once I was in the spirit, and lo, a throne stood in heaven..." He goes on to describe meeting 24 elders.

I think that religious leaders and ufologists today should not be so afraid of telepathic communications. I have found that most of them contain more wisdom than most human writings; and, like human writings, some is garbage. We each have to choose what is meaningful to us.

## THE KORAN

In the year 610 AD, Mohammed had repeated encounters with an angel thought to be Gabriel as he meditated in a cave near Mecca. Through Mohammed, all 78,000 words of the *Koran* were transcribed over a period of 22 years. Mohammed was an illiterate camel driver and shepherd who had recently married a wealthy older woman, and the words he spoke to the scribe were considered to be the word of God. Perhaps his words were accepted as the word of God because he was illiterate. I wonder if he was channeling. The *Koran* was a unifying force that stopped the continual bloody wars of the desert tribes of that time.

## OAHSPE

OAHSPE[3] is a word meaning earth (O), sky (AH), and spirit (SPE). It is a history of the human experience on the earth and in the heavens associated with the earth. It is written from the perspective of the Gods. It covers the period of Lemuria and Atlantis and the progression to the current technological period. Most of the 884 pages of my 1935 edition have a horizontal line across the center of the page. Below the line is a history of events on the surface of the planet, and above the line is a description of the events taking place in the heavens associated with earth. I found it interesting that occasionally interaction by the higher Gods, in both arenas, was necessary to ensure the continued evolution of the human soul.

The manner in which OAHSPE was written should be considered. Dr. John Ballou Newbrough was an American with degrees in medicine and dentistry. He was also a seeker of spiritual truth. In 1871, an "angel" appeared before Dr. Newbrough and asked if he would stop eating meat, fowl, and fish for 10 years. He agreed. Ten years later the angel instructed him to buy a typewriter. Typewriters had just been invented. On January 1, 1887, he was awakened at night and asked to sit with his fingers on the keys. Something seemed to control his fingers, causing him to type several pages. He was asked to place them face down and not look at them until told to do so. He was awakened one hour before sunrise for the next 350 nights to type several pages in the dark. When he had 1008 pages he was told to read them and publish them. The first edition was published in 1882.

This book has been advertised as the world's most challenging book. It may be. Before you start, I recommend you study both the glossary and index to familiarize yourself with the strange words used.

## THE URANTIA BOOK

Urantia is a word meaning planet Earth. This book was published in 1955 by The Urantia Foundation. It contains information acquired telepathically during the preceding several years. No human author is acknowledged because the Foundation wants the book to be judged by its own content. It contains over 2000 pages of information with many scientific explanations. As with OAHSPE, there are study groups that meet to discuss and digest the information. I have not read this entire book, but I did read Joe Dundovic's 1981 lecture about it to a Unitarian church. The book is about many things. In one paragraph Joe said, "The life of Jesus is described year by year, including the years of his twenties when he traveled with caravans to the centers of Greece, Rome, Carthage, Crete, and Mesopotamia. It agrees in general with the four gospels except for the additional details. Basically, the teachings of Jesus stress the Fatherhood of God and the Brotherhood of Man, and that if we truly relate to each other, person to person and nation to nation, as brothers, then strife and bickering will cease. Concerning wars, national sovereignty is blamed for causing them, and the following statement summarizes the discussion of the paper entitled *Political Sovereignty*."

"Peace will not come to Urantia until every so-called sovereign nation surrenders its power to make war into the hands of a representative government of all mankind. Political sovereignty is innate with the peoples of the world. When all the peoples of Urantia create a world government, they have the right and the power to make such a government SOVEREIGN: and when such a representative or democratic world power controls the world's land, air and Naval forces, peace on earth and good will among man can prevail—but not until them." (p. 1489)

## THE KEYS OF ENOCH

*The Keys of Enoch* is another thick book of 564 pages with another 48 pages of glossary. It contains a lot of Hasidic and new-age language, so you should study the glossary first. It was first published by James J. Hurtak in 1973, and is now published by The Academy for Future Science. Hurtak's 12-page introduction starts with these two paragraphs:

"While I was in the act of prayer calling upon the Name of the Father, asking to know the meaning of life and for what reason I was called into the world, my room suddenly became full of a different type of light. And in the presence of this 'Light' a great being stood before me who announced that he was Master Ophanim Enoch. This being had so much Love and Light, I felt as if I were a child in the presence of this divine Master Ophanim.

"The being asked if I were ready to go with him into the Father's midst, and I said I was. And with that, a great field of Light was placed around my body and I sped upwards into the heavens; first into a region of stars called Merak and Muscida. And while I was in this region of the heavens, I was told about the earth and my temporal homeland upon the earth."

Hurtak's introduction ends with this sentence, "The opportunity to walk like Enoch with The Most High is now extended to all peoples!"

## A COURSE IN MIRACLES

*A Course in Miracles* was acquired by Helen Schucman, through a telepathic process in 1975. It is published by The Foundation for Inner Peace. It was reviewed by Willis Harmon, President of the Institute of Noetic Sciences. He wrote, "Although the Course deals with the same discoverable psychological and spiritual truths as the New Testament, it presents them in a form that is harder to evade because it is more specific and less liable to various interpretations, and also because the psychological exercises employed are so effective in helping us elude our normal defenses against self-discovery." I have not taken the course, but I think it helps people to perceive reality from the perspective of their soul and to avoid being caught up in a lot of unpleasant human dramas. The course is taught at some churches in our area.

## CONCLUSION

I would like to close with Carl Sagan's statement on science and theology from his 1986 book, *Contact*, p. 142:

"There were many interpretations of Scripture and many interpretations of the natural world. Both were created by God, so both must be mutually consistent. Wherever a discrepancy seems to exist, either a scientist or a theologian—maybe both—hasn't been doing his job."

## REFERENCES

1. *The RA Material:* L/L Research, P.O. Box 5195, Louisville, KY 40255, $11.50

2. YC 1-ASHTAR (two-tape set) available from Connecting Link, 9392 Whitneyville Road, Alto, MI 49302-9989, $19.23.

3. *OAHSPE:* New Leaf Distributors, (800) 326-2665, $30.50.

## ⊕ John Hunter Gray, Ph.D.

*John Hunter Gray, Ph.D.*

Dr. Gray has recently reclaimed his original family name replacing his adoptive name, John R. Salter, Jr. He is Professor Emeritus American Indian Affairs at the University of North Dakota. Of Micmac/Abenaki/Mohawk and Scottish ancestry, he grew up in Northern Arizona. He was involved for forty years in community organizing in the Southwest, the South, Chicago, upstate New York, the Plains, interspersed with college and university teaching. Conscious involvement in ET matters began in 1988, with now famous and very friendly CEIII and IV experiences in Wisconsin and Illinois. He is a spokesperson for the friendly view of ET encounters and interaction. John authored the book, *Jackson, Mississippi* and the monograph, *An Account of the Salter UFO Encounters*, and many articles. He is married and has four children.

# Thoughts On Fear, Extraterrestrials, and Healthy Minds

*John Hunter Gray was invited to the Conference to participate as a member of the Fear Panel. Unfortunately, a family medical emergency kept him from attending the Conference. He is well known in the UFO community as John R. Salter, Jr. Recently he reclaimed his original family name. His father, an American Indian on both sides of his family, was born Frank Gray—but was adopted and partially raised by a family named Salter. Gray, the original family name, is Scottish, but now thoroughly Indianized over many generations. Hunter is a name from his mother's side. By any name, John is a thoughtful participant and observer of the UFO scene. In this paper the reader will discover an interesting parallel to the recent attack on John Mack's academic freedom at Harvard. The forces of ignorance and defenders of the status quo appear to be equally distributed across the nation.*

As an agitator and somewhat unconventional academic, I am taking the liberty of avoiding the format of a purely "proper" tome and instead I am doing this rather informally.

It has been seven years since the March 20-21, 1988, UFO encounter experiences of myself and my son John III. Since then, a great deal of recall has occurred with me. Some of this has involved three previously submerged encounters in 1941, 1952 and 1957. John III also has had much recall. The many positive physiological changes which began in me following the 1988 experiences, and several in my son, are continuing.

We see all of this, including the ETs, their motivations and their effects as very friendly and positive. We certainly hope and expect to see them again. I have written about our experiences in: *An Account of the Salter UFO Encounters of March 1988: Their Background, Development, and Ramifications*; and "Extraterrestrial Contact and Human Social Justice Sensitivity and Action," (International Association for New Science, 1992), and "No Intelligence Life is Alien to Me," *Contract Forum*, July/August 1993.

A few portions of this last article are incorporated into this paper.

Most of the people I have met or from whom I have heard who have had convincing CE III or CE IV experiences share a positive view.

I am not a naive, starry-eyed creature. A half-breed Indian who grew up in Northern Arizona, I have encountered various forms of danger and much violence from early years on. Some of this was in deadly and sanguinary settings. A few examples: I have been shot at, been on the Klan's death lists in the Deep South of the 1960s, sustained serious injuries following an assassination attempt, and lived through comparable targeting in Chicago and elsewhere. For reasons comprehensible to itself, the FBI listed me on its high priority sheet of dangerous agitators, Section A of the Reserve Index, while I was in my early 20s.

In sum, I have had my share of "earned paranoia" garnered long before my first <u>conscious</u> UFO perceptions in 1988. But I have always known that you cannot let fear turn you around. You have to proceed ahead, step-by-step, never recklessly, often deliberately, occasionally with dispatch.

To Leo Sprinkle and Betty Hill I am greatly indebted. I connected with them early after our 1988 experiences. Their good sense and positive, forward-looking analysis and vision have been a great help to me and to my family. This points up the needs always for ethical, sensible, and effective mutually supportive relationships anywhere on life's trail.

188

Early on I encountered the writings of the "doom and gloomers." These bleak souls, sometimes crudely and sometimes with relative finesse, proclaim various degrees of alien perfidy. This includes Lucifer, underground bases, sexual mesmerization and obsession, and half-breed takeovers. This material is variously presented by obvious extremists and occasionally in the clothing of ostensible moderates. They offer little or no evidence. Indeed, their contentions fly in the face of the overwhelmingly non-fearful and usually positive perceptions of genuine CE III and CE IV experiencers.

There is in American culture a paranoid tradition. Perhaps this is also generally true for much of contemporary human, mass populated urban/industrial culture. I am convinced this has a great deal to do with imperialism, certain kinds of corporate capitalism, government bureaucracy, guilt, and interpersonal and value alienation. I have addressed this in "Reflections on Ralph Chaplin, the Wobblies, and Organizing in the Save the World Business—Then and Now" (*The Pacific Historian [Special Issue: Voices of Western Labor]*, Summer 1986).

A gloom-doom case in point is sociologist Ron Westrum's strange article in the October 1989 issue of the *MUFON Journal*, "Abduction Research: The Challenge Ahead." In this article he talks about vast numbers of "abduction." Personally, I see these encounters as rare, but not super-rare. Westrum warns ominously of intellectuals and artists who may be witting and unwitting tools of the aliens. His concern is that in Hollywood and elsewhere they are creating a situation where "we are bathed in a sea of abduction-infected thoughts, emotions, and messages." He cites as examples the films *ET* and *Close Encounters of the Third Kind*. Shades of the Red Scares earlier in this century!

In an exchange of letters a few years ago with UFO abduction researcher Budd Hopkins, I commented: "When you use terms like 'deception,' 'disturbing,' 'lies,' 'dangerous,' 'subversive'—under titles such as 'What They're Doing to Us' and *Intruders*; imply that those of us who have a positive view of all of this (and we are a great many indeed) have simply been programmed in a Machiavellian sense: well, it's very obvious where you stand."

Another example of the sinister view involves the alleged alien bases. Claims have been made that some are located near Dulce, New Mexico and Sedona, Arizona. I know the Southwest well indeed. That is my home. The area around Dulce is Jicarilla Apache country. In this area are many Hispanic and Morman ranchers and farmers. It is tight and insular. There is no chance a sparrow could fall without being noted by half the population.

As far as the alien bases near Sedona are concerned, and the claim generally places them in Boynton Canyon, this is personally very interesting to me! My home town is Flagstaff, which is close by. In the 1950s I hunted in the upper reaches of that canyon and later trapped in the lower regions. Any ET who set up a base in that mess of boulders and pine log wreckage would need a psychiatrist. A few miles west of there is an ideal area for a base if the ETs really wanted one—which I am sure they do not. The people who write glibly of Boynton Canyon don't know the secluded area to the west and hopefully never will. They really don't know anything about the entire region.

Going deeper into some of the specifics of the paranoid cant, I have some observations about the setting of some of the scared people. I am convinced that those who are frightened of UFOs and ETs come mostly from backgrounds where people are inclined to be afraid of anything strange. These would be people from urban/industrial settings, enmeshed in interpersonal alienation, subject to high crime rates, afraid of anything after dark and often caught up in just plain racial bias. From the late 1960s well into the 1970s, I directed the grassroots organization of almost 300 block-clubs in Southside Chicago. I know whereof I speak. I saw the same thing in only a little more relaxed Rochester, New York, in the late 1970s when I directed Catholic social justice activities for that diocese.

Let us take a closer look at race. In various television programs by gloom-doomers, e.g., Hopkins, the term "abduction" is always used. Some "abductees" often refer to the "aliens" as "so ugly." This reminds one of just how racist some human views can be. I remember whites perceiving a group of blacks (in this case, nice black college kids) as "mean looking" and "dangerous." In another situation, some whites observing a group of vigorous American Indians of various ages and backgrounds commented that "they all look so much alike, I couldn't tell one from another," and "they are so impassive, so stolid and solemn."

A certain amount of fear, I suppose, is involved for some people observing UFOs and ETs in CE III and CE IV situations. When this occurs, the fear generally passes quickly enough unless the wrong kind of researchers and/or the wrong kind of hypnosis establishes a dogmatic fix at the fear point. I appear to have been initially frightened when my first encounter experience occurred at age 7 in 1941. But I was not very frightened at all in 1952 and not a bit in 1957 and 1988. My son, who appears to have had only the 1988 encounter, took his cues from me.

Fear, of course, can be big business. What Hollywood did to the very bona fide Travis Walton case provides a hell of a sad example. Walton, as many know, was one of several Northern Arizona woodcutters who, in 1975, accidentally encountered a hovering ET craft. Going closer to it, Walton was "beamed up" into the craft while his more cautious companions fled. Aboard, the frightened Walton seems to have been treated well and several days later was gently returned to the proximity of a town not far from the encounter.

His account remained reasonably prosaic and laid-back until several years ago. Then Hollywood produced a film, *Fire in the Sky,* ostensibly based upon the case. It was thorough distortion. The ETs, who in reality had been non-hostile, calm, and matter-of-factly professional, were depicted in the movie as quasi-insects, diabolically hideous creatures operating a craft littered with rotting pieces of humans. Walton's home town, Snowflake, was mostly Mormon. In fact, they had shown a fair amount of open-mindedness about the original event in 1975. In the movie they were depicted as a nest of red-neck bigots. I happen to have nieces and nephews who are members of the Church of Latter Day Saints in that general Northern Arizona setting, and know the region very well.

I am a long-time community organizer. Like all good organizers, the ETs are working at the grassroots. I very much believe they are involved in a long-term endeavor which is focused on: (a) helping some people on this Earth "keep on keeping on" in the Save the World business, and (b) sensitizing humanity, on a step-by-step basis, with regard to the presence of friendly ET life in our solar neighborhood. To the gloom-doomers, whoever and whatever, I question. If the alien intent is interest in securing our "genetic materials" for selfish reasons, why weren't they getting those 100 years ago, or further back than that? Physiologically, the people of Earth were no different then, or 25,000 years ago, than they are now. If the ETs are building toward a takeover of Earth (and what rational being would want to run this mess?), then why go to the trouble of a mass half-breed creation? Why not take over at any point prior, say, to 1914, when relatively all we had were bows and arrows? There may indeed be some ET/human half-breeds. In fact, I am quite certain that there are. Whenever races and cultures begin coming together, half-breeds play important, often very critical, roles.

It seems very probable that the social/political system or systems of the ETs are democratic and strike a balance between collective and individual well being. To do this they would be drawing from the best of the group and the best of the individual creativity. A significant indication that their ethos is not authoritarian lies in the occasional reports of disagreements between crew members and leaders. More to the point, they could never have accomplished what they have attained and are attaining if they have a totalitarian or "hive" super-collective mentality, or are individualistic in a cutthroat fashion. They are distinctive, individual personalities, working together.

Ultimately, the ETs can offer us many things. Among them are health advances and much longer life which, in turn, will help us, the human race, grow up and mature as a people. But one of the most valuable gifts would be insights, not formulas, into balancing collective and individual well-being. We can, I am sure, offer them many worthwhile things, both tangible and intangible.

Most of the CE III and CE IV experiencers from whom I have heard are involved in meaningful social justice pursuits. For example, the enhancement of the human condition with respect to material, libertarian, and spiritual factors, and involvement in environmental and ecological positive activities. Others are active in the formulation of non-violent approaches to human problems.

Cosmic citizenship, sensitization and good works, for us make up the only logical explanation for ET involvement.

It certainly seems clear that the long-term sensitization endeavors of the ETs are, step-by-step, proceeding effectively. Belief levels in the United States have climbed over the decades to the point where a majority of U.S. citizens believe some UFOs to be real in the extraterrestrial sense. After our 1988 experiences I slowly began talking openly about them. This surprised some people who were aware that I had never shown a whit of conscious interest in the subject. I had, as things developed, no problem of any sort with most people who were quite open-minded, often interested, and not afraid. This includes genuine liberals, conservatives, Christians of various kinds (including many fundamentalists), and non-Christians. The most problematic folks have fallen into two categories: the narrow kind of "secular humanist" (not the William James sort who always sees a pluralistic universe), but the deep-down-into-the-dark-canyon person who has not really had a new idea in 50 years or so, and does not want anyone else to have one. The other category is the person who isn't afraid of the UFO/ET topic itself, but who is scared of what he/she thinks other people may think of him or her if too much interest is revealed.

At the request of the University of North Dakota students, in the Fall of 1990, I began teaching a three semester hour undergraduate course called "UFOs, ETs and Close Encounters." All of the students had heard of my experiences, and although I made no secret of my position, I vigorously encouraged active skepticism. The course boomed. This is a tribute to the total lack of fear and the genuine open-mindedness of younger people, and some older ones as well. I taught the full semester-long version of the class four times and at each run it drew about 180 students from 65 different majors, heavy from the sciences and Aerospace Studies. I also taught a well-received version of the course on state-wide interactive television, and also did two non-credit mini-versions. It was the most popular elective course in the history of the university. At one point we brought the always excellent UFO researcher Stanton Friedman, to the university for a major lecture. Competing with the World Series, Stan drew almost 800 people, young and old, from school and community and hinterland, for a fascinating four hours. It was on a snowy night as well!

But there were enemies about. Behind the scenes, fear and jealousy sharpened knives. I was the only full time Native American regular faculty member, not only in the Indian Studies Department, but in the entire university. Eventually, after several years of increasingly open hostility from "colleagues" and some frightened administrators, I took early retirement and have gone on to other things.

Oddly, even though I publicized this unfortunate internal situation, and its attendant academic freedom issues, to the UFO community and its connections, none of the UFO research organizations nor their journals showed any tangible interest in the University of North Dakota situation and the plight of one of the country's first for-credit UFO/ET courses.

I am an optimist, and think things will work out well in the bigger panorama. There is no question in my mind but that, at some point down the trail, we and they—the not-really-so-alien ETs—will come together in mutually positive and productive intercourse. Thomas Merton, monk, priest, and theologian, recognized that (as John Donne had earlier put it) "no man is an island." Tribal religions have always seen the interrelationships between all components in the Universe.

Humanity always has, sooner or later in its long odyssey, put aside its irrational fear and learned to accept a great many new things. We can, and we will, accept our brothers and sisters in the Creator's Great Work as we all forge ahead with faith in ourselves, faith in our destiny, and faith in That which lies above and beyond all of the stars.

# ⊕ Elisabet Sahtouris, Ph.D.

*Elisabet Sahtouris, Ph.D.*

Dr. Sahtouris is an American Greek geobiologist, futurist and author of *GAIA: The Human Journey from Chaos and Cosmos*. She is a co-founder of the Worldwide Indigenous Science Network, and a consulting expert on indigenous peoples for the United Nations, Geneva. She has lectured and appeared on radio and television in North, Central and South America, and in Europe. Dr. Sahtouris worked with the NOVA-Horizon science series produced by WGBH/BBC TV, and has taught at the Massachusetts Institute of Technology and the University of Massachusetts. She has lived extensively in Greece, and now resides in Peru where she is assisting in the developement of an Andean/Amazon Institute of Indigenous Culture.

# Expanding Our World View To Other Dimensions

*On the subjects of the prominence and irreducible spiritual component of the other-dimensional phenomena that Cosmic Cultures present, Dr. Sahtouris' presentation was prescient of the attitudes later revealed in the responses to the questionnaire completed by over 100 of the participants in the conference.*

## INTRODUCTION

Experiences and reports of other-dimensional and other-planetary encounters here on planet Earth are still strange to most people. So strange, in fact, that many, if not most people in industrial cultures, do not even believe they occur. But this failure of belief is in turn strange to cultures outside western scientific/industrial culture, to whom other dimensions are as familiar as the basic four of spacetime.

It is not my intention to try to prove the reality of such encounters. I merely wish to explain why our culture finds them either strange or incredible—i.e., not believable—while other cultures find them normal. For when something is strange, it tends to inspire fear and hostility, and one purpose of this conference is to shift our attitudes away from fear and hostility to a reasonable human warmth and welcome of other-dimensional and other-planetary cultures, not to mention *this*-planetary human cultures different from our own.

## MORE THAN FOUR DIMENSIONS

What I *would* like to show is that the universe is composed of ten or more dimensions, known to most cultures, while the western scientific worldview limits itself to four. This limitation necessarily obscures most of the existing universe. When phenomena of other dimensions insistently intrude on the four-dimensional world, they are seen as magical, miraculous, fearful or dangerous, or they are denied existence and thus viewed as the fantasies of disturbed minds. Readers familiar with "Flatland," the hypothetical world of two dimensions, will recall how magical the passing of a three-dimensional ball through that world appears: a point appears from nowhere, expands into an ever-growing disc, then shrinks back to nothing and disappears. There is no way in a two-dimensional world to properly perceive or explain a three-dimensional phenomena. Likewise, fifth-dimensional phenomena (such as Sai Baba's materialization of objects from apparently thin air, for example) are mysterious and inexplicable to those who live in a four-dimensions-only world. And so, if inter-dimensional visitors suddenly appear in our skies and then disappear again, we find it hard to accept them as real. Should we encounter beings who simply "cannot be here," we are likely to encounter them with fear and hostility. This will continue to be the case until we can accept the normalcy of passage in and out of our four dimensions from or by way of others.

What do I mean by "from or by way of other dimensions?" Most people nowadays do believe that there must be other star systems that have planets with intelligent inhabitants. Serious scientists such as Carl Sagan and many others have for some time been engaged in various projects trying to contact them. I share the belief that they exist, but I believe that the only way they can transport themselves about the universe is by entering and exiting other dimensions that have no spacetime limitations. It is simply not possible to travel the distances involved in three-dimensional ships using three-dimensional fuels. I further believe that the only way they are likely to communicate over interstellar distances is by using other dimensions for that purpose as well. That is, they will communicate telepathically, as is the experience of most contactees, or by some other interdimensional technology. They will not communicate by signals discernible to radio telescope, as in our projects still being initiated—the biggest and newest begun in Australia within the past year. Such projects will likely seem very primitive to those we are trying to contact.

To sum up, interdimensional and interplanetary travels and communications are not possible, in my opinion, within a four-dimensional world.

## MORE THAN ONE SCIENCE

Interestingly, we pursue these very expensive technological communications attempts on the assumption that our present-day material technology is far superior to anything so-called "primitive peoples" could have developed. Yet, through my work with indigenous people, I have come to believe that those who have had the longest history of interstellar or cosmic communications and travel are in fact indigenous peoples without any kind of *material* technology. They have been practicing such communications and travels for thousands of years, and to such an extent that they are a normal part of life in many cultures.

It is of the utmost importance, from a number of perspectives, for us to combat our own prejudices in believing western science to be the only, or the most superior, science of all human cultures. For western science is a newcomer on the world scene, and an upstart newcomer to boot. In its immaturity, however brilliant, it has lacked even the wisdom to ensure that the basis of human life is conserved. This puts into question whether the destructive technological culture it has spawned can be legitimately considered an intelligent culture. Perhaps extraterrestrials are studying us to answer this puzzling question: are Earth humans an intelligent species or not?

As a trained western scientist who has become ever more aware of the limitations of my own science, I have looked at length to the sciences of other, much older, cultures, including many indigenous cultures. I now live in the South American Andes, where, for example, the extent an ancient agricultural experiment, ecological understanding and sustainable development exceeds that of any other culture in the history of the world. Most of the world's food today is the product of this Andean science, yet it continues to be unrecognized as such by the dominant scientific culture, to the great disadvantage of all the world. Andean agricultural science, if practiced by the world at large, might well make the difference between the survival or extinction of our human species over the next few decades.

However, our concern here is with other aspects of such sciences, in particular with their acknowledgment of a more-than-four dimensional world. But before we can consider whether those sciences or ours are right about this cosmic composition, I would like to give you a glimpse of what it is like to live and work within such non-western sciences, and be disrespected by the dominant western scientists.

In the introduction to Carlos Milla Villena's book, *Genesis de al Cultura Andina* (Fondo Editorial C.A.P. Coleccion Bienal, Lima, 1983), Salvador Palomino and Javier Lajo write, as I have translated it into English, the following passage:

"Does Andean science exist? It has always been considered in the circles that manage Western culture that other cultures either have not had a scientific development or that their systematized knowledge has been so poor that it was easily assimilated into the hegemonous world culture. Thus it is in America, particularly in the Andean region which in ancient times was based in Tawantinsuyo [the name of the Inka nation, meaning 'four directions or parts'].

"Among the principle causes of this undervaluation of the non-Western, we can identify ignorance of other cultures, but there also exists, without a shadow of a doubt, an accumulation of prejudices which, as principles or dogmas, the West uses to preserve its senile hegemony. Principles that when applied to the study of occidental reality explain it objectively, but when applied to non-Western realities degenerate into norms or molds whose narrow frameworks attempt vainly to repress objective phenomena or knowledge that escape the rationality and the methods of the West. What these principles cannot make simple, is denied, silenced, or disqualified as obscurantism, esotericism, charlatanism or witchcraft.

". . . As is logical and customary, with the publication of this book we expect, without disdain, and proud reaction of the ordinary Western person. . . we hope for a positive reaction, a calm and high dialogue, as is suited to their own high station, with the priests of the northern sciences."

Put ourselves into the position of people who practice a science vastly older than our own, which has long *known* things western scientists are just beginning to discover and are claiming as though they were *not* known before. Then we should be able to sympathize with the nature and tone of this critique.

Western science limits not only its own reality or worldview, but presumes to limit science itself, as a human endeavor, to its own practitioners. In other words, it acknowledges no other science as valid or even possible. It should not surprise us that this attitude is seen as intolerably arrogant by the scientists of other cultures. In recognition of the importance of this issue—of whether science is unique to the "west" or whether different sciences exist legitimately—let us look briefly at the west's own definition of science.

*Science* is defined by Merriam Webster's Collegiate Dictionary (10th edition, 1993) as "the state of knowing" or "a department of systematized knowledge as an object of study." This definition certainly includes the knowledge of most indigenous cultures as well as the more urban knowledge on non-western cultures around the world, past and present (all of which we intend by "non-western cultures" from here on).

The American Heritage Unabridged Dictionary of the English Language (3rd edition, 1992) defines science as "the observation, identification, description, experimental investigation and theoretical explanation of phenomena." A bit more precise, yet a good description of what non-western cultures have done that is appropriately dignified with the label "science." As defined by the Oxford English Dictionary, science is "the state of knowing," or "knowledge as opposed to belief or opinion," knowledge, that is, "acquired by study." The OED continues explaining that science is "in a more restricted sense: a branch of study which is concerned either with a connected body of demonstrated truths or with observed facts systematically classified and more or less colligated by being brought under general laws, and which include trustworthy methods for the discovery of new truth within its own domain."

Detailed as this definition is, there is nothing in it to exclude indigenous and other non-western sciences. So let us proceed to discuss other cultures with due respect for their sciences, and greater impartiality in judging which culture's sciences have the best explanatory power for describing human experience. If we are to encounter other-planetary and other-dimensional cultures with respect and good will, let us practice encountering those of our own Earth which differ from our cultures with the same respect and good will.

## How Many Dimensions?

As far as I know, no culture has ever recognized fewer than three physical dimensions extended by motion into a fourth we call "time." That puts western culture at the minimalist end of the scale. At the other end of the scale, some cultures may posit an infinite number of cosmic dimensions, but the usual range is from seven to less than twenty.

The exact number of dimensions beyond the familiar four is not important to this discussion, but the existence, as reality, of other dimensions is critical. This is because the Cosmic Cultures we are here discussing necessarily exist, as we have said, in these other dimensions or pass through them in order to move about the cosmos from one three-dimensional location to another. Again, if other dimensions do not exist, I know of no reasonable way that there could be sophisticated interplanetary communications and other forms of encounter between different star systems.

Now I will propose *that such communications and encounter in or via other dimensions is essential to a living Cosmos*, which I believe our universe to be. In light of this, it is worth trying to understand the normalcy of the multi-dimensional universe in other cultures, and the reluctance of western science to accept a multi-dimensional universe.

## Separation/Integration

The method of western science is the analysis of natural phenomena by isolating them from their context (that is, into laboratories whenever possible) and dissecting them into their component parts. Parts are everything to western science. No wonder, then, that the west sees the natural world as an assembly of parts into a kind of giant three-dimensional mechanism with moving parts, and our constructed human society as an assembly of parts, such as politics, economics, science, art, industry, agriculture, education, etc, etc.

Let me sidetrack for just a moment to illustrate this. Last year, here in Washington D.C., the President's Council on Sustainable Development met and discussed whether or not economics should be part of their discussion. No one doubts that ecology is essential to a discussion of sustainable human life, but highly educated and well-positioned members of this eminent group were seriously asking what has economics got to do with ecology? As a Greek, I could only respond that *ecology* literally means the organization of the world "household" (from *logos*, organization and *oikos*, household) while economics literally means the law of the household (from *nomos*, law and *oikos*, household). Clearly one cannot separate the law of a "household" from its organization. Imagine, for example, trying to understand the laws by which your body functions without understanding how your body is organized, or vice versa.

What I am trying to do is clarify the difference between a culture that works at understanding the world mechanically, that is, by separating it into parts, and cultures that work to understand the world organically, that is, through its inseparable interrelationships. My Tewa friend, Dr. Greg Cahete, from the Santa Clara Pueblo in New Mexico, author of *Look to the Mountain: an Ecology of Indigenous Education*, (Kivaki Press, Durango, CO, 1994), has put it this way. The white man isolates parts of nature in laboratories to study them because he wants to control them, while the native person goes out into nature to study it because he wants to integrate himself harmoniously with it. Only out in nature, where the phenomena under study are not torn from their contexts, is it possible to understand the vital interrelationships of parts or aspects of nature?

Even as a western scientist I have come to understand the Earth and all the Cosmos to be alive, which means among other things that no part of it can live without the rest. I want to integrate myself harmoniously with the rest of nature and want to see the rest of my human species do likewise so that we can all survive harmoniously within it.

## EARTH LIFE

I will not go into great detail to show that the Earth is a living planet within a self-creating living Cosmos, as I have done that in my book *GAIA: the Human Journey from Chaos to Cosmos* (Simon & Schuster Pocketbooks, New York, 1989). This book is now difficult to find in English except for an expanded version called *Earthlife: Our Life*, available free of charge through the electronic network TMT—The Moccasin Telegraph—(inquire Michelle, mosa@netcom.com). Let me briefly give the essence of the argument.

Teachers of biology used to teach a list of properties of living things to distinguish them from non-living things. This list included such properties as irritability (reactivity), mobility, growth and reproduction. A few decades ago, two Chilean biologists, Humberto Maturana and Fransisco Varela, gave us our first basic definition of life as *autopoiesis*, a Greek word meaning "self-creation." The definition that goes by this name is as follows: A living entity is one that continually creates it own parts. Note that this basic definition says nothing about growth or reproduction, which may or may not be properties of a living system. Some of you may be happy to know that you can be alive whether you reproduce or not. In any case, this definition seems to apply admirably well to our planet Earth, which scientists used to think of not as a living entity, but as a non-living geological ball upon the surface of which, by some miracle, life sprang from non-life.

Now we know that the Earth constantly creates itself from the inside out. Lava erupts from its molten insides to form new rock, while old rock is eroded, carried to the oceans and remelted at the subduction zones of tectonic plates, where the edge of one slides beneath the edge of another. This great recycling system of magma to rock to magma is joined by those of Earth's waters and atmosphere as the sources of endless creativity, endless supplies of materials to be incorporated into microbes, plants and animals. The entire planet regulates its temperature like a warm-blooded creature, which indeed it can be seen to be, as well as regulating the delicate chemical balance in the composition of its atmosphere, seas and soils, further evidence that it is a great living cell or body. Note well that it can function as such only because all its parts are in constant communication and because of the ceaseless planetwide flow of its energy and materials. Life will never evolve naturally on one part of a planet; planets either come to life as wholes or do not come to life at all.

The statement that the Earth is alive is, to me, not a hypothesis or theory, as in the case of the Gaia Hypothesis of James Lovelock. Rather it is a conceptualization to replace the conceptualization of the Earth as a non-living mechanism. By the *autopoiesis* definition of life, the Earth is indeed alive, and not a machine or collection of machines.

## COSMIC LIFE

If the Earth is alive, can we not assume that other planets as well have come alive? Our known four-dimensional Solar system was born from the scattered gaseous materials of a Supernova some five billion years ago. It is generally accepted that only one of its planets came alive and remained alive from this four-dimensional perspective (leaving open the possibility of life in other dimensions associated with the other planets). I like to think that the Cosmos scatters planets like star seed, much as plants and animals here below scatter *their* seed. In both cases, only few seeds in this prolific venture of life actually come to life themselves—those that land in the right conditions to support life. And so it makes sense that only a few of many planets can come to life—"a few" meaning untold billions given the scope of the universe.

What about the stars that give birth to these planets? A star is a self-organizing entity, keeping itself alive by drawing in new material and sloughing off old, with a series of life stages often ending in its explosive reproduction as a new star system including planets. And what about entities larger than stars? A protogalactic cloud itself is a huge whirlpool of gaseous matter. Now a whirlpool, whether in a river or in outer space, is an entity that takes in matter, holds it in a more-or-less constant form, and ejects matter no longer needed. In other words, it is the simplest form of a living entity that constantly creates itself! A galaxy is a protogalactic cloud that has elaborated itself into a more complex living entity. At every level of the four-dimensional universe, then, we see living entities, and so it makes sense to propose that the entire universe is and always has been a living, self-creating entity. One of the great advantages of doing so is that we need no longer pursue that endless confusing search of western science to determine how life can come from non-life.

Note that all these arguments have been made within the four-dimensional worldview of western science. This self-creating universe or Cosmos seems quite logically to have begun with unity that gradually diversified, with simple cosmic whirlpools in which smaller whirlpools become stars, which in turn generate new stars and ultimately star systems including planets. Some of which in their own turn self-create as extremely complex material beings.

## Cosmic Interaction

If I am right that this cosmic evolutionary process has always been "of a piece," in other words, the natural evolution of a single great living entity, then it follows that the parts of the cosmos are essentially inseparable—note that I do not say interconnected, as is usual, but inseparable—in the same sense that the parts of your body are inseparable, no one of them capable of living on its own. And just as in your body the parts communicate with one another constantly—how else would the complex organization of all parts be possible?—So all parts of the Earth and of the entire Cosmos are necessarily in communications with one another. "As above, so below," so to speak. The next question we face, then, is "How can this constant communication take place?" One requirement is intelligence, the prerequisite for coherent information exchange. Another is the means, the channels, by which such exchange can occur. Let us take these one at a time.

## Cosmic Intelligence in Western Science

With this model or conceptualization of the entire cosmos as a living entity containing the smaller living entities it continually creates, ideas of an intelligent universe begin to make much more sense than within the old mechanical model of a nonliving universe. In the old model the obvious intelligence of the universe could only be explained by proposing a *Deus ex-machina*, or God outside the great mechanism. God, its inventor, or as Descartes called him, "the Grand Engineer"—a God whose existence western science denied, while keeping the idea of His machinery, which led to an illogical science, since machinery by definition *cannot* exist without an inventor.

Now certain leading western scientists have been talking about the universal intelligence of the material world for some time, despite the "official" view that such notions are heretical. To wit, Nobel laureate George Wald, the Harvard biologist, in his foreword to L.J. Henderson's *The Fitness of the Environment*, has written that "A physicist is the atom's way of knowing about atoms." Quoting this in his article *Life and Mind in the Universe*, he continues, arguing that:

The stuff of this universe is ultimately mind-stuff. What we recognize as the material universe, the universe of space and time and elementary particles and energies, is then an avatar, the materialization of primal mind. In that sense, there is no waiting for consciousness to arise. It is there always.

Wald points out that in 1928, Eddington said "the stuff of the world is mind-stuff. Wolfgang Pauli suggesting in 1952 that "*physics* and *psyche* (i.e., matter and mind) could be seen as complementary aspects of the same reality." And von Weizacker in 1971 added that "consciousness and matter are different aspects of the same reality."

Note that these statements on the part of highly respected western scientists show the clear link between the notion of an intelligent universe and the existence of other dimensions. The "mind-stuff" of the universe is clearly not locatable in the basic four dimensions of space extended into time. For that matter, neither is any thought you have at any time, including your dreamtime, showing that all of us live in more than four dimensions night and day!

## New Dimensions in Western Science

In 1994, the theoretical physicist Michio Kaku's book *Hyperspace* (Oxford University Press, 1994) made waves with its proclamation that the deeply ingrained prejudice that our world consists only of three spatial dimensions and one of time is "about to succumb to the progress of science." Eloquently, and at length, he explains that the laws of nature, when expressed mathematically under the assumption of a four-dimensional world, are crude and unwieldy. At the same time, the elegance with which they can be expressed and united under the assumption of ten dimensions, is extremely strong evidence for the existence of these other dimensions.

Unfortunately, to this western scientist, the mathematical "existence" of these other dimensions is puzzling in that they appear very tightly curled, to the point of impenetrability, or inaccessibility. Physicists are actually suggesting we may have to blast our way into them, though that would require, they say, more power than we can presently generate on Earth. My friend Tanai Starr, a chemical engineer who learned nuclear physics from ETs claims this strange mathematical view of higher dimensions as due to the simple error of limiting the speed of light in higher dimensions as it is in fact limited in our familiar four. Whatever proves to be the case, western science is at least on the edge of acknowledging what other cultures have always taken as reality.

## Old Dimensions in Other Cultures

Adnanb Sarhan, a Sufi Master with whom I studied, says that "the universe, space and nature are the sources of intelligence and if you do not communicate with them, you cut yourself from the source of intelligence."

In Brazil, I spent time with Sapain, a *pajay* or medicine man of the Amazon *Xingu* nation to whom I gave a gift of sage from my island in Greece. He indicated to me that he wanted to sleep with, to dream with this plant. The following morning he came to me very excited, saying, "Your plant and my plant are so happy—they came so far to be together. They have been talking all night and still aren't finished." I asked him whether the trees in the Amazon talked with each other. "Of course," he said, "all the time!" When I asked what they talked about, he said, "They plot survival strategies." And will enough of them survive? I asked. "Yes," he said, though sadly, clearly feeling their painful struggle.

Macsuara Kajiwel, another Amazon friend with whom I traveled, told me that all natural beings, the trees, the herbs, the birds and animals are in constant dialogue and that humans need only to be quiet and listen to understand what is being said. Don Faustino, a ninety-year-old Andean elder showed me how rich the *Q'eswa* language is in the sounds of nature (what we call *onomatopoeia*) because it was given to *runakuna* (people) by the beings of nature whose language it first was.

These are various examples of how indigenous cultures see their natural world as an intelligent, intricately interconnected web of beings in constant communications with each other and with humans. They are the kind of examples often used by anthropologists to describe people considered to be less sophisticated than our "scientific" and technologically "advanced" society. They are the kind of examples used to identify "primitive animism," a worldview considered to be inferior and backwards. But these cultures, unbeknownst to most of us, look very seriously at us in turn and wonder about *our* backwardness, as in the following quote from Nicolas Aguilar Sayritupac's prologue to *Genesis de la Cultura Andina*, reprinted in full at the end of this article.

I know a little of the customs of the men who come from the place where the Sun puts itself down, and their mentality is as confused as a tangled ball of yarn as day by day they become more entangled without relief. . . The human being of the West has abandoned being human and has turned himself into an individual: man, woman, child, elder, separate; community has died in them, the "ayllu"—the essential unity of humanity. The existence of Western people and society has been destroyed by their egoism.

Please note this view of community as human, and individualism as non-human. The failure of community in the west is seen as the failure of human society as a living, loving interdependent system.

In the Andean culture, an example of the role other dimensions play in the daily life of ordinary communities lies in the all-pervasive coca ceremony which is an integral part of everyday life, of basic social amenities. (The World Health Organization [WHO] of the United Nations has clearly stated the health benefits of coca chewing to the Andean peoples and pointed out the dangers to them of making it illegal. Coca leaf should no more be confused with cocaine that should rye bread be confused with rye whiskey.) Catherine Allen, an anthropologist at George Washington University who has studied the Andean social role of coca intensively, points out in her book *The Hold Life Has*, that the social interaction of the coca ceremony includes not only the persons present but:

"entities immanent in the living Earth as well: Mother Earth, the Mountain Lords, the ancient dead. Understanding the nature of this communicative bond, forged by coca chewing, means exploring an attitude in which land is experienced as animate, powerful, and imbued with consciousness—a parallel society of Earth Persons with whom one is in constant interaction." (p. 25)

When you blow on coca leaves, performing *phukuy*, you blow their animating essence, their *sami*, into the Earth Mother, the *Pacha Mama*, or to the *Apus*, the mountain Lords, directing the *sami* to them by calling their names. In the same way, the *sami* of alcoholic beverages passes into the ground as you pour libations. *Sami* is also the animating, creative essence found in humans. In the Earth it is manifested physically as water and light. This animating essence *sami* is known in many cultures by many names, such as *prana* in India. In the Andes, as Allen describes, it is consciously directed by humans to other parts of nature in recognition that humans have received it and must circulate it. Thus we have a clear example of other-dimensional communications used consciously by humans.

When Amazon healers use the hallucinogen known widely as *ayahuasco* in the diagnosis of illnesses, they are facilitating their ability to see the other-dimensional aspects of the human body, also known as subtle bodies or auric, mental, psychic, etc., bodies in other cultures. Many cultures understand that illnesses begin in these other-dimensional bodies and can be cured there before they even manifest physically, and that curing illnesses in the physical body alone does not prevent their recurrence. The Brazilian/Peruvian healer, or *curandero*, Manual Cordova, whose biography has been written by Bruce Lamb (*Rio Tigre and Beyond: The Amazon Jungle Medicine of Manuel Cordova*, North Atlantic Books: Berkeley) worked in this way and was offered a chair in the Medical School at the University of Lima for his abilities to cure diseases incurable by western medicine, including that of the Chairman of the Medical School itself!

I could give innumerable other examples, as no doubt my readers can do as well. The point is that other-dimensional communications channels clearly exist among our various physical and subtle bodies, as well as between ourselves and the rest of nature. These are no doubt similar, at least in principal, to the communications channels that exist throughout the cosmos.

## Multi-dimensional Timespace in the Andes

If you imagine a woven fabric of a very complex pattern in ten colors, and then imagine that everything woven in six of the ten colors disappears, would you not miss most of the pattern? Western science, by limiting itself to acknowledging and exploring only four dimensions of a multi-dimensional reality, has been unable to perceive most of the universal pattern with its rich interconnections. The older Indian, Arabic, Chinese, Greek, Mayan, Inca and other indigenous sciences of the world had and still have a broader understanding of the multi-dimensional cosmos and thus were and are able to explore and use higher dimensions for many purposes, including those just cited. Yet the difference between the worldviews of western culture and others is far more than a question of the number of dimensions acknowledged.

For example, even within four dimensions there is the question of how they are related. While western science has been working very hard to integrate them, other cultures have never separated them. In the *Q'eswa* (Quechua) language of the Andes, for example, there is but a single word for time, space, Earth and cosmos: *pacha*. This is not a matter of linguistic poverty, for *Q'eswa* is as rich, detailed and expressive as any other language. It is a matter of direct experience in nature, of the observation that timespace is of a piece and that it is everything observable: the timespace events of all the Earth and all the Cosmos. You yourself cannot perceive any event in which time is separate from space, as all spatial events occur over time if they occur at all. It is the *separation* of time and space that is abnormal in human experience, an abstraction from reality, not reality itself.

In our western culture, we make this abstracted time into a line. Far more cultures, including the

Andean cultures, perceive time in terms of cyclic or spiraling events that take place spatially. Thus cycles of events such as daily dawn-sunset-dawn cycles and annual ones marked by such spatial events as the disappearance and reappearance of the Pleiades from the Southern skies, are superimposed on the thousand-year Great Solar Years of the Andes, and their half-length 500 year cycles, marked by huge upheavals such as earthquakes, floods, etc. These catastrophic transitional events, called *pachacutis*, punctuate the cycles but do not destroy them. Past cycles do not disappear completely, but exist beneath or behind or within present reality such that they can powerfully influence it, as can future events not yet realized but also near everyday surface reality. Think of a spiraling model of timespace in which from any single point considered as the present, the past and future loops of the spiral lie close enough to affect each other.

Another Andean example of timespace interconnection is in the belief that the new, like the Sun always comes from the east, which is the past, and moves toward the west, which is the future. East Andean *paqos* or spiritual practitioner/healers are thus sent to the *selva*, the Amazon which lies to the east and below the mountains, to study for a year in order to bring up fertility and new growth. Robert Randall (Qoyllur Rit'i, An Inca Fiesta of the Pleiades, Bull. Inst. Francais des Etudes Andines, XI, No. 1-2, pp. 37-81) has pointed out that the Creator God, *Wiracocha*, comes from the past in Lake Titicaca and moves into the future of the Pacific Ocean. Again, an east to west timeline. He also mentions that high places overlooking the east, the Amazon, are for seeing into the past. Those that look west, over the ocean, look to the future. In the 16th century play in which the Inca *Atahualpa's* seer-prophet and high priest, *Huaylla Huisa*, sees the Spanish as bearded men in iron ships coming from the future out of the Pacific. Alejandro Ortiz Rescaniere (De Adaneva a Inkarri, Lima 1973) reports that in Inca tradition, mountains can see into the future—for example, to the return of the Inca (*Incarri*)—because of their height.

## As Above, So Below

*Qosqo*, modern Cusco, the center of the Inca nation, was divided or ordered into a complex system of radiating lines called *ceques*. According to Tom Zuidema (Bureaucracy and Systematic Knowledge in Andean Civilization, MS Urbana, 1978), this is an organization of space intended to control time—the unknown past and future worlds. He also draws attention to the Inca search for the true Axis Mundi to connect Earth with other Cosmic levels. This theme is pursued as well by Palomino and Lajo, cited above, in the same introduction to Carlos Milla Villena's book, *Genesis de la Cultura Andina*, where they quote John Earls (The Organization and Production of Ancient Tawantinsuyo, Lima, 1977):

"To connect the cycles of the social system as tightly as possible to the astronomic cycles, major control was exercised over the incremental social entropy. In the hypothetical case (impossible to suppose) in which it succeeds: The Incas have succeeded in unifying social science with astronomy in a single science. Or, they have wanted to create a society in the image if the celestial universe."

and then continue:

"To conclude, we will say that we are in agreement with Earls when he indicates that it was impossible for the Incas to succeed in creating a society in the image of the *entire* celestial universe, but, and herein lies the importance of the book here presented, everything seems to indicate that they did succeed in creating a society in the image of and like the *Southern* celestial universe."

The town of Ollantaytambo, in the Sacred Valley northwest of Cusco, where I happen to be writing this, is laid out in the form of a tree that represents the same shape seen as a black or empty space in the Milky Way just below the Southern Cross, which is directly overhead at this moment. It is thus easy for me to identify with the reality if Andean integrations of timespace above (*pacha* as Cosmos) and below (*pacha* as Earth). This constant awareness of human connections to the Cosmos—as above, so below—is truly something missing entirely from northern industrial culture.

## SCIENCE AND THE SACRED/FACT AND FICTION

Mechanical linear logic, like linear time, seems impoverished beside the cyclic organic logic and time of other cultures which have developed all sciences except mechanical technology—biology, astronomy, medicine, physics, agriculture, architecture, and social sciences—without separating any of them from concepts of the sacred.

Cultures that know the Earth and all the Cosmos as alive and intelligent, recognize all this as sacred. Western science, on the other hand, has regarded nature as a vast resource to be exploited for human benefit. It has relegated the concept of the sacred to religion which has firmly been separated from, and is not to be confused with, science. In fact, from a western scientific perspective, science is about facts, while religion—and all the world's vital teaching "mythology"—is considered a great fiction.

Traditionally, anthropologists separated the myths, religious beliefs, dreams, etc., of cultures they studied from their objective observable artifacts and behaviors. That was because that is how the world of human experience is divided in western culture—a division into fact and fiction, real and unreal, the obvious and the mysterious. One of the so-called Andean "shamans" (a title unknown in native communities before anthropologists introduced it), a man who is also a university-trained anthropologist, told an interviewer here in the North that in the Andean world "*Yoqe*" and "*Panya*" realities are what we would call "ordinary" and "non-ordinary" or "mysterious" realities. No one I have met in Andean communities uses such language. I have been told, on the contrary, that *lloq'e* and *panya* are more like "left" and "right" in the same sense as *hanan* is "up" and *urin* is "down," without any implications of mystery.

The Andean world is divided into *hanan pacha*, which we can now understand to mean literally "upper world," represented by the condor or intelligence, *kay pacha*, the middle or surface world, represented by the puma or balance, and the *uhu pacha*, the lower or inside world represented by the serpent or wisdom. This inner world is not only inner to the individual but represents the inner Earth, from whence Andean people are said to originate and where ancestors continue to dwell. There is nothing mysterious about this concept, or about that of the upper world. These other dimensions of experience are simply accepted as part of everyday reality, as is the existence of the *Apus*, the living Andean gods or lords associated with the mountain peaks of the same names. In other words, other-dimensional realities are perceived as no less real than our familiar four dimensions. In this Andean culture no one seems to be very surprised—though some people admit to being impressed—when they encounter UFOs, known in Spanish as OVNIs.

The obsession of western culture with distinguishing between fact and fiction, as well as between science and religion, is unique to it and is considered by it to be one of its marks of superiority over other cultures. In fact, it may prove to be the downfall of this culture while others survive. For the exclusion of everything not measurable in four dimensions from factual human experience has cut western culture off from the very life of the universe as we have been describing it. Such isolation of a part of a living system leads to its death.

Zuidema, cited earlier, has pointed out that "mythstory," as opposed to "history," may contain contradictions and inconsistencies which should not be interpreted as lies. There is a big difference between intentional distortion of history, such as when white conquerors wrote Native American history in the United States, and the mythstories of cultures that make them for teaching purposes. There the strict observation of what we call fact matters less than the message conveyed. This message may have far more historical cultural value than the "facts" with which the west is so obsessed.

## CONCLUSIONS

Fortunately, western scientists are slowly coming to conclusions that have long been obvious to the cultures they view as "primitive" or less advanced. Unfortunately, these conclusions are being presented as something new, as important discoveries of western science itself, rather than being acknowledged as acceptance of matters known earlier in other cultures. This prevents western scientists from learning more rapidly the rich integration of science, myth and ethic that is so vital to healthy human survival, as was well known by the Incas and other advanced world cultures in ancient times.

I find that western science, while brash and brilliant in some ways, is extremely illogical and immature in other ways. For this reason I have sought better understanding and greater wisdom in the science of other cultures, indigenous and ancient. I now understand the universe as having multiple dimensions beyond our familiar four and being essentially spiritual in the sense that intelligence is a fundamental characteristic of the universe in both its material and non-material or other-dimensional expressions. Trees and rivers and mountains appear to me now as more intelligent than my own kind. In turn, those of my own kind who do not know and experience their intelligence seem sadly backwards.

Today's indigenous peoples, as well as the adepts of ancient cultures such as the Andean, Indian and Tibetan, have traveled in and mapped other dimensions for as long as we know anything about their beliefs, sciences and practices. But what they say about the other dimensions has been classified by western science as religion, imagination, sorcery, childishness, non-reality or utter nonsense as in the quotes given earlier. In the Andes, pre-Inca cultures from the Chimu and Mochica of the north to very ancient Tihuanaco in the south, as well as the Inca themselves, seem to have worked closely with extraterrestrial and other dimensional beings, some of whom, such as the *Apus*, are still around.

The point is that there is really only one reality which has many dimensions. Those sciences which recognize them all are aware that the universe is fundamentally sacred, that the highest dimensions contain non-material beings of light, of very fine vibrations, of cosmic sound, of pure love. Thus, in such knowledge systems, science is not separated from the sacred, nor are any aspects of human and nonhuman experience separated from one another. We are all related, as the Lakota and many other say, and our relatively dense material dimensions are simply part of a vastly great universal whole.

I believe that Earth, in all its human conflict, reflects the conflicts of the greater living Cosmos. Yet, I find it interesting that extraterrestrial visitors in this western culture are so often perceived as hostile, while I have heard of no hostile encounters in the Andes. I believe the Earth has been visited and experimented with for thousands of years, yet that most of our visitors, as well as our own ancestral spirits, are benign and loving—call them angels, ETs or spirit grandmas—and that many are here explicitly to guard against nuclear accidents and to help us learn to walk in love and service to others, the secret of happiness for us all.

When I asked an Andean friend about her experiences with ETs, she shared this story. In the remote village where she grew up there were people in white who came whenever a truck, the only vehicle in most of the Andes, had broken down or a person was ill. After they fixed the vehicle or the person, they went back to their base in the mountains where no one disturbed them. They were known by the villagers simply as "the doctors." They were well loved.

I believe such experiences of indigenous peoples, who have long lived with other-dimensional beings and welcomed extraterrestrials, can help us newcomers to these experiences encounter Cosmic Cultures intelligently and peacefully as they enter our familiar dimensions.

# Genesis de al Cultural Andina
### by Carlos Milla Villena, Lima 1983

Prologue: Nicolas Aguilar Sayritupac (translated from Aymara/Quechua)

From Chucuito, my village, at the edge of the sacred lake, the nights of May are beautiful and dazzling. As it has always been, our elders showed us the Southern Cross, with its two guiding stars, as four small suns that guide our community and our thoughts through the black nights and passages in which our happiness and faith sometimes fall. I am old now and too tired to walk strange roads. Many times I have lost tranquility and hope when so often I saw my community and my culture crushed and destroyed.

How many times have I also wept at the bitterness of death and have seen in these stars my only consolation and my faith. To ask why these images and emotions are fixed in my most inner self would be to ask why the stars are fixed in the firmament. The odor of wool and of rain is our peace and the voice of the mother in this image of the Cross of May.

Since reading and seeing the figures of our brother Carlos Milla's book, an infinity of ideas have occurred to me; dreams and thoughts flower like a new dawn. I know a little of the customs of the men who come from the place where the Sun puts itself down, and their mentality is as confused as a tangled ball of yarn as day by day they become more entangled without relief. What will they think of the things in this book? There is abundantly clear evidence, such as they cannot negate, that our indigenous people made it all and made it well and that what *they* made was made badly.

Our Andean culture attained its complete development with nothing lacking. We knew this long ago, because we felt it, but now we know it definitely. The Amautas will remain, caring for our people, firstly so we can survive physically, secondly so our spirit and culture do not die. Today our indigenous people grow large and, yes . . . yes! It is time for all the knowledge of the Haqes and Runas to come out of their caves where they have been hidden so they would not disappear.

In the hearts of the Westerners there are no feelings that can resolve their conflicts; their hearts go in one direction and their minds in another. It follows that men, women, children and old people do not work together collectively. On the contrary, that which man cannot see, alone can help him to see the woman, the child and the old one, maybe most important is that we see them all together. The human being of the West has abandoned being human and has turned himself into an individual: man, woman, child, elder, separate; community has died in them, the "ayllu'—the essential unity of humanity. The existence of Western people and society has been destroyed by their egoism.

On the contrary, we Indians have things well in our heads, our feelings in order, determined to do what we can; it is for this reason that we do not go away much from our home and family, for this reason that we have kept ourselves away from the equivocal ideas of the men who find themselves in the place where the Sun hides itself. When our feelings are confused, when we are attracted by strange lights, more brilliant than they are, let us go toward this light, but let us go together.

We cannot, in the universe of ideas, distance ourselves alone for our story, we must divide the light of wisdom, and to do it Western writing is not a good road. Our brother Carlos Milla with his book has opened a new road for recording our knowledge, work, life . . . all.

Since having read this book it seems to me I have slept many years and have dreamed a black nightmare in which stars of the night collided with each other, in which there was no hope for light in the obscurity, in which everything was a black and turbid river of pain and sadness. I was desperate and I came back to see in May, and in all the nights of the year, the four beautiful stars and their two star guides, as when in the nights many years ago, my father, looking with his good eyes, said to me: Look at the "Chacana" . . . now be certain that if the West wants to totally destroy our community and our culture it will first have to destroy the Cross of May in the heavens.

*The Aymaras are eternal people.*

# ⊕ James J. Funaro

*James J. Funaro*

James J. Funaro is the founder of CONTACT, an international, interdisciplinary conference which brings together some of the foremost scientists, writers and artists to exchange ideas, explore possibilities and stimulate new perspectives about humanity's future. He is an instructor of anthropology at Cabrillo College and holds his degrees from the University of California at Davis and Ohio State University. A recent publication demonstrating his research interests is "Anthropologists as Culture Designers for Offworld Colonies." He also received a BA with honors in literature and creative writing from Dension University, and is a published poet.

# On The Cultural Impact of Extraterrestrial Contact,

# With Special Attention To Religion As An Adaptive Response

*In 1960, research done by the Brookings Institution for NASA speculated that of all groups, scientists and engineers might be the most devastated by the discovery of relatively superior extraterrestrial intelligence, since these professions are most clearly associated with the mastery of nature, rather than with the understanding and expression of man. How would institutionalized religions fair? Anthropologist James J. Funaro provides an assessment of the critical role that religion may play.*

## INTRODUCTION

There is a satisfying diversity represented by the participants at this gathering, and I think it may be useful to begin by discussing why I myself was invited—or, at least, why I think I was invited.

First, I am the founder of an organization called CONTACT. Now that sounds pretty central to a conference entitled "When Cosmic Cultures Meet," doesn't it? In fact, over the past 12 years, CONTACT has produced dozens of simulated contacts between humans and aliens, as professional thought experiments, as media features and as educational curricula. But though CONTACT does deal with the possibility of extraterrestrial encounters, that is not its primary interest, despite what may seem to be the implications of our name and some of our activities.

CONTACT is a unique interdisciplinary organization and annual conference which brings together some of the world's foremost social and space scientists, science fiction writers, and artists, to exchange ideas, stimulate new perspectives and encourage serious, creative speculation about humanity's future ... onworld and offworld. One of our primary goals—motivated by my commitment to anthropology— is to develop ethical approaches in cross-cultural contact, whenever and wherever it occurs.

So the "contact" in CONTACT really signifies the primary obsession of anthropology with new connections between peoples and things, demonstrated by its century of professional and personal focus on the interactions between cultures. However, I believe that this actual fieldwork with encounters between humans ought to embrace, by logical extension, potential intercultural interaction between humans and extraterrestrials.

In fact, the discipline's perspective of cultural relativity, its broad data base on biological and cultural adaptations, and its methodologies of cross-cultural comparison and ethnographic field work developed here on this planet, may have made anthropologists the most appropriately-trained, "field-tested" scientists to deal with extraterrestrial cultures should we encounter them.

Which brings me to the second reason (I think) I've been asked to be here. I'm an anthropologist. Anthropology produces, among other things, experts on human alternatives. It is part of our discipline to become fluent in the immense variety of ways that people do (and have done) things. Thus, our speculations on what people are likely to do in the future are based not just on a specific culture, like our own, or on a group of cultures, like Western civilization or the "major powers," but on an overview of our species as a whole. Any particular cultural system is bound to be specialized and limited compared to the full range of known or conceivable alternatives produced by a true representative sampling of humanity.

So, when you ask an anthropologist about the world reaction to some global crisis like an extraterrestrial encounter, don't expect a discussion of the "international scene," such as you might find on Meet the Press or the 6 o'clock news. Most of the real world is peopled by folks, browner than most of us, who spend their days, not browsing a mall, worrying about their bank accounts or fighting a war, but trying to raise their families on small resources, working hard at their trades to make sure there is enough food to eat, and worrying about getting along with the others members of their communities upon whom they depend for emotional and physical support.

To me, the "world" means the whole world, which includes, but is by no means limited to, the specialized, compartmentalized and institutionalized media view we are familiar with. I point this out particularly because some of the things I will say later in this paper, especially with regard to science and religion, may otherwise sound exceedingly unfamiliar.

Forewarned, then, let us without further ado imagine the public announcement that we are not alone in the universe. I will start by exploring the impact on some of the major interest groups in the international scene. Their general reactions should be somewhat simpler and more predictable to the degree that they can be expected to react as whole institutions. This discussion will also incorporate some of the primary human motivations that are likely to be elicited in individuals as well as in the groups in question—fear, greed, hope.

I will then turn to the impact of the news on the smaller communities which I believe will provide the basic social, political and economic units for most of our planet's people in the future. Here I anticipate a more complex responses and great resilience; and I will concentrate particularly on religion (in contrast to science) as an adaptive resource for dealing with an extraterrestrial encounter, perhaps even the most valuable tool in our species' survival kit. And remember ... it's all just my best guess!

## GENERAL REACTION OF GLOBAL INTERESTS

### 1. Nation-states: Fear and Defense

During the past millennium, the nation-state has provided the primary basis for political boundaries and the dominant model for political entities, both of which had been previously founded on imperial, city-state or tribal traditions. However, these entities have increasingly been showing sure signs of failure; and the twentieth century—with the advent of world-wide wars, the withering of colonialism and the emergence of global economies and communications networks—may become known to future historians as the century which ensured the demise of the nation-state. Nonetheless, as we enter the next millennium, nation-states still exert primary influence on the lives of most people of our planet.

Given the long-standing and time-tested concerns of nationalism with vital national security, we shall not be surprised by a reflex reaction of paranoia, with respect to both the perceived external threat and the competing interests of other nation-states. Attempts to provide local or global defense capabilities (even in the face of overwhelmingly superior technology) and to gain and restrict access to the new information are likely responses. We may also expect certain nations to try to seize the opportunity to enhance their prestige by claiming to represent all of Earth or to attempt to strike separate alliances with the aliens which will favor their own interests and constituents at the expense of others. It is not impossible that the presence of an external threat may even cause internecine wars of dominance, to guarantee the precedence of one nation or faction of nations in dealing with the new outsiders.

I should point out that such a defensive posture, though often labeled paranoid, is not irrational, though it is based on the knowledge of human, and not alien, motivation. History on this planet shows that exploitation is the most usual motive that one society has for establishing contact with another: Somebody wants something somebody else has, whether it is land, food, material wealth, knowledge, souls, or just plain "human resources". We should not assume that a visiting extraterrestrial civilization will have the same motives, but the possibility cannot be ignored.

### 2. Supra-National Entities: Greed and Expansion

To fill the increasingly larger gaps that will be left by the waning nation-states, other entities are emerging. The supra-national corporations are becoming the major players on the international scene, with their primary concern being global economics. These entities, which seem to include in their ranks many of the most powerful political leaders, could become the foundation for a truly world-wide human community based on world peace and cooperation, because they rise above divisive national interests (though not necessarily above personal interests) and, at least in theory, are able to operate on the basis of economic sanctions, without the necessity of depending on the application of physical coercion to gain their ends. The bright side of this future is the possibility, through centralization and equitable redistribution of resources, of an increased standard of living for all humankind.

The dark side portends much worse: The precipitation of all wealth to a thin layer at the top, and its resulting solidification into a small privileged class in control over the masses of humanity abandoned to their fate without recourse. Politics, and the government of people at large, are of interest only insofar as they are seen to enhance or interfere with the flow of economic resources. Without the support of strong nation-states, the United Nations, as a body representing the interests of all, could be financially forced to become a puppet to ensure these mercantile goals.

Such a supra-national coalition, with little investment in human rights or welfare and lacking any effective system of checks and balances, may resort to using military forces previously established by defunct nation-states or recruited from the vast ranks of the impoverished unemployed to act as mercenaries to enforce its "global" will. This would indeed be an ironic perversion of the worldwide human community of the flower children's dreams.

In either case, however, supra-national entities can be expected to have less concern about national interests (since they operate between rather than within them) and may even perceive the advent of visitors from outside as furthering their desire to bring about a global unity more conducive to trade. Information about the aliens, however, could become a commodity among the elite, restricted to increase its value and sold to the highest bidders. And, of course, should the contact turn out to be friendly, the opportunities for tourism, brokerage, and expansion of markets beyond our planet will surely not be missed by enterprising entrepreneurs, who will likely try to drive hard bargains and negotiate exclusive franchises with their new, and possibly inexperienced, trade partners.

### 3. Science: Hope and Welcome

Unlike national governments or supra-national corporations, the "scientific community" is not a real group and is therefore hard to delineate, even by those who consider themselves a part of it. It has no formal membership and may be considered to include any professional scientists in the world, whether in academia, government or business. They profess to share a commitment to a common methodology and typically belong to their respective local or international organizations and perhaps to more general multi-disciplinary groups.

Their interests are unofficially represented by a shifting core of vocal, well-known and well-published individuals who maintain their ties with one another and are typically contacted by the media to speak for the whole on particular issues. The community is as multi-faceted as its many disciplines, the specialized segment invoked shifting with the particular scientific focus under public scrutiny.

Because it tends to see itself as a consciously ecumenical group with interests and loyalties that override political and economic boundaries and allegiances, the scientific community, unlike either nation-states or supranationals, generally favors the widest possible dissemination of information about a confirmed alien contact, specifically in order to deter special manipulation by private or national interests. In contrast to nations, the projected scientific response has been labeled "pronoid," holding that the results of extraterrestrial contact will not be threatening but therapeutic. Various manifestations of this position I have heard range from optimism to naivete.

A moderate and fairly widespread perspective suggests that we would benefit from the contact because a presumably older and more sophisticated civilization will have solved our problems and moved beyond our motives and will thus be interested in sharing their knowledge with less-advanced intelligent species. A somewhat subdued variation on this theme is expressed in the supposition that their technology is likely to be so far in advance of our own that we have no choice but to hope they are benevolent.

At the other extreme, a highly idealistic view (which I have perhaps too sardonically dubbed the Quetzalcoatl complex) imagines that the aliens will be wise and selfless teachers who come to us across the vastness of space to offer the wonders of their advanced science and technology in order to heal the ills of a needy and grateful Earth. In this belief, those scientists approach some of their fellow theorists in religion, perhaps lured by a wistful projection of our own future role as scientific missionaries to underdeveloped worlds.

Finally—though this does not exhaust the spectrum—a more cynical but not necessarily malevolent suggestion is that we may be the subjects of legitimate and ethical scientific study, though whether the alien scientists are the equivalent of anthropologists, biologists, epidemiologists, medical researchers, museum curators or zoo staff ought to be a matter of concern to us.

Because the scientific community operates in a somewhat rarefied atmosphere with respect to subject matter and personnel, its expectations are sometimes idealistic to the point of failing to take proper measure of the mundane or unpleasant realities of human behavior in general; and, historically, scientists (or groups like them) have rarely had much political or economic power or been influential in determining significant policy.

Realizing the potentiality of a remote contact as the result of its work, SETI solicited a group of scientists in appropriate areas to develop a protocol for dealing with an extraterrestrial message should it be detected. The goal was admirable and the result exhibited excellent thinking and considerable erudition; but it seemed incomplete, because it did not anticipate the impact from various, and especially "unofficial," groups outside the scientific community, like hackers, crooks and fanatics, which would surely intrude.

In fact, an extensive project was carried out by CONTACT to construct a reasonable and realistic simulation that might be of practical value in the event of an actual first contact and to provide a test of the protocol created for such an eventuality. Over a period of three years, a team of scientists, writers and artists created a credible and coherent extraterrestrial civilization. Its representatives produced and sent messages from their home planet light years away. An Earth receiving team, representing various local, national and global communities of interest, attempted to simulate our world's reactions, via Internet and connected virtual networks and in two real-time demonstrations. Several of the scientists involved in devising that protocol were present for the presentations in 1992 and 1993.

### 4. "Grass-roots" communities: Any and All of the Above

As the nation-states fail over the next century, it does not seem to me that—barring the imposition of a single totalitarian system on the entire planet—humanity as a whole is likely to be moving toward greater unity of interest, purpose or action, despite the above-mentioned global trends and the high hopes of many individuals and groups.

It has been suggested that the one thing that could finally get all of humanity together into a single global community would be the arrival of extraterrestrials—that is, nonhuman Others. In fact, some people have even suggested creating a fraudulent simulation of such a contact—ala Orson Wells, but with space age special effects and virtual reality technology—precisely in order to bring about such a world-wide unity.

An actual, undeniable encounter, then, especially if it provided a common threat, might have such an effect. But I doubt that it would, without some pre-existing infrastructure for support and course of action to follow. At this point in time, the United Nations is the only possible candidate, and its effectiveness would depend on the cooperation of its members, whereas, in reality, it is their competition that will more likely intensify as their own local sovereignties diminish. Could the UN—which is now often forced into the unpalatable solution of killing people to keep them from killing people—mobilize, or provide the mechanisms for mobilizing, the world population?

In actuality, then, I anticipate less unity and more, rather than fewer, communities in the future. While the supranationals may provide a powerful but impersonal architecture above, most of the populations of disintegrating nation-states will be re-organized, or re-organize themselves, from below.

This process is already in progress. New communities of interest based on communications technology are replacing some of the older communities based on residence (e.g., Internet, the Iridium project) and, perhaps more commonly because they require no capital, other rising communities are reverting to sub-nationalistic forms of affiliation such as tribe, ethnicity, religion, etc. (e.g., USSR, Yugoslavia, Rwanda). For people who may be unsuccessful in joining these communities, life could become very brutal; they may find themselves disenfranchised, alienated and even outlawed.

These grass-roots movements may provide the source of community for most of humanity in the future. In contrast to most theorists on the subject, I think it is here—and not among the major movers on the international scene—that we will find the most surprises and the greatest resilience in the face of alien contact.

And what would be their reaction? In the first place, there would be no united response, but a multiplicity of responses, varying from fear to habituation or denial to welcome, and everything in between. This ought to reveal to any alien—far more than the reactions of national governments, supranational corporations, the scientific community or any other institution—our true multicultural nature.

By contrast, then, the other "institutionalized" approaches to the extraterrestrial visitors we have already discussed constitute artificial monolithic facades, subterfuges only effective until the aliens—like those institutions themselves—come into contact with real people and learn the truth: Humanity is not a unified, predictable species.

In fact, this behavioral flexibility is one of the main reasons for our biological success. So, the visitors might as well find that out sooner than later. If they possess superior intelligence, they may appreciate the honesty. If they are benevolent, they may be better able to help us if they know what they are dealing with; and finally, if they are not, they may realize that we could be a difficult species to manipulate as a whole to their ends, and perhaps not worth the trouble.

## RELIGION AS AN ADAPTIVE RESPONSE

### 1. Science and Religion

Among the many responses expected, religion will surely provide a wide spectrum. A common notion I have heard expressed by many in our society who have speculated on the impact of an extraterrestrial encounter is that religion would be devastated, whereas science would be vindicated. This belief, I think, is a fallacy and springs from both a limitation in the field of religious experience and an inexperience in the limitations of science. I am not suggesting that religion is better than science, or vice versa, but simply that they have different contexts of maximum effectiveness. And I intend to argue that religion may have some tools that are superior to those of science in dealing with the specific impact of cosmic contact on our species.

We in the secular West are confident that science and technology can solve most of our problems. We distrust or ridicule religion, secure in the belief that science is the superior system for acquiring knowledge about everything. This belief is based not on evidence alone but on an intellectual tradition that was born in the Enlightenment (our word for it)—with its trust in Reason and its concept of the Noble Savage—and was then nurtured on the success of European Colonialism, and finally came of age with the theory of Evolution. This perspective leads us to assume that progress is inherent in the nature of the universe and that we, as the technological leaders, are demonstrably the end product of that glorious march, the goal of evolution.

But evolution does not have such a specific goal. If it could be said to have any, it is a general and impersonal goal of adaptation, increased fitness in meeting the current conditions of a given environment. And what constitutes increased fitness is different for each environment and has nothing at all to do with concepts like "winning" or "truth" or "right" or any of our usual culturally-defined goals; the only criterion is the survival and transmission of the species' genetic information.

In such an emotional and conceptual crisis as cosmic contact is likely to bring to Earth, science may not offer the most satisfying answers to most of the people on this planet, or even to everyone in our own society. And perhaps, more surprisingly, religion may turn out to be, at least in some scenarios, a superior overall adaptive tool. Especially if the encounter occurs during the additional power surge generated by the turning of the millennium.

### 2. The Adaptive Advantages of Religion

Over the past four million years, our species has evolved many resources besides science for dealing with the unknown and accommodating to change. For example, our tool chest includes religion, philosophy, warfare, art and many others. Of these, perhaps the one with the longest tradition and widest distribution of enduring success is religion, which often incorporates the others as aspects. Our earliest prehistoric evidence of religious behavior may date back as far as 100,000 years and, on the basis of more controversial data, perhaps hundreds of thousands. And very likely, religion was an essential component of the human experience long before there was any physical evidence of it.

So, it's old. That seems to confirm our culture's belief, mentioned above, in an evolutionary progression: Religion was what we were stuck with before we discovered science, which will gradually replace religion as we learn more and more about the nature of the universe. But is that really true?

a) Religion answers questions science cannot answer.

I suggest that, as long as we are human, religion will be with us, paralleling and maybe even outliving science. Why? Because religion answers some important questions humans will always ask, the kind of questions that science cannot answer. And though science may discover ever more precisely how to explain why, and predict when, we ask these questions, it will likely never be able to give satisfactory answers to people forced by their intellectual or emotional crises to ask them.

Here's a sample list, for the selection or grouping of which I claim only convenience, and not logical, consistency. Any of you could add to it at will.

Problems of explanation:

What are we here for?

Who created the universe, and how was it done?

What is the order in the universe, or does God play dice with it?

What is an idea, love, creativity or the human spirit?

What is charisma, animal magnetism, the twinkle in a child's eye?

Problems of causality:

Why did that have to happen to me? Why doesn't it feel like a coincidence?

What causes a coincidence? What causes luck?

Why do only some people get cancer; and of those, why do only some die?

In a natural disaster or accident, why were only those certain people killed?

And what was special about those who survived that saved them?

Problems of suffering:

Why is there suffering in the world?

If we cannot always avoid suffering, how can we make the pain bearable?

Does our suffering have any use, value or meaning?

How do we endure the loss of someone we love?

Why do some people give up their lives for love, or for an idea, or for God?

Problems of evil:

Why is there evil and injustice in the world?

How can people do such hurtful things to others, especially to children?

Why am I having such troubles, when I didn't do anything to deserve it?

Why do good people sometimes have terrible lives?

Why do bad people sometimes have wonderful lives?

Certainly, many scientists would retort that most of these are questions without answers, or coincidences, or propositions not subject to objective testing by the scientific method. But this is surely an insufficient response, if people persist in demanding answers anyhow. Thus, in some vital areas of human needs, science may continue to be a lesser tool, as long as it remains committed to the limits imposed by the rigors of its method and the laws of physics. Religion, with no such compunctions, can consequently encompass more things in heaven and earth than are dreamt of in science's philosophy.

It could be argued that the effectiveness of a tool for answering questions is dependent, not on its absolute competence, but on its relative competence within the context of the questions asked, just as a hammer may be good for driving nails but poor at mending pottery or providing comfort to an injured child.

Recently, science has been quite successful in answering our questions about the universe, but this may be partly due to the particular questions that we in Western culture today have the luxury to ask. It may be equally true that religion was just as successful in answering the questions asked by the more inwardly-directed, spiritually-oriented society of Medieval Europe, whose creatural viability was perpetually threatened by famine, plague and other evils whose causes were invisible to the physical eye, while science and magic alike were distrusted because they misguidedly sought to manipulate the mere external world of illusion.

With most of our basic needs for survival and security met, our attention in modern Western society is directed externally, toward the world outside ourselves. Therefore, science's apparent effectiveness in our society may also be due in part to the important questions it does not have to answer for us, such as those listed above. But these may be exactly the kinds of questions that most members of our species would ask when confronted with aliens beings from outer space.

Isaac Asimov, in the final book of his original "Foundation Trilogy," offered us two different answers to the mystery which was the central theme of the whole epic. The next-to-the-last chapter was entitled "The Answer That Satisfied" and the last chapter, "The Answer That Was True," the latter being given higher priority by its ultimate position. Asimov's literary reasons for this order are certainly understandable. However, a scientist of human behavior (a true psycho-historian) might argue that he had the priorities backwards: What real people outside of novels seem to want is not the answer that is true, which may offer no recourse, but the answer that satisfies, which is its own recourse. Sometimes the truth is less than what we really need.

b) Religion has had more experience with extraterrestrial contact than science has.

I have already suggested in my introduction that the science of anthropology has amassed a century of field experience in dealing with contact between human cultures which may provide relevant training and methodologies for dealing with the meeting of cosmic cultures. But religion may offer even more pertinent experience.

Like all humans, I have the ability to believe. All I need is the evidence in the right context. So far, I don't believe there's anyone on this planet that didn't evolve here, but only because I haven't encountered convincing evidence that can't be otherwise explained in the context of similar experiences familiar to students of human behavior. For at least thousands of years, innumerable people have reported their meetings with unearthly beings and visits to otherworldly places. In fact, the efflorescence of UFO sightings and alien abductions over the past few decades is thoroughly expectable at the end of a millennium, with a new generation of heavenly emissaries transmogrified into high-tech space explorers.

This wealth of information on unearthly beings and otherworldly places has, of course, usually been relegated to what the secular world views as the unreliable realm of religious experience. This could also, however, constitute a convenient justification for nonbelievers not to investigate further; "unreliable" could simply mean "unexplainable;" i.e., it doesn't fit the secular model of reality.

The fact is that we already have a great deal of evidence throughout human history and prehistory of contact with other worlds and peoples; science just doesn't accept its validity. But to the believers, their encounters have been just as real as those of more recent believers in aliens, and their reactions therefore are legitimate field-tests and can provide models for speculation on the results of cosmic contact. In other words, rather than a deficit, we actually already have a profusion of data on the impact of extraterrestrial encounters on human culture, if we are willing to consider it.

216

What does this data tell us about how people react to such encounters (whether empirically verifiable or experiential only)? Typically, cultures accommodate, producing an eclectic religion more vital than the original. Herein lies much of religion's capacity for adaptation; a religion that doesn't change will die. We in our secular society tend to view religion as a conservative force, the staunch defender of the status quo; but it can also, because of the emotional power and intellectual validation it can mobilize, be the strongest force in the world for change.

Contacts with non-ordinary beings have commonly provided strong motivation, even crusades, as in the case of Islam; but even here there was considerable tolerance of similar "peoples of the Book," Judaism and Christianity, and, in sub-Saharan Africa, its enthusiasm was embraced but its doctrines tailored to fit the different cultural context, the jinn becoming local spirits. In its missionary quest in pagan Europe, Christianity was itself converted, adopting many native heathen beliefs and practices; even today, most English-speaking Christians do not realize that their central festival, commemorating the triumphant resurrection of their Savior, takes its name from a pagan Teutonic fertility goddess.

Such syncretism seems to be the lifeblood of change. I have attended a "year after" ceremony for my Native American brother which featured the smoking of the pipe to the four cardinal points led by a Lakota medicine man followed by Holy Communion administered by a Catholic priest. The blending of West African beliefs with Roman Catholicism by slaves in the New World has resulted in some of the most exciting and fastest-growing religions in the world, Santer'a from Cuba, Vodun from Haiti and Macumba, Umbanda, Condomblä and others from Brazil, each springing from a different European tradition. Orthodox Christians might be disconcerted at seeing a dog or chicken sacrificed on an altar with a crucifix on it, but then the Buddha would no doubt be disappointed by the proliferation of gods in village Buddhism. Religions live, despite efforts, even by their adherents, to restrict change.

Such examples of accommodation could be multiplied endlessly. The point is that, though some of the world's hundreds of religions may have trouble dealing with an extraterrestrial encounter, most would probably find a way to incorporate the new information into their belief systems. Indeed, many religions will surely see the presence of extraterrestrials, not as a threat, but as a long-awaited confirmation of their belief in supernatural beings. For example, it would be perfect timing for Christianity, with its millennial beliefs in the Second Coming and Last Judgment.

c) Religious hypotheses are strengthened by disproof.

A puzzle which emerged from research on a religious movement, described in the book *When Prophecy Fails*, led psychologist Leon Festinger to propose his theory of cognitive dissonance: Individuals try to maintain consonance among their cognitions (their ideas, beliefs, opinions). Therefore, the intrusion of dissonance (non-fitting relations among cognitions) triggers a strong drive to reduce dissonance and increase consonance. To accomplish this, the individual can dismiss cognitions, change them or acquire new ones.

So what else is new, you say? The most interesting part is yet to come. When a dissonant cognition is proved false by objective testing, the scientific solution would be obvious: Achieve consonance by discarding the unconfirmed hypothesis. But this is often precisely what individuals and groups do not do. The probability of rejection is not based on the disproof of the hypothesis but is inversely proportional to the individual's investment in it. In fact, in some of the most important issues humans face, failure may motivate an increase in the belief. Not very scientific, but true. Clearly, science is not always the method by which people choose their behavior.

The religious group in question was based on the prophecy by one of its members that the Guardians from outer space were coming in flying saucers to rescue the believers from a cataclysm scheduled for a particular day that would destroy most of the continent. They did not keep the prophecy secret; but, before the event, they had little motivation to attract new members or gain publicity, since they were among the chosen few. By the time they gathered together on the predicted day of deliverance, most of the members had made irreversible commitments, such as exposing themselves to public ridicule, quitting their jobs and divesting themselves of goods and property. With the media and hundreds of curious onlookers present, the appointed time came and passed, and no cataclysm, no flying saucers.

It might be expected that the followers would disband in dismay when the prophecy failed, but they didn't. Indeed, from then on, the cult began actively proselytizing to gain converts. In other words, the failure of the primary doctrine, far from discouraging enthusiasm, actually provided the impetus for expansion. Since they were prevented from repudiating the beliefs by their heavy personal, social and economic commitments, the believers were forced to seek to reduce the dissonance created by the disconfirmation of their prophecy by convincing more and more people that their beliefs were valid. And it worked.

This theory of cognitive dissonance may be used to explain the rise and success of many religions. A familiar model is provided by Christianity, which started as a movement to reform Judaism and probably would have remained a small and unsuccessful attempt. However, the "failure" of Christ's predicted return forced the early church to seek new cognitions: A reinterpretation of the doctrines of salvation and final judgment, an expansion to include gentiles, and the glorification of martyrdom (which itself demonstrated increased commitment, by act and example). The church emerged victorious, to become the state religion of the Roman empire and of Christendom, and ultimately one of the world's most widespread faiths.

What could be the value of a tool for acquiring knowledge that is based on disproved hypotheses? It allows humans to survive the truth, if that truth would precipitate despair which could impair species survival. In an encounter with aliens of an advanced civilization, their motives and methods are unknown quantities; if their goals are exploitative and their means superior, religion may provide a more effective defense for humanity than our science or military technology.

d) Culture has a built-in, self-activating religious mechanism for adapting to stress.

In comparable contact situations on this planet, religious responses have preserved many populations threatened by others with superior resources, especially if direct physical retaliation is impossible, because they can infuse people with hope in objectively hopeless situations and provide a mechanism for adapting to stressful conditions or threats to survival by reformulating their cultures.

How do religious systems accomplish this? Anthropologist Anthony F. C. Wallace has produced a general theory on the process of major cultural-system transformation, which gathers together under a single heading phenomena that have been variously labeled revivalist, messianic, reform, utopian, charismatic, revolutionary, nativistic and millenarian movements. He proposed that all of these are characterized by a uniform process which he calls "revitalization."

He defines a revitalization movement as a deliberate, organized, conscious effort by members of a society to construct a more satisfying culture. He suggests that most religions, world or local, have originated by this process; and though revitalization movements are primarily religious, application of the model to other more secular movements like the Communist revolution or the rise of Nazism are quite appropriate and instructive. The McCarthy era brought us witch hunts and the Kennedy era got us to the moon.

A society is a homeostatic system, with feedback loops that automatically detect and respond to changes. Stress, a condition in which the society is threatened with potentially dangerous damage, is one of the environmental components to which the social organism is particularly sensitive; and, under increasing stress, the system will initiate emergency measures to preserve itself. Revitalization is one of these built-in, self-actuating measures.

The structure of the process is as follows: (I) In the steady state, the culture satisfies the needs of the majority, and stress remains within tolerable limits. (II) However, if the stress increases over time, individuals begin to find the normal stress-reducing mechanisms insufficient to meet their needs and look for other alternatives. (III) If the increasing stress persists and becomes widespread, enough individuals will eventually be so severely affected that the culture itself becomes internally distorted. My metaphor for this: Picture a pool. It begins to rain, but the drops are few and sporadic enough so that the splashes, though visible, do not obscure the surface; but when it begins to pour, the drops ultimately hit so fast and furiously that the surface is no longer recognizable.

This period of cultural distortion may ultimately trigger (IV) the revitalization movement, which follows a remarkably uniform pattern over time and space. First, a prophet (almost always a single individual) has a vision, which transforms him and provides a guide for reformulating the culture. Next, he communicates his message to others and gains converts. Then, the converts develop an organization—usually prophet, disciples and followers—which begins to administer the action program.

As the movement becomes more public, it will usually encounter some resistance, to which it responds by modifying its doctrines and activities, adapting to better fit the overall cultural context. Over time, as a significant portion of the population accepts and begins to benefit from the superior stress-reduction mechanisms of the new religion, the culture is transformed . Finally, if it remains effective, the movement becomes the religion of the society. This leads to the development of (V) the new, and more satisfying, steady state of the reformulated culture.

The outcomes of revitalization movements have been various and often spectacularly successful, producing new vitality and societal reform: Christianity and Islam won empires, Mau Mau won Kenyan statehood, Gandhi's application of Hinduism to politics won Indian independence. However, at other times, they seem to have been inadequate to sustain the new vision, sometimes through their own doctrinal deficiency, more often because the external threat was too powerful.

For example, the Ghost Dance, a last-ditch religious response by the Plains Indians to military defeat and cultural disintegration, was crushed by superior manpower and weaponry. Yet even here the culture, though considerably diminished, did not die; the success was simply delayed, and has reemerged a half-century later, considerably transformed by reservation life and new native religious practices, as a pan-Indian revitalization movement with some political clout.

Whether the encounter is with terrestrial or extraterrestrial strangers, we must remember that "success" must be seen not in terms of winning but of survival; the intruder may win the battle and lose the war. And, especially if winning is impossible due to the overwhelming power of an alien culture, religion may provide more effective survival mechanisms than science. Religion, when faced with intolerable conditions, has the resources to create for its members a more satisfying world—a world, if necessary, beyond objective reality. And, another world to live in, says Santayana, is what we mean by having a religion.

## Epilogue

It is by no means certain that extraterrestrial visitors to Earth will be either intelligent or technological. Certainly these traits are rare as significant adaptive mechanisms among the life forms on this planet, and there is no indication that evolution here or elsewhere has these adaptations as goals. If the aliens are neither, the interaction could be especially difficult and frustrating (if indeed we are even aware of each other's presence).

However, if a species has evolved both intelligence to solve adaptive problems and the biological structures to physically manipulate the environment, it is not unreasonable that it would develop technology, as we did. And if that technology were used to travel here, it is almost certain to be vastly superior to our own. Arthur C. Clarke's well-known (but rarely sourced) statement may turn out to be appropriate to our cosmic encounter: Any sufficiently advanced technology will seem like magic. Indeed, the aliens may match more closely humanity's images of supernatural deities than of "ultra-natural" scientists.

In such a situation, it is likely that our level of science and technology will seem to them primitive and uninteresting by comparison, except for its historical value. Instead, they may be more fascinated by our ability to create artificial (virtual) realities in our individual or collective consciousnesses, such as art or religion. It might be that we were wiser than we had imagined when we put Bach aboard Voyager as an ambassador to civilizations in space—perhaps we should have included the B-minor Mass.

Before closing, I want to reiterate that, as a scientist, I agree that science is the most reliable method so far devised for understanding objective phenomena and should be utilized to the utmost in dealing with the problems of contact within its expertise. However, when cosmic cultures meet, some of the needs of humanity at large may require the kind of subjective—and even non-objective—understanding provided by religion.

In the final analysis, whatever the impact on us of an extraterrestrial contact, we may not have much choice in our response; and, if our science ultimately proves inadequate or inferior, we may find ourselves relying on the intrinsic value of what may be unique and surprising non-scientific characteristics we have evolved. Given the number of unknowns in the equation, we should not preclude the value of any of our adaptive resources in establishing and maintaining successful and mutually-beneficial relations when we meet others who share the universe with us.

## References Cited

Because this paper consists largely of my opinions about a highly speculative topic and is intended for a general audience, the bibliography is minimal and includes only those works from which I directly drew quotations and ideas.

Asimov, I. *The Foundation Trilogy*, New York: Doubleday, 1964

Festinger, L. *A Theory of Cognitive Dissonance*, Stanford, 1957

Festinger, L. *When Prophecy Fails*, University of Minnesota, 1956

Santayana, G. *Reason in Religion*, New York: Collier, 1906

Wallace, A.F.C. "Revitalization Movements," *American Anthropologist*, LVIII, 264-281, 1956

# ⊕ Jerome C. Glenn

220

*Jerome C. Glenn*

Jerome C. Glenn is Executive Director of the American Council/United Nations University. This organization provides a point of contact between the United Nations University (the U.N.'s think tank) and the United States. He is coauthor of *Space Trek: The Endless Migration*, and author of *Future Mind*. He is also coordinator of the Millennium Project (on Global Future Studies) for the United Nations University's World Institute for Developing Economies.

# So What Do We Do Now? Ten Points to Consider

*Is Earth a womb to protect us, or a home to leave when post-adolescent hormonal activity is matched by technological know how? Or is it both and more? Glenn sees peril in casting our lot to remain on Earth. But would the outcome of contact in space be any more predictable than contact on Earth?*

**Point #1:** The faster we get off Earth the better. We're sitting ducks in the cosmic ocean of uncertainty. Why shouldn't there be a vast range of extraterrestrial life?

Hitler demonstrated that advanced technology and intelligence does not automatically imply advance morality. Hence, if we wait on earth to be contacted, we have no control over whether we are contacted by friendly or hostile beings. If we get out of our solar system and have contact in galactic space, then at least there is the possibility of intelligence and technological parity in case we need to defend ourselves. If the comet that hit Jupiter last year had entered the solar system at less than 1% different, it would have hit us and we would not be talking today.

**Point #2:** If contact occurs **before** we leave earth, fearing contact is probably counter-productive, and trying to avoid it is irrelevant. So it is right for us to think together about what we do now. If we are found first—here on earth, then we are less technologically and intelligently advanced; and hence, have no chance of defending ourselves if the first extraterrestrial contact is hostile. The faster we prepare our minds to think beyond previous norms of life, the better. Attempts at communications with dolphins, apes, and other terrestrial species are good beginnings. Another good beginning is the experimentation with the many new multi-computer user-created simulations to stretch or expand our minds. But imagine communicating with beings with the equivalent of IQ's possibly in excess of several hundred points?

If full cultural contact occurs—not contact with one individual or isolated contact which is **NOT** acknowledged by the dominant culture—but if humanity is contacted and knows it, prior to our departure from earth, how can we prepare? Should the United Nations Office of Outer Space Affairs and United Nations University conduct training programs in cyberspace, on CD ROMS, on educational television? What should be taught? Who gets to decide? We don't have to wait for that. We could begin with ourselves, by encountering ourselves in new ways. We are all part mystic and part technocrat, but tend to favor one side more than the other. Throughout all ages and cultures the more mystically inclined and the more technocratically inclined have disdained each other's views of metaphysics, epistemology, and aesthetics. Merging these two facets of our personalities is one challenging technique to begin to prepare for the unknown.

Should the United Nations be the point of communications? Isn't that a bit beyond our control? Wouldn't the ETs make their own presence known their own way? Or would they respect our social order and assume that the Secretary-General of the UN to be the point of contact? If so, then who would the Secretary General turn to for support? UN Peace Keeping/ World Bank? UNICEF? No, more likely he will ask UNESCO or the UNU to study the issue. And what within the UNU does the long-range thinking? The Millennium Project, which is also supported by UNESCO. So, if you would like to have this issue addressed within the UN system, then the normal procedure is to have your Ambassador at the

UN General Assembly bring it up. The request for study of this issue could then be sent on to the UNU and the Millennium Project.

**Point #3:** Some like George Wald, Harvard University biologist, claimed that contact with advanced extraterrestrial intelligence would destroy human dignity. A free ride on the advanced extraterrestrial knowledge starts the decay of human culture. If this view became dominant, then it could set up the subconscious reflex that once contact occurs, the human brain would no longer seek its own development. Wald's view ignores that the interaction between technologically different cultures here on Earth provided the basis for culture hybrids and scientific progress. Fear of the unknown insults the inquiring human spirit. Are not, teachers sometimes more advanced than their students? And has that caused the decay of students' dignity?

Depending on the kind of Contact, it could be a new lease on life. It could serve as stimulation for intellectual, spiritual, and physical development beyond current understanding. Even the concept of Contact as a myth serves human cooperation and educational goals. Trying to understand how to communicate with an intellectually and technologically advanced culture should stimulate our own evolution.

**Point #4:** Some like Ashley Montagu, Rutgers University anthropologist and social biologist, believe that contact is unlikely since humans would be perceived "as a highly infectious disease that is best quarantined from the rest of the universe." Oh come on now! As if humans are not interested in the smallest and seemingly most insignificant forms of life. Are extraterrestrials less curious than we? This also contradicts anthropocentric theologies as fraudulent opiates for the masses. This view, like the previous one, could create a negative self-fulfilling prophesy.

**Point #5:** One fear is that our future technology will leave us in the dust bin of evolution. Human-created artificial life adapted to outer space might leave the solar system and make the contact, rather than with us as a biological species. If so, well, tough! If humans don't get with the program, we'll be deselected. The program clearly states that stars and orbits decay. So we don't have all day—cosmically speaking. Either we accept we are a transition species evolving into a space-faring one, or we share the earth's fiery fate—assuming no friendly extraterrestrial bailout.

Although our species may not be enlightened enough yet for a healthy contact, we do seem to be getting little beacons or hints of presence to warm us up. Our response to the radio show *War of the Worlds* just one generation ago was much different than the current response to *The X Files*. We are clearly getting warmed up for contact.

**Point #6:** Of course, people should be free to think and say what they want. But as futurists we have a responsibility to point out potential consequences of beliefs.

**Point #7:** Contact via our unconscious mind. Creating an extraterrestrial threat has been proposed as a strategy to unite humanity. The suggestion that Contact could be made via human unconscious minds could have the effect of creating an unconscious consensus that humanity will be united. This could be seen as a legitimate view to popularize. Surely, our conference organizer, who served the previous Senate Foreign Relations Chairman knows, such views were proposed as cost-effective compared to conventional Pentagon expenditures for the prevention of WWIII. Should we consider unconscious contact as a way to reduce ethnic conflict today? And maybe the idea of contact via the unconscious mind has some value; why wouldn't an ET want to do a little safe feasibility study of human responses to contact? We can all imagine many strategies for such a feasibility study. The Soviet science fiction movie *Solaris* proposed contact via taking the form of unfulfilled love found by the ET in the human dream state. I have no idea if this is possible, but contact via the unconscious mind could have the effect of making ethnic conflict less significant. Is it right to manufacture and deploy such an idea to prevent ethnic conflict, as nuclear weapons were at the ready to prevent national conflict?

If the distances are too vast for Contact and communications within the three dimensions of space, then hyper dimensions might be more likely. Could the mind be a link between the three dimensional brain and hyper dimensions for ET contact?

**Point #8:** Many have speculated that a source of religion and stories of extraterrestrials could be the same. Historians tell us that Spanish Conquistadors were viewed by the less technologically advanced South Americas as gods. How would we distinguish between a divine presence and a friendly extraterrestrial? ...May we be so lucky.

**Point #9:** Astrophysics gives us two rather miserable long-range futures: either a cold entropic death as the universe expands to oblivion or a hot kinetic death as the universe contracts to the next big bang. To keep our options open, we might expand beyond our star, merge with cosmic cultures, and permeate the universe with consciousness—as does gravity today—and become a permeating force to hold the universe long enough to create a third alternative.

**Point #10:** To repeat the first point: The faster we get off Earth, the better. Unfortunately, we have no consensus on this point and are a long way from it. We need a global system to bring together the range of views of the future, global problems, and potential solutions in such a way that we are neither over pessimistic or optimistic. A three-year feasibility study of such a system is nearing completion. Called **The Millennium Project**, its purpose is to help humanity think together about the future by connecting futurists, scholars, policy analysts, and activists around the world and from many disciplines via modern computer communications and software; and to have public access to find those ideas, individuals, and research not found through the traditional means. If an ET were to be asked to report on what humanity thought about its future and how it came to those conclusions, where would it go for the answers? There is no global system to answer such questions. Once successfully established, The Millennium Project would be able to answer questions like that and to feed back such answers to civilization so that we can improve thinking. Many want to create a global consensus to create a more peaceful world and migrate beyond our womb solar system. One definition of consensus is that which becomes obvious after sufficient information has circulated and been acknowledged.

The Millennium Project is a tool within the United Nations to help create global consensus among many different systems necessary to address such issues as space migration, and how to prepare for cosmic cultures meeting. The Millennium Project is an activity of the United Nations University's World Institute for Development Economics Research. It is one answer to the question: "What do we do now?"

Some of these points were drawn from Glenn's books: *Future Mind: Artificial Intelligence: Merging the Mystical with the Technological in the 21st Century*, and from *Space Trek: The Endless Migration* (Stackpole Books) co-authored with George Robinson. More information on the Millennium Project is available on Internet via gopher futures. wic.epa.gov or on the World Wide Web via links at: http://undcp.or.at/unlinks, html, select UN Organizations and then select UNU/WIDER Millennium Project.

## ⊕ John E. Mack, M.D.

*John E. Mack, M.D.*
*(photo ©Karin Rosenthal 1994)*

Dr. Mack is Professor of Psychiatry at the Cambridge Hospital, Harvard Medical School, and founding director of the Center for Psychology and Social Change. His earlier books include the Pulitzer Prize-winning *A Prince of Our Disorder, a biography of T.E. Lawrence*. His most recent book is *Abduction: Human Encounters with Aliens*. Current activity is with the Program for Extraordinary Experience Research (P.E.E.R), in Cambridge, MA.

# Studying Intrusions From the Subtle Realm: How Can We Deepen Our Knowledge?

*This paper was adapted from a talk given by John Mack at a conference of the International Association for New Science on September 16, 1995. Focused on his experiences in working with alien abduction phenomena, he observes that we may be getting near the moment when that small percentage of elites that determine what we are supposed to think is real, wake up to the fact that the consensus view of reality is gone.*

I want to talk with you about what I have been finding over the past, now nearly six years, in studying the alien abduction phenomenon. In the context of this meeting I wish to talk particularly about the ways that we know, how we actually know anything. What is the appropriate epistemology for a particular subject? It seems to me that all science, all knowledge really, is about the discovery of patterns, and that includes patterns of meaning. But how we know, the approach that we use, depends on what the matter at hand happens to be. For the sake of clarity, I would divide the realms that we are considering here between what has been called the gross material world on the one hand, and the subtle realms on the other, or, in [psychiatrist] Stanislav Grof's language, the hylotropic versus the holotropic world, or in [physicist] David Bohm's terms, the explicate or manifest order or the implicate, or hidden, order, by which he means the structures, deeper reality and meaning in the universe.

By and large, science, as it is traditionally spoken of, has addressed, and its methodology has been appropriate to, the gross material, the physical or manifest world, and the approach to this world has been largely dualistic: an observer studies something from outside of, or separate from, that person or phenomenon. We know that some of the best scientists do not think of their work in that way, but, nevertheless, that is the standard that we often think we mean, or are told we mean, by the "scientific method." I might add that in the focus on the material realm to the exclusion of the subtle realms, we have virtually rid the cosmos of nature, rid nature of spirit and, in a sense, denied the existence of all life other than that which is physically observable here on earth.

What do I mean by the subtle realm? As I began to think about it more deeply, I realized this is not so easy to pin down. It has to do with phenomena that seem to come from another dimension: information obtained by telepathy; clairvoyance and the whole psi realm; out-of-body experiences; near-death experiences; telekinesis and the alien abduction phenomenon itself—i.e., phenomena that may manifest in the physical world, but seem to originate in another dimension, to come from a place unseen. We are speaking of matters which are not readily observable under ordinary "separatist," dualistic, scientific or methodological conditions, but make their presence known more subtly through an opening of consciousness or more receptive perception.

One of the fundamental tenets of the mechanistic or dualistic approach is that consciousness is seen as an epiphenomenon of the human brain. This is one of the basic assumptions we have to challenge if we are going to be able to study the subtle realms, which not only involve consciousness itself, but the relationship of consciousness to the material world. We have to consider the possibility that consciousness—spirit, self, soul—all have a life, an existence, separate from the physical body. That, for me, was once a very great leap, and I had to do my own self-exploration through work with Stanislav Grof, and a great deal of challenging of my own materialist scientific and clinical upbringing, to come to appreciate the fundamental parting of the ways required between the materialist scientific approach and one which can begin to allow us to study more profoundly these subtle realms.

226

The Western world view, what Tulane philosopher Michael Zimmerman calls anthropomorphic humanism, has reduced reality largely to the manifest or physical world and puts the human mind, or the human being, at the top of the cosmic intellectual hierarchy, eliminating not only God but virtually all spirit from the cosmos. The phenomena that really shake up that world view are those that seem to cross over from the unseen world and manifest in the physical world. That is why someone like Uri Geller may be hounded from pillar to post. That is why people like Brian O'Leary, who studies free energy, or people who study phenomena that seem to challenge the great divide we have created between the unseen realm and the physical world, are given such a hard time in this society. By the 17th century, theologians and other "spiritual people," perhaps even psychologists, were given a mandate over the subtle or unseen realm and scientists were given jurisdiction over the physical, or material, world. There was not a great problem as long as phenomena seemed to array themselves neatly on one side of the divide. But if a phenomenon appears to cross over, if it will not stay on one side or the other, this raises a big problem in our culture.

The matter that I am studying is just such a phenomenon. There are others—the near-death experience, materializations, telekinesis. But this is the one that I have been studying, and I think it is one that by its very nature seems to "grab" us where we live just <u>because</u> it crosses over and manifests in the form or language that we do understand in this culture—spaceships, abductions, implants, instruments, surgery, hybrids, babies, reproduction, etc. All that seems very physical and ought to be reducible, or at least possible to study, by the dualistic methods of traditional science. But the alien abduction phenomenon does not seem to yield its secrets to that approach. The phenomenon challenges vigorously that sacred barrier we have created between the unseen and the material world. It undermines the fundamental world view of the Western mind.

I believe we need to consider another frontier, which I am only going to be able to touch upon briefly here, namely what makes us so attached to a particular world view. Why do we cling so tightly to a world view in general, and the materialist paradigm in particular? What makes our world view so fundamental to our existence? I do not believe it is just the huge economic investments—which there are, of course—that derive from the materialist view. Indeed, the whole materialist marketplace mentality of technology and science, as we know it, is threatened by a world view that tells us of vast realms unavailable to our direct observation. In fact, a result of the world view in which we are embedded is, ultimately, the destruction of the material playground, the earth itself as a living organism.

But there is more to it. A world view organizes our sense of self. It can give us the illusion that we have some control of ourselves and of nature, that we are in charge, that we are safe. Never mind that we all must die, and perhaps die more lonely deaths, for in this particular world view we have rid the cosmos of all consciousness, of spirit, of God him or herself, and thus can hardly come to grips with the notion of death except as a bleak end to everything. There is, therefore, a terrible loneliness in this world view.

Nevertheless, the materialist world view, like any paradigm, organizes our sense of self, and constructs reality. When this, or any world view is challenged and shattered, it creates terror. I think that some of the resistance that I have encountered, and which, naively, I rather underestimated, derives from this threat. People have said to me "Well, didn't you know if you started saying that little green men or spirits or funny beings were taking men, women and children away and doing things to them, didn't you realize that you would run into trouble?" But, like the frog who dies in gradually heating water, I think it kind of snuck up on me. I had been doing this work for several years, and had not said anything publicly until I was pretty clear about what I was doing. Perhaps you have to be a little naive to wander off into these insecure realms of knowledge, or you will not go there at all. For if you know in advance the opposition you are going to encounter, you might not choose to take on the adventure of such exploration at all. If what Bertrand Russell said about resistance being proportional to the square of the importance of what you are studying is true, I must be studying something very important indeed.

Finally, in one sense I appreciate the criticism, even the attacks I have encountered, for it is, I believe, useful for all of us to know more deeply about what resistance our work is stirring up. For then, if we can embrace the questions and polarities that the critiques represent, perhaps we can go to a deeper level of understanding instead of finding ourselves, as we tend to, in opposition to the people that will not take in what we are trying to communicate.

I would like to say one more word about the challenge to our world view that crossover phenomena like the alien abduction story represents. Consider the blows to the collective egocentrism of humanity starting with Copernicus and Galileo and going on to Darwin and then Freud, wherein little by little we had to face that not only were we not at the center in terms of the geography of the universe, we were not the only God-given ones among the earth's creatures, and, with Freud, we were not even in charge of our own psyches. Now, finally, we are learning from the abduction phenomenon that we may not be the smartest guys in the universe after all. In fact, we may not even be in control in any sense. Other beings—funny-looking ones at that—little creatures with big black eyes can come and do what they will with us and render us helpless. That is truly a fourth blow after what Copernicus, Darwin and Freud had already done to our collective arrogance. I must admit to being a bit perverse, actually, for, as a psychiatrist, I believe that anything that can be a big blow to the human ego can only be a good thing in terms of our collective development. Such shocks can perhaps help us to grow as a species.

Before speaking of my specific work, I want to say another word about how a world view is maintained in a given culture. For this consideration, I have suggested the idea of the "politics of ontology," which has to do with how a society organizes itself, particularly through a certain elite group, to determine for the rest of that society what is real. The politics of ontology is a kind of governance of ideas. In this culture, there may be a very small group of scientific, governmental, religious, and corporate elite that determine the prevailing boundaries of reality. The forces that surround the determination of reality is an area of politics that we have not really thought about that much. We think about the politics of economics, of the governing of communities and the creation of a social order, but not much about how we are governed with respect to what we are supposed to think is real.

An interesting thing is happening, however, in this culture, as Michael Zimmerman has pointed out. With so much information available through the media, computer networks, and extensive public education, everybody is getting kind of smart. People know their own experiences and when what they have undergone does not fit the prevailing mechanistic world view. Whatever polling methods you may use, it is apparent that large percentages of people seem to know there is an unseen world, or hidden dimensions of reality. They may not call it that, but they know that the subtle realms exist. They know their own experiences and trust them. They are not fooled by NBC or the *New York Times* or *Time* or other official arbiters of the truth and reality. We have a kind of samizdat going on here, an underground of popular knowledge about the world and the universe. But this universe is not the one we are being officially told about. It is really going to be interesting to see when the official mainstream, the small percentage of elites that determine what we are supposed to think is real, wake up to the fact that the consensus view of reality is gone. We are, I think, getting near that moment.

228

In 1974, Margaret Mead wrote in *Redbook* magazine, "People still ask each other, 'Do you believe in UFOs?' I think this is a silly question, born of confusion. Belief has to do with matters of faith. It has nothing to do with the kind of knowledge that is based on scientific inquiry... When we want to understand something strange, something previously unknown, we have to begin with an entirely different set of questions. What is it? How does it work? Are there recurrent regularities?" (Mead, 1974). I resonate with that, because I am always being accused of being a "believer," somebody who has come and gone over the edge from rationality to belief. My work has nothing to do with belief. It has to do with what I do as a clinician.

I began to see people in 1990, who seemed of sound mind but were describing experiences which simply did not fit into any kind of psychiatric category of which I could conceive. Child abuse, psychosis, neurosis, organic brain disease, fantasy-prone personality, you know the litany here. No diagnostic category came close to explaining what I was seeing. I often say this to audiences: there is not a single example of an abduction case that fulfills my rather simple criteria for an authentic case, (the person reports, with or without hypnosis or a simple relaxation exercise, observing some sort of humanoid beings, being taken against their wills into some kind of enclosure, and subjected to traumatic and sometimes enlightening procedures which has been shown to have a cause other than what the person says happened.) There are now thousands of cases described in the literature that fulfill these criteria. These patterns are clear, down to quite specific details. No case, for example, has revealed that behind the reported experience is some kind of strange depression, or child abuse, or something else. Clinicians have made intense efforts to find this "something else," because the motivation is very strong to shoot this phenomenon down, to find another cause, what I call the "anything but syndrome"—anything but that we are being visited by some unusual intelligence that is entering our world.

The methodological issues are important. On what basis do I ask that these experiences be taken seriously? In some ways, it is easier for a psychological clinician, like a psychiatrist, to use these methods because, in a sense, that is the way we always work. We are not basically people who get anywhere by standing back from other people and observing them as specimens. The way we need always to work, to be helpful to our patients, is by entering into their worlds through a kind of intuitive use of our total self—intellect, inspiration, and intuition. We use the total psyche, our total consciousness. In effect, trained <u>consciousness</u> has been our instrument of knowing from the beginning of the discipline when we were doing it right and not trying to act like physicists or pharmacologists. Our true roots as psychological professionals come from the use of consciousness, including non-ordinary states. We learn by methods that are participatory and non-dualistic. This is a "relational" way of knowing.

It is easy for people who use a dualistic approach to say, "You're contaminating the field. You're influencing, you're leading," when, in fact, you are joining the other person in bringing forth experiences. But you cannot get away from the fact that in any exploration of human experience two consciousnesses, two energy fields, are interacting or connecting and that what emerges is out of that participation, out of the relationship. Then, after that, you look at what you have found and apply rational judgment in analyzing the material. You ask, was this person trying to please? Was this authentic? What was the emotional intensity that came with the communications? Was this emotion appropriate to what the person was talking about? These are the yardsticks that psychological clinicians apply in assessing what a patient or client is reporting. It has nothing to do with belief. In my abduction cases, with few exceptions, I have felt people were describing as best they could what had occurred. In fact, they doubt as much as I do what they have undergone. They tend to come to me saying, "Can you make this go away?" Or will report waking experiences as dreams if they occurred at night. They want the experiences to be found to be a product of their psyches, not to be "real." In case after case, I have seen the lips quiver or tears come down the cheeks when the person realizes that he was not asleep and that what occurred was not a dream. I might then say, "Yes, I'm sorry, but I know many people who have had experiences like yours." One woman who came to me a few days ago, and was eager to believe her experiences were dreams, said to me sobbing "But if it's real, then it can happen again. And I can't stop it and you can't stop it." These individuals prefer that this be a clinical phenomenon that will go away, or that I might cure it by giving them a pill, or talking them out of it or interpreting it in some dynamic sense which, of course, is what many of my colleagues want to do as well.

So the method used here is to employ consciousness, my total self, my whole background or being, to be with a person, to create a safe environment in which the individual can share and bring forth that which is the most sensitive, most troubling, most confusing, most extraordinary kind of experiences that are imaginable, at least in the world view of this culture. I have worked intensively now with over a hundred people and done a modified hypnosis or relaxation exercise in which the person closes their eyes and just "goes inside" in about seventy cases. Contrary to what is said about hypnosis bringing distortions of memory in such cases, I often trust what comes out in the relaxation sessions more than in face-to-face interviews because the feelings are so intense and less acceptable. The person is able to bring forth more ignoble, more humiliating experiences, than in conscious, more social, kinds of interaction. When the individuals tell what they have consciously recalled, they tend to organize their thoughts in a way that is more palatable and appropriate to their positive self-regard and world views.

The basic phenomena associated with abductions seem to be consistent worldwide. At the same time, paradoxes abound, and it is difficult to make statements that apply in all cases. For example, I do not believe that in every abduction case the physical body is taken. Yet, there are cases in which the person is witnessed to be not there. A child, for example, may go into the mother's room at night and the mother is gone, and the mother reports an abduction experience that occurred at that time. But there are also cases where the person reports experiencing an abduction and other people have observed seeing the person still in place. But the basic phenomena: seeing a beam of light; the intrusion of humanoid beings into the person's life; the experience of being paralyzed and taken through walls into some kind of enclosure and subjected to a variety of procedures with the creation of a "hybrid" species; the conveying of powerful information about threats to the planet such as nuclear war and vast ecological change; the evidences of an expansion of consciousness that occurs for the people that undergo these experiences, for people that work with them and for those who will attend to what this appears to be about— these all seem to be quite consistent findings. Furthermore, the experiences seem also to be consistent worldwide. My colleague, Dominique Callimanopulos, and I have traveled to South Africa, to Brazil, and a number of countries in Europe. We are also getting reports from all over the world and learning that the basic phenomenon appears to have a consistent core. I have worked with a South African medicine man, Credo Mutwa, a Zulu leader now 74, who had a classic abduction experience when he was 38. This occurred during his training as a shaman. Mr. Mutwa was in the bush when suddenly he found himself in an enclosure surrounded by humanoid beings with large black eyes. He was terrified, and underwent the range of traumatic, educational and transformational experiences described above.

He believes the "mandindas," as his people call these beings, are trying to teach us about the threat to the earth that our mindless destructive actions are causing.

I would like to turn now to what appears to be the basic pattern and meaning of the abduction phenomenon. First, abductees are being told over and over that this phenomenon is occurring in the context of the threat to Earth as a living system, a response to the ecological devastation that our particular species has undertaken. Credo Mutwa told us that, according to African mythology, Earth is one of what his people call "mother planets." There are twenty-five mother planets in the cosmos, he said, and we may be destroying life on one of them. As one of the abductees I have worked with put it, the phenomenon is an effort to bring about "a cosmic correction". For Earth, evidently, has a place in the larger fabric of meaning and significance in the cosmos, and this one species cannot be allowed to destroy it for its own exploitative purposes.

Second, this other intelligence appears to function as a kind of intermediary between the Source of creation and us, emissaries perhaps, of that correction. This does not mean that every kind of alien being is involved in that mission. But the beings are often perceived in this way.

Third, a message is coming through to us—I will shortly provide some clinical material related to this—that we have lost connection with what some aliens, humans who have had these experiences, call Source, or Home, the divine core of creativity, the light—different traditions have varying ways of talking about this realm. We are being told that we have grown too far from that Source and have lost our connection with it.

Fourth, these encounters are changing the consciousness of the people that are undergoing them, and, I believe, influencing consciousness on the planet as the power and implications of the abduction phenomenon are becoming more widely recognized. The phenomenon seems to hold the potential of reconnecting us with our divine Source.

Fifth, the hybrid "program," which can be deeply traumatic for mothers and fathers (particularly when they are brought back to see and hold these odd children, especially as they cannot know when they will be able to see these creatures again), seems to be a kind of awkward insurance policy for the next step of evolution. We do not, of course, know in what reality these hybrids exist. It could be an intermediate realm between the material world and the unseen world. A number of abductees have been told that the hybrids represent a step in evolution that is being created for the time when we have destroyed ourselves so that some aspect of our genetic structure or nature can be preserved.

Finally, the human-alien relationship, which is not simply good or bad, is, nevertheless, reciprocal. We do not know from what dimension or Source the whole connection is being orchestrated. Perhaps it serves them and us. It may emanate from another dimension, inviting us to explore its mysteries.

Now I will tell you about the case of a woman who we will call Ifyani, a name derived from her alien encounter. She is a 34-year-old mother of three children. Her oldest son was killed in an automobile accident several months ago, and her abduction encounters have been important in enabling her to integrate that terrible loss and to put it in a larger cosmic perspective. Ifyani has had a wide range of abduction experience, from being "used" for the breeding project to having a dual identity, seeming to work along with the aliens, identifying with them and at the same time experiencing the trauma of her encounters. She has a complex religious background. She is an artist and writes poetry. These talents are utilized as a therapeutic outlet for her emotions and experiences. Ifyani is a native of a Central American country, where she experienced Mayan-derived folklore influences while also being raised in a strict Christian atmosphere. Her mother was a Pentecostal deaconess and her grandmother and great grandmother were devout Catholics. We have been working toward enabling her to overcome the victimization aspect of her abduction experiences. Ifyani has undergone profound personal growth in the context of her encounters.

The session from which I will quote occurred on July 31, 1995. The transcript has been edited by Ifyani herself to clarify what meaning she intended, and in some instances to correct what she felt was awkward phrasing. Ifyani had been having ongoing encounters with the beings during the days before that, and was struggling to change these encounters into more reciprocal exchanges. She sensed that the beings were struggling to connect with her on a soul level, even to take her soul, or to connect with her, body and soul. She found that by emanating love towards them, the demonic or dark dimension of their being was affected. They seemed to pull back from the love she sent them, and, at the same time, to thrive from it. Thus, a kind of loving connection seemed to grow out of that struggle. This was not a regression but a regular interview.

Ifyani, referring to love, says:

> "I believe that love is the most powerful force in the whole universe, or in every other universe that might exist. I think it's what everything originated from. I think it's what created everything, and I think everything has love in it."

Ifyani's beliefs seem to stem directly from her on-going life-long experiences. She continued:

> "I look at love as an extension cord that connects my soul to the main major Source, a sort of umbilical cord that provides me with spiritual nourishment."

Speaking of the aliens, she says:

> "They seem very frail. I think they feel a sort of envy toward us. Maybe if they are creating these half-and-half babies, using our bodies for themselves, trying somehow, to get enough human qualities to nurture themselves, to be mothered and reconnect with the Source of love."

I hear this in a number of cases, i.e. that the alien beings envy our dense, physical embodiment and seem to treasure our sexuality, our nurturance, our intense physicality. This is something that they want from us, while they, in turn, crack our barriers, breaking down the egoism that distances us from our Source. In Ifyani's words:

> "They're like starving children who are trying to sneak in with the other babies who are being breast fed. I think that they remember what this felt like. They know what it feels like, and I think they want to go back to that, but for some reason unknown to us, they can't connect to the Source without physical bodies."

This is paradoxical, because in another sense the beings seem to function like emissaries from Source. But what I think she means here is that the beings do not have the kind of deep, rich physical, emotional and spiritual experience of connection with Source for which we long. She continues:

> "I would have to grant them permission to use my body and give up soul willingly (which I don't intend to do), for them to connect with the Source. To me, it's like they're trying to use tricks and I don't know why. I don't consider them evil in the way that we look at evil. I think that they're just interested in self-preservation. I do believe we all originated from the same Source. I believe if we look back on ancient myths and religious beliefs, many of the answers are there. But we've gotten to the point here where we consider ourselves so technologically advanced and educated, just "up there," that we don't even think it's necessary to remember where we came from. We've become educated fools.

232

I feel religion has been made into a tool that keeps us blind and ignorant, keeping us from remembering where we came from. I think Source's purpose for allowing these encounters to take place—perhaps this is totally weird, was to let us remember things, to bring back to us the memory of Source so we can empower ourselves. It's not like Source is giving you this power now. It's always been there. It's self-realization. It's to open up our consciousness more. I think it's almost like a baby going from crawling to walking and realizing that I am. That's what I think Source's reason for, was for this. I am...

I think there's so much more to this body then we are aware of. We don't even know a lot about our DNA. I think we have the ability to restructure our DNA. We only need to remember how. I think we can become what the Bible said; in the last days people will have new bodies, indestructible bodies. They will be new beings, and I think it's all inside of us. It's all here, this package, and I think the mind is the key. I feel that our minds will expand and open, and a percentage of the brain that we don't currently use will become accessible to us. Then we will be truly free, because I don't think humans are free now.

We tend to look at everything as good or bad and say, "Oh, how can God let this happen?" We look at things from our perspective only and think, "Oh, my God, how horrible, how terrible," but that's because we're looking at it through these eyes. We're not looking at the whole picture. I don't think there's ever an end to anything or a real beginning to anything—everything just is. Every action you look at, even sending a little kid to school for the first time, everything we do just mimics the way Source does things. If you take a good look at society and our individual lives you will notice that patterns are always being repeated—in the way we raise our children, and the way government treats us. Everything mimics over and over and over. Where is that pattern coming from? I think it comes from the main Source. I guess in a way we're like a small replica of what goes on everywhere else. I suppose we are baby Sources and we come here to mature...

We're getting ready to graduate... A lot of us are starting to wake up and remember and realize, I think graduation time is coming up... Our Mother Earth has gone through a lot. She's gone through having to support a whole race of kindergarten kids and juvenile delinquents who've mauled, raped and spray painted it, disfiguring and totally disgracing it. All of this was done in the name of technology and advancement.

I think this class is gonna graduate, and I think the earth will have to go through a cleansing period.

Poison in the water. Poison in the air. Poison in the food. I keep having these visions and dreams about the water and other resources being deliberately poisoned. Just by being the way we are, here we are poisoning the planet. We are giving off negative energy, and we're poisoning the planet by giving off these repelling energies, we're killing our Mother Earth. Our thoughts can destroy or create by the energies they produce. It affects the animals. It affects the insects. It affects everything. Everything—all of it, the trees and everything. If we continue to give off this negative energy, after a while the earth will look at us as something like a harmful bacteria and repel us. It will fight back. I think Mother Earth is actually fighting back. These blue baldies [that's what she calls the alien beings]—I won't say they own this earth, but they see it as their home. I think they were here before we were made. They are the true keepers of this earth... Whether they mean to or not, they're here to help us in this growth period, to help us to mature.

This, I would remind you, is a person who has been highly traumatized by her experiences, but with the trauma, or perhaps as an outgrowth of it, she has demonstrated personal growth and knowledge.

I would say we're getting to a point where we're becoming more aware, waking up, but I think these blue baldies were put in charge of Mother Earth, and I think they're the ones that are going to clean it up after we have been dealt with. It seems to me that I'm becoming more conscious of things around me. It feels like there's an actual chemical reaction happening in the lower back part of my brain, something is changing, and I am being changed by it.

In conclusion, I would begin by paraphrasing what the American Catholic bishops said at the time in the early 1980s when they took a policy stand against nuclear deterrence: We could destroy God's work. Also, the Dalai Lama, when a group of researchers met with him around the alien abduction phenomenon in 1992, suggested that, "These beings, these creatures, they are very upset. We are destroying their physical and spiritual homes." They have no choice, he added, but to become physical and come back and try to stop us.

Next, the alien abduction phenomenon appears to be a kind of spiritual outreach program from the cosmos for the spiritually impaired.

Third, we and the beings, evidently, come from a common Source and that love is at the core of the cosmos as its essential creative power.

Fourth, to know in the domain of our relationship to the subtle realm requires, paradoxically, (and this phenomenon is filled with paradox), an attitude of not knowing, what the Buddhists call empty mind. Knowledge here seems to come like the creation of the universe itself. As the universe emerged from nothing, so knowledge in matters such as this seems to emerge from radical not knowing. The new paradigm we have heard so much about has to do, I believe, with a different notion of our relationship to reality, one that is co-creative and evolutionary, as if we were co-creating with nature and with God.

Fifth, and finally, our job at this time, for all of us, appears to be to overcome the dualism, the separateness, that has characterized not only our world view, but our scientific approaches to all the realms that have been studied up to this point. The task now is to integrate the polarities at every level. At the intrapsychic level this means the darkness within us, as well as our loving spiritual selves. At the interpersonal level we have to overcome the polarized individual and collective human relationships that find expression, for example, in "ethnic cleansing," an instance of extreme polarization within the human community, what Erik Erikson called "pseudo-speciation," feeling and behaving if we were not even a single species.

Finally, we need to transcend the separateness that disconnects us from nature. If we could transcend this division, we might then explore, enjoy, and travel ecstatically, lovingly, materially and non-materially, among the unique particularities of our own being, our own natures within the cosmos, experiencing at the same time an essential unity and sacredness of creation. That possibility is, I think, what this extraordinary phenomenon has to teach us.

Reference: Mead, Margaret (1974) UFOs—Visitors from Outer Space? Redbook, September 1974.

⊕ Keith Ferrell

234

*Keith Ferrell*

Keith Ferrell, Vice President and Editor of *OMNI* magazine, also has served as Vice President and Editorial Director of *COMPUTE* magazine and General Media Online Services (including *OMNI*, *Longevity*, and *Saturday Review Online*). An author of a dozen published books, he has written biographies for young adults on H.G. Wells, Ernest Hemingway, George Orwell and John Steinbeck. Forthcoming are biographies of Jack London and Robert Oppenheimer. He has written computer hardware and computer software articles for *World Book Encyclopedia* and *World Book Science Year*. He appears frequently on television and radio, and lectures on a broad range of subjects including the future of business and the dangers of censorship.

# "If We Can't Talk to Each Other, How Can We Expect to Talk to Them?"

Omni Magazine *editor Keith Ferrell provides an inside view of Project Open Book, a continuing and developing dialogue on all aspects of UFO phenomena. One of the few responsible print media undertakings in this field, in over three years it has become a highly interactive dialogue. Beyond this,* Omni *is using the information it is developing in attempts to engage multiple levels of government on the subject.*

What I want to talk about is something we call Project Open Book. It is our attempt to provide an area for dialogue or communication about the very topics we've been discussing all through this wonderful weekend. Because of what we've learned, and because of what we've seen as a result of endeavoring to create this dialogue space, I'm calling my talk, "If We Can't Talk to Each Other, How Can We Expect to Talk to Them?" Project Open Book, it seemed like a good idea at the time—about two and one-half years ago. *Omni* was as *Omni's* been since October 1978—really on a roll. In light of the badly reviewed film, *Johnny Mnemonic* opening last Friday, I will make a point that this film is based on a story that first appeared in *Omni*, and the word 'cyberspace' of which we hear constantly, also appeared first in *Omni*.

That role, that posture we have taken, of being in the forefront, of looking ahead, of being the first magazine of the future, of providing our readers, over 750,000 of them, with what we call tools of the 21st century, had continued to gather steam, gather force, gather momentum. Over the last 3-4 years we have won any number of journalism awards. I cite them to reflect well on the staff, not on me, but these range from the American Institute of Physics, the Distinguished Science Writing Award, which is the biggest of all the science writing awards, to the one that really I think flattered us the most, which was New York University's Olive Branch Award for contributions to international security and world peace, journalistic contributions. *Omni's* scientific credibility, I think, had never been higher than in the last 2-3 years; our journalistic credibility is through the roof, our sales were higher, our advertising was higher, which made my employers happy.

We have been historically the one science magazine that has been willing to look and look seriously at non-traditional topics, look at them in a scientific way. Whether that is UFOs, or nano-technology, which was laughed at when we talked about it in *Omni,* or the global telecommunications network in computers which actually we have some files on hilarious correspondence from people arguing things like electronic mail would never happen.

We noticed, over the last 4 to 5 years, the response when we would do an article or take a look at the possibilities for the communication or contact with extraterrestrial beings was increasing. There was more and more interest. Simultaneously, we saw what I think of as an unfortunate concomitant media explosion, which is the trivialization of the subject. It was either mocked in the mainstream press or exploited in the "Rush Limbaugh and Newt Gengrich are both the products of alien incest" press, as I think of it. So we decided it was time to put *Omni's* reputation, prestige, power, and reach on the line. We created something I call Project Open Book. That's a little bit of a nod to Blue Book; it's a lot of a nod to what we wanted to create, which was a place, a dialogue space, where we would serve several goals. One was to be a clearing house, central area where people could come to share their ideas, insights, theories, yell at each other, pat each other on the back. Two, we wanted to put together a review board that would look at the most interesting of the cases we receive. We wanted to put together the tools for our investigation, journalistically, and to share those tools with our readers so that they could further investigate. Obviously, because we were in the business, we wanted to provide a publication platform. Finally, and above all, we wanted to do what *Omni* has always done. We have a hero at *Omni*. That hero is called human consciousness. We need to know, we need to imagine, desire, stretch our boundaries. So our final and overriding goal was education. I've made it clear or tried to—that we had no agenda at the magazine. We're neither believers not disbelievers, whatever we are personally. I'm talking now about the platform, the magazine, neither believer nor disbeliever. Indeed, our staff is half and half. I made it clear that we were coming to everything that came in with a certain scientific skepticism, and by God, that has got to be the most misunderstood word in the language. It does not mean debunking. We're not interested in debunking. There are plenty of debunkers around, and they annoy me as much as I'm sure they annoy a lot of you. What we did want to do was set up a set of parameters for the material we would cover and debate and publish that we're guided by that skepticism. It's not enough to say "I believe, here it is," or "I've experienced, here it is." We wanted to set up a set of parameters and guidelines that would give our readers and the participants in Project Open Book a chance to offer proof. Proof is what we were after.

Let me do a little experiment as you just did. How many of you think in the way we go through our daily lives the government serves us well, works well, is efficient and effective? Very good. We have one and he's in charge. We have two. How many of you believe (and you may not want to raise your hands, I think my point will become clear quickly)... how many of you believe there is a secondary, shadow, or secret government that is effectively suppressing information? I think we should all get together and get that second government in charge, because obviously it works!

We announced in the middle of 1993 our intentions to proceed with this. The mail started flowing in. We were prepared for an interesting response, we were prepared for a high volume of response. We were not prepared for crates of mail, and I mean the word *crate* in its most literal sense. Tens of thousands of letters, examples; we called for instances, and anecdotes, reminiscences, pieces of evidence, and we received tens of thousands of pieces of mail. *Omni's* always been a very interactive magazine. We printed the Roswell Declaration, agreeing to forward the responses to the government. We got so many responses I had to justify the mail bill to my finance department, because it cost us hundreds of dollars to forward the tens of thousands of responses we got.

We got a lot of attention, we got a lot of controversy. Probably my favorite moment of all was the day that within the space of an hour I heard from both Carl Sagan and Richard Hoagland both of them saying I was wrong; Carl saying I was too credulous, and Dick saying I was too skeptical; which led me to believe that probably our posture was right on target, for what we are: a *mass* media magazine. We're not an enthusiasts' magazine, we're not a believers' magazine, we have no ax to grind. We want to provide those tools for the 21st century to give people something to think about.

We called for incidents, anecdotes, examples, cases we could investigate. In the space of the first month or so—and this is why I asked the question about the government—we learned there was a shadow government run by the CIA suppressing information, a shadow government run by the FBI suppressing information, and one the Treasury was running that was suppressing information because it had so much financial impact. There was the Trilateral Commission running a shadow government to suppress information, and on and on. We found that fascinating, and have talked about that in the magazine. We got a lot of stories that were moving, and touching, and some that were heartbreaking about contact, or about experiences, or about abductions, but that were not investigatable, which was our goal—to put together a program that could be investigated. We got a lot of things that could be investigated, however, and that's where things have started to get very interesting with *Omni*. These have ranged from observations made by groups of people who have contacted us, who have outside verification, to a range of materials. The one that was the funniest to us was some material that was sent that had been found in a child's ear one morning. It struck us as a little amusing, and a little bit of concern until we did have it examined, and there was a little bit of a mystery in it. We weren't sure what the material was, so we hired a team of chemists and researchers to look into that. We have hired private investigators. We have taken Roswell, for example, from the top as though we were starting from scratch. This Fall will be publishing our results which I think will surprise a lot of people. It's been a little scary, quite exciting to dig into the material.

I will say there's one other word that causes as much controversy as when we say 'UFO' or 'alien'. We got a lot of controversy. The only other thing that causes as much controversy with *Omni*, is the word *evolution*. When I put evolution on the cover two or three years ago—we did a wonderful issue on evolution, scientific evolution, and it was pulled from newsstands. Chicago, surprise, not the deep South, but Chicago. Certain newsstands removed the magazine because of that word. With this sort of material, cosmic material, encounter material, the controversy tends to stem from the more traditional or conservative scientific community who enjoy making a lot of fun of us. *Time* magazine's had a lot of fun making fun of us in various areas. I've enjoyed many wonderful conversations this weekend. One that's stayed with me for a couple of days was someone talking about the *conservatism* of the magazine. She made some very wonderful points.

I want to talk about why we are as conservative as we are, and it is precisely because of the sort of media exploitation that is going on right now, as this topic is used solely to drive ratings points. Now I have been accused of using this topic solely to drive our circulation up. If that were true, there are things I could have done that would have taken our circulation much higher than it did go. Indeed, I think, or fear, a lot of the people who watch *Sightings* or some of the other programs I think are more exploitative would, when encountering *Omni's* material, feel that we're not open minded enough—that Project Open Book is not open enough. If I was simply trying to send our ratings sky-high, we would not have that level of skepticism. Our conservatism is prompted by our belief that this sort of material is under a certain type of assault right now, and the assault comes from two or three areas. One is that very type of exploitation, the non-critical acceptance of every single story that comes along. If you watch some of the programs or read some of the publications consistently, it can't all be right, yet everything carries the same weight. Here's this experience, here's this experience, here's this experience: put them all three side by side and they tend to contradict or even conflict with one another. But they don't do that. They space things out on the short-term memory of the wider viewing public.

The other side of it is, what's happened to the serious speculation about the future in the media, and that is what I call the 'star-trekkization' of the future, which tends to present images of what we've talked about this weekend—the wholly hopeful futures and contacts; or wholly fearful futures and contacts; no sense of what we're bringing to the party; what we have to contribute. That's why we've been so conservative. We're simply trying to provide tools for thought. If you disagree with what we're saying at *Omni*, terrific. That's why we publish in the way we do, and are doing as much on-line as we are, to give people the opportunity to have that back-and-forth. We are very serious about taking seriously the interest in this topic and the sense that something is going on in our consciousness, something is happening, some curiosity is being raised. That's the purpose of the clearing house. Our review board has gotten a lot of controversy because our review board has enthusiasts, believers, experiencers. It also has James Oberg, which has resulted in a lot of interesting debates. But again, if you have a panel looking at the prospects for the baseball season and every member of the panel is a big fan of the New York Yankees, odds are you know what result is going to come out of that panel. The Yankees are going to go all the way. I think the Yankees are going to go all the way, but I also think my mutual funds are going to grow at 27% this year so... again, no agenda. We wanted to offer all sides a chance to be involved, to present their points of view.

We also wanted to make overt and solid some of these tools we talked about, these tools for the 21st century. The most fun we had with that was our January cover story this year: What would you say to an alien? What message would you send if you had the opportunity to make contact, if you were the one writing our message? My favorite of all was the funny one which came from Harlen Ellison, the science fiction writer. His message to the aliens was, "You've come a long way, come into the house, you're dehydrated, have a little fruit, suck on a lemon." It was a lot of fun. I thought the most poignant was the one that said, "Go away, we'll kill you." That spoke again to some of the questions we've addressed this weekend. Will we shoot? Will we shoot first? Consistently, the message most people wanted to send was, "Teach us. We're open. We want to learn." More consistently than that was the people who would not comment. We sent the questionnaire well in advance to every member of Congress, to every world leader, to the Supreme Court justices, to the heads of the cabinet, the heads of the military, to their peers and compatriots world-wide. Out of Congress we got one response—the senator was taking the question under advisement and would get back to us. George Bush's office called. I'm not sure he's ever really forgiven *Omni* for printing his fax number about four years ago. His office called to thank us for the letter but to let us know that his speaking schedule would not allow him to respond. The poet Lawrence Ferlinghetti, typical I think, of a lot of artists in this age of language and transition, wanted to know who would do the translation of his poetry, but he wouldn't give us the poetry he wanted to send to the aliens.

We in turn have opened this project, "What would you say to an alien?" up to the readers, to the general public. The messages they're sending are more eloquent, more thoughtful, more profound, than anything we got or didn't get, from officialdom, the recognized brains of the business.

Additionally, we started what we call the field investigators handbook, because one of the things I think breaks a lot of people's hearts is when there is a terrific incident, or experience, or encounter, and it is not recorded in such a way, or noted in such a way, as to make it convincing to anyone who doesn't share that New York Yankee belief, as I call it; in other words, to the larger public. So we wanted to put together the sort of tools that would, for our readership, for the general public, give them the methodology to present to the debunkers, or the skeptics first, because we're open-mindedly skeptical, but also to the debunkers, and that has been phenomenally well received. How to do a ground-to-air sight measurement so you can determine altitude; how to take photographs and capture images that will stand up; how to write down your observations; how to make your report. Concurrent with that, are the other tools— how to lobby the government for release of information; how to use the Freedom of Information Act; how to spend most of your life using the Freedom of Information Act to no avail!

For my sins I've been promoted to senior vice president of our corporation, and even that doesn't help me because I keep getting called into the finance department to justify the amount of money we spend on Freedom of Information Act requests—reviewing them and tracking things down. It seemed like a good idea, the response certainly has been gratifying as has been the type of dialogue we've raised. One of the things that concerns me most is the trivialization of this topic by the wider general media. I think most of what passes for science fiction on television these days, and science fiction has traditionally been a tool for teaching us how to think about the future, how to think about other cultures, and most of it today is trivial and its effect has lapsed over into the way science fiction is published in this country. This Star-trekkization of the universe again. The willingness to think about alternatives. I am convinced that Frederick Poll, in many ways the greatest of our satirical science fiction writers, hit it on the head in 1967 when he wrote a story called 'The Day After the Day the Martians Came.' He nailed our culture pretty well because what do you get the day *after* the day of contact? You get the alien jokes. You get the alien T-shirts. You get *Oprah* with real aliens. That denies what we've learned at *Omni*. I think we have a very special readership. As I think those of us here are engaged in a very special level of conversation and communication, but I also think this type of conversation, communication, discussion with each another about the wonderousness of the universe, whether you are someone who has experienced a higher plane of reality, whether you are someone who has been abducted, whether you are someone who has seen the saucers here, whether you are someone who has not seen the saucers, whether you are someone like me who believes more in the New York Yankees than the spiritual side of my life, which is unfortunate. We deserve better from our media than we've gotten. We deserve these tools of communication. That's what we try to provide.

What have I learned? I have truly learned over the last two years to be more open to spiritual questions. I was trained at a distance, but seriously trained by the greatest hero of my life, Dr. Isaac Isomov. I was privileged to get to know Isaac pretty well the last couple of years of his life. I can still hear him, "Hello Keith, you need 2000 words, you need it in an hour, you need it in two." That was Isaac. But Isaac was too dismissive of spiritual quests, of non-hard scientific looks at things. So I've learned. I think our readers have learned to be a little more skeptical. I think we've learned to be a little less skeptical, a little more interested. What we wanted to avoid and what we've succeeded in avoiding, I think, is any blanket endorsement of sky hooks. That's all we're trying to do with our skepticism. Sky hooks are anything that moves miraculously. *Miraculously* out of the blue, lifts us up, out, and away from where we are and delivers us *Snap!* to where we want to be, and it's that "want" and that *"snap"* that gives us pause, and that's why Project Open Book is as rigorous as we try to be, as methodological as we try to be, and as conservative as we seem to be. Because no matter how much we want something to be true, if we're trying to communicate it to a mass audience, we have to be able to share evidence, to make a case, to be convincing. Otherwise, you're in the business of preaching. That is a wonderful business to be in, but it's not the business of *Omni* as I run it.

The business of *Omni* as I run it is to serve my other great hero, the greatest futurist of all, H.G. Wells. He said that Civilization is a race between catastrophe and education. I have tended in the past to see more catastrophe ahead than education. That's why with Open Book we've tried so hard to serve the cause of education—of giving tools, of providing an area for people to talk. A funny thing happened on the way to Open Book's great success, which is that last month *Omni* ceased monthly publication. After 17-1/2 years, we're no longer coming out every month. Except for the day we would have shipped to the printer, I really miss it. On deadline day I didn't miss the monthly magazine. But the response we got to Project Open Book has led us to look at new ways to handle *Omni*. Let me stop right here and say to any of you who may have heard the rumors, that it is absolutely not true that the government, either overt or secret, put *Omni* out of business. We're getting a ton of mail to that effect. Which leads me to believe that we're raising the sorts of questions people are interested in, in the larger community. The 2-3/4 millions of copies per month. *Omni* is very successful. We just finished the best year we've had, but simultaneously we saw the explosion going on in interactive media, the telecommunications medium concurrent with financial questions about what's happening to the old medium, paper, paper costs, postage costs, and the timing seemed right to us. It seemed to me that someone was going to make that first leap of a mass magazine away from the dead tree business into the live electron business.

It's hard to take your computer to bed with you, and dangerous to take it into the bathroom with you. To that end, we will be four times a year publishing a big, thick, glossy paper *Omni*. It was not a question of *Omni* staying in the paper business. What I think is ahead for paper magazines: thinner and thinner paper. Then you're cutting corners, and those of you who have been with *Omni* for a long time, and there are a lot of you here who have told me you've been with it from Issue 1, know that *Omni* was always a gorgeous, slick, wonderfully produced magazine. I have a deal with Ben Bolva, who was one of the editors of *Omni*. The deal is if there's anything to reincarnation, the next go-round he gets *Omni* in the '90s and I get it in the early '80s when things were cheaper.

So let me talk a little bit about what we're doing on-line and how that affects the dialogue. Again, our attempt to spread the tools for real communication about this topic. We've been very successful with our area at America On Line. One of the most active areas within that area of America On Line has been our Project Open Book. It is amazing to me to watch this daily evolution of hundreds or even thousands of messages flying back and forth. People sharing information, debating, offering ideas, offering a lot of angry debunking, name-calling which we try to contain as much as we can without censoring—we're not in the censorship business. So our America On Line area has been very successful.

One of the reasons we ceased publication last month—and as we begin our transition—is that I wanted to free the editors up to have a couple of months to work on what we'll be unveiling by mid-summer, which is *Omni* site on the World Wide Web, the multi-media if you will, section or aspect of the Internet, and that's going to be a wonderful area. Central to it will be what we're calling the Chronosphere, which will look at the entire 18-year history of the print magazine and have as many of the past articles as we can republish from authors who don't have agents. Authors with agents are all convinced that we need to pay 12 times as much for the electronic one-time publication as we did for the paper piece. We're more than happy to pay, but it's not worth that much money. Also, a timeline of science, and also what we're building now is a timeline of contact-related materials, weird things that have been seen, what's happened.

We're going to have an on-line university to look at these topics, to offer places for people to share ideas, to debate, again to criticize, to extol, to communicate, and I hope carefully and rationally. Along with other things; there will be areas to talk about science-fiction and pure science and sociology, and all of the things that *Omni* has been, *Omni* will continue to be. Above all, we will continue, I hope, to be the one place where the seemingly irrational, at least to the larger world, can be discussed rationally, carefully, clearly, and I hope intelligently and politely, because that sort of courtesy is what is most missing in this dialogue with the larger general public. It's one of the things we try hardest to bring to the party. I don't agree with everything, even most things that are raised in certain areas. I'm sure most of you non-Yankee fans would not agree with many of the things I believe. That does not mean that we cannot discuss them, learn from them, share them, respond to them, and together whether in paper or over the wires on the net go onward doing more of the same. Thanks a lot.

I will take questions.

*Are you going to continue to publish Richard Hoagland's material?*

No, Dick and I are certainly in contact, and it was made clear to him that we are publishing the magazine four times a year. It will be bigger and thicker, and we'll get to Dick's material as we can. I can't give a specific issue because we've had so much Hoagland over the last year and a half. I want to give some other people a chance too...

*Are you planning on translating* Omni *into other languages?*

Yes, we're in discussions and negotiations with various translation bureaus and licensees, which is what we're really looking for. Translations are a very expensive business. But we certainly want this to be as global as we can, and ultimately as universal as we can make it.

*In the interim, what will happen to current subscribers to* Omni*?*

Subscribers to *Omni* will be receiving *Discover*, or your money back.

*Has* Omni *tried any contact with anyone in government who claims to have inside government information and are willing to talk about it?*

We have of late, in the last few months, been contacted by some people who are actually, as you'll see this fall in our September issue, willing to go on record for the first time. I think that's a tribute to the credibility we've brought to the table, again to that conservatism which we brought which is that people know that it's not going to be exploited, or turned into a feeding frenzy for the media sharks.

*What is Open Book's future, do you have a timeline on it? How long are you going to go?*

Open Book will be around as long as I'm the editor of the magazine. I will say that right now. My greatest hope as a skeptic would be that it is..also as a magazine publisher, that it would be *Omni* that would arrive at the sort of proof, incontrovertible, inarguable proof, that could be shared with the larger general public, in other words, that scoop. But even if we had that tomorrow, I don't think that Open Book would go away, again because it's a forum and a tool as much as it is an impulse. I mean Open Book exists as a place for people to talk about things that aren't talked about in polite scientific circles. We're having a lot of fun with it; we're raising some good questions, we're raising them in ways that are journalistically valid. In ways that make for good reading and education. So Open Book, I hope, will be a part of *Omni* as long as there's an *Omni*, and I hope there's an *Omni* forever.

*For historical purposes, what is happening to the thousands of letters you are receiving?*

We archive them. We store them very carefully. We're looking at different ways to do things and getting back in touch with a lot of people. Because when you write a letter, and we made it clear with Open Book, that the material would belong to us once they mailed it in, unless they said otherwise. But when that disclaimer was published, it was before we'd really made the decision to move to the Web, and my hope is we can get the permission of these people to let us reproduce these letters and have a real treasure trove, both for the interested and for scholars looking into this phenomena, and as a phenomenon. But we'll see about that. It's a lot of work, and I've got to justify it to finance.

*How has the responce to Open Book impacted on you personally?*

I guess my concern, and this again is coming from someone who comes from a very rationalist scientific point of view, is that it seems to me, narrow-minded as I may be, that it cannot all be right. Yet the level of sincerity, belief, and faith evinced in the correspondence we've gotten has moved me to rethink some of my thinking. I think I'm more open-minded now. Again, I pass no judgment. I've never seen that as my job as editor. My readers are smart enough to make up their own minds. But that's what's been giving me the greatest pause—that level of sincerity.

*Are you doing anything to encourage leaks in the shadow government?*

All the time. But it's a real good government. I mean, they just don't talk. They're very good at what they don't do.

*What characteristics do you value in the dialogue, the* Omni *Log?*

I love that—*Omni* Log! Can I have that? In an *Omni* Log we would value a sense of our place in the universe and in time, of the various traditions from which we have sprung. Of that human quest for knowledge and for belonging, that's one of the things that I've become far more open to and have fallen more in love with. Our species does need that sense of belonging to something larger than just the rational or materialist, material world. Above all, an openness to the dialogue, to the *Omni* Log, to the various points of view, can't all be right, but aren't necessarily all wrong either, is what I think we're trying to get at in the magazine.

*You mentioned the Trilateral Commission. What role are they playing in this field?*

We have no information on it. We had someone write us a four-line letter saying that surely anyone knows it's absolutely proved beyond a shadow of a doubt that the Trilateral Commission is keeping the aliens secret in a cave in Peru. They also assassinated Jack Kennedy. It's another conspiracy theory. This one wasn't even a theory, I used that perhaps too facetiously. But again it's what I'm talking about. Not every one of these theories can be right. Unless there are a bunch of shadow governments. Then that means there's probably a bigger shadow government controlling all the little shadow governments.

*Is anyone else in the media taking this subject seriously?*

There's certainly some talk radio that's willing to look hard at it. The television coverage of the phenomenon seems to me to split into two camps. One is where even at a serious conference such as this or the contact conferences, when the news bite comes on with the (silly sounds) and they make fun of it with snide comments. But the other side of it is what I think is equally or perhaps even more dangerous, or of more concern, and that is the hyper-romanticization of the stories, such as we see on some of the tabloid programs where it's true, it's wonderful, it's moving for 9-1/2 minutes. There's no follow-up , no deeper investigation; it's whatever can give you the best shot generally through gossamer. Watch the camera tricks that are being used. Again, that ethereal sense. So no, I don't see a lot of serious media attention to this issue. But nor do I see on the purely scientific side, a lot of serious media coverage of real science, of what a bargain SETI is, how cheap it is to scan for messages. You're not getting that either. I don't mean that to sound arrogant—it's not *Omni* alone out there. It's just that *Omni's* always been a little bit off the conventional path, and more than a little willing to look at topics that I don't think are looked at seriously.

*Omni has a wonderful reputation for the use of art. How are you going to keep that alive with your electronic edition?*

That's one of the reasons that four times a year we'll have the paper version. Despite the wonderful evolution of computer technology and display technology and how quickly that's evolved; 500 years of putting ink on paper, lets you get a different, and I think richer, experience of visual art. But we will be putting the art on line as well. Thank you. I'll pass that along to the artists because I think they do a wonderful job in the magazine, and *Omni* has never really looked like anything else, nor do we intend for it to in the future.

*In your Anti-Matter section of* Omni *you recently had a well-known critic who knew nothing about the subject.*

I appreciate that criticism. Obviously we do what we can by the lights that guide us, and that does open us up to criticism which we welcome. We're as balanced as we're able to make it. The magazine does have a perspective. *Comment from the audience: "I could identify some qualified critics."* Thank you. *Omni* could probably get them cheaper, too. Having invoked one last time my beloved finance department, I thank you again for your attention today. Thanks.

⊕ Michael Michaud

# A Unique Moment In Human History

*Recommended by John Peterson, member of the conference's Future Panel, this article is a careful presentation of the major issues that an Earth government would logically consider in anticipation of contact with alien civilizations. One hopes that such serious thinking has been going on inside government for many years.*

*Michael A.G. Michaud was director of the Office of Advanced Technology at the U.S. Department of State when this article was written. In that position he was responsible for the foreign policy aspects of space activities and other advanced technology issues. He is the author of eighty-five published works, sixty-two of them on space or extraterrestrial intelligence. He holds a master's degree in political science from the University of California at Los Angeles.*

Consciously and unconsciously, we are making contact with extraterrestrial civilizations more likely. The evolution of our technological civilization is making Earth electromagnetically noisier, with radio signals, television carrier waves, and radar pulses radiating outward into the Galaxy. Though we may not intend to call the attention of other civilizations to ourselves, we have been doing so for most of this century. We are making it more likely that other intelligences "if there are any" will find *us.*

At the same time, we have embarked on our own searches for life and intelligence beyond Earth, first with optical telescopes, then with planetary probes and radio observatories. So far, we have failed to find convincing evidence of another civilization. But, by extending the sensitivity and duration of our searches, we are making it more likely that we will find them.

Because we search for others, we tend to assume that they search for us. If we scour the skies with our instruments, send automated probes to other planets in this solar system, and imagine sending such probes to the planets of other stars, we assume that others are doing the same.

Yet this search for others may be an episodic cultural phenomenon in our own civilization, dependent on the values and perceptions of the time. The idea of a plurality of inhabited worlds has had its ups and downs throughout recorded human history; sometimes it was widely believed, and at other times it was widely rejected. This implies that other civilizations, if they ever start such a search, may not give it continuing attention over the millennia, particularly in the absence of a positive result. Thus the detection of another civilization, by us or by them, may not be the result of a thoughtfully planned search conducted by astronomers sympathetic to it; it may come as a *surprise.* It may be the unintended by-product of other activities, such as astronomy, planetary or interstellar exploration, or the gathering of military intelligence. While there are strong arguments for radio as the preferred method of search, we should not exclude the possibility of other scenarios, such as finding an artifact of another civilization in our own solar system, or spotting the exhaust trail of an interstellar spacecraft. Those too would be forms of detection.

Given the youth of our own technological civilization, probability suggests that alien civilizations capable of detecting or communicating with us would be older than ours and technologically superior. This suggests that they are likely to find us before we find them.

## The Consequences Of Contact

What happens if we do detect others, or meet them face to face? Because of the probable technological superiority of the alien civilization, there is a presumption that the relationship will be an unequal one, implying a submissive reaction on our part. But the consequences of contact depend heavily on the circumstances of the detection, and the state of our own civilization at the time.

At one extreme is the classic radio astronomy scenario, in which our radio astronomers detect a faint signal that is the product of another intelligence. After lengthy efforts, a message is deciphered, and the wisdom of a superior civilization is revealed to us. The remoteness of the aliens, perhaps hundreds or thousands of light-years away, implies that they will be no threat to us, and that an exchange of information may be the major outcome of contact.

At the other extreme is the direct contact scenario, in which an alien spacecraft touches down on Earth, and we encounter extraterrestrials face to face. As envisioned in science fiction, the aliens could be as benevolent as the cute alien botanist E.T., or as malevolent as the marauding invaders depicted in the paranoia-charged atmosphere of the early 1950's.

In our thinking about aliens, we reveal our emotional selves—our predilections, our preferences. We are variously hopeful, naive, hostile, intolerant; we display idealism, wishful thinking, insecurity, fear, defeatism, even self-loathing. At one extreme, we think of aliens as altruistic teachers who will show us the road to survival, wisdom, and prosperity, or God-like figures who will raise humanity from its fallen condition. At the other, we see the aliens as implacable, grotesque conquerors whose miraculous but malevolently applied technology can only be overcome by simpler virtues.

These images are determined largely by our cultures, and by the circumstances of the time. Consider how American film and television portrayals of extraterrestrials changed from the weird and horrible invader of the 1950's. *(The Thing, Invasion of the Body Snatchers)* to the benign aliens of the 1970's. *(Close Encounters of the Third Kind)*, and then back to the repugnant aggressor of the 1980's. television series *V* and *War of the Worlds*. We carry these images around in our heads, and they will influence the way we react to contact. (Of course, in other cultures people may carry other images.)

Our emotional and intellectual predispositions could be reinforced strongly by contact. Those humans who suffer deeply from guilt, who think that our species is uniquely evil, may fear retribution, a chastising of humanity; some may even welcome it. Those who despair at humanity's lack of wisdom, or who are frustrated by important unanswered questions, may see in the aliens a long-desired source of guidance and solutions, a living, law-giving deus ex machina. Those who perceive contact in the context of the more brutal episodes of human history may fear attack, invasion, or enslavement. We are likely to attribute motives to the aliens before we have real evidence.

Contact almost certainly would cause many more humans to attribute events on Earth to alien intervention (some already see this in the UFO phenomenon). There might be an upsurge in conspiracy theories, witch-hunting, and UFO sightings. But many of us would simply be excited by this new outside stimulus, with its suggestion of a break with conventionality and of new prospects for the future. Contact could be shared adventure for a species that badly needs one.

## ANTHROPOCENTRISM GOOD BYE

The most profound message from the aliens may never be spoken: We are not alone or unique. Contact would tell us that life and intelligence have evolved elsewhere in the Universe, and that they may be common by-products of cosmic evolution. Contact would tend to confirm the theory that life evolves chemically from inanimate matter, through universal processes implying that there are other alien civilizations in addition to the one we had detected. We might see ourselves as just one example of biocosmic processes, one facet of the Universe becoming aware of itself. We would undergo a revolution in the way that we conceive our own position in the Universe; any remaining pretense of centrality or a special role, any belief that we are a chosen species would be dashed forever, completing the process begun by Copernicus four centuries ago.

The revelation that we are not the most technologically advanced intelligent species could lead to a humbling deflation of our sense of self-importance. We might reclassify ourselves to a lower level of ability and worth. This leveling of our pretensions, this anti-hubris, could be intensified if we were confronted with alien technology beyond our understanding. (Arthur C. Clarke has observed that any sufficiently advanced technology would be indistinguishable from magic.) We could feel even more deflated if the aliens, after contact, showed no interest in talking to us.

Contact also could be immensely broadening and deprovincializing. It would be a quantum jump in our awareness of things outside ourselves. It would change our criteria of what matters. We would have to think in larger frames of reference. Continuing communication with an ancient civilization would strengthen our sense of our own genetic and historical continuity, and could encourage us to take on longer-scale projects than we do now. Awareness of extraterrestrials would help to establish a new cosmic context for humankind; we would leave the era of Earth history and enter an era of cosmic history. By implying a cosmic future, contact might suggest a more hopeful view of the Universe and our fate, one less alienating than the cynical, materialistic, and limiting visions of the present.

Contact would remind us, as nothing else could, of our identity as a species. We would see the common nature of human beings defined by contrast with the aliens; the racial, religious, linguistic, and cultural differences among humans would seem minor by comparison. This could have a considerable unifying effect on humanity, easing tensions and encouraging cooperation within our species. But this new unity could be based as much on shared fear as on a sense of human brotherhood. If direct contact occurred, it could lead to a new racism, directed against the aliens.

Contact would give us the satisfaction of making others aware of our existence. If we detected extrasolar aliens, we would be strongly tempted to send a signal immediately to announce our presence, tell the aliens about ourselves, and begin spreading our own culture and values. But we have many causes for embarrassment about human civilization and behavior, and we might be tempted to disguise our problems and engage in posturing, inflating our stature and conveying an image of perfection. The aliens might not be above doing this themselves.

Contact also would be very reassuring to a species as doubtful about its future as we are. It would tell us that life and intelligence had survived and prospered elsewhere, even after acquiring powerful technologies. If the alien civilization were superior to ours, contact would suggest that intelligence is not an evolutionary dead end, and that the present state of human development is not final. More than any other event, contact could motivate us to transcend our present condition.

Contact would end the isolation of our species from other minds, giving us a new perspective on intelligence and on ourselves. At last we would encounter other beings who also worry about their survival, who feel the pain and joy of awareness, and who seek answers to many of the questions we ask about the purpose and destiny of intelligent life. We might enter a community of intelligence, gaining access to new knowledge and sensibilities, participating in a vast commerce of ideas among disparate minds. And we might join together with other civilizations in a mutual effort to assure the long-term survival of intelligence in the Universe.

## THE KNOWLEDGE REVOLUTION

Contact could bring a knowledge revolution. Simply detecting aliens would bring us new knowledge about the evolution of life and intelligence, especially if we could identify the characteristics of their home star and planetary system. Even undecipherable signals could tell us much about their technology and their command of energy. Radio communication could allow extraterrestrials to transmit vast quantities of information deliberately. Philip Morrison has suggested that aliens might send us a volume of information greater than that transmitted to medieval Europe from the ancient Greeks, stimulating a new and even greater Renaissance. By entering a communications net, we might receive maps of the Galaxy, and elaborate descriptions of the physical Universe and how it works. We might learn the histories of civilizations stretching far back into the galactic past, and become aware of alternative cultures, arts, social and economic systems, and forms of political organization. Deliberately or by implication, the aliens might tell us how they had survived. It is intriguing to consider how much we could contribute to the other side of the dialogue.

Alien knowledge, integrated with our own, could generate a dramatic forward leap in our sciences and our other academic disciplines. For the first time, we could compare our information and our perceptions with those of other minds in different environments, illuminating voids in our own knowledge and suggesting new generalizations. This almost certainly would lead to new syntheses, a boom in interdisciplinary studies as we perceived new linkages, and new branches of science. Dealing with this influx of new knowledge could force us into mind-stretching responses. Our curiosity would be stimulated by finding out how much we had not known. Contact also could reveal areas of shared knowledge, supporting our own conclusions; this might include religious concepts such as creation or a Supreme Being.

But we should beware of excessive optimism about this exchange of information; communication with an alien civilization may not be easy. No matter what we *wish* to believe, aliens, by definition, will be very different. While they may share some of our perceptions of physical reality and some of our evolutionary experiences, their evolutions would differ from ours in many ways, and we might share little in philosophy and culture. There could be serious problems of mutual unintelligibility, or misunderstandings caused by different ways of perceiving reality and by different cultural frames of reference. We might find that our own concepts of language, including mathematics, are narrow and idiosyncratic.

We also should not assume that the aliens will want to tell us everything. Transmitting the species data bank might not be the aliens first priority. They might want to know first our capabilities and our intentions to assure themselves that their security would not be threatened. There might be things they would not want to tell us, such as how to achieve interstellar flight or how to create more powerful weapons.

Receiving knowledge much more advanced than our own, and the solutions to problems we have struggled with for years, could break the intellectual morale of some scientists and other scholars, and undermine support for some forms of research. Instead, we might simply wait for alien answers, and translate them into our terms. Humans concerned about their personal and institutional interests might resist the dissemination of some alien information, or seek to brand it as dangerous, immoral, or subversive.

Receiving, interpreting, and disseminating information from extraterrestrials could be a major enterprise for humanity, almost certainly requiring new institutions. Since control over this information could bring great power and status, there would be a strong temptation to monopolize the channel and to limit access by others. Individual nations or groups might attempt to conduct separate dialogues with the aliens to exploit contact for their own purposes. Political and governmental leaders would be concerned about the impact that contact could have on their populations, and might try to let through only those ideas they considered safe. National security policy-makers might argue for classification of the contact and the information received. Some scholars, particularly those personally involved in the first contact, might be equally possessive about the information and the channel, especially if they distrusted governments and held a low opinion of the general population. Entrepreneurs might compete to get first access to alien ideas and to monopolize or patent those with commercial value.

## The Fatal Impact

The more intense forms of contact could have a fatal impact on our culture. Human history is littered with examples of cultural shock, of cultures that were destroyed or absorbed by other civilizations. An encounter with superior aliens could disorient our thinking, diminish our achievements, and shake our confidence. Even if the aliens meant well, their impact on us could amount to cultural imperialism; the missionary mentality may not be uniquely human. If the aliens were experienced in contacts with lesser civilizations and were concerned about the damage they might do, they might seek to reduce the shock of contact, or even avoid continuing it. But our own record in dealings between unequally powerful cultures gives us no reason for optimism.

In the cultural sense, contact could be the beginning of the end of humanity as we have known it. Contact's stimulus could produce a new cultural synthesis, leading to a new human civilization. Over time, our separate human culture might fade and vanish, becoming a quaint historical memory as it merged with a superior culture. Our anthropocentric religions might crumble, as superior aliens became our new gods, or as we adopted their religious concepts.

We have learned from our own history that a receiving culture cannot take in only those practices it likes from another culture; it is affected by the context of those practices, including the broader culture. Alien ideas could influence our codes of behavior and styles of social interaction, our arts and our tastes. Humans might emulate alien ways, as we rush to fads and fashions now; this impulse could be stronger if we thought we were imitating superiors. There probably would be a reaction against this, a sort of nativist movement and counter-reformation combined.

Alien technologies and new ideas about the possible forms and purposes of economic organization could spur economic change, perhaps suggesting new opportunities for innovation and growth, or less damaging prosperity. But they also might disrupt our economies, undermining the spirit of invention and independent initiative, forcing massive readjustment and unemployment, and threatening existing economic institutions. Fear of such possibilities could provoke a new Luddite movement against alien technologies.

Encountering an alien civilization also could force us to consider more universal bases for our laws, which would encompass alien concepts as well as our own. If direct contact were to occur, we would need to adjust our conception of the legal status of non-human life forms.

## DANGERS

One of the things we tend to forget in our thinking about contact is how the aliens might react to *us*. Many scholars who have written on SETI have argued that there would be no danger in the remote contact scenario in revealing ourselves to aliens because: (1) More advanced beings would be peaceful and benign; (2) interstellar travel is so difficult and expensive that we would be insulated by distance, making direct contact impossible. These assumptions need a closer look.

Extrasolar aliens may not share the ethical standards of fairness and regard for all species. They may show no more concern for alien intelligences than we show for whales and dolphins. They may think us unintelligent. They may have had violent histories, ascending the slippery slope from barbarism to civilization several times. Their experience with competition and conflict may have instilled in them a deep concern for security. They may have had bad experiences with earlier contacts, and might "at least at first" regard us as a potential threat. Contact might come as an unpleasant surprise to a species that had believed itself to be unique and superior; learning of another technologically advanced civilization might violate the integrity of their belief system and provoke a strong reaction. Even after the communications process started, misunderstandings could provoke a nasty response. And there is the danger that Freeman Dyson is right "that we may first encounter a species in which technology is out of control, a technological cancer spreading through the Galaxy.

Contact might bring the aliens here, at least to look us over. Studies such as the British Interplanetary Society's Project Deadalus indicate that interstellar flight might be possible (though by no means easy) even for a species only slightly in advance of our own. If we are already giving serious thought to interstellar travel, it may be commonplace for more advanced beings, who might enjoy longer life spans and access to more powerful means of propulsion. Contact with us might provoke even a non-star-faring species to interstellar travel, possibly bringing eventual direct contact. Even if attack or invasion are unlikely, the aliens might wish to confine us to our own solar system, and prevent us from achieving interstellar flight, as if they were isolating a virus. That could close off human expansion, and set a final limit to our growth.

Contact with extrasolar aliens, especially a star-faring species, could be the greatest possible stimulus to the human expansion into space. Finding that another species could travel across interstellar distances would suggest that we could too; it would draw us outward, first into our solar system and then to nearby stars. We might be motivated to spread human colonies away from Earth to broaden our options for survival, should contact imply possible eventual conflict with another species. Ultimately, the existence of an alien civilization would imply a limit to our expansion, at least in one direction.

Contact might draw us into some form of interstellar politics. We would have to think about how we should relate to other cultural and political entities, and ask what role *Homo Sapiens* could play in a galactic society. We must hope that relations among civilization in our galaxy are not based on some sort of interstellar social Darwinism. As a newcomer, with limited capabilities to affect anything beyond near-Earth space, we might have little influence at first. Galactic geopolitics might be meaningful only if contact was with aliens whose technologies were not much better than ours.

Contact, then, could be the most important event in the history of human civilization. Its effect on us could be both positive and negative, a gigantic stimulus and a demoralizing revelation; it could stir both hopes and fears on an unprecedented scale. It could involve us in a dialogue of centuries, bringing an incalculable richness of knowledge, physical instrumentalities, and cultural growth, and opening the door to a galactic society—or it could wreck our cultures and endanger our survival. Since we are in the process of making contact more likely, we need to prepare.

## ORGANIZING FOR CONTACT

Despite the popularization of the idea of extraterrestrial intelligence, we are not ready for contact. We have not created the philosophical context or the institutional framework for a calm and rational relationship with aliens. That relationship will require a broad view of the importance of life in the Universe, and of its forms and its purposes. It will require us to accept the worth of beings sprung from different evolutions. It will require political and cultural sensitivity, and tolerance for differences. It will require a long perspective on the history of our own species, and a sure knowledge of our purposes. Successfully dealing with contact will require a significant degree of consensus among human beings, and a means for expressing it.

In 1972 humanity made its first deliberate attempt to communicate with extrasolar aliens when NASA attached plaques to the Pioneer 10 and 11 spacecraft that were launched that year to swing by Jupiter before heading out of the solar system. The plaques were intended to tell any alien civilization that found them about the nature of our species and our location in the Galaxy.

Given the unlikelihood that these probes will be found in the vastness of interstellar space, the act of sending this message is more symbolic than practical. However, thinking that any contact with an extrasolar species would only be the beginning of a much larger process, I published an article in 1972 that speculated about how we might manage our relationship with an alien civilization. I argued that we could learn much by studying relations among different civilizations on Earth, and by considering the lessons of diplomatic history. I concluded that we must be as ready as possible before interstellar negotiations begin. When a group of scientists led by Frank Drake sent a powerful radio message from the Arecibo observatory in Puerto Rico in 1974, I was one of those who raised the question of what right such a small group had to speak for the entire human species without broader consultations or prior agreement.

Further developing ideas about interstellar politics in published articles over the next decade, I discovered that lawyers Andrew Haley and Ernst Fasan, among others, also had given thought to these issues. But there was no detectable interest in this subject in the world's foreign ministries, or in the United Nations.

In the absence of convincing evidence of extraterrestrial civilizations, we are unlikely to engage the sustained attention of most humans in such sweeping issues, so removed from ordinary life, or to create a permanent global institution for contact. But there may be ways to start modestly, by seeking agreement among the searchers on how we would handle the *detection* of an alien civilization.

In March 1985, Professor Allen Goodman of Georgetown University began circulating drafts of a paper titled "Diplomatic Implications of Discovering Extraterrestrial Intelligence," which included a proposed international "Code of Conduct" for SETI. That code contained four principles: (1) Anyone who discovers evidence of extraterrestrial intelligence will publicly report the contact; (2) any response will be formulated by a process of international consultation; (3) visiting extraterrestrial will be regarded as envoys entitled to diplomatic immunity, protection, and aid in the event of accident; (4) in the event that extraterrestrials appear to pose a threat to human health or peace, no nation shall act without first consulting the United Nations Security Council.

At the Congress of the International Astronautical Federation in Stockholm in October 1985, John Billingham, then chief of the extraterrestrial research division at the NASA Ames Research Center in California, proposed that a session at the next Astronautical Congress address the question of international agreements on four points: The need to distribute the details of the discovery of all nations; the establishment of a mechanism to distribute this knowledge; how to determine if a response should be made and who should make the response; and how to determine the content of the response. At the October 1986 Astronautical Congress in Innsbruck, Austria, Goodman presented a revised version of his paper, titled "Diplomacy and the Search for Extraterrestrial Intelligence." It included his proposed code of conduct for relations with extraterrestrial civilizations.

Goodman and several other authors addressed the issue in papers presented at the next Astronautical Congress, in Brighton, England, in October 1987. As co-chairman of the SETI session, I noticed that there was considerable overlap among the papers. I synthesized elements from the various proposals, boiling them down to one text. As the issues associated with handling a detection appeared to be quite different from the issues associated with sending a communication, I then produced separate drafts, one a proposed agreement on detection, and the other a proposed agreement on sending a response. I presented these drafts for discussion at a session of about twenty-five interested people at Brighton. We made good progress on the detection agreement, but discussions on the communication agreement quickly bogged down in broad moral and philosophical issues.

It was clear that it would be much more feasible to reach agreement on how to handle detection than on how to handle a reply. Volunteering to act as coordinator, I circulated drafts of an agreement on the detection of extraterrestrial intelligence to interested persons over the next year, making numerous minor revisions in the text as a result of their comments but preserving its basic principles, on which correspondents generally agreed. That draft agreement was endorsed by the International Academy of Astronautics in April 1989, and by the International Institute of Space Law shortly thereafter. It also is being submitted to the International Astronautical Federation, the International Astronomical Union, and the Committee on Space Research of the International Council of Scientific Unions for their endorsements. The agreement then will be opened for signature by all of those engaged in the scientific search for extraterrestrial intelligence, hopefully in time for the planned start of NASA's expanded radio search in 1992.

The detection agreement is to be among the *searchers* not among governments, as some institutions involved in the search, such as the Planetary Society, are not government-sponsored. Thus the agreement has no diplomatic status and is not an international agreement like the Outer Space Treaty. In fact, at the request of Czech legal scholar Vladimir Kopal, former head of the Outer Space Affairs Division of the United Nations, the agreement is now called a Declaration of Principles. The Declaration implicitly accepts an astronomical detection as the most likely scenario, but its principles could be applied to contact with another intelligent species on Earth, such as (possibly) intelligent dolphins.

The basic principles of the Declaration are those laid out by astronomer Peter Boyce in his 1987 Brighton paper: Verify the evidence in cooperation with other observers, and then tell the world. The Declaration spells out procedures for handling the detection, including the recording of the evidence and the protection of the appropriate electromagnetic wavelengths. Many of the procedures were developed by astronomer Jill Tarter, now chief scientist of NASA's SETI program. The Declaration also provides that no response to a signal or other evidence of extraterrestrial intelligence will be sent until appropriate international consultations have taken place, but leaves the mechanism of those consultations to another agreement, which could be developed from the second Brighton draft.

That draft addresses the profound questions of who should speak for Earth, and what should be said on behalf of our species. It states that communications with extraterrestrial intelligence will be undertaken on behalf of all mankind and provides that an international group will be formed to deal with the question of whether such communication should be sent and, if it is, what its content should be. This proposed agreement is not essentially a matter of scientific research; it involves social and political questions of considerable magnitude. Refining it and gaining its acceptance by governments will be difficult. But that effort will force us to think big about our nature as a species, our shared interests, and our vision of the future.

## DECLARATION OF PRINCIPLES CONCERNING ACTIVITIES FOLLOWING THE DETECTION OF EXTRATERRESTRIAL INTELLIGENCE

We, the institutions and individuals participating in the search for extraterrestrial intelligence,

Recognizing that the search for extraterrestrial intelligence is an integral part of space exploration and is being undertaken for peaceful purposes and for the common interest of all mankind,

Inspired by the profound significance for mankind of detecting evidence of extraterrestrial intelligence, even though the probability of detection may be low,

Recalling the Treaty on Principles Governing the Activities of States in the Exploration and Use of Outer Space, Including the Moon and Other Celestial Bodies, which commits states as parties to that treaty "to inform the Secretary General of the United Nations as well as the public and the international scientific community, to the greatest extent feasible and practicable, of the nature, conduct, locations and results" of their space exploration activities (Article XI),

Recognizing that any initial detection may be incomplete or ambiguous and thus require careful examination as well as confirmation, and that it is essential to maintain the highest standards of scientific responsibility and credibility,

Agree to observe the following principles for disseminating information about the detection of extraterrestrial intelligence:

1. Any individual, public or private research institution, or governmental agency that believes it has detected a signal from or other evidence of extraterrestrial intelligence (the discoverer) should seek to verify that the most plausible explanation for the evidence is the existence of extraterrestrial intelligence rather than some other natural phenomenon or anthropogenic phenomenon before making any public announcement. If the evidence cannot be confirmed as indicating the existence of extraterrestrial intelligence, the discoverer may disseminate the information as appropriate to the discovery of any unknown phenomenon.

2. Prior to making a public announcement that evidence of extraterrestrial intelligence has been detected, the discoverer should promptly inform all other observers or research organizations that are parties to this declaration, so that those other parties may seek to confirm the discovery by independent observations at other sites and so that a network can be established to enable continuous monitoring of the signal or phenomenon. Parties to this declaration should not make any public announcement of this information until it is determined whether this information is or is not credible evidence of the existence of extraterrestrial intelligence. The discoverer should inform his/her or its relevant national authorities.

3. After concluding that the discovery appears to be credible evidence of extraterrestrial intelligence, and after informing other parties to this declaration, the discoverer should inform observers throughout the world through the Central Bureau for Astronomical Telegrams of the International Astronomical Union, and should inform the Secretary General of the United Nations in accordance with Article XI of the Treaty on Principles Governing the Activities of States in the Exploration and Use of Outer Space, including the Moon and Other Bodies. Because of their demonstrated interest in and expertise concerning the question of the existence of extraterrestrial intelligence, the discoverer should simultaneously inform the following international institutions of the discovery and should provide them with all pertinent data and recorded information concerning the evidence: the International Telecommunication Union, the Committee on Space Research, of the International Council of Scientific Unions, the International Astronautical Federation, the International Academy of Astronautics, the International Institute of Space Law and Commission 51 of the International Astronomical Union.

4. A confirmed detection of extraterrestrial intelligence should be disseminated promptly, openly, and widely through scientific channels and public media, observing the procedures in this declaration. The discoverer should have the privilege of making the first public announcement.

5. All data necessary for confirmation of detection should be made available to the international scientific community through publications, meetings, conferences, and other appropriate means.

6. The discovery should be confirmed and monitored and any data bearing on the evidence of extraterrestrial intelligence should be recorded and stored permanently to the greatest extent feasible and practicable, in a form that will make it available for further analysis and interpretation. These recordings should be made available to the international institutions listed above and to members of the scientific community for further objective analysis and interpretation.

7. If the evidence of detection is in the form of electromagnetic signals, the parties to this declaration should seek international agreement to protect the appropriate frequencies by exercising the extraordinary procedures established within the World Administrative Radio Council of the International Telecommunication Union.

8. No response to a signal or other evidence of extraterrestrial intelligence should be sent until appropriate international consultations have taken place. The procedures for such consultations will be the subject of a separate agreement, declaration or arrangement.

9. The SETI Committee of the International Academy of Astronautics, in coordination with Commission 51 of the International Astronomical Union, will conduct a continuing review of procedures for the detection of extraterrestrial intelligence and the subsequent handling of the data. Should credible evidence of extraterrestrial intelligence be discovered, an international committee of scientists and other experts should be established to serve as a focal point for continuing analysis of all observational evidence collected in the aftermath of the discovery, and also to provide advice on the release of information to the public. This committee should be constituted from representatives of each of the international institutions listed above and such other members as the committee may deem necessary. To facilitate the convocation of such a committee at some unknown time in the future, the SETI Committee of the International Academy of Astronautics should initiate and maintain a current list of willing representatives from each of the international institutions listed above, as well as other individuals with relevant skills, and should make that list continuously available through the Secretariat of the International Academy of Astronautics. The International Academy of Astronautics will act as the Depository for this declaration and will annually provide a current list of parties to all the parties to this declaration.

Annex: Addresses of Institutions named in this declaration.

# ANNEX

## List of Institutions

Central Bureau for Astronomical Telegrams of the International Astronomical Union, Center for Astrophysics, 60 Garden Street, Cambridge, Massachusetts 02138, U.S.A.

Secretary-General of the United Nations, United Nations Headquarters, New York, New York 10017, U.S.A.

Director General, International Telecommunication Union, Place des Nations, CH- 1211, Geneva-20, Switzerland

Secretary, Committee on Space Research, 51, Boulevard de Montmorency, 75015 Paris, France

Secretariat, International Astronautical Federation, 3-5 Rue Mario Nikis, 75015, Paris, France

Secretariat, International Academy of Astronautics, 3-5 Rue Mario Nikis, 75015, Paris, France

Secretariat, International Institute of Space Law, 3-5 Rue Mario Nikis, 75015, Paris, France

Secretariat, International Astronomical Union (IAU-UAI), 98 bis, Boulevard Arago, 75014, Paris, France

## PROPOSED PROTOCOL FOR THE SENDING OF COMMUNICATIONS TO EXTRATERRESTRIAL INTELLIGENCE

The signatories agree that communications with extraterrestrial intelligence will be guided by the following principles:

1. Communications with extraterrestrial intelligence will be undertaken on behalf of all mankind, rather than specific nations, groups, or individuals.

2. Nations, organizations, and individuals will not unilaterally send communications to extraterrestrial intelligence until appropriate international consultations have taken place.

3. The signatories will not cooperate with attempts to communicate with extraterrestrial intelligence which do not conform to the principles in this protocol.

4. An international group including representation from all interested nations will be formed to deal with the question of whether such a communication should be sent and, if so, what its content should be.

5. If a decision is made to develop a communication to extraterrestrial intelligence on behalf of all mankind, the following principles will be observed:

    a. Respect for the value of life and intelligence.

    b. Respect for the value of diversity, including respect for different customs, habits, languages, creeds and religions, approaches to social organization, and styles of life.

    c. Respect for the territory and property of others.

    d. Recognition of the will to live.

    e. Recognition of the need for living space.

    f. Fair play, justice, mercy.

    g. Reciprocity and quid pro quo.

    h. Non-violation of others.

    i. Truthfulness and non-deception.

    j. Peaceful and friendly welcome.

    k. Cooperation.

    l. Respect for knowledge, curiosity, and learning.

6. The drafters of a communication to extraterrestrial intelligence will consider detailed information about mankind to be a commodity of high value which will not be transmitted without due attention to human security and well-being, and to reciprocity.

7. In the event that extraterrestrials appear to pose a threat to human health, well-being, or peace, no nation shall act without consulting the Security Council of the United Nations.

## The Panels

# Fear, Hope and Future

The three panels, Fear, Hope and Future, were designed to provide an opportunity for interaction between the audience and speakers and panel members. At the time of their registration, each conference participant was invited to submit in writing a question no longer than 40 words, and then to take the remainder of the page to argue why that question should be selected and responded to as the most important question for the panel to consider. Conference participants were additionally informed that each of the three panels would select the most pertinent question submitted to it and the author of that question would receive a refund of his or her conference tuition. There was an excellent response to this invitation.

For the Fear Panel the chosen question was submitted by Chloe Diroll:
**To eliminate fear of the unknown, is it not necessary to reconcile religious beliefs with the nature, origin and purpose of Space Beings?**

The winning question for the Hope Panel was created by Jeanne Noble:
**In anticipating the benefits of dialogues with Cosmic Cultures, how can we ensure that we remember and represent the positive interests of all Earth's inhabitants (plant, animal, geographic, spirit) and not the interests of human alone?**

Trish Pfeiffer provided the question selected by the Future Panel:
**In anticipation of the time when Cosmic Cultures meet, what long term endeavors should be undertaken now, and by whom, to prepare humanity for such an eventuality; and what steps are presently being undertaken?**

# Fear Panel:
# Baldwin, Funaro, Hunt, Underwood

**MODERATOR (JIM FUNARO):** **It appears that the cosmic visitors have been studying our human psyches along with our bodies. They may use our own emotional pathologies against us in order to further their own agendas. How may we prevent this possibility from occurring?**

**UNDERWOOD:** That's easy. The media does it to us all the time. We call it advertising. I think that the easy way to prevent this from being used against you is to be aware of your own emotional pathologies. Then you drop your hooks, you don't have any hooks, and there you go.

**BALDWIN:** How can they use our emotional pathologies against us, I think they're already doing it. Any excess of emotion whether it be fear or anger or jealousy can be used against us. Anybody here who doesn't have such, you can raise your hand—that's OK. That renders us vulnerable in a way, at least this is what I find in clinical practice. My wife Judith does a lecture on protection and one of the main points in there is PAY ATTENTION. Pay attention. And how little we pay attention to our own feelings, our own needs, our own desires, our own excesses. Certainly this can be used against us by those who are clearer and less emotional, and some of the extraterrestrials do seem to be much less emotional.

**HUNT:** Well, we haven't of course, agreed on who these ETs are, what powers they have. It would seem to me that if they are really making contact and the next closest star to us is a mere four and a half light years away, which would take Pioneer—one of our space vehicles— 90 thousand years to reach it, at the rate it's traveling, and our galaxy is 100,000 light years across, so if you just went 1% into our galaxy, that's not very far; that's 1000 light years—it would take Pioneer 2 million years to traverse that space. If there are some creatures that have the capability of actually reaching us and are in contact with us, I don't think they need to use our pathologies against us. The second speaker, the gentleman from Germany, used a brave phrase. He said he doesn't believe in fear, but a challenge. I think we would have reason to fear technologies that are that far beyond us. I don't think they need to use our pathologies; I think they have something else they could use.

**FUNARO:** I suspect that it wouldn't be impossible in their interpretation of us to misinterpret our pathologies, as we have often done when looking at our own pathologies. They may find themselves in a peculiar turnabout position of having us use our pathologies against them. One of the particularly interesting things about human beings to me as an anthropologist is that we have this ability to believe anything and that could likely work to their disadvantage. I think that one of the intents of the question was, for example, would they be able to use human characteristics to increase the divisiveness among ourselves, and clearly we don't need anything from outside to make ourselves more divisive.

I was involved in a simulation a few years ago in which there was an attempt to create a scenario where some aliens had come to this planet, actually on the moon—they were watching us—and what happened was that although the earth teams representing particular interests originally started out very unified, they all started cutting their own deals eventually with the aliens, against one another, and the aliens got scared and thought we had a global multiple personality deficiency and left!

**MODERATOR:** **Since the cosmic visitors have greater technological and psychic abilities, will earth's government be able to maintain a balance of power, or will the visitors dominate us by favoring those governments who are most receptive and useful to them?**

**UNDERWOOD:** That's assuming several things. One is that they have superior technology; and I for one disagree. I think one of the disadvantages of linear thought is because you get one expertise, you put it in front of all the other possibilities.

Earlier Mr. Hesemann was talking about how, for instance, the Conquistadors were technologically superior to the Aztecs. No. They just had certain things that the Aztecs didn't necessarily realize. The Spanards absolutely did not win because of superior technology. The Aztecs could have piled on top of them and crushed them to death. They won because, and I have a different view of who won, the Aztec had a prediction that right about this time Quetzalcoatl was coming back. And Quetzalcoatl came over the ocean from the east and was pale of skin. So when the Conquistadors showed up, they said, "Oh gosh, is this or is this not Quetzalcoatl?" It froze them into place. Otherwise, those Conquistadors wouldn't have stood a chance. They would have been dead in 15 minutes if the Aztecs had decided to do that, which wouldn't prevent the next group from coming over.

I see a lot of similarities between the mismatch of technologies which is what I would prefer to call it, between Europe and so-called Native America and the Visiting Others—assuming there are such—and ourselves. I don't believe for a minute coming out of a Shamanic tradition that they have superior psychic abilities. I think in the West we have been purposely stamping out our psychic abilities for a few hundred years now and we've done a pretty good job. In a Shamanic tradition that doesn't happen and I fail to see in all the reports I've read, anything listed as "a something they can do" that isn't a common practice in one or another Shamanic traditions here on Earth. So what's the big deal?

**BALDWIN:** I think we need to get out of our current scientific envelope. Elisabet Sahtouris mentioned this morning the possibility of 10 dimensions, and we're certainly on the low end of the scale when we're studying our three dimensions and time. Regarding the distances—indeed if there are beings from different places, they are not coming across those distances as we know them with Einsteinian physics or anything else. If they are indeed other-dimensional, what does that mean? Are the other-dimensions outside of us or are they within us? There are certainly mind technologies in our 3-D world. But the greater technology that might in fact be a threat to us is that mind-control technology.

If we think of the 3-dimensional world and recall back to 1945 when this country that had the atomic weapon technology and dropped two bombs on Japan, it wasn't that Japan was receptive. They surrendered. I don't know that they've ever been receptive but they certainly surrendered in that time. So I think there're some assumptions in that question—which isn't a question, but a statement—and that the technology that will control us is at the level of the mind. Again, from my clinical practice I deal only with people's experience and with people's narratives when they are in the altered state which is, of course, a dissociative state. But so are Bud Hopkins' book, and John Mack's and David Jacobs' accounts of people's experience that we can take as real to them. But I wouldn't correlate that to reality in the physical world at all.

Many people have certainly been taken over by what appear to be other energies. I wouldn't begin to define what those other energies are. There are procedures—loving, gentle, persuasive procedures—that can release the holds of those particular energies on people, and they are back to where they were before those energies took effect. I'm beating around the bush because I don't want to come out and say what it appears to be because I don't believe in appearances either. But I think the technology will be of the mind, not of the atomic bomb style, or the Europeans that eventually conquered the natives on this land. The technology will be at a far subtler level. The subtle level most of which most humans don't focus on, at least in this country.

HUNT: I don't think we really are sure and I can, with all due respect to my colleague here, imagine the Shamans somewhere saying the same thing. What we're talking about, superior technology, it's not a question of the quality of it. Is it kinder, or is it better, or is it more human? But the question is—I would take a .45 over a bow & arrow. I think an atomic bomb is more powerful than a poison dart. Not a question of whether it's good or bad. And I would agree, I don't think these beings are coming across this kind of space.

Robert Jastrow said that evolution could have been going on some distant planets 10 billion years longer than on Earth. I cannot believe in evolution; I cannot believe that life and intelligence sprang spontaneously from an empty space and that the words I'm speaking right now are simply the result of and antecedent motions of the atoms in my brain that all began with the big bang 18 billion years ago. You shouldn't even be listening if that's what it is. There's no purpose or meaning in that. Sir Fred Hoyle said "What is the probability that by chance evolution could produce just the basic enzymes of life. He said that's one over one with 40,000 zeros after it. You can't even imagine what that fraction is so let me give you an idea of what it is. What is the likelihood that you could reach out and by chance pluck a particular atom out of our universe? That's merely one over one with 80 zeros after it. Let's make another universe out of every one of those atoms and what is the likelihood that out of all those universes you could reach out and pluck a particular atoms out of it—that's only one over one with 160 zeros after it. Now you got one over one with 40,000 zeros after it, forget it! You can't even get the basic enzymes of life and the you've got to make cells and brains, etc. Or take Jacques Monod, Nobelist, in his book, *Chance and Necessity*—he gives you 20 reasons at least why evolution couldn't happen. Just one of them—DNA—the thing about DNA is that it must exactly replicate itself, and the only way you could have an evolutionary process would be a foul-up in the DNA complex. And you're going to produce the human brain out of a series of harmful, accidental foul-ups in the DNA? It doesn't make sense.

But anyway, going back to Robert Jastrow, he said evolution could have been going on some planets out there 10 billion years longer than planet Earth. Those beings would be as far beyond us on the evolutionary scale if you want to believe that, as man is beyond a worm. And they would have powers that would seem like gods to us. I mean if those creatures—if there are such creatures— they have the capability of getting here to planet Earth, I don't even think we'd make good pets for them! They wouldn't want to make slaves out of us because their robots would be a whole lot more efficient and less expensive to maintain. This is the Fear Panel—if you believe in that, I think we've got some reasons to be afraid and I think our discussion could be rather academic.

FUNARO: Well, there's a lot to respond to besides this question. Personally I happen to use evolution as a model in what I do and you got about 100 building blocks and given a fairly compatible environment, and just randomly putting those 100 building blocks together, you should be able to come up with organic compounds—a little less than that, but that's my view of it.

With respect to technology, I simply want to point out that there may be other ways of traveling besides technology. There certainly are on this planet. I mean a snail can get from here to there. You can do it faster, so the snail is slow, but it's faster than a tree in movement at any rate. Maybe we're just talking about scale and since we happen to do most of our things using technology we assume other entities might do the same. I'm not just necessarily talking about anything metaphysical here. Perhaps super-physical is all I'm referring to, although you might do whatever you want to with it.

Again, the Conquistadors, there's also some other things like war dogs and war horses and most importantly, diseases, that seem to attack the native Americans but not the Spaniards. This is going to be very demoralizing to the people who feel their gods have betrayed them. These are diseases white men brought there that they were already immune to or were childhood diseases. So it seems very specific as to who was getting attacked here.

Finally, back to the question about our governments, I think one of the things I see happening, and it's nice all this is happening at the second millennium—at least in some linear time scales. The millennium has been within the Christian world an important time for things to be expected. What we're seeing politically, I think, is the demise of the nation state after about 1000 years or so. These entities we thought were monolithic are disintegrating and what we're seeing is the development in a hierarchy of multinational entities that do not have national allegiances or a national security to worry about. I think this could create a global society that will not be the dream of the flower children, but a rather different one in which we might have extreme class differences between those people that are involved in the multinational level and the rest of humanity.

I can imagine these corporations seeing themselves as having more in common and perhaps more to gain by dealing with extra-terrestrials than they would with the rest of the people on the planet. I can also imagine that some religious systems will find in an encounter, if it occurs, a validation of their beliefs rather than a denial of them, a validation in a belief of supernatural beings. It also can prove that there may indeed be a universal God that has more to deal with than just this planet. We may have responses that are quite surprising out of religion because I have a feeling that religion may have some tools to deal with this contact that are superior to those of science.

**MODERATOR: To eliminate fear of the unknown is it not necessary to reconcile religious beliefs with the nature, origin, and purpose of space beings?**

**UNDERWOOD:** Well, if you have them I suppose, perhaps. One of the assumptions Dr. Jones wrote us originally, we are assuming there is a common basis in this group that we are afraid of the unknown, and of course, I have to be one of the more alone voices protesting that we don't have to be afraid of the unknown. I remember my son talking about a major automobile accident in which he was involved where he was sound asleep, and he suddenly woke up and saw the world whizzing by the windshield. And then he said to himself, "No, that can't be what's going on. Oh, I see the car is rolling." (Which it was.) "Oh," he said, "this must be what it's like to be about to die. How interesting!" Because his first reaction was what is in my tradition—where you perceive difference, there's a possibility of learning. So as soon as you see something new, you're cautious about it because you don't know what you're about to learn. But on the other hand, as soon as you see something that is different, you go, "Oh, wow!

Something is different! Come over here and tell me about yourself." So you're not afraid of the unknown. And it's not disinterested curiosity. It's really interested curiosity. Along with it goes a healthy dose of caution which you get trained into from the time you're a little child. So we don't have to be afraid of the unknown, period. My tradition also—doesn't believe in belief. The idea is you should not stick to one answer for anything. If you don't stick to one answer to explain everything, then you don't have to accommodate new information as strange. In my tradition there's no such thing as an anomaly. The only thing you've got is more information.

BALDWIN: Again, it's not really a question, but a statement with several assumptions. The fear of the unknown is not universal, but many of us do have a fear of the unknown or fear of the dark or whatever. That stops some people. Other people form a series of beliefs around it. The Lord of the Flies, the Cargo Cult in the Pacific, a system of beliefs around the unknown attempting to explain it and bring it under control. What we're really fearing is loss of control, and fear of the unknown is loss of control.

Reconcile religious beliefs—which religious beliefs would this questioner want us to reconcile with? Which among the world's many religious beliefs would they consider would have to be reconciled? And again a system of beliefs, whether it's about the world is flat, or religion, or science or whatever else is a belief to be expanded against, upon, beyond. To be transcended—John Lilly's words, to a new set of beliefs. What else do we have? That's the way the mechanism works. But a strong, limiting belief system stops critical thinking and I think it's essential that we continue to think critically and move outward. The spirituality within us, which is the core of the being, will not change, will not be destroyed in any case. So I think the fear of the unknown for some people is a challenge to be overcome. Some people have said a fear of flying—well, take that fear of flying aboard the airplane with you like a football under the arm, just take the fear of flying with you. Simply overcome it. I had a client once who had a fear of falling, so he joined the paratroopers and overcame that fear. He really took it in hand, and he got over his fear.

I'm not that brave, but I have certainly moved into the areas of the unknown and have discovered many interesting things and I certainly don't know the answers, nor the truths. But it's fun to explore, whatever we come up against. The whole field of UFOs, or ETs, or aliens or alien abductions, are really based on people's experience and people's narrative. We can't go farther than in saying what it is or trying to explain it. So fear of the unknown, fear of control, fear of lack of control, reconciling beliefs—it's a statement, and I wonder what the author had in mind rather than ask any question that really has some assumptions there that are stretches.

HUNT: To eliminate fear of the unknown. It sounds to me like Roosevelt who said, "We have nothing to fear but fear itself." That's a brave statement, but I think there are some things. A healthy fear is worthwhile. A child has to learn a healthy fear of heights, for example. They might just think they can jump off. You might try to teach the child positive thinking, and he might step out of an airplane at 37,000 feet and say, "Well, grandma believed in the law of gravity, but I don't. The birds can fly, why can't I? Let's be positive about this." Talk about fear of the unknown assumes that there's something to be afraid of. Maybe there are some things to be afraid of. I don't want to keep sounding like a broken record. An earlier speaker referred to the European civilizations coming here to the new world. I think the natives had some things to fear. I think that Bosnians have some things to fear about Croatians and Croatians have some things to fear about Bosnians. The Tutsies and the Hutus, have had something to fear from one another. So I don't think we can just dismiss legitimate fear by saying it's the fear of the unknown. If we knew what it was, we might be even more afraid.

Maybe caution is a better word. Is it not necessary to reconcile religious beliefs with the nature origin and purpose of space beings? If space beings exist and they really represent a higher truth than we have, and your or my religion whatever it is hasn't acknowledged that or recognized that, then I think religious beliefs have to be brought into agreement with whatever is truth. On the other hand, to say there is no truth, that we just simply are trying to discover more and more, I think that's rather discouraging. What's the point of discovery? What's the point of working on it, if we've been discovering, been getting a little closer to truth for the last 1000s of years, and we haven't gotten there, and you can't say anything is truth anyway, then what's the point? I believe Jesus knew what he was saying when he said "I am the truth." Probably most of you disagree. But nevertheless, it's a question of fact.

My oldest son is a philosophy professor. He gives a little quiz to his opening class each year. Do you think truth is absolute or relative? Invariably, he says, about 80% of the respondents say it's relative. About 20% say it's absolute. Then he makes an offer to them. I don't know about our other philosophy professors here, but he makes this offer. He says, "If you can prove to me that truth is relative, that what is true for you is not true for me, that what was true yesterday is not true today, that what is true on this planet is not true everywhere in the universe, I'll give you an A in this course and you don't even have to do another thing. He's never had anybody, at least not an undergraduate, able to get an A on that basis. I happen to believe truth does exist. That truth is absolute. If it doesn't, there is no purpose or meaning in life. So if we don't have that truth and extraterrestrials have it, then we're going to have to bring it in line with that. But if there is truth, then it's not going to change, whether the extraterrestrials come or if they don't.

**FUNARO:** There's always a lot to follow. I don't think we're afraid of the unknown. I think we're afraid of the unknowable. I think human beings have shown a lot of evidence all the way through history at least, maybe there's even prehistoric evidence for this, of being able to come with an explanation for anything because we need an explanation. In the third book of Isaac Asimov's trilogy, the last two chapters I thought were very interesting. His second last chapter was called *The Answer that Satisfies*. And the last last chapter was called *The Answer that Was True*. I think that what's behind this is a fairly traditional western view that truth is more important than satisfaction. Whereas I think human behavior indicates that as a matter of fact, satisfaction is more important than truth. What we really want is the answer that satisfies, and we'll define that as truth, no problem. But it's our ability—borrowing back from Dennis Rohatyn a phrase of mine—we have an incredible ability to 'eff' the ineffable. To come up with an explanation that gives us a feeling that we understand something. I don't like the idea of the unknown because it suggests to me that there is a truth, and that means that somebody's right and therefore somebody is wrong.

I have this nagging feeling that if human beings have been looking for the truth for at least several thousand years you would have thought there would be some agreement on it by this time. There doesn't seem to be much agreement. In any case, it seems to me that many other cultures have come up with their explanations for various kinds of phenomena that today we may be talking about. At least in part, people have believed in supernatural beings of all sorts that do all kinds of things. Maybe in our society, since we have no gods we have created our own way of 'effing' the ineffable. Certainly ETs are quite in context of the space race, our movement out into space, and even comes from heaven although heaven is defined a little differently this time.

**Moderator: Why is the USA a leader of negative and fearful information about ET contacts, while European contacts are positive and even European military does not spread fearful disinformation? It is not possible that ETs have made a deal only with America. Only the UN can represent planet Earth.**

UNDERWOOD: Which gets back to one of our basic questions according to the brochure, which is who represents us? I'm not really sure that Europeans do not get into negative disinformation. I don't have any information on that. In speaking with European scientists, they are judged to be just as stupid and ridiculous if they get into UFO phenomena as American scientists are. It's a real problem for them. So the judgmentalism I'm told in Europe is even worse than it is here. The thing of it is, if you're a participant in the community that looks at these phenomena as a possibility, the information you get from Europe, by in large, is information from people who agree with you. OK? It's been almost impossible to report on British crop circles because everybody giggles and hehaws so much and as soon as two guys show up with nails and boards the entire British press believes them just ipso facto. They're even worse than American press. So I guess it depends on where your disinformation is.

However, the points about fearful information I think are very well taken. Perhaps European military does not spread fearful disinformation. Well, who can represent us? I'm not sure the UN can represent us until we have a clearer line between individuals in the United Nations. There are a couple of movements afoot to have some of the UN representatives elected directly. I participated in a replanning of the United Nations. How's that for ego? I participated in a replanning of the United Nations which had a Senate and a House much like ours, and the Senate represented the nations and the House represented the people according to a certain number per representative, and were directly elected. Now don't you think it would take us more than 5 minutes to get to such a point? But until we get to such a point I'm not sure the UN can really represent us either. It does represent our national governments. It absolutely does. But the question is, What does that mean? It means one thing in the United States and something quite different in Somalia, for instance.

BALDWIN: I have no information or very little information on the European reactions to UFOs. I don't know how much information the government has leaked directly. So it may indeed be a product of the media. There's certainly alot of talk about disinformation being leaked by the government and this is part of the hearsay and part of the conspiracy, and I certainly don't find any truth in any of that. I can't comment on the difference between European and American. Certainly there have been alot of painful experiences by people in this country and there seem to be explanations of that by various people. But the people who have had the painful experiences certainly don't go along with the explanations of people who say they are not painful, but benevolent. Who would lead us in this representation? How many saw *The Day the World Stood Still*? Michael Rennie, black and white, in 1951, when the UFO landed on the White House lawn and the alien came out of the craft with a device in his hand. Unfortunately, he held it in his right hand and it went *pop* and everybody thought "gun," and a soldier with an itchy finger in the crowd, with all the guns trained on this alien visitor, not attacker, but a visitor, shot him. The alien in the hospital with a bullet wound in his body was healed the next day by his robot companion Gort.

It won't be the patriarchal society that meets these beings with any success. That's my feeling. I'm going to go out on a limb and say, yes, I have an opinion about this. This is my opinion. That the patriarchal will get in just as much trouble as they did in *The Day the World Stood Still*, in that movie. It will be inner spiritual experience. According to some sources they tried contacting government officials and that didn't work, and now they are going to the grassroots. Acknowledging this is information coming from somebody else or somebody's imagination, I wouldn't begin to say which. But it will be a gentle forthcoming. It will be showing the gentle side. The patriarchal institutions are dying. Anyone just has to look around our culture to see that.

That patriarchal culture is not going to be the one that receives amicably other beings, other voyagers, if indeed they do bother to come to this planet. Many of them have been seen as physical on radar and some claim to have samples of the metal from the craft, and yes, there are lots of rumors about the bodies at Roswell, and so forth. But far more have come in consciousness to people. So maybe that's where the meeting will be. Maybe that is where those who can connect with their own consciousness— and many are separated from their own consciousness, I see the women nodding, very few men. This is where the meeting must take place in order that things don't come tumbling down. That's my opinion and only my opinion.

HUNT: OK, that's what we're all giving. Our own opinions. Well, why is USA a leader of negative and fearful disinformation about ET contacts while European contacts are positive, and so forth? Again, I probably put myself on the other side of the chasm from most of you, but I'm troubled by those words "postive" and "negative." If we're talking about electricity, if we're talking about magnetism, we're talking about chemical bonding, positive and negative have some meaning. But if we're talking about morals, about truth, we're talking about whether somebody is a threat to us or not. It seems to me, so far, we're approaching this from as though we are going to determine what is going to happen.

We talk about these beings—again my views are considerably different, I don't think they have come across this space—doesn't mean there might not be beings who theoretically could do that. But, for example, one of the earlier speakers said something about they will probably ease us into this gently, we don't want to shock anybody, create a culture shock and so forth. We don't have anything to say about this, folks. This is the Fear Panel again, OK? It's like the Japanese after the bombs were dropped, talking about whether we would go about this gently, or not. I mean, they met on a ship out there in Tokyo Harbor and they signed some surrender documents. I'm probably older than most of you here so I am old enough to remember, peace in our time. Anybody remember that one? Chamberlain with his umbrella goes to see Hitler. He was very positive. But it didn't help. Positive and negative has nothing to do with it. We have to deal with the facts. Are there such beings? Do they have these powers? If so, it's like, do I dare take a moment, to lighten it up here for a minute? There was this fellow that was a bit overweight. His doctor suggested he do 18 holes of golf twice a week to reduce. But at the same time you got to visualize because exercise is not enough. Don't take your clubs with you, you just visualize going around the course. He'd never done this before, and he went to the driving range and took an imaginary ball out of an imaginary bag of clubs and put it on an imaginary tee and took an imaginary driver out and took some imaginary swings and after 10-15 minutes, he was hitting it pretty well. So he headed over to the first tee, and on the way to the first tee he was tapped on the shoulder and a guy says to him, "You must be Dr. Bartovsky's patient," and he said, "Yes I am. How did you know?" And he says, "Well, I'm one of his patients too and he suggested that I join you in a twosome."  The second fellow says, "You know, I have never parred this course in my life. I got a feeling today is going to be my day." Well, to shorten this up, as you can imagine, it was a very close match. In fact, by the time they reached the 18th hole they were tied. It was a 450 yard dogleg, par 4. The first guy put his imaginary ball in the imaginary tee, imaginary driver, whacked that thing 280 yards straight down to where it jogged off and the other guy did the same thing, and the first guy goes down and says, "I can do this with a 9-iron! You know, 170 yards, but I can do this with a 9-iron." He pulls the imaginary 9-iron out of his imaginary bag of clubs and whacks that ball and he calls it, "It's headed for the green! It's on the green! It's headed for the pin, it's in the cup!. An eagle! Beat that!" And the other guy said, "I don't have to beat it. I win. You lose. You hit my ball."

I get a little bit disturbed by people who think they can create their own realities with their minds. "I visualize that Cadillac, I'm gonna get it." Hey, you're only visualizing the gross outlines of this thing. You don't know what the subatomic particles look like in that thing. It sounds to me like we're engaging in that sort of thing. Negative, positive, fear of the unknown, is there something really out there? Then maybe we better bring our reality in line with it.

Is it possible that ETs made a deal with America only? I don't think so. I don't think they have made a deal with anybody. That is one of the things that disturbs me a little bit, causes me to have some different ideas on this subject. I don't think they are going to come across hyper-space with all the technology that takes, or the psychic powers, however you want to look at it, and contact some little old lady on a typewriter and talk through her, or some guy's gonna get this through hypnotic regression, I think they'd be a little more forthright. I really think they would approach the leaders, and I think they would have the chutzpah and the capability of doing what I don't think has been done yet.

FUNARO: I perhaps should say I don't know whether they're here, to preface my remarks. I don't really think they are, but that's only because I haven't had evidence that convinces me. So the question about the US repressing information, I don't know whether that's true, whether they're really repressing it. However, I think we have some way of judging why they might. National governments on the planet right now have the most to lose if we encounter a higher technology because they're in competition with other such groups and so the attempt to limit distribution of such information would be in the interest of national security. Since we have the biggest military on the planet, it's no surprise why if there was information to be held back, that our society would be doing that. It also is no surprise why other nations who have lesser militaries would be interested in giving all they could because it might simply be a strategy to get the U.S. to open up. Because the US has the most to lose and other militaries would have more to gain. That part of it doesn't bother me, although as I say, I don't really know what's happening.

As to the question as to who will lead, I agree with David although for somewhat different reasons. I do not think it will be a matter of our choice, although I'm not sure it'll be a matter of the extra-terrestrials' choice either. It'll be a matter not of choice but of access. I think as I've pointed out, multi-national corporations, if there is a good deal to gain, will preempt the UN no matter what the UN wants to say about it. And they have the clout to do it. It's the economic clout, not military clout. Also, I think one other thing we can't overlook is the communication revolution that has changed our lives so much in just the last few years, has allowed individuals—who can afford personal computers—access to the world. Access in a way that it's going to be very difficult for national and multi-national interests to preempt that access. Because hackers are very, very good at getting around whatever needs to be gotten around.

I suspect that one of the unexpected—at least in most of the scenarios I've seen so far—one of the most unexpected, but most likely results, is that everybody who can get on line is going to try to talk to them. It will be an even more obvious example of what might be seen as a multiple personality syndrome for the whole planet. When a civilization comes here and tries to talk to Earth and gets not one, not ten, but millions of answers, what will it make of this? I think we will probably have more difficulty speaking as a world than we've ever had before. Partly because of our access to communication tools.

HUNT: Can I just add a comment, how many of you've read *Childhood Zen* by Arthur C. Clarke? In that book—I would recommend it—giant UFOs station themselves over Washington, London, Paris, etc. and they impose peace on this earth. It's not a question, I don't think, whether the U.S. for its own self interest wants to suppress this. We're not dictating to them if these beings have this power. I happen to believe there are some beings out there, but taking Robert Jastrow's step farther he said some of these beings could have evolved beyond the need of bodies. He says they would be what old-fashioned religious people call spirits. Then, he says, how would we know they're there? Maybe they can materialize and dematerialize and do all kinds of things that seem like magic to us. I happen to believe such beings are out there. I don't think they evolve out there. I think they have some evil designs. I wrote a novel that military intelligence have read and asked me where I got my information—called the *Arcon Conspiracy*, where I give you what I think might be the way it would happen.

BALDWIN: Can we do more comments on that? *Arcon Conspiracy* is worth reading. In the work we do with altered state of consciousness, we deal with nonphysical beings largely and my paper, that will show up in the proceedings some time in the future, has this scenario. I cannot give you a synopsis here in two minutes nor in 10 pages in the symposium proceedings, but this is what we've found over several thousands of cases. There are patterns in this. I don't believe a thing when I hear once or twice or ten times, but it gets my attention. Now, when it comes through hundreds of times and we see the pattern over thousands of individual cases and these people have not conspired to make up stories to bring into me and my wife and tell us in session that there's some similarity to what you've described in *Arcon Conspiracy*. So I'll leave you to read the symposium paper on that particular subject. It's the briefest outline of a small section of the work that we do.

UNDERWOOD: Well, a couple of things, I guess. One is, what does conquest mean? Someone pointed out to me a long time ago that the Chinese were never really conquered. I thought, "What about the Manchu Dynasty?" When the Manchurians and Mongols came in and conquered them. Ah, but he said, as soon as they were conquered the new Chinese emperors became more Chinese than the Chinese. So what happened was that they conquered theoretically, they had the power theoretically. In fact, it destroyed their own culture. Not the Chinese culture. Their own culture was gone down the tubes.

To a certain extent that's what happened here on Turtle Island, North America, with European cultures coming in—what my dad used to describe as two great waves washing around the world to meet, foam, join, and eventually one blue, one green, become together blue-green. One of the things he also used to say, the differences you see in America that you cannot identify as European are probably all Native American. He said, who are they teaching you in class taught you how to be American? ..I was in fifth grade and said, "Daniel Boone." Who do you think Daniel Boone learned from? The west is deeply involved with concepts of technology, I loved the phrase this morning—techno-barbarism—I just thought that was great, and we need to think which technologies are good and which are barbaric. But in addition to that, I ran across some research several months ago, where they did an experiment with people on diets. They put them all on the same diet. They all got the same food. One group was invited to visualize salad with no dressing when they ate their food. The other group was invited to visualize whipped cream with strawberries when they ate their food. The latter group lost less weight. Ok, so what you see is to a certain extent what you get.

Of course, my tradition doesn't think in terms of dominance or conquest at all. Power is considered to be something different, there being two forms of strength. One being strength and the other being endurance. They're both important. Not just one or the other. Women, minorities, tend to have the latter—endurance, rather than that kind of power. So the whole concept of what conquest is isn't totally different. Instead, we are mutually modifying one another. And that's just the way it works. Anybody who wants to ask me about the Iroquois roots to the Constitution, do be sure and do that.

FUNARO: Just one comment before going on. Something Dave mentioned, *Childhood Zen*. I teach a course called Anthropology for the Future. And that's one of the textbooks I use in the class.

MODERATOR: **It has been noted that the gray species of visitor have appeared with every species of alien type. Since they appear to be without sexual organs, they must be clones or androids. Does the ubiquitous gray indicate a soul alien creator?**

UNDERWOOD: It depends upon where you get your information. I've been collecting samples of direct experiences from individuals for a while, not assiduously and not as an avocation, but just when I happen to run across them. Some of the people I've been talking with tell me the grays do indeed have sexual organs. They're just not external. They have to be externalized, so are they clones or androids? I don't know. I have trouble with concepts. We in the western world tend to put things in boxes and slam down the lid and tie it fast really quickly. So we say OK if you move slowly; if you don't seem to have an emotion or sexual organs, then you're an android. Well, kind of, who said that? Who gets to make the rules here? In my tradition I would be asked to say, I understand you as an android,not—you are.

Try this one, as Elisabet Satouris will tell you, Hopi has no nouns. None at all. You have to describe a life totally in terms of verbs. It does something to your thinking. The term Great Spirit comes out of our ancient tradition where you are talking about that which in the West is sometimes called God. The words coming out of your mouth are All things, All things, All things. One's for body; one's for mind; one's for spirit. All things got translated into Great Spirit.

BALDWIN: In our experience with persons who have experienced abductions, in a number of cases people who have no prior knowledge of this, have never cared to read anything about UFO abductions, or alien beings, or have not seen the movies depicting these various things will come up with similar scenarios. I wouldn't say this is part of the collective unconscious, they're having a memory or connecting with somebody else that has a memory. It may be their memory, I don't really know. But with people who don't know this and don't have an agenda, don't have preconceived notions, it's interesting that several of these people have said, when these little gray beings are around poking them, and one woman says, "They're poking me and running, stepping back and laughing," It's like we used to do in science class with a bug on the table, and she felt like a bug on this table as these little things were poking her. But then they got quiet and backed away when the door opened and the taller one came in which looked like a dentist, which is interesting since I had been a dentist in my earlier incarnation in this life for 12 years. She felt definitely that the dentist or the doctor as David Jacobs describes it, was definitely a superior being and had the responsibility, and the others were just sort of underlings, even mechanical.

Another fellow more recently suggested, and he was terrified, he came up for a demonstration in a class we gave a short time back, no knowledge, no interest, but recently his wife who was affectionate and fondled him across the back of his head when they were driving, suddenly realized after 30 years of marriage he has this groove across, just the base of his skull, and it had not been there before. This groove was about a ½ inch deep and ¾ of an inch high and it's definitely there and it hadn't been there before. She was curious; he was curious and volunteered for the demonstration. Indeed, we found an abduction scenario, sometime within the past year, and it was a new technology implant that was not visible on X-ray or any other method that we have existing now in our medical repertoire for discovering. We did discover it and what he felt was these little gray ones that were doing the menial tasks before the big guy came in and put the thing in that hurt like crazy. He felt again that these were just little mechanical beings, android-like, as the question comes here. He had no experience before this at all, never had read anything about this. His experience, his memory of that, was that they were android-like, mechanical. He had a hard time describing it, but that was the feeling.

There's a stretch there and we can call it channeling or communication or other dimensional communication or whatever you might want to call it in the techniques of spirit releasement therapy. We can ask questions of the other, whoever the other may happen to be. Asking questions of the one who was placing the implant, finding out what it was for, why it was new technology, what he had done, what was the purpose, what was controlling them, and so forth. He finally agreed to remove that implant, to let go of those... actually release them in our terminology, releasement, not exorcism, but releasement of the dark energies that were controlling that entire civilization, and this Being removed the implant. So this is a different type of implant, this is a different type of experience for this man, for sure. He felt, indeed, his first contact with these little gray beings, that they were mechanical. Again, I share clinical experience; not labeled the truth or facts, but people's experience.

**UNDERWOOD:** Which are true facts?

**BALDWIN:** Facts can change; truth doesn't. Right?

**Hunt:** Well, I think it's important to remember where these experiences come from. Sir John Echols, Nobel Prize winner for his research on the brain, describes the brain as "a machine that a ghost can operate." I think that some of us would agree to that. I don't think we're just pieces of educated beefsteak wired with nerves, lumps of protein molecules, you know. I think that there is a spirit inside and in the normal state of consciousness, psychokinesis is going on right now in all of us. You would find, if you haven't listened to some of his tapes, or read some of his books, you would find Sir John Echols' lectures fascinating. For example, he wired the brain to follow the neural activity, gave orders that you couldn't just do like piano playing, but it took some thought, and he followed the neural activity. When he would give the command to someone who had Parkinson's or who had had a stroke, and who was paralyzed and who couldn't do that, he said in every case the SMA, the supplementary motor area of the brain, fired. But nothing else happened. He believed that was where the spirit of man has the connection with the body to operate it.

Now in an altered state, and we are in what the New Agers call a consciousness revolution where altered states, not just the Shamanic state of a Shamanist, but alter states are being encouraged. We're being trained to enter into these altered states. Dr. Echols would say the normal state between the spirit and the brain is loosened. That allows another spirit to interpose itself, tick off the neurons in the brain, create a universe of illusion.

I happen to think that's what is happening. There's not a genuine memory. I have some friends.. I'm thinking of a man in New York, a loving family. His daughter went to a therapist and came to the conclusion, came out with alleged memories that he had sexually abused her. Father says no, mother says no, siblings say no. But she has believed this and has destroyed the family. There are thousands of families who have that. I'm not saying that sexual abuse doesn't take place, but the courts are turning against this now. There was a reversal of a man who was put in prison for murder on the alleged memory of a daughter that came out under hypnosis and the court has now reversed that. It was back in 1982 that the California Supreme Court outlawed all testimony by witnesses who had been hypnotized regarding anything about the case in court. Arizona, Maryland, other places have followed suit. So I have serious questions about the validity of these memories.

I've traveled around the world, I've interviewed people by the hundreds, and I have found out that whether they're on LSD, whether they're in yogic trance, whether they're under hypnosis in a psychiatrist's office, or however that altered state of consciousness, there is a consistency not only in the experience, but in the message. There's not only a phenomena, but there's a philosophy. I have found it interesting that it conforms precisely to what that book that some of you probably don't believe in, the Bible says. You want to know who the first ETI was way back there? There was a talking serpent, and what do you know, he said exactly the same thing that is coming out in all these instances. Four points: God is not personal but a force; it's the whole universe and because this force is in everything, you don't die, you just get recycled, reincarnation. And furthermore, we're all being recycled higher and higher to Godhood; you don't have to wait for that evolutionary process to take place; you can accelerate that through yoga, thru TM, through an initiation into this secret tree of knowledge, with a dark and a light side. The enlightenment will suddenly catapult you into this state of consciousness where you will have these powers. I think that gives us a clue where this is coming from.

FUNARO: My position on the material we've been talking about, and will be talking about this whole conference, is that I don't deny at all the manifestations, but I have a need to believe they can be fit into a western explanatory model. In other words, I don't think that you need to postulate anything external to explain why human beings have always believed in supernatural beings of one sort or another. I think that the similarity in response worldwide then has to be placed into the category of the fact that all human beings have basically the same physical equipment and evolutionary background that they share. This equipment when stimulated in a certain way responds in a predictable way. I'm glad someone asked this question because it is something I wanted to play with you with. I think one of the things we can see if we just look at the history of not just proposed extraterrestrial contacts, but the public image of extraterrestrials in this century. It's changed considerably. We've had a sort of evolutionary process from what are first perceived as being essentially malevolent beings to benevolent ones. We can see this even when we talk about robots. The first robots were seen as coming out of the notion of the industrial revolution and machines as being competitors with human beings, to eventually a place where human beings have gotten used to their machines, and have begun to use them as partners rather than as competition. In fact, in my own opinion, I don't believe we are a species, we're a partnership with our technology; and that human beings aren't human without their technology; I don't mean computers; I mean any inorganic thing that we use to extend or expand our bodies. So this connection with our tools, our machines, our technology, is part of being human. In fact, I think that our machines make us more human, not less human. What we're really mourning, our nostalgia, is not for our lost human nature, but our lost animal nature as we become more human, as we blend with the products we produce.

I think we can also see this evolution at least in what I see as our perception of aliens. They were originally more malevolent as manifested in science fiction films of the 50s and 60s. They've become more benevolent: ET and the gray people. I assume this question has to do with these particular rather small beings compared with us, with large heads, large eyes, small faces. This really can be explained. I'm not suggesting it's the only explanation. One of my favorite mottoes is: theories are made by desperate people. We're all of us in our own ways desperate to have our theories be right.

But there's a peculiar thing called the Cute Response, which I suspect many of you have heard of. It may indeed be the trigger for our human parenting response. It springs out of our biological background, although I'm not suggesting it's totally biological. But we have an emotional response to certain proportions of faces. These are faces which have large heads in proportion to the size of the face, large eyes in proportion to the size of the face, small faces in proportion to the size of the head. This cannot be simply our own idea of what our babies look like because it seems to be trans-pacific. We have the similar kind of parenting response if we look at a puppy or a kitten or a baby bird, and adults of many of those other species also have the same emotional response to our young, as for example, an adult dog who will treat our young differently than animals, less rough. Now, this I think could be very important, because in the first place, these precise proportions that I've discussed are first of all characteristics that the young of many species share with one another. And secondly, they are exactly the proportions that change as the young mature into adults. That is, as adults our faces look larger in proportion to our heads, the eyes look smaller in proportion to the size of our faces, and the adaptive value of this is clear enough.

It is hopefully some kind of guarantee that the young of a species will not be brutalized. They will be taken care of in a positive emotional response, a beneficial emotional response. Now I'll draw this for those who have not seen it, here is a child. OK. Watch me make it younger. Here is a baby. Did you see it get younger? There have been tests on this that show human beings when confronted with pairs of drawings which show the actual proportions of the young of an individual of either our species or other species, that the humans.. and they're asked to pick the cutest one, they almost always pick the exaggerated one over the true responses. So there's something going on here that we need not go to the actual presence of something that conforms to this externally in order to explain it. As I say, it's not the only explanation. But we can see this, for example, in the evolution of Mickey Mouse. Mickey Mouse was a rat when it started out. Some of you may remember. They made him more and more human. In fact, he hasn't had a tail since 1960. Walt Disney taught a whole generation—mine—that deer look like Bambi, and rabbits look like Thumper, and the *Lion King* is doing the same thing with Simba. The Japanese comics are experts at utilizing this parental response to make their characters more identifiable. So that's my schtick on it. At least it so far convinces me there are explanations I can utilize within my own scientific context. I need not go outside to explain manifestations, and the manifestations are real. That certainly does not make those experiences unreal.

HUNT: Can I just add one thing here? I have to keep reminding my panel members that this is the Fear Panel.

Look at the metamorphosis from 1938. The Invasions of the Martians, Orson Wells, created terror, down to ET, that nice-looking gila-monster. I think that could be a little bit dangerous. If I dare say, it reminds me of a story of a missionary going through the jungles of Africa and he came out around a corner confronted by a lion, and he gets down on his knees to pray. And he was praying and nothing happened and he looked up and the lion is praying. And he says, Praise the Lord, it's a Christian lion! The lion says, Shut up. I'm giving thanks for my food. Anyway, its the Fear Panel, folks.

**MODERATOR: Most Americans speak only English and are unfamiliar with other Earth cultures and languages, unlike Europeans. Could this be a reason for the American ego not to accept so readily more advanced ETs with different looks and technology?**

UNDERWOOD: Remember I said a few minutes ago about how Hopi doesn't have any nouns? There's a saying in my tradition, which is basically Iroquois, that language predicts the conclusions that we reach therein. Which it does and unless you're trained to notice this you have no idea that's happening. You think you're talking truth when actually you're just labeling things. Deciding, this is an android, that is a clone. Well, you know, those are the definitions of western science, android and clone, or western science fiction as the case may be. Not necessarily relevant to the whole earth experience, and a lot of cultures don't do that at all.

I think Americans are particularly susceptible to this because we precisely have not been a bi-lingual, tri-lingual nation. In many places, Holland for instance and Norway; Holland especially, English is the second language; it's taught as the second language; in Norway it is also. Because they say, if you only speak Norwegian, you have 4 million people you can talk to, period. So they assiduously teach English which has a similar language base. Specially if you get totally outside of European languages you really get exposed to different ideas, and I think that's profoundly valuable. It wakes you up as to what might be truth and what might be linguistic assumption.

BALDWIN: I think there are many reasons why American ego might not accept the reality there are more advanced ETs than we are. After we are Americans, right? Who has an ego in here? Ego aside, and it's interesting when one studies the dolphin, there's very little ego involved. A great deal of altruism and cooperation. An open, loving sexuality. If a female jumps in a pool in Florida with male dolphins, they are very eager and sexual. But a lot of altruism, a lot of caring, a lot of compassion. And a lot of *selflessness*. I don't know if we'd be accused of that as a people. We do need to pay attention, not only to our own feelings and many of us deny our own feelings. But to pay attention to those who come to us, before we shoot like the soldier shot Michael Rennie in *The Day the World Stood Still*, before the soldier got frightened at that little thing that he had in his hand.

To pay attention, to find out, to gather information, to be open, not to think we have the answers, or we know the truth. Language is just one way. We're very arrogant about our language, and I understand French people are very arrogant about their language, and their money. So maybe the European Common Market will have difficulty in both arenas—language and money. But there must be some commonalties. This is what we must look for in the aliens, not differences in languages or differences in ideologies, or differences in emotions. Some of them seem to have no emotions whatsoever. But they have an interesting spiritual outlook, which is *oneness*. If they are all one, why would we object to being experimented upon? This is one of the statements that comes through by some of the aliens that do seem to do some of the experimenting in people's experience. I think we can't go away from taking full responsibility for own self, not looking out there, but our own self here, paying attention to our own self and what's out there. Not giving our authority away: here's our great big brother from the sky, space brothers, they're going to rescue us. That's giving away authority. There's a question that didn't come on the panel, about authority. What about giving our authority away? Absolutely not. Whether it's to any authority figure: to our parents, or police officer or school, medicine or religious figures, or extra-terrestrials, or government, we can't give our authority away. We are sovereign beings and we must hang onto that; above all, to pay attention, to remain sovereign, to remember who and what you are. If there is a one God, then we are part of that one God; we are derived from that one God, and so are the aliens. Yes, there's a oneness, and we are still a separate being. Here we are sovereign. So giving away our authority, no. Give away our arrogance, but just pay attention, to remember who and what you are always.

HUNT: Could this be the reason for American ego not to accept so readily more advanced ETs? Well, I'll be very brief. I don't think it matters what our ego wants to accept, or doesn't want to accept. I'd have to go back to it again. If these beings are who people think they are, they have the capabilities either technologically or psychically of getting here and contacting us. I think they're going to dictate the terms. It's beside the point whether our ego wants to accept it or not. And we could be humbled very quickly.

FUNARO: Actually, I don't really think we need to go to dolphins really, although dolphins do have egos. Like humans also have egos but we also have the ability to be loving, altruistic. It's just that in the society we live in we don't get much chance to do that. That's because of the peculiar nature of our society. It's very typical for people to think the way they live is normal and representative of the way all people live. So I'm not faulting anyone for that. Anthropologists are used to this. This is partly biological in nature. The evolutionary theory at least says that chimpanzees and humans had their last point of separation of common origin perhaps as recently as 5 or 6 million years ago.

We see a number of characteristics that modern chimpanzees and humans share that most likely derive from that mother society. One of them is the community, which is a group of individuals which has very definite boundaries. Strangers are recognized as strangers, and are dealt with a range of reactions from curiosity and suspicion to hostility. I think it's part of our biological background to see things in terms of US and THEM. This is also why not just Ronald Reagan, but before Ronald Reagan, at least as early as Andre Malraux, the idea of creating an extraterrestrial invasion in order to make us all "us," because there would be a THEM out there, makes sense. Although I don't know whether it would really work, but it's a good idea. The point I want to make is a point Elisabet brought up today, and that we're guilty of using it today. We call ourselves Americans, how arrogant. There're a whole bunch of people outside the United States who call themselves American, too. Plus the people who really have the right to call themselves Americans aren't even given that priviledge, unless Indian is tacked onto the end of it. So we, even in trying to deal with the questions of our egos, betray our arrogance. Most of the various kinds of human consciousness movements, group therapy movements, that I have come across in recent years in the United States, have the same tenet at base. It's individual responsibility. We need to be responsible for ourselves.

274

This is often promulgated as if it were some kind of enlightened view, that the linear universes which seems to make progress inherent in the universes got us too, above all the other cultures who haven't quite got the fact that individual responsibility is the answer. The fact is, it's not the answer, at least not the human answer. In most societies individual responsibility is called selfishness. People in other societies are not raised to be responsible for themselves, they're raised to be responsible for one another, because in a real community you can know that other people are being raised to be responsible for you. Mother is not a responsibility for self; mother is a responsibility for children. Father is not a responsibility for self; father is a responsibility for family. So we've got it all backwards in thinking we're normal. The reason for bringing this up is to try to explain from an anthropological point of view to us why what many questioners are noticing is how come we seem to have difficulty dealing with these notions. I mean it's very obvious if you look at it from an anthropological perspective, and perhaps other perspectives as well.

# Hope Panel:
# Montgomery, Ware, Boylan, Sprinkle

**SCOTT JONES:** I've asked Don Ware to be the moderator. In that august and very responsible position, it means that he is asked to read the questions. Also, I will give him another assignment. Ruth Montgomery is notoriously a panel hog, she likes to take all the time. If Ruth gets out of control, Don, I'll ask you to please tell her that the fellow panel members need a fair shot at the questions.

**MONTGOMERY:** With that, I refuse to go on.

**WARE:** I guess the general question is why I'm here. Let me start with the evolution with my thought on this subject. I saw the lights over D.C. in 1952 on 26 July, that made headlines around the world. I was 16 years old, walking down the street in Arlington, Virginia. I stopped and looked at them for ten minutes. They appeared about as bright as Venus at its brightest but reddish in color, very much like the things that appeared in Gulf Breeze 180 times in an 18th-month period earlier this decade. I asked myself, is that what I read about in the newspaper the previous Sunday morning? Sure enough, the next morning I got up and there were UFO's in the headlines. They repeated the thing two Saturday nights in a row, and in hindsight I think they did that so there would be the subject "flying saucers" in the headlines around the world.

I have always had a great interest in all the mysteries of mankind, but that caused me to read everything I could find on UFO's for the last 43 years. It took me two years, primarily in the Duke University library, reading reports in the American Rocket Society, etc., to come to the conclusion that some UFO's are vehicles controlled by more advanced intelligence. It took me ten years in the Air Force working with top secret data to figure out that somebody in our government has known that for a fact since at least 1947, perhaps earlier. When I retired at age 47, thirteen years ago, and didn't have to work for a living, I expanded my reading into other peripheral areas, like ancient astronauts, and soon learned that someone has been watching us for a very long time. I came to the realization that I'd always known there was some connection between UFO's and religion, but I didn't know what it was. I came to the realization about then—ten-twelve years ago—that both the UFO phenomenon and religions are avenues through which we get a glimpse of a much larger reality. I ask myself, what other avenues are there that we get a glimpse of this larger reality? I assumed—this is my logical mind working, now—that it probably included all the persistent mysteries of mankind and I set out to do a rather decent literature search on those mysteries, starting with reincarnation. My personal view is that, unless you accept reincarnation as part of your reality, you will *never* understand what's going on concerning our alien visitors—very important to do that—and the book I recommend in that respect is—if you just read one book—is *Exploring Reincarnation* by Hans Ten Dam. That's the fellow who had it republished in English in 1990.

I studied telepathy because I realized that telepathy was the normal means of communication among higher intelligence. I studied out-of-body experiences, near-death experiences, spiritual healing, and in

1989, started receiving messages that appeared to me to come from higher intelligence. They didn't come directly to me; they came through seven other people, using three different telepathic processes. They all came to me because they mentioned my name. I started paying attention.

I was fairly well known among people in the field in that I had been a—since the day I retired—a field investigator for MUFON and a state section director in five counties. I was the state director for MUFON in Florida for six years; the Eastern Regional Director for four years; and I managed the investigative activities in eighteen eastern states, so to speak—that is, I critiqued the reports and wrote one-paragraph summaries for publication, some of which didn't get published.

On January 28, 1992, I got a direct message. I woke up at exactly 2:00 in the morning and it was like a video screen in my mind with two sentences on it, two lines, each one above the other. No room in my mind for any other thought until I got up and wrote those two sentences down. The first one had said, "Unconditional love is becoming a driving force on this planet." The second sentence said, "I am trying to learn to express unconditional love." As soon as I wrote those down, my mind cleared up and I could think about other things and go back to sleep. I took that as confirmation, perhaps from my spirit guides, that I had arrived at some valid conclusions.

I realized that I probably knew more about our alien visitors than I did about those people representing this planet that they were interacting with, because I accepted alien liaisons as part of reality. I chose January last year to start focussing my attention on world government. I've studied many aspects of it, not just the UN, but all those organizations in many countries where people are inspired to work toward a democratically elected government that can speak for all the people of the planet. That is a prerequisite to joining a galactic society, from what I've learned.

Then I studied what I've been advised to refer to as a not-so-secret world government, which I think includes the people that have the resources to bring about major change on this planet—resources being the money and the influence. I've been watching the newspapers carefully to see just what those individuals are doing, and I'm encouraged; it makes me hopeful. For example, the co-founder of the Trilateral Commission was Zbigniew Brzezinski, if you recall, was a national security advisor for Carter. In 1970 he co-founded that organization—that's a world level, not-so-secret world government, as I see it—with David Rockefeller, and in 1973—in 1970 he wrote a book called *Between Two Ages*. Read it. It's interesting. It told me that Zbigniew Brzezinski had a real good handle on the supernational problems of the world, many of which were environmental in nature. He understood that we were destroying the environment that supports us. That gave me some warm feeling that maybe the Trilateral Commission was founded to help resolve some of those problems that threaten all mankind.

Then, when I see what Jimmy Carter did in the last year or so—you know, he and Colin Powell and Sam Nunn went down to Haiti and pulled off a minor miracle, all members of the Council on Foreign Relations, the U.S. branch of that group. Then, Carter went to North Korea to work on the number one problem from their perspective and from ours, nuclear proliferation. Next he went to Bosnia and got a four-month truce called. Then he went to Africa where people are slicing each other up with machetes. Now, watch what they're doing.

One more conference I wanted to mention. I was in Madagascar recently. The only newspaper I had was the *International Herald Tribune*, and I read about the Casablanca Conference, which was sponsored by the U.S. Council on Foreign Relations, who apparently had enough influence to get the head of state of Israel to sit down with the heads of their Arab neighbors and talk about economic cooperation. They had enough influence to get representatives from all the major economic powers there, and they set up a regional development bank. They wanted to get ten billion into that account, and they got two billion in that meeting. So, the newspaper says it wasn't really all that successful. But any time you call a meeting and get two billion dollars to help solve a problem, I think that can be called sucessful. Tom, the Galactic Council representative who influenced Gene Roddenberry so much—taught him about reality— said the number one problem that humanity has to resolve before we can get on with the transformation is, that Jewish folk and the Arabs have to learn to live with each other. That's a species karma thing that we have to get over.

That meeting, by the way, was hosted by Paul Volker, member of the Trilateral Commission.

BOYLAN: Why am I here? Well, that's a long journey. I'm old enough to remember the headlines in 1947 when Kenneth Arnold saw a squadron of UFO's over Mt. Ranier, Washington state. That was the day that reporters coined the term, "flying saucer." And, also, the headlines in the western U.S. papers before the wire service news embargo set in about the Roswell saucer crash, Army Air Corps retrieved saucer. I was a very disappointed eight-year-old, semi-literate school kid when the next day the newspaper said, "Oops, it was just a weather balloon." But by the time I was in eighth grade, I was very much hip to the news story that Don just reminded you of in 1952, the repeated overflights of UFO squadrons over the nation's capital here that pushed the Democratic National Convention off the front page and became world headline news, complete with photographs. I remember a nice night photograph in my humble hometown paper at the time, showing lights in formation over the nation's capital, photographic evidence. All the skeptics yell for photographic evidence. They need to go to the newspaper archives. Anyway, after that light settled down, the cover-up settled in, and everybody got on with their lives.

To fast-forward, in 1989, I had long since gotten to the point where I was doing psychotherapy as a licensed clinical psychologist, counseling people for a variety of garden variety of problems, when that year four different people in my case load, after we'd settled the issues they basically came in for, each separately decided they would trust me with a very sensitive aspect of their lives, namely, along the lines of—you probably won't believe this, Doc, but back some years ago I had a visitation by somebody who didn't come from here—and proceeded to launch into an account of ET visitation. This sparked my interest, needless to say, and I then read the scant literature available on the topic and decided the proper thing to do, if these kind of cases were going to continue to come forward, was to do a little research project, which I began and which is still ongoing. I have now talked at length to over 155 such persons and gathered a fair amount of information, and have also conferred with other colleague researchers and psychotherapists in the field, and quite a bit is now known.

The panel today is about hope, and we might just as easily call it the consciousness panel, perhaps even more to the point, because as we get involved with the ET-human contact phenomenon, it becomes much more than an exercise in interesting anthropology, about "Gee, isn't this nice, quite different looking people. Neat!" As will become clear from this conference and certainly from this panel, such meetings are transformative of the individual, and we have every reason to believe that, as time goes on, the meeting of cultures on a large scale between humanity and the peoples of space will be transformative of us as an earth society. And so, part of that transformation is not just nuts and bolts, technology or even our history, but ET's bring to us very much an emphasis from their own cultural development and what we would be pleased to call metaphysics and spirituality and consciousness at a high level, and that will indeed be what we will be speaking to in some measure today.

The Cosmic Cultures conference, as Scott has wisely set up, is not to argue about the reality of

UFO's or ET's but to move to the question of getting ready for the prospect of open engagement between our society and the society from space. And so, I would invite all of you to join with us in tuning in for the next two or three hours to this kind of consciousness, because it's much more a consciousness shift than it is an empirical event of some dark-eyed individual walking down the carpet here. I would argue that the transformation that goes on within us is the larger event and will be ongoing. There is some indication that we may have some sense of energy presence in this conference before it's all over, and I would invite those of you who are unusually sensitively attuned to see if you detect that. With that, I think I'll close for now and pass the baton.

MONTOGOMERY: Why am I here? That's what I asked Scott Jones. I still think of myself as a newspaper reporter after having been one for most of my adult life. But everything that has happened to me since then seems to go back to that, so that must have been what I was meant to do when I got here. The psychic all began for me when I was asked to do a syndicated series, that turned out to be eight-part series, that newspapers carried all over the country that they entitled, "What happens to a girl reporter when she goes to seances?" I was the most skeptical Washington newspaper reporter you could imagine. I didn't believe anything unless it happened to me personally. I went to these seances and I became intrigued by some and turned off by others and then wrote that just as it befell me. In this series I told the things that I thought were phoney or that could have been staged, and then I told other things that seemed inexplicable, but I felt sure there was an explanation if I were just smart enough to know it. That's the way it turned out. Well, this was for International News Service and they said that they'd never had so much reaction to anything in all of their many years of existence because mail bags full of mail came in by the bundlefulls from all over the country from the newspapers who forwarded them. They started sending them down to me here in Washington, and I said , "Stop! Stop! Just prepare a form letter saying thank you for your letter."

I did research for that series at the Library of Congress. There wasn't too much written about this in those days, if any of you are old enough, as I am, to remember those days. But in the things that I did read, a lot of them were scoffing or exposés, but nobody seemed to have a bad word for Arthur Ford. I'd never met him and that was my first encounter, even with his name. About a year later, I read an ad in *The Washington Post* that said that Arthur Ford would be giving a speech about a new foundation that he was associated with—A.R.E., it's called now—and I was intrigued enough to persuade my husband to go with me to hear him that evening at Universalist Church, and afterwards I went up and introduced myself and told him that I had written a series about mediums and seances and could I interview him? He said, "Fine." So I went in. The other seances and the other mediums that I'd been with were all in dark rooms. After I'd finished interviewing him for my syndicated column, he said, "Would you like me to go into trance and see if there's something that transpires?" I said, "Oh, great!" and I jumped up and—we were in a suite—and I said, "I'll help you pull the curtains down." And he said, "No, that isn't necessary," and he just tied a handkerchief over his eyes and leaned back. Pretty soon my deceased father was talking to me and all kinds of things were occurring out of his throat, out of his larynx. When I reviewed my notes afterwards, I thought, well, some of this is really startling, but there's no way in the world he could have known about these things. I wrote a big Sunday piece about that interview.

Then I really thought that I was through with it, but all kinds of things began to happen. Every time Arthur Ford came to Washington after that, he would call me and we'd get together, and we became very good friends. One day he said, "Ruth, I'm getting psychically that you can do automatic writing."

I said, "What's that?" He explained it, and told me how to go about it. So I began trying that every morning at the same time, at 9:00, sitting at my desk with my eyes closed, holding this pencil lightly over paper, and absolutely nothing happened. I would grin to myself and throw down the pencil, and go on to make an honest living at the White House or at the Capitol. Finally, on the tenth day, I was just sitting there half asleep like I usually was, and suddenly it was as if a great hand put it over mine, and this began going round and round and round in figure 8's and circles and I couldn't drop the pencil. I thought, "What in the world is going on?" Finally, it let go of my hand and I went on to the office. That afternoon an old, much older friend of mine who told me that she gets automatic writing, called me and she said, "Oh, Ruth, I'm so excited! I was doing automatic writing today and it said, 'Now Ruth can do this. Now Ruth can do this.'" I said, ya, I'll tell you what Ruth can do. She can make circles and figure 8's. And she said, "That's wonderful! That's the way it always starts. That's their way of expressing glee that they've finally made contact. Now, don't fail to do this tomorrow morning." So I said, OK.

The next morning I was sitting there and the pencil began to move. Pretty soon I opened my eyes and looked at it, and it was drawing little figures. Then it was writing "I love you, I love you, I love you. Aunt May." Well, the only Aunt May I'd ever had died when I was three years old, so I didn't really remember her. But every morning it would do the same thing. It would draw little figures of children, dogs, animals. Finally, I wrote to one of her sisters, an older sister who, of course, was my aunt, and I didn't—believe me—tell her why I was asking. But I said, "Did Aunt May ever show any interest in drawing?" She wrote back and said, "Oh, yes, she loved to draw little children and animals." I thought, well, allright. I just kept on for awhile, and finally I threw down the pencil one morning and said, "Aunt May, if you have any messages for me, I'll take them, but I will *never* draw another picture for you." That's the last I heard from Aunt May. This is true.

The next morning, though I didn't know that I was through with Aunt May, I was sitting there and suddenly it started drawing something. I thought, "Oh, no, not again!" Then, it began to do some writing and I thought, well, you know, sort of half of me was in a medium state and half of it was conscious, as it always is when I do these. I thought, "Well, at least she's starting to write a message." When I opened my eyes, it had drawn a lily, and then, with a continuous action from the pencil had written L-I-L-Y, and then said, "This is how you will identify me from now on. I am your guide." That was the advent of Lily and my automatic writing.

From then on, every day, Lily came in and always first drew the lily—maybe Aunt May was teaching Lily to draw! But, anyway, from then on I began to hear from Lily all the time. Of course, Arthur Ford became quite interested in the fact that I was getting this automatic writing, and the messages were beautiful. They could not have come from my mind because I was just a cynical, hard-bitten newspaper reporter and these messages were beautiful. They had wonderful philosophy.

One morning I had overslept. They were always bawling me out when I did that. One morning I just sat on the side of the bed and reached over for a pen or pencil and sat there writing, eyes closed, of course, and suddenly it was as if something had grabbed my hand again and it wrote something real, real heavy. I opened my eyes and it said, "We said, go to your typewriter!" Then I read what they had been writing, which I was not conscious of, and it said, "We think we have now developed enough strength to type through you. This scrawling is becoming illegible." I went across the hall to my typewriter and sat down and put my hands in typing position on it, closed my eyes, and it was very faint at first, and then it began going click-click-click.

From then on, I began getting all this what *I* think is beautiful philosophy, which came about in a search for the truth. Well, then, of course, I was telling my family about it now and then, and Mother was just thinking, "How did I ever give birth to that!" But finally the guides began writing, "This information is not just for you, young lady. It's meant for everybody. We want you to publish a book." I thought, "Oh, that's all I need to tell Mother." So I finally did tell Mother and she said, "Oh, Ruth, please, I *pray* you don't do it!" She said, "People respect you." She said, "You're invited to the White House to dinners and presidents call you by your first name. Honey, *don't* do that. What will the church people think?" Which was Mother's real concern.

I delayed a year. I was writing at it but I was not going to publish it. Then I decided that I had to because the guides were even more persistent than Mother. So I did turn it over to a publisher, who brought it out, called *Search for the Truth*, and immediately afterwards I began getting calls from ministers all over the country asking if I would address their congregations from the pulpit. Notre Dame University asked me to address its student body. I did address several other university ones, including another Catholic one, which amazed me. I mean, I was more surprised than Mother! But the thing that really sold it to Mother was that my mother's older sister called her one Sunday all excited, and she said, "Bertha, our minister preached his whole sermon today on Ruth's new book, and it seems that he knew Arthur Ford, and it was just the most wonderful sermon!" So from then on, Mother let me off the hook. Now, if it weren't for Don, I could tell you the rest of my life, but he says stop.

**Ware:** In the interests of time, I strongly recommend all of you, if you haven't read it, read the book *Ruth Montgomery, Herald of the New Age*. It's a wonderful book. Thank you, Ruth.

SPRINKLE: I'm here because I have the opportunity to sit next to this golden lady. I thank Scott, the Human Potential Foundation, and all you good people who are here, and the people who have written questions. I'm enjoying the opportunity to interact with people about these questions that we are posing for ourselves.

I do want to comment on the experience that happened to me when I was about ten or twelve years old, sitting on a chicken house in our yard in Rocky Ford, Colorado. I looked up in the southwestern sky and I thought to myself, "My mother and my father are up there somewhere." Then my rational side took over and said, "What are you talking about, Leo? Rex and Anna Sprinkle, they're your parents; Bob and Gene, brothers; Faye is your sister. You were born here on Earth." And so I let go of that strong feeling that I had.

There are many other experiences I could share, but in general, what it boils down to are these conclusions. I state my conclusions first because when I gave a talk at the University of North Dakota— I was an assistant professor back there in 1961—and I went through some preliminary arguments about communication and human evolution, wound up arguing for psychic abilities as part of human evolution. The head of the psychology department gently chastised me. He said, "Leo, you should warn the audience what you're going to talk about," because, well, you know, I was almost persuasive. So, my conclusions are that UFO phenomena, ET intelligence are here. They're engaged in a gigantic educational program. In '76 I suggested the possibility it could be called CCC, the Cosmic Consciousness Conditioning program. You know, whenever there's an educational program, where you always have a book that outlines three levels: there's the philosophy, that's what is stated is believed; and the policy, the way it goes about it; and then the practice, what actually happens. Sometimes they're closely intertwined and sometimes they're not.

What's the philosophy? It can be—my philosophy about these phenomena can be stated in a story. A young man went through an abduction experience in hypnosis with me, I don't know, back in the '60's sometime. He returned to the normal state. His eyes were big and he said, "Leo, is this war?" Then I said, "No, I don't think so. I think it's worse." He said, "Worse?" I said, "Yes, I think it's education."

And what's the policy? How does this educational program work? It can be illustrated by a story of a woman who went through her experience. She returned to the normal state. She was upset. She'd been groaning and moaning, going through the various kinds of medical—what she perceived to be medical experimentation, examination, sexual examination, and so forth—and she was writhing and groaning. When she returned to the normal state, she opened her eyes and she wept awhile. And then pretty soon she said, "Leo, do you think they're going to come back and take me away?" I said, "I don't think you'll be that lucky; I think you'll have to stay here and work like the rest of us."

Well, what's the practice? The practice is to provide a person with a puzzle, a Mission Impossible. In my opinion, there are two aspects: the individual initiation and the social stimulus. I think they're interacting, although this is the puzzling question and I wish I could talk more about it with other investigators. For example, the hypothesis that, first of all, those of us who claim to have UFO experiences, first of all were psychotic. Well, then, we're neurotic. Well, then, we're kooks. Well, then, we don't understand natural phenomena. Then, we are experiencing memories of our birth experience. Then we are confusing child abuse—you know, anything but the actual hypothesis. (Oh, my god!) So, in my opinion, the individual initiation and social stimulus sometimes work together. We have to find out whether we have been abused as children, those of us who are UFO experiencers. As we do, we uncover a social mystery: Why did we refuse to talk about ourselves as a society that allowed children to be abused? When people talk to me about how fearsome these events are, I sometimes acknowledge their pain, their misery, but also I sometimes acknowledge to myself that I've heard this before from people who claim they suffered these same things from the hands of humans.

When I went in the service, some of my friends said, "This is the worst experience of my life!" I said, "This is the easiest time in my life!" "Easy?!" I said, "Yes, we get five minutes of free time every hour." My dad didn't want us to lean on the shovel or to take five minutes every hour, so the experience depends upon the person's view of whether it's horrible or not. As one person said, (whispering) "Leo, do you realize these ET's, they come down and they grab cattle, and they mutilate 'em!" And I said, (whispering) "Yes, and do you realize we mutilate cattle and we eat them?"

So, what's it all about? Well, I don't know. That's why I'm hanging around, and I exercise, I eat right, work right, you know, sleep right, do all the good things so that I'll be here long enough to find out. But I like two hypotheses, and I think that they are on the right track. Maybe in a few years we'll know. Jim Deardorf, who will be speaking, has the leaky embargo hypothesis, and, of course, with a name like Sprinkle, I like the leaky embargo hypothesis. I don't know whether to say more about it or not, but I'll just mention that it's the idea that there's an embargo in information, and so we aren't going to know about the ET's. The ET activity is to hold up a mirror, and we see ourselves. So if you have a nice, friendly physical experience, fine. If you have a nice, friendly spiritual experience, fine. Or if you have a horrible physical experience or a horrible spiritual experience, then it gives you an opportunity to look into the mirror and say, "Why would I have this kind of particular experience?" So, as an individual we can learn more about ourselves, our past lives, and why we're here on the planet at this particular time.

From a social standpoint, the model I like is the one by Jessup—Morris K. Jessup. Some people say he died by suicide. Other people said he had help. His model, which I appreciate and I think it still follows, is that there are three groups: There are the higher forces, there are the humans, and there are the ET's. The higher forces are the shepherds, the humans are the sheep, and the little ET's are the sheep dogs. If we follow the shepherds, all is well. If we don't, the sheep dogs come along, they nip at our heels, and it hurts!

282

MODERATOR: WARE: Now let's get into the questions from the audience. The way we'll do this is I'll take the first one, and we'll all have a chance to respond on it; and then Richard Boylan will start with the second question and we'll work it on down the table so we all don't have to be the first to speak.

The first question is, **"In anticipation of the benefits of dialogue with cosmic cultures, how can we insure that we remember and represent the positive interests of all Earth's inhabitants— plant, animal, geographic, spirit—and not just the interests of humans alone?"**

I feel that if we can view the universe from the perspective of our spirit, then we will really have a better understanding of what's going on. I think a lot depends on our concept of God, and I was very fortunate to hear a lecture at the International UFO Congress last December by Daniel Sheehan, who is a fairly well-known Harvard Law School graduate who founded the Christic Institute here in Washington a few years back, represented major cases that involved cultural issues—Three Mile Island, Karen Silkwood, KKK, Greensboro, that kind of case, Watergate. He gave what appeared to me to be a classroom-type lecture on why people think the way they think. It starts off with our personal cosmology. You know, he tried to rank-order people's thinking on the subject of UFO's, or almost any other subject as to the right systemist and the—you know, on down the line—the middle and to the left. So, he's going to make either rightists or leftists out of all of us, I guess. He said our personal cosmology, whether we view the universe as an everlasting, pulsating, living universe, eternal universe, or whether one that is guided by the forces of entropy and is ever expanding and will die out. That basic cosmology greatly affects how we think about many different subjects, like our alien visitors. I found that on his scale, I was a leftist. I never thought of myself as a leftist before, but apparently I was on this subject. If we can accept God as being Universal Consciousness or Christ Consciousness or All That Is, define it by one of those terms rather than a personage sitting on a cloud somewhere, and if we can recognize that there is some form of consciousness in everything, in trees, plants, animals, and the Earth itself is a living part of this universe, then it is much easier for us to learn to love everything, to learn to love God. I think that's one of the things that we need to do to join a galactic society, and I think a lot of us are getting help in that direction. That gives me great hope.

BOYLAN: Well, of course you can have the benefits of dialogue with cosmic cultures and making sure that there's positive benefits for everyone—plant, animal, geographic, spirit, and not just humans alone. I think the question assumes perhaps that there's a risk of a one-sided engagement between human beings and extraterrestrials. The risk being that somehow the rest of the Earth equation being left out of the deal—animal, plant kingdoms, Earth, atmosphere, water, and so forth, spirit force. I think there are enough people now on this planet with a holistic understanding of the way things are put together—some people come at it by the code word "ecology;" some people come at it by systems theory; some people come at it by a spiritual perspective that understands it's in spirit, or consciousness, or the underpinning being that makes everything what it is, pervades everything—that you can't escape the holistic understanding of things. Some people do not have a university level vocabulary for that consciousness, but they have it nonetheless.

We know that some of the people that industrialized nations might consider primitive have this most securely within their grasp of understanding. Certainly from the many cases I've dealt with experiencers reporting out their dialogue with extraterrestrials, it is—and from other researchers of great soundness that I've collaborated on data comparison with—it is very clear that the ET message is one of an ecological sensitivity. It is a holistic understanding of the way the world is put together, indeed, the cosmos, and furthermore, a spiritually imminentist understanding of the way things are. I guess the short answer to that question is, I don't think that there is any possibility of a one-sided or lopsided engagement between the peoples of Earth and the peoples extraterrestrial and possibly interdimensional because both sides have plenty of representation that understand things holistically.

I'm put in mind of the Native American tradition, and I think some of the wisdom of the Native American tradition comes from the fact that Native American peoples of North, Central and South America have a long history of contact with space people or star people. It is tempting to hypothesize that some of their deep grounded learnedness and wisdom comes from those contacts. But be that as it may, the Native American peoples have a very good understanding of the fact that humans are but stewards of this Earth and a part of a greater whole, and that to defile one's own nest is to commit suicide. While we find ourselves in the industrialized countries, ones that are doing the major Earth pollution, and by our reach into the third world and economically create incentives for ecological destruction there, nevertheless, while these portions of the world are the chief practitioners of what the Hopi call *kiamasquasi* (world out of balance), we recognize it as such. We've had the Rio de Janeiro conference and others, and even the most obtuse materialistic societies on this earth are beginning to get the message. It is, of course, the same message the ET's are bringing us. So I, despite the data to the contrary, maintain a consciousness of hope that this dialogue will only accelerate, play into the hand of the better elements of consciousness on both the ET and the human side to move this planet, this space we occupy, around.

MONTGOMERY: Well, I think that since everything was created by God, in my opinion, that the animals are just as important as the humans, I think it's a laugh for us to think that the highest creation of God's ability was the human being.

The most remarkable person I have ever known is William Goodlett who has lived down here in Salem, Virginia for a couple of decades. In my opinion, he is the only real space traveler I have ever known. I have a chapter about him in *Aliens Among Us*, and how he suddenly transverses himself almost without his own knowledge to other planets. The minute he returns to his body he describes all that he has seen there. He is also an artist, he paints pictures of how the costumes were. I think some of the most engaging ones were from a Galactic Conference which didn't look at all like this one. He was describing all the different form of Beings. Some of the delegates from other planets were what we would call chickens, except that they were much bigger than our chickens. He described an engaging little episode with one of them. She was kind of naughty, I thought. Also, some of them have pig faces but pony bodies.

In order to believe any of this you really have to know William Goodlett. He is the most authentic man I have ever known in my life, after I could get by my native skepticism to what he was telling me. He is Cherokee on this father's side and descends from the Royal House of Hess in Europe on his mother's side. He is a marvelous admixture.

The Guides have told me recently that this actually is the nearest that we are going to realize what we are all going to be doing in the next century. We will not be building fancy machines to get to other planets, but learn this perception of putting yourself there through thought.

He is not just there in thought, he actually is there. He describes what he is wearing. It may not be anything like he is wearing here, or his body. I think he is experiencing now what those of us who survive this century and those who come back to be reborn in the next century, discovering that we can project ourselves there instantaneously. We are not going to need those expensive machines any more.

SPRINKLE: As I read the question, I recognize that the questioner has prefaced in anticipating the benefits of dialogue with Cosmic Cultures, how can we ensure that we remember and represent the interests of all of Earth, recognizing with the comment that sometime our society has interpreted the Biblical mandate of dominion over all creatures as meaning the right to exploit the planet. That seems to be one of the messages that many UFO experiencers claim they receive from ETs. That ETs are here for two purposes: to help rejuvenate the planet, and to help humankind in its evolution. Ecological and environmental issues seem to be very important ones. In that regards, my own take on it is that the male dominated mechanical, mechanistic, materialistic viewpoint is going to be replaced by a more combination of god/goddess technology, spirit, and so forth. So, I think that it is already happening. But how do we insure? This may be simplistic, but it seems to me just like physicists talk in term of particles and waves in sub-atomic activity, UFOs appear to be both physical and psychic. I think that every time we talk in terms of ET interaction with humans that we recognize that there is both the external and the internal. The view I have is that mediation is the way in which we deal with the political problems of including everybody, and meditation is the way we remember that we are part. I recall a woman who had written some years ago, talked about various experiences, came to the UFO conference in Laramie and returned again. After a few years she felt bold enough to tell me what she had initially felt when I wrote to her. She said, "You sent me some good information and some ideas, but you also said to meditate." She said to herself, "Meditate! I've got some wild stuff going on here."

Well, that's what many people feel, that they have some wild stuff going on. Yet, I think that the benefit as well as perhaps the requirement, whenever we are experiencing fear, anger, distress, skepticism, is that after awhile we close down and we go into meditation, and perhaps that's the whole purpose of this nonsense that's played out in front of the experiencer. Either way, I think the only way we can share it is to mediate politically and meditate spiritually.

MODERATOR: **Dr. Rich Boylan will start the second question, and the question is fairly short. "What can you hope your reaction will be when you first make contact?"**

SPRINKLE: Eee Hah!

BOYLAN: That would be a good one. This is sort of a trick question. To some measure, it describes for me an event in the past. In 1992, I had an encounter while I was doing some field reconnaissance on some UFO and StarWar bases in the Southwest of the United States. It was heavily blocked from conscious memory, and partially retrieved with the aid of some hypnotic block removal. I suppose the fact that it was partially—mostly blocked from memory is some kind of a reaction, not the one I hoped for, but maybe you think you're big and brave and ready, and you're not. I guess the psychologists believe the unconscious mind knows best when you're on overload. So, let's just say, I blew the first one.

Let's move to the future, a more conscious state, open kind of encounter and assume the question is dealing with that, and answer that. I certainly hope the reaction will be one of warmth. I guess we have two choices when we meet a stranger from a strange land, and that is to be apprehensive, withdrawn, guarded, cautious, or to be open, friendly, almost hand outstretched, and let them teach us that that isn't what they're here about. I guess I'd rather err in the direction of the latter approach. I'm not quite naive on this topic because I have the benefit of several hundred other human beings' track record with encounters and multiple encounters, and as a research scientist, I've already long since come to the conclusion that we're dealing with a benign and highly advanced series of races working in concert to understand us and to engage us gradually. So optimism and openness seem to be the proper emotional response. I would hope that I would be humble. I don't think there's much need for anything else. It's not like we're dealing with an inferior species. So I think that, if not, they have a good way of reminding you of your place. I think the openness should be there, openness to what they have to bring and openness to what they might be interested in, of what we are as individuals and as a society. I think there's every reason to believe that this coming event—some of us think it's already an ongoing event, somewhat in the closet—should be and is a mutual exchange of benefit for both sides. So, openness certainly helps that agenda to move forward and make sure that we don't miss something that they would like to learn about us or miss something that they have to share with us. And a readiness not to miss clues. I've been speaking of humility, reminded by several psychic colleagues' experiences I've worked with, that they have seen ET's around me that I haven't seen, and it's sort of like "You dummy," you know, so I guess one needs to attune one's consciousness as much as possible so as not to miss the subtle precursor signs and approach signs that the ET's often use. I think this physical showing up in conscious state is for the most obtuse or for the very select few, and so it's wise to be sensitive ahead of time and catch some earlier signs.

MONTGOMERY: Well, I have a feeling that my first reaction would be to say rather indignantly, "Well, where have you been? It's about time!" Because when I was writing, at the urging of my guides, *Aliens Among Us*, I kept saying, "But I've never *seen* an alien. I've never seen a *space* ship." And they said, "That's all right. Just begin writing it like you have the others and the material will be brought to you." Well, then they brought in through automatic writing some aliens who said, "Don't worry, we'll be seeing you before you've finished the book so that you will have that material." If I'd waited for that, that book would never have been born because, to my knowledge, I have not yet seen a UFO or an alien. But I would *love* to. And, after I'd finally finished the book, they explained that, "Well, we can't get to you where you are now," 'cause I was living right over here on Connecticut Avenue, three blocks from here, and they said, "There's no place—" I was in 2101 Connecticut, a very large apartment building, and they said, "We can't get *to* you there, but we *will* get to you." Well, I wasn't about to drive alone out on some country road, hoping that they'd show up, and my husband certainly was not interested enough to go with me, so I have not seen them yet, although I now live in Naples, Florida, and it seems to me that they could get to me there if they really wanted to. So, I may not be on their A list to contact. But I certainly, *if* I contacted one, I would do it with loving welcome because I think that they're wonderful, and the guides say that they do not mean any harm when they come here. That doesn't mean that they can't now and then *do* harm, because they said that so many of them are scientists who are taking little samples, investigating what it's like to occupy our bodies, and also taking the cows, the plants, the humans who are willing to go, to put on *other* planets, where they could be restocking us because, according to the guides, they foresee this shift of the earth at the end of this decade and there's no time to lose. So I'm surprised that they haven't abducted more of us. Although I'm not volunteering now. But I do think that their purpose is good, that they're trying to help us and at the same time they're trying to help to preserve the wonderful life that we have here on this earth, and not to let it all be destroyed. Not that—the shift is not going to destroy everything and many millions will survive it, but it is going to make drastic changes. Some animals, particularly, will be going out of existence for awhile until they can be replanted, resurfaced somewhere else.

SPRINKLE: "What do I think my reaction will be when I first make contact?" Well, if I block off the historical aspects and the consciousness awareness aspect, which I think are important, I do believe that the evidence is impressive that we came to the planet many, many thousands of years ago. If you're interested, there's some evidence that—available in not only the books by Sitchin, by Richard Thompson, but also Arthur Horn, cultural anthropologist using biological and cultural evidence, and Maurice Chatelain, *Our Ancestors Came from Outer Space*, a NASA engineer who uses mathematical and physical evidence. So if you're interested in evidence, well, then you can read the evidence and recognize that not only have *we* made contact, *they've* made contact; we all together have made contact, and that's why we're here on the planet. Also, if we minimize the importance of meditation, which I think is a hasty thing to do, but look at just the political external question, I'm assuming that the question has to do with formal public contact, because some of us have already had informal, individual contact. I hope that my reaction will be to point in the direction of my former colleagues at the University of Wyoming and say, "I *told* you!" I hope I won't become saintly and humble, and ignore that opportunity.

WARE: My response to this is a one-liner, so let me take my three minutes to tell you a short story. On the 14th of March, 1992, I had attended Dr. Steven Greer's lecture in Gulf Breeze and sat through his day-long workshop, and that evening at the field exercise—there were 39 of us who for 30 minutes sat down in a parking lot, deserted parking lot to the east of Pensacola Beach, just north of the Villa Vinice section of Gulf Breeze. For 30 minutes we did some meditation and sent out our thoughts of love and friendship and welcome and depicted exactly where we were on the planet and on the continent and in Florida and right—narrowed it down to this little parking lot and invited their presence. Dr. Greer had chosen me to be one of the boarding parties, so I'd given the subject some thought. After that we stood up and he took his powerful 500,000 candle power light and started drawing triangles over Gulf Breeze in the sky. Shortly thereafter, he said, "I sense their presence." Then he said, "There's more than one of them." Then three of them appeared in a triangular formation over Gulf Breeze right where he had been drawing triangles, and people were excited. There were three teams, three sections of the Gulf Breeze research team in the field that night, some with us—we had two video cameras and still cameras—some at Shoreline Park South with a video camera; and some at the Delchamps parking lot on U.S. 98. The UFO's showed up right in the middle between all three sections of the Gulf Breeze research team. We had them cross-referenced in video cameras, so we can plot their position in space. We all started screaming, "Come closer! Come closer!" because they were still almost two miles away from us, the other side of the Sound. These three kind of faded out. It was like they were drifting with the wind. We could see the star background. They faded out and two more appeared down lower. Before they faded out, Dr. Greer put his light on the lower right one and flashed it three times, and it brightened and dimmed three times. This is a type of a reaction. He did that several times with different numbers of flashes on different vehicles, and they responded, and we were really excited. We started saying, "Come closer! Come closer!" and they did come, according to our analysis, eight tenths of a mile closer to us and faded off of the camera and my vision at about the same time at 1.3 miles. A formal MUFON report on that evening had seven UFO's seen from seven different locations. Only five, I think, from any single location at the same time was the maximum number. There were 52 people that signed statements describing what they saw. It was kind of neat. We were hoping they would land on the beach and get out, you know, invite us for a tour of the ship or something. I like machines, as an ex-fighter pilot; I wanted the real tour of that. I've been told, by the way, that it will happen when the time is right, and I'm ready.

What I would say is—I hope this is what I would say—is, "Hello. I love you. What can I do for you?" Dr. Greer, by the way, teaches us to be real positive in our relations with them. Perhaps they will reciprocate.

**Moderator: The next question, we'll start with Ruth Montgomery, and the question is, "Do you anticipate that substantially larger numbers of people will experience personal contact or encounters with multidimensional or non-Earth intelligence in the short or long-term future?"**

MONTGOMERY: I think definitely that more and more people are experiencing it now. Look at these other three at the table. I'm the only dummy here. They've all had it already. But I think as people's minds open up, their whole countenance opens up. They're easier to contact. They're more free and aware of what's going on. But I have a feeling that the real opening of the universe is not to occur until after the shift because I happen to believe the guides that there will be a shift of the earth at the end of this century or thereabouts. I think that once that occurs, it's really going to become a one-universe people instead of just a one-people Earth. I think that it's coming, that we should prepare ourselves, that those of us who do not survive the shift will certainly survive in spirit. We'll be coming back as bodies become available 'cause there won't be as many then available as there have been in the last 200 years or so, with the baby boom and all of that. I do think that we are headed within the next at least couple of hundred centuries into a complete interchange on a galactic level, that it's all going to suddenly be discovered that we're all brothers and sisters, that God made us all and probably made us all at the same time, and that we're simply part of the whole.

SPRINKLE: I answer affirmative. I think that the presentation this morning of Señor Maussan showed that many, many people in Mexico are experiencing encounters, at least with the ships. Whether there are personal encounters with ET's or not is a question that may take some time before it's answered. Of course, the question always is, "What is an encounter? What is contact? Is it a physical-to-physical encounter, or is it out-of-body, or is it mental programming?" But certainly it seems the upswing of reports is increasing. I can recall the time in the sixties when not only was it rather lonely to be involved in these kinds of investigations, but also each report was carefully scrutinized and evaluated. One time the UFO panel of the *National Enquirer* had a meeting in Florida, and Dr. J. Allen Hynek and Craig and Salsbury Harder, we were involved in writing down the criteria by which we thought we would be able to evaluate a good report. For example, if there were more than a few witnesses, if they were in more than one location, if there were photographs or film, radar, various messages back and forth, various kinds of things that might be involved in a good report. So we were satisfied that we had developed a little scheme by which we could evaluate good UFO reports. I recall some years later, after the panel had been dissolved, we—it wasn't even a good marriage, maybe not a good affair between the newspaper, the *National Enquirer*, and the panel. They wanted more stories. We wanted more research. But anyway, I was sitting at my desk at home one time and Bob Pratt had sent a letter describing his investigation of a case in Colorado with a so-called mother ship and smaller ships and policemen and various people, photographs, different location. I read it and I put it aside. I kept on reading, responding to the correspondence that Ruth had caused me to suffer, and so, and—

MONTGOMERY: He's the star of my book.

SPRINKLE: And I kept getting upset and irritated, and I thought, "What's wrong?" And I closed my eyes and I did a little meditation and I saw the image of Bob Pratt's letter. I went back to it and I realized that the criteria that had been developed years before about what would be a good UFO report was being fulfilled by that report and it was just another UFO report. So, I sometimes tell my friends that when it used to be "What?! You think you've seen a UFO?!" it will be replaced by "What? You mean you *haven't* seen a UFO?" Well, then I'll tell you a story about how to do it.

I was at a conference in '75 and a friend of mine who's an engineer came up and he said, "Leo, I've been an investigator for fifteen years; never had a sighting!" I told him about my sightings and experiences, and he kept on complaining. I said, "Well, you know there are two ways of having a sighting. The first one is to go out where there are a lot of sightings being reported; you camp out; you watch night after night after night; you'll get a sighting." He said, "I tried that; it didn't work." And I said, "Well, the other method is you sit in your room, your apartment; you meditate; you say, 'I'd like to have sighting; I'll do something for you guys; you do something for me.' And you'll get a sighting." He said, "I tried that and it didn't work." I said, "You tried that method and it didn't work?" "Ach—" I said, "I've never heard of that method not working." I said, "Are you *sure* that you haven't had a sighting?" "Nah." "Or something that *might have been* a sighting?" "Oh, well—" And he looked over his shoulder. He didn't want anybody to listen. He said, "Well, these two guys and I, we were out camping one night out in the woods, and along about dusk, there were two lights on the horizon. As they came overhead, there's no sound, so I knew it was no airplane, no helicopter, just these two satellites." I said, "Two satellites?" He said, "Two satellites." I said, "Two?" He said, "Two!" like, listen dummy. I said, "I've never heard of two satellites traveling at the same time. Have you?" (Trained engineer). He said, "That's *strange*." I said, "Yes." He said, "Another strange thing, just after these two satellites came overhead, two more came from this direction." I said, "Two, and then two?" I said, "Doesn't that sound weird to you?" He said, "That's *weird*." He said, "What do you suppose that was?" I said, "Maybe you had a case of misidentified UFO's."

MONTGOMERY: You sure have dumb friends.

WARE: This question reminds me of a document I received in the mail from John Schusler a few years back. We call it the Warwick Research Institute Document. It was about the public acclamation program. It was directed to the policy committee, "Attention MJ 8, 'whoever he is.'" I presume, perhaps, one of the—if that wasn't the disinformation part of this message, one of the members of MJ 12—There is some disinformation in there in that the date had no day on it. It just said "November 1990—I can't remember, 90 something or other. There was no signature, just said on the bottom, "Warwick Research Institute" with WRI initials. What the letter said, basically, was that the public seems to be digesting fairly well the information that has been given to them; that the UFO research groups are about two years ahead of the mainline media, the major media, in being able to assimilate it, which might give some guidelines to when they want to put further information into the system; and that the UFO support groups are doing a reasonably good job of assisting those who need it, and that's important because the numbers of those who will require such assistance is rapidly growing. This message was sent with a fairly thick package annonymously to a lot of UFO investigators. The Mid-Ohio Research Group did a fair job of investigating, I think, that message and found out that there was a Warwick Research Institute associated with the University of Warwick—Warwick, England; that their receptionist says, when asked who their primary clients were, were told the United Nations, the World Bank, and the International Monetary Fund, which I thought were very interesting folks, since they all represent the world and nation. So that was somewhat intriguing to me, especially in my studies. I think that the numbers are very—I think Dr. David Jacobs is probably correct when he thinks that at least ten million Americans have been on board alien vehicles, whether they know it or not, all involved in the hybridization program. You know the interactions that are taking place, for other reasons, by other perhaps more spiritual beings, are tremendous in number and increasing as our consciousness is expanding.

BOYLAN: The question really has a couple of parts to it about whether we anticipate substantially larger numbers of people having an encounter in the short or long-term future, the larger part in the short or longer future. As regards larger numbers, it's very clear to a number of researchers in this area that more and more people are coming forward with their accounts of extraterrestrial encounters. Now, to be scientifically precise about it, it's hard to tell whether that represents absolute more numbers of folks having encounters or whether it represents more people now coming forward who have had them in the past and are now, because of the climate of the times, finding it permissible to identify themselves and the strange experience they've had. While it's hard to nail that down, because we don't have any timeline of data to measure the before and the after with any reliability, it's my impression from my own research and talking to others that what we have is a combination of people coming in from the past now surfacing with their accounts *plus* more people being contacted. As to whether there's going to be yet more in the short or long-term future, I think the answer to that would appear to be yes, that there's a crescendo going on and it shows no sign of slacking off. If anything, it shows signs of an increase. As to the long and short-term future, I would think that in the short-term future is what we're talking about, because the point of individualized, closet or covert encounters is only to a point, as I think Jaime Maussan made a good point this morning. You don't get secretive close encounters in Mexico with the population because it's out in the open what's going on. There's no need to educate the populace one by one the way the ET's need to do in the information-suppression society in the United States. So, since it appears that the one-to-one covert encounters are for the purpose of educating us despite the cover-up, it would seem that as the manifestation of ET presence comes out in the open that there will be little or no need for such encounters on an individualized basis and we can export more of a society-wide kind of engagement between those peoples and ourselves. I think, in terms of the question of the personal encounter, that we should look at it with a very wise perspective as not a meeting between two interesting peoples but, in view of the historical evidence, as a family reunion. I would offer you four dates that have some basis in ET experiencer reports, psychic predictions, futurist analysis, that obviously we won't have to wait very long to find out if they have any substance or not to them. Between now and October, I would think we could look to an ongoing crescendo of the UFO fly-overs over populated centers. I think in October we can anticipate, or thereabouts, certainly this fall and early winter, a world announcement of UFO presence. I would think in 1996, more likely the first half than the second, that we can look forward to an official meeting between Earth and ET ambassadors during a public UFO landing. And I would think by the end of 1997, we would be at a point where there would be an announcement of establishment the following year of the first official opening of a declared ET community on Earth. Those who operate from that kind of sense of timetable realize that we haven't any time to kid around and that we'll either be prepared for events or they will catch us in progress. So I congratulate all of you for educating yourselves.

MODERATOR: Thank you. I think we have time for one more question before the scheduled break. So I will start that. The question is, "In your opinion, why are the masses being contacted on such a large scale by ET's?"

As I understand what's going on, I think it's transformation, both of the human species and of the planet. One step is what we have normally thought of as the human free-will choice experience, where we make choices that orient us at the soul level toward service to others and service to self, that experience. There are a number of us who are ready to graduate from that and get on with the experience of developing unconditional love of others, a normal step in the evolution of the soul, as I understand it. This planet is going through something that it has never gone through before, even though intelligent species have developed up through the technological stage on two or three times in the past. The planet has never graduated from being a home to that level of experience to being a home for the next level, let's say, being changed from a third grade classroom to a fourth grade classroom. I think the planet will be a place where people will be developing unconditional love of others. Those people that *do* that, those souls ready to do that, will be fortunate that they won't have to do that on the same planet where people are learning to develop unconditional love of self. There is negative influence throughout the universe that continues through the experience of developing true wisdom and on up into, some of us say, halfway through the galactic teacher level before there's no more need for that polarity. I think that right now we have a dual experience taking place on the planet. There's one segment of society, I think a growing segment, that are either here to assist in the transformation process—that is, their souls, from wherever they graduated from, are here on this planet to assist in the process—or maybe they were from this planet and came back to assist by carrying the hybrid babies and stuff, knowing that they wouldn't remember that was their mission here. There are a number of us who are just *becoming* ready to graduate, just becoming sufficiently polarized toward service to others to be ready to graduate. Their souls, I'm told, will reincarnate in these hybrid bodies, along with Zeta Reticulan souls. I think at the soul level, these little, these little grey guys with big heads and big eyes will physically be our brother and sister in some future incarnation on this planet. That may be a real scary idea to somebody. We won't have a better world until we have better people on it. I think we're going to get it, and I think we're getting celestial assistance.

BOYLAN: As to the question why the masses are being contacted on such a large scale by the ET's, I addressed that mostly in my previous remarks. I would add that if the questioner thinks we're being addressed on a large scale by the ET's now—I assume that means individual contacts, in growing numbers—you ain't seen nothing yet! We may very well see the day when it's CNN material and that global satellite hookup would be large scale. I think we'll live to see that day.

MONTGOMERY: Well, I think that the reason we're being contacted on such a large scale now is that everything is being speeded up in preparation for the short time remaining to us before the shift occurs. I think that they realize, whether we do or not, that time is of the essence and that if they're going to save their, perhaps some of their own planets or celestial bodies, so that we don't destroy them with what we're doing to the earth that's causing the shift, that then they *must* rush here, they *must* contact some people of some kind of influence like these and not me.

FEMALE VOICE FROM AUDIENCE: They're all going to land at your house tonight.

MONTGOMERY: I won't be home 'til tomorrow. That would be just like them, to come when I wasn't there. But I really do think that everything is being speeded up because of that cosmic event, that it *is* going to occur, whether it's right at the end of the century or not too long thereafter. They want to save our species, save it from ourselves, and save these wonderful dogs, for instance, who are the only ones I know who really give unconditional love. I'm a dog lover, of course. And all the other—the beautiful plants, the fruits, the vegetables, the cats, the horses, everything that needs to be spared destruction when the shift occurs, they're trying, I think, to transplant segments of them to other planetary systems so that we don't destroy everything along with ourselves.

SPRINKLE: The opinion about why are the masses being contacted on such a large scale by ET's— well, once again, within the assumption of an educational model, it seems to me that there's a two-pronged program going on. Individuals are being tested, you know, each soul is being tested, as well as the social stimulus. But assuming that the question deals with public displays for common people all over, as reported in various countries—my opinion is that it's part of that enlightenment and part of that political awareness which has a double-barrel effect. Not only are more and more people invited in to be examining the evidence about UFO's and ET activity, but also the question of governmental secrecy becomes less important or more important, depending upon your political point of view.

JONES: Before we take a break I would like to share a story about Leo Sprinkle and Ruth Montgomery. Leo called me from Wyoming, said he was coming to Washington. Among other things, he was going to meet with Ruth Montgomery and wanted to know if I knew her. I said, "I've read a lot of her books, but I've never met her." He said, "Why don't you come and we'll have lunch together?" I said, "That seems to be OK with *you* and certainly with *me*. How will *she* feel about it?" Leo answered, "I think she wouldn't mind." So the three of us met in a hotel not far from here and not far from where Ruth lived at the time. It turned out that the purpose of the meeting was that Ruth had asked Leo to write a little blurb for the jacket of one of her books soon to be published. The waitress came and we ordered, and Ruth said, "Well, Leo, do you have the statement?" He said, "Yes," she took it from Leo and she read it, and she looked up at him and said, "Oh, Leo, that's a wonderful statement, except there's one word. Would you mind if we changed such-and-such a word to so-and-so?" Leo, of course, said, "That would be fine with me, Ruth." She said, "Fine," she read it again, and then said, "Well, that's—I think that's a little better statement, don't you? Now, do you feel all right about this?" Leo said, "Certainly, I do." Then she said, "Well, you know, if we sort of altered this—" Now, this went on a little while longer—it didn't take long, believe me, she can skin a mule in a hurry. Pretty soon they were both very pleased with what she got—what she wanted. That part of the business meeting was over. Then Ruth looked at me and said, "What do you do?" I said, "I work up on Capitol Hill for Senator Pell." She said, "Oh, you do? What do you do up there?" I explained, and she got very interested, still in her reporter mode. I said, "You know, Ruth, there's something I would like to ask you." She said, "What's that?" I said, "You know, I'm working on a little project involving the Soviet Union and the current leadership, and it's getting quite involved. It involves using spiritual contacts, one thing and another, and I'm having second thoughts, and I really don't know whether I should be continuing this, and I'd like you to ask your guides for a little input." She quickly responded, "The guides are too busy! We are working on the next book!" She was emphatic. I accepted that. We had a short, enjoyable lunch. The next day, I was at work in the office, and the phone rang. When I answered I recognized it as Ruth. She said, "All right, here's your answer!" I never really asked her, but I take it that the guides were listening at that time and *they* had an answer, even though Ruth didn't want to give time for it. So, I thanked the guides.

MONTGOMERY: I get a word in here. I told those two guys several things that happened during that lunch. Neither one of them remember it. I've never heard of this. It's all new to me. It's like when I reread one of the books I've written. I think, well, where did that come from? I don't remember that either. But I tell you, this one is a new one to me.

MODERATOR: **We'll start the questions with Dr. Sprinkle leading this time. The question is: "Many experiencers have gotten the message that they had ET heritage. Does this mean when the ET's show up that it will be a family reunion?"**

SPRINKLE: Well, as we were being cautioned yesterday about the fear panel—remember, this is the hope panel—I hope so! I had mentioned earlier some of the books that, to me, show evidence not only of humanity's extraterrestrial origins but also talked about the feeling that many UFO experiencers have described to me over the years about the feeling that they come from other planets, that they lived other lifetimes, sometimes on ships, that they came to the planet Earth. My wife and I have conducted over 160 reincarnation workshops in the last 15 or so years with over 2,000 participants, and sometimes their stories are fascinating, not only about the possibility of other lives on this planet but possible other lives elsewhere. One story I always like to tell, about a young man who told her that when she gave a suggestion that he could look down and he could see his experience, his birth experience starting to happen, he said he looked down, he saw a woman that he recognized to be his mother-to-be and felt like there was a tube going down toward this pregnant woman, and he was going to jump in that tube and his soul, his essence, was going to join that of the fetus in the pregnant woman. He said, "I remember just before I jumped into that tube, the thought, oh yes, this is the time of forgetting." I think that is so marvelous, "the time of forgetting." What I'm excited about and hopeful about as this writer has asked, "Many UFO experiencers have gotten the message they have ET heritage. Does this mean that when the ET's show up it will be a family reunion?" I'm hopeful that this is the time of remembering.

WARE: My answer is yes. And I would like to get in about three stories in my three minutes. A lady just earlier this week told me that in February two Beings appeared in her living room that told her that they were her sons, her hybrid sons. These were grown up folks. Earlier this week, she was sitting on the beach down there where I live in Florida, inviting a contact, and a being—this is a very brief, uninvestigated story, now; keep this in mind—a Being appeared who said that she was the hybrid daughter and introduced three hybrid granddaughters, all with very large, round blue eyes with whites around them and very thin blonde hair, that the hairline didn't start here, but it started back here somewhere.

Next story is about a lady who was an observer at the Face to Face Invitational that I host once a year after the Gulf Breeze conferences Project Awareness puts on. She was going through considerable stress even in that room as she participated because she's been picked up by folks who look like reptilians, and were trying to convince her that she is one of them and she was having a hard time dealing with this. But the implication is that in her past incarnation she, her soul, inhabited a reptilian form, which many other investigators or experiencers have indicated are very intelligent beings. And the only case that I've personally investigated concerning the reptilian forms was a person in Pensacola who was lying on his bed and saw the lights of a UFO that he recognized out of the window, and he was paralyzed. He said it was the strangest thing, because he could also see the light coming from under his fifteen-year-old daughter's bedroom door.

He wanted to know what happened so he went through hypnotic regression. The first time it didn't work. The second time he recalled that two reptilian beings came through the wall between his daughter's room and his, and one stood by the foot of the bed and one leaned over the side of the bed and said, "We just want you to know we're not going to harm your daughter." And that's all he could remember.

Next story was the wife of an F15 pilot at Eglin AFB who has had two very strong feelings. One is that the reason she is on this planet is to care for special kids. Both of her kids are immaculate conceptions, that is both mother and father know that there's something paranormal about their birth because the father had been out of town, out of the country for a year when the first one was born, and she hadn't been messing around. They're just angelic kids. They're being home schooled for good reasons. They both have full recall of many on-board experiences. One of them calls one of the guys on board 'granddaddy.' They both call these little gray guys 'yucky monkeys.' It's kind of a pet name, not showing any fear. They both say they're picked up frequently and taken to the garden behind the house—or occasionally I guess would be more accurate—to play with the strange little kids. It's what the UFO investigators feel is known as the 'children's circle' experience. There is a great deal of cosmic cultures meeting and they're starting it at very young ages. They have full recall of it until they get to be school-age. When they go to school they don't let them recall, because even little kids can be cruel if they tell their friends those stories. Their mother will pass it off as a dream and still treat them nice, but the other little kids don't, so they're blocked.

BOYLAN: When we take on the question of ET heritage, I think it pays to look at past, present, and future. If we look at the historical record we see examples of ET contact going back 4-10,000 BC; I'll certainly defer to Zecharia Sitchin who is much more up on that topic than I. But I would honor that research. Then, we can look at the Native American tradition, both oral tradition and inscribed in petroglyphs, historical records on rock faces. Again, recording the visitations of the star people, the interpenetration of the two cultures, enrichment, consciousness expansion, using our terms, and the expectation that they would come again. If we look at the South American tradition as Puma reminded us this morning, the Andean cultures also recognize visitors from the stars. Many , many other civilizations around the world have long-standing historical indications: the Aborigines of Australia, etc. I think it's safe to say there's not a continent except maybe Antarctica that does not have such tradition.

Let's move fast-forward into current events. While the majority of extraterrestrial contacts with human beings in the U.S., anyway that's my research sample, seem to have the agenda of education and consciousness-building, there is a minority of such meetings where some reproductive processes are involved. Either harvesting of reproductive material or the reimplantation of fertilized reproductive material. These seem to go on two tracks. Part of the agenda seems to be to do what seems to us in our terms some genetic engineering that results in the offspring of said human being. Very much indistinguishable from any other human kid, except that they happen to be a little brighter, a little more cosmically aware, or more metaphysically attuned or psychic than you would expect the average kid to be. The other stream of outcome seems to involve the ETs coming back and taking a partially gestated fetus and finishing its growth and development off planet, and the ensuring product of conception being an individual who has both ET and human features, usually more ET than human, but some of both. Subsequently, experiencers have gotten the message that this child couldn't survive on earth. You can look at him, hold him, but they need to stay here. Some of this seems to be due to hybridization and the delicacy of the child versus earth's atmosphere and biological environment, viruses and so forth. But I think some of it is also due to the fact that such a child put out in current society that isn't prepared for ET reality would be reduced to the level of a monster or a government exhibit or something even worse. So that has been in abeyance. But not for much longer.

Then let's look to the near future. I think that some of these hybrid individuals who can honestly say to everybody — to the ETs, "I'm part you;" and to the humans "I'm part you" will make very efficient and credible ambassadors, as the two societies begin to openly engage. So I think that we're looking at a family reunion. In some cases, of distant cousins from our historical past; in some cases, very closely related descendants.

MONTGOMERY: While I agree with what you've said, I'd like to approach it from just a little bit different angle. I think we may be having a family reunion right here now. Because the guides say the more advanced human beings have lived on many different planets in past life times and between life times, and we're advanced or we wouldn't be here. Let's face it. I mean our minds have been opened up. We're opened up to this and the guides in the *World Before* described a number of their lifetimes on different planets and have told me about some of mine and where I came from; I forget where it is but it's in one of my books. But I think we've all had that experience; of course we admit we're all space people because we're all whirling in space, but I think that we've had previous lifetimes, we've been on different planets, and we're drawn together again just as people who have known each other in past earthly lifetimes are often drawn together. We either instantly like somebody or we feel repulsed by them—if we've had a warring existence with them before. I think that many of us here, if not all, have probably been together on another planet and I hope it's not Uranus because they said, I remember in that book, that Arthur Ford says he (he'd been telling about the different planetary lifetimes that he'd had) and he said that Arthur doesn't ever want to go back to Uranus again. So I don't know what it's like, but kids, let's don't meet there the next time!

**Moderator: When do you expect US government agencies officially to announce our contacts with cosmic civilizations?**

BOYLAN: I think they'll be the last in line. I think historical and recent history and current events would indicate to us (I said this for some time) that the game plan appears to be, is going to go like this: I think the ETs are playing the hand because they're good at looking at the crystal ball even better than we are. A prestigious group of scientific professionals, the academicians, such as gathered here, such as gathered at MIT in 1992, and have gathered at other places overt and covert, will and are the bearers of the official dimensions of what's going on. Anybody with an open mind could go to this conference and deduce from the presentations and the credentials and the backgrounds of these individuals involved that we are not the propeller-beanie crowd—that we are a serious gathering of learned folks who bring together a great deal of wisdom and experience from a lot of time and a lot of research, and that any fair-minded person ought to conclude that ETs are real, UFOs are real, and that while the conference is engaging the question as a future probable about cosmic cultures encountering, that the evidence that the speakers keep bringing up has a remarkable similarity to current events. Therefore, one could reasonably deduce that it's going on and so all we need, really, is the union of one of these learned gatherings with some media that are prepared to put it out there in the public domain and we have the announcement. The government is not about to give you a 'My Fellow Americans' speech...I hope Bill Clinton makes us wrong or shows up or sends an emissary, but I don't think that may be in the cards for this particular round. But it could be. But so far it looks like we're doing the lead; ETs are playing to us. I don't see anybody inside of government who seems to have the huge privileged edge on the information over and above what I see in learned colleagues. Therefore, I think the momentum will continue as it has been. I want to honor the international community that's here, too, and those who aren't here who are also at work. I don't know if the US private sector scientists and professional community is going to be the one who is finally to get the camera and the microphone internationally, or whether it will be our distinguished colleagues in South American, Latin America, Europe, or elsewhere. But somebody will. Then the governments will reluctantly come along—last—I think what they're doing now is slipping evidence to various researchers, leaks, informational documents such as Don has alluded to, so that they're setting us up to take the fall so they don't have to. Then, I think the whole thing'll get punted to the UN so that no one will have to eat crow, and frankly that's a good move, cowardly as it is. Because the UN is exactly where this matter belongs. It's global. It's not one country's little game to get the edge on the ET contract. So I think we'll go from private researcher groups, to the UN, and the national governments will be last in line.

MONTGOMERY: I certainly agree that the government may be last. But the guides for many years, as some of you know, have been saying that before the shift occurs, or shortly before it occurs, that we'll have a walk-in president who will be so aware that although he's not going to announce, "Hey look, I'm a walk-in from another planet," he's going to know about the shift, he's going to be preparing us for it, he's going to create jobs in the areas that he considers to be safe, and people can move there in time if they want to survive the shift, because we may not survive in body; we will survive in soul and spirit. But I don't know whether the government will even announce that unless the shift occurs. Because then they say our consciousness, our everything will change so totally as the earth is cleansed of all the evil and the concrete that paves our whole planet, that we'll be ready for it then. But I keep griping to Scott about when Jimmy Carter was running for president that he said, told about seeing a UFO with a group of people, and he said 'If I'm elected president I'm going to release all this material they have on it.' And Jimmy may have been going around solving some of the other crises of the world, but he certainly has not come through with that one yet. And I'm mad!

SPRINKLE: I wish to respond to the question, when I might expect government agencies to officially announce contacts, but I have to wear three hats; the psychologist, the UFO researcher, and the UFO experiencer. Let's see if I can do that. I conducted a little study in '85-86, with three groups of people, essentially asking them if they perceived themselves to be left-brained or right-brained in their perception. The work of David Loye, psychologist, found that left-brained types and right-brained types use different methods of predicting or forecasting, but they do a good job, and together they do a better job. Then I asked questions about nuclear war, President Reagan being re-elected. Most people said no to nuclear war; yes to Reagan being reelected; and then the third question about a UFO announcement by a public UN official. They were asked to guess the color of a paper clip inside a plastic paper cup. They were given three color choices, each color representing a time period which was not identified to the participants. The times were '85-95; '95-2000; 2000-2005. Left-brained types had normal distribution of responses or guesses; and right-brained types, 40%, rather than 33% chose blue which was associated with the time period 1995-2000. So there's a part of me that hopes that's correct. I'm skeptical though because when people ask me, 'When do you think an announcement might be made?' I said I thought it was going to be 1967 and then 1977, and then it was going to be 1987, so now I believe it's going to be 1997. And, of course, if I continue, then 2007, and ...so the psychologist part of me doesn't know. The UFO researcher part of me—I've talked with many, many people, and some of them say they are told there will be an announcement; some of them are told there will be no announcement. That it will continue on this way, so that the Phil Klasses and the James Randis will continue to question and doubt, and the other believers will continue to believe, and we'll just keep on going, kind of like Snoopy and the gang, in Peanuts—we never see the parents, we never see the teachers, we just see the kids. And yet we know the parents and teachers are around. And so in the same way, some UFO experiencers have been told there will never be an official landing, that we will develop flying saucers; we'll be going out, we'll become the ETs for some other planetary system in our flying saucers; and it will continue on just like kids grow up to be teachers and adults...and yet that's another scenario. The UFO experiencer part of me doesn't know either; but oh, my, how I would like there to be official announcement and an official landing. Eee hah!

MONTGOMERY: Which side of your brain did that come from?!

SPRINKLE: That was the reptilian part.

BOYLAN: Now let's hear from the praying mantis part.

WARE: Well, my short answer to this question is that I think the US government will follow the UN lead. But I think the US government policy was codified in 1953 by the Robertson Panel, which generally recommended it is in the national interest to keep the public from getting too excited about our alien visitors. I think that policy is still in effect, and I think it's driven by what you might call, if you watch

*Startrek*, the prime directive. That is, the rule of engagement among higher intelligences is that they're not supposed to interfere with the normal course of events of the lesser evolved society, and that's all those free-will/choice people on this planet, the vast majority of the people here. I think there is a dual society taking place, a growing fourth density society who are here on soul level to develop unconditional love of others, and that's growing, and the free-will/choice society is on the way out. I think the majority of souls on this planet have not made enough choices to be sufficiently polarized one way or the other to graduate from the human experience, and won't in this lifetime, and when they die for whatever reason, they're going to reincarnate somewhere else and get another chance at it, but it's not going to be the planet Earth, from what I've been told.

Now that might be scary to some people, but not to me. Who knows, those other planets might be better than what we're turning this place into.

I'm really anxious to read Budd Hopkins' new book on the Linda Cortile case, because apparently in November 1989 they stopped the Secretary General of the United Nations at 3 o'clock in the morning in Brooklyn so that he could observe three little alien folks and Linda floating out of the 12th floor room of her apartment and up into the UFO, up the blue beam into the UFO. They stopped 12 cars along the Brooklyn Bridge so they also could watch, and some cars directly above them on the Roosevelt Parkway so they could watch it, also. The only reason I could think of that they would want this to happen, why they would stop all those other cars, besides the leader of the UN, is so that when the time is right for him to talk about that there will be somebody to back up his story. I can't think of any other reason why they would do that. I'm anxious to get that book. That might inspire him to come forward and say something about it, now that he's no longer running for office down in Peru.

I think that there will continue to be small steps toward our awareness and acceptance by government, but I think there're already many joint programs. I think the hybridization program, the basic authorized hybridization program, is a joint human-alien program. If any of you recall the Parade magazine article by Carl Sagan that had on the front cover *Are They Coming For Us?* Highly educational about the UFO abduction phenomenon it showed three really interesting pictures from three movies that I think had government assistance and I've been told there were government intelligence agents on the sets in the making of those movies for a reason, for specific purposes. One being *The Day The Earth Stood Still*—to help us overcome this 'shoot first, ask questions later' attitude most of us have, and *Close Encounters of the Third Kind*, because it represented something that had already happened, and *ET* because we need to teach the kids not to be afraid of strange looking creatures, because a lot of them are meeting them. You know it's absolutely amazing what's going on. I think there is a fourth-density technology program that somebody is real serious about not allowing into the human experience until all national leaders choose peace. I think there's a moratorium on any technology breakthrough and has been for a number of years, until they're ready for the final steps in the transformation. There're too many Sadam Husseins in the world who would use that technology, whether it's zero-point energy sources, or whatever, to find better ways to kill each other. That's not supposed to happen now.

**Moderator: What personally gives you hope for cosmic cultures meeting peacefully and hopefully?**

MONTGOMERY: I always have hope. I've always been a very sunny person who always looked for the best and never thought anything bad would happen to me. Ha ha. But I think probably the thing that gives me the most hope is that people are awakening so much in recent years. I've seen such a change. When I first started, when I did that series on going to seances, there were just some little old ladies in tennis shoes and a few old men with beards and maybe their elderly children who were with them, who wanted to contact the dear one who had passed over—look what's happened since. First in the '60s and '70s people were swamping to seances and to mediums and to awakening, and now they've gone beyond that. They're making their own contacts; they're meditating; they're opening their minds and their whole aspect of being to a whole new conception. I think it's all because of the way time is speeding up because of this prophetic shift—if it comes; I can't guarantee it, now. But I do think that people are developing emotionally and spiritually much faster than they were in the many generations ahead of us, and they're all being prepared for this that I feel will occur before long: the contact with other civilizations and other galaxies.

Female voice from the audience: "Thanks to you, the planet will choose."

SPRINKLE: Let me give some comments that speak toward the down side. We understand from a variety of traditions; the Vedic traditions, Mayan perhaps, many others that we're not aware of from various cultures, but Sitchin and other scholars have pointed out that the wars of the gods, the ancient Greek culture, mythologies, speak to the possibility that not only have there been wars between gods, but also between humans and gods in terms of our being generated and being maintained by our creators, or creator. And so, I recognize the possibility that if those traditions are accurate that it may well be that in our coming scenario there may be more trouble, more difficulty, more conflict. One researcher asked me, in kind of a chiding tone; he said, 'Leo, what if you're a Judas goat leading the lambs to slaughter'. I shrugged and said, 'Well, if I am, then I hope we dance.' Because I don't know at this point. Part of that not knowing is the terrible task. So not knowing historically, not knowing scientifically, not knowing politically, I'm glad that the question is: What *personally* gives you hope for cosmic cultures meeting peacefully and hopefully, because so far my experience both in terms of personal experience as well as in terms of meeting with people who claim to have contacts, both dimensional and physical, is that these contacts are preparing the way for us to grow up so that *we* are the ones who are peaceable and hopeful. That's what gives me hope.

WARE: What gives me hope is the 70-some people I know personally, some quite well who have had on-board experiences; and although most of them initially had some fear as a result of that—and some of them had a lot of fear as a result of that—the vast majority now that they have a better understanding of what's going on have overcome that fear. Many of them would be very disappointed if the encounters stopped. They've accepted the folks they interact with as maybe not fellow human beings but as fellow cosmic beings. And a very loving relationship has been established with quite a few of them. That gives me a lot of hope.

BOYLAN: As for the cosmic cultures meeting peacefully and as a basis for hopefulness, I think there're three reasons for having such a hope. The first being the nature of the ETs. There are a number different races, civilizations, visiting us, depending on how you measure anatomical differences, anywhere from 8 to 15 on up possible distinct species using our traditional terminology; and some that don't fit physiological categorization. But the range of their engagement with us is everything from somewhat scientifically detached to opening loving and anxious for encounters on all levels including the more physical. So the spectrum is from neutral to extreme positive. I find no credible research data for menacing or sadistic ETs. So that would seem to give some basis for hopefulness. The second basis would be the changing nature of humans, as has already been mentioned by some on the panel. We are slowly awakening to a larger world out there, to see our own self-interest as defined by being a global population rather than little splinter groups. That the issues that will define us go beyond power and territoriality conflicts, that we need to pull together. On a metaphysical level many people are sick to death of the emptiness of the materialistic and are ready for something better. It's sort of the fertile void before something marches in to fill that void. I think the nature of the phenomenon itself is causing people to wake up. We see a lot more play of it on the media now. People—this is Leo's little line—people used to when they saw a saucer land, ran away yelling, "Jesus save us." Now they ran towards the craft yelling, "Save us, save us!"

The last of the three bases of hope is the press of events. The openness we have now, the constant bombardment of new events such as you have seen in video tape today and discussed, UFO showings up, ET encounters with humans, people coming forward saying what their experiences have been like, all over the world, that this environment and the unsteadiness of world events, the upcoming cataclysms, the destabilization of certain societies, the hope for a better life, a more globalized mentality—all these pressures make for a unusual readiness for extra-terrestrial contact on a global level. So I think the openness is there; the timeliness is there; and certainly the ETs are here.

**Moderator: We're down to this question. Can we solve energy, pollution, overpopulation problems easily if we make contact with alien beings?**

SPRINKLE: Can we solve energy, pollution, overpopulation problems easily if we make contact with alien beings? That's an excellent question. I don't know the answer, so I should shut up. But I feel obliged to comment about one aspect of it. Many of the contactees, the UFO experiencers that I've talked to over the years have described their abduction or as I sometimes think of it—ad-duction—an abduction is moving away from the planet, from home. Adduction is moving some place towards the stars, towards the ETs, and many of these people feel that they've not only had the on-board experience, but they've been given a task, a mission, or a purpose and a duty. A couple of examples: I've known some people who felt they were given information about a cure for cancer. And I've known some people who were given information about a propulsion system that would be better on the environment than the kind of propulsion system we have—the automobile, petroleum, and so forth. Yet, in many of these cases these persons seem to have an incomplete theory. Or a wrongness about it. So therefore the conventional scientist could dismiss it, this is nonsense. And yet there'd be a little puzzle within that story, within that information, that would intrigue a physicist, or an engineer, or a physician, or whoever. I've often wondered if there were funds available where it might be possible to bring together some of these people and like a template, have one contactee story put on top of another, I wonder if the whole story would emerge about a cure for cancer, or for a propulsion system, or whatever. It seems as if this being done deliberately, according to many UFO experiencers, for a couple of reasons. One is to protect the individual because if the individual had this kind of information, he or she could be taken and could be tortured or forced to release the information, or whatever. So from the individual standpoint there's a reason; and from the social standpoint there's also a reason; the Jim Deerdorf Leakey Embargo theory that the embargo on information, but it gradually is being provided so that gradually we become aware and able to make use of it; and then we can claim we did it. It's like a good counselor who sits there and says Uhm, uhm; and I ask questions and I get some information, but most of the information I get is about myself as a client rather than information from the counselor. So it seems as if I don't know if the word *easily* is something I can handle. Can we solve energy, pollution, overpopulation problems if we make contact with alien beings? I think that would be an excellent beginning. Whether it will be easy or not—well so far, the suggestion according to UFO experiencers is that it's not easy; it's hard work, but it's good work.

WARE: I agree with Leo. The answer to that question is, 'No, it will not be easy.' But we can do it. We must do it. It will require a change of consciousness to make it happen, and for a few years now I've been a member of the Institute of Noetic Sciences founded by ex-astronaut Edgar Mitchell, which when I joined it 3 or 4 years ago had, I think, 13,000 members, and now membership is over 60,000. It's rapidly growing and I think it will continue to grow; and they're doing a great job of raising consciousness. The Omega Project: how many of you have read that book by Dr. Kenneth Ring at University of Connecticut? He did a real good study of two different groups of people. People who've been on board UFOs, and people who had had near-death experiences. His findings basically were, although those experiences are quite different in nature, they had the same effects on the people. They caused the people to be more spiritually aware, more environmentally concerned. It's not by accident. About a year ago, I was at a conference in Kalarny, Ireland, a week-long conference run by the International Transpersonal Association. There were 1,500 people from 75 countries talking about how to solve these problems that have been mentioned in this question. I saw Ram Das walking around the grounds picking up little pieces of paper and putting them in the trash can—teaching by example. There were lots of people there that were learning. We left that place, I think, cleaner than when we found it. Which is amazing for 1,500 people for a week. You know I married a golfer a while back—and I get my exercise by playing golf whenever I can find time, whenever I'm home. it's caused me to start picking up the paper on the golf course instead of just complaining about it, and it makes the experience of being out there in nature much more enjoyable, and I hope you will all do the same whether you're golfers, or not.

BOYLAN: As to the question of whether we can expect ET assistance with energy, pollution, and overpopulation problems—let me say a word to each of those. I think the ETs are well-positioned to offer us some solutions of soft technology that will help us meet our energy needs in less environmentally damaging ways. However, as has been alluded to before, it's difficult to implement that right now while there's the denial of ET presence, because while some experiencers are being provided information about advanced technologies and about advanced physics principles and other information necessary to move towards more efficient energy pathways, those people are not free to come forward on a society-wide basis and implement what they know because of the societal denial. So, if we want that better future we have to get past the societal denial phase.

As for pollution, much of that has to do with our own consciousness. We have not as yet, as global people, totally understood that everything is a closed cycle. That recycling is not just a trendy word, it's the way nature is organized. Until we get that, we're going to spiral in linear ways towards death sequences. The ETs can somewhat inform us that those are the consequences of our behaviors, but that will really be a human transformation. We already know the answer, that pollution isn't good for us, it doesn't take any visiting star civilization to tell us that. Perhaps the jolt of them coming and seeing ourselves more as a global people in a finite environment in a much larger world of intelligent civilizations out there, may help us a bit towards that consciousness, but that's still our own discipline to take it, as Don has well indicated.

As to the overpopulation problem, I think there are two things we can say with some likelihood are going to happen. First of all, the coming earth changes are going to winnow out the population that's somewhat apparently going to be done on a consciousness-sorting level. The ETs have already indicated to many experiencers that these events are coming. And it's not just ET information; many psychics and indeed many scientists and futurists have seen the same events coming. It is indicated that the ETs will be somewhat of a help as these events get to be harrowing. But I think that it will be the nature of society that there will be those that pay attention to them as helpful fellow intelligent humanoid beings as we face these crises, and there will be those who say, 'To hell with them' or get out a shot gun and chase them off and say 'We can take care of ourselves just fine.' I think the latter group will go down more or less in flames and the former group will, by its own self-sorting, be more likely to survive these winnowing times. That isn't a complete solution to the overpopulation question. There is a question of more choiceful childbearing, and a lot of other things that I think derive from developing consciousness as we form our society more in a globally mutually-caring area, the dynamics and psychology and resource distribution will put population pressures in a more homogeneous place.

MONTGOMERY: Well, you've sort of stolen my thunder. I don't want to oversell the shift. But if we have the shift, that takes care of the overpopulation, believe me. Because there'll be just—if the guides are correct—a few many millions left, and there won't even be many available bodies for us who want to come back for a good while until it builds up again. The guides say the shift is needed because of all the pollution, that it's a cleansing the earth needs to go through. So I think the pollution and overpopulation will be solved in the next century. As for energy, according to the guides, we're not going to need the kind of energy that we have in such desperate need of now because instead of motors and machines and all that sort of thing, which of course, adds to pollution, we'll be out of body transporting ourselves, which serves us right, believe me, because we've been sort of abusing these bodies, and requiring too much to take care of them. But if we can do all this by projection as the guides say William Goodlett and some who are forerunners of the New Age are doing, then I think those three problems are eliminated.

# Future Panel:
# Petersen, Glenn, Sitchin

**MODERATOR, PETERSEN:** We will start with Jerry Glenn. If panel members want, they can say anything specifically about themselves to embellish the bio that was in the program and then anything else they want to say.

**GLENN:** Details of the following ten points will be reproduced in another part of the Conference Proceedings. In summary, here are points to consider in anticipation of Cosmic Cultures meeting.

1. The faster we get off the Earth the better. There are too many uncertainties to think we can safely hunker down on Earth and wait for things to happen.
2. It is important to think together now about what we would do if contact occurs before we leave Earth. Use computer simulations to stretch and expand our minds.
3. Depending upon the kind of contact, it could stimulate intellectual, spiritual and physical development and our own evolution.
4. Acknowledging that ETs very likely may be vastly more intelligent than us, they probably will be no less curious that us. Differences between us should not be the determining factor whether contact is made or not.
5. Either we accept that we are a transition species into a space-faring one, or we are destined to end up in the dust bin of evolution.
6. Thoughts have consequences. As futurists we have a responsibility to point out potential consequences of beliefs.
7. Could the mind be a link between the three dimensional human brain and hyper dimensions for ET contact?
8. Are ETs the source of our religious beliefs?
9. Expand beyond our star, merge with cosmic cultures. Buy time to address current predictions for the future end of Earth.
10. The faster we get off the Earth the better.

**PETERSEN:** Jerry and I are both confessed card-carrying futurists. He came at it a long time before I did. But about five years ago, after spending a little bit of time in the White House looking at defense policy, I became convinced that there was a big change coming down stream, that there was a fundamental shift going on in the world—that the government in general and the military in particular really didn't have any idea about what was happening.

So I started a little non-profit organization called the Arlington Institute which is the little think tank that I hang around—it's a think tank of one most of the time unless I hire other people for projects. My particular interest was in the area of national security. I was convinced that we were at a period where the fundamental idea of security was changing and becoming something quite different than it has been in the past. I went off to try to understand what it might become so I could help some of my friends in the military understand how the military had to change in order to adjust to this new reality.

About a year later I found myself being a futurist like Jerry. People started saying, "you are a futurist" and I said, "OK, I am a futurist". And, in fact, I was a futurist, because if you are going to try to help people look downstream a long way, then you necessarily have to try to have some kind of concepts and ideas about the future—when you start thinking about methodologies, about how you look at the future and you start looking at the driving forces and other such things, you find out you are a futurist.

I've had a number of people ask—'how do I go to school to become a futurist?' Generally speaking, you can't go to school to become a futurist. I started looking at all of this and trying to make sense out of what the world might look like 20, 30 years hence. I became convinced that we are at a period of a fundamental shift in history that has been unequaled any time before. The closest analog was the time of the shift between the middle ages and the industrial age, where the very essence of science—remember when Copernicus and Newton came in with whole new ideas of science—came together with an enabling information technology, the printing press, and it took these ideas and duplicated them and distributed them and communicated them in ways many, many times more efficiently than ever before. What it produced was the enlightenment, revolution in every aspect of life. It changed the reality of how we understood how physical things worked. It changed how humans worked between themselves, amongst themselves. It changed how we educated, how business works. It changed every aspect of life.

As I look at all of this, I believe that we are at an equal kind of junction in history. Only there are about five different converging trends that are coming together at the same time, and they are almost certain to produce bigger changes than ever before. One is science, quantum mechanics, some of the underling physics about how things work. Then, there is extraordinary technology, driven by the microprocessor primarily, but variations of microprocessors in other areas. There are things like zero point energy, nano-technology, and stuff that will just make the world in twenty years quite, quite different than it is now. There are fundamental changes in social values that are happening—both positive and negative, a lot of fragmentation within societies, within our society and the world in general. There are some contextual issues, primarily having to do with the environment, and also about population. All of these are coming together at the same time. These are big driving forces and they have deep, significant implications.

They are certain to produce a world in conventional terms, in a decade or less that is really quite different than anything we've seen before. The amount of information in the world, for instance, is doubling every 18 months, and it's accelerating. If you just held it at that rate, in about ten years you'd have close to something over 20 times more information in the world, and in 15-17 years you'd get like 200 times more information in the world. When you get out to 22 years, it gets exponential and it goes up to about 20,000 times more information in the world. Now, you can be off by a factor of five or whatever you want to be, but I'm here to tell you that a world that has 20 times more information or a 100 times more information is just a dramatically different place than we have now.

What you find when you go back and look at the transition between the dark ages, the medieval time, and the industrial age is that you put yourself in a castle or hovel back in the dark ages and you try to picture airplanes or atomic bombs or whatever you want to talk about—people would say, 'that's all magic, that's all mystical, that's impossible'.

The grid that you look through from that position, from that paradigm, would make this new future, this new era, almost unbelievable. I frankly believe that we are at a time where we are sitting at a transition that is far more compressed than the 150 years or so it took to come between the dark ages and the industrial age. It's more like maybe 50 years. The implications, the amount of change, is many times more.

We're obliged, if we want to hold things together, to begin to look out on the horizon and try to make some sense out of it. But there is a fundamental problem, and that is that it all looks weird and it looks strange. We look at it from this history and the experience that we bring to the table. Furthermore, there are wild cards. There are those things that come out of the side, come blowing in, have a low probability and a very extraordinary kind of implications. They always come along, but you have no idea what they are. For my money, the UFO subject is a wild card. It's more than a wild card . You can look at Jaime's pictures and say, 'there is something there. This is not going to surprise some of us. But the point to all of that is that if you go to the major futurists, names like Toffler, Peter Schwartz, and some other folks who are friends of ours and you ask them if they have ever been surprised, everyone of them will tell you that, "Yes, I've been surprised. There is something that has happened big time in the world that I didn't anticipate." Most of them will tell you that having been surprised, they walk themselves back in history and see that there were early indicators that such a thing was coming along.

The problem with the futures business, is that it, like so much of society, has a relatively narrow focus. My friends in the military look at technology and geopolitical kinds of stuff. If you look at most futurists—they look at economics because they are working with companies and other such things. We necessarily constrain our view into some kind of a box. I would suggest that the ET/UFO subject is a genuine, significant, wild card. The most profound thing that ever happened and frankly, there are all kinds of indicators that suggest that it might be coming along. That is why I, as a futurist, keep an eye on this and am interested in it.

You are going to have this big paradigm shift—we're going from one period to another one—and everything is going to look like magic; I mean in conventional terms even, not counting some of the metaphysical and extraordinary kinds of things. There are two kinds of underlying models for looking at this. One of them is that you have to look at everything as a system, everything is kind of organic. What we are finding out is—as above, so below. I never knew what that meant, but suddenly it clicked in because everything works like an organism. It works like nature. All of these linear mechanistic industrial age models that we've all used are an anomaly because that's not how it works. Everybody is figuring that out on the edges. Economists and scientists all over are figuring out that it really doesn't work the way we thought it does. So, first of all, you have to look at this all as a system—that everything is interconnected with everything else. That's what quantum mechanics says.

When you look out at the future, when cosmic cultures meet, you have to look at it from a systems point of view. Furthermore, it seems to me that the only way that you get from here to there is a fundamental shift in the way we all think. In conventional terms, I think that is just that. How do you think? You don't think in linear kinds of ways, you think in systems ways. You have to look at all of the component parts. You have to juggle them all at the same time and see them all, and understand that if you push here it might shove up two or three different other ways. Even if you go down this traditional line and talk to companies and conventional kinds of people, you have to think in quite a different way.

I think it is obviously more than that. Most of us in this room understand that there is really a mind set change, a rather fundamental kind of shift in the way that we understand reality and humanity, and how we all work together. In my mind, it is a shift from competition toward cooperation. I see no way to get from here to there—with all of the big problems that are right in front of us, kind of waterfalls and rapids that are out on the horizon—without a fundamental shift in the way we all deal with each other—

environmental problems, and so on. We have to understand that we are all in this together. If our alien friends show up then we are **all** in this together, and we have to approach it differently. I see it all in terms of a system, and that we have to think differently about it.

SITCHIN: I find myself in the position of the speaker/lecturer who said, "Before I start talking I have a few words to tell you." The first thing which I assume has become obvious to you by now is that we were given a set of questions ...and at the end of this panel discussion, we are required to select the best questions so that there will be a winner of some prize. I assume that you realize by now, that there will be no winner, because we don't intend to answer your questions. We just intend to share with you what we came to share with you; and it's highly interesting, and I'm glad that we have this extra time due to several factors, which gives us the opportunity to have these extensive opening remarks, and I'm not going to deprive myself of the opportunity, either.

The second preliminary words I wanted to share with you is that I've been asked many times during the last couple of days the same two questions. With the organizer's permission I'll say that people who want to reach me or write to me, my address is: P.O. Box 577, NY, NY 10185, so I won't have to give the information to each one of you individually.

The other question which has not been asked repeatedly, but has been asked, and that is, 'Will I speak English or Sumerian?' That's a true question and I assured the questioner, if that's what I talk, then it's English. Because having been born in Russia and raised in Palestine, and educated in England and lived in the United States, I don't know what kind of English I'm talking by now. But I hope it's understandable.

Now, the theme of this conference, as you know from the program, is "When Cosmic Cultures Meet." It is very cleverly worded, because it does not say, "When Cosmic Cultures Will Meet," so Scott and the others, who helped put this together, don't commit themselves and don't say it will happen. It does not say, "When Cosmic Cultures Are Meeting," because I think if you listened to the speakers the past two days about abductions and UFO sightings, etc., it seems that it is taking place. So it should be, "When Cosmic Cultures Are Meeting." But when it comes to me from my six books what I would have said is, "When Cosmic Cultures Met," because the meeting has been taking place and has begun almost 450,000 years ago. It is all recorded in text, some of them very detailed and pictorially, and some showing what we would call today UFOs, some showing what we would call today—those little gray men—and some showing the actual visitors to earth themselves. According to the Sumerians, whose culture I have studied and described in my books, I'm one of about 200 scholars who can read the Sumerian tablets.

About 450,000 years ago, people from another planet arrived on earth. The Sumerians called them Anunnaki which, in Sumerian, means literally, "Those who from heaven to earth came." They say they originally came for their own purposes in search of gold because they needed the gold not for jewelry, not for making coins or medallions, but that they needed it for the survival of their own planet, where the atmosphere, or the heat, was dissipating. The only way they could protect their planet was by creating a shield of gold particles to keep the heat and the atmosphere in. At first, they landed a group of 50, splashed down in the Persian Gulf. They waded ashore. There is a very long text, very detailed.

By the way, all of the text that I will mention in these few minutes and the hundreds of them that are in my six books, none of them have been discovered by me. I do not claim anywhere that I went to one of the ancient sites, like Mesapotamia, and poking with my stick in the ground, I found a tablet and look what it says—nobody knew it before but I now discovered it. Every text, every depiction, were discovered by others. They are all in well-known and prestigious museums. The text, the pictures were published, republished, translated, transliterated by others. Except that through my knowledge of Sumerian, Akkadian, early Hebrew, and other languages, I was able to read them and judge the accuracy for myself. So, they are very detailed. The only difference between me and all of the scholars who are aware of them is that all of these tablets, all of these texts, are called mythology. For example, the text that describes the first splash down, how they waded ashore, who their leader was, and how he assigned tasks in order to start the process of extracting gold from the waters of the Persian Gulf,—the leader's name was Enki, meaning "Lord Earth"—the scholars call the text the myth of Enki and the earth. So, on every text that describes what they were doing here is called a myth. And I asked, my writing on the subject was published in the *Archeological Society* and other magazines "What if these are not myths? What if all this really happened?" According to this, if you treat it as essentially what had happened on earth beginning some 450,000 years ago, then they tried to get the gold from the waters. It did not work out. They then had to do it the hard way by mining gold in Southeastern Africa. By then, there were only 300 of them, eventually 600, but by then there were only 300 of them on earth. Those who were assigned to the mines after a certain period, which is stated in the Sumerian writings, said they mutinied. They said, "We cannot continue."

Then, their chief scientist came up with a solution. He said, "We can create a primitive worker, a Luluamalu, somebody who will do this work for us." When they said to him, "How will you create such a thing?" He said that, and this is a quote from the text, "This being already exists. All that we have to do is put our mark on it." Then the text, in great detail, described the process that the only modern parallel to it is that of bringing about test-tube babies. Because they mixed the genes of one of their young males with the egg of—lets call her—an ape woman at the time or one of the early hominids brought about by evolution, and after mixing the two, reimplanted the fertilized eggs in the wombs of some of their own females. Now, some biologists and other experts in fertility tell me that this little detail, the fact that I quoted it from the text, that the fertilized eggs of the ape woman was reimplanted in the wombs of females who arrived on earth, lets say the ancient astronauts females, Anunnaki, has great significance to the nature of the being that was finally created, so apparently it's important. And that as we, Homosapiens, not the hominid race which appeared on earth through evolution, but we appeared about 300,000 years ago through the efforts of someone who jumped the gun on evolution through genetic engineering.

After I had written my first book, *The Twelfth Planet*—published in 1976, and this book *Genesis Revisited*—which is subtitled, 'Is modern science catching up with ancient knowledge?' I deal with the information about Eve, because most geneticists and others agree now that all mankind, no matter of race or location, stems from one female, an Eve, and that all begin about 250—270,000 years ago (I said 300,000). Only a few days ago I read it in the New York Times, but I was told here that the story was also in the Washington Post, that also the existence of such an Adam, one Adam, one first male from which we all stem, has been confirmed scientifically, and the date again is 270,000 years ago, which is basically my date. So this is how we were brought about.

At first we were brought about to be workers, to work for them. But as time went on, and especially in the aftermath of the deluge, which was a watershed more than figuratively, they made us partners with them on earth and started to give us civilization. If you check the progress of human culture and civilization from the million years old stone age—lasted maybe 2 million years—into the middle stone age, Mesolithic, and then the new stone age, Neolithic and then the Sumerian civilization, about 3,800 BC, you see that the time span always is about 3,600 years, and this coincides with the orbit of the planet from which those Anunnaki had come to earth.

The orbit according to the Sumerians, is 3,600 earth years. To them, by definition, it's just one year which explains the so called immortality of the gods, but that is another subject. So they started to give us civilization each time more or less coinciding, with the time that their comings and goings have taken place. Now, the key difference between all this Sumerian information is not only that it explains many enigmas facing our astronomers—the origin of the asteroid belt, why Uranus lies on its side, and so on and so forth, but it touches on the issue that we are not alone in the universe. First of all, because even mathematically there're so many galaxies and in each galaxy are star systems, and each star which is a sun may or may not have so many planets, and then one of them is in the right place to have life on it. So even mathematically, there ought to be millions upon millions of planets bearing life and somewhere there intelligence is developed.

This is the reason for the search called by its initials, S.E.T.I., which means Search for Extraterrestrial Intelligence. I almost chuckle when I see the search continues, though it's under a different name now. They're not looking for other beings; they're looking for intelligence. In other words, rocks that are clever or some such other thing, they don't dare even say 'intelligent beings'; but they're looking for them OUT THERE. Not near us, but out there. Five light years away, or whatever. In this book, *Genesis Revisited*, towards the end in the chapter entitled, *In Secret Anticipation*, I deal with a document that is now a little better known but which was totally unknown when I wrote the book. It's called Declaration of Principles. The White House may have come across it, but it was an international effort coordinated by the State Department. During the cold war the Soviets were part of it, the French, etc. and the purpose of it was to establish principles of what should be done, or not done rather, because most of the clauses deal with what should not be done, when a contact is made, when we get a message from some intelligence. The import of all this, about 10-12 clauses, was how to suppress the information, if possible, for 48 hours. Not to release it because there will be panic, and who knows what. I was thinking to myself, if the contact as the SETI people are supposedly telling us, is with someone who is 5 light years away, (not a light year is a measure of distance, not the time, because it's the distance light travels in one year—it's fantastic) if this is where the message would come from what's the difference of delaying the information for 48 hours? So obviously, they're talking about somebody closer at hand.

I believe what they're talking about is this planet the Sumerians called Nibiru that astronomers who have been searching for, and some apparently have located, refer to as Planet X. It is a member of our own solar system and people from it have been coming and going for almost half a million years. They had a space base or way station on Mars, and I think all that which is past is significant not only to the future, which is the subject of this panel, but also to the present. If you want to understand what is going on nowadays and what we could expect, which I hope will tell you as we tackle the questions unwillingly, that we are not alone. We are not alone in our own solar system.

MODERATOR: I've had a number of people saying this has really been a fascinating conference but nobody's talking about 'When Cosmic Cultures Meet,' and probably the best exhibit of this is this plaintive question from Suzie Smith who says, **"Please address the premise of this conference. What do you envision the ramifications to be when cosmic cultures meet? Be specific!"**

308

GLENN: Rapid neurological connectivity. Simultaneous hypothalamus activity, and probably after that a bit of shock. I think it's going to be a stimulus to our evolution. If we are smart about it in preparation ahead of time. To me, the best way to prepare for it is get the hell out of town. I really do like the analogy of life being life; but instead of life being the way we know it. Imagine life being a zygote and the placenta being the earth, and you're born off in the universe. It seems to me that's reasonable. You sort of do your adolescence as you leave the solar system, and the galaxies, try on different roles and then get married, other terrestrial existences, and grow up and go on. We say that you're not an independent living entity until you've gotten at least out of the womb, and we say you're not ready to leave home (solar system) until you're at least independent of your parents when you go to the bathroom. If contact happens right now, what would be the impact? Extraordinary perceptual evolution—no question about it. The faster we think that through and prepare our minds for that, the better we are. In the mean time, get out of town and grow up.

PETERSEN: What are the ramifications of when cosmic cultures meet? I think they could be one of two things. They could be obviously very detrimental, very negative. All the present systems are built around a set of realities, a set of assumptions that don't work in that kind of context. By the way, I think that works if you just consider this convergence of all these forces together, even if you don't have cosmic cultures meeting. It's all of the old framework, all of the old institutions fall down. I think government gets redesigned within 15 years, but in any case, you'd have no method, no framework from which to support all of that. On one hand—and I suspect there are a lot of people who are very concerned about this—is the economic system could go sideways. The religious and belief systems of lots of people could be threatened rather significantly. If lots of people jumped out of the windows because the stock market fell, what would they do if the whole essence of what human beings are was called into question?

On the other hand, I think it's a function of timing. Let me say it two ways. It seems to be a window that's opening here, and it's enabled by technology. This is the first time in the history of the planet that we're essentially wiring up the planet so that we're building almost a global nervous system. Information and messages and means and ideas can suddenly run their way round this planet almost immediately and inform people very quickly, and inform them very deeply about things—pictures, films, and so forth—and that's never been doable before.

You always had the problem in the past if something of this scale happened. It would kind of roll its way through the world, filled with all kinds of eddies of rumors and problems. But now you're getting to the place very soon—you're literally within years—to where you can communicate to anywhere on this planet instantaneously. You can do that in a 24-hour period. I think there are enough of us who have considered what the implications might be, have thought through maybe how the process might be, of how you deal with the underlying problem, or how the institutions deal with it. But more than that, how you communicate the ideas and how the concept is brought together. How the images are set out. We've got a period of time here where you can literally pull this off, and you could pull it off far more benignly than you could in the past.

SITCHIN: The question specifically is what we envision the ramifications to be when cosmic cultures meet. At the risk of repeating myself, the cosmic cultures have been meeting and obviously one of the things mankind has done about it is to call a conference like this one. That is not said sarcastically or in an amusing way because I think the more we meet and the more we discuss and the more we accept the possibility and reality of such meetings with others, the better we will be prepared for the meetings and the more benevolent the results might be, because they were not always benevolent.

I mentioned the instances where we were given more and more civilization and knowledge and technology each time. But there was one time, and that's the Biblical tale of the deluge told in the Sumerian writings in much, much greater detail, that one of the leaders of the Anunnaki, his name was Enlil meaning Lord of the Command, ordered drastic action. He was the chief commander on Earth and did not like the way mankind had turned out. The deluge was a natural calamity that was anticipated by them. It was actually the slippage of the ice cover over Antarctica into the oceans creating a tremendous tidal wave. He had called all the other leaders to a conference, actually they called it a council, and made each one swear that they'll keep the coming calamity a secret from mankind. One of them circumvented the oath, and thus the story of Noah and the Ark. The remnants of mankind were saved after all. But at one time the leader was not happy with the way it turned out, and sought the total annihilation of mankind. The Noah, or mankind, was not aware at the time of what was going to happen, except that Noah was told in secret. The more we know and the more we discuss it, the better we will be prepared for the next encounter, and ensure a benevolent result.

MODERATOR: How do you educate people for this kind of transition? One said in anticipation of an overt contact, what types of educational programs do you believe would be implemented in the schools to prepare young people for this eventuality? Another question along this line said, **'Is it possible to convey benevolence, or is our planet so filled with conflict that our first task prior to meeting is to work throughout the world to educate that our planet's survival ultimately will come from unity rather than separation?'** So the whole issue of education, Jerry, how might you approach that?

GLENN: Is Jim Furano here? Boy is he going to be angry. I'll give him a big plug. The Contact group that Jim coordinates can help. I understand they're putting together some materials that can go from elementary schools to graduate school. That's one place you might go to. The United Nations University itself is supposed to be a backbone support system for education by interface between the UN systems and the education systems. I think it would be fascinating if you got the United States Ambassador to the General Assembly to say, "what is the US doing to support the UN University's development of curriculum for these issues." I think it'd be a real problem for us to answer, and we'd enjoy that one.

I think there's a lot of this data on *Omni* on line they've talked before, and they are putting more information on Omni and making it available for discussion groups. I think that's great. I think there is a tremendous amount of education that you guys can pull together yourselves that way. Have you ever gone to a PTA meeting and asked about this subject? I don't know. Call up your principal. Do you have children in school? It might be interesting.

SITCHIN: Learn Sumerian!

PETERSEN: The whole educational problem is an interesting one because you need to teach people to think differently, to understand that this is not just a random event that's happening, that it's linked to a larger system, to a larger plan, perhaps to a larger view of the cosmos. Some would argue, I'm sure, that all the things we're seeing in the newspapers, tabloids, and films is perhaps an educational process. Maybe, in fact, that's the best way. A lot of folks in education are finding out that the entertainment industry and the amusement business is the best way to move ideas and to change things.

310

That brings me to another question along that line. Fears can be eased in our experience with enjoyment in a safe atmosphere, i.e., roller coasters and horror movies. Could entertaining movies, TV, theme parks, and books be used to soften the eventual reality of other worlds and cultures for humanity? I want to take that another step and say 'virtual reality and other kinds of devices.' Are they coming along at the appropriate time to be able to effectively communicate in the way that needs to be implicated, and the profound nature of all this?

GLENN: I don't know what the deadline is. But I'm very pleased that the radio show, *War of the Worlds,* got one response a long time ago and that ET got a completely different response. I think most of us in this room are aware of the global opinion <u>shift</u> on this issue. I mean how fast is a fast global change? I think we're moving along at a pretty good clip. If I had a parallel universe or a separate world of evolution to compare with, I could give you an idea of how we're doing. I think it's going pretty damn fast to the point that ...it may have gone to the point of "Oh, wow, let's go out and contact." Remember the *War of the Worlds*, and it was the first one that went out there and *whsszt.* I assume that's not the way it's going to go, but the idea of the public being warmed up for contact has been extraordinary, I think, by any measure.

I haven't measured it myself, but I'm very pleased with the speed it's going. It could be faster, but I think it's going fast. Obviously, movies like ET and Star Wars played a big role. I track technology relationships and take a lot of flack on all sides of that issue. I remember there was a shift—my own observation—on the movie Star Wars. The idea of that little droid being asked to find the vulnerable point in Death Star and going Weee! Shoo! At that point, I saw a quantum shift in consciousness towards technology, at least in this society, and I think that is related to the idea of being the conscious contact as well. I think we're moving along very fast in a lot of films.

PETERSEN: Absolutely. There are CD-ROMs out already, and there are new films supposedly in the works, major feature films, supposed to come out next year or the year after, that have to deal with Roswell in new ways that haven't been done before, and so on. What anybody who's in either the military or in business will tell you is that kids coming out of school think and learn in a different way now than they did in any other time, that they've done in the past. I think this new technology is probably some of the key tools to being able to effectively communicate these things.

GLENN: A friend gave me a little dune program in virtual reality. One of the problems with it is that it is an extraterrestrial killer sort of deal. We have to figure out how we let the producers know that there is a market for peace and beauty as well as death and destruction. Don't applaud. Take your energy and send postcards to those producers. I mean if the market doesn't let it be known that it's there, production will not occur.

MODERATOR: The problem is not just educating in the conventional sense, but also the issue with the existing form of leadership. We have a question here that says, **'How do you explain to world leaders as well as average people what happens if, in fact, a contact comes?'** How do we get ready for that? How do you explain to world leaders and to average people how this works?

GLENN: Put together an interactive communication system to pool our intelligence and ideas and methods about future thinking, and this is certainly a major phenomena to consider.

PETERSEN: My take on that is a bit different. I've been involved in three presidential campaigns. I'm here to tell you that presidents and presidential candidates never make decisions on their own. They respond to people. They put their finger in the wind and find out which way the wind's blowing. That decides what policy they will have. I think the way you explain a lot of this to world leaders is that the average people probably explain it to them, the threshold of interest in these subjects, the significance of interest. I think *Omni* is playing a very interesting, maybe subversive role in the way they're increasing the exposure here. I think there will come a time when this starts showing up on the polls and politicians can't ignore it any more, and then they suddenly become receptive to it.

How you explain it to them after that is probably a kind of conventional marketing plan, or campaign plan or any of the other ways we do. You go around and take the essence of the exhibits of what you know of what's real and what the implications might mean. It's going to take a whole lot of thinking. By the way, let me underline that we haven't even begun to start to understand what the potential implications of this might be and how you move from here to there with a whole planet. Obviously, we've never done anything like this before. You have to do a whole lot of homework and try to understand and consider what the alternative ways it might play out. Then, you take it out and sell it in a kind of a conventional way you sell anything.

SITCHIN: The question really has two parts. They don't deserve the same answer. One is how to explain this whole business to world leaders and to the average people. The average people—we covered that in a previous question, and that is as best as possible—education, movies, television, whatever means are used these days to convey information and educate the public at large. As far as the world leaders are concerned, that, of course, raises the first issue of who are the world leaders? There could be some debate or disagreement on that, not just between the remaining major powers. I once heard a committee on the subject say that those visitors to earth who finally decided to show themselves and make official contact, etc., first of all they debate where to land; in Moscow, in Washington, the UN, the Vatican, and they land in Washington and the being comes out and says, 'Take me to your leader' and they take him to Hillary. So there could be some disagreement who the world leaders are today. Though I see many, many faults in the UN organization that need a good revamping, perhaps this is the only place that we can look to once it's put in shape. The world leaders already know the truth. They know who's out there, whether contact the way we're discussing it here has been made or not. I'm talking **these** days; I'm not talking in the past. The planet is on its way back. It's robotic emissaries are here or on the way back. This is well-known. In my opinion all evidence points to the fact that their way-station or space-station on Mars has been reactivated.

I would draw the attention of all here, and if you're not familiar with the details, it's in one of my books—the so-called Phobos Incident—in 1989 when two Soviet spacecraft were sent to Mars. One of them was lost on the way, they said, because somebody leaned on the console and pushed the wrong button in Moscow. I've never been at the launch site, but I saw it on television and the movies with the hundreds of people who have to do something so the next one could do something. So how could one just lean on a button and lose a spacecraft? But that's what was claimed—that Phobos One was lost. But

Phobos Two did make it to Mars, orbited Mars for about a month in March of that year, sent back incredible photographs of features on Mars that appeared both in visual light, meaning regular camera film, and infrared. Among them was a shadow of an elliptical object, according to all those who were willing to make comments at the time on the subject, and some of them appear on camera in a video documentary based on *Genesis Revisited*. The video title is, *Are We Alone?* They said it's the shadow of an object that should not be there.

After orbiting Mars for 26 days and sending some of those unbelievable photographs, the spacecraft was redirected to its main objective. Mars has two small moons or moonlets, the larger of them is called Phobos. There are many indications that it's an artificial object, not a natural object, hollow inside. One of the first things that Phobos Two, after leaving Mars orbit and examining the Phobos moonlet, was to fly in tandem with the moonlet, or this artificial object about 35 meters above it, and bombard it with laser beams. As it neared Phobos Two, some object that looked like a missile, and the Soviets, finally, after two years of not releasing the photograph, released it, hurdling toward the spacecraft, at which point it went out of commission, fell silent, and disappeared. Obviously, it was shut down.

When we sent in two years ago, Mars Observer, —I was asked by some of my friends, I was then talking in London, 'Well, what will it find?' I said—and that was in July—'first let's see if it gets there.' A month later it did not get there. Again, something happened as if somebody there says, 'I don't want you to take a look at me.' 'You can fly to Venus, but not to Mars.' I think the world leaders are aware of what's going on. I think that some of the changes in the geopolitical situation, the dissolution of the Soviet Empire, the end of the Cold War, has to do with their knowing what's happening. We don't have to explain it to them. Whether they're making the right decisions based on their information or not, this I don't know.

MODERATOR: The problem of education and communication is laced with the underlying issue of how do you explain all this in ways that are compelling and understanding? That comes out in a question from Trish Phiffer who says, **'One answer to reducing the fear response involved in cosmic interchange might lie in a new interpretation of quantum mechanics which posits an intellectually acceptable model of reality capable of demystifying some of the phenomena associated with the manifesting of other intelligences which are unexplainable within the parameters of conventional science.'** What that says in real nice language is, how do you explain this, and how do you make sense of it so people can understand it? That's a real good question, because if they don't fly with jet engines and aerodynamics as we understand it, how do you get common people to understand it? What would you deal with, how would you react to the underlying science issues, Jerry?

GLENN: Well, the short answer is, I don't know. But what hit me when you were explaining that was I remember what a relatively well-known German rocket scientist at Huntsville, Alabama, said when asked what he thought the next fundamental breakthrough in science would be. He said he thought in the fields of gravity. There's been great breakthroughs in certain parts of physics, and certainly in biology and mathematics and material science, but we really had *squat* in the last 100 years when it came to gravity and that whole realm of force. He thought there would be some breakthroughs in that area that could explain these things. But beyond that, I don't know.

PETERSEN: Some of this is happening already. Within the last nine months in the mainline physics journals there are proposals about new interpretations in quantum mechanics, that there is no mass, there is no inertia, suggesting that the fundamental pieces of Newtonian physics don't exist as such but they're a by-product of consciousness interchange with probably the zero-point energy field (underlining <u>field</u>) from which everything supposedly all comes. The fact that this shows up in mainline scientific journals, peer reviewed of the highest order is really quite intriguing to me. The first of those articles came out in February of last year in *Physical Review*. By the end of the year there were already two or three follow-on articles, one of which said, 'Well, if that is the case, then what we're talking about here is being able to control not only mass, but then, gravity.' I have a copy of an article, again in a mainline type science journal, which says, 'If you can do that, then the possibility exists that you can engineer space-time in order to influence this mass, run it down to zero, change the amount of mass, and therefore you can go into speeds higher than the speed of light.' Arthur C. Clarke then wrote an article in December saying, 'Look, warp drive might really be here. The possibility we could move from here to here instantaneously, we could decrease mass down to zero, that will let you do whatever you want to do and then bring it back up again.'

The point to all this is, suddenly in the last nine months or so, there are some new ideas starting to work their way in. They are starting to explain new variations of quantum mechanics. Again, this will be on the Internet. It's going to be the device that will function the same way the printing press did the last time and these new ideas will be able to be communicated and distributed many, many times faster, almost instantaneously. So guys like Keith Ferrell will have them in their magazines two months later than the time somebody first picked it up. That, again, is one way these questions might be communicated.

SITCHIN: Well, I don't view science as an obstacle to understanding, discovering, and preparing humanity for what is undoubtedly about to happen. I think, on the other hand, science is the key and the means and the clue to understanding and achieving what the question puts the finger on. The only problem with science is that there's so much establishment, that the dogma can be challenged or changed only at the risk of the innovator. I think that while science is the key to the future, scientists should have more open minds.

MODERATOR: All right, I'm told in the break that a lot of people are interested in photon belts. I don't own any photon belts, all mine are leather or something. We had a couple questions here; I'll use one as being representative: **'It's been predicted that we'll be moving through a photon belt probably within the next year and a half; prior to that event mass landings of extraterrestrials are to occur to assist and educate humans through this transition.' How does the panel view this potential event?**

GLENN: I suppose I'll have a lot of neural connections, and my hypothalamus will be excited when it happens.

Petersen: You know somebody called me once about six months ago and said something about a photon belt and I went back years when I was younger, had more hair and I'd studied electrical engineering, and so I thought I understand the basic words. I called up a scientist friend of some renown and said I'm going to fax to you some pages out of this book that explains what a photon belt is. I sent it to him and he called me back and said, 'I don't know how any of this makes sense, photons as we understand them don't do this, and I don't understand how they could stay in a belt, and I don't know what it means. I'm afraid that's where I am. I don't know what a photon belt is, I don't know that we're getting near one, and I don't know how they work.

314

SITCHIN: I'm in the same place.

MODERATOR: There are some interesting questions that ask about the best possible future that might be out there. What should we be doing in order to get to that. One question says **'What do you project is the best possible future? Do you believe it is in each of us to create it?'** An important phrase, I think. Another one says, **'What's the most important thing each of us can do to help prepare for the cosmic cultures to meet peacefully and joyfully?'** Jerry, what's the best possible scenario that you've got? And how do we get there from here?

GLENN: Well, one I offered before, is get out of town. Grow up in the galaxy, merge with extraterrestrial intelligence and permeate the universe with consciousness to hold off either the big expanse to a cold and tropic death, or the big bang of a kinetic burst. So the best I can hope for is, we permeate the universe, merging with cosmic cultures, and we get a good overview of the situation and then invent the next step. Do I have it within me to do that? Not alone! Best I can do is help humanity to consider its own options through an interactive system so that we can make our logical and positive futures.

PETERSEN: One of the tools that futurists use, and is probably the most effective tool for trying to make some sense out of what might be on the horizon, is the use of scenarios. Scenarios are kind of mental pictures of alternative futures. It's almost certain that you can't predict anything, at least predict it in any kind of conventional terms. There are too many variables. Everybody who's ever tried to predict something straight on in conventional terms has almost always been wrong. So the approach to this that's most used, and used quite effectively, is to spend the time to think about how the different kinds of driving forces might come together and what kind of worlds they might produce. How they might branch in one way or another. You get a spectrum of the future as a series of scenarios, images about what might happen. I've always thought at least in the last few months that this would be a wonderful way of trying to look at what the implications of contact with extraterrestrials might be. How might it play out in what kind of images. Once you have those in your mind and see them as alternatives, then you have a basis on which not only to plan for the different ones, but also when events happen in life you can look at them to evaluate them to decide which kind of future it's pointing us to.

I think that knowing what the best possible future might be is a serious undertaking, but in general it would seem trite: light, love, happiness, and everybody lives together and we don't pollute the earth, and things like that. But, essentially, the best future seems to me to be if we had a benign transition between the old era to the new one, that we understood the implications of systems and how we're all connected together, so that when the next extraterrestrial team showed up we saw them in the best positive light. That we tried our best to communicate to them the best of what we have and to learn from them what we could do.

The other part of the question to me is more interesting. 'Do you believe it's in each of us to create it?' Yes, I think that's the only way you get there from here. I think this is all about us. It's not about governments. It's not about institutions. It's all about us. I think the very notion of national security is fundamentally shifting. In the past, we've all been dependent on governments and big institutions for providing consistency and predictability, that we translate into security. We're all here today because we don't think the world is going to blow up tomorrow, or that there's going to be an earthquake. If we really thought there was going to be a earthquake tomorrow, we'd all go off and do something to plan it. So we've got this sense of predictability, and that's what gives us security. In the past, that's kind of the principal role of government—to provide that predictability and make sure the economy works and nobody attacks, and those kinds of things.

But what's happening here in this transition from one era to another is that the very ability of these institutions to provide that predictability is eroding. In the past, all of us as individuals have been dependent upon and always felt we were dependent upon the government for our sense of security in the future. It's not going to work that way. We're going to be more and more dependent upon ourselves, our reserves, what's inside ourselves, to deal with an environment that's very uncertain, very chaotic. I think that in terms of building the possible future, therefore, that the essence of getting from here to there is that if you again get this broad change of attitude, this broad change of the way we think, believe, I think that's the only way we get from here to there. What's the most important thing each of us can do to help prepare for it? Work on ourselves. I think it's all about us.

SITCHIN: I concur wholeheartedly with John's last remarks. But, again, from an historical or prehistorical vantage point, look at the lessons of the past and for the present and future. On several occasions, as I mentioned, each time the contact was close, they gave us more knowledge, more civilization, more ways to improve ourselves, to heal ourselves. At least on one occasion, which is recorded not only in the Sumerian and Babylonian texts, but those in the Bible, that of the great flood, the deluge, the commander in chief on earth, Enlil, sought to wipe mankind off the face of the earth. There are two reasons given for that decision, that he tried to enforce on his colleagues. In the Bible, which is the one most of you are, or should be familiar, the reason given is, and I quote, "Because the wickedness of men was great on earth." This is the reason the Bible gives for the decision to do away with mankind. In the Sumerian texts, which are much more extensive and are the origin of the tale of the deluge, the reason given is that Enlil could not stand the noise of mankind. He complained to his colleagues that mankind increased in numbers too much, it is filling the earth, it is making a tumult and sort of enough is enough. I've had it. Now, if you try to assess the prospect of the next close encounter, not just the signals and the preliminaries for it, and what might happen—first of all the question is: Who is now in charge?

On Nibiru, and thus on the decisions affecting us, ...there was a constant divergence of opinions, a conflict when Enlil who was strict, who wanted things to be right and exact, and according to the rules and regulations. His half-brother, and sometimes adversary, Enki, the first one to land on earth, the chief scientist, the one who created us through this genetic engineering, considered mankind as his children, as his offspring. He was responsible for mankind, and thus he connived, and the tale is told in great detail in Sumerian text—he connived with his faithful servant called Noah in the Bible, to save him and family and thus the seed of mankind and other life on earth, and preserve it even during the deluge.

Now who is now in charge? Enlil or his line of descendants? There was a conflict about the succession, or that of Enki, whose successor on earth was Marduk, the Babylonian national god. Many adverse occurrences happened after the rise to supremacy of Marduk in Babylon. So who is in charge and thus what kind of attitude would be taken, I don't know. But if the criterion would be one of the two, or both— one is the increasing wickedness of mankind, and the other is the proliferation, the getting out of hand, the number of humans on earth, I think we are guilty of both of those deficiencies.

Certainly after WWII and the Holocaust, what ensued afterwards, and even in Chechnya and so on, you can compare human wickedness and not compare it, but certainly mankind has illustrated that it's wicked, or capable of wickedness. This probably did not go unnoticed. The other is the proliferation, the increase in human population that is really the cause of so much poverty, suffering, and disease in so many parts of the world. Few efforts have been made to contain or control the growth of mankind. Some of those under the auspices of the UN have been thwarted by other powerful entities—in human affairs—religious and others. So it is quite possible we will find one thing on both counts, and this part— and here I agree with John—this part is entirely up to us. I mean, none of those who are in Nibiru is forcing mankind to get out of hand in numbers, or to slaughter each other. Whether this is up to governments, or the change is to begin with individuals, each one should decide. If we are to do anything in preparation for the encounter, meeting no doubt with superior beings, let's recall that these are the two areas: human wickedness and human uncontrolled proliferation, and it's up to us to prepare for a more benevolent result, or a less benevolent result of that encounter.

GLENN: One of the primary impediments that I've experienced in bringing about the positive future is prejudice—and I don't mean racism or sexism or ageism, but the concept of prejudice is wrong in the same way the concept of the earth as flat was wrong. Of course, we had someone to go around the earth to verify that, so how do we do that with prejudice? Prejudice means prejudging the future. That's an illogical concept when you think about it. There's true or false past; true or false present; but there's not true or false future. At least as far as we know. So prejudice is an illogical concept. It really is. And it used to annoy me because I'd find myself working for one think-tank that might be right-winged, and then for a left-winged think-tank, and an up-winged think-tank and then a down-winged think-tank, and have friends across the spectrum who said, 'How can you like X when you work for Y?' As if it's a mono-future. It just really drove me nuts to keep hearing people who would immediately reject something because it came from University X or Think-Tank Y. That prejudging just drove me nuts. I got sick of answering the question, 'How can you be friends with Timothy Leary, you work for the Hudson Institute,' or 'How can you be friends with Timothy Leary and actually get paid by the Hudson Institute? I mean, there's a contradiction here somewhere, kid, you're really confused.' I would explain piece by piece along the way. Finally, I got sick of it, and said I'm going to sit down and write a book to resolve what I consider to be the largest prejudice that I could find, which I considered to be between the mystically-oriented and the technocratically-oriented people. By mystic, I simply mean one whose first response to a problem is shear consciousness; and a technocrat is someone whose first response is shear technology. You can give a more detailed definition of both of these, but then you would be dealing with prejudice all over again. So I said better to define it very simply where we can get universal agreement and then resolve these, too. It became very clear to me that there's two major trends that are becoming forefront in present tense, and may eventually merge. Humans are becoming integrative technology at the same time technology is becoming, or appearing, sentient, and these two begin to merge somewhere off in the future as George Robinson earlier this morning talked about.

If you want a detailed answer to your question about what I think is a positive future to the future, read my book *Future Mind*. I spent a lot of detail going into what about crime, what about laws, what about the logic. I even took mystic notation and related it to Boolean logic so you can do this in a more regular sort of way. That would be the long and short of my answer on how, on what kind of a nearer term future, but I still buy a longer term future. That entropy stuff is serious to deal with down the road. In the mean time, the merger of consciousness and technology is the way to go. The implication for prejudice fighting is that we're all part mystic and we're all part technocrat. Each of us tends to be a little more on one side than the other. If you can resolve your own prejudice in your own mind, come to terms with your own mystic self and technocratic self, merge that, then I think you develop, commercially speaking, a future mind. And you'll move along, and it'll be better.

PETERSEN: Commercially speaking, I want to identify my book. It's called *The Road to 2015*. It's a green book out there. Get it if you're interested in the underlying, driving forces across the whole spectrum, and now they're coming together. Tagging along on the same question—I want to try something here—and we'll go through and answer, and then if any of you have some questions about this subject, and only about this subject, then we'll take a couple of them, and then I will, in the interest of keeping it moving, I may stop that one and go on to the next one, but let's generate a little interaction here if you have some pressing questions about this? But there's a series of them, again, that have to do with 'Who are we and how do we deal with all this.' One says **'Do you think our ability to communicate with and travel to cosmic cultures in the future depends upon a change of consciousness?'** And another one says **'Do we need other new values to make contact and do aliens have values that we don't understand?'** Another one says, **'Many of us in various walks of life on this planet base our lives on service to others; yet there are many on the same planet who are self-focused and fear-based. How do you convey dualities that are integral to the nature of our planet?'** The underlying point in the question is, is there a new set of values; is there a new set of ideas that need to attend this transition or this kind of epic event in time.

GLENN: I answered this question with what I just said. The mystic self and the technical merges, so that would be my answer to the question. New values is that you create technology to enhance consciousness and enhance consciousness to design better technology, and its a positive feedback loop.

PETERSEN: It should be self-evident from what I've seen that this is all about trying to learn who we are in new ways and a new set of values. I have no idea what the values of aliens are. I've never met an alien. I don't know if they like art, music, I mean it's kind of interesting because the stuff you hear about them is fairly narrow. You never hear about whether they have pictures on the walls of their space ships, or any of that kind of stuff you take for granted is an integral part of what humanity is. I don't know.

SITCHIN: I do.

PETERSEN: Good.

SITCHIN: As a matter of fact, when I arrived and spoke briefly to Scott, I said the subject, 'When Cosmic Cultures Meet,' implies one party to the meeting is us, people, humanity, earthlings. Now two questions; one—who are we going to meet, and here I want to comment that for the first time I disagree with you, John, because you use the term *aliens*, and this term *aliens* immediately implies something different, something to be afraid of, it doesn't look like us, you know—watch ET or other movies, ...it

318

is this, it is that, it has other emotions, etc. The text, again I keep returning to my sources, which are the sources for the Bible and for the so-called myths and knowledge of the ancient peoples, that knowledge, or depiction of what happened, is summed up in the Biblical verse where Elohim, which is translated God, with a capital G as a singular, but literally in Hebrew it's a plural term meaning the Deities. Elohim said to unnamed colleagues who must have been there according to the Sumerians, even their names are given, said, 'Let us make the Adam in our image and after our likeness.' In our image means physically to look like them, and after our likeness means internally, emotionally, intelligently, etc. Therefore, when people ask me frequently 'How do they look? Do they look like us?' I say No, we look like them. So they're not aliens. In some respects they are not just our creators; we are their offspring. Especially in the story of the deluge where it was proceeded by the intermarriage between some of their young ones; the Bible calls them **Nefilim,** those who have come down, with the daughters of men and they had children. So mankind, Homo sapiens, are their offspring, in more ways than one. From the initial mixing of the genes to the intermarriage, through what mostly the Egyptians call the demigods, who were offspring of some of the **Anunnaki** who were mostly females, but not always. Some of their females also had human mates. So they are not aliens.

Now when we then discuss 'When Cosmic Cultures Meet,' whom are we discussing at this conference, and we're all from the same side. Now to whom are we talking? I think I'm the only one who is capable of being their spokesman. Not because I've met them, but because I've read the records of those who have met them and listened to them and wrote down the tales, the records of those ancient events. If you compare even biologically, humans, Homo sapiens, with earlier hominids, with our apelike cousins, you find that first the ability to speak makes us different due to the structure of the larynx, etc. I'm not talking about the brain, which of course, is different. The ability to speak, the ability to have a language. According to the Sumerians, they are the ones who taught us music. So they like music. They wanted the people to play for them, to dance for them. They are the ones who taught mankind art, plastic art, painting, other works of art. So when the question arises, 'Whom are we going to meet,' we are going to meet ourselves. But at a much earlier and more advanced stage.

PETERSEN: Do you know if they like rock 'n roll?

SITCHIN: I wouldn't be surprised.

MODERATOR: Anybody else have a question about this specific area? Yes ma'am. I already did photon belt.

...The question was **'There are a lot of books out from Pleidians and Arcturians and all kinds of other folks who explain how the essence of what ..other..our culture is, and do you agree with that?'**

SITCHIN: It took me literally a lifetime, because the whole thing started when I asked my teacher when we were studying the Bible in Hebrew, "Why does it translate Nefilim 'those who came down', as giants," and I got reprimanded and thus the whole study started. I devoted a lifetime to the subject; ended up with six and a half books; six are unpublished and the other one has been written. At the end of the year there will be seven, and I don't think I mentioned in any of them Pleidians or others. I think it's tough enough to prove there's one group coming from one planet. So as far as I am concerned, there's one group from one planet. If others have other ideas and substantiate them, then I do not have a monopoly on wisdom or on truth. You can accept what they say, too, if you want to.

**MODERATOR**: OK, anybody else quickly. We'll move on. In the back, yes sir. **So far I haven't heard much about the cosmic cultures from a futurist perspective, ...future, talk about extrapolation of higher technology and education which you seem to dance off of the ET presence among us in the sociological and cultural implications of that interface. I'd like to get engaged in that ..those are established factoids you'd just as soon not deal with.**

**GLENN**: You know, I thought I had that in my notes in the opening comment. I thought I'd talked about that. It would be an extraordinary stimulus to rapid neural development, to ethnic conflict reduction. But to me it's a quantum growth. I made the comments before, we want teachers who know a great deal more than we do. I talked about all those implications. One thing futurists do, is to posit a future event and then say, 'What are the impacts?' Which is essentially your question as I understand it. Yes, we should prepare, but how do you prepare the negative scenarios, you get the hell out, so you have technological parity. Thinking about the negative scenario being here sets up negative self-fulfilling prophesies. We talk about the psychological impacts. The others would be the very rapid growth patterns, and the more quickly we prepare our minds for that idea—rapid, intelligent growth--the better off we are. There's a whole range of kinds of contacts. There's a difference between working through the mathematics of the contact and saying, 'Ladies and Gentlemen, we now have proof in the Academy of Science that there's a signal we can verify that it's from another source than the natural phenomena we've studied. That's a much different kind of impact on civilization than XYZ Joe showing up on top of UN Building. And simultaneously, in a bunch of other places around the world. It's a different kind of contact.

**Question, comment from audience.....We have thousands of UFOs over rural cities every year; we have millions of citizens around the world being visited by ETs on a regular basis. If you take those as givens you don't have to worry about a signal from space. That's irrelevant. Deal with the evidence right in front of us, credible witnesses, and extrapolate into the future from that.**

**PETERSEN**: I don't know what the strategies are of the extraterrestrial visitors. What is the purpose of all this? The stuff that I read gives me any of a number of variety of reasons including the very compelling kinds of things that Zechariah talks about. I don't really understand if there are those amongst us who come from these other civilizations. If there are, they are probably here for a reason, and I am frankly not familiar with what that reason might be. It seems like a relatively benign reason, or at least a low-key kind of reason, an infiltration kind of thing. You'd think if you're smart about this and maybe if you'd been involved in it somewhere else before, maybe they've done this somewhere else before, then you wouldn't want to come in waves and throw everything up in the air. You'd want to work yourselves in, learn how it goes, try to influence thoughts and ideas, and so on, so maybe that's the kind of thing that's going on. If they are coming here to mine minerals in order to support life somewhere else, then it might be a transient thing that has nothing to do with interfacing with humans. So maybe they're trying to do their thing and get off and go somewhere else. If they're trying to crossbreed, then what can I do about that? I don't quite know how to deal with it. Maybe you can focus it a little bit more. It's an interesting question.

320

**Moderator**: Yes ma'am. Over to the right. **Through history when things that we're not familiar with or changes that are coming in, it seems to be apparent to us that much of the information comes through grass roots, there are people here today who have studied with the tools, that have been accepted within the framework of our scientific study. We also have techniques to add to that telepathic communication have been studied, we need to listen to those in a spiritual, not religious, context, channeling and other information and give out and then to take the information from around the world...and to see how similar it is..and do we have a gulf of information that must be looked at outside of the regular scientific tools that we have today?**

PETERSEN: I think you make a good point. I have suggested to Jerry that an interesting study would be to look at the indigenous-kind of predictions and alternative points of view, if we're looking at the future, and put that in a UN study. But as my friend Willis Harmon said once when I was talking to him about this, 'Shoot, there's so many people channeling so many different things, who knows what is right any more, and I don't know who they're plugging into, and who's got credibility, and not.' Certainly there are a lot of people with different perspectives on this and, but, what's the quality control?

SITCHIN: I think that was a very important question ...which implied an answer or a way to plug into the information that we seem to be seeing but missing. As I think is clear to all of you, I'm plugged into the past, trying to find there the answers for today and for tomorrow. Specifically in connection with the last question, I take the opportunity to tell you the book that is due later this year, titled *Divine Encounters* deals exactly with how did the so-called divine beings, the ancient gods, or the God of the Bible, how did they communicate, how did they deliver their messages or instructions, etc.

We have in the Bible many instances that the communication was through the medium of dreams. People dreamt that the deity or its emissary, the so-called angels, appeared to them and stood sometimes at the foot of the bed, sometimes at the head of the bed, and gave them a message while they were asleep. The question was how authentic the dream was, etc. which is what you said, how do we know? What to believe or what to accept, but that happened. I have a chapter in the book that deals with other forms of encounters, which I call encounters in the twilight zone. Because, if you recall the series, *The Twilight Zone*, which I liked to watch at the time, sometimes at the end, the conclusion, both the viewer and the hero of that particular tale was not sure whether he was witnessing reality or unreality.

In some of them, to the surprise of the hero of the tale, himself, the viewers of course, he finds that during the incident in the Twilight Zone—true, imagined, or hallucinated—the other being, visitor, whoever, the miraculous personage, gave him an object. Then the man or woman or child puts his hand into the pocket and finds that he has the object that supposedly he just dreamt about. So this is one of the episodes, or a few of them, that's really left a great impression on me. There were such instances reported in Sumerian writings, in Hittite writings, in Babylonian and Egyptian, etc. So I devoted chapters to that calling it *Encounters in the Twilight Zone*. It supposedly never happened, just imagined, but how did they come to possess the objects, so it must have happened. So there were dreams, there were instances where the person, many times of royalty, received a communication and was shown something, not as if it was a holographic image, but that the person was inside the holographic image. And then POOF! it all disappeared.

All these things that the lady is asking or pointing to, and many more, took place in antiquity, and that was the way the visitors, the divine beings, because they were revered, communicated with mankind. The problem was, at the time, as time went on, and it was the age, or era, of the Biblical prophets, there was a lot of contention between the true prophets and the false prophets. Somebody came and said 'I received the word of God.' Did he or didn't he? So this is what you pointed to, John, how do we know who is the true prophet, who is the true channeler, etc. But what you are pointing at was in antiquity one of the methods of communication, and this is the subject of my book, and whichever conclusions or lessons could be drawn from it, I hope some will draw lessons and will apply them to the present.

PETERSEN: Let me make just one follow-on point. I grew up in a conservative religious traditional Protestant household where our whole family revolved around the church. I memorized whole books of the Bible. There was a very clear interpretation about what all this meant, and there were no alternatives. It was really quite clear, and it was beat into me year after year after year, what it all meant. I found out later on, or at least I believe there are other ways to look at some of the ideas in the Bible, and they're still as powerful and important, but they might mean something different than I thought otherwise. Jim Hurtek's coming up here and he has a wonderful book. It's been very important to me. But do you believe Jim's book, or do you believe the *Only Planet of Choice,* or do you believe the Pleidians, or the Arcturians, or a friend of mine across the river who started channeling and quit doing it because she was getting such negative ideas, and so on? In the end for me, I've come to believe that it's all about the only thing I can control, the only responsibility I've had, is for me. For my money; it all means something different for everyone else. We're all supposed to see and hear or what we're to hear or see, and we're supposed to go out and try to figure out what that is. We're not supposed, necessarily, to have somebody tell us, "This is...read my book...all the answers are here..." I think this is about us, and about ourselves, and getting to a different place of understanding and awareness, and I don't think you could buy a book from Kay Allison out there that tells you exactly what your awareness is supposed to be.

GLENN: On the business about how to judge, we wrestled with this in the Morning Project daily for years. We've come to the conclusion that we want to do some mapping of the future, and this way we in a sense bypass the issue of judgment by clustering the views. There's a range of views about the future. Well, what is it? Remember, in the beginning, when I made some comments, I said, What if an extraterrestrial had to come through the solar system and report on sentient views of the future, you know—where's the home page on the World Wide Web for range of human views of the future? Well, OK, we'll do that. We're not there, yet; we're in the process of getting to that. One of the products we'd like to have is a map of the future, the range of the views. So this way, we don't have to judge. The difficult part will be the groupings. We also have maintained the idea of having public interaction on the Internet, as well. People can put their views in there, so our approach is not to judge but to have feedback systems and charting systems. That is our approach to the question about judgment, or channeling, and so forth.

PETERSEN: What are the aliens coming for? Maybe they're coming to help us learn how to love and teach others. Absolutely. Again, this business of being a teacher/futurist is to look for patterns and shapes. Many of you are navigators, you look for a number of different lines of position, from this perspective you go through there, and from this perspective, ..and all of a sudden you say there's something right there. And that's, for my mind, what you've got to do. I don't think you buy into anybody being the gospel, or anybody not being the gospel. I think you look and you have to be curious, and you have to be objective, and you have to be honest with yourself.

MODERATOR: There are a couple of interesting questions that probably best should have been on the Fear Panel. But since we're kind of a pattern and a shape, ...**Once contact is made and accepted and we're working together as coworkers, assuming with our extraterrestrial friends, and not as pawns, toward a common purpose to save a race and planet from self-destruction, how public should we be in sharing the information with others we come in contact with? What are the dangers and repercussions, especially if you work for the government?** Here's another government question. **If the Government has been covering up and keeping alien contacts secret, how justified have they been? Is it something truly terrible out there that we can't handle?** How much might the problem be power and control orientation in people in major nations? Could power and control be so important to them that they're terrified by civilizations and beings that are far more powerful than they, and that they have trouble seeing that much of the rest of the population might be able to handle it better than the leaders? So here's an issue about how do you handle the essence of this relative to power and control in government, and dangers and repercussions.

GLENN: I haven't studied this issue personally: I haven't done the Freedom Of Information Act requests, and done the normal sorts of things. I like the idea of the conference organizer which will appear on a video tape documentary of this conference, saying like, "Show what you got. Bring it up." Put some public pressure on people to show it. I mean, whatever is held back, let it go out. Why not? Who has the right, anyway? Ultimately, who has the right, anyway?

PETERSEN: Let me just say something about government. I work with the government. You know there are some really nice, good people in the government, wonderful people in the government; there's millions of people in the government; the government is not the government. The government does not have a conspiracy about this. I mean, if you've ever spent any time in government, it's so inefficient, they can't communicate to the guy next door, and they're all full of bureaucratic kind of problems everybody else has. In one sense, it's pretty naive to think that they can keep a secret. My friend who has the highest clearances in the world will tell you that you can't keep a secret. It doesn't make any difference what the secret is.

I got a wonderful story about a friend of mine who was responsible at a very high level for intelligence, not an appointed official but a civilian in a large organization. He said, "We can't keep a cotton-pickin' secret. I just had Tom Clancy in my office sittin' here tellin' me what he's going to say in his next book," and we were saying, "Please don't say that, please don't say that!" "Please hold off at least six months so we can fix it before you go public with it!" He found out all this stuff by just going around talking to people and reading open sources. I mean, I don't see the government in quite the terms that a lot of folks do. Perhaps some of you in this room do. I perceive them as people, and some of them are wonderful people, some of them are very dedicated people, and some of them have made extraordinary kinds of contributions to do what they absolutely think is right. My approach to all this is that if you change their motivation and change their orientation they will put the same kind of effort into a new direction, and that's the kind of effort I'm talking about.

**QUESTION from audience: ..you say it's so easy, the government can't keep secrets; then why, when I ask for FOIA stuff, why does it come back blacked out?**

PETERSEN:  I've been involved with that. Sure they keep secrets, and they have reasons to keep secrets. A well-known UFO researcher gave me whole pages blacked out, and I had somebody check on it. The blacked out sections had nothing to do with UFOs. It had to do with sources, or some other kind of thing. There are secrets, and they have good reasons to have secrets. Just because they don't tell you the secrets doesn't mean they're holding something back that you're supposed to know. Sometimes, they may well be. They are bureaucrats and operate like any other big organization does. It is not fair to assume across the board they know anything about UFOs, or they are keeping anything away from you that you otherwise would like to see.

MODERATOR: One more question. **In anticipation of the time when cosmic cultures meet, what long-term endeavors should be undertaken now, and by whom, to prepare humanity for such an eventuality, and what steps are being taken now? What long-term endeavors should be undertaken?**

GLENN:  If you already know what my answer is would you put your hand up? Very good. I think a long-term endeavor is to create a system for humanity to assess the past and forecast a range of possible futures and learn together to set our priorities. Who should do it? The United Nations. What part of the United Nations? The United Nations University. They're one step from politics. Really. That's why I do it. I'm trying to live consistently with all this jazz. That's why I say it. The UNESCO funds us but doesn't do the work because UNESCO has countries on the board. If you have countries on the board, then you have to work through their politics.

PETERSEN:  Well, I agree there should be an educational program, and put into place soon. It needs to be coupled with new ideas in terms of science; new ideas in terms of who we are has to be coupled with ideas about how do we determine who we are, and what's our sense of security.

# A Special Search for Knowledge

Since the Conference, it has become evident that among the large but unknown number of individuals who have memories of sustained personal contact with ET's and UFO phenomena, there is a very small number of individuals who have become guardians of special information and skills. This gifted knowledge, and the skills springing from it, appear to be important in solving some of Earth's endemic and dangerous problems. Locating these people and working with them to bring their knowledge into global service is a program that the Human Potential Foundation is undertaking. The assumption is that they are rather evenly distributed around the world, and that there is redundancy and overlap between what each of them may know. If this is correct, we anticipate a particularly powerful outcome by bringing them together in an exchange of knowledge. Anyone reading this who feels they have a role to play in this program is encouraged to contact the Human Potential Foundation.

# ⊕ Appendix A

# Completed Composite Questionnaire

The questionnaire was included in the registration packet of everyone who attended the conference. The questionnaire was not a simple one. It was designed to provoke introspection on a confusing and to many an unknown, and to some a fearful, phenomenon. Additionally, most of it required a narrative response. It seemed fair then to offer a reward for the work required to complete the task. Out of 175 registered attendees, 102 returned a questionnaire. What follows is a composite completed questionnaire. Analysis and editorial comment is given in *italic* font. **Bold font** is used to present responses taken from the returned questionnaires.

Questionnaire
When Cosmic Cultures Meet
May 27-29, 1995, Sheraton Washington Hotel, Washington, D.C.

As a registered participant in the conference, when you complete and sign this questionnaire, you may designate anyone in the world to receive a copy of the Conference Proceedings.

You are part of a unique group assembled for a very particular purpose: to stimulate a dialogue anticipating that some day there will be unambiguous evidence that Cosmic Cultures are meeting, and that Earth is one of the meeting grounds.

The purpose of the questionnaire is to hear from you, to give you an opportunity, personally, to join the dialogue we are trying to stimulate. The results of the questionnaire will be reported in the Conference Proceedings.

Obviously, this is not a scientific survey of attitudes. While the subject is very important, very challenging, and from many aspects very serious, if we do not approach it with a cultivated sense of humor, it may well be overwhelming. Facing this possible future will take courage. But courage without the moderation of humor can easily turn into fanaticism, and an unhealthy and unjustified desperateness may appear to rule the day. Loosen up, give the role-playing questions your best shot—be President Clinton, Newt Gingrich, Bob Dole, and the others. Believe me, they need your help!

1. What are the dialogue's most important components? Rank in order of importance the following components. You may, of course, add additional ones of your own. Educational, military, philosophical, political, scientific, spiritual, whole being, _____, _____ , etc.

*With 93 responding, the rank order of the seven listed components is as shown. A modest number of additional components were provided by respondents. They are not included in this compilation. The numerical values were obtained by assigning a score of 7 to a respondent's top listed item, 6 to the next listed item, etc. By a factor of nearly 5 to 1, the most important component was considered spiritual rather than military.*

| | | | |
|---|---|---|---|
| a. Spiritual | 504 | e. Scientific | 283 |
| b. Educational | 439 | f. Political | 201 |
| c. Philosophical | 344 | g. Military | 105 |
| d. Whole Being | 317 | | |

2. Until they identify themselves and inform us what they want to be called, what is your preference for a collective name for the other Cosmic Cultures? Aliens, Enlightened Entities, Intergalactic Travelers, Visiting Others, or any other term of your choice _____.

*Sixty different names were offered, with some respondents giving more than one name. A number in parenthesis indicates the number of times that name was cited. The impact of Hollywood's ET is apparent.*

Advanced Souls
Aliens (2)
Beings (5)
Celestials (2)
Company
Comrades
Cosmic Beings (2)
Cosmic Brothers (3)
Cosmic Cousins (3)
Cosmic Cultures (2)
Cosmic Entities (2)
Cosmic Kin
Cosmic Siblings
Cosmic Visitors
Curious Ones
Demons
Dimension Travelers
Distant Cousins
Energy Explorers
Extraterrestrials (15)
Extraterrestrial Arrivers
Extra-Dimensional Beings (2)
Friends (6)

Friends and Educators
    from Cosmic Cultures
Friends-to-Be
Galactic Entities
Guests
Higher Intelligences
Honored Guests
Inter-dimensional
    Chatter-Boxes
Intergalactic Beings
Intergalactic Emissaries
Intergalactic Explorers
Intergalactic Travelers (9)
Intergalactic Visitors
Interstellar Citizens
Light Beings (4)
Living Presence
Love and Light
Multi-Dimensional Beings
Nattering Nabobs
Non-Terrestrials
Other Civilizations
Other Conscious Beings

Other Friends

Other Terrestrials

Other Worldly Beings

Sentient Beings

Sol Brothers

Space Beings

Space Brothers & Sisters (4)

Star Being

Star Brother and Sister

Star Lights

Star People

Universal Beings

Universal Friends

Universal Others (5)

Visiting Others (5)

Visitors (5)

328

3. Sketch the symbol that for you represents interactions with other Cosmic Cultures. *A sample of the many symbols created included:*

4. In relation to **actually** meeting members of other Cosmic Cultures, on the following scales indicate where you currently are in terms of the attitudes or emotions indicated. Mark somewhere on the line. *Out of 102 returned questionnaires there were 96 responses for each of the three scales. The values are given from the mid-point on the line from zero to five in each direction.*

**Very fearful**                                                              **Absolutely no fear**

5_____|_____|_____|_____|_†__0_____|_____|_____†|_____|_____5

*With 14 respondents the average value toward "Very fearful" was .7. With 82 respondents the average value toward "Absolutely no fear" was 2.9*

**Very hopeful**                                                              **Despair, no hope**

5_____|__†__|_____|_____|_____0_____|_____|_____|_____|_____5

*With 95 respondents the average value toward "Very hopeful" was 3.4  There were no respondents marking a value toward "Despair, no hope"*

**Dim future**                                                              **Brightest future**

5_____|_____|_____|_____|_†__0_____|_____|_____†_____|_____5

*With 9 respondents the average value toward "Dim future" was .7. With 87 respondents the average value toward "Brightest future" was 3.0*

5. You have been asked to give President Clinton a short introduction to his official announcement that the United States government is now ready to share with the world all special knowledge it has concerning interactions with Cosmic Cultures. What are the first five sentences of that introduction? You may omit "Good evening, my fellow American citizens, and citizens of every culture of the Universe."

*Out of 102 returned questionnaires, 91 responded to this question/situation. The original plan was to select one response for each question/situation to make up a composite completed questionnaire. After reading all the responses and laboring with the difficult task of selecting the "best" one, it was decided to share several.  Respondents frequently came from decidedly different philosophical positions.*

*The first example provided more detail than most:*

**"As hard as it may be to believe, approximately fifty years ago our military became aware that our country was being visited by flying craft of a high technology, piloted by beings of another race who had traveled billions of miles from another planet to make contact with us.**

**Our government at that time made the decision to classify this subject until we could determine if their motives were friendly or dangerous, and because their technology was far superior to our own.**

**Our nation had just finished World War II, and had just entered the Cold War and the beginning of the Korean conflict, and it feared that releasing its knowledge about such strange visitors might create a panic similar to the one which occurred in 1939 due to Orson Welles' radio play, "War of the Worlds."**

**We have now established that these visitors are friendly, and come out of concern because we**

had developed nuclear weapons and rockets, and used them in warfare. Left to our own, we faced the likelihood of destroying our planet in future wars, or destroying our environment through the misuse of our new technology.

They came to help us learn to live peacefully with our new and powerful technology, and to educate us so that we might someday enter into trade and relationship with races from other worlds. This is the reason for their display over Kansas, and it is my privilege to formally welcome them to the earth and ask all Americans welcome them as well."

*The second example probably would throw the nation into panic;*

"You have all imagined the day when there would be global peace, health and happiness for all peoples. You have prayed for God to melt all the guns and weapons of death, war and destruction. You have imagined greeting peaceful peoples from distant worlds with stories to tell of other beautiful planets populated just like ours. This morning you awoke to a new day, a new reality, a new world. . . the best of all possible worlds. Sit down and take a very deep breath and clear your mind of everything you know to be true. I have the difficult job of telling you everything you know is wrong!"

*The third example is more politically feasible and practical:*

"I have an announcement that is likely to be the most important that a president of the United States will ever make. It is my honor to announce what many of us have believed for a long time: God's marvelous creation includes other beings not unlike ourselves. Leaders on the planet Earth have now been formally and openly contacted by visitors from other parts of the Universe and we have welcomed their representatives to visit the White House. Many citizens in government and private organizations have been preparing for such an eventuality and we appreciate their efforts. Let us all join together in learning what our visitors have to teach us."

6. There are a number of participants in the dialogue we are trying to stimulate. One group is earth-based actors. Indicate your view of the importance of each of the following actors in the dialogue. The scale is 1 to 10. One equates to "insignificant role." Ten equates to "critically important role." Numbers in between are on a changing scale between these two positions. You may use the same number more than once. How important to the dialogue are the following?

*On a scale of 1 to 10, responses from 102 returns rated the "individual" as the most important actor. I wonder what response national leaders and organized religions will have to this assessment?*

| | | |
|---|---|---|
| a. | Individuals | 8.24 |
| b. | United Nations | 7.36 |
| c. | Educational | 7.14 |
| d. | National Governments | 7.02 |
| e. | Families | 6.88 |
| f. | Religious Institutions | 6.37 |
| g. | Government Intelligence Agencies | 6.14 |
| h. | Local Governments | 5.54 |
| i. | State or Provincial Governments | 5.19 |
| j. | Military Organizations | 5.03 |

7. Another component of the dialogue is communications with members of other Cosmic Cultures. Some have suggested that these communications primarily will be accomplished via direct mind-to-mind links, i.e., what we currently call telepathy. The following questions are about telepathic communications and how to feel about this subject.

a. Do you think it would be a worthwhile undertaking at the present time quietly to sit and attempt to make a telepathic link with other Cosmic Cultures? _____ (Yes or No)

*Out of 102 returned questionnaires: Yes—88 (87%), No—10 (10%), Maybe—1, No response—2.*

b. If you answered "yes" to the above question, what would be the first thought message you would send?

*By using the concept of telepathic communications, the intent of this question was to get from the respondent what she or he allowed themselves to "think" versus asking them what they might verbalize. The hope was that thereby a deeper articulation of true feeling would be made. The responses were in various forms: one word, a short phrase, one sentence, several paragraphs. Out of 107 separate statements, "love" was mentioned 28 times, and "peace" 23 times. A sample of distinct ideas is presented below. Numbers in parentheses indicate the frequency of use.*

- **Welcome, how can I help? (11)**
- **I/we send you love and peace (10)**
- **Welcome—I/we love you. (7)**
- **Welcome, we are ready to meet you. (3)**
- **Please come and help us. (2)**
- **I will listen. (2)**
- **Teach us to live our lives more peacefully and understand values that are important to survive. (2)**
- **Love, but beware because some humans are violent and aggressive.**
- **Peace. I welcome your presence but caution you to approach humans with care.**
- **I am scared but welcome you. I hope we can be friends.**
- **I do not trust you, therefore I will remain armed against you. Perhaps through cooperation things may change.**
- **A warning: I fear some humans may not respond with friendliness.**
- **I am curious. I grant and ask for respect.**
- **Explain yourselves.**
- **Please help neutralize the human tendency toward violence and destruction.**
- **Our finest expression of life is love. We seek to share with you what this means.**
- **I greet you in love and peace, but wait till you meet some of your relatives. You might rethink your decision to come here.**
- **I'd like to introduce you to my family. They think you are just a myth!**
- **Welcome to Planet Earth where belief masquerades as knowledge.**
- **How can I best serve my people, the planet, and divine order of things?**
- **Let us work together on advancement of our Universe.**
- **Accept my limits as I shall accept your limitlessness or lack of boundaries.**
- **Thank you for your loving guidance over the years.**
- **We want this to be a peaceful, joyful interchange.**
- **If there is someone out there, we need help.**

333

- Peace and friendship. Please reply.
- I am ready to receive, I think.
- Who are you. What is your purpose?
- Thank you for reaffirming I am not alone.
- If you work in the light, share with me that which I need to know.
- Establish peace. Teach our children well.
- I communicate to you in peace. This is my clear intent for any contact between us.
- I am eager to be in open communication.
- I send you love and trust and the spirit of unity.
- For a while send the frequency of unconditional love, then the thought "come."
- We need ground rules for interaction, understanding of definitions of time and distance, and to establish a mutually agreeable "virtual" meeting place.
- Communicate in peaceful and non-threating ways.
- I send love and compassion for all living things.
- The majority of this civilization believes in coexistence of all cultures.
- Communicate openly, honestly and with sincere, non-hostile intentions.
- I come in peace seeking your experience of life and wisdom.
- We wish to share our culture.
- We are open to learn and desire to share.
- Give us instructions beneficial to both parties and that will not interfere with free will or choice, hinder or harm us as well as you in any way.
- We want to get to know you better.
- We realize you are trying to help us help ourselves and our planet.
- What are you doing here? What is your mission?
- I offer myself as a conduit for information exchange.
- I am a realist. We are all links in the food chain! We need time to get acquainted.
- Here is a friendly, interested, aware reception. I am open to your approach.
- If just one of our species can open his/her mind and heart, putting fear aside—we all can.
- I am ready to work for positive change on this planet.
- I am open to guidance.
- I miss you. I need closer contact with you lest I falter or fail in my mission due to loneliness and isolation.
- We wish to establish a meaningful, interactive, peaceful dialogue to mutually expand awareness of life forms outside of our planet.
- We make this opening in peace and mutual respect, willing to inquire into possible relations between us.
- I love you and desire to meet you, yet feel awkward and fearful at our first meeting.
- I invite you into my heart and mind, and request an invitation from you to be in communion as well.
- Please come now and teach us to save ourselves and our Earth.
- Namaste. Let us begin the renewal.
- Reveal yourselves to us. We are Earthlings on the threshold of cosmic consciousness.
- I ask that only beings of the highest light who seek the highest good for self and others, make appearance to me at this time.

- **Our planet and people are beautiful but troubled. We have much to share on a physical level but often experience conflict.**
- **Peace. I wish to communicate to those beings of the highest level of spiritual development.**
- **Send simple, repeated images of our galaxy, major constellations, humanoids with tools, embracing, welcoming, waiting.**
- **What wisdom do you have for me to share?**
- **There should be a coordinated world-wide meditation to send a simultaneous thought message conveying love, openness and cooperation.**
- **We are open, ready to receive. Please communicate to us.**
- **Share whatever you can which would assist human beings to experience harmonious existence.**
- **We love you as a fellow child of the Creator. We wish to be part of the Galactic Federation of cosmic cultures.**
- **An openness of mind and spirit, unafraid and patient.**
- **I am open to receive your guidance with love and to learn how our interactions might benefit all sentient beings.**
- **I affirm love, peace of mind, joy, health, patience, happiness and kindness.**
- **Could we talk?**
- **Show yourselves.**
- **We ask for assistance and guidance in healing our planet and working with and serving divine purpose.**
- **Let us share our thoughts, our desires, our intentions together in peace.**
- **If you come from love and light we welcome you.**

c. If there was a major, sustained sighting of space craft over a large metropolitan area, would you be more interested in trying to establish telepathic communications with the Cosmic Cultures in these craft than in the general situation of "a" above? _____ (Yes or No)

*Out of 102 returns, Yes = 74 (72%), No = 16 (16%), No response = 12 (12%)*

d. In the scenario of "c" above, what would be your first thought message?

*In 7a and b above, the situation was passive and not associated with an immediate situation. In 7c, the situation is active, immediate. We wanted to see if that made any differences in stated interest in trying to establish telepathic contact. There actually was a drop in the number of "yes" responses. Some respondents pointed out that use of the phrase "would you be more interested" required them to answer "no," in that they would be just as interested as previously indicated in answer to 7a and b. Seventeen respondents simply referred to their answer to 7a and b. Six respondents who had no interest in the passive situation of 7a and b, were willing to make contact under the changed situation. Their comments are given first. There was a reduction by 50% in the use of the terms "peace" and "love," although they were still the most frequently used terms.*

- **Go slowly, give us time/opportunity to understand. Be careful, there may be danger here.**
- **Cool it guys**
- **What the f _ _ _ _ you doing here?**

- Thanks for contacting us. Be careful, you are in danger from our military and others who will respond with violence.
- In the spirit of peace and cooperation we ask you to join us in dialogue to educate and enlighten both our species.
- The law is one. Greetings in the love and light of the one infinite Creator. Teach us, we are open to you, and closed to you and unsure of you. The ball is in your court.
- Why are you here? (5)
- What do you want? (3)
- Who are you? (3)
- Please remain calm, you are in an unstable environment where clear communication may be difficult.
- Some of us will be fearful. Do not dismay. They will understand you come in peace, but it will take time. Please be patient. For those who cannot be persuaded—be gentle.
- Peace! Be cautious, I welcome you but many of our people are fearful. Can you give us a clear sign of peace? Can we offer you rest and respite?
- Please be patient with our backward and fearful ways. We have lived a long time in a world with conflict, competition and warfare.
- We are suspicious of anything strange, especially if it is powerful. We have seen how the powerful treat the weak in our world, and we fear that you will do the same to us.
- Welcome, wear breathing masks, the air and water are polluted. I hope you got your vaccinations and have medical coverage.
- Peace or war — think now!
- Peace, we are one.
- Greetings Cosmic Cousins. Why are you here? For what purpose have you come?
- We are here. Where are you?
- Are you coming down, or what?
- Welcome. Smile a lot. Observe our gestures before making a lot of gestures yourself. Note the many frequencies we use to communicate.
- We welcome your arrival.
- Welcome, I envision a union of peaceful balance between both races.
- I love you very much. I am sorry for the state of our home, can you help?
- We love you. If it is in the interest of the highest good of all concerned, we are ready and willing to have more open contact.
- How can we create a receptive, safe place for you to join us?
- Please land, reveal yourselves and participate with us in peaceful, friendly communications.
- Would you like something to eat and drink?
- Send a group message of love, openness and cooperation.
- Thank you for your courage and compassion in presenting yourselves to us.
- I both admire and fear your advanced technology.
- I am attracted and repelled by the various forms that are reported by other humans of your presence.
- Assist us to become aware, to accept, and to acknowledge our past, present, and future connections with you.

- **Picture the craft, then send images of acceptance (embrace), feelings of love.**
- **Welcome! Who are you and how may I help you? I send you blessings and love.**
- **Teach us how to evolve beyond competition and warfare, to empathy, love and cooperation.**
- **Come now, we are open. We are ready to receive and accept.**

336

- **Welcome to our material home.**
- **How can I help?**
- **Who do you represent?**
- **May we creatively and peacefully communicate in another more remote location?**
- **Hey guys, be cool! Don't scare these people. Feel them, be aware of how much they can handle.**
- **When do I get the tour of your ship that I was promised?**
- **Please help fellow Earthlings by some formation of your craft in an easily understood sign of peaceful goodwill.**
- **Why did you let us destroy our plane of existence if you knew darn well we could produce unlimited non-poluting energy to develop our technology?**
- **Are we witnessing the start or the end of an intergalactic clan struggle?**
- **Nothing about this is benign and lambs get taken to slaughter for taking down their guard.**
- **Welcome, how can we work together to save the Earth?**
- **I greet you with light and love. Why have you come?**
- **I've been waiting for you. What took you so long? You guys need some new clothes. Grey does not look good on you.**
- **Hi!**
- **We welcome you to our three dimensional world. We do not wish to harm you or to be harmed. It is our desire to share with you our rich heritage of life and to learn about your life.**
- **What are you trying to teach us?**
- **My concern is a flooding of thoughts from a fearful Earth population.**
- **I am curious about your culture and the place from which you come.**
- **I am visualizing a virtual (mental) space where we can meet and compare common concepts such as time, space, energy, emotion, etc.**
- **Love. Welcome. We are one. We are open to receive your message.**
- **We send you our love and friendship. We are so happy you have finally come to us—visibly.**
- **Impress all the world leaders with these messages: neutralize/destroy all weaponry, redistribute food resources so all have some, stop harming other living things.**
- **Try to balance press fomented hysteria and the government's overreaction.**
- **Join with us in growing close in an understanding of one another that honors the best in our natures.**
- **How can we communicate with you?**
- **Welcome Brothers. Come closer!**
- **First, I would want the actual experience to see and feel the impact. Than I would be very interested in telepathic communications.**
- **Let's get together, talk and be diplomatic about the situation.**
- **My objective would be to be quiet, receptive, attentive and actively listening.**
- **Love, joy, glad to see you. Come on down!**
- **I would want them to land to meet them face to face.**

- Explain yourselves. Tell us your secrets.
- State your motives and plans before any further flybys.
- Suggest you land in country area. Warning, all people carry guns.
- Will I be going home now? Have I fulfilled my purpose according to the plan? I am excited to meet you.
- We are friendly. Please send a message that will help us know of your good intentions. Be patient with us.
- Beam me up.
- You are accepted with love and we expect the same in return. How can we help you? What are your needs? What are your plans for us?
- We ask and grant respect.
- Tell them who I am and mention the names of the ET's I know to explain my connection.
- Please establish contact with us. We request your assistance.
- Welcome aunts, uncles and cousins. It has been too long.

e. Would you be interested in trying to develop telepathic skills? _____
*Out of 102 responding, Yes = 93 (91%), No = 5, (5%), Maybe = 3 (3%), No response = 1 (1%)*

f. If a drug was available that in a very short time gave you perfect telepathic skills, i.e., you could read the mind of any person by simply looking at them or envisioning them in your mind's eye, and that your mind similarly would be an open book to others, would you take the drug? _____.
*Out of 102 returns, Yes = 34 (33%), No = 58 (57%), Maybe/Conditional = 5 (5%), I don't know = 3 (3%), No response = 2 (2%)*

g. Would you take such a drug if a permanent side affect was that the condition of "perfect telepathy" was irreversible and that no shielding was possible? _____.
***Out of 102 returns, Yes = 28 (27%), No = 64 (63%), Not sure = 5 (5%), No response 5 (5%)***

h. How would you describe your feelings about the possibility that most, if not all, of the Cosmic Cultures who have a capability of interacting with Earth have the capacity of "perfect telepathy"?
*There were 93 responses to this question. A majority, 55 (59%) expressed delight over this possibility, while 15 (16%) expressed considerable unhappiness over the potential loss of privacy. In another category there were 6 (7%) who argued that "perfect telepathy" was not a possibility. The remaining 18% were either ambivalent or made another comment that could not be categorized as either being pleased or displeased with the prospect of "perfect telepathy."*

- Intimidated.
- Nothing to worry over.
- Okay with me. Nothing to hide.
- Free at last.
- At ease. They would know of soul's essence of love.
- Very concerned. We are not a people coming from a place of love and altruism.
- Acceptance.

- Concern about the ethics of perfect telepathy.
- Excitement.
- I want to be able to shield, to protect myself at will.
- They will work with those whose heart is "right," warts and all.
- It gives me hope that there could be so many teachers.
- That is great. This means that we have to develop our moral values and positiveness.
- Gratitude for the honesty such a gift requires and bestows.
- It seems to be a likely possibility.
- I do not believe it. All forms of consciousness are self-delimiting, and we have some power of shielding.
- I would be concerned that "they" may be overwhelmed by our emotions.
- Neutral and positive. There would be more balance and harmony—no deceit.
- This is true. Accept it and deal with it.
- Curiosity.
- All evolved species have full intuitive and telepathic abilities. Few on this Earth take time to listen to the wisdom imparted.
- We had better get to work on ourselves. It is sad to realize how behind we are in our development.
- They know me better than I know myself. I am accepted as I am. I'm ok with this.
- Nothing is perfect, all things have limits. Perfect telepathy can only exist between like beings.
- No problem. Earth beings do this too, just not Earth-wide.
- I totally accept this as true.
- I suspect this is the case.
- I believe this and it is ok.
- It has to be that way to overcome language barriers. An impression of feeling is more effective than words. Telepathy is a healing tool of the future.
- I'm not sure I like the idea of not having any privacy at all.
- Strange at first, then of trying to communicate.
- Very happy because it would eliminate different languages.
- A challenge to adapt to, but not unacceptable if safeguards against reprisals existed.
- I would want them to land and meet face to face.
- It is exciting to me. It would make life more interesting and, once people resolved their issues with it, relatively stress free. I would not like it if they were the only ones who were telepathic.
- If they use it for a positive and peaceful motive, I have no problem.
- If true I would feel fear, fascination—and comfort.
- I'm not surprised about this. It is a fact for me!
- Curiosity, trust.
- We have the ability to both open and close our minds.
- Rejoicing in what this would mean for promoting full life. "Perfect telepathy" would manifest unconditional love.
- I welcome it.
- Intimidated. I have a lot of mental and emotional housecleaning to do. But ultimately the aliens would see my true nature—an honest person with spiritual values.
- Yes! Wow! Wonderful! Effortless communications finally. Feel the energy.

- I agree.
- Perfect telepathy between humans and visitors would need continuing interaction to account for individual differences.
- This will happen in the future so we may as well get use to it.
- I believe they do it now. I have no concerns with this.
- Wonderful, it cuts right through the bullshit! It would be a real surprise to get a printout of what they learn telepathically from our world leaders.
- Very excited, provided they are friendly.
- I would welcome this phenomena and attempt to learn all I could from it.
- Scared.
- Wonderful! Can we talk? No more phone bills.
- I am an artist and believe that something is working through my hands. I feel that something out there has this capability, I call them Angels, but I don't know for sure who they are.
- This would be to their advantage because they are not fooled by spoken words or deceived by appearances. I would like living in such a world.
- Emotions are contagious. Empathy responds to distress. Feel it yet?
- It appears to be a wonderful social shaping phenomena that creates a trusting open society.
- No problem. I'm just not sure that I am ready for that capacity.
- I don't mind them knowing. It is the small human minds that frighten me, not the Aliens.
- It is my belief that they do. I feel that it is far more effective and creates a more intentional language, communications without misunderstanding. It would encourage us to discipline our mental apparatus.
- What is, is. We shall have to adjust. Ultimately, I believe it would make life more wholesome.
- Very positive. Trust would no longer be an issue or question. We would know where they stand and they would know where we stand.
- My feelings are mixed: delighted in the fact that telepathy gives us all a common language, and disappointed that I have not developed those skills more diligently.
- Perfect acceptance, understand that this is a given of these advanced cultures.
- On a planetary scale telepathy probably is essential for survival of a technologically advanced society. Once a technologically advanced society achieves success on a global scale, if they still operate on the basis of competition, they will destroy the planet's environment as well as each other. Races with a high degree of empathy or telepathy will avoid this fate be cause they will sympathize and relate to the victims, either plants, animals, other races, or the planet itself.
- I have good feelings. I would explain that it is not lack of interest or desire, but lack of skill development on my part that blocks total communication.
- Possible, but not necessarily probable. Perfection is rare.
- If "perfect" means control, focus, discrimination, then I have no problems. In fact, I would welcome such. I do not believe in "secrets," therefore I welcome a more advanced interaction such as a cosmic culture would have to be.
- Warm, receptive, thankful. It makes communication easier.
- Maybe it would clean up our thoughts to an amazing extent. To move toward effective communication we would have to acquire this skill as well.

- I accept the probability and welcome the opportunity to learn more about that capacity.
- Mixed. Open communication is good, but balance is essential, and personal boundaries need to be respected as well.
- Since I prefer to be a co-creator and not a perennial apprentice, I would be inclined to developed my own ability. Until that time, I find that that possibility assists me in cultivating greater humility, clarity, integrity, openness.
- I believe this type of communication is the most natural and advanced form of communication. When we are prepared for the complete openness and honesty required, we will be ready for telepathic communication.
- It would be painful because I do not think that the general population is in a position to totally change their ways and let go of their barriers. Total honesty and unconditional love would have to exist for telepathy to work in our society.
- A clearer form of expressing ideas. It is not a form of communication that can express feelings.
- Ambivalent.
- I would be encouraged that they would be able to teach me that same capability.
- I would hope that this is not true. In any important interaction I would want moments of privacy to collect, sort, evaluate information received as well as to be given. I would expect others would want the same courtesy.
- Fine.
- I think it is highly probable.
- Great. O.K. Why not?
- Telepathy, like anything else, can't be perfect! Subtle nuances of meaning will always draw a "blank" out of context of understanding the total picture—or the whole culture, personality, experience of the being who is subject. I think there is also the ability to block being "read" by someone else's mind.
- I feel the term "perfect" telepathy is a relative one, and that most of these cosmic cultures are at various stages of ability. The possibility that they do have the capability of interacting in this way seems to be good reason for beginning focused efforts in this direction.
- I feel that while telepathy is probable, I doubt if "perfect" telepathy exists. Indeed, I feel that such intertwining of minds could lead to one losing one's individual identity to a group mind, or perhaps schizophrenic disorders.
- I would find it an interesting possibility to ponder, as it would mean that such a culture was incapable of being insincere or hypocritical.
- Not overjoyed about it. What is "perfect?" What is the range?
- Invasion of privacy.
- Hopeful trust in their capacity for understanding and perspective.
- No feelings
- Delighted
- No feelings. My comprehension of the dimensional travelers is that they are very far in advance of us, that they are in control, and that I might as well just sit back and watch the show.

• **This is my major interest and concern. There is a fundamental difference between visitors in a vehicle in the sky and visitors in our minds. As a Christian, I have never considered my thoughts to be entirely private, but rather accessible to the spiritual realm. I am comforted to know God is aware of my thoughts and that I can commune with Him, but disturbed at the thought of any material being with telepathic capability. There is great potential for abuse, which seems to be the case with some experiencers.**

8. In 1984, the U.S. Army Research Institute gave the National Academy of Science $500,000 to have a committee of the National Research Council investigate issues of enhanced human performance. One of their findings was, "In the committee's view, the best scientific evidence does not justify the conclusion that ESP—that is, gathering information about objects or thoughts without the intervention of known sensory mechanisms—exists."

In view of this conclusion by the nation's most prestigious scientific body concerning telepathy, one form of ESP, what comments do you have about the possibility of telepathic communications with other Cosmic Cultures?

*Out of 102 returned questionnaires, 97 (95%) answered this question. While it was not asked for, 50% of the responses commented about the National Research Council's findings. These comments were all negative. No one supported the Council or its findings. A few showed very specific knowledge about the Council's report. There was near unanimity on the possibility of telepathic communications with other Cosmic Cultures. A few examples of each category of comment are provided.*

• **The possibility is independent of what a "most prestigious" scientific body concludes.**
• **The NAS blew $500,000 by not knowing how to open their minds and finding people who can discover new and better forms of natural communication.**
• **The NRC report is the most biased review of psi I have seen outside of CSICOP! I suspect that telepathic contact has occurred with Cosmic Cultures, but we have been unable to interpret these messages clearly. They have been framed with our fears and thus grossly distorting them.**
• **I worked for the NRC for two years. Their work is strongly biased by the selection of individuals to form their panels. I place no weight on their conclusion compared to my own experience to the contrary.**
• **The conclusion was criticized by a number of prominent people on scientific grounds. The NAS study hardly proves that telepathy is not real. While one series of studies may not support a given hypothesis, other studies may provide support using other procedures. Daryl Bem's work on the Ganzfeld study of telepathy is good evidence in favor of it.**
• **My experience is that ESP is alive and well, and it is the most effective means to communicate with others who may not speak your language.**
• **Empiricism is a religion and belief systems predict conclusions.**
• **ESP/telepathy exists. Use of this capability may serve us well in communications with other Cosmic Cultures.**
• **I should hope so.**
• **UFO aliens seem to communicate to abductees using direct brain transmission. Therefore, they must know something about our brains that we don't know.**

- Scientists have also held other views that later were completely overturned.
- The military would have reason to deny to the public that ESP existed, while studying military applications of it in secret. I have no problem of psychically aware E.T.'s.
- The truth is that these types of communication have been going on for some time.
- I think that this is a quality of experience that is God-like. Man trying to become God—yet again.
- If science does not open up, other people or institutions must—like this one.
- With training, certain highly developed humans should be able to communicate telepathically.
- I do it, therefore it is possible.
- Just as I pay no attention to movie critics, I pay no attention to the conclusions of this scientific body. One way or another, mind-to-mind is the way it will be.
- Telepathy is as real as voice communication. Our growth into telepathy is related to keeping our minds focused and quiet.
- With the increase of human consciousness and vibrational level of Earth, there is definitely the possibility of communicating with other Cosmic Cultures. Telepathy will be a true form of communication.
- This statement reinforces the view that our official governmental and educational institutions are not yet evolved enough to participate in these communications. Communications are best carried out through individuals open to this responsibility.
- These Beings have a telepathic capability, and there are many earth citizens who also have developed this ability. I yearn for the same ability.
- Oh sure, the government and the Army are the last word on what is possible and what is not.
- The National Academy was wrong. Telepathic communications will progress without a hitch.
- I doubt that those conclusions are based upon the actual evidence of various studies. For example, Robert Rosenthal's paper was rejected by that body. I accept the evidence of many papers about GESP, healing at a distance, etc.
- Many, if not all ,bureaucracies and academics are the most obtuse of all. I have no problem accepting telepathy. My mother always knew who was calling before she answered the phone.
- They are using traditional, unenlightened reasoning. Bias is strong. Do not rely on the expert establishment unless individuals in it are willing to use alternative methods for data collection and analysis.
- If you have no faith in the technique, it will not work. When individuals work together in a mental and spiritual endeavor, the intensity of the experience is greatly increased as is the possibility of successful communication.
- I know, personally, it is possible, and use it with ETs, my son and other members of my family.
- My daughter telepathically communicates with her children and several children with whom she cares for daily.
- ESP, telepathy is real and has been proven in many experiments. The work of Jahn and Dunne for example. Someday, hopefully, the NAS will catch up. However, it does highlight the fact that few people have developed this skill to a high degree, and there is no widespread educational or training program to assist the population in learning ESP.

- This information was probably politically jaded to hide actual findings. Many people all over the world experience it daily and use it to communicate with other human beings as well as other Cosmic Cultures.
- Councils and organizations as currently structured do not possess the vision to expand conscious exploration of additional dimensional reality. It is an individual—one to one, or One and One.
- I believe that there is a 100% possibility of telepathic communications with other Cosmic Cultures.
- My personal experience, and that of countless others, does not support the NAS findings. Telepathy is the natural mode of communication for the Cosmos on mental levels. There are higher levels and modes.
- It will be a challenge to the academician who up to this point has used verbiage to convey his superiority of mind, to take on a language that has no words but encompasses all things that are knowable. Denying the existence of that which is not provable proves nothing.
- They are the ones who will not hear the telepathic call put out by the ET's.
- Those who hear and respond in a positive manner are contacted at some point.
- Many scientific organizations continue to demonstrate the closed mindedness of the past. I see frequent demonstrations of a sixth sense.
- The NRC's findings are not sincere and serve to provide cover for the Army Intelligent Command's continuing research into parapsychological abilities and applications. Their behavior belies the press release. Despite the NRC, telepathy exists as demonstrated in psychological literature, and available to communicate with extraterrestrials.
- What the Green Machine says and the Green Machine does are two different priority lines. We are now officially controlling triggers with DTAB (Delta Theta Alpha Beta), research begun 25 years ago at the Idaho National Engineering Labs (SQUID) by Howard Hughes.
- Their findings are understandable for the scientific world is hindered by their limited standards and influenced by what is politically correct.
- The National Research Council should go back to school so they can communicate better.
- The Nation Research Council had better get real. The world knows what they are thinking— even if it isn't much.
- We will learn.
- The Army Research Institute has not explored the indigenous cultures among us that have already developed this ancient, present and future communications technique.
- I feel good about it because I hope they (Cosmic Cultures) don't only live by analyzing experiments, but by living in a society where the most important thing is love. All else would not be important.
- I've been a professional clairvoyant for several years, working with medical professionals and researchers. I'm a proficient hands-on energy worker and have absolutely no doubt of my capacity to read past, present and future events as well as the human aura and subtle bodies. The government needs some updated material to work with.
- I do this regularly with Beings from various realms in our universe.
- Great.
- On the one hand the evidence of perfect ESP by Cosmic Cultures would lead to an acceptance by earth science. Skeptics would still remain convinced that ESP is baloney but might accept that the visitors have ESP if they can accept the possibility of alien life.

344

- Telepathy exists. I am a scientist-physician who has explored energy and the unexplained. Present day science has closed to new knowledge as they believe their own dogma and intelligence. We are ignorant as we have cut ourselves off from the creative energy: vital energy—archeus—spirit force—zero point energy. This energy must be the focus of a new science as the old institution of science is already dying (as are other institutions). We must accept energy in all forms to bring knowledge in. Individuals, not institutions, must do it.

- The other Cosmic Cultures read my thoughts all the time. I'm use to it. I read theirs. I love it. Truth—all day long. Mutual understanding—all day long. Sharing and growth—all day long. Love and compassion—all day long. Non-judgment—all day long. All of the above as long as I maintain my vibration and remain aligned with my Inner Core, my Higher Self and them.

- It was a placebo Committee. $500,000 is nothing to the Army. It probably covered the cost of advertising, phone bills, xeroxing, fat salaries and bribes. ESP is too threatening a concept because they can't control it. They can't own it. They can't make a profit from it. Therefore, they deny its existence

- I don't give a shit about "prestigious" scientific bodies. I know telepathy exists but I have yet to be in telepathic communication with a Cosmic Culture—at least to my knowledge.

- I believe there are many individuals who have ESP capacity and that they could very well open themselves to communicate telepathically with other planetary cultures.

- Possibility lies in going beyond the politics of the NRC committee. This report of findings should be instructive in seeking more promising understanding of telepathy. Government reviews should be explicit about their assumptions, so value of reports can be related to the appropriateness of promises used (how they framed the problem space).

- The Council was wrong, lied or obviously used the wrong techniques or measurement instruments.

- Probable—likely. (We should get our $500,000 back).

- We can only establish contact when we overcome the dogmatism of the scientific establishment and the Newtonian/Cartesian paradigms. We need a paradigm shift towards a holistic world view.

- I don't think the Army knows how to research ESP in ESP terms.

- Might as well try! We may benefit from the experience.

- ESP or telepathy is only valid if we are willing to do the cleansing work in order to become clear channels. Garbage in—garbage out. The need is to cleanse all prior conditioning. The NRC doesn't have any idea of what that entails.

- I think the above august group doesn't know what it is talking about. They will never learn to communicate with ET's. I have had telepathic communications with many types of Beings, so I know it works.

- I find that a person is born with the art of telepathy and ESP.

- Not likely to be fostered by official bodies. However, individuals with capacity are likely to produce results in this field.

- Ignore what any military government-sponsored body says. Keep doing ESP communications. If they are right, we have nothing to lose. When we prove we are right, they have every thing to gain.

- I believe it would be difficult but perhaps since they are another species, and it isn't known how they communicate, it would be possible.
- I think it is probably possible. Perhaps the committee didn't interact with people who have developed these skills, or who may have had and used them from birth.
- With a closed mind you are not capable of mind/thought communication. Scientific methods are full of limitations, that is why the metaphysical exists.
- Telepathic communications are possible. We need to quiet the mind and body. Enlightening the body, mind and soul. Listen to peace within and say, "Peace be still." Give thanks and honor all creation.
- I know we can and do, so it is hard to comment.
- Just because science can't validate something doesn't mean it doesn't exist.
  It won't stop natural telepathy. The dominating culture has been trying to stamp out natural skills for hundreds of years. Its major effect has been to blind the dominators. Its secondary effect has been to create social trauma. It is profoundly dysfunctional and will die out.
- What evidence exists to demonstrate the trustworthiness of the U.S. Army or any (by extension) of those with whom it conducts business? Can this evidence withstand the assault from evidence to the contrary?
- My personal experience tells me telepathic communications is possible. I have telepathic communications with some ETs, and to a lesser extent, some humans.
- All abductees or experiencers of UFO contact engage in telepathy. I believe we need to establish educational programs to generalize this into our world culture.
- You mean after I have stopped laughing, and then crying, that I had to give up my hard earned tax dollars to idiocy? If I let "experts" do my thinking for me, or even influence my thinking, I wouldn't be answering this questionnaire. Their opinions don't influence what comments I've already made.
- The above conclusion will have to be eliminated and a new grant be given so ESP will be taught to the masses. There is no other choice as the "Space Brothers" telepathic communication is the only way it can be done.
- I think 'the committee' did not fully examine the phenomenon.
- The NAS finding is irrelevant. The power exists among humans and probably all conscious beings, i.e. consciousness is indivisible and therefore universally accessible.
- If I understand the question or the result of the committee's findings, is that they could not substantiate ESP. I, myself, would not stop work on, or belief in telepathic transmissions.
- One cannot assume that human laboratory performance is the criteria and standard for all cultures in the universe. The arrogance of such a position places it beneath consideration. From personal experience I know that telepathy exists, and wish that it were more consistent in human endeavors. I can only pray that it will be the mode of communication chosen in all cultures someday—Cosmic or otherwise.
- There are very many cases that tell us that telepathic information is coming directly into our brains.
- It certainly is possible. Perhaps we close ourselves because of the probable judgment that would come from this society. I believe an entire, more advanced culture would be capable of

generating enough non-conditional love and non-judgment to open up those with
developing abilities.

- Each person must start with himself—then it will reach critical mass.
- Until we ourselves recognize these ESP abilities, we would not be able to open "all channels" to communication. We must first recognize and acknowledge these capabilities in ourselves in order to understand Cosmic Cultures. I believe they are assisting mankind to raise their conscious levels to include various types of communication, to regain what we have had and to make effort to develop these on this universal language.
- A biased review of the literature can give any result. Telepathy with other Cosmic Cultures is a reality to those who have experienced it.
- The "possibility" still exists in my view, particularly given the strong possibility that the Committee's views are based on "probability." New dimensions could well mean new possibilities, including enhanced ESP and/or consciousness.
- Telepathic communications in the other Cosmic Cultures exist. The scientific body on Earth presently holds "proven" viewpoints about their "knowledge." The bridge between the two awarenesses can be reached when a critical mass of telepathic believers exercise their abilities in unison to manifest physically what the "scientists" are to learn. The need is to assist in raising the level of consciousness for all.
- Scientific evidence for ESP? How about psychic studies/evidence? Many of us have the capabilities and others of us may or will develop them.
- Just because their methods aren't built on a reductionist model or theory of scientific evidence does not mean that ESP isn't a reality or phenomena that some people have or are currently using with Cosmic Cultures. Western science is merely representative of a world view held by certain people. It is only a perspective, it isn't necessarily a truth that exists for everyone.
- As we move into the photon belt of light and time seems to have speeded up, the veils that kept us in the dark are opening and new paradigms and shifts in consciousness are happening to everyone, telepathy and ESP begins to open within all of us. In my opinion this allows mind control to be less effective and truth be known. I feel in a very few years we will all be able to communicate through telepathic means.
- Too bad that "scientists" disregard anecdotal evidence at times.
- If that is the way to communicate with other beings, then that's what I'll do.
- The $500,000 grant was a waste of money. You can have a pretty good party with that kind of money. Most of man's most advanced, if undeveloped talents, cannot be tested within the limits of scientific methods and thought. Stay tuned. In Galileo's time this committee would have found the planet Earth to be flat and the center of the universe. They would also consider bathing unhealthy.
- If and when we are exposed to any other Cosmic Culture we should immediately communicate on whatever plane is common and begin the learning process. What do we, individually, know that we both can benefit from sharing?
- There is and will continue to be communication with demonic entities by those who seek such communication or otherwise enter altered states. It works, it happens, it is dangerous for the individual and a channel for delusion.

- **It is less than 50/50 probable.**
- **There is plenty of evidence of ESP in our world culture, especially in the female side of our collective race. Our ESP may be at a very primitive state, or it may be something we are not allowed much access to at our stage of karmic development. ESP is very strongly indicated in many native cultures.**

Here is the scenario for the final series of questions: a large number of space craft have appeared over Kansas City. They are in a high altitude hover between 20,000 and 50,000 feet. When they arrived a message appeared on all television and computer screens: "We do not have any hostile intentions, and we will leave in ten days. Observe us but do not attempt to approach or to damage us. We can adequately defend ourselves."

9. Speaker of the House Newt Gingrich immediately called a news conference and after telling reporters that no one in the current Congress previously had been briefed by the White House on this phenomena, made the following opening statement to the American public:

*There is no public record of Mr. Gingrich's interest, knowledge or attitudes about UFO phenomena. In giving voice to Speaker Gingrich, the first example is spoof as the medium.*

**"Do not panic, good citizens of this country. The White House is surrounded so I am in charge! Ralph Reed is rushing to be at my side. He is activating his Legions of troops to pray this evil thing away. All local militia are on alert. All members of the NRA are asked to have their assault weapons at the ready. Some of the creatures seen marching out of their huge ships are said to have extra large, long ears, rather like donkeys. So we know this is a pure Democratic plot to take over. I will not let that happen. This will all be documented in a new book. I have just signed a contract with Rupert Murdock."**

*A second response for Mr. Gingrich was straight, full of the Speaker taking a responsible role.*

**"We don't know why they are here. The leadership of the Congress has sent the President a list of questions to find out what the Executive Branch knows and if they have kept information from us. So far these space craft have taken no hostile action. My office is arranging a meeting of experts including military and intelligence personnel, scientists and UFO researchers to attempt to establish contact with them and to ascertain their true motives. I am sending down to the floor a joint House-Senate Resolution welcoming these visitors to our planet, if that is indeed what they are. In this resolution we will include a guarantee that we take no hostile action against them if they take none against us."**

10. When reporters pressed Speaker Gingrich for details he did not have, Newt turned on them and asked what the press had been doing about this issue for the last forty years. Connie Chung, (formerly CBS TV News), gave the following response:

*There were a number of one-liners given for Ms Chung's response:*
- **Just between you and me, Newt, it has been a bitch.**
- **For the last forty years? Are you kidding? Why don't you ask Barbara Walters?**
- **Please don't let this hoax distract you from the OJ trial.**
- **I've called Barbara Walters in case the alien commander needs someone who speaks another network.**

*More serious responses raised real issues:*

**"We in the press have failed to take seriously the reports of many people on the possibility of other intelligent life. We have followed the lead of public officials and now have been proven wrong. The fact that so many in America are ready for such contact is due to the alternative media who have dared publish so-called unscientific information. We owe a lot to them for their courage."**

**"Mr. Speaker, the press corps has questioned the U.S. Government many times over the past forty years about the reality of these incidents. When Tass reports about a landing in Russia made the headlines a few years ago, the Reagan and Bush administration ridiculed it, and told us they had no evidence of such contacts, that it was a hoax. The U.S. Military has repeatedly discouraged us from investigating such topics, describing them as hoaxes and misidentifications. Scientific spokesmen such as Carl Sagan have publicly ridiculed such incidents as impossible. Our editors have not allowed us to follow up on these stories in the face of such blanket denial and ridicule by government and scientific spokesmen."**

11. Senator Bob Dole was in Kansas on the campaign trail as part of his bid to win the Republican party nomination to oppose President Clinton in 1996. In his best "presidential persona" he had this to say about what millions were seeing on television around the world:

**"We now have public proof of what many of you have suspected for so long: we are not God's only creation in the universe. We must take this opportunity to learn from our visitors to the extent they will permit us, and offer our cooperation as appropriate. America must show the universe the best of our people, our aspirations and our capabilities to meet any challenge before us."**

*Another respondent decided to put Dole in a hair shirt and confess:*

**"I'm heading into the twilight years of my life, having served my country to the best of my ability. Now I believe that to serve it best in this moment is to serve myself and my God by telling the truth. This government has hidden the truth from you for too long now. We have covered up, ridiculed our citizens, closed you out of our process, betrayed our positions, abused our power and thought we could get away with it forever. Forever is now, this development is the result of our duplicity."**

*Several responses included a sentence such as this:*

**"Well, we don't know where these folks are from or why they are here, but if they have come to see if there is intelligent life on Earth, we are complimented that they chose to look first in Kansas."**

12. On January 20, 1993, Billy Graham stated in an interview that he emphatically believed in the existence of other life in the universe. Now, in response to the evidence of this belief being seen over Kansas City, he had the following message to Christians and non-Christians alike.

*Throughout the questionnaire respondents were asked to provide statements for a total of seven prominent public figures, and one lesser known academician. Some of these were a challenge that not all were willing to take. Only President Clinton drew more responses than Billy Graham. Three Graham responses are provided:*

**"For those of us who are Christians, security comes from knowing that in God's Universe there is perfect order. We cannot be separated from the love and care of God because we are inextricably connected to Him by the love and power of Jesus Christ. There is nothing to fear. We welcome this revelation that God's Universe is truly a wonder to behold and that we are at long last worthy to see an even greater part of that Wonder. Let us all thank God for this unique privilege in the history of humankind."**

**"I thank God for the presence of our cosmic brothers. We know they are of the same origin as mankind and serve the same Creator as we on Earth do. We open our hearts in brotherly love and compassion and stand ready to be of service to our Father who art in Heaven. Let us pray for peace and for joy among all of God's children."**

**"Keep God in your hearts and pray for God to be in their hearts. Have faith that God will help you understand this new phenomena—these new beings in our lives. Keep the faith that they too are God's children—as all of us, and that we will find ways to reach out to each other."**

13. From the Vatican, Pope John Paul II, spiritual leader of over a billion followers of the Roman Catholic Church, had this to say to the world:

*There were surprises in the 82 responses given for Pope John Paul II. Of these, 36 (44%) took the opportunity to make a comment, usually negative, about the Catholic Church and one or more of its policies. These subjects included church land holdings, abortion, purchasing ablution, celibacy of the priesthood, birth control, marriage to non-Catholics, primacy of the Church to decide the reality and response to UFO phenomena, proselytizing the alien heathens, and women in the priesthood. There were other, more generous responses. Three examples of these are:*

"God is love. Love is open to all diversity. Accept God's love in all its forms. Pray for them. Pray for us. Call God into our midst and sing for joy, praise Him. Be not afraid, for He is with us. Extend your embrace of love to these other beings. God provides for us all. Be not afraid."

350

"Jesus, our dear Savior, the supreme Shepherd, offered His precious blood to save us from our sins. The loving Father sent his only Son out of His infinite love for us. Strengthened by this faith, we have the courage to face the many trials of life. Today we face cosmic visitors who have come, apparently in peace. Let us face these visitors with Christian calm, serenity, faith and fraternal love and hope as befits the sons and daughters of God."

"These events have been foretold in the prophecies of the Blessed Lady of Fatima. We are approaching a time of signs and wonders when events long foretold by our Lord in the Book of Revelations are coming to pass. It is a message and warning to all Christians to make yourselves right with God and with the Holy Church. The Day of Judgment and the day of His return is drawing close. Let us welcome these visitors but be wary of their message. There are dark forces which our Lord has told us will come into the world in the end times. Beware of following such forces. Place your trust in Him, in the Holy Mother, and in the Holy Catholic Church. May God grant us strength and courage to keep our faith in these times to come."

14. From Dharamsala, India, His Holiness the Dalai Lama made the following statement:

*In the 85 responses there was a similar generosity of spirit to that demonstrated in the responses given for Billy Graham. Three examples are given:*

"Let each of us hold a vision of peace in our consciousness. Hold a continuing meditative peaceful wave over the course of the next ten days. It is within our ability to manifest a lasting evolutionary step as we complete this initiation of peaceful interaction with our celestial brethren."

"I implore all humans to honor and respect our sacred visitors and to exercise great compassion for them. We will need to be patient and humble and allow them to acclimate to our planet and to our energy. Hopefully, they will quickly feel safe and will move beyond their need to be on guard. We must love them and bless them as fellow beings on this journey."

"Dear Masters, for that each of you are, should we be surprised that we have brothers and sisters from other places and spaces? You have within you all knowledge of all things. Unless you learn to love and respect yourself, learn your Mastership and live your birthright of love, the arrival of these brothers and sisters can only portend fear and more war will continue. It is your choice. Meditate, pray and become the full benevolent, loving Masters you are. Welcome them and learn from one another."

15. When a reporter called Paul Kurtz, Chairman of the Committee for Scientific Investigation of Claims of the Paranormal (CSICOP), for a statement about what was being seen over Kansas, this staunch defender of the current Western scientific paradigm made the following short comment:

*Respondents were not unkind to Kurtz, but out of 80 responding, 46 (57%) had him explain what was being reported in terms of either natural phenomena, fraud/hoax, hysteria, illusion/hallucination or that he doubted the reports. Another 17 (21%) had him say that it required or deserved more investigation. A small group, 11 (14%) had him acknowledge that the reported event was real, and 3 (4%) gave him words of apology for lying or being wrong in the past. The remainder were short expletives with ambiguous intent. The following short examples are typical of those who gave Kurtz a voice without trying to make him sound like an intellectual Luddite. The first example is a spoof of triteness and an example of creative clichés.*

**"We must analyze before we act, think before we speak and line up our possibilities before we let down our guard."**

**"When the perpetrators of this hoax have been discovered, people will be ashamed of their gullibility. The Amazing Randi is investigating."**

**"Until the scientific community has hard evidence of the reality of this phenomena, it is highly probable that this is nothing more than some vast, common hallucinatory experience. I suggest that we check out all the evidence before coming to a conclusion!"**

16. To whom do you want a copy of the Proceedings of the conference sent in your name? Why did you select this person?

*Half of the respondents designated themselves. The various reasons given for the choice of the person designated were diverse and logical.*

This questionnaire is copyrighted by the Human Potential Foundation. However, its reproduction and use is encouraged in order to stimulate the dialogue on this subject. Some users of the questionnaire certainly would want to substitute names of other countries' national leaders. Clinton, Gingrich and Dole are not household names around the world, and this is not an issue for just one country. The best lampoon of the questionnaire will receive a free copy of the Conference Proceedings. That should sober you up.

If you would like a copy of the questionnaire, or to communicate about it, write us at:

Human Potential Foundation
P.O. Box 6
Falls Church, VA 22040

# ⊕ Appendix B

# Invitation Letter to President Clinton and White House Response

Three letters were sent to President Clinton inviting him and encouraging him to participate as a speaker to the Conference. The first invitation letter, dated December 9, 1995, indicated that other heads of state and former heads of state also had been invited to speak at the conference. In less than two weeks the White House responded with their letter dated December 21, 1995. It is a cleverly worded letter, leaving a shadow of hope that he night ultimately be able to accept the invitation to speak.

A second and third letter was sent to the President on March 31, 1996. The first of these sent him a conference flyer that identified the twenty-three speakers and panel members who had committed to participate at the conference. We gave him an out by suggesting that if he could not make it, he could send either Vice President Gore or Chief of Staff Penetta in his place. Additionally, we sent him a copy of the invitation letter we had mailed to all of the foreign ambassadors assigned to Washington, D.C. [See Appendix E].

In the second letter of March 31, we informed him that each member of Congress had been sent a personal invitation to the conference.. [See Appendix D]. The purpose of this letter was to give him additional incentive to participate in the conference by making sure he knew that an effort was being made to educate Congress about the issue and to encourage them to become active players on the subject.

The White House responded to these two letters two months later on June 2. They didn't completely close the door in this final letter, but it was obvious that this was a style issue. What it means is that the thousands of people who invite the President to attend a function can say that he "never said no," implying that there was a real attempt by the White House to get the President to attend the Annual Knuckle Cracking Convention.

**Human Potential Foundation**

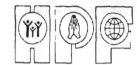

December 9, 1994

William J. Clinton
President of the United States
The White House
1600 Pennsylvania Avenue NW
Washington, D.C. 20500

Dear President Clinton:

The Human Potential Foundation invites you to be a principal speaker at the international conference: *When Cosmic Cultures Meet.*

The conference will be held May 26-29, 1995, at the Sheraton Washington Hotel in Washington, D.C.

Attached is a copy of the letter sent to other conference invitees and a list of those who have been invited. In addition to these individuals, special invitations have been sent to Hillary Rodham Clinton, First Lady, Boutros Boutros-Ghali, Secretary-General of the United Nations, Boris Yeltsin, President of the Russian Federation, Mikhail Gorbachev, former General Secretary of the Soviet Communist Party, and Jiang Zemin, President of the People's Republic of China. Beyond these individuals there is another list of foreign and U.S. academicians, spiritual leaders, and civilian government and military personnel who are also being invited to participate as speakers and panel members.

Your participation is considered particularly important. It is assumed that your staff has briefed you concerning what is popularly called UFO phenomena, and the U.S. government's policy concerning this information. There is some indication that the policy of secrecy and silence on this subject that you inherited when you came into the Office of the President is under consideration to be changed to one of openness. If that is correct you may want to use the venue of the conference to inform the American public and the world of this decision. If you are not ready to direct and announce such a full policy change, the conference could be used as a step in that direction. For example, you might indicate that the subject of interaction with non-earth cultures is so important that you strongly endorse a high order of serious academic and public inquiry and dialog on the subject. Beyond that, you could also indicate that to assist in these processes you have ordered the release of meaningful government held data on the subject.

P.O. Box 6 • Falls Church, VA 22040-0006 • USA • Tel. 703/534-8566 • Fax 703/534-8569

If it turns out that you have not been fully briefed on this subject, and this letter gets to you, something much more important than your participation in the conference will have been accomplished.

We sincerely hope that you have been fully briefed and that you are leading the decision process that will change the policy of secrecy to the needful one of openness. This will be an act of courage, but following a short period of surprise and shock, you will be honored for it.

It is intended that this conference be as responsible as it will be vital to the future of earth's cultures. Your participation will assure both objectives.

If you believe that the Foundation can be of assistance to you in this area, we are ready to help in any reasonable effort toward openness. The facts are that individual governments are quite limited in possible responses to the phenomena, whatever its source. As impracticable and unpalatable as it may appear to some political and military leaders of the world, this is a "people" thing. The understanding and final resolution will come from the spiritual strength of individuals. To play their critical part they need to know all the information available and be welcomed into the dialog.

Respectfully,

C.B. Scott Jones

Attachment as stated

## THE WHITE HOUSE

WASHINGTON

December 21, 1994

Mr. C.B. Scott Jones
Human Potential Foundation
Post Office Box 6
Falls Church, Virginia 22040

Dear Mr. Jones:

Thank you for inviting President Clinton to speak at the international conference of the Human Potential Foundation. The President has asked me to convey his appreciation for your kind offer.

At this time, it seems that the tremendous demands on the President will not give him the opportunity to attend this special event in May of 1995. However, I will keep your invitation on file and will be sure to contact you if any changes in his schedule allow him to accept.

Once again, thank you for your thoughtful letter. Your continued interest and support are deeply appreciated.

Sincerely,

William M. Webster, IV
Director of Scheduling and Advance

WMW/inc

**Human Potential Foundation**

March 31, 1995

William J. Clinton
President of the United States
The White House
1600 Pennsylvania Avenue NW
Washington, D.C. 20500

Dear President Clinton:

This is a follow up to the letter we sent you on December 9, 1994, inviting you to be a principal speaker at the international conference: *When Cosmic Cultures Meet.*

Your office responded to that invitation on December 21, 1994, indicating that at the time it seemed that the tremendous demands on your schedule would not give you the opportunity to attend the May conference. The door was left very slightly open by Mr. Webster with the comment, "*However, I will keep your invitation on file and will be sure to contact you if any changes in his schedule will allow him to accept.*"

Attached to this letter is a copy of conference promotional material recently mailed. We expect a large turn out for the conference. Twenty-three speakers and panel members have committed.

As you can see from the program schedule, we have built in flexibility for all three days anticipating that you will decide to join us. You may speak at any time on any day. We will simply reschedule the other speakers. Your appearance will not cause anyone who has committed to the conference to be canceled.

In the event that for scheduling or perceived political reasons you feel that you cannot participate in the conference, a high level administrative surrogate for you would be acceptable. We have in mind Mr. Penetta or Vice President Gore. Dr. Gibbons certainly also would be acceptable, but he has already been invited and has declined. A separate, private letter is being sent to Mr. Gore about the conference.

Recently we sent letters to heads of all the diplomatic missions in Washington, inviting them to attend the conference. One of the ambassadors responded by saying that it was the most interesting letter that he has ever received in Washington.

You might be interested to know that in recruiting some of the academic participants, the issue of the nature of the conference was critical. They had to be convinced that it was not a "UFO conference." I mention this because of the unfortunate irony that you are a victim of previous administration policies that has successfully used a strategy of ridicule to keep this issue out of the public domain.

It will take political guts to start to reverse this old dysfunctional and dangerous policy. The conference provides you with as safe an opportunity as possible to take important first steps on this path.

I close with a repeat of the final paragraph of our previous letter. If you believe that the Foundation can be of assistance to you in this area, we are ready to help in any reasonable effort toward openness. The facts are that individual governments are quite limited in possible responses to the phenomena, whatever its source. As impracticable and unpalatable as it may appear to some political and military leaders of the world, this is a "people" thing. The understanding and final resolution will come from the spiritual strength of individuals. To play their critical part they need to know all the information available and be welcomed into the dialog.

Respectfully,

Scott Jones

C.B. Scott Jones

Attachment:  Conference announcement

**Human Potential Foundation**

March 31, 1995

William J. Clinton
President of the United States
The White House
1600 Pennsylvania Avenue NW
Washington, D.C. 20500

Dear President Clinton:

This is a follow up to the letters we sent you on December 9, 1994, and March 31, 1995, inviting you to be a principal speaker at the international conference: *When Cosmic Cultures Meet.*

Recently letters were sent to all members of Congress inviting them to the conference. A copy of one of those letters is enclosed along with the attachments that were sent to them. These attachments are the questionnaire that all participants at the conference will be asked to complete, and a copy of a talk I gave last year that provides background about the apparent government role concerning UFO phenomena, and the related issue of mind control technology. Up to this point Congress has failed to focus on these issues. We hope that they soon will realize that they have a responsible constitutional role to play, and get fully engaged.

As was indicated in previous letters, the conference program remains flexible to accommodate your participation. It is our sincere hope that you will take advantage of this opportunity. As difficult as this decision may be, it is far better than being placed in a defensive role, responding for the first time to events about which no country will have any control. It would also appear to be to your advantage to keep ahead of the Congress on these issues.

Sincerely,

*Scott Jones*

C.B. Scott Jones

Enclosures as stated

P.O. Box 6 • Falls Church, VA 22040-0006 • USA • Tel. 703/534-8566 • Fax 703/534-8569

360

## THE WHITE HOUSE

WASHINGTON

June 2, 1995

Mr. C.B. Scott Jones
Human Potential Foundation
Post Office Box 6
Falls Church, Virginia 22040

Dear Mr. Jones:

Thank you for your kind invitation to President Clinton.
The President has asked me to convey his appreciation for your
offer.

At this time, I am unable to make a commitment to your
request. However, please be assured that I will keep your
invitation on file for further consideration.

On behalf of the President, thank you again for your
thoughtful invitation and best wishes.

Sincerely,

William M. Webster, IV
Director of Scheduling and Advance

WMW/inf

## ⊕ Appendix C

# Invitation Letter to Senior Executive Branch Personnel

Forty of the most senior civilian and military leaders in the executive branch of the government were sent personal invitation letters to attend the conference and to pass the word about the conference within their departments, office or agencies. There were two different types of letters sent. The first covered the situation where it was considered unlikely that the department, office or agency head being addressed had any official responsibility or knowledge about government involvement with UFO phenomena. The example letter for this situation is to Robert Reich, Secretary of Labor.

The second situation was when it was a reasonable assumption that someone in the agency, office or department being addressed would have reason to be knowledgeable about government involvement with UFO phenomena. An example of that letter was sent to Daniel S. Goldin, Administrator, National Aeronautics and Space Administration.

There were only two responses to these forty invitations, one from the Department of Defense and the other from the National Aeronautics and Space Administration. The letter from the Pentagon is straightforward, acknowledging that Secretary of Defense Perry had received the invitation.

The letter from NASA appears to have been written by the "Gang who couldn't shoot straight." The invitation letter didn't ask or talk about evidence of UFOs. It invited Goldin to participate in a conference that would address a future when there was no ambiguity about the existence of extraterrestrial intelligence. It was appreciated to have in writing the statements from NASA that "the investigation of UFO's does not fall under the governmental jurisdiction of NASA. NASA has no factual evidence that life exists on other planets, nor that UFO's are related to aliens." The defensive tone of the letter is that 'NASA is sick of this subject, it has cost us politically and we wish it would go away.' In fact, NASA is up to its arm pits on the subject and cannot let go of the tar baby.

**Human Potential Foundation**

362

May 18, 1995

Robert B. Reich
Secretary of Labor
200 Constitution Ave., NW
Washington, D.C. 20210

Dear Secretary Reich:

It seems reasonable that less than 1% of the federal government would have any official responsibility or official knowledge about what popularly is known as UFO phenomena.

Logic suggests that the Department of Labor is not part of that very small fraction. However, there certainly are thoughtful people in your department who may have a personal interest in this phenomena, or who have enough vision to see how the phenomena will impact your department. It may be large. They are invited and encouraged to attend the conference, *When Cosmic Cultures Meet.*

Wherever they are, those who labor with the dysfunctional policy concerning secrecy of UFO phenomena that the current administration inherited from previous administrations, they should be interested to know about the efforts under way to have this policy reviewed and reversed to one of openness.

- A direct approach has been made to the White House to accomplish this end.
- Congress has been given several reasons to become involved.
- A dialog at the grass roots level is being stimulated.
- The media is being challenged to wake up and play a responsible role.

If national leaders fail to lead on this subject they will earn, deserved or not, a place in history that has yet to be labeled in terms of deceit, indecision, arrogance and cowardliness. It may appear to be a no win situation, but to delay being open and honest will inevitably end up with the initiative being taken away from the president and place the government in an impossible defensive catch-up mode.

Sincerely,

*Scott Jones*

C.B. Scott Jones

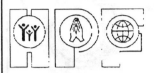

# Human Potential Foundation

May 18, 1995

Daniel S. Goldin
Administrator, National Aeronautics and Space Administration
Washington, D.C. 20546-0001

Dear Mr. Goldin:

It seems reasonable that less than 1% of the federal government would have any official responsibility or official knowledge about what popularly is known as UFO phenomena.

Logic suggests that part of NASA makes up some of that very small fraction. Please direct the enclosed material to that select group. They are invited and encouraged to attend the conference, *When Cosmic Cultures Meet.*

As they labor with the dysfunctional policy concerning secrecy of UFO phenomena that the current administration inherited from previous administrations, they should be interested to know about the efforts under way to have this policy reviewed and reversed to one of openness.

• A direct approach has been made to the White House to accomplish this end.

• Congress has been given several reasons to become involved.

• A dialog at the grass roots level is being stimulated.

• The media is being challenged to wake up and play a responsible role.

If national leaders fail to lead on this subject they will earn, deserved or not, a place in history that has yet to be labeled in terms of deceit, indecision, arrogance and cowardliness. It may appear to be a no win situation, but to delay being open and honest will inevitably end up with the initiative being taken away from the president and place the government in an impossible defensive catch-up mode.

Sincerely,

Scott Jones

C.B. Scott Jones

**OFFICE OF THE ASSISTANT TO THE SECRETARY OF DEFENSE**
1400 DEFENSE PENTAGON
WASHINGTON, D.C. 20301-1400

**PUBLIC AFFAIRS**

25 May 1995

Dr. C. B. Scott Jones
Human Potential Foundation
P.O. Box 6
Falls Church, VA 22040

Dear Mr. Jones:

Thank you for your letter of May 18, 1995, to Secretary of Defense Perry concerning your forthcoming conference, *When Cosmic Cultures Meet*. It was good of you to bring this information to the Secretary's attention.

Sincerely,

Harold Heilsnis
Director for Public Communication

National Aeronautics and
Space Administration

**Headquarters**
Washington, DC 20546-0001

Reply to Attn of:

P

June 6, 1995

Mr. C.B. Scott Jones
Human Potential Foundation
P.O. Box 6
Falls Church, VA 22040-0006

Dear Mr. Jones:

I am writing in response to your letter to Administrator Goldin concerning evidence of UFO's.

The investigation of UFO's does not fall under the governmental jurisdiction of NASA. NASA has no factual evidence that life exists on other planets, nor that UFO's are related to aliens. NASA's only assignment on UFO's was in October 1992, when we began a detailed search for artificial radio signals from other civilizations under the NASA High Resolution Microwave Survey (HRMS) program. Congress directed NASA to end this project in October 1993, citing other pressures on the U.S. Federal budget.

The HRMS did not detect any confirmed signal before it was stopped. However, similar work will continue in a more limited manner through efforts of private groups and through academic institutions. For further information on the Search for Extraterrestrial Intelligence, please contact:

The SETI Institute
2035 Landings Drive
Mountain View, CA 94043

Thank you for your interest in NASA and its programs.

Sincerely,

Elsie Diven Weigel
Special Assistant for Communications
Office of Public Affairs

### ⊕ Appendix D

# Invitation Letter to Members of Congress

Two separate mailings were made to each member of the House of Representatives and the U.S. Senate. The first mailing on May 16, 1995, was an invitation to attend the conference. Five specific reasons were given why this would be a reasonable and important thing to do. Out of 435 letters sent to members of the House, only two responded with letters regretting that they could not attend. Out of the 100 letters sent to members of the Senate, only one Senator sent his regrets. There is no evidence that any Congressional staff members attended the conference.

The second mailing went out on August 23, 1995, three months after the conference. Attached to each letter was a stick-on hand written note addressed to the Administrative Aid or Chief of Staff of each Member. This was an attempt to get the letter out of the mail room and into the hands of someone senior on the staff who might actually read the letter and consider passing it on to the Member. In this short note it was suggested that if they did not already have one, that they establish an office UFO/ETI file. Attached to the letter was a "Less than one minute to complete poll." They were given seven statements to respond to with either "Yes, No or Uncertain," and two opportunities to identify personal staff and committee staff members who could be contacted on the subject of UFOs. The last of the "Yes," No, or Uncertain" statements was "Do not send any more letters on this subject."

There was zero response to this mailing of 535 letters. Later I talked to a few friends on Capitol Hill about this result. One told me that there wasn't a big enough club to use on a Member to get his attention on anything other than the budget and the upcoming 1996 elections. It appears that for the very largest part of Congress, the UFO issue is simply invisible. That would change quickly if the folks back home started writing letters and making phone calls about the subject.

## Human Potential Foundation

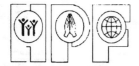

May 16, 1995

Rep. _____
Room _____ HOB
Washington, D.C. 20515

Dear Mr. _____:

Attached are flyers announcing the conference "When Cosmic Cultures Meet." This conference will be held at the Sheraton Washington hotel on May 27-29. Also attached is a questionnaire to be completed by everyone attending the conference. In it, Newt Gingrich and Bob Dole have a voice. Also attached is a speech I gave last year that gives adequate reason for you and Congress to pay attention to this conference and the issues it raises.

While it is likely that you will be in your district for the Memorial Day weekend, I urge you to arrange for personal and committee staff participation at this conference. The reasons for this recommendation are simple and compelling:

•      National polls have indicated for years that a majority of your constituents have an interest in this subject.

•      There is a high probability that Congress has been kept out of the information loop on this subject by both Republican and Democratic presidents for over forty years.

•      There is some suggestion that the current administration is in the process of reassessing the policy of secrecy and silence that it inherited from previous administrations, and changing it to one of openness.

•      This is a politically safe conference to attend. The thesis and assumptions transcend party and ideology.

•      It is an important conference. Congress as an institution and you as an individual member have important and responsible roles to play in developing the dialog.

Sincerely,


C.B. Scott Jones

P.O. Box 6 • Falls Church, VA 22040-0006 • USA • Tel. 703/534-8566 • Fax 703/534-8569

368

COMMITTEES:

TRANSPORTATION & INFRASTRUCTURE
SURFACE TRANSPORTATION
PUBLIC BUILDINGS & ECONOMIC DEVELOPMENT

VETERANS' AFFAIRS
HOSPITALS & HEALTH CARE

# Congress of the United States
## House of Representatives
### Washington, DC 20515

## CORRINE BROWN
3D DISTRICT, FLORIDA

May 20, 1995

REPLY TO:

**WASHINGTON OFFICE:**

☐ 1610 LONGWORTH BUILDING
WASHINGTON, DC 20515
(202) 225-0123
Fax (202) 225-2256

**DISTRICT OFFICES:**

☐ 314 PALMETTO STREET
JACKSONVILLE, FL 32202
(904) 354-1652
Fax (904) 354-2721

☐ 75 IVANHOE BOULEVARD
CHAMBER OF COMMERCE
ORLANDO, FL 32804
(407) 872-0656
Fax (407) 872-5763

☐ 101 SE 2ND PLACE
SUITE 106
GAINESVILLE, FL 32601
(904) 375-6003
Fax (904) 375-6008

DAYTONA BEACH AREA
TOLL-FREE (904) 254-0914

Mr. C. B. Scott Jones
Human Potential Foundation
Post Office Box 6
Falls Church, Virginia   22040-0006


Dear Mr. Jones:

Thank you for your letter of May 14 inviting me to attend a a conference from May 27-29.  I regret that I will be unable to attend because of prior commitments.  I do, however, appreciate your thinking of me in this.

With kindest regards, I am

Sincerely,

Corrine Brown
Member of Congress


CB:des

L D. COVERDELL
GEORGIA

## United States Senate
WASHINGTON, DC 20510-1004

May 24, 1995

Mr. Scott Jones
Human Potential Foundation
Post Office Box 6
Falls Church, Virginia  22040

Dear Mr. Jones:

Thank you for your kind letter inviting me to attend a Human
Potential Foundation Conference May 27-29, 1995.  Unfortunately,
I have a prior commitments on those dates.  I will, however, pass
this invitation to a member of my staff.

Please extend my best wishes for a most successful event
to your guests.  Again, thank you for thinking of me and for your
interest in my work.

Sincerely,

Paul D. Coverdell
United States Senator

PDC/saj

## Human Potential Foundation

370

August 23, 1995

Rep. _____
Rm ____, _____ HOB
Washington, D.C. 20515

Dear Mr. _____:

Three months ago you were invited to a conference held in Washington, D.C. A copy of that invitation letter is attached. This conference, *When Cosmic Cultures Meet*, was judged by those who attended to have been very important and successful. Since the conference was held on the Memorial Day weekend, we understand why it failed to compete for your attention compared to what was going on in your district and state that weekend. We regret that you did not send a staff person to the conference.

The purpose of this letter is to provide you with a copy of the conference program and a composite copy of the questionnaire completed by those who attended, and to ask you if you are going to carry out your constitutional responsibilities on this issue.

The conference was part of a process to make it politically safe for Congress to get involved in a subject that from all available evidence has been the secret purview of the executive department for nearly fifty years.

Along with others, we have been urging the executive branch to change their policy of silence, secrecy and disinformation to one of openness with Congress, the American public and the world.

How do you feel about this? We would like to work with Congress and see it play its normal constitutional role of checking the executive branch and being involved in vital policy issues. In our opinion the issues are too important for a few in the executive branch to presume to make decisions about it for the rest of us.

Will you please complete and return the attached questionnaire? **It will take less than one minute to complete.** Based upon your answers we will either leave you alone or if it is your desire, work with you to help get the information out and help prepare for an extraordinary future.

Sincerely,

C.B. Scott Jones

Attachments as stated

P.O. Box 6 • Falls Church, VA 22040-0006 • USA • Tel. 703/534-8566 • Fax 703/534-8569

### Questionnaire for Members of the 104th Congress

**Subject:** Position on Release of U.S. Government-Held Information Concerning Extraterrestrial and/or Other Dimensional Intelligence (popularly known as UFO phenomena)

Please mark each statement with one of these responses: Y = yes; N = No; U = Uncertain, and return to the Human Potential Foundation: P.O. Box 6, Falls Church, VA 22040.

_____     1. There is an oversight role for Congress to play on this subject.

_____     2. I expect Congress to carry out its oversight role on this subject.

_____     3. As a member of Congress I want to be involved in this process.

_____     4. The person to contact on my personal staff on this subject is:

**Name:**_____**Telephone**_____

    5. The person to contact on my committee about this subject is:

**Committee:**_____

**Name:**_____**Telephone**_____

_____     6. This subject is of no interest to me.

_____     7. This subject is of no interest to my constituents.

_____     8. I want to leave this issue to the White House to handle.

_____     9. Do not send any more letters on this subject.

We request that you complete and return the questionnaire so that there is no ambiguity about your position on this subject. If you decide not to return the completed questionnaire we will assume that the unstated answer to 9 is "yes," and that you are going to be a spectator rather than a participant. There could be a number of reasons why you would not return the completed questionnaire. These include: a. You don't know and don't care what your constituents know or feel about the subject. b. It could be possible ammunition in the hands of the "other" party and/or your next primary opponent. c. You can't see any political gain for getting involved. d. There is no PAC support involved. If any of these apply, you might try looking beyond your district, state and nation to see if there is a vision in which you appear. We have no doubt that everyone spends some time thinking about the future and a larger reality. We are asking for one minute of thoughtful time from you and the courtesy of a reply. All responses will be kept private. The number of responses and non-responses will be reported in the Proceedings of the recently completed conference.          [8-17-95]

**Member:**_____

**Address:**_____

_____

_____

**Telephone:**_____

372

⊕ Appendix E

# Invitation letter to the Washington, D.C. Diplomatic Corps

Washington D.C. has a large diplomatic corps. Invitation letters were sent to 167 Ambassadors, Counselors, or Chargé d'Affaires ad interim, whomever was in charge at the various embassies. Approximately a dozen responded either in writing or by phone. A specific issue raised in the invitation letter was whether they would support the establishment of a non-government organization (NGO) with a working name of the Center for Cosmic Culture Interactions. Such an organization would be associated with the United Nations system. Two responses, typical of the others, are reproduced. As may be seen, unlike the U.S. non-response, the conference and the subject of the conference was not simply fobbed off.

Contact continues with the diplomatic community. There is some interest in establishing a salon format where members of the diplomatic corps could come together to discuss UFO phenomena under the tutelage of individuals who have given the subject considerable thought. These would not be open to the press or the public.

**Human Potential Foundation**

374

March 27, 1995

His Excellency _____
Ambassador [Country]
[Address]
Washington, D.C. 200XX

Dear Ambassador _____:

The purpose of this letter is to invite you to participate in the international conference *When Cosmic Cultures Meet*. This conference will convene in Washington, D.C., May 27-29, 1995. The attached pamphlet provides details about it. We expect the conference to be well attended and therefore recommend your early registration.

The purpose and expectation of the conference is that it will facilitate international dialog concerning a most profound but currently enigmatic subject. The thesis of the conference is that some day there will be unambiguous evidence that cosmic cultures are meeting and that Earth is one of the meeting grounds. These cosmic cultures may be extraterrestrial or other dimensional in nature, or both. Anticipating that time, what questions should we be asking? What basic and reasonable preparations should we be making?

One of the products of the conference will be a book of the proceedings. Also included in this book will be invited think pieces from international contributors. We invite you to make such a contribution or to arrange for a contribution from someone in [Country's name] who you feel also would make an important contribution to the international dialog.

The Human Potential Foundation is a public non-profit research and educational organization chartered in Washington, D.C., USA. We are considering establishing within the Human Potential Foundation a special unit that will seek non-governmental organization (NGO) status with the Economic and Social Council of the United Nations. A working title of this unit is the Center for Cosmic Culture Interactions. It would be structured to provide a repository of special knowledge on the subject of cosmic culture interactions, and the problems and opportunities attendant thereto. It would additionally convene seminars, symposia and conferences of interest to components of the United Nations and to associated member nations.

P.O. Box 6 • Falls Church, VA 22040-0006 • USA • Tel. 703/534-8566 • Fax 703/534-8569

The structure of this unit is still in formation. At the present time we anticipate that it will have the following sections:

o Library and archives

o Oral traditions, folklore and science of indigenous cultures

o Theological and spiritual issues

o Philosophical considerations

o Current western scientific paradigm

o Developing multidimensional science

o Extended perception communications

o Cultural impact assessment

o Formerly classified information

Would [Country's name] be interested in the existence of such an organization with a mission of providing consultant support to the United Nations system, and to individual associated countries? Would [Country's name] support the NGO status of such an organization?

We have asked much from you because we believe that this subject now deserves serious attention from all of the world's cultures.

If you have any questions about the conference or the proposed NGO we would be pleased to meet with you and discuss these matters.

Sincerely yours,

C.B. Scott Jones

Attachment as stated

376

**EMBASSY OF JAPAN**
*2520 Massachusetts Avenue N.W.*
*Washington, D.C. 20008*
Tel. (202) 939-6700
Fax. (202) 265-9484

April 3, 1995

Mr. C. S. Scott Jones
Human Potential Foundation
P.O. Box 6
Falls Church, VA 22040-0006

Dear Mr. Jones:

I would like to respond to your letter of March 25 at the behest of Ambassador Kuriyama, who directed it to my attention.

He asked me to thank you for the information you provided and the invitation to participate in the *When Cosmic Cultures Meet* international conference, an unusual, albeit potentially interesting conference. Unfortunately, the press of official duties will prevent the Ambassador from attending, but we wish you the best in generating international interest.

At the present time, Japan is not prepared to provide specific support for your organization as a consultant to the UN or as an international NGO. We will, however, take note of any progress your organization might make toward establishing an international presence and reevaluate our position as required.

In the meantime, please accept my most cordial regards.

Sincerely,

Tsukasa Uemura
First Secretary

AMBASSADE VAN HET KONINKRIJK DER NEDERLANDEN

ROYAL NETHERLANDS EMBASSY
4200 Wisconsin Avenue, N.W.
Washington, D.C. 20016
tel. 202 244 5300
fax. 202 537 5124

Washington, D.C., April 10, 1995

Dear Mr. Jones:

Thank you for your letter to Ambassador Jacobovits inviting him to participate in the Human Potential Foundation's conference *When Cosmic Cultures Meet*.

After reviewing the conference brochure, I was impressed with the diverse qualifications of your presenters and your goal of probing challenging topics from a variety of disciplines. Much to my regret, I must inform you that a scheduling conflict will prevent the Ambassador from attending the conference.

The Embassy cannot answer your question regarding support for NGO status within the U.N. at this time. A prospective answer would be difficult to give considering that the entity in question does not yet exist. I can assure you, however, that the Netherlands Government will continue to monitor developments in this field.

Sincerely,

Dale T. Morris
Press and Cultural Affairs

Mr. C.B. Scott Jones
Human Potential Foundation
P.O. Box 6
Falls Church, Virginia 22040-0006

# ⊕ Appendix F

# Exchange of Correspondence with Carl Sagan

On December 23, 1994, Carl Sagan was invited to the conference as a speaker. In his response of January 16, 1995, he observed that it was premature to plan a conference on meeting with extraterrestrial civilizations, but more importantly because of the assumed vast difference between their advanced status compared to current Earth dwellers, the conference "would be tantamount to ants planning a meeting on what to do should they ever encounter humans."

I felt that Sagan had underestimated both ants and humans and responded telling him so. In a later letter I invited him to write a paper on the subject that would be published in the conference proceedings. He opted not to write a paper and regretfully did not attend the conference thereby missing a great learning opportunity and depriving us of his wit and wisdom.

# Human Potential Foundation

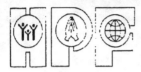

December 23, 1994

Professor Carl Sagan
Cornell University
Center for Radiophysics and Space Research
Laboratory for Planetary Studies
Space Science Building
Ithaca, New York 14853-6801

Dear Professor Sagan:

You are invited to participate as a speaker in the international conference: When Cosmic Cultures Meet.

The object of the conference is to advance a dialog that will lead to constructive action by the world's cultures concerning preparation for the time when there is no ambiguity that cosmic cultures are meeting, and one of the meeting places is Earth.

The above objective also tells us what the conference is not about. We are not meeting to discuss the evidence, however compelling, that cosmic cultures have already met. This is a separate important continuing debate, and one that deserves its own venue.

However, we are looking to a time in the future when knowledge known to governments will be made public and the issue will take on a different aura of reality.

The conference is not a trivial undertaking. A former president of the United States while in office expressed the idea that contact with off planet cultures constitutes a threat to the world, and that the response should be for the world to unite against such an eventuality.

Whether the above action was based upon knowledge or conjecture is unknown. However, it would appear that attempts either to make demons or angels of non-earth cultures and the consequences of meeting with them should carefully be preceded by reflective contemplation of ourselves and a future that includes a probable meeting and living with cultures currently beyond our ken.

P.O. Box 6 • Falls Church, VA 22040-0006 • USA • Tel. 703/534-8566 • Fax 703/534-8569

One of your fellow invited participants, Michael E. Zimmerman, Professor of Philosophy at Tulane University, has recently commented why many social leaders refuse to publicly discuss any aspect of the subject of this conference.   He observed that leaders fear that they will lose social status because of the ridicule and skepticism usually directed at people who take the possibility of extraterrestrial intelligence, and particularly contact with it, seriously.   Additionally, some social leaders cannot tolerate the possibility of superior non-earth intelligence, because their identity is bound up with a patriarchal, anthropocentric worldview that might not survive if faced with such intelligence.   And finally, still other leaders fear potentially calamitous social disruptions that might follow if establishment figures were to confirm that technologically advanced non-earth intelligent beings are visiting.

Dr. Zimmerman's assessment presents a real challenge.   How do we get from where we are in a fear based, patriarchal dominant society to where it seems reasonable to some of us to go?   Throw in a dash of the possibility that regardless of both the formidable obstacles our culture presents, and the strong desire of some of us to do better, we may learn that our options are rather limited because of the capabilities and propensities of the visiting others.

Now you can understand why you have been invited as one of a select group bringing a broad range of academic disciplines, professional and personal attainments and courage to advance this dialog.   Your participation would be particularly important.   No other scientist to our knowledge has given this area as much consideration as you have.

The conference will be held May 26-29, 1995, in Washington, D.C. The site is the Sheraton Washington hotel.   Attendance is expected to be approximately 900.   The Foundation will cover your travel and conference expenses and offer a modest honorarium.

We will be pleased to discuss any aspect of the conference with you, and look forward to an early decision on your part to join us in this path finding undertaking.

The last time we communicated was back in July and August of 1993 when you were invited to participate in a roundtable discussion on UFOs hosted by Laurance Rockefeller in Wyoming.   One direct result of that meeting has been a low profile effort with the White House get them seriously to address the government classification policy concerning UFO phenomena.

The Human Potential Foundation was co-founded in December 1989 by Senator Claiborne Pell and the undersigned to look into all aspects of the human condition.

Sincerely,

*Scott Jones*

C.B. Scott Jones

Attachment:

List of invited participants

# CORNELL UNIVERSITY

*Center for Radiophysics and Space Research*

SPACE SCIENCES BUILDING

Ithaca, New York  14853-6801

Telephone (607) 255-4971

Fax (607) 255-9888

Laboratory for Planetary Studies

January 16, 1995

Dr. Scott Jones
Human Potential Foundation
P.O. Box 6
Falls Church, Virginia 22040-0006

Dear Dr. Jones:

Thanks for your interesting invitation. As we have, in my view, no even moderately suggestive evidence that humans are encountering or have ever encountered a non-primate technical civilization, it seems premature to plan a conference on the subject. As far as extraterrestrial civilizations on planets of other stars are concerned, I think there is a quite compelling argument that any contact we make will be with a civilization immensely more advanced than we are, in which case the conference you propose would be tantamount to ants planning a meeting on what to do should they ever encounter humans.

With best wishes,

Cordially,

Carl Sagan

P.S. Nevertheless, I would appreciate being kept apprised of progress in the planning of the meeting.

CS:lkp
cc: Laurence Rockefeller

**Human Potential Foundation**

January 30, 1995

Dr. Carl Sagan
Cornell University
Center for Radiophysics and Space Research
Space Science Building
Ithaca, NY 14853-6801

Dear Dr. Sagan:

Thanks for your reply to the invitation to participate in the *When Cosmic Cultures Meet* conference. I find your comments about the conference stimulating and regret that you will not be with us in a capacity to advance your unique and important perspective.

You noted the compelling argument that any contact we make will be with a civilization immensely more advanced than we are, and in which case the conference we are holding would be tantamount to ants planning a meeting on what to do should they ever encounter humans.

I know nothing of ant consciousness, but assume that they operate on instinct rather than the cognitive processes associated with holding a planning meeting. In any event it appears that the Army Ant (Dorylinae) and the Fire Ant (Solenopsis geminata) have worked themselves into rather impressive and protected niches, and when present in numbers are prudently avoided by humans who have knowledge of their capabilities. Who knows, maybe the galactic reputation of Earthlings is comparable to the junk yard dog: don't mess with him. Even if we are not the the toughest son of a bitch in the cosmos, we could take the ant strategy. After all, there are billions and billions of us.

We will keep you apprised of the Conference progress. If you would like to attend we would be pleased to have you as a guest of the Foundation.

Cordially,

*Scott Jones*

C.B. Scott Jones

P.S. I can imagine the excitement when Jill Tarter and the SETI crew get a message and then realize that there is no protocol for the next step because they had previously agreed that it was too premature to think about such things.

cc: Laurance Rockefeller

**Human Potential Foundation**

384

February 28, 1995

Dr. Carl Sagan
Cornell University
Center for Radiophysics and Space Research
Space Science Building
Ithaca, NY 14853-6801

Dear Dr. Sagan:

As you requested in your letter of January 16, 1995, this is a progress report of planning for the May 27-29, 1995 conference, *When Cosmic Cultures Meet.*

Twenty-three speakers and panel members have signed on. The attached draft ad announcing the conference identifies these outstanding folks. There are three more speaker slots to fill. I have a list of people who have asked to be included, and several invitations out for which response has not yet been received. I will keep one of the speaker positions open anticipating a late decision from the White House on the invitation extended there.

You are still welcome to participate in the conference either as a speaker or guest in the audience. Whether you attend or not, I invite you to provide a short written piece which will be published in a book containing the papers presented at the conference and contributions from other world scientific, business, political, spiritual and literary leaders.

Cordially,

C.B. Scott Jones

cc: Laurance Rockefeller

P.O. Box 6 • Falls Church, VA 22040-0006 • USA • Tel. 703/534-8566 • Fax 703/534-8569

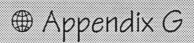

⊕ Appendix G

# UFO and New Frontiers: Connecting with the Larger Reality

This paper was given by the editor at a Tampa UFO Conference a year prior to the Conference. Inasmuch as it contained a number of points considered germane to the government's current policy of secrecy, silence and disinformation on the subject of UFO phenomena, copies of it had been provided in mailings to members of Congress, members of the diplomatic corps, and to the forty senior executive branch personnel invited to the conference.

In some respects it was a tough speech, and probably upsetting to some old hands in the intelligence community. Upsetting or not, the issue of excessive government secrecy is critical to the survival of democracy.

You will note that in the talk I link a particular aspect of UFO phenomena, mind influence and mind control, with an earth-based capability in the same area. More is known about the earth-based capability than the reported UFO capability. The point is this: when the full earth-based capability in this area is known to the Congress and the American public, it should be an adequate wake-up call to get serious about the dialogue on UFO phenomena.

If Congress wants to continue to dodge its responsibilities concerning UFO phenomena, perhaps it will be willing to look under the rock that covers our nation's activity in mind control technology.

[This paper was previously published in the book, *Phoenix in the Labyrinth*, Human Potential Foundation Press, 1995]

# Tampa UFO Convention

"UFOs And New Frontiers:
Connecting With The Larger Reality"
May 20-22, 1994
Holiday Inn Tampa International Airport, Tampa, Florida

C.B. Scott Jones, Ph.D.

# MATRIX OF UFO BELIEF

The Directors of Project Awareness have selected a provocative and appropriate theme for this convention: UFOs and New Frontiers - Connecting with the Larger Reality. My contribution to this theme will be centered around an anchor the Human Potential Foundation has found useful in its work in the UFO field for the past several years. Its current articulation is largely the work of Dick Farley, until recently a colleague at the Foundation.

The main thrust of the Foundation's involvement in the UFO field has been a low key approach to the current administration, encouraging it to review the policy it inherited concerning secrecy about UFO phenomena, and urging it to change the policy to one of openness - sharing with the American public and the world what special knowledge it may have on the subject.

As I suspect most of you know, there is a world of opinions about UFO phenomena, but we could not identify any body of evidence that would be generally accepted as proof of any hypothesis concerning that phenomena. We felt, therefore, that it would be helpful to have a starting point for discussion that generally defined, in summary, where we are on the subject. We were not seeking a consensus of belief, but rather a statement about the spectrum of beliefs. Personally I think that there currently is only one reasonable consensus: there is not sufficient information in the public domain to support a logical and rational belief structure. I also believe that somewhere there is enough information to support a logical and rational belief structure concerning what we call UFO phenomena. I don't want to disappear into a semantic fog, but it would probably take a good deal of effort to get agreement on what exactly is considered to be "UFO phenomena." I know for sure that we have our labels wrong. The issue is not Unidentified Flying Objects: discs, triangular, cigar or other shaped craft. That is at best merely one possible manifestation of what we really are interested in. Abduction phenomena is another poor and misleading label. Again, I suspect that it is another manifestation of a more encompassing phenomena that so far no one has been smart enough or bold enough to identify. I'll give it a try later because it is one of our Matrix entries.

The UFO Matrix of Belief presents the spectrum of scenarios found in current literature which are used to explain so-called UFO or ETI activity, or the lack thereof. Each matrix item has a supporting constituency. Some of these constituencies are quite vocal and apparently confident that the data with which they are familiar are adequate to support their belief systems in these areas. Others are less vocal, but no less confident that their current belief structures are the most reasonable, given the data which are generally accepted. There most certainly is a large minority which is not willing to commit to one matrix entry over another, or in combination, until additional data are available. The following are Matrix of Belief entries which purport to explain UFO phenomena.

0. All sightings except for a small minority which lack detail can be explained in terms of naturally occurring phenomena.

1. The phenomena are explained by craft from off planet, but from the visible universe.

2. The phenomena are explained by interdimensional penetrations by other intelligences or life-forms, based in or operating from another (parallel) overlapping dimension than our own time-space.

3. The phenomena are explained by earth-based "others," referenced throughout history, who may be other life-forms, or predominately resident in realms or dimensions we term spiritual.

4. The phenomena are explained by hoaxes or dramatic scenarios perpetrated by various intelligence organizations as part of broader security or disinformational campaigns.

5. The phenomena are broader social engineering, or population mind-influencing programs designed to promote a more universal planetary consciousness and to reduce the influence of nationalistic or religious traditions.

6. The phenomena are examples of technologies springing from multi-dimensional science, either Earth-based and surrounded by a bodyguard of lies, and/or non-Earth-based but rejected by most as outside the current scientific paradigm.

7. The phenomena are any combination of the above, including "all of the above." Intent: unknown.


A second part of the Matrix concerns possible U.S. Government levels of awareness, involvement and/or control of the phenomena termed UFO.


0. There is no government activity inasmuch as the phenomena are explained by naturally occurring events.

1. The government is aware, but not directly involved or in contact with the perpetrating forces.

2. The government is in contact to some degree, and cooperating with at least some of the source-phenomena or intelligences, either for technology trading or because government believes it has no choice.

3. The government is the perpetrator of at least some of the phenomenology, perhaps drawing on the source experience for ideas and methods, but employing the events for other purposes such as intelligence, disinformation, or to alarm other nations.

4. At least some UFO phenomena are results of government or other agency sponsored experiments in mind-control, or social control experiments or initiatives.

As an institution, the Human Potential Foundation does not endorse any of the Matrix entries. As we have distributed it over the past months, we have stated that it was prepared to stimulate discussion and research into the broad spectrum of ideas that are represented in current literature addressing what are popularly known as UFO phenomena. Of course, everyone in the Foundation has his or her favorite Matrix entry, but I have observed that these change from time to time. There has always been agreement in the Foundation that we need more data, and that the U.S. Government and other governments of the world can and should play a positive role in sharing what they know, and openly to assist in gathering more information and to be a full partner in interpreting all available information. As tax payers we have paid billions to develop, deploy and maintain land-based, sea-based and space-based sensors. There can absolutely be no doubt that some of these systems have engaged and recorded some aspect of UFO phenomena. Where is the data, what does it mean?

There are several Matrix entries that I want to discuss, and I also want to share some thoughts about the Cold War and what impact it may have had on decisions to withhold information about UFO phenomena from the general public.

It is generally accepted in Washington that the cold War is over, and that the West won. Personally, I think a better assessment is that humankind won. However, the point I want to make is that the energy that went into fighting the Cold War was huge on both sides. It was ultimately a cost that the Soviet Union could not continue to carry, and exhausted itself in the attempt. The economic burden of sustaining an empire and maintaining a huge military establishment was crushing. As William G. Hyland and other close observers of the world scene have observed, the Soviet system failed because it was inherently and fatally flawed. Its political philosophy was oppressive and supported a rigid hierarchy. Its economic system was inefficient and suppressed incentives to perform at anywhere close to normal potential. The Communist Party in the Soviet Union was mirrored in Eastern Europe. The system had become thoroughly corrupt. Communist leadership had degenerated into a venal, arrogant oligarchy, living like oriental potentates while their own people were desperate. However, if the system had been efficient, the Cold War would either still be going on, or the West would have lost. There was no lack of intent to defeat the West.

What does this have to do with UFO phenomena? I am suggesting that in both the Soviet Union and the United States, decisions were made to place on hold any effort to respond to UFO phenomena while the Cold War was raging, and its outcome unsure.

I assume that throughout the period of the Cold War, both countries were experiencing similar UFO phenomena, and very likely their assessments and responses were also similar.

An argument can be made that due to cultural differences, the Soviet and U.S. responses to the same UFO phenomena would be different, not similar. I would agree that there would be some differences, but suggest that there would be more similarities than differences, and absolutely no differences in the area of vital national interests. Most of us remember Winston Churchill's elegant and famous phrase that described the Russian as "a riddle wrapped in an enigma;" but the second half of his statement is usually overlooked. Churchill added that the secret to the riddle was the Russian national interest. The primal national interest of all countries is to survive as a national entity, i.e., the protection of their existing territory, and the preservation of their prestige from a massive loss of face. These are interests in common with all nations, and the prestige issue on the subject of UFOs is a current one for the U.S. government.

In regard to observed UFO phenomena, I imagine during the Cold War that in both countries questions such as the following were raised:

1. Is this a threat to sovereignty and national security?

2. Even without a direct physical threat, is our country and culture somehow in peril from the source of this phenomena?

3. What are the threat components from UFO phenomena?

4. Can any of the threat components be neutralized, or do we have to learn to live with them?

5. Is this a separate threat, or in some way associated with my Cold War adversary?

6. Is there some way that UFO phenomena can be used to my advantage against my Cold War enemy?

7. Can we be sure that our Cold War adversary won't be able to use it against us?

8. What are the technological significances to be learned from UFO phenomena? Can we capitalize on these in any way?

9. Will our Cold War enemy be able to capitalize on these UFO technologies?

10. Should we consider ending or setting aside the Cold War relationship in order to have unilateral or joint resources available to address possible threats from the source of UFO phenomena?

11. How do we handle the "threat capability verses intention" issue, and finally -

12. In view of the Cold War economic and psychological burdens being carried by our citizens, would additional knowledge about the reality of UFO phenomena be more than the citizenry could handle?


There is no evidence that I know of in the public domain about how these questions may have been answered. There is, as Zecharia Sitchin has documented in his book, *Genesis Revisited*, the provocative statements of President Reagan and Mikhail Gorbachev concerning the possibility of joint response to some outside threat to the Earth. Following their meeting in Geneva in November 1985, Reagan told about one part of their private discussions. Reagan, speaking of their meeting said: "Just think how easy his task and mine might be in these meetings that we held if suddenly there was a threat to this world from some other species from another planet outside in the universe. We'd forget all the little local differences that we have between our countries and we would find out once and for all that we are all human beings here on this earth together." Over a year later in February 1987, Gorbachev confirmed what some up to that time had considered to be merely Reagan's musings.

At a conference in Moscow on the "Survival of Humanity," Gorbachev said: "In our meeting in Geneva, the U.S. President said that if earth faced an invasion by extraterrestrials, the United States and the Soviet Union would join forces to repel such an invasion. I shall not dispute the hypothesis, though I think it's early yet to worry about such an intrusion."

By this time, the Cold War actually was over, and the leaders in Moscow knew that. My personal contacts in the Soviet scientific community had been telling me that this was the case and the scramble for personal survival was on. They could not predict if the pending revolution in Eastern Europe and in the Soviet Union would be bloody or not. I will leave this side bar of Cold War history, with some observations.

During a visit to Moscow, at the Institute of Theoretical Problems, I was informed by the director that a very senior scientist wanted to meet with me on an important subject. At the Institute we had been discussing its parapsychological and UFO research. I was informed that the scientist was a respected Hero of the Soviet Union, and was responsible for the huge phase array radar near Krasnoyarsk. That particular radar had been cited by the United States as a violation of the Antiballistic Missile Treaty. The Soviets had denied this and were going through extraordinary contortions to make their case. For thirty minutes I was lectured on the short sightedness of the U.S. in trying to force the Soviets to dismantle the radar. The insistence was that it was a vital installation, and technically not in violation of the treaty. I countered by saying that I was not knowledgeable enough with details of the treaty to make a judgment whether or not there was merit to his argument, and observed that he obviously was not making a technical case to me, but simply asserting that the radar was important and needed. I conceded that the

Soviet military and scientists would naturally feel that it was important, and be resentful that their diplomats had given it away. I asked what he wanted me to do about it. He requested me to carry his message to Senator Claiborne Pell, Chairman of the Senate Foreign Relations Committee. I promised him that I would. The broader issue was the Strategic Defense Initiative (SDI), the child of President Reagan, and the principal sticking point that Bush and Gorbachev had to negotiate away.

When I briefed Senator Pell and senior members of the Foreign Relations committee staff about the conversation I had in Moscow, it meant nothing special to them. Looking back on that incident, it is obvious that I missed an opportunity in Moscow to question whether the importance of the radar site was related to UFO phenomena. I now suspect that it was, and that they made the assumption that Senator Pell would make the link. Alas, the Soviets did not know how compartmentalized UFO information is in the U.S. government, and that the Congress has not been determined to have a "need to know."

Except for a small number of unreconstructed Cold Warriors in the U.S. and Russia, the Cold War is over. That means that the energy and treasure previously dedicated to that issue has become available for other uses. However, don't spend too much time looking for the Cold War dividend. The nature of the bureaucratic beast assures that nothing will be refunded to the tax payer. Recently the Campaign for New Priorities (an organization I know nothing about) announced that the Clinton budget for Star Wars and related programs is still larger than the combined federal outlays for small business loans, Head Start, child immunization, mass transit, summer youth jobs and Pell educational grants. Such a statement doesn't mean much without the availability of actual figures. However, parts of Star Wars do survive. The question is why? The power of some Congressmen to keep military spending in their home districts is part of the answer. The known successes in developing various Star Wars technology is so marginal, that it is hard to believe that another answer is that a pending technological breakthrough justifies continuing R&D expenditures. The acknowledged value of Star Wars was its use as a bargaining chip in getting the Russians to agree actually to destroy missiles and nuclear warheads. Was there, is there another reason for Star Wars technology that is intended to address UFO phenomena? I don't know, but we must think about this because of the assumptions that drive such a consideration.

Reagan made two more public statements on the subject. In September 1987, in an address to the General Assembly of the United Nations, he said: "In our obsession with antagonisms of the moment we often forget how much unites all the members of humanity. Perhaps we need some outside, universal threat to recognize this common bond. I occasionally think how quickly our differences would vanish if we were facing an alien threat from outside this world."

Reagan's last public statement on the subject came seven months later in May 1988, in Chicago at a meeting with the National Strategy Forum: "What would happen if all of us in the world discovered that we were threatened by an outer - a power from outer space - from another planet."

What is important about these statements? A number of things, but looking carefully at Reagan's assumptions, they tell us much about the man and about possible government policy on the subject. The most important assumption is that there is a "threat" to the world. Explicitly it is an "alien" threat, from some "other species," not human.

This was the president of the United States speaking publicly for the record, and the subject was confirmed by another head of state. How many lead stories in national newspapers and weekly news magazines picked up on this? How many editorials were written exploring the subject and the president's concerns? Zero. The reason for that will be discussed later. But what about the assumptions of a threat from a non-human alien species? Where did that information come from? We can look at this two ways. Either Reagan had slipped a cog (after all, he was the person who said that trees are a primary source of pollution!), or he was making a statement based upon information he received as the president of the United States. Because it was repeated three times over a period of nearly two years, it has the earmarks of an official statement. It may be official, but is it accurate? Not knowing what the government knows, it is impossible to answer that question. However, the same question can be asked of the private UFO research community. Based upon what they know about UFO phenomena, do you think that they would agree with Reagan that the world faces a threat from non-human aliens? You would get three different answers to this question: "yes," "no," and "I don't know." In my view the most reasonable answer is "I don't know." Of course, the "yes" answer is correct for those who are seeking a new enemy to replace the old Soviet Union, even if there is no evidence of hostile intent on the part of the visiting others. That may have been Reagan's attitude. I would assume that those who would answer "no" would include those who believe they have had a personal interaction with the visiting others, and on balance feel that the interaction was positive.

Without an informative data base, we should be conservative in making judgments concerning the "threat" potential from UFO phenomena. If any country of our contemporary world was capable of extending its human presence to an inhabited planet of another star system, I would be fearful for that community, given the general track record of violence on earth. I don't know who may be interacting with us, but if we try to meet them with aggressive Star Wars technology, the hopeless outcome is easy to predict.

On the other hand, if we meet visiting cultures with fearless curiosity and a genuine willingness to try to understand their needs and offer what we can, and to ask for assistance that we need, the outcome may be uncertain, but the dance will have begun.

The point is that this critical decision is too important for any government to make in secret. I am sure that the counterpart to the "Better Dead than Red" group has already been formed.

I am certain that a major problem the government faces concerns how to handle the "capabilities versus intention" issue. Those of you with government intelligence experience know what this issue is. A major responsibility of the intelligence community is to estimate a potential enemy's military capability. For example, how many ICBMs, what range, what size warhead, what reaction time to launch, what accuracy, what reliability, etc. However, political leaders routinely ask additional questions. "Given that the enemy has 1,000 ICBMs, under what conditions will he use them, does he intend to launch a pre-emptive strike, etc.? In their minds is the apparent logical link that the reason a country has a certain military capability is that it intends to use it. This is always easy to believe about an enemy state, while on the other hand, your country has military capabilities for defensive use only.

We have to wonder how the world's intelligence communities have assessed UFO phenomena. What capability assessment have they made? From public reports, craft can hover and then accelerate at such a rate that they fly out of visual range in a matter of seconds. Alternatively, they can "blink out" without obvious movement. This is the ultimate stealth technology. There are reports that when the pilot of an intercepting aircraft starts to arm his weapon systems, he immediately looses other critical aircraft systems that keeps him from pressing home his attack. The suggestion is that somehow his aggressive intent is immediately known to his potential target, and effective countermeasures are instantly engaged. Then there are numerous reports that the Visiting Others are capable of taking over the mind of an individual and obtaining a complete data dump. Communications is also reported in terms of robust parapsychological phenomena, for example, telepathy.

If they can control our weapon systems and take over our minds, they apparently can do anything they want to do. But do these monster powers make them monsters? And what are their intentions? If you had the responsibility of briefing the president on these issues, what would you tell him? Knowing the president, would you tell Jimmy Carter one thing and Ronald Reagan another? And who are you, a faceless bureaucrat in an unnamed agency?

The issue is too important to be handled by a faceless bureaucrat in an unnamed agency. The American public and the U.S. Congress must be involved.

Earlier I asked the question why there was no press response to Reagan's extraordinary statements concerning a space threat to the world. The short answer is that the press has effectively been taken out of the loop by the success of a counterintelligence program targeted against the American public and the press. The government wants no restrictions on how it attempts to handle what we are calling UFO phenomena. To get this freedom of action, a clamp of secrecy and stealth intimidation of the press has been employed. The program has been so successful against the press, that it doesn't even recognize the wound. The process apparently was to stage a number of "UFO events," get the press charging to the bait and then with fanfare show that it was either a hoax or misinterpretation of natural phenomena. When print editors hear: "UFO," "UFO," we get the same response from them that the village finally gave the young sheep herder who cried "Wolf" too many times.

This program of ridicule along with super secrecy and an aggressive way of dealing with individuals who officially know something about the facts and begin to talk have been adequate to keep the lid on what the government really knows and what it is doing about it. Of course we all wish them well in whatever they are doing, but with the pressures of the Cold War gone, and for the first time in over forty years the Executive can turn fully to this "problem," I frankly am very concerned about what decisions are being made without involvement of the normal democratic process.

Now, it may not be as critical as we fear. There is the possibility that a few government scientists and outside aerospace contractors are still staring intently at some assumed or known other-worldly crash material and continue to be unable to reverse engineer it. If that is the case, the super secrecy is based more on embarrassment than anything else, and to admit this would be a huge loss of face by some part of the government.

On the other hand, there are a host of scenarios that presume a rich interaction between the government and various off-earth cultures. The facts are that the public does not know what, if anything, has been going on, and president Reagan's ravings or trial balloons didn't move the mark one millimeter. What probably did happen was that the director of the counterintelligence program was staggered at the effectiveness of his efforts.

Here are two simple scenarios to consider:

1. UFO phenomena are real and a counterintelligence operation involving disinformation has been employed to protect this fact.

2. UFO phenomena, real or not, are also part of a counterintelligence operation of disinformation to protect something of greater value, e.g., multi-dimensional science and technology. (The ultimate stealth—invisibility; through the earth communications; greater than the speed of light propulsion; remote mind control; unlimited, non-poluting energy.)

One of the Matrix entries concerns itself with multi-dimensional science. It reads, "UFO phenomena are examples of technologies springing from multi-dimensional science, either Earth-based and surrounded by a bodyguard of lies, and/or non-Earth-based but rejected by most as outside the current scientific paradigm."

Most of the literature on this subject comes from Russia, and parts of Eastern Europe. In the hours of briefings and discussions I have had with Russian scientists, the subject frequently arises. They seem to be both comfortable with it and knowledgeable about it. Only a few U.S. scientists appear to have much interest in it. For both U.S. and Russian scientists, the work of Tesla is a touchstone for the subject. A few U.S. researchers have told me that when they became involved in this type of research, serious problems developed and persisted until they dropped their efforts. That suggests that a classified program exists with military applications, and that these particular scientists were not among the few to be allowed to work in the area.

The Foundation has followed several of these trails. The easiest one was mind control technology, and this, as you may recall, is one of the Matrix entries for possible Government involvement and/or control of UFO phenomena. This is a little discussed and disturbing area of government activity. Stan Friedman talked a little bit about this yesterday when he told about the success that John Marks had under the Freedom of Information Act in obtaining documentation about the CIA MKULTRA program. Perhaps in the style of Paul Harvey's "Now, the rest of the story," later I will pick up where Stan left off on this particular case.

Over the years, a number of citizens have reported that following what they thought and reported was a UFO sighting or some sort of interaction with UFO phenomena, they were visited by "government personnel" and questioned about their experience. Some also claim that evidence in the form of photographs was either asked for or demanded by these alleged agents of government. More extreme claims have been made, including various forms and intensity of harassment. This data supports the existence of government policy to discourage activity and discussion by private organizations and individuals on the UFO subject. If this is true, then it predicts the existence of a government organization to implement this policy. While there may be no evidence concerning what level in government such a policy may have been articulated, there can be no doubt that such a policy and every enforcement action of it is illegal and a gross violation of the rights of U.S. citizens.

It seems fair for anyone who is making an effort to get the White House to change its inherited policy of secrecy to one of openness, to know the type of personnel who play the important counterintelligence game. In a Colloquium on Counterintelligence they were described by Major General Edmund R. Thompson, U.S. Army, former Assistant Chief of Staff, Department of the Army, this way:

*I too have long believed that successful deception or counter-deception efforts require that kind of outlook, skills and especially operational mind that intelligence and counter-intelligence people have —or as Eric Ambler has described us: "the most suspicious, unbelieving, unreasonable, petty, inhuman, sadistic, doublecrossing set of bastards in any language."*

If a counterintelligence program has been in effect against the American people, it is so abhorrent that it virtually assures, in my opinion, that its development and implementation is layers below the White House. There have been enough men of integrity in the office of the president to believe that they would not have allowed such a program to continue if they had known about it.

This is not to suggest that the President is not briefed on the subject of UFO phenomena when he comes into office. However, there is speculation whether or not such a briefing is automatic with every incumbent, and how complete each briefing may be.

   If the above is correct or even partially so, how could the government get into such a mess? It very likely had an innocent beginning, but over the years has become a problem within and outside of government, the extent of which is known to very few. Here is one scenario. In the late 1940's or early 1950's, there was one or more UFO incidents that convinced people in authority that earth was in interaction with cultures of unknown origin. The response was predictable. The military insisted upon absolute secrecy while attempts to assess potential threat to national security were being made. Whatever tangible items for investigation were available, possibly material from a crashed vehicle and bodies of crew members, either failed to yield unambiguous evidence of a threat, or defied our best efforts to reverse engineer the material in order to reach some conclusion. A decision, not unreasonable, was made to keep the secret in anticipation that future additional evidence would add clarity to a confusing picture, or that our own future engineering and technological advances would allow us to begin to solve the mystery. Over forty years later we are essentially in the same position, hoping that the next piece of evidence will be critical to a denied understanding, and still blocked from penetrating technology that may be ten thousand or hundreds of thousands of years in advance of ours, or simply based upon another metaphysics that we cannot handle.

   The above is a simple scenario and it needs no embellishment to explain the government's continued want for secrecy on the subject. What does need to be explained is what someone in government may have been willing to do in order to keep the secrecy lid in place.

   Concurrent with this there may be at least two opportunistic coattailing programs, attempting to use the government's policy of UFO phenomena secrecy and the public's interest in UFO phenomena to cover other activity. One of these is essentially benign; research and development programs of the military services and possibly NASA, on advanced air and space systems. The attempt here is to shield R&D programs for as long as possible from foreign intelligence penetration. The motivation is not to keep U.S. taxpayers in the dark, but rather the realization that if the information is available to them, it is also available to other countries' intelligence services. This would be a legitimate counterintelligence program, and the people running it, probably the Air Force, need not know anything about real UFO phenomena. It is associated in name only.

   The second program that may be cruising along with UFO phenomena cover is not benign. The subject is mind control and mind influence technology. It may be an unrevealed facet from one of the "family jewels" from the mid-1970's when the CIA was plunged into purgatory by the investigation of the Senate's Select Committee to Study Government Operations with Respect the Intelligence Operations (the Church Committee), and the Rockefeller Commission established by President Ford. These investigations uncovered Project MKULTRA, the CIA's program of research and testing the use of drugs in behavioral modification.

   The Senate Committee report on MKULTRA is critical reading for anyone becoming educated on how a black (secret) project is run, and why it is so difficult to locate the records.

   Few accounts of the MKULTRA program fully identify what is available in the public record about it. Most attention is given to the use of LSD, and the tragic loss of at least one life as the result of it. Attention has been focused on the drug component of the program. There were other identified components, and some subprojects that never were identified.

   The subjects of identified subprojects are: effects of behavioral drugs and/or alcohol; research on hypnosis and drugs and hypnosis in combination; aspects of magicians' art useful in covert operations, e.g., surreptitious delivery of drug-related materials; studies of human behavior, sleep research, and behavioral changes during psychotherapy; library searches and attendance at seminars and international conferences on behavioral modification; motivational studies, studies of defectors; polygraph research; research on drugs, toxins, and biologicals in human tissue; provision of exotic pathogens and the capability to incorporate them in effective delivery systems; unspecified support for activities connected with the Army's Special Division at Ft. Detrick, MD (this included project MKNAOMI, wherein the Army developed darts coated with the biological agents, and pills containing several different biological agents which could remain potent for months); electroshock; harassment techniques for offensive use; analysis of extrasensory perception; gas propelled sprays and aerosols; crop and material sabotage; "Blood grouping" research; energy storage and transfer in organic systems; stimulus and response in biological systems; examination of techniques to cause brain concussion and amnesia by weapons or sound waves; and controlling the activity of animals. Additionally, there were three other subprojects about which there are no public details.

A reported 185 non-government researchers worked on the 149 subprojects in 44 colleges and universities, 15 research foundations, chemical or pharmaceutical companies, 12 hospitals or clinics, and 3 penal institutions.

The argument inside the Agency for this research was the belief that hostile powers had used chemical and biological agents in interrogations, brainwashing, and in attacks designed to harass, disable, or kill. This was part of the legitimate fear and paranoia of the cold war. The Chief of the Medical Staff of the CIA noted in 1952.

*There is ample evidence in the reports of innumerable interrogations that the Communists were utilizing drugs, physical duress, electric shock, and possibly hypnosis against their enemies. With such evidence it is difficult not to keep from becoming rabid about our apparent laxity. We are forced by this mounting evidence to assume a more aggressive role in the development of these techniques, but must be cautious to maintain strict inviolable control because of the havoc that could be wrought by such techniques in unscrupulous hands.*

From the record, there is no evidence of attempts to secure approval for the most controversial aspects of this program from the executive branch or Congress, and that even some of the various Directors of CIA during the period of MKULTRA were uninformed about the details of the subprojects. It was also deemed imperative that these programs be concealed from the American people. The CIA Inspector General wrote in 1952:

*Precautions must be taken not only to protect operations from exposure to enemy forces but also to conceal these activities from the American public in general. The knowledge that the Agency is engaging in unethical and illicit activities would have serious repercussions in political and diplomatic circles and would be detrimental to the accomplishment of the mission.*

The list the MKULTRA subprojects provides a vital insight. Even though some of the cryptic descriptions fail to reveal what the subject really was, it is the absence of a specific subject that is most important. For discussion let us grant that the CIA's prime motivation for this undertaking was as stated. It is believable that there was genuine concern about Communists capabilities in these areas. It follows then that the Agency would be thorough in its investigation of all relevant technologies. The list belies thoroughness. What is not mentioned is any subproject addressing electromagnetic technology. The reason this is significant is both historical and contemporary. It is known from open source literature that during the time of project MKULTRA, scientists in several countries were reporting research about using electromagnetic energy to influence the mind. It is not believable that the CIA was unaware of this research. Moreover, we now know that perhaps the largest effort in this area was in the Soviet Union and Eastern European countries. We also know that the Soviet Union achieved success and the assessment from Russian scientists who have been interviewed is that they were operating at least a third-generation system of the technology when the Soviet Union imploded.

The MKULTRA Family Jewel may well have been a throwaway to protect something much more valuable. We will all know someday what accuracy there is in this speculation. As will be addressed below, there appears to be more than one link to UFO phenomena and mind control technology.

Contemplation of the broader meaning of UFO phenomena easily leads to serious philosophical and practical areas. Two obvious ones are the implications for organized religion and the current scientific paradigm. These and other implications are the vital issues, but it cannot be assumed that in the case of government these are the first issues to be considered. It is likely that the government's first cut of the situation is a few notches below that level. More likely, it is much more bureaucratically visceral: how can we handle this and keep on doing what is normally expected of us? This is not an unimportant observation. It may be that the determining factor in the policy of government secrecy about UFO phenomena is that they have not been forced to say anything about a subject that probably will be very awkward to discuss with the American public. As long as they can keep the media neutralized and either successfully ignore or intimidate the few serious researchers in the field, they do not have to face the issue of disclosure. There is nothing particularly mean spirited or conspiratorial about this. It simply is delaying facing a problem that they imperfectly understand, and about which there is only one major area of agreement: they can't do anything about it.

In some parts of government, the intelligence community for example, there probably are some very practical concerns about the UFO phenomena being observed. This is where the link between what undisclosed mind control technology the CIA may be been investigating (and may have gone operational), and UFO phenomena takes place.

One of the most prevalent phenomena reported by participants who claim UFO interactions is mind to mind communications. Additionally, some participants report that the most commonly observed visiting other, the short Grays, have an ability to take over a mind, apparently empty it of all knowledge, then later replace the data base. During this process the mind may temporarily be given a different data base which supports in the mind's eye a complex scenario of cataclysmic world ending. Any agency that has an interest in mind control and mind influence technology would have to be concerned about that alleged capability. The interest may be high enough to make doubly sure that any independent success the agency had in this area was still deeply hidden, and that its new interest in this component of UFO phenomena was also out of public view. When you think this out, and accept that the mind control phenomena being presented in UFO phenomena may be real, the potential impact on the intelligence community would be nothing short of devastating. The foundation of intelligence activity is secrecy. What happens when there is a potential to remove that foundation?

The manipulation of truth to maintain secrecy can be seen in the 1977 joint hearings of the Senate Select Committee on Intelligence, and the Senate Subcommittee on Health and Scientific Research, chaired by Senator Edward Kennedy. The director of the Central Intelligence Agency, Admiral Stansfield Turner, was being questioned concerning aspects of the MKULTRA program.

Senator Huddleston: How about record keeping?

Admiral Turner. Yes; I can't imagine anyone having the gall to think you can just blithely destroy records today with all the attention that has come to this, and certainly we are emphasizing that that is not the case.

It wouldn't be "gall" that was the operative factor. It would be a rich mixture of belief that "this nasty job has to be done by somebody, and no one else is more qualified," and an addictive willingness to bask in the rush of the power that secret knowledge provides. Of course, the practical tradecraft explanation is that everything works on a need-to-know basis. That is, all information is compartmentalized. This is buttressed by the rule of never putting anything in writing that is vital to the survival of the organization. But, if you must, never allow more than one copy to exist.

The next example is very important. If you don't ask the right question, particularly about classified information, you cannot expect to get the information you are after. The intelligence community is bred to survive on limiting access to the next layer of knowledge. Part of the issue is "need to know," of compartmentalization of information and operations.

Senator Huddleston: Is there any indication that knowledge gained as a result of these experiments has been useful or is being applied in any way to present operations?

Mr. Brody: (Senior CIA employee) Senator, I am not sure if there is any body of knowledge. A great deal of what there was, I gather, was destroyed [by orders of the Director of CIA] in 1973. I would like to defer to Frank here. Do you know of any?

Mr. Laubinger (CIA Office of Technical Services). I know of no drugs or anything like that developed under this program that ever reached operational use or are in use today.

Senator Huddleston: So apparently any information that was gathered was apparently useless and not worth continuing, not worth further development on the part of the Agency.

Admiral Turner: I think that is basically correct.

Look at Laubinger's narrow, conditioned and therefore probably truthful answer. It was focused strictly on operational programs using drugs, and his knowledge about that. Brody's response was disingenuous. It denied the possibility that the scientists doing the contract research would have their own documentation. And, if that had been swept up by the Agency (a real possibility), at least they would have memories of their work. But there is another issue that fleetingly surfaced and disappeared. Huddleston was the first questioner to ask about "operational" use of these technologies, versus "experimentation" with them. If an experimental program had gone operational, continuing questioning about the experiments would not easily lead to knowledge about its operational status. There is more than a hint in this short exchange of CIA counterintelligence at work. The objective is to move the issue to a safe part of unimportant history. The tactic is part of hiding in the light, to be alert to every opportunity to turn truth, natural good fortune, bad fortune and luck to maximum advantage. Reality really sells. It requires little explanation and no defense. The Agency had established an eager willingness to share all it could find about a program that actually wasn't very successful. That part was most likely verifiably true. But this truth shadowed more important truth that would not be volunteered.

Another trace of possible counterintelligence activity can be found in this last question and answer example.

Senator Schweiker: Mr. Gittinger, a moment ago you mentioned brainwashing techniques, as one area that you had, I guess, done some work in. How would you characterize the state of the art of brainwashing today. . .

Mr. Gittinger (former CIA employee) . . . By 1961, 1962, it was at least proven to my satisfaction that brainwashing, so called, as some kind of an esoteric device where drugs or mind-altering kinds of conditions and so forth were used, did not exist even though "The Manchurian Candidate" as a movie really set us back a long time, because it made something impossible look plausible. Do you follow what I mean? But by 1962 and 1963, the general idea that we were able to come up with is that brainwashing was largely a process of isolating a human being, keeping him out of contact, putting him under long stress in relationship to interviewing and interrogating, and that they could produce any change that way without having to resort to any kind of esoteric means.

Gittinger was sharing accurate information about brainwashing techniques. But did it also mean that while "esoteric means" were not necessary to achieve the effect, that such means did not exist? That certainly is the thought left dangling by his statement. What makes this whole episode especially interesting is that the reason the Agency went back to the records one more time after exhaustingly searching for MKULTRA records for the Church Committee set up in 1975, is that they were responding to a FOIA request brought by John D. Marks. Marks was perceived by the Agency as an indefatigable foe. With co-author Victor Marchetti (who spent 14 years with the CIA), they had written an extraordinary expose of the CIA. Their book, *The CIA and the Cult of Intelligence*, was touted by the publisher as the first in American history to be subject to prior government censorship. In a brilliant move, they printed the book with exactly the same amount of white space of the censored lines and words. Nearly 200 passages were printed in boldface type. These were lines first censored but subsequently yielded up by CIA in legal proceedings. The net result was to highlight what the Agency wanted to keep secret.

Now, John Marks was at it again. Very likely the CIA actually did surprisingly discover seven new boxes of MKULTRA documents in the Retired Records Center. They said that for the first time they checked the retired records of the Budget and Fiscal Section of the Branch responsible for the research, and — there they were! Actually it makes little difference whether they were salted there or truly located for the first time. From a counterintelligence perspective it was an opportunity to get back on top after being upset. Marks "won" his FOIA battle, was given some of the newly discovered material, but was denied the critical data that may have led him to the fullness of all MKULTRA research. It was determined by Admiral Turner that the Privacy Act and the moral obligation to protect the researchers and their institutions from any unjustified embarrassment or damage to their reputations, kept him as Director CIA from revealing their names to the public. However, they were identified to the Senate committees on a classified basis. Now, seventeen years later in 1994, how many of these researchers are alive? How many of them are willing to remember details about research not yet in the public domain? What did this do to Marks? It substantiated that he was able to use the system to get theretofore classified material, and that there was still something to learn about MKULTRA. Importantly from CIA's view, it kept him on a trail that they had marked and could grumble about while inwardly smiling.

It should be considered that a variety of fears on the government's part probably have played a role in maintaining its policy of secrecy. One wonders whether the level of fear has remained essentially the same over the last forty years, or whether it has increased or decreased because of additional knowledge or lack of additional knowledge?

We think that it is responsible to encourage the White House to change its policy, and suspect that until the public is fully informed, that no process will be identified that will bring the phenomena out of the apparent "magic" category. Whatever its source, the phenomena is leading in this dance. We only get what is offered, and understand little of that. And to the frustration of the nation-state system, the source of UFO phenomena appears to have a preference to deal with individuals, not governments.

There is no evidence that the Congress has been informed by the Executive branch about information it may have concerning UFO phenomena. If that is correct, and Congressional interest in the subject can either be identified or developed, this would nominate a strategy to influence the White House to change its policy of secrecy.

There is a specific issue that should provide a strong incentive for Congress to get involved. On the subject of mind control technologies, Congress was probably misled during two separate hearings about the MKULTRA program, and it is possible that an operational mind control system has been in the inventory of some government agency for a number of years. The Congressional intelligence committees may or may not see a link between mundane mind control technologies and UFO related mind control, but I would be surprised if questions along that line were not asked if hearings were held.

In summary, do we see government secrecy? Lots of it, and probably most of it is the common garden variety. Are there secrets about UFO phenomena? Absolutely. At a minimum are the lines censored out of FOIA released documents. And, if there wasn't more, then the government's policy of silence and counterintelligence activity would not be justified. Remember that the government has never said that there is no additional information. However, government silence and secrecy does not prove the reality of any UFO phenomena. What is needed is all the data.

What to do about this? I suspect that in the end all of the fringe speculation will be lopped off as simply nuts. The truth will be exciting enough without trying to force-fit UFO phenomena with the fear based cries of those against income tax, the Federal Reserve System, international Jewish bankers, the Club of Rome, the Council of Foreign Relations, etc, etc. These fear mongers have a variety of other agendas which have nothing to do with UFO phenomena.

Let us work together responsibly to encourage and to allow the White House to face its responsibilities on this issue. Additionally, the U.S. Congress needs to be brought into the loop, first to assure that it has all the information available on the subject, and then to perform its constitutional role as a check on the executive.

Whatever the truth on this subject, it is time to face it.

---

End Notes:

U.S. Senate, *Foreign and Military Intelligence, Book 1, Final Report of the Select Committee to Study Government Operations with Respect to Intelligence Activities,* 94th Congress, April 25, 1976. See pp. 385-422.

U.S. Senate, *Project MKULTRA, the CIA's Program of Research in Behavioral Modification,* Joint Hearing, 95th Congress, 1st Session, August 3, 1977.